THE ROUGH GUIDE TO

Croatia

written and researched by

Jonathan Bousfield

roughguides.com

Contents

OPPOSITE PLITVICE LAKES **PREVIOUS PAGE** ŠIBENIK CATHEDRAL

Introduction to **Croatia**

Despite being one of Europe's hit holiday destinations, Croatia doesn't feel like a place that has been thoroughly worked over by the tourist industry. Though development continues apace along the more commercialized stretches of the coast, Croatian tourism has spun off in a number of positive directions. Whether backpackers or touring families, long-distance cyclists, yachters or spa-hotel surfers, all travellers have seen a big leap forward in the range and quality of what the country has to offer.

A renewed respect for natural ingredients has become the watchword of Croatian **cuisine**, with locally sourced foodstuffs, wines and olive oils standing up increasingly well to globalization. Croatia has a growing reputation for niche **festivals** – not just in the party-the-weekend-away music events held on beaches and in abandoned factories and ancient sea-forts up and down the coast, but also in the mushrooming number of arts festivals and small-town cultural shindigs. And in Zagreb and elsewhere, a raft of new **galleries** and art attractions has given the country a cool and contemporary sheen.

Croatia is blessed with a wealth of **natural riches**, boasting almost 2000km of rocky, indented shore and more than a thousand islands, many blanketed in luxuriant vegetation. Even during the heavily visited months of July and August there are still enough off-the-beaten-track islands, quiet coves and stone-built fishing villages to make you feel as if you're visiting Europe at its most unspoiled. There's plenty in the way of urbane **glamour** too, if that's what you're after, with swanky hotels, yacht-filled harbours and cocktail bars aplenty – especially in à-la-mode destinations such as Dubrovnik and Hvar. Wherever you go though you'll find that Croatia retains an appeal for independent travellers that's in short supply at more package-oriented destinations elsewhere in the Mediterranean. Most budget and mid-range accommodation is still in the form of private rooms and apartments, and there has been an explosion in the number of backpacker-friendly hostel-type establishments in the major cities.

ABOVE RECTOR'S PALACE, DUBROVNIK **RIGHT** VIS

The country has certainly come a long way since the early 1990s, when within the space of half a decade – almost uniquely in contemporary Europe – it experienced the collapse of communism, a war of national survival and the securing of **independence**. Two decades on, visitors will be struck by the tangible sense of pride that independent statehood has brought. National culture is a far from one-dimensional affair, however, and much of the country's individuality is due to its geographical position straddling the point at which the sober central European virtues of hard work and order collide with the spontaneity, vivacity and taste for the good things in life that characterize the countries of southern Europe – a cultural blend of **Mitteleuropa** and **Mediterranean** that gives Croatia its particular flavour. Not only that, but the country also stands on one of the great fault lines of European civilization, the point at which the Catholicism of Central Europe meets the Islam and Orthodox Christianity of the East. Though Croats traditionally see themselves as a Western people, distinct from the other South Slavs who made up the former state of Yugoslavia, many of the hallmarks of Balkan culture – patriarchal families, hospitality towards strangers and a fondness for grilled food – are as common in Croatia as in any other part of southeastern Europe, suggesting that the country's relationship with its neighbours is closer than many Croats may admit.

Where to go

Croatia's underrated capital **Zagreb** is a typical central European metropolis, combining elegant nineteenth-century buildings with plenty of cultural diversions and a vibrant café life. It's also a good base for trips to the undulating hills and charming villages of the rural **Zagorje** region to the north, and to the well-preserved Baroque town of **Varaždin** to the northeast.

Villach & Salzburg
Maribor, Graz & Vienna
ITALY
SLOVENIA
Varaždin
Krapina
Lepoglava
ZAGORJE
LJUBLJANA
Sava
Venice
ZAGREB
Trieste
Samobor
ŽUMBERAK
Velika Gorica
TUROPOLJE
Umag
RISNJAK NATIONAL PARK
GORSKI KOTAR
Novigrad
ISTRIA
Opatija
Karlovac
Sisak
Poreč
Pazin
Rijeka
Ogulin
Crikvenica
Krk
Novi Vinodolski
Korana
Rovinj
Slunj
BRIJUNI NATIONAL PARK
Cres Town
Krk Town
Senj
Pula
PLITVICE LAKES NATIONAL PARK
Cres
Rab
Kvarner Gulf
VELEBIT
NORTHERN VELEBIT NATIONAL PARK
Rab Town
Bihać
LIKA
Lošinj
Mali Lošinj
Pag
Karlobag
PAKLENICA NATIONAL PARK
N
Gospić
Pag Town
(MAGISTRALA)
DALMATIA
Nin
Zadar
Ugljan
Dugi Otok
KRKA NATIONAL PARK
Pašman
Biograd-na-moru
Knin
Murter
Vodice
Ancona
KORNATI NATIONAL PARK
Šibenik
Trogir
Solin
Split
Šolta
Supetar
ADRIATIC SEA
ITALY
Hvar Town
Vis
Vis Town
Pescara
0
50
kilometres
E65
E71

Budapest
Budapest
Čakovec
Koprivnica
PODRAVINA
Drava
HUNGARY
Pécs
Danube
Metres
1500
1000
500
200
100
0
Bjelovar
Virovitica
Slatina
LONJSKO POLJE
NATURE PARK
SLAVONIA
Drava
KOPAČKI RIT
NATURE PARK
Daruvar
Osijek
Kutina
Našice
Sava
Novska
Požega
Đakovo
Vukovar
Bačka Palanka
Slavonski
Brod
Vinkovci
Danube
E70
E70
Belgrade
Banja Luka
Sava
BOSNIA -
HERCEGOVINA
Tuzla
SERBIA
Travnik
Zenica
Bugojno
SARAJEVO
Sinj
Cetina
Imotski
Omiš
Brela
Makarska
BIOKOVO
NATURE
PARK
Mostar
Brač
Međugorje
Hvar
Korčula
Ploče
Vela
Luka
Korčula
Town
Pelješac
Peninsula
MONTENEGRO
Ston
MLJET
NATIONAL
PARK
Lastovo
Mljet
E65
(MAGISTRALA)
Dubrovnik
Cavtat
Podgorica

FACT FILE

• Croatia (**Hrvatska** in Croatian) is a crescent-shaped country of 4.3 million people. Roughly 89 percent of the population are **Croats**, who speak a Slavic language akin to Serbian and Bosnian, and mostly practise the **Catholic Christian** faith. There is also a sizeable **Serbian** population (about 4.5 percent of the total), who largely belong to the **Orthodox Church**.

• Politically, Croatia is a two-chamber **parliamentary democracy** with a directly elected – though nowadays largely ceremonial – president as head of state.

• Opinion surveys conducted throughout the 2000s repeatedly revealed that locals consider Croatian-born, ethnic Serbian inventor **Nikola Tesla** (1856–1943; see box, p.75) to be their greatest national figure of all time, closely followed by communist strongman **Josip Broz Tito** (1892–1980; see box, pp.102–103).

• The average Croat consumes over 5kg of **coffee** a year (almost twice as much as the average Brit), and spends an estimated 183 hours a year drinking it.

• Croatia's **Janica Kostelić** is the most successful female Olympic skier of all time, winning a total of four gold and two silver medals at the 2002 and 2006 Winter Olympics.

• The total length of Croatia's dramatic mainland **coastline** is 1777km. The highest **mountain** is Dinara (1831m) on the border with Bosnia-Hercegovina, and the longest **river** is the Sava, which rises in Slovenia and passes through Croatia for 562km before joining the Danube in the Serbian capital Belgrade.

The rest of **inland Croatia** provides plenty of opportunities for relaxed exploring. Stretching east from Zagreb, the plains of **Slavonia** form the richest agricultural parts of Croatia, with seemingly endless corn and sunflower fields fanning out from handsome, Habsburg-era provincial towns such as **Osijek** and **Vukovar** – the latter, almost totally destroyed during the 1991–95 war, is now in the throes of total reconstruction. Inland Croatia also offers numerous **hiking** opportunities: **Mount Medvednica**, just above Zagreb, or the **Samoborsko gorje**, just to the west of the capital, are good for gentle rambling. Also lying between Zagreb and the coast, and easily visited from either, are the deservedly hyped **Plitvice Lakes**, an enchanting sequence of forest-fringed turquoise pools linked by miniature waterfalls.

Croatia's lengthy stretch of **coastline**, together with its **islands**, is big enough to swallow up any number of tourists. At the northern end, the peninsula of **Istria** contains many of the country's most developed resorts, along with old Venetian towns like **Poreč** and **Rovinj**, and the raffish port of **Pula**, home to some impressive Roman remains. Inland Istria is characterized by sleepy hilltop villages, often dramatically situated, such as **Motovun**, **Grožnjan**, **Roč** and **Hum** – each mixing medieval architecture with rustic tranquillity.

The island-scattered **Kvarner Gulf**, immediately south of Istria, is presided over by the city of **Rijeka**, a hard-edged port city with an energetic cultural life. Close by are a clutch of resorts that were chic high-society hang-outs in the late nineteenth century and retain a smattering of *belle époque* charm, including quaint, diminutive **Lovran** and the larger, more developed **Opatija**. Not far offshore, the Kvarner islands of **Cres**, **Lošinj** and **Krk** have long been colonized by the package-holiday crowds, although each has retained its fair share of quiet seaside villages and tranquil coves; while the capital of the

CLOCKWISE FROM TOP LEFT ARCH OF THE SERGIANS, PULA; FISH MARKET, SPLIT; WATER POLO IN ZADAR

island of **Rab**, south of Krk, is arguably the best-preserved medieval town in the northern Adriatic.

Beyond the Kvarner Gulf lies **Dalmatia**, a dramatic, mountain-fringed stretch of coastline studded with islands. It's a stark, arid region where fishing villages and historic towns cling to a narrow coastal strip rich in figs, olives and subtropical vegetation. Northern Dalmatia's main city is **Zadar**, whose busy central alleys are crammed with medieval churches. From here, ferries serve a chain of laid-back islands such as **Silba**, **Olib** and the ruggedly beautiful **Dugi otok** – none of them sees many package tourists, and they're enticingly relaxing as a result. The site of an unmissable Renaissance cathedral, middle Dalmatia's main town, **Šibenik**, is also a good staging-post en route to the waterfalls of the **River Krka** just inland, and the awesome, bare islands of the **Kornati archipelago**.

Croatia's second city, **Split**, is southern Dalmatia's main town, a vibrant and chaotic port with an ancient centre moulded around the palace of the Roman emperor,

NATIONAL PARKS

If untrammelled nature is what you're after, then Croatia certainly offers variety, with stark mountains, forest-cloaked islands and wetlands teeming with wildfowl all vying for your attention. Several unique locations enjoy national park protection: most celebrated of these is **Plitvice**, a descending sequence of clear blue lakes punctuated by a stunning series of terraced waterfalls and foaming cataracts.

One must-visit offshore attraction is the **Kornati archipelago**, an extraordinarily beautiful group of largely uninhabited islands whose sparse covering of shrubs and sage produces an unearthly palette of grey, green and purple shades. A major target for yachting folk, the Kornati can also be reached on day-excursions from the mainland.

Sweeping views of the coastal islands can be enjoyed from the desolate grey slopes of the Velebit mountains, where the **Northern Velebit** and the **Paklenica** national parks offer trails along cliff-enclosed gorges and scenic ridge-top hikes. And those who make it to the far east of the country will be rewarded with a glimpse of the mysterious sunken forests of **Kopački rit**, a renowned haven for wading birds.

ABOVE VELIKI TABOR CASTLE

Author picks

Our indefatigable (if occasionally grumpy) author, Jonathan Bousfield, has travelled the length and breadth of Croatia to bring you some unique travel experiences. Here are some of his personal favourites.

Offbeat attractions Discover why Croatia is at the forefront of Balkan arts and culture with trips to the Museum of Broken Relationships (p.66), Krapina's Neanderthal Museum (p.104) and Zadar's *Greeting to the Sun* (p.249).

Classic journeys To experience unforgettable landscapes hike up the Velika Paklenica gorge (p.226), cycle the Parenzana trail through inland Istria (p.174), or weave your way through the Elaphite islands on the Dubrovnik–Lopud–Šipan ferry (p.421).

Amazing views The Adriatic is so full of them that it's difficult to make a choice, although the maritime panoramas offered by Vis's Mount Hum (p.364), Orebić's Franciscan Monastery (p.380) and Dubrovnik's Mount Srđ have few equals (p.406).

Car-free islands Enjoy a traffic-free paradise on islands like sandy Susak (p.213), sleepy Zlarin (p.274) or snoozy Silba (p.259) – where even bicycles are banned.

Deli delights Stock up on olive oil in Vela Luka (p.374), biscuits and sweets in Korčula (p.371) and fruity preserves in Šolta (p.331).

Boutique festivals Hobnob with the literary set at Zagreb's Festival of the European Short Story (p.91), watch cartoons in the open air at the Supertoon Animation Festival (p.339), or rock in an abandoned paper factory at Hartera (p.197).

Adriatic icons Share a pint with James Joyce in Pula (p.145), go skinny dipping with Edward and Mrs Simpson on Rab (p.230) and talk movies with Orson Welles in Split (p.298).

Croatian wine Sip medium-dry whites in Ilok (p.134), knock back rich fruity reds on Hvar (p.341), and taste autochthonous oddities like Grk on Korčula (p.366).

> Our author recommendations don't end here. We've flagged up our favourite places – a perfectly sited hotel, an atmospheric café, a special restaurant – throughout the guide, highlighted with the ★ symbol.

FROM TOP KRAPINA NEANDERTHAL MUSEUM; HIKING IN PAKLENICA NATIONAL PARK; GRAPE HARVEST, HVAR

Diocletian. It's also the obvious jumping-off point for some of the most enchanting of Croatia's islands. The closest of these are **Šolta** and **Brač**, where you'll find lively fishing villages and some excellent beaches, while nearby **Hvar** and **Korčula** feature smallish towns brimming with Venetian architecture and numerous beaches. The cocktail bars and beach parties of **Hvar Town** have earned the place a reputation for chic hedonism, although the rest of the island offers plenty of soothing corners. Slightly further afield, the islands of **Vis** and **Lastovo**, which were closed to tourists until the late 1980s, remain particularly pristine.

South of Split lies the walled medieval city of **Dubrovnik**, site of an important arts festival in the summer and a magical place to be whatever the season. Much of the damage inflicted on the town during the 1991–95 war has been repaired, and tourists have been quick to return. Just offshore lie the sparsely populated islands of **Koločep**,

CROATIA'S TOP FIVE BEACHES

Although there are a handful of genuinely sandy beaches in Croatia, most are pebbly or rocky affairs. Some beaches have a sandy sea floor suitable for paddling around, others are stony and uneven underfoot – so plastic sandals or swim shoes are a must. What you'll find pretty much everywhere is clean, clear water and raw Mediterranean nature – here are a few recommended places in which to enjoy them.

Susak Not so much a sandy beach as an entire sandy island, distant Susak rewards the journey with a succession of bewitching silvery-grey coves. See p.213

Kraljičina plaža, **Nin** One of Croatia's few sweeping sandy beaches, in a beautiful location. See p.258

Zlatni rat, Brač Very much the poster boy of Dalmatian beaches, with a long tongue of shingle extending into a turquoise sea. See p.339

Proizd A sequence of sloping stone-slab beaches on a compact unspoiled islet off Korčula. See p.376

Kupari, Župa Dubrovačka The derelict hotels of a deserted resort form the surreal backdrop to this sublime crescent of smooth pebbles. See p.416

ABOVE ZLATNI RAT

Lopud and **Šipan** – oases of rural calm only a short ferry ride away from Dubrovnik's tourist bustle. Also reachable from Dubrovnik is one of the Adriatic's most beautiful islands, the densely forested and relaxingly serene **Mljet**.

When to go

Croatia's climate follows two patterns: **Mediterranean** on the coast, with warm summers and mild winters, and **continental** inland – slightly hotter during the summer, and extremely cold in winter, with average daily temperatures barely scraping freezing from December to February. **July and August** constitute the peak season on the Adriatic, and this is definitely the time to visit if busy beaches and lively café society are what you're looking for. Many Croats make their way to the coast at this time, and social and cultural activity in the inland cities tends to dry up as a result. Peak-season daytime temperatures can be roasting, however, both on the coast and inland, and dawn-to-dusk sightseeing can be a gruelling experience. Hotel accommodation soon fills up at the height of summer, and it may be more relaxing to travel in **June** or **September**, when there is significantly less pressure on facilities. From October to May the coast can be very quiet indeed, and many hotels and tourist attractions may well shut up shop for the winter. **Autumn** is a good time to enjoy inland Istria and national park areas like the Plitvice Lakes and the River Krka, when the woodland colours produced by the mixture of deciduous and evergreen trees are at their best. Given the innocuous **winters** on the Adriatic coast, urban sightseeing in historic centres such as Zadar, Split and Dubrovnik can be enjoyable at this time, and it's also worth bearing in mind that hotel prices on the Adriatic may be up to fifty percent cheaper than in peak season. Winters inland are a different kettle of fish entirely: snow is common here over this period, and transport in highland areas is frequently disrupted as a result – though it can also be a picturesque backdrop to sightseeing. **Spring** is well into its stride by mid-March: warm, dry weather makes this a great time to go cycling, hiking or touring the cultural sights, and in southern Dalmatia the sea might be warm enough to swim in by mid- to late May.

AVERAGE TEMPERATURES

	Jan	Feb	March	April	May	June	July	Aug	Sept	Oct	Nov	Dec
DUBROVNIK												
°C	8.3	9.1	11.2	13.9	17.8	22.2	25.6	25.0	22.3	17.8	12.9	10.2
°F	46.9	48.4	52.2	57	64	72	78.1	77	72	64	55.2	50.4
SPLIT												
°C	7.5	8.5	11.5	12.8	18.9	23.9	26.7	26.1	22.8	16.7	12.5	9.5
°F	45.5	47.3	52.7	54.7	66	75	80.1	79	73	62.1	54.5	45.1
ZAGREB												
°C	0	1.2	5.5	11	16	18.7	22.3	21.8	15.6	12.3	5.4	2.3
°F	32	34.2	41.9	51.8	60.8	65.7	72.1	71.2	60.1	54.1	41.7	36.1

25

things not to miss

It's not possible to see everything Croatia has to offer in one trip – and we don't suggest you try. What follows is a selective take on the country's highlights, from unspoiled islands to buzzing festivals. Each entry has a page reference to take you straight into the Guide, where you can discover more.

1

1 SUNSETS IN ZADAR

Page 249

Alfred Hitchcock raved about them, and you will be bowled over too, especially now sunsets in Zadar are accompanied by the complimentary sound-and-light effects of the famous *Greeting to the Sun* and *Sea Organ* art installations.

2 WALKING DUBROVNIK'S WALLS

Page 391

The briefest of trots round the battlements will serve as a breathtaking introduction to this ancient city.

3 PLITVICE LAKES NATIONAL PARK

Page 114

A bewitching sequence of foaming waterfalls and turquoise lakes, hemmed in by forest-clad hills.

3

4

4 KORNATI ISLANDS
Page 265

Largely uninhabited and with tourist facilities limited to a handful of shoreline restaurants and the odd yachting berth, the Kornati represent the Adriatic at its most untouched.

5 MUSEUM OF BROKEN RELATIONSHIPS
Page 66

This mould-breaking museum of the human emotions is witty, well designed and wryly philosophical at the same time.

6 PEKA
Page 244

Slow-roasting lamb, octopus or other local goodies under the ember-covered metal lid known as a *peka* is the traditional route to a deliciously succulent meal.

7 WALKING THE PREMUŽIĆ TRAIL
Page 223

Croatia's most exhilarating long-distance hiking route takes in mountain ridges, dense forests and awesome views.

8 ROVINJ
Page 156

Riviera-town chic collides with fishing-port charm in the most Italianate of Istria's coastal resorts.

9 VARAŽDIN
Page 105

A postcard-perfect Baroque town, complete with opulent squares, crumbling palaces and a unique garden cemetery.

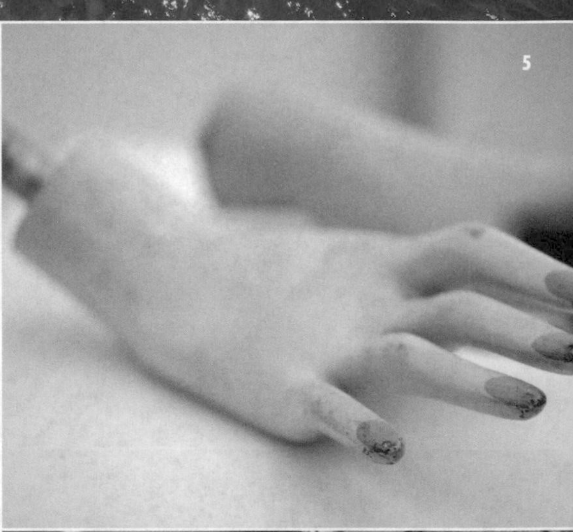
5

6

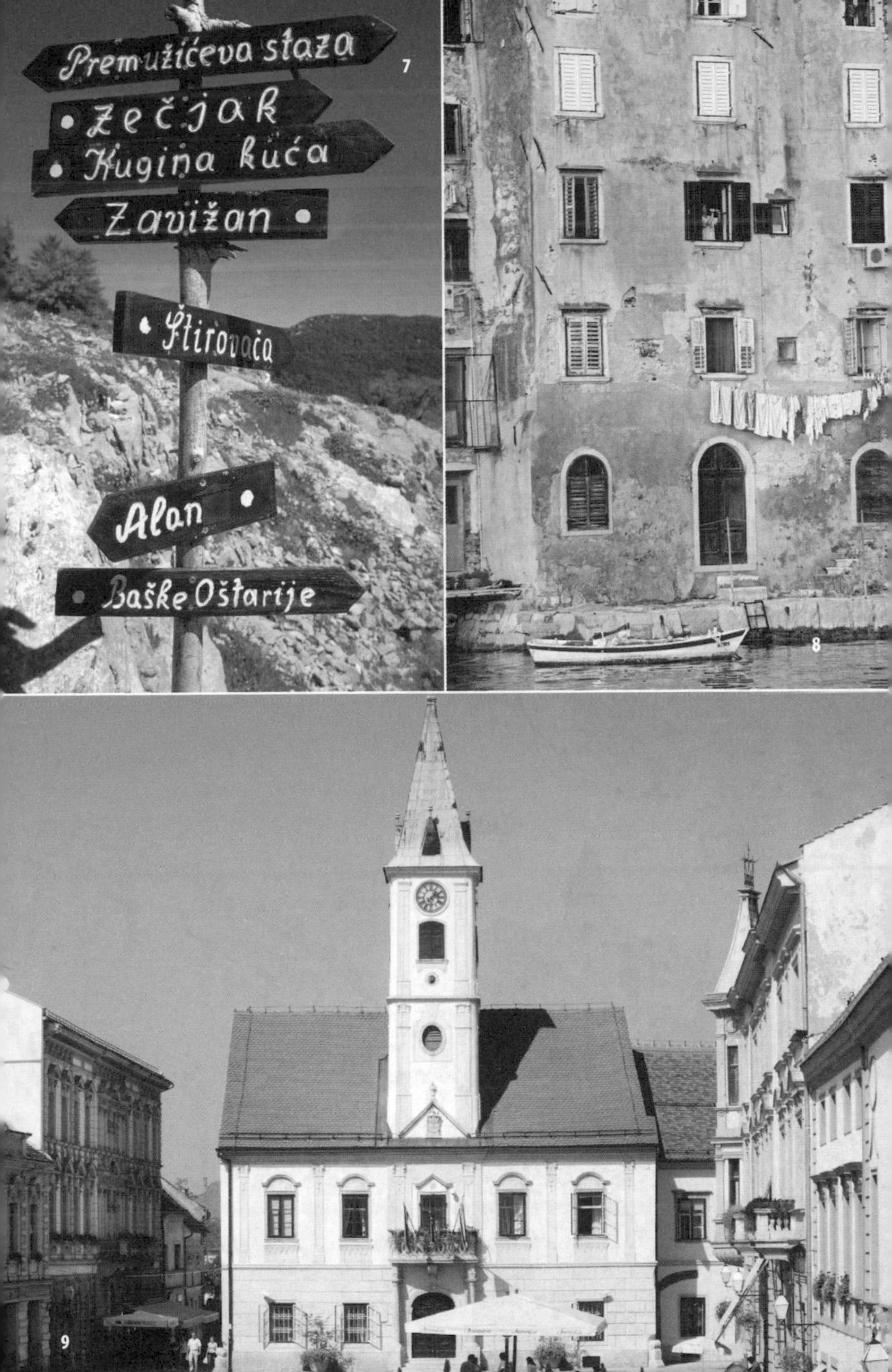
Premužićeva staza
Zečjak
Kugina kuća
Zavižan
Štirovača
Alan
Baške Oštarije
7
8
9

10

11

12

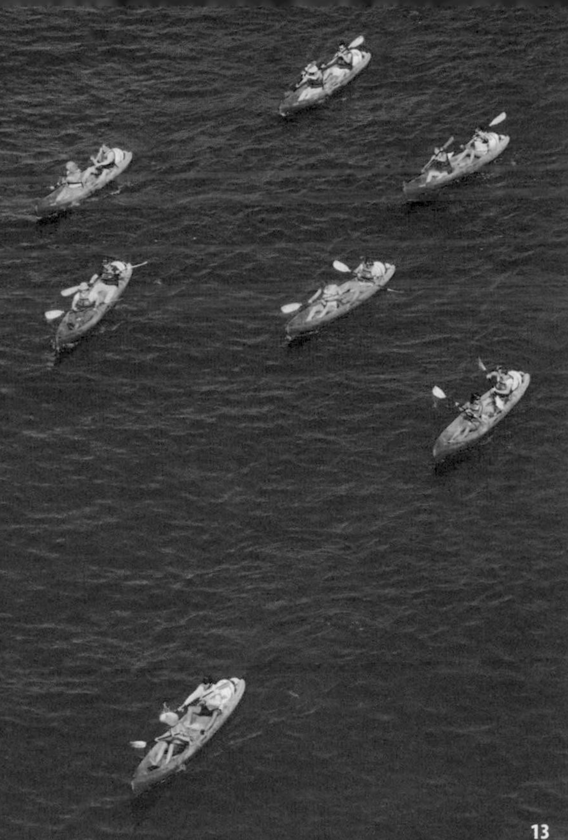

13

10 SCALING MOUNT SRĐ
Page 406

Whether you walk, cycle or take the cable car, Dubrovnik's very own neighbourhood mountain offers stupendous coastal views.

11 THE ELAPHITE ISLANDS
Page 421

These easy-to-explore, largely car-free islands offer great hiking, sandy beaches and plenty of peace and quiet.

12 PULA AMPHITHEATRE
Page 142

Imperial Rome's greatest gift to the eastern Adriatic, this awesome arena still serves as the venue for pack-'em-in summertime concerts.

13 SEA KAYAKING
Pages 48 & 394

The Dalmatian coast is often best enjoyed from the water, and what better way to see it than by taking a leisurely paddle.

14 TRUFFLE DAYS, ISTRIA
Page 178

The start of the truffle-hunting season is marked by festivities throughout Istria in September – especially in Buzet, where the world's largest truffle omelette is eagerly scoffed by an army of celebrants.

14

15 PELJEŠAC PENINSULA

Page 379

Explore rugged mountain scenery, quiet coves and unspoilt seaside villages in a region renowned for its robust red wines and fantastic seafood.

16 RAKIJA

Page 42

There's nothing like a shot of *rakija* (grape brandy) to oil the wheels of social intercourse. Try herb-infused *travarica* or carob-flavoured *rogačica* for a truly heart- and soul-warming experience.

17 MUSEUM OF CONTEMPORARY ART, ZAGREB

Page 79

Always a hotbed of cutting-edge culture, Zagreb has burst confidently onto the European arts map with this exciting new building.

18 STARI GRAD

Page 349

Stone houses and Renaissance palaces help make this as restful a spot as you will find on the Dalmatian coast.

19 ČIGOĆ

Page 118

This bucolic timber-built village in the Lonjsko polje wetlands is the famed nesting-ground of white storks.

20 HVAR: THE TOWN

Page 342

The swankiest resort on the Adriatic is full of temptations, whether you're a culture vulture, Mediterranean foodie or cocktail-bar cruiser.

17

18

19

20

21 HVAR: THE ISLAND
Page 341

Beautifully unspoiled and pitted with a wealth of bays and coves, the island of Hvar still has what it takes to enchant the seclusion-seeker.

22 SUMMER FESTIVALS
Page 45

Pretty much every genre of music is catered for in Croatia's summer-long festival calendar, with indie rock at Terraneo (pictured), cutting-edge dance music at Garden Tisno and dub-to-dubstep extravaganzas at Outlook, near Pula.

23 SKRADINSKI BUK
Page 277

Head for Krka National Park to admire this stunning series of waterfalls. Don't forget to take your bathing costume.

24 DIOCLETIAN'S PALACE, SPLIT
Page 286

Taken over by the townsfolk centuries ago, the Roman emperor's pied-à-terre now forms the chaotic heart of the modern city.

25 TRSTENO
Page 415

Relax in Renaissance gardens in this beautiful coastal village just north of Dubrovnik.

22

23
24
25

Itineraries

These three itineraries will give you a taste of Croatia's variety and diversity. Our Grand Tour concentrates on the country's historic cities and the most rewarding of its Adriatic locations. The other tours focus on aspects of Croatia that are increasingly important to the country's appeal – get-away-from it all islands and quality culinary treats. The Grand Tour will easily take up two weeks, while the other two could each be squeezed into a ten-day trip – although you may well be tempted to lounge around for longer.

GRAND TOUR

❶ **Dubrovnik** Every bit as beautiful as the brochures say it is, Dubrovnik is the obvious place to begin or end your travels. It's choked with trippers during the day – save yourself for the evenings and early mornings and let the town work its magic. **See p.386**

❷ **Korčula** An obvious next stop from Dubrovnik, Korčula is a green island studded with pebbly coves and sandy bays; a reputation for good wines and rustic cuisine ensures there's lots to enjoy. **See p.365**

❸ **Hvar** A rising jet-set reputation is yet to dent Hvar's essential charm, and it remains southern Dalmatia's all-round best-of-everything island. Get set for historic towns, unspoiled beaches and the Adriatic's best nightlife. **See p.341**

❹ **Split** A play-hard Riviera town built on top of a Roman palace, Split is more than just the main gateway to the south Dalmatian islands. **See p.282**

❺ **Zadar** An obvious stopover on any coastal trip, the main city of northern Dalmatia is oozing with both history and contemporary style. **See p.244**

❻ **Pula** Scattered with Roman-era oddities, including one of the best-preserved amphitheatres in the Mediterranean, Istria's self-possessed port city never feels like a resort. **See p.142**

❼ **Rovinj** A pretty peninsula town of sloping alleys, Venetian architecture and outstanding seafood, Rovinj is the most laid back and chic of the settlements along the tourist-thronged Istrian coast. **See p.156**

❽ **Zagreb** Croatia's understated capital's combination of café society, contemporary art and cultural energy more than merits the trip inland. **See p.56**

❾ **Plitvice Lakes** The sequence of lakes and waterfalls that make up Croatia's most publicized national park is truly stunning; it's an essential journey-breaker between Zagreb and the coast. **See p.114**

A FOODIE'S TOUR

❶ **Baranja** In the flatlands of eastern Croatia paprika is king; the region's signature dish is *fiš paprikaš* – freshwater fish cooked up in a cauldron of spicy red liquid. **See p.126**

❷ **Zagreb** The capital is home to the best of Croatia's new gastro-bistro culture, with a clutch of small, affordable and creative restaurants leading the way. **See p.84**

ABOVE TRADITIONAL DANCERS, ZAGREB; FIŠ PAPRIKAŠ, OSIJEK; WATERFALL, PLITVICE

❸ **Inland Istria** Good home cooking is very much the rule in inland Istria. Local truffles grated sparingly over home-made pasta are the standard treat, and outstanding wines provide the icing on the cake. **See p.169**

❹ **Volosko** Some of the Adriatic's best restaurants are squeezed into this seaside village, with freshly caught fish and delicious local scampi the stand-out choices. **See p.201**

❺ **Skradin** Located where the Krka river meets the Adriatic, Skradin offers the best of both coastal and inland Dalmatian cuisine, with a mouth-watering array of unique local recipes. **See p.276**

❻ **Mali Ston** There's something special about eating oysters and mussels mere metres away from where they were harvested, and Mali Ston is the best place to do it. Red wines from nearby Pelješac vineyards are irresistible. **See p.382**

IDYLLIC ISLANDS

❶ **Silba** A ferry ride from Zadar, Silba has no cars and no hotels – just a sleepy village linked to scattered beaches by a network of country lanes. **See p.259**

❷ **Murter and the Kornati** Slow-paced Murter is a great place to chill out, and is the obvious departure point for the Kornati archipelago, a maritime national park that can only be visited by boat. **See p.263**

❸ **Šolta** Despite being the nearest island to Split, Šolta remains totally absent from the package-tourist map. The cute harbour village of Maslinica is the place to wind down. **See p.331**

❹ **Hvar** Hvar has a well-deserved reputation for hedonism but still provides plenty of places for a quiet getaway: head for Stari Grad for a taste of seaside life without the nightclubs. **See p.349**

❺ **Vis** A magnet for independent travellers and lotus-eating Zagreb folk, Vis combines unspoiled beauty with seriously good restaurants and a discreet beach-party vibe. **See p.357**

❻ **Mljet** Most people visit this national-park island as a day-trip from Dubrovnik, and miss out on the benefits of a longer visit: village accommodation, nature walks and a multitude of quiet bays. **See p.425**

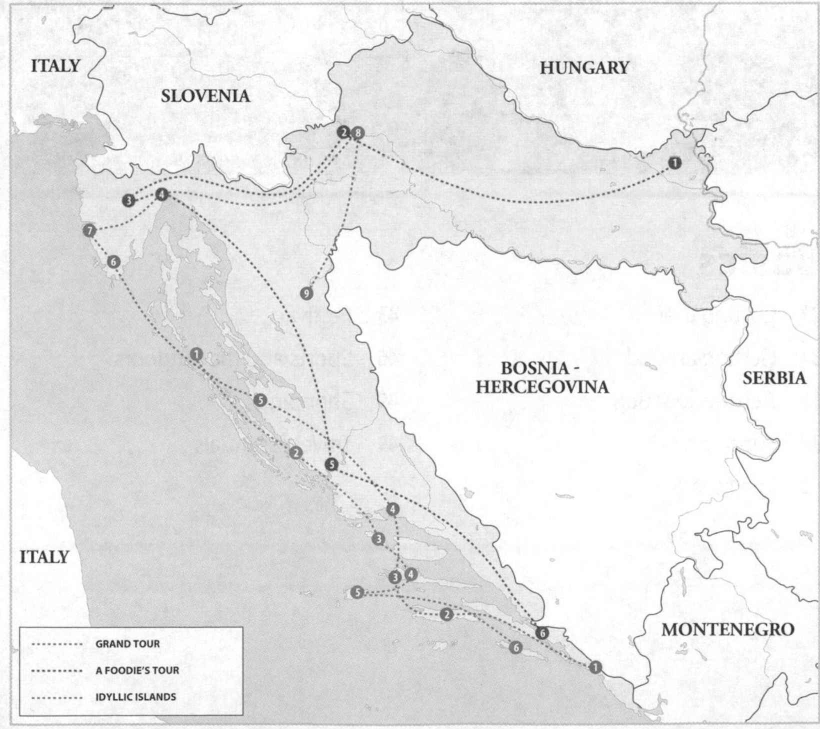

TRAM, ZAGREB

Basics

Getting there

The easiest way to get to Croatia is by air, and during the summer season most parts of the country are accessible by flights from the UK and Ireland. Though there are a few direct flights to Croatia from outside Europe fares can be expensive; a cheaper option may be to fly to a major Western European city and continue by air, train or bus from there.

Airfares always depend on the **season**. Peak times for flights to Croatia are between May and September, and around the Easter and Christmas holidays; at these times be prepared to book well in advance. Fares drop during the "shoulder" seasons (April and October), and you'll usually get the best prices during the low season (Nov–March, excluding Easter and Christmas). Many of Croatia's cities are served by **budget airlines**, although flights may be limited to the summer tourist season (May–Sept). The best deals are usually to be found by booking through discount travel websites or the websites of the airlines themselves.

You may sometimes find it cheaper to pick up a bargain **package deal** from a tour operator (see p.29). The main advantage of package holidays is that hotel accommodation is much cheaper than if you arrange things independently, bringing mid-range hotels well within reach and making stays in even quite snazzy establishments a fraction of the price paid by walk-in guests. The season for Adriatic packages runs from April to October; city breaks in Zagreb and Dubrovnik are available all the year round. Croatia is also the venue for an increasing number of **maritime packages** – ranging from sailing courses for beginners to boat charter for the experienced (see p.29).

Flights from the UK and Ireland

Flying from the UK to Croatia takes between two hours fifteen minutes and two hours forty-five minutes. Direct **scheduled flights** are operated by Croatia Airlines, which flies from London Heathrow to Zagreb, and British Airways, who run year-round direct flights from London Gatwick to Dubrovnik and London Heathrow to Zagreb. EasyJet operates from London Gatwick to Zagreb throughout the year, while seasonal (usually May–Oct) services run by Wizzair, easyJet, Jet2 and Ryanair) fly to Dubrovnik, Split, Zadar, Rijeka and Pula from a wide range of UK airports. Travelling **from Ireland**, Aer Lingus fly from Dublin to Dubrovnik, while Jet2 fly to Dubrovnik from Belfast.

Expect to pay around £150 return low season, £220–280 return high season if travelling with Croatia Airlines or British Airways, although bear in mind that prices rise drastically if you don't book well in advance. Tickets with budget carriers can be significantly cheaper – again, you have to book well in advance to take advantage of the lowest fares.

Package deals

The widest range of **package deals** is offered by Croatia specialists (see "Travel agents and tour operators"; p.29), who can put together customized flight-plus-accommodation deals; in high season (June–Sept) expect to pay from around £650 for a week, and from £800 for two weeks. As for **city breaks**, a three-day stay in Zagreb or Dubrovnik will cost £400–500 per person depending on which grade of hotel you choose. A few specialist operators offer **naturist holidays** in the self-contained mega-resorts of Istria.

Motorsailer cruises in Dalmatia start at around £620 for seven days. To learn the rudiments of **sailing**, you can arrange a one-week beginner's course – prices start at about £660 per person. The cheapest seven-day holiday in an eight-berth yacht is typically around £550–650 per person (rising to £750–850 in a two-berth yacht), depending on the season. Prices rise steeply for fancier yachts. You won't be able to charter a smallish three- to four-berth bareboat yacht for much under £700 per week, while prices for larger craft can run into thousands; a skipper will cost upwards of £120 a day extra.

A BETTER KIND OF TRAVEL

At Rough Guides we are passionately committed to travel. We believe it helps us understand the world we live in and the people we share it with – and of course tourism is vital to many developing economies. But the scale of modern tourism has also damaged some places irreparably, and climate change is accelerated by most forms of transport, especially flying. All Rough Guides' flights are carbon-offset, and every year we donate money to a variety of environmental charities.

Flights from the US and Canada

There are currently no direct flights from North America to Croatia, though most major airlines offer one- or two-stop flights via the bigger European cities, often in conjunction with Croatia Airlines, the national carrier. **From the US**, a midweek round-trip fare to Zagreb in low season starts at US$750 from New York (US$1200 from US West Coast cities), rising to US$1300 (US$1800 from the West Coast) during high season. **From Canada**, round-trip fares start at Can$1450 from Toronto and Can$1900 from Vancouver during the low season, rising to Can$1800 and Can$2300 respectively during high season. Note that the above prices are for tickets bought from airlines directly, and the pricing varies hugely depending on the route and the carrier combination; discount agencies usually have lower fares.

Specialist travel agents such as TravelTime (see p.30) offer air-inclusive **independent packages**. Expect to pay about US$1100 for eight days in Dubrovnik or Dalmatia in low season, $1650 in high season. There are also several North American tour operators offering escorted and independent tours and activity holidays to Croatia (see opposite) – a number of which also include Slovenia in their itinerary.

If you're planning to visit Croatia as part of a wider trip across Europe, you may want to get the cheapest transatlantic flight you can find, and continue your journey overland – in which case it's worth considering a **Eurail pass** for train travel (see p.30).

Flights from Australia and New Zealand

Flying to Croatia **from Australia and New Zealand** with major airlines usually involves two stops en route and can work out quite expensive – fares hover around the Aus$2800 mark from Australia, NZ$3400 from New Zealand. It probably makes far more sense to aim for a big European city such as London or Frankurt and then travel on to Croatia on a local budget airline. This can work out quite cheaply if booked well in advance over the internet.

A small number of **package-tour operators** offer holidays in Croatia from Australia and New Zealand, including accommodation, cruises along the Dalmatian coast, sightseeing packages and rail passes (see p.30).

Flights from South Africa

There are no direct flights to Croatia **from South Africa**, but plenty of airlines offer one-stop flights via European hubs such as London, Frankfurt or Paris. Flying with an airline such as Lufthansa from Johannesburg to Zagreb via Frankfurt costs around ZAR9200 in low season, ZAR10,720 in high season, and takes around eighteen hours. Flying to Split or Dubrovnik usually involves one more stop and costs ZAR1500–2500 extra.

AIRLINES

Aer Lingus Ⓦ aerlingus.com. Direct flights from Dublin to Dubrovnik.

Air Canada Ⓦ aircanada.com. Flights from Canadian airports to Zagreb, with a change of airline in Frankfurt or Munich.

Air New Zealand Ⓦ airnewzealand.co.nz. Flights from New Zealand to major European cities.

American Airlines Ⓦ aa.com. Flights from North America to European cities.

Austrian Airlines Ⓦ aua.com. Flights from New York to Zagreb with a change of plane in Vienna.

British Airways Ⓦ britishairways.com. Direct flights from London to Dubrovnik and Zagreb.

Cathay Pacific Ⓦ cathaypacific.com. Flights from Australasia to Hong Kong, with onward connections to major European hubs, then Croatia.

Continental Airlines Ⓦ continental.com. Flights from North America to Zagreb with a change in Frankfurt.

Croatia Airlines Ⓦ croatiaairlines.com. Direct flights from London to Zagreb, with onward connections to Dubrovnik, Rijeka, Split and Zadar.

CSA (Czech Airlines) Ⓦ czechairlines.com. Flights from North America to Prague with onward connections to Zagreb.

Delta Ⓦ delta.com. One- and two-stop flights from North America to Zagreb involving Delta and a partner airline.

easyJet Ⓦ easyjet.com. Year-round flights from London Gatwick to Zagreb, and summer-season flights from Edinburgh, London Gatwick and London Stansted to Dubrovnik, and from Bristol and London Stansted to Split. Also operates flights to Dubrovnik from Berlin, Geneva, Madrid, Milan and Paris.

Flyglobespan Ⓦ flyglobespan.com. Seasonal flights from Aberdeen to Dubrovnik.

Germanwings Ⓦ germanwings.com. Flights to Dubrovnik, Pula, Zadar and Zagreb from Berlin and several other German cities..

Jet2 Ⓦ jet2.com. Seasonal flights to Dubrovnik from Belfast, Edinburgh, Leeds-Bradford and Manchester.

Lufthansa Ⓦ lufthansa.com. Flights from Australia, Canada and the USA to Frankfurt, with onward connections to Dubrovnik and Zagreb.

Northwest/KLM Ⓦ nwa.com. Flights from several North American cities to Croatia, with a stop-off in Amsterdam.

Qantas Airways Ⓦ qantas.com. Flights from Australia to a European hub with onward connections to Croatia.

Ryanair Ⓦ ryanair.com. Seasonal flights to Pula, Rijeka and Zadar from London Stansted.

South African Airways Ⓦ flysaa.com. Flights from Cape Town and Johannesburg to Frankfurt and London Heathrow.

United Airlines Ⓦ united.com. One-stop flights from North America to Croatia, changing planes in a European hub such as Frankfurt.

Virgin Atlantic Ⓦ **virgin-atlantic.com.** Flights to London from North America, Australia and South Africa.

Wizzair Ⓦ **wizzair.com.** Seasonal flights from London Luton to Split.

TRAVEL AGENTS AND TOUR OPERATORS

Adriatic Travel US Ⓣ **1 310 548 1446,** Ⓦ **adriatictours.com.** Croatian travel specialists offering escorted tours, pilgrimages and activity holidays.

Adriatica.net UK Ⓣ **020 7183 0437, Croatia** Ⓣ **00 385 1 241 5611;** Ⓦ **adriatica.net.** Enormous range of accommodation-only deals and activity holidays throughout the country, from Croatia's biggest travel agent.

Adventure World Australia Ⓣ **1300 295 049,** Ⓦ **adventureworld.com.au.** Accommodation, sailing, hiking tours and more.

Affair Travel UK Ⓣ **020 7616 9990,** Ⓦ **affairtravel.com.** Accommodation in apartments and villas along the Adriatic coast.

Balkan Road Trip UK Ⓣ **0845 257 8289,** Ⓦ **balkanroadtrip.com.** Guided tours of three- to seventeen-day duration taking in Croatia/Slovenia, Croatia/Bosnia or Croatia/Bosnia/Montenegro combinations.

Concorde Ireland Ⓣ **01 775 9300,** Ⓦ **concordetravel.ie.** Holidays in Dalmatia and charter flights from Dublin and Cork from an operator with long-time Croatian experience. They also deal with accommodation, flights and car rental.

Croatia for Travellers UK Ⓣ **020 7226 4460,** Ⓦ **croatiafortravellers.co.uk.** Tailor-made packages and activity holidays using a wide range of hotel and apartment accommodation along the Adriatic coast and in Zagreb and the Plitvice Lakes.

Croatia Tours Ireland Ⓣ **01 878 0800,** Ⓦ **croatiatours.ie.** Destinations in Istria, Dalmatia and the Dubrovnik region, plus tailor-made itineraries, from a specialist operator.

Croatia Travel Agency US Ⓣ **1 800 662 7628,** Ⓦ **croatiatravel.com.** New York-based agency specializing in all things Croatian, including packages, airfare, cruises and car rental.

Croatian Villas UK Ⓣ **020 8888 6655,** Ⓦ **croatianvillas.com.** Tasteful apartments and holiday houses throughout Dalmatia and the Kvarner region, with a particularly good choice of properties in Lovran and on the island of Veli Brijun.

Discover Croatia Holidays Australia Ⓣ **1300 660 189,** Ⓦ **discovercroatia.com.au.** Dedicated specialists offering packages and tailor-made arrangements to pretty much everywhere in the country.

Eastern Eurotours Australia Ⓣ **1800 242 353,** Ⓦ **easterneurotours.com.au.** Holidays in Dubrovnik, Split and Zagreb, plus multi-centre Adriatic tours and sea cruises.

Exodus UK Ⓣ **0845 863 9600,** Ⓦ **exodus.co.uk.** Guided cultural tours, walking trips, mountain biking and cycling expeditions along the Croatian Adriatic.

Explore Worldwide UK Ⓣ **0845 291 4541, US** Ⓣ **1 800 715 1746, Canada** Ⓣ **1 888 216 3401;** Ⓦ **exploreworldwide.com.** Cultural tours, cycling, hiking and Adriatic cruises.

SAILING AND YACHTING PACKAGES

Croatia's island-scattered littoral is the perfect place for sailing and yachting, the season usually lasting from early May to early October. The most basic form of sailing holiday, for which you need no nautical experience, is a cruise in a **motorsailer** – basically a large, engine-powered yacht with simple bunk accommodation and a crew to do the work. If you already know the ropes you might consider **flotilla sailing**, in which a group of yachts with an expertly crewed lead boat embarks on a set seven- or fourteen-day itinerary. Flotilla yachts usually range from two-berth to eight-berth, so per-person prices decrease according to the size of your group. At least one of your party will have to have sailing experience – exactly how much differs from one travel company to the next.

Yacht charter can either be "bareboat" (meaning you have to sail it yourself) or "skippered" (which means you pay for the services of a local captain). Prices are subject to many variables, the most important being the model of yacht and the number of berths. For bareboat charter, at least one member of the party has to have about two years' sailing experience – again, precise requirements differ from company to company. To find out more, you can contact a specialist agency in your home country.

SAILING HOLIDAYS AND YACHT CHARTER CONTACTS

Activity Yachting UK Ⓣ **01243 641304,** Ⓦ **activityyachting.com.** Learn-to-sail packages, flotilla sailing and bareboat charter out of Murter in central Dalmatia.

Cosmos Yachting UK Ⓣ **0800 376 9070,** Ⓦ **cosmosyachting.com.** Individual yacht charter or skippered charter out of Zadar, Pula, Split, Dubrovnik and other ports.

Interpac Yachts US Ⓣ **1 619 222 0327,** Ⓦ **interpacyachtcharters.com.** Yacht-charter specialists offering customized Adriatic cruises.

Nautilus Yachting UK Ⓣ **01732 867445,** Ⓦ **nautilusyachting.com.** Learn-to-sail packages based in Murter, plus bareboat yacht and motor-yacht charter from various Dalmatian ports.

Sail Croatia Croatia Ⓣ **00 385 21 494 888,** Ⓦ **sailcroatia.net.** Skippered and bareboat charter from a wide range of Dalmatian island bases.

Sail Croatia Adventures UK Ⓣ **0845 257 8289,** Ⓦ **sail-croatia.com.** Motorcruiser tours of Dalmatia, sailing-plus-cycling combinations.

Seafarer UK Ⓣ **020 8324 3117,** Ⓦ **seafarercruises.com.** Bareboat charters and flotilla sailing based in Dalmatia.

Setsail Holidays UK Ⓣ **01787 310445,** Ⓦ **setsail.co.uk.** Bareboat charter, and two-week flotilla sailing in Dalmatia.

Gateway Australia 0612 9745 3333, Ⓦ **russian-gateway.com.au.** Flight-plus-accommodation deals, and cultural tours of the Adriatic coast.

Headwater Holidays UK Ⓣ **0845 154 5253,** Ⓦ **headwater.com.** Light walking tours taking in nature and culture in Dalmatia.

Kompas US Ⓣ **1 954 771 9200,** Ⓦ **kompas.net.** Various packages including city breaks in Dubrovnik, Split and Zagreb, yachting trips and customized tours.

Peng Travel UK Ⓣ **0800 171 2153,** Ⓦ **pengtravel.co.uk.** Naturist packages in the major Istrian naturist resorts.

Ramblers Holidays UK Ⓣ **01707 331133,** Ⓦ **ramblersholidays .co.uk.** Cultural tours with a bit of easy walking, centring on Split and Dubrovnik.

Road Scholar US Ⓣ **1 800 454 5768,** Ⓦ **roadscholar.org.** Specialists in educational and activity programmes, cruises and homestays for senior travellers, including Croatia, Hungary and Slovenia combo packages.

Simply Travel UK Ⓣ **0871 231 4050,** Ⓦ **simplytravel.co.uk.** Upmarket tour company specializing in charming villas and hotels in the less touristy parts of Croatia.

Skedaddle UK Ⓣ **0191 265 1110,** Ⓦ **skedaddle.co.uk.** Biking tours in Istria, staying in rural accommodation.

TravelTime US Ⓣ **1 800 354 8728,** Ⓦ **traveltimeny.com.** The main Croatian specialist operator in the US, with a wide range of packages including guided tours, city breaks, kayaking, wine-tasting and culinary tours, plus programmes for senior citizens.

Vintage Travel UK Ⓣ **01954 261431,** Ⓦ **vintagetravel.co.uk.** Apartment holidays with small-town Istria a speciality.

Trains

Travelling to Croatia by train **from the UK** is unlikely to save money compared with flying, but can be a leisurely way of getting to the country if you plan to stop off in other parts of Europe on the way. It's certainly simpler and more cost-effective to buy a rail pass (see below), invest in an international rail timetable and plan your own itinerary than to try and purchase a rail return ticket to Croatia: most ticket agents deal exclusively with premier express services, and fares often work out more expensive than flying – a London–Zagreb return will set you back something in the region of £230–300. The high cost is at least partly explained by the fact that almost all through-tickets from London to European destinations now use Eurostar trains, rather than the (traditionally cheaper) ferries. It's still possible to travel by rail from London to the continent via ferry, but (unless you have a rail pass) you'll probably have to buy individual tickets for each stage of the journey.

There are two main London–Zagreb **rail itineraries**: the first is via Paris, Lausanne, Milan, Venice and Ljubljana; the second via Brussels, Cologne, Salzburg and Ljubljana. The total journey time on either route is around thirty hours, depending on connections – considerably longer if you cross the Channel by ferry rather than taking the Eurostar. If you're making a beeline for Dalmatia, consider heading for **Ancona** in Italy (16hr from Paris), the departure point for ferries to Zadar, Split and Stari Grad (see opposite).

Rail passes

If you're planning to visit Croatia as part of a more extensive trip around Europe, it may be worth buying a **rail pass**. Croatia is covered in the Inter-Rail pass scheme, which is available to European residents.

Inter-Rail passes can be bought through Rail Europe in the UK (see below) and come in over-26 and (cheaper) under-26 versions. They cover most European countries, including Croatia and all the countries you need to travel through in order to get there. A pass for five days' travel in a ten-day period (£225 for adults, £148 for those under 26) will just about suffice to get you to Croatia and back; although a more leisurely approach would require a pass for ten days' travel within a 22-day period (£321 and £216 respectively) or a pass for one month's continuous travel (£537 and £355). Inter-Rail passes do not include travel between Britain and the continent, although pass-holders are eligible for discounts on rail travel in the UK and on cross-Channel ferries.

Non-European residents qualify for the **Eurail Global pass**, which must be purchased before arrival in Europe from selected agents in North America, Australia and New Zealand or from Rail Europe in London. The pass allows unlimited free first-class train travel in twenty European countries, including Belgium and Germany. The pass is available in increments of fifteen days (US$800), 21 days (US$1034) and one month (US$1270). If you're under 26, you can save money with a **Eurail Global Youthpass** (second-class travel only; US$530 for fifteen days, US$830 for one month, or US$620 for ten days' travel in a two-month period). Further details of these passes can be found on Ⓦ raileurope.com.

RAIL CONTACTS

CIT World Travel Australia Ⓣ **02 9267 1255,** Ⓦ **cit.com.au.** Eurail passes.

Deutsche Bahn UK Ⓣ **0871 880 8066,** Ⓦ **bahn.com.** Timetable information and through-ticketing on European routes.

Eurostar UK Ⓣ **0843 218 6186,** Ⓦ **eurostar.com.** Passenger train from London St Pancras to Paris (2hr 15min) and Brussels (1hr 51min).

Rail Europe US Ⓣ **1 800 622 8600, Canada** Ⓣ **1 800 361 7245, UK** Ⓣ **0844 848 4064;** Ⓦ **raileurope.com.** Agents for Eurail, Inter-Rail and Eurostar.

Rail Plus Australia ⓣ 1300 555 003 or ⓣ 03 9642 8644, ⓦ **railplus.com.au.** European rail passes.
The Man in Seat 61 ⓦ **seat61.com.** Enthusiast-run site packed with information on all aspects of international rail travel. Far more reliable than many official sites.
Trainseurope UK ⓣ **0871 700 7722,** ⓦ **trainseurope.co.uk.** Inter-Rail passes and through-tickets on European routes.

By car from the UK

Driving to Croatia is straightforward. The most direct route from the UK is to follow motorways from the Belgian coast via Brussels, Cologne, Frankfurt, Stuttgart, Munich, Salzburg and Villach as far as the Slovene capital, Ljubljana, from where you can continue by ordinary road south to Rijeka on the Adriatic coast or southeast to Zagreb. An alternative approach is through France, Switzerland and Italy as far as Ancona on Italy's Adriatic coast, from where there are ferries to various points on the Dalmatian coast. Farther down towards the heel of Italy there are ferries from Bari to Dubrovnik.

Note that if you're driving on Austrian motorways you'll have to buy a vignette (a windscreen sticker available at border crossings and petrol stations; €8 for ten days, €23.40 for two months). In Slovenia you'll need to buy a vignette to drive on all but minor country roads (€15 for one week, €30 for one month).

By bus from the UK

The bus journey from London to Zagreb (changing in Frankfurt) takes 34–38 hours and is slightly cheaper than the train, with a return costing £160 (£140 for under-26s and seniors).

BUS CONTACT

Eurolines UK ⓣ **0871 781 8181,** Ireland ⓣ **01 836 6111;** ⓦ **eurolines.co.uk.**

By ferry from Italy

Seasonal ferry services (usually spring to late autumn) run from Ancona to Split, Stari Grad and Zadar; and from Bari to Dubrovnik. passengers can usually buy tickets on arrival at the relevant ferry port, but if you're travelling with a vehicle it's wise to book in advance, especially in July and August. Services to Split and Dubrovnik usually take eight to twelve hours; services to Zadar slightly less.

From northern Italy, **Venezia Lines** serve Mali Lošinj, Poreč, Pula and Rovinj from Venice; while **Emilia Romagna Lines** operate passenger-only services from Cesenatico, Pesaro and Ravenna to Mali Lošinj, Rovinj and Zadar.

Simple deck passage from Ancona or Bari to Croatian ports costs about €65–70, but as most crossings are overnight, consider investing an additional €30 for a bed in a basic cabin. Pushbikes are free, motorcycles cost about €45, cars €85. Return tickets are usually twenty percent cheaper than two singles.

FERRY CONTACTS

Blue Line ⓣ **00 45 3672 2001,** ⓦ **blueline-ferries.com.** Italy–Croatia ferries (Ancona–Split, Ancona–Stari Grad and Ancona–Vis).
Direct Ferries UK ⓣ **0871 890 0900,** ⓦ **directferries.co.uk.** Online booking for Italy–Croatia ferries.
Emilia Romagna Lines Italy ⓣ **00 39 547 675 157,** ⓦ **emiliaromagnalines.it.** Passenger ferries (summer only; from Cesenatico, Pesaro and Ravenna to Mali Lošinj, Rovinj and Zadar).
Jadrolinija Croatia (Split) ⓣ **00 385 21 338 333,** Italy (Ancona) ⓣ **00 39 071 204 305;** ⓦ **jadrolinija.hr.** Italy–Croatia ferries (Ancona–Split, Ancona–Stari Grad, Ancona–Zadar and Bari–Dubrovnik).
SNAV Italy ⓣ **00 39 712 076 116,** ⓦ **snav.it.** Ancona–Split ferries.
Split Tours Croatia ⓣ **00 385 21 352 533,** ⓦ **splittours.hr.** Croatian agents for Blue Line.
Venezia Lines Italy ⓣ **00 39 418 821 101,** Croatia ⓣ **00 385 52 422 896;** ⓦ **venezialines.com.** Italy–Croatia ferries (summer only; Venice to Mali Lošinj, Poreč, Pula and Rovinj).
Viamare UK ⓣ **020 8206 3420,** ⓦ **viamare.com.** UK agent for SNAV, Jadrolinija and other Italy–Croatia ferries.

Getting around

Croatia's indented coastline and mountainous topography conspire to make travel a scenic but sometimes time-consuming experience, although a growing network of toll motorways has sped up journey times for drivers. Croatia's train system covers the north and east pretty well, but is little use on the coast, where the country's extensive and reliable bus network comes into its own. As well as providing the only route to the islands, ferries offer a leisurely way of getting up and down the coast, and island-hopping by boat offers some of the most memorable journeys Croatia has to offer.

By train

Croatian Railways (Hrvatske željeznice; ⓦ hznet.hr) run a reasonably efficient service, and it is slightly cheaper than using buses in those areas where routes overlap, though trains are usually both slower and less frequent than buses. A single Zagreb–Split ticket will cost around 180Kn. Around Zagreb and in the north the network is pretty dense, and you can use trains to visit most places of interest in inland Croatia. Trains also run from Zagreb to Rijeka and Split on the Adriatic, though there are no rail lines running up and down the coast. Both **Inter-Rail and Eurail passes** are valid for Croatia (see p.30).

There are two types of train (*vlak*, plural *vlakovi*): **putnički**, slow ones which stop at every halt, and **IC**, inter-city trains which are faster and more expensive. **Tickets** (*karte*) are bought from the ticket counter at the station (*kolodvor*) before boarding; those bought from the conductor on the train are subject to a surcharge unless you've joined the train at an insignificant halt that doesn't have a ticket counter. On some inter-city routes, buying a return ticket (*povratna karta*) is cheaper than buying two singles (*karta u jednom pravcu*), although it often makes no difference. Seat reservations (*rezervacije*) are obligatory on some inter-city services. The only journey on which **sleeping car** (*spalnica*) or couchette (*kušet*) accommodation is available is the overnight service between Zagreb and Split.

Timetables (*vozni red* or *red vožnje*) are usually displayed on boards in station departure halls – *polasci* or *odlasci* are departures, *dolasci* are arrivals. Timetable information on the German **bahn.com** website is far clearer than that on Croatian Railways' own site.

By bus

Croatia's **bus network** is run by an array of different companies, but services are well integrated and bus stations are generally well organized, with clearly listed departure times and efficient booking facilities. Buses (*autobusi*) operating inter-city services are usually modern air-conditioned coaches, and travelling long distances is rarely uncomfortable; stops of ten minutes or more are made every ninety minutes or so. The buses operating shorter routes on the islands or in the provinces are more likely to be ageing and uncomfortable vehicles which can get unbearably stuffy in summer – but you're unlikely to be spending a long time in them.

There are few places in the country that you can't get to by bus, and departures on the principal routes (Zagreb to the coast, and routes up and down the coast) are usually hourly. Rural areas, however, may only be served by one or two buses a day, and maybe none at all at weekends. Out in the sticks, the bus timetable is much more likely to correspond to the needs of the locals: there'll be a flurry of departures in the early morning to get people to work, school or market, and a flurry of departures in mid-afternoon to bring them back again, but nothing in between.

Tickets and fares

If you're at a big city bus station, **tickets** must be obtained from ticket windows before boarding the bus, and will bear the departure time (*vrijeme polaska*), platform number (*peron*) and a seat number (*sjedalo*). Your ticket will also carry the name of the bus company you're travelling with: two different companies might be running services to the same place at around the same time. If you're not getting on at the start of the route, tickets might not go on sale until the bus actually arrives. If there's nowhere to buy a ticket, sit on the bus and wait for the conductor to sell you one. It's a good idea to buy tickets a day or two **in advance** in

CROATIA DISTANCE CHART (IN KM)

	Dubrovnik	Karlovac	Osijek	Pula	Rijeka
Dubrovnik		526	521	711	601
Karlovac	526		336	236	126
Osijek	521	336		572	462
Pula	711	236	572		110
Rijeka	609	126	462	110	
Šibenik	305	282	494	406	296
Slavonski Brod	472	246	91	482	372
Split	216	309	505	503	393
Varaždin	630	154	236	390	280
Zadar	377	232	559	334	224
Zagreb	572	56	280	292	182

summer if you can, especially for any services between Zagreb and the coast – though bear in mind that buying advance tickets from a station midway along the bus's route may not guarantee you a seat.

Fares are a little cheaper than in Western Europe, although costs differ slightly according to which company you're riding with and what part of the country you're in. Long inter-city trips like Rijeka–Zadar or Split–Dubrovnik weigh in at around 180Kn one way; Split–Zagreb will cost around 210Kn. **Return tickets** are sporadically offered by some companies on a selection of their inter-city routes – they'll work out slightly cheaper than buying two one-way fares. On bus journeys that involve a ferry crossing (such as Rijeka–Lošinj or Rijeka–Rab), the cost of the ferry will be included in the price. You'll be charged extra for rucksacks and suitcases (7–10Kn per item).

Tickets for **municipal buses** in towns and cities should usually be bought in advance from newspaper kiosks and then cancelled by punching them in the machine on board. You can buy tickets from the driver, as well, in most cases, although this might be slightly more expensive and you may have to provide the correct change.

By ferry

A multitude of **ferry services** link the Croatian mainland with the Adriatic islands. Most of them are run by **Jadrolinija** (see p.31), the main state ferry firm, although private operators are beginning to offer competition.

All ferries, apart from simple shuttle services, will have a **buffet** where you can buy a full range of drinks, although food may consist of crisps and unappetizing sandwiches, so it's best to bring your own. The main coastal ferry has a restaurant with a full range of reasonably priced food; breakfast is included if you book a cabin.

Island services

Short hops to islands **close to the mainland** – such as Brestova to Porozina on Cres, Stinica to Mišnjak on Rab, or Orebić to Domince on Korčula – are handled by simple roll-on-roll-off ferries, which either operate a shuttle service or run fairly frequently – every hour or so. Prices for foot passengers on such routes rarely exceed 20Kn (this will usually be incorporated into your fare if you're crossing by bus). A car will cost about 100Kn extra, a motorbike 40Kn.

Departures to destinations slightly **farther offshore** run to a more precise timetable. The ports offering access to the most important groups of islands are Zadar (Silba, Dugi otok), Split (Šolta, Brač, Hvar, Vis and Lastovo) and Dubrovnik (Koločep, Lopud, Šipan and Mljet). **Fares** for foot passengers are reasonable; approximate prices are: Zadar–Silba 30Kn, Split–Stari Grad 50Kn, Split–Vis 55Kn, Split–Supetar (Brač) 30Kn, Dubrovnik–Mljet 50Kn. Island-hopping with a vehicle involves much more of an outlay: travelling from Split to Stari Grad costs (on top of the passenger fare) 45Kn for a bicycle, 80Kn for a motorbike, 320Kn for a regular car, 600Kn for a large saloon car, jeep or SUV. If you're travelling without a vehicle, look out for **catamarans** linking Zadar with smaller islands like Silba and Olib, and Split with destinations on Šolta, Brač, Hvar, Korčula and Vis. Although slightly more expensive than ferries, they'll be twice as fast. Beware however that tickets for catamarans are only sold on the day of departure and can't be booked any earlier – so if you're travelling on a summer weekend go to the ticket office as early as possible.

Šibenik	Slavonski Brod	Split	Varaždin	Zadar	Zagreb
305	472	216	630	377	582
282	246	309	154	232	56
494	91	660	236	559	282
406	482	503	390	334	292
296	372	405	280	280	175
	97	436	72	338	
403		448	239	468	190
97	448		463	169	378
436	239	463		386	98
72	468	169	386		253
338	190	365	98	288	

Coastal services

Jadrolinija operates a **coastal service** from Rijeka to Dubrovnik, calling at Split, Stari Grad (Hvar) and Korčula on the way. This only runs twice a week in summer (June–Sept). Travelling from Rijeka to Dubrovnik takes twenty hours and always involves one night on the boat. Prices (often quoted in euros but payable in kuna) vary greatly according to the level of comfort you require. The cheapest Rijeka–Dubrovnik fare (which involves spending the journey either on the open deck or in smoky bar areas) is 230Kn; you'll pay double that for a couchette-style bunk bed and three times as much for a bed in a well-appointed cabin. Taking a car on the same journey will cost an extra 620Kn, a motorbike or bicycle 200Kn. Return tickets are twenty percent cheaper than the price of two singles, and prices fall by up to twenty percent in winter. Tickets are sold at offices or kiosks near the departure dock. For longer journeys, book in advance wherever possible; Jadrolinija addresses and phone numbers are given in the text where relevant.

By plane

The obvious attraction of flying is the time it saves: the plane journey from Zagreb to Dubrovnik takes an hour, compared to a whole day to get there overland. **Croatia Airlines** (Ⓦcroatiaairlines.com) operates domestic services between Zagreb and Pula (1 daily), Split (summer 4 daily; winter 3 daily), Zadar (summer 2 daily; winter 1 daily) and Dubrovnik (summer 3 daily; winter 2 daily). Between May and October there are flights (weekends only) to Bol on the island of Brač. The price of flights vary enormously according to time of year and how far in advance you are booking – Zagreb–Dubrovnik can cost as little as 350Kn if booking online, months ahead of travel; otherwise expect to pay three times this amount.

By car

Croatia's **road system** is comprehensive, but not always of good quality once you get beyond the main highways. Major additions to the motorway – **autocesta** – network in recent years ensure that it's now much easier to get across country from east to west. The main stretches run from Zagreb to Županja on the Serbian border, Zagreb to Goričan on the Hungarian border, Zagreb to Macelj on the Slovenian border, Zagreb to Rijeka, and Zagreb to Ploče (passing Zadar, Šibenik and Split on the way). Parts of the Istrian "Ipsilon", a Y-shaped network of high-speed roads, are dual carriageway, parts are single lane. The Zagreb–Ploče motorway is an exhilarating ride through karst terrain, and is due to be extended southwards to Dubrovnik in the future. All the above are subject to tolls – take a ticket as you come on and pay as you exit. The toll for a car from Zagreb to the Split exit is currently 181Kn. Elsewhere, the main routes (especially the coast-hugging **Magistrala**) are single carriageway and tend to be clogged with traffic – especially in summer, when movement up and down the coast can be time-consuming. Note that everywhere in Croatia, roads in off-the-beaten-track areas can be badly maintained.

To drive in Croatia, you'll need a driving licence, and registration documents if taking your own car. A Green Card is not required for Croatia itself but is needed for the short coastal stretch of Bosnia-Hercegovina at Neum, between Split and Dubrovnik. **Speed limits** are 50kph in built-up areas, 80kph on minor roads, 100kph on main roads, 130kph on motorways. It is illegal to drive with more than 0.5 percent alcohol in your bloodstream. Headlights should be switched on at all times between October and March. **Petrol stations** (*benzinska stanica*) are usually open daily 7am–7pm, although there are 24-hour stations in larger towns and along major international routes. If there's anything wrong with your vehicle, petrol stations are probably the best places to ask where you can find a mechanic (*automehaničar* or *majstor*) or a shop selling spare parts (*rezervni dijelovi*). A tyre repair shop is a *vulkanizer*. If you **break down**, contact the Croatian Automobile Club (HAK; Ⓦhak.hr), which has a 24-hour emergency service (Ⓣ987); their website is also a good source of **traffic news**.

Finding **parking** spaces in big cities can be a nightmare, and illegally parked vehicles will be swiftly removed by tow truck (known locally as the *pauk*, or "spider") and impounded until payment of a fine. Most cities have garages where you can leave your car for a small fee. Hotels usually have designated parking areas for their guests – some offer free parking, others charge a daily rate. Private apartments usually come with a parking space, unless they are located in the middle of a historic town, in which case available parking may be quite a walk away.

Car rental

Car rental in Croatia works out cheaply if you rent the vehicle for a reasonable period of time –

costing around 820Kn per day to 1600Kn a week for a small hatchback with unlimited mileage, depending on the season. The major rental chains have offices in all the larger cities and at Zagreb airport; addresses are detailed in the Guide. Most travel agents in Croatia will organize car rental through one of the big international firms or a local operator. It's usually cheaper if you arrange rental in advance, either through one of the agents listed below or with some of the specialist tour operators (see p.29).

CAR RENTAL AGENCIES

Avis ⓦ avis.com.
Budget ⓦ budget.com.
Europcar ⓦ europcar.com.
Hertz ⓦ hertz.com.
SIXT ⓦ sixt.com.
Uni rent ⓦ uni-rent.net.

Accommodation

There's a growing choice of accommodation in Croatia, but summer-season prices are growing too: travelling in July or August will not yield any bargains. There is an increasing number of well-equipped four- and five-star hotels but a relative shortage of boutique hotels and B&Bs. For the moment, the apartments and private rooms offered by local families represent the country's best-value accommodation. The Adriatic coast is well provided with campsites, and hostels are increasingly evident in the major centres.

Hotels

The tourism boom of the 1960s and 1970s gave Croatia an impressive number of large seaside **hotels**. Most of these have been renovated and upgraded in the last decade or so, and recent years have also witnessed the building of new, top-range hotels in key resort areas.

Croatian hotels are classified according to the international **star grading** system, although some of the grades might seem a little generous – many of Croatia's four-star hotels would only qualify for three stars in Western Europe, and so on down the scale. Generally speaking, one-star hotels (of which there are hardly any left nowadays) have rooms with shared WC and bathroom; two-star hotels (also increasingly rare) have rooms with en-suite facilities but little else; three-stars have slightly larger en-suite rooms and, most probably, a television; four-stars correspond to comfy business class, and will have plush carpets, bath tubs in most rooms and a range of other facilities (such as gym or swimming pool); and five-stars, most of which are in Zagreb or in and around Dubrovnik, are in the international luxury bracket.

There's a small number of small **family-run hotels** aiming to conquer the mid-range market, offering the comforts and level of service of a good three-star hotel but in cosy, informal surroundings and at a slightly cheaper price. They don't crop up in all parts of the country, but we've recommended them throughout the Guide wherever they exist.

In addition, a growing handful of establishments deserve the "**boutique hotel**" tag, most of which occupy restored houses and palaces on the Dalmatian coast and islands.

Seasons and prices

Croatian hotel rooms are priced according to season. In **high season** (usually July and August, although it may cover June to September in the more popular areas) prices are at their highest and standards are at their lowest – hotels are crowded at these times and the staff are overworked. **Spring and autumn** frequently offer better value for money, when prices may be 30–50 percent lower. Dubrovnik and Hvar are currently the most fashionable – and consequently most expensive – parts of the country. Many hotels on the Adriatic coast are closed from November through to April, although there is usually at least one hotel open all year round wherever you are.

In two-star establishments you can expect to pay 450–600Kn for a double in high season, but it's worth bearing in mind private rooms and studio

ACCOMMODATION PRICES

Throughout this guide we have quoted a headline price in each accommodation review. This is based on the cost of each establishment's **least expensive double room** (or two-person apartment) in high season (July and August), excluding special offers. Where single rooms exist, they usually cost 60–70 percent of the price of a double. Hotel prices almost invariably include **breakfast**.

TOP 5 UNIQUE PLACES TO STAY

Hotel Lone Rovinj. An artwork in its own right, the *Lone* is everything that modern architecture should be. See p.160

Goli & Bosi Hostel Split. The white-and-yellow decor may be too much for some, but this designer hostel-cum-B&B is very much a one-off. See p.301

Martinis Marchi Maslinica, Šolta. Baroque palace kitted out with contemporary comforts, sitting above an exquisite harbour village. See p.333

Dešković Palace Pučišća, Brač. A lovingly restored Dalmatian island retreat in a restful small town. See p.337

Lešić-Dimitri Korčula Town. Historic stone houses and modern design brought beautifully together. See p.371

apartments offer similar comforts for less money. Three-star hotels are the hardest to predict, both in terms of quality and price, and you'll pay anything from 600Kn to 1200Kn, depending on whether it's just a glorified two-star with an extra lick of paint, or a genuinely comfortable and well-managed outfit that meets international standards. Rooms in four-star hotels will normally go for around 1000–1600Kn, while a five-star will cost you 1400Kn a double and upwards.

Many of the hotels on the Adriatic also offer full-board (*pansion*) and half board (*polupansion*) deals for a few extra kuna, but bear in mind that you'll be eating bland, internationalized food in large, institutional dining rooms.

Private rooms and apartments

The vast majority of tourist accommodation in Croatia comes in the form of **private rooms** and **apartments**. They might be located in a family house where the owners still live, or in a separate building built or renovated specifically for this purpose.

Private rooms

Private room (*privatne sobe*) standards vary widely, but rooms are usually grouped into three **categories** by the tourist association in each area. Category I rooms are simple affairs furnished with a couple of beds, a wardrobe and not much else, and you'll be using your host's bathroom. Category II rooms have en-suite bathrooms, and category III rooms will probably come with TV and plusher furnishings, as well as en-suite facilities. In high season **prices** start at around 150/200/250Kn for a category I/category II/category III double in a smallish resort, rising to about 250/330/400Kn in relatively expensive places like Dubrovnik, Hvar Town and Korčula. Prices in spring and autumn can be thirty percent cheaper. Many families don't let out rooms over the winter, although local travel agencies will probably come up with something, providing you contact them a week or so in advance. Prices are subject to a 30–50 percent surcharge if you stay for fewer than three nights. **Single travellers** usually have to pay the full price of a double room.

As well as the price of the room itself, you will be charged a fee of about 10Kn to cover the cost of **registering** you with the police (see p.50), and a **residence tax** (*boravišna pristojba*) of 7–10Kn per person per night, which is the local tourist association's main source of funding.

Apartments

Apartments (*apartmani*) usually consist of a self-contained unit or floor of a house with its own kitchen and bathroom, maybe a small lounge and possibly a terrace for sitting outside. **Two-person apartments** often provide much more convenience, comfort and value for money than a double room in a hotel, and even single travellers – who will have to pay the price of a double – may find apartments favourably priced compared to bland hotel rooms. For those travelling as a family or in a group, apartments offer excellent value, providing that sleeping quarters are not too cramped – check how many beds are crammed into a single bedroom before accepting.

Two-person apartments generally cost around 350–500Kn per night in high season. Where available, four-person apartments cost around 450–800Kn, six-person apartments 600–900Kn. The higher the price, the more likely you are to get a central location, TV and a parking space, should you need it.

Finding a room

Bookings for rooms and apartments are traditionally administered by **local travel agencies**, who normally have several properties on their books. Agencies are usually very happy to take advance bookings for rooms and apartments by phone or by email, although they will probably ask you to pay a deposit by bank transfer or to provide your credit card details as a guarantee. In cases where there is no established travel agency, the local **tourist office** will help out by providing a few relevant addresses and telephone numbers, although they are unlikely to make bookings on your behalf.

An increasing number of room and apartment owners have registered their properties with well-known international **internet booking sites** – with the result that many rooms and apartments are listed as "hotels" on hotel booking sites, and as "hostels" on hostel booking sites. This is especially true of popular destinations such as Dubrovnik, where the role of the local travel agency has all but disappeared. There are no inherent risks in booking private accommodation online – providing you read the descriptions and customer reviews carefully.

If you arrive in your destination **without a reservation**, it is frequently easy to turn up a private room by asking around or looking for "sobe" or "Zimmer frei" signs posted up outside local houses. You may also be offered rooms by landladies waiting outside train, bus and ferry stations, especially in Split and Dubrovnik. Rooms obtained in this way sometimes work out significantly cheaper than the agency-approved ones, but equally leave you prone to rip-offs. There's little chance that your hosts will be passing on registration fees or tourist tax to the relevant authorities (they'll charge you for them, then pocket the cash themselves), and they may exploit your naivety by inflating these additional costs, or inventing new ones of their own. However you find a room, it's acceptable to have a look at it before committing yourself.

B&Bs, rural homestays and pensions

The development of **B&Bs** in Croatia has been held back by red tape. A lot of private-room owners are dissuaded from serving breakfast by the amount of paperwork it requires, and only a small number of people have registered their properties as B&Bs, although a much larger number of private-room owners provide breakfast facilities on an unofficial, optional basis. Surprisingly perhaps, B&B culture is most developed in the rural areas of inland Croatia (such as inland Istria, the Zagorje, the Plitvice Lakes, Lonjsko polje and the Baranja), where an increasing number of **rural homestays** offer family accommodation and locally produced food and drink. A **pension** (*pansion*) is somewhere in between a B&B and a small hotel: usually (though not always) family run, equipped with a breakfast room and maybe a reception desk.

In all of the above cases **prices** are slightly more than those in private rooms and apartments, and (naturally) include breakfast; half- or full-board arrangements featuring home-cooked food are often available for an extra cost.

TOP 5 HOMESTAYS AND B&BS

Studio Kairos Zagreb. Outstanding little B&B in a city that has been crying out for this kind of accommodation for years. See p.83

Crvendač Bilje. Cute village guesthouse a short hop from Kopački rit Nature Park. See p.127

Art Hotel Villa Ines Zadar. Charming and friendly bed and breakfast in a quiet part of town. See p.253

Fregadon Silba. Homely accommodation with attention to every comfort, above a soothing garden restaurant. See p.260

Karmen Dubrovnik. Cosy and welcoming rooms in a cosy and welcoming house in the heart of the Old Town. See p.410

Hostels

There has been a boom in backpacker-oriented accommodation in Croatia over recent years, and major centres such as Zagreb and Split now offer a wide choice of **hostels** offering dorm beds and frequently a handful of private doubles too. A double in a hostel will probably be around the same price as a double private room, except in a handful of boutique hostels (such as *Goli & Bosi* in Split) where it might be more similar in style and price to a hotel room. Be aware that many popular hostel-booking websites list an extraordinary number of establishments in Croatia that call themselves "hostels" but are really private rooms in disguise. If you want the genuine backpacker experience then it's probably a good idea to read our reviews first. Per-person prices hover between 140–200Kn in high season (June–Sept), falling to around 100–120Kn in winter.

There's also a small network of **HI-affiliated youth hostels**, run by the Croatian Hostelling Association (Hrvatski ferijalni i hostelski savez; T 01 482 9291, W hfhs.hr). Some of these are a bit old-fashioned and institutionalized in comparison to the new generation of backpacker-oriented places, but they are still habitable and friendly on the whole.

Campsites

Campsites (*autokamp*) abound on the Adriatic coast, ranging from large-scale affairs with plentiful facilities, restaurants and shops to small family-run sites squeezed into private gardens or olive groves. Check out Ⓦcamping.hr, a comprehensive resource for the best Croatian campsites. Sites are generally open from May to September and charge 30–80Kn per person, plus 30–80Kn per pitch and 30–50Kn per vehicle. Prices are significantly higher in fashionable destinations such as Dubrovnik. Electricity in the bigger sites costs a few extra kuna. Bear in mind that the stony ground of the Adriatic coast often makes it difficult to hammer in tent pegs – spare rope comes in handy to fasten your canvas home to nearby rocks and trees. **Camping rough** is illegal, and the rocky or pebbly nature of most Croatian beaches makes them uncomfortable to sleep on anyway.

Naturist campsites are a common feature of the northern Adriatic resorts, with big, self-contained complexes outside Rovinj, Poreč and Vrsar in Istria, and Krk, Baška and Punat on the island of Krk.

Food and drink

There's a varied and distinctive range of food on offer in Croatia, largely because the country straddles two culinary cultures: the seafood-dominated cuisine of the Mediterranean and the filling schnitzel-and-strudel fare of Central Europe. Drinking revolves around a solid cross-section of wines and some fiery spirits.

Main meals are eaten in a **restoran** (restaurant) or a **konoba** (tavern) – the latter is more likely to have folksy decor but essentially serves the same range of food. A **gostiona** (inn) is a more rough-and-ready version of a *restoran*. For Croatians the most important meal of the day is lunch (*ručak*) rather than dinner (*večera*), although restaurants are accustomed to foreigners who eat lightly at lunchtime and more copiously in the evening, and offer a full range of food throughout the day.

Because many Croatians eat lunch relatively late in the afternoon, restaurants frequently offer a list of **brunch-snacks** (called *marende* on the coast, *gableci* inland) between 10.30am and noon. These are usually no different from main meat and fish dishes, but come in slightly smaller portions, making an excellent low-cost midday meal. Details are often chalked up on a board outside rather than written on a menu.

No Croatian town is without at least one **pizzeria**, and most of them serve Italian-style, thin-crust pizzas made to reasonably authentic recipes, and seafood pizzas are quite a feature on the coast.

Breakfast and snacks

Unless you're staying in a private room or a campsite, **breakfast** will almost always be included in the cost of your accommodation. At its simplest it will include a couple of bread rolls, a few slices of cheese and/or salami, and some butter and jam. Mid- and top-range hotels will offer a buffet breakfast, complete with a choice of cereals, scrambled eggs and bacon. Few Croatian cafés serve breakfast of any kind, and they don't usually mind if you bring along bread buns or pastries bought from a nearby bakery and consume them alongside your coffee.

Basic **self-catering** and picnic ingredients like cheese, vegetables and fruit can be bought at a supermarket (*samoposluga*) or an open-air **market** (*tržnica*). Markets often open early (about 6am) and begin to pack up in the early afternoon, though in well-touristed areas they sometimes keep going until late evening. Bread can be bought from either a supermarket or a **bakery** (*pekara*). Small outlets may offer a simple white loaf and little else, although you'll usually be offered a wide choice of breads, ranging from French sticks (*francuski baton* or *francuz*) through to wholemeal loaves (*bio kruh*) and corn bread (*kukuruzni kruh*). You'll have to point at what you want though: names of different loaves differ from one place to the next. A *pekara* may often sell sandwiches – filled most commonly with ham, cheese or *pršut*. Most bakeries and *slastičarnice* sell traditional Balkan pastries such as *burek* (filled with minced meat or cheese), *zeljanica* (filled with spinach) or *krumpiruša* (with potato).

For a more substantial snack, try the traditional southeast European repertoire of grilled meats: *ćevapi* (rissoles of minced beef, pork or lamb), *ražnijići* (shish kebab) or *pljeskavica* (a hamburger-like

At the start of each chapter in the Guide we have included a feature box on regional food and drink, which provides a rundown of local specialities. A comprehensive list of Croatian food and drink terms is given in the Language section (see p.459).

PRŠUT

Croatia's most celebrated hors d'oeuvre is *pršut*, home-cured ham served in thin, melt-in-the-mouth slices. **Pršut** is mainly produced in inland Istria and Dalmatia, where it's common for families to own a handful of pigs. The unlucky porkers are slaughtered in late autumn, and the hind legs from which *pršut* is made are laboriously washed, salted and flattened under rocks. They are then hung outside the house to be dried out by the *bura*, a cold, dry wind that sweeps down to the coast from inland Croatia. After that, the ham is hung indoors to mature, ready to be eaten the following summer. *Pršut* from Dalmatia is usually smoked at some stage during the maturing period, while that from Istria is left as it is, producing a significant difference in flavour between the two regions' produce.

minced-meat patty), all of which are often served in a *lepinja* – a flat bread bun.

Main meals

Any list of **starters** should begin with *pršut*, Croatia's excellent home-cured ham (see box above). It's often served on a platter together with cheese: *paški sir* from the island of Pag is the most famous – a hard, piquant cheese with a taste somewhere between Parmesan and mature cheddar; *sir sa vrhnjem* (cream cheese) is a milder alternative. *Kulen*, a spicy, paprika-laced sausage from Slavonia, is another local delicacy. Soups (*juha*) are usually clear and light and served with spindly noodles, unless you opt for the thicker *krem-juha* (cream soup).

One starter that is stodgy enough to serve as a main course is **štrukli**, a pastry and cheese dish which is common to Zagreb and the Zagorje hills to the north. It comes in two forms: *kuhani* (boiled) *štrukli* are large parcels of dough filled with cottage cheese, while for *pečeni* (baked) *štrukli* the dough and cheese are baked in an earthenware dish, resulting in a cross between cheese soufflé and lasagne.

Meat dishes

Main meat dishes normally consist of a grilled or pan-fried *kotlet* (chop) or *odrezak* (fillet or escalope). These are usually either **pork** or **veal**, and can be prepared in a variety of ways: a *kotlet* or *odrezak* cooked *na žaru* will be a simple grill, *bečki odrezak* (Wiener schnitzel) comes fried in breadcrumbs, *pariški odrezak* (Pariser schnitzel) is fried in batter and *zagrebački odrezak* (Zagreb schnitzel) is stuffed with cheese and ham. *Mješano meso* (mixed grill) appears on all menus and will usually consist of a pork or veal *kotlet*, a few *ćevapi*, a *pljeskavica* and maybe a spicy *kobasica* (sausage), served alongside a bright-red aubergine and pepper relish known as *ajvar*.

Lamb is usually prepared as a spit roast. In sheep-raising regions (Cres, Rab, the hinterland of Zadar and Split) it's quite common to see roadside restaurants where a whole sheep is being roasted over an

CROATIA'S BEST RESTAURANTS: A ROUGH GUIDE TOP 20

Our Rough Guide Top 20 (arranged by area rather than by ranking order) lists the twenty most enjoyable places to eat we experienced while researching this guide, based on quality of food, value for money and general ambience. It's by no means a guide to the fanciest gastronomic addresses in Croatia, though haute cuisine – as well as good home cooking – is well represented in the list below.

Takenoko Zagreb. See p.86
Lari i Penati Zagreb. See p.86
MaliBar Zagreb. See p.86
Žar Zagreb. See p.87
Bistro Apetit Zagreb. See p.87
Tač Zagreb. See p.87
Gostiona kod Ribiča Jasenovac. See p.120
Kovač Čarda Suza. See p.129
L Rovinj. See p.161
Wine Vault Rovinj. See p.161
Plavi podrum Volosko. See p.201
Tic Tac Murter. See p.265
Noštromo Split. See p.302
Giaxa Hvar Town. See p.348
Macondo Hvar Town. See p.348
Turan Jelsa, Hvar. See p.355
Pojoda Vis Town. See p.361
Konoba Mate Pupnat. See p.374
Bota Oyster and Sushi Bar Dubrovnik. See p.411
Galija Cavtat. See p.419

VEGETARIANS IN CROATIA

Vegetarian cuisine has never been one of Croatia's strong points, but there's usually enough to choose from on restaurant menus if you look hard enough. Strict vegetarians should exercise caution however: many items that look like good vegetarian choices – the various risottos and bean soups are invariably made with fish or meat stock. Even in well-meaning restaurants, it's not uncommon to find dishes advertised as "vegetarian" that turn out to have ham or chicken in them. Yummy-looking grilled vegetables may have been cooked on the same grill as the meat dishes, so be sure to ask.

Vegetarians can however construct a handsome meal from the meat-free dishes listed as starters or side dishes. **Pastas** with various sauces, mushroom dishes and sizeable **salads** are rarely hard to find. Mushroom omelettes (*omlet sa gljiivama*) and cheese fried in breadcrumbs (*pohani sir*) are fairly ubiquitous. Italian-influenced **pizzerias** and spaghetterias are perhaps the best bet: most pizzerias offer a *pizza vegeterijanska* featuring a selection of seasonal vegetables, and there's usually a choice of meatless pasta dishes including, if you're lucky, a vegetarian lasagne. One traditional meat-free dish is the cheesy *štrukli* (see p.39) although this is a north Croatian speciality that can rarely be found on the coast.

"Ja sam vegeterijanac" (*vegeterijanka* is the female form of the noun) means "I am a vegetarian." To ask "Have you got anything which doesn't contain meat?", say "Imate li nešto bez mesa?"

open fire in the car park to tempt travellers inside. One way of preparing diced lamb that's typical of Istria and the Adriatic islands is to slow-bake it underneath a *peka* – a metal lid that is covered with hot embers.

Stewed meats are less common than grilled or baked ones, although **goulash** (*gulaš*) is frequently employed as a sauce served with pasta, and *čobanac* (a fiery red stew) is a staple of the southeast. *Grah* (or *fažol* in Dalmatia) is a delicious **soup** of paprika-spiced haricot beans (*grah* literally means "beans") with bits of sausage or *pljeskavica* added.

A main course associated with Dalmatia is *pašticada* (beef cooked in wine and prunes). The most common **poultry** dish is *purica s mlincima* (turkey with baked pasta slivers), which is indigenous to Zagreb and the Zagorje. Other meaty mains include *punjene paprike* (peppers stuffed with rice and meat) and *sarma* (cabbage leaves filled with a similar mixture). *Arambašica*, a version of *sarma* found in the Dalmatian hinterland, contains more meat and less rice.

Seafood dishes

On the coast you'll be regaled with every kind of **seafood**. Starters include *salata od hobotnice* (octopus salad) and the slightly more expensive *salata od jastoga* (nibble-size portions of lobster flesh seasoned with olive oil and herbs). **Fish** can come either *na žaru* (grilled), *u pečnici* (baked) or *lešo* (boiled). Grilling is by far the most common way of preparing freshly caught fish, which is sold by weight (the best fish starts at about 300Kn per kilo in cheap and mid-range restaurants, 400Kn per kilo in top-class establishments). Waiting staff will tell you what fish they have in stock, or will show you a tray of fish from which to choose. A decent-sized fish for one person usually weighs somewhere between a third and half a kilo, although you can always order a big fish and share it between two people. Fish dishes are invariably accompanied by *blitva* (Swiss chard), a spinach-like plant indigenous to Dalmatia, served with boiled potatoes and garlic.

Among the tastiest white fish are *kovač* (John Dory), *list* (sole), *brancin* (sea bass), *komarča* or *orada* (gilt-head sea bream) and *škrpina* (scorpion fish), although the range of fish caught in Adriatic waters is almost limitless. *Oslić* (hake) is slightly cheaper than the others, and is often served sliced and pan-fried in batter or breadcrumbs rather than grilled – when it will be priced per portion rather than by weight. Cheaper still is so-called *plava riba* (oily fish), a category that includes anchovies and mackerel. Another budget choice is *girice*, tiny fish similar to whitebait, which are deep fried and eaten whole. *Brodet* (also spelled *brudet*) is seafood stewed in red wine and spices. Two ubiquitous and inexpensive staples are *lignje na žaru* (grilled squid) and *crni rižot* ("black risotto"; made from pieces of squid with the ink included).

The more expensive or specialist establishments will have delicacies such as crab, oysters, mussels and lobster. Scampi usually come as whole prawns which you have to crack open with your fingers, rather than the sanitized, breadcrumbed variety found in northwestern Europe. They're often served with a *buzara* sauce, made from garlic and wine.

Accompaniments, salads and desserts

You'll usually be offered a choice of accompaniments with your main course: boiled potatoes, chips, rice and gnocchi are the most common. Indigenous forms of **pasta** include *fuži* in Istria (pasta dough rolled into a cylinder or folded into a twirl, and occasionally filled), *šurlice* on the island of Krk and *mlinci* in Zagreb and the Zagorje – the last are lasagne-thin scraps of dough which are boiled, then baked. Additional vegetables can be ordered as items from the menu. Croatians eat an enormous amount of **bread**, and you'll be expected to scoff a couple of large slices with your meal regardless of whatever else you order.

The most common **salads** are *zelena salata* (green salad) and *miješana salata* (mixed salad). Other popular side dishes are gherkins (*krastavci*) and pickled peppers (*paprike*).

Typical restaurant **desserts** include *sladoled* (ice cream), *torta* (cake) and *palačinke* (pancakes), which are usually served *sa marmeladom* (with marmalade), *s čokoladom* (with chocolate sauce) or *s oresima* (with walnuts). In Dubrovnik, try *rožata*, the locally produced version of crème caramel. A **slastičarnica** is a place to find ice cream, cakes and pastries, including *baklava*, the syrup-coated pastry indigenous to the Balkans and the Middle East.

Drinking

Drinking takes place in a **kavana** (café) – usually a roomy and comfortable place with plenty of outdoor seating and serving the full range of alcoholic and non-alcoholic drinks, as well as pastries and ice creams – or in a **kafić** (café bar), essentially a smaller version of the same thing. The word "**pub**" is frequently adopted by café-bars attempting to imitate British, or more often Irish, styles. Both cafés and café-bars open extraordinarily early (sometimes as early as 6am) in order to serve the first espresso to those catching the early-morning ferry, although alcohol isn't served until 9am. Closing time is usually 11pm–midnight, although regulations are relaxed in summer, when café-bars in resort areas may stay open till 2am. Few Croatian cafés of any kind serve substantial food except for the odd sandwich.

TOP 5 SWEET-TOOTH TREATS

Torte i to Zagreb. Cakes and tarts to die for. See p.85

U prolazu Samobor. Best place to sample the town's famous *kremšnite* (creamy custard slices). See p.113

Grand Café, Opatija. Once you've tried their home-made chocolates you'll be back for more. See p.202

Cukarin Korčula. Unique handmade treats from Croatia's most famous sweet shop. See p.371

Sugar and Spice Dubrovnik. Divine, inventive and irresistible cakes and muffins. See p.412

Beer

Most Croatian beer is of the light **lager** variety. Mass-market brands Karlovačko and Ožujsko are pretty unexciting, and it's well worth seeking out the more flavoursome Velebitsko pivo from Gospić, or the malty, unpasteurized Vukovarsko from Vukovar. Ožujsko produce a decent **wheat beer** (pšenično pivo) and a fine **porter** called Tomislav. Kasačko pivo is a palatable blend of light and dark beer made by the Velebitsko brewery. Whether you're drinking beer in bottles or on tap, a *malo pivo* (small beer) usually means 30cl and costs 12–25Kn, a *veliko pivo* (large beer) is a half-litre and will set you back 15–30Kn.

Wine

Croatia's wine industry has come on in leaps and bounds in recent years, with a new breed of boutique wineries and family businesses leading the way. Although there are plenty of decent-quality Chardonnays, Cabernets and Merlots in Croatia, it's really the indigenous or near-indigenous grape varieties that are worth exploring.

Of the main wine producing regions, **Istria** is renowned for its dry white Malvazija, and for the tannin-rich reds Teran and Refošk. More excellent reds are to be found in **Dalmatia**, where Babić is king in the Primošten-Šibenik region, while Plavac mali (a distant cousin of Zinfandel) predominates on the south Dalmatian islands and the Pelješac peninsula. The Plavac wines from Pelješac's Dingač and Postup vineyards are among Croatia's finest reds, and command the highest prices. The island of Korčula is home to the excellent light whites Pošip and Rukatac; Krk is renowned for the medium-dry Vrbnička Žlahtina, while Vis is famous for the more flowery white Vugava. Hvar offers an embarrassment of riches, with Plavac mali, Pošip and indigenous white Bogdanjuša. White Graševina (Welschriesling) and Traminac (Gewurztraminer) cover much of **eastern Croatia**, with the cellars of Kutjevo and Ilok traditionally producing the best wines.

Wine sold in shops and supermarkets is **graded** as stolno vino (table wine), kvalitetno vino (quality wine) or vrhunsko vino (supreme wine). Basically, anything in the stolno category (20–40Kn/bottle) is cheap and drinkable, although the kvalitetno category (40–70Kn/bottle) usually delivers higher quality for a very reasonable price. Anything in the vrhunsko band (120–140Kn/bottle) is really quite special.

Popular **wine-derived drinks**, all served cold, include *bevanda* (white or red wine mixed with plain water), *gemišt* (white wine and fizzy mineral water) and bafflingly popular summer tipple *bambus* (red wine mixed with cola).

Spirits

Most local spirits (*žestoka pića*) are grouped under the term **rakija** (brandy), which covers all the indigenous fruit-derived firewaters. Most *rakijas* are produced from grapes, and are called *loza* or *lozovača* unless they are flavoured with an additional ingredient, as is the case with *travarica* (herb brandy), *medica* (honey brandy), *rogačica* (carob brandy) and *orahovača* (walnut brandy). *Rakijas* made from other fruits include plum brandy (*šljivovica*) and pear brandy (*vilijamovka*). **Other local aperitifs** you should try are *pelinkovac* (a juniper-based spirit similar to Jägermeister), *borovnica* (blueberry liqueur), *maraskino* (a cherry liqueur from Zadar) and *biska* (a mistletoe-flavoured spirit from Istria. Foreign brandies and whiskies are available pretty much everywhere.

Coffee, tea and soft drinks

Apart from the vast urns of overstewed brown liquid served up by hotels at breakfast time, **coffee** is usually of a high quality. It is served as a strong black espresso unless specified otherwise – *kava sa mlijekom* or makijato comes with a drop of milk, *kava sa šlagom* comes with cream, and *bijela kava* (white coffee) is usually like a good *caffè latte*. Cappuccino is also fairly ubiquitous. **Tea** is usually of the herbal variety; ask for *crni čaj* (black tea) or *indijski čaj* (Indian tea) if you want the Brit-style brew. *Čaj sa limunom* is with a slice of lemon, *sa mlijekom* comes with milk.

Tap water (obična voda) is usually free, and comes automatically if you are drinking an espresso. **Mineral water** and other soft drinks are often served in multiples of 10cl or *dec* (pronounced "dets"). If you want 20cl of mineral water ask for *dva deca*, 30cl is *tri deca*. If you want **fruit juice**, note that the word *đus* ("juice") usually means orange juice.

The media

Having enjoyed a lively media scene in the 1980s and 1990s, when political and social changes were reflected in a startling array of opinionated and often subversive newspapers and magazines, Croatia has settled down to something approaching central European sobriety.

Newspapers and magazines

The most widely read daily **newspaper**, *Jutarnji List*, is breezy and populist, but contains decent cultural content in the weekend editions. The most influential of the weeklies is *Globus*, a glossy news magazine that reflects the broadly pro-liberal attitudes of Zagreb's emerging middle class.

An increasing range of **foreign-language newspapers** is available from news kiosks in Zagreb and on the coast. Many of the best-known English, German and Italian dailies are on sale within 24 hours of publication, and are usually two or three times more expensive than in their home countries. International fashion, lifestyle and computer magazines are fairly ubiquitous.

TV and radio

Of the three main state-owned **television channels**, HRT 1 is primarily known for its plodding diet of political discussions and singing-dancing reality shows. HRT2 dishes up liberal servings of live sport, while HRT3 concentrates on culture and arty films. Private stations RTL and Nova TV have more in the way of imported soaps and feature films – the latter are usually shown in the original language with Croatian subtitles. The majority of private households and hotels have access to cable TV packages, which usually include English-language documentary fodder, news from CNN or BBC (sometimes both), and several international sport and movie channels.

With a shortwave **radio**, you can pick up the broadcasts of the BBC World Service (W bbc.co.uk /worldservice), Voice of America (W voa.gov) and

Radio Canada (Ⓦ rcinet.ca) among others; check their respective websites for frequencies and schedules.

Festivals

Croatia offers an increasingly crammed festival calendar, with rock and DJ events, annual beach parties, niche art gatherings and folksy fairs taking place up and down the Adriatic throughout the summer. The bulk of the "serious" cultural festivals take place in Zagreb in spring and autumn, although Dubrovnik, Split and Rijeka offer a lot in the way of heavyweight drama and music, and almost every region of the country offers a film festival of one sort or another. In addition, the Croatian year is peppered with religious holidays, featuring church processions and celebratory feasting.

Cultural festivals

Croatia's **film festivals** represent high-quality culture at its most accessible, attracting enthusiastic audiences and a healthy diet of drinking and DJs after the screenings themselves. Motovun (July/Aug) and Zagreb (Oct) are the big two, although specialist events such as Zagrebdox (Feb) and Animafest (June) offer an equally intriguing blend of high-art seriousness and post-show partying.

Zagreb is very much the centre of Croatia's highbrow culture for most of the year, with spring and early autumn being the busiest times. Among the most prestigious festivals are the Biennale of New Music, a festival of cutting-edge contemporary classical work held in April in odd-numbered years; the Contemporary Dance Week in May/June; Eurokaz European Theatre Festival in late June; and the Festival of World Theatre in September.

Croatian culture heads for the coast in summer. Almost every Adriatic town organizes a cultural programme, usually featuring outdoor concerts of pop, classical music or folk. Most important of the heavyweight events is the **Dubrovnik Summer Festival**, six weeks of classical music and drama beginning in early July, much of which is performed in the squares and courtyards of the old town. The Dubrovnik Festival's only real rival in the high-culture stakes is the **Split Summer**, which offers a varied diet of top-notch music and theatre. Historical buildings also form the backdrop for a number of other classical music events, including the Osor Music Evenings on the island of Cres; St Donat's Church in Zadar; and the Varaždin Festival of Baroque Music, which uses many of the city's fine churches.

Rock and DJ festivals

Recent years have seen Croatia muscle its way into the European party calendar in a major way. From late June to early September big-name DJs perform every weekend at the dance clubs along the Adriatic coast. The events organized by the **Garden** organization in Tisno throughout July and August have quickly established themselves as some of the Mediterranean's coolest DJ festivals, although visitor numbers are limited and tickets should be bought well in advance. The **Seasplash**, **Outlook** and **Dimensions** festivals are fast turning Pula into the unofficial summer capital of reggae, dub and dubstep. In addition, the beach bars of Zrće on the island of Pag (see p.238) are famous for generating a summer-long atmosphere of hedonistic excess.

Croatia was always a hotbed of punk, new wave and alternative music, and this is still reflected in the range of rock events on offer. **Terraneo** near Šibenik (Aug) is the leading alt-rock event in this part of Europe; **In-music** in Zagreb (June) is the other main rock and indie event, though the city has a year-round schedule of gigs. Live music events elsewhere are pretty sporadic.

Folk festivals

The country's main folk festival is the **Inter-national Folklore Festival**, held over a weekend in July and traditionally the best place to see songs and dances from all over the country. The tradition of the Dalmatian *klapa* (male-voice choir) is preserved in numerous festivals up and down the coast, the biggest being the one held in Omiš in July. The remaining big folk events are all in Slavonia and have a more regional character, although the **Brodsko Kolo Festival** in Slavonski Brod (mid-June), **Vinkovci Autumn** (late Sept) and **Đakovo Folk Festival** (end Sept) are all worthwhile shindigs. Guests in Adriatic hotels will be treated to folklore shows, often over dinner, throughout the summer season. Local songs and dances are performed outside the church in Čilipi, near Dubrovnik, every Sunday morning.

Traditional events and religious festivals

The most important event in the early part of the year is the pre-Lenten carnival (*karneval*; often known as *fašnik* in inland Croatia, *pust* on the Adriatic), which actually begins before Christmas but does not reach a climax until **Shrove Tuesday** or the weekend immediately preceding it, when there are processions and masked revelry in towns all over Croatia. A lot of places organize parades with floats, the participants donning disguises which frequently satirize local politicians or comment on the events of the past year. Rijeka, Samobor and Velika Gorica (just south of Zagreb) host the biggest events. In smaller places carnival practices are still linked to pre-Christian fertility rites: in the villages near Rijeka groups of men (called *zvončari* or "ringers") don sheepskins and ring bells to drive away evil spirits, while in many areas a doll known as *pust* (or *poklad* in Lastovo) is ritually burned in order to cleanse the coming agricultural year of bad luck.

The next big event is **Easter week**, characterized by solemn processions in many towns, especially Hvar and Korčula. Most important of the summertime religious holidays is the **Assumption** (Aug 15), when churches throughout the country hold special services, and large pilgrimages are made to Marian shrines such as Marija Bistrica near Zagreb, Krasno near Senj, Sinj in the Dalmatian hinterland and Trsat near Rijeka. The **Birth of the Virgin** (Sept 8) is only slightly less important in the Catholic calendar, and is celebrated in similar fashion.

All Saints' Day (Nov 1) is one of the most important Catholic feasts of the autumn, when families visit graveyards to pay their respects to the departed. By the evening, many big-city cemeteries are transformed into a sea of candles. **St Martin's Day** (Nov 11) is traditionally the day when the year's wine is first tasted, and is often used as an excuse for revelry in wine-producing areas. In accordance with a widespread central European tradition, St Martin's Day is also marked by the slaughter and roasting of a goose. A slaughter of a more widespread kind takes place at the end of November, when many rural families (especially in Slavonia and the Dalmatian hinterland) set aside a weekend in order to carry out the annual **pig slaughter** (*svinokolja* or *kolinja*), and begin preparation of the sausages and hams which will be consumed over the next year.

On **St Nicholas's Day** (Dec 6) children leave out stockings and are rewarded with small presents. They are also threatened by visits from the monster Krampus, a kind of St Nicholas in reverse, who takes away bad children in his bag. **Christmas** itself is much the same as anywhere else in Europe, with presents laid out under the family Christmas tree. The main family meal is eaten on Christmas Eve (*Badnja večer*), and traditionally consists of fish (often carp), after which everyone attends midnight mass.

A festival calendar

Festivals marked ★ are especially worth checking out.

JANUARY

Snow Queen Trophy ⓦ **snowqueentrophy.com.** World Cup downhill skiing on Mount Sljeme, with a big-screen broadcast on the main square. First and second weekends in Jan; Zagreb.

FEBRUARY

Feast of St Blaise (Sveti Vlaho) ⓦ **tzdubrovnik.hr.** Processions and pageantry in honour of Dubrovnik's patron saint. Feb 3; Dubrovnik.

Carnival (Karneval; fašnik; pust). Processions, fancy dress and festivities in Rijeka (ⓦ www.tz-rijeka.hr), Velika Gorica (ⓦ tzvg.hr) and Samobor (ⓦ tz-samobor.hr). Weekend preceding Shrove Tues.

Zagrebdox ⓦ **zagrebdox.net.** A feast of documentary films from around the globe, with a packed week of screenings. Late Feb/early March; Zagreb.

MARCH

RAF (Review of Amateur Films) ⓦ **revijaamaterskogfilma.hr.** Celebration of amateur, student and no-budget film-making, showing work in all styles and of all lengths. Zagreb.

APRIL

Easter Religious processions on the islands of Hvar, Korčula and in many other parts of Croatia. April or late March.

★ **Music Biennale** (Glazbeno biennale) ⓦ **mbz.hr.** Ten days of contemporary classical music featuring new work by major international composers. Every odd-numbered year; Zagreb.

Test! ⓦ **test.hr.** Festival of Student Theatre, with a healthy dose of experimental performance. Zagreb.

Days of Croatian Film (Dani hrvatskog filma) ⓦ **dhf.sczg.hr.** Major review of Croatian films made during the previous twelve months, including features, shorts and documentaries. If you are on the lookout for new talent, this is the place to find it. Zagreb.

MAY

Feast of St Domnius (Sveti Dujam) Church processions, craft fairs and feasting. May 7; Split.

Subversive Film Festival ⓦ **subversivefestival.com.** A wide range of films and lectures on contemporary political topics, followed by the usual after-party drinking. Zagreb.

Roč Accordion Festival (Z armoniku v Roč) Ⓦ tz buzet.hr. Accordion bands from Croatia and beyond. Second weekend in May; Roč.

Festival of One-Minute Films (Revija jednominutnih filmova) Ⓦ crominute.hr. Exactly what it says in the title, with plenty of eccentric, experimental work. Late May; Požega.

Jewish Film Festival (Festival Židovskog Filma) Ⓦ jff-zagreb.hr. A week of feature films, documentaries and post-screening concerts addressing wider issues of race and tolerance. Co-founded by Holocaust survivor and Oscar-winning producer Branko Lustig. Late May; Zagreb.

★ **Festival of the European Short Story** (Festival Evropske kratke priče) Ⓦ europeanshortstory.org. Engaging and accessible lit-fest attracting major international participants (and big-screen English-language translations). A two-centre festival based in Zagreb and at least one Adriatic city. Late May/early June.

Contemporary Dance Week (Tjedan suvremenog plesa) Ⓦ danceweekfestival.com. Croatia's premier dance event, with a strong contemporary edge. Late May/early June; Zagreb.

JUNE

Cest is d'Best Ⓦ cestisdbest.com. Live bands and street entertainment on stages throughout the city centre. Early June; Zagreb.

Mediterranean Film Festival (Festival mediteranskog filma Split) Ⓦ fmfs.hr. New features from the Mediterranean region, screened on Split's Bačvice beach, with an accompanying after-show DJ programme. Early June; Split.

★ **Strossmartre** (Ljeto na Štrosu) Ⓦ ljetonastrosu.com. Summer-long sequence of gigs, puppet shows and open-air art in Zagreb's Gornji grad. June to early Sept; Zagreb.

Animafest Ⓦ animafest.hr. Among the animation world's most important and longest-running festivals, screening a week's worth of arty and edgy films. Early June; Zagreb.

★ **Dan-D** ("D-Day"). A long weekend devoted to contemporary design, with local creatives displaying their wares and DJ events in the evening. Mid-June; Zagreb.

Summer Nights (Riječke ljetne noći) Ⓦ rijeckeljetnenoci.com. Classical music and drama in a variety of indoor and outdoor venues. Mid-June to late July; Rijeka.

Eurokaz Theatre Festival Ⓦ eurokaz.hr. Challenging avant-garde drama with an impressive roster of international guests. Late June/early July; Zagreb.

Valamar Jazz Festival Ⓦ valamarjazz.com. Top international names performing in atmospheric indoor and outdoor venues. Late June; Poreč.

★ **In-music** Ⓦ inmusicfestival.com. Three-day rock-and-pop fest on the shores of Lake Jarun, featuring major international bands and DJs. Attracting a daily average of 30,000 people, it's big enough to feel like a major event but small enough to preserve a laid-back vibe. Late June; Zagreb.

International Children's Festival (Međunarodnji dječji festival) Ⓦ mdf-sibenik.com. Puppet shows, street entertainers and musicals, with a young audience in mind. Late June/early July; Šibenik.

Hideout Ⓦ hideoutfestival.com. Festival of cutting-edge DJ music takes over Zrće beach for a long weekend. Late June; Novalja, Pag island.

Fantastic Film Festival Ⓦ fantastic-zagreb.com. Week-long event devoted to fantasy, horror and sci-fi genres, with open-air screenings and DJ events. Late June/early July; Zagreb.

JULY

Kastav Cultural Summer (Kastafsko kulturno leto) Ⓦ kkl.hr. Concerts in the streets and squares of Kastav, near Rijeka. July/Aug.

St Donat's Musical Evenings (Glazbene večeri u sv. Donatu) Ⓦ donat-festival.com. Classical soloists and ensembles performing in an early medieval church. Early July to early Aug; Zadar.

Đakovo Embroidery (Đakovački vezovi) Ⓦ tz-djakovo.hr. Folklore groups from all over Croatia celebrate traditional costumes, music and dance. Early July; Đakovo.

★ **Garden Festival** Ⓦ thegardenfestival.eu. Eight-day DJ-driven extravaganza with a capacity of 3000 and a beach-party feel. Early July; Tisno.

Omiš Klapa Festival Ⓦ fdk.hr. Traditional choirs (*klape*) from all over the country, with prizes for the best performances. Omiš.

Dubrovnik Summer Festival (Dubrovačke ljetne igre) Ⓦ dubrovnik-festival.hr. Prestigious classical music and theatre event that makes full use of Dubrovnik's historic buildings and atmospheric open spaces. Early July to late Aug; Dubrovnik.

Electric Elephant Ⓦ electricelephant.co.uk. Five-day fest for connoisseurs of quality dance music old and new, based at the Garden summer HQ. Mid-July; Tisno.

Vanka Regule ("Outside the rules") Ⓦ vankaregule.com. Sports- and activity-based festival with an imaginative range of everybody-can-join-in competitions, followed by outdoor gigs. Mid-July; Sutivan, Brač.

★ **Hartera** Ⓦ hartera.com. Weekend rock-fest in an adapted old factory complex. Mid-July.

Split Summer (Splitsko ljeto) Ⓦ splitsko-ljeto.hr. Opera, orchestral music and a host of other high-cultural delights, with many performances taking place in Split's ancient piazzas and squares. Mid-July to mid-Aug; Split.

International Folklore Festival (Međunarodna smotra folklora) Ⓦ msf.hr. Highly enjoyable display of ethnic music and dance from all over Croatia, plus a range of international guests. Mid- to late July; Zagreb.

Seasplash Ⓦ seasplash-festival.com. Reggae fest in the Punta Christo fortress, just north of Pula. Late July.

Ethno Ambient Live Ⓦ ethnoambient.net. Two-day world music festival with a mix of Croatian and international stars, in ancient Salona's amphitheatre. Split.

Soundwave Ⓦ soundwavecroatia.com. Another long weekend of DJ-orchestrated bliss at the Garden's Tisno site; late July.

Osor Music Evenings (Osorske glazbene večeri) Ⓦ osorskeveceri.org. International chamber music. Late July to late Aug; Osor, Cres.

Night of Diocletian (Noć Dioklecijana). Locals dress up as ancient

Romans for a night of city-centre swords-and-sandals partying, symbolically welcoming third-century Emperor Diocletian back into town. Late July; Split.

★ **Pula Film Festival** Ⓦ **pulafilmfestival.hr.** The country's annual crop of feature films, screened in the Roman amphitheatre. Pula.

★ **Rab Fair** (Rapska fjera) Ⓦ **tzg-rab.hr.** Huge medieval pageant featuring parades, archery contests, fine victuals and hearty drinking. July 25, 26 & 27; Rab.

SuncéBeat Ⓦ **suncebeat.com.** The Dalmatian offshoot of well-known UK DJ event the Southport Weekender, held at the Garden. Late July; Tisno.

Motovun Film Festival Ⓦ **motovunfilmfestival.com.** High-art film festival that also functions as a five-day open-air party. Late July/early Aug; Motovun.

Supertoon Festival Hugely enjoyable animation fest with outdoor screenings of kids' films, music videos and arty stuff. Late July/early Aug; Bol.

AUGUST

Stop Making Sense Ⓦ **stopmakingsense.eu.** The cream of cutting-edge London club culture descends on Dalmatia for another long weekend of round-the-clock partying. Early Aug; Tisno.

Saljske užance Ⓦ **dugiotok.hr.** Seafood feasts, donkey races, island madness. First weekend in Aug; Sali, Dugi otok.

Alka Ⓦ **alka.hr.** A sort of medieval joust held in celebration of the 1715 victory over the Ottomans. Early Aug; Sinj.

★ **Terraneo** Ⓦ **terraneofestival.com.** With international indie-rock and alternative DJs, this is the Adriatic's premier hipster hop, with decent food and camping on site. Early Aug; Šibenik.

Zadar Dreams (Zadar Snova) Ⓦ **zadarsnova.hr.** Festival of alternative drama and performance art. Early to mid-Aug; Zadar.

Neretva Boat Marathon (Maraton lađa) Ⓦ **maraton-ladja.hr.** Teams in traditional rowing boats race through the Neretva delta towards the sea. Second Sat in Aug; Metković.

Tilting at the Ring (Trka na prstenac) Ⓦ **barban.hr.** Competition in which horsemen attempt to spear a ring on the end of a lance. Third weekend in Aug; Barban, Istria.

★ **Špancirfest** Ⓦ **spancirfest.com.** One of the few festivals to light up inland Croatia during the month of Aug, Špancirfest takes over the centre of Varaždin with a week of outdoor variety performances alongside pop, rock and folk concerts. Late Aug; Varaždin.

Vukovar Film Festival Ⓦ **vukovarfilmfestival.com.** New features from southeastern European countries, screened on a barge in the River Danube. Late Aug; Vukovar.

Outlook Ⓦ **outlookfestival.com.** A spectacular treat for fans of jungle/dub/dubstep and beyond, with sound systems and live music stages in and around the Punta Christo naval fort. Late Aug/early Sept; Pula.

SEPTEMBER

PIF International Festival of Puppet Theatre (Međunarodni festival kazališta lutaka) Ⓦ **pif.hr.** Puppet productions from all over Europe. Early Sept; Zagreb.

Dimensions Ⓦ **dimensionsfestival.com.** Held the weekend after Outlook on the same site, here is more of the same, but with a more eclectic, experimental line-up. Early Sept; Pula.

Korkyra Baroque Festival (Korčulanski međunarodni barokni festival) Ⓦ **korkyrabaroque.com.** Ten-day festival of early music, with many of the performances taking place in historic churches. Early to mid-Sept; Korcula Town.

Buzet Saturday (Buzetska Subotina) Ⓦ **tz-buzet.hr.** Gastronomic and musical fiesta dedicated to the opening of the truffle-hunting season. Second weekend in Sept; Buzet.

Festival of World Theatre (Festival svijetskog kazališta) Ⓦ **zagrebtheatrefestival.hr.** Seriously worthwhile drama festival attracting the big European names. Mid- to late Sept; Zagreb.

Split Film Festival Ⓦ **splitfilmfestival.hr.** Shorts, documentaries and art-house films. Mid- to late Sept; Split.

Varaždin Baroque Evenings (Varaždinske barokne večeri) Ⓦ **vbv.hr.** One of Europe's most prestigious early music events, with performances in Varaždin cathedral and other city churches. Mid- to late Sept.

International Festival of Experimental Film and Video (Internacionalni festival eksperimentalnog filma i videa) Ⓦ **25fps.hr.** Moving pictures from the cutting edge. Late Sept; Zagreb.

OCTOBER

★ **Perforations** (Perforacije) Ⓦ **perforacije.org.** Top regional showcase for performance art and genre-bending theatre, from Croatia and southeastern Europe. Zagreb.

BIT (Blind in Theatre) Ⓦ **novizivot.hr.** International festival for visually impaired theatre groups. Extraordinary and unique. Odd-numbered years only. Early Oct; Zagreb.

★ **Zagreb Film Festival** Ⓦ **zagrebfilmfestival.com.** Outstanding documentaries and art movies from around the world. Generates a genuine festival atmosphere: free access to the late-night DJ parties is well worth the price of your cinema ticket. Mid-Oct.

NOVEMBER

St Martin's Day (Martinje). Festivities in all wine-producing regions of the country, with the chance to taste and buy the season's new produce. Nov 11 or nearest weekend.

DECEMBER

Human Rights Film Festival Ⓦ **humanrightsfestival.org.** Politically engaged documentaries from around the globe, plus the inevitable after-parties. Early to mid-Dec; Zagreb and Rijeka.

Sports and the outdoors

Croatia is an increasingly versatile destination for adventure tourism, with plentiful outdoor activities on offer, from hiking in the hills of the interior to scuba diving in the Adriatic. Sailing is best organized before you arrive (see p.29). Croatian team and

individual sports occupy an important position in society, not least because of the significant role they have played in enhancing national prestige abroad – one outstanding example being former Wimbledon champion Goran Ivanišević.

Spectator sports

Football (*nogomet*) is the most popular spectator sport and an important badge of national identity. The Croatian national team is one of the most successful in Central-Eastern Europe, consistently qualifying for international tournaments since their first appearance at the European Championships of 1996. Finishing third in the 1998 World Cup was Croatia's best-ever result.

While the exploits of the national team remain a national obsession, the domestic league is hampered by a lack of real competition. The big teams Dinamo Zagreb and Hajduk Split have more or less monopolized domestic honours since 1991, but rarely make a significant impression in Europe – Hajduk made the quarter finals of the UEFA Champions' League in 1995; Dinamo qualified for the group stages in 1998, 1999, 2011 and 2012. Matches between the big two can attract large crowds, but otherwise Croatian league attendances are poor, with most fans following their favourite European teams on TV instead.

After football, the most popular sport is **basketball** (*košarka*), with teams like Split, Zadar and Cibona Zagreb enjoying large followings and a Europe-wide reputation. Like football, it's a sport in which Croatia exports its best players, with performers like Tony Kukoč, Dino Rađa and the late Dražen Petrović (see p.76) finding big-time success in the NBL. **Ice hockey** is a major spectator sport in Zagreb, with local team Medveščak playing in the pan-Alpine EBEL league, and **handball** (*rukomet*), **volleyball** (*odbojka*) and **water polo** (*vaterpolo*) all get a good deal of newspaper and television coverage. One sport which is definitely not televised – although you'll see a lot of it in Dalmatia and Istria – is a form of bowls known as **bočanje** (derived from the Italian *boccie*), which is played in villages on a sandy outdoor rectangle by local men on summer evenings.

Hiking

Hiking was first popularized in Croatia in the late nineteenth century, when the exploration of the great Croatian outdoors was considered a patriotic duty as well as a form of exercise. It's still a popular weekend activity, especially in spring and early summer, before the searing Mediterranean heat sends people scurrying for the beaches.

Easy rambling territory in inland Croatia is provided by wooded **Mount Medvednica** and the **Samobor hills** (Samoborsko gorje), both close to Zagreb and criss-crossed by well-used trails. On the Adriatic coast, **Učka**, immediately above Opatija and Lovran, is one of the most easily accessible mountains, and can be safely bagged by the moderately fit hiker. Farther south, the more challenging **Velebit** range stretches for some 100km along the eastern shore of the Kvarner Gulf; its main hiking areas are around the Zavižan summit, near Senj, and the Paklenica National Park at Velebit's southern end. In Dalmatia, the principal peaks are **Kozjak** and **Mosor** (immediately west and east of Split respectively) and, most challenging of all the Adriatic mountains, **Biokovo**, above the Makarska Riviera.

Ranges such as the Velebit seem to invite extended expeditions, but unfortunately hut-to-hut walking in Croatia is still in its infancy, and no local travel agencies organize it. **Mountain refuges** (*planinarski dom*) run by local hiking associations do exist, but they're usually only open at the weekend, making anything longer than a 36-hour trek unfeasible.

Detailed **hiking maps** are published by the Croatian Hiking Association, Kozarčeva 22, Zagreb (Hrvatski planinarski savez; Mon 8am–6pm, Tues–Fri 8am–3pm; Ⓣ01 482 3624, Ⓦplsavez.hr), although they're only sporadically available in bookshops and you'll have to visit the association in person to inspect the full range. Tourist offices sometimes sell hiking maps of their own area (for instance the tourist information centre in Zagreb sells maps of Mount Medvednica), but don't bank on it.

Cycling

Several parts of Croatia are ideally suited to cycling holidays, with inland Istria, the Dalmatian islands, the Lonjsko polje and the Baranja region of eastern Slavonia topping the list. Cycle routes are increasingly well marked and several local tourist organizations have published cycling maps. **Hiring a bike** is easy in the bigger Adriatic resorts, but can be tricky elsewhere. A number of local bed and breakfasts have begun stocking up on bikes that their guests can use – and we have mentioned these in the Guide wherever relevant. An initiative called **Bike &**

Bed (mojbicikl.hr) publishes a series of brochures detailing regional cycling itineraries, along with details of bike-friendly B&Bs that can be found along the way.

Bikes can be transported in designated luggage vans on certain inter-city **trains**, notably those operating on the Zagreb–Split, Zagreb–Rijeka, Zagreb–Osijek and Zagreb–Varaždin routes. There's a flat fee of 30Kn for each bike. If cycling in a group of more than four people you should contact the station of departure five days in advance to book your space.

Bikes can in theory be stowed in the luggage compartments of inter-city **buses** for a small fee, but many drivers are bad-tempered about this – and the amount of luggage stowed by your fellow passengers often ensures that there isn't enough room anyway. Your best bet is to confirm regulations governing carriage of bikes when buying your ticket, and arrive in good time at the bus departure point so you can be among the first to stow your gear.

Rafting

On the coast, tourist agencies organize **rafting trips** down the River Cetina, southeast of Split, and the River Zrmanja, just east of Zadar; you'll find contact details in the relevant sections of the Guide. The rafting **season** usually runs from May to September, although trips on the Zrmanja may be suspended in July owing to low water levels. **Prices** vary according to the duration of the trip – expect to pay 230–260Kn per person for a day's excursion.

Diving

Thanks to the crystal-clear waters of the Adriatic and the diversity of the local marine life, Croatia has become one of the most popular scuba-diving venues in the Mediterranean over the last few years. There's a growing number of **diving centres** along the Adriatic coast offering lessons, guided expeditions and equipment rental. Most resorts will have somewhere offering one-day introductory **courses** for 250–350Kn, as well as a range of other courses for all abilities. If you already hold a diving certificate, you need to pay a registration fee (100Kn), available from registered diving centres or from the local harbour master's office (*lučka kapetanija*), before being allowed to dive in Croatia.

Two of the most rewarding areas for diving, with clear waters and rich marine life, are the **Kornati islands** in mid-Dalmatia and the island of **Mljet** near Dubrovnik. Both have National Park status and diving here can only be arranged through officially sanctioned operators – see the relevant sections of the Guide for details. For general information, contact the Croatian Diving Federation at Dalmatinska 12, 10 000 Zagreb (01 484 8765, diving-hrs.hr).

Windsurfing

There are really only two places to go in Croatia for serious windsurfers. The best is **Bol** on the island of Brač, which stands on the northern side of the narrow channel dividing Brač from Hvar, providing calm waters and channelling the right kind of winds. Second best is the **Kučište–Viganj** area just west of Orebić, which occupies a similar position on the Pelješac channel dividing the mainland from Korčula. Bol is a fully developed package resort with all the accommodation and nightlife opportunities one would expect; Kučište and Viganj on the other hand are unspoilt villages equipped with a few private rooms and campsites. Whichever you choose, you'll find plenty of people renting out gear (boards 200–250Kn/day) and offering courses (about 600Kn for 8hr tuition).

Sea kayaking

Sea kayaking is an increasingly popular way of exploring the coast around Dubrovnik, the Elaphite Islands and Hvar. It's extremely easy to organize, with several Dubrovnik- (see p.394) and Hvar-based travel agents (see p.346) arranging half- or full-day tours. Kayakers are led in a small flotilla by the tour leader, and apart from the few short minutes required to learn how to use a paddle, no training or previous experience is required.

Skiing

Croatia has two main skiing areas: **Sljeme** on Mount Medvednica, just outside Zagreb, and **Platak**, just inland from Rijeka. Although both are fun venues for occasional skiing if you're already visiting Croatia, neither is worth planning a holiday around. Altitudes (1035m and 1363m respectively) are too low to guarantee long periods of adequate snow cover, and most Croats treat skiing trips as spur-of-the-moment events if the weather is right. You can rent gear at either place.

Shopping

The best destination for shopping in Croatia is Zagreb, which offers a range of retail experiences you won't find along the Adriatic coast. The capital has regular flea and collectors' markets, second-hand clothes shops and plenty of stores selling old books, records and CDs.

Zagreb also has more in the way of boutiques selling household goods and **fashion accessories** made by Croatian designers, although these are beginning to crop up in Rovinj (see p.162), Dubrovnik (see p.414) and Split (see p.305) as well.

Many of Croatia's best souvenir ideas involve **food and drink**. Top Croatian wines can generally be picked up at high-street supermarkets, although a specialist wine shop (*vinoteka*) will stock a broader choice. Bottles of herb-flavoured *rakija*, often featuring fragments of herb in the bottle, also make good gifts. Widely available delicatessen products include truffle-based sauces and pâtés, *pršut*, figs in honey and other fruit based preserves. Extra-virgin olive oil is as good as any in Europe. **Soaps** made from olive oil and fragranced with local herbs are also a good buy, as are bags of lavender, harvested on the island of Hvar.

Intricate **embroidery** featuring folk motifs is still produced in many areas of inland Croatia, and in the Konavle region south of Dubrovnik. Even the smallest pieces make gorgeous souvenirs, but can be very expensive. Finally, **lacemaking** is still a traditional occupation in the Adriatic town of Pag, where lacemakers are frequently encountered selling their wares from doorways and living room windows.

TOP 5 PLACES TO SHOP

Britanski trg Zagreb. This Sunday-morning collectors' market is a rummager's delight. See p.92
Lega-Lega Osijek and Dubrovnik. Quirky, Croatian-designed T-shirts and stationery, with outlets in Osijek and Dubrovnik. See p.126 & p.415
Sheriff & Cherry Rovinj. Wacky sunglasses, casual shoes and accessories courtesy of local designers. See p.162
Zadar market Zadar. Local cheeses, home-cured meats and seafood galore in one of the Adriatic's most animated markets. See p.250
Damacijaland Jelsa. Deliciously weird T-shirts, postcards and graphic art from Dalmatia's strangest souvenir outlet. See p.354

Travel essentials

Addresses

The Croatian word for street, *ulica,* is either abbreviated to *ul.* or omitted altogether if the meaning is clear enough without it. The street name always comes before the number. Buildings that don't have a street number are often designated by the letters "bb", meaning *bez broja* or "without a number".

Costs

Croatia is by no means a bargain destination, and the cost of accommodation – on a par with Western European countries for most of the year – shoots upwards in July and August. Eating and drinking, however, remain reasonably good value.

If you're staying in hostels or private rooms, self-catering and travelling by public transport, then bargain on spending at least 500Kn/£50/€60/US$80 per person per day. If you are staying in a decent apartment, eating out once a day and enjoying yourselves in the evening, then 850Kn/£85/€100/US$130 per day seems more reasonable. Staying in a good hotel, eating in nice restaurants, hiring a car and not skimping on the cocktails will involve a daily outlay of 1500Kn/£150/E180/US$240 or above.

Accommodation will be your biggest single expense, with the average private room weighing in at around 250Kn for a double, rising to 375Kn in fashionable places like Dubrovnik and Hvar. In high season the cheapest doubles in three-star hotels hover around the 800Kn mark, although they can be significantly cheaper in spring or autumn.

As for **transport**, short journeys by ferry and bus (say from Split to one of the nearby islands) cost in the region of 40Kn, while moving up and down the country will naturally be more expensive (a Zagreb–Split bus ticket, for instance, costs upwards of 210Kn. The prices of accommodation, ferry tickets, international bus tickets and tourist excursions are often quoted in **euros**, although you can pay in kuna.

About 200Kn per person per day will suffice for **food and drink** if you're shopping in markets for picnic ingredients, maybe eating out in inexpensive grill-houses and pizzerias once a day, and limiting yourself to a couple of drinks in cafés; 400Kn a day will be sufficient for breakfast in a café, a sit-down lunch and a decent restaurant dinner followed by a couple of night-time drinks.

Prices often include a **sales tax**, known locally as PDV, of up to 22 percent. Visitors from outside the EU can claim a PDV tax refund at the Croatian Customs Service for goods over 750Kn, as long as they have kept all original invoices – though the refund can take up to a year to arrive.

Crime and personal safety

The crime rate in Croatia is low by European standards. Your main defence against petty **theft** is to exercise common sense and refrain from flaunting luxury items. Take out an insurance policy before you leave home (see opposite) and always stow a photocopy of the crucial information-bearing pages of your passport in your luggage – this will enable your consulate to issue you swiftly with new travel documents in the event of your passport being stolen.

Croatian **police** (*policija*) are generally helpful and polite when dealing with foreigners, and usually speak some English. Routine police checks on identity cards are common in Croatia: always carry your passport or driving licence. If you get into trouble with the authorities, wait until you can explain matters to someone in English if at all possible. The police are not allowed to search your car or place of abode without a warrant. Should you be **arrested**, you can be held in a police station for 24 hours without charge. The police are supposed to notify your consulate of your arrest automatically, but often fail to do so.

There are few specific situations in which **female travellers** might feel uncomfortable and no real no-go areas, although some of the more down-at-heel café-bars can feel like male-only preserves. By Western standards, Croatia's streets are relatively safe at night, even in the cities.

EMERGENCY NUMBERS

Police T 112 or T 192
Ambulance T 112 or T 94
Fire T 112 or T 193
Sea rescue and diving alert T 9155

Electricity

Wall sockets in Croatia operate at 220 volts and take round, two-pin **plugs**. British travellers should purchase a continental adaptor before leaving home.

Entry requirements

Citizens of EU countries need only a valid passport to enter Croatia. Citizens of the US, Canada, Australia and New Zealand are allowed to enter Croatia without a visa for stays of up to ninety days. Citizens of other countries should check visa regulations with the nearest Croatian embassy or consulate before leaving home.

Visitors to Croatia from non-EU countries are required by law to **register** with the local police within 24 hours of arrival. If you're staying in a hotel, hostel or campsite, or if you've booked a private room through a recognized agency, the job of registration will be done for you. If you're staying with friends or in a room arranged privately, your hosts are supposed to register you. In practice, however, they very rarely do so. This only becomes a problem if the police have reason to question you about where you're staying, which in well-touristed areas is very rare. Even if they do, official attitudes to registration are flexible: the police often turn a blind eye to tourists and hosts alike if you're merely enjoying a short holiday on the coast, but can throw you out of the country if you've been staying in Croatia unregistered for a long period of time.

There are no **customs restrictions** on the kind of personal belongings that you need for your holiday, although you are limited to two hundred cigarettes, one litre of spirits and 500g of coffee. It's a good idea to declare major items – laptop computers, televisions and other electronic equipment, boats – to ensure that you can take them out of the country when you leave. Pets are allowed in, providing you have a recent vaccination certificate. Note that when leaving you can only take 2000Kn of currency with you.

CROATIAN EMBASSIES AND CONSULATES ABROAD

Australia T 02 6286 6988, E croemb.canberra@mvep.hr. Also consulates in Sydney, Melbourne and Perth.
Canada T 613 562 7820, W ca.mfa.hr.
Ireland T 01 476 7181, W ie.mfa.hr.
New Zealand T 09 836 5581, E ecro-consulate@xtra.co.nz.
South Africa T 012 342 1206, W za.mfa.hr.

UK ⓣ **020 7387 2022,** ⓦ **uk.mfa.hr.**
US ⓣ **202 588 5899,** ⓦ **croatiaemb.org.** Also consulates in New York, Chicago and Los Angeles.

Gay and lesbian travellers

Although **homosexuality** has been legal in Croatia since 1977, it remains something of an underground phenomenon, and public displays of affection between members of the same sex may provoke hostility, especially outside big cities. The younger generation is more liberal in its attitudes to homosexuality, and though there are few recognized gay hangouts, some of the more alternative clubs in Zagreb have a reputation for attracting a tolerant, mixed crowd. Adriatic beaches where same-sex couples will feel comfortable include those around the Istrian resorts of Rovinj and Poreč, on Sveti Jerolim near Hvar, and on Lokrum near Dubrovnik.

A **Zagreb Pride** march has been held every June since 2005 and, despite the presence of counter-demonstrations in the early years, has become a regular feature of the city's calendar. The first **Split Pride** procession, in June 2011, was notoriously halted by a mass demonstration of an estimated ten thousand homophobes, but passed off without incident in 2012.

The website ⓦ friendlycroatia.com offers useful travel tips on various Croatian destinations.

Health

No inoculations are required for travel to Croatia. Standards of public health are good, and tap water is safe everywhere. However, anyone planning to spend time walking in the mountains should consider being inoculated against tick-borne encephalitis.

Minor complaints can be treated at a **pharmacy** (*ljekarna*); in cities, many of the staff will speak some English, while even in places where the staff speak only Croatian, it should be easy enough to obtain repeat prescriptions if you bring along the empty pill container. A rota system ensures that there will be one pharmacy open at night-time and weekends – details are posted in the window of each pharmacy.

For serious complaints, head for the nearest **hospital** (*bolnica* or *klinički centar*), or call an **ambulance** (ⓣ 112 or ⓣ 94). Hospital treatment is free to citizens of EU countries, including the UK and Ireland, on production of a European Health Insurance Card (EHIC; available online in the UK from ⓦ ehic.org.uk; in Ireland from ⓦ ehic.ie); nationals of other countries should check whether their government has a reciprocal health agreement, or ensure they have adequate insurance cover.

Insurance

You'd do well to take out an **insurance policy** before travelling to cover against theft, loss and illness or injury. A typical travel insurance policy usually provides cover for the loss of baggage, tickets and – up to a certain limit – cash or cheques, as well as cancellation or curtailment of your journey. Most of them exclude so-called dangerous sports unless an extra premium is paid: in Croatia this can mean scuba-diving, whitewater rafting, windsurfing and trekking, though probably not kayaking or jeep safaris. If you need to make a claim, you should keep receipts for medicines and medical treatment, and in the event you have anything stolen, you must obtain an official statement from the police.

Internet

An increasing number of hostels, hotels and cafés offer free **wi-fi** access to their customers, and **internet cafés** are common in cities and Adriatic resorts. Prices are generally reasonable: expect to pay around 20–30Kn per hour online. Some internet cafés require customers to register as members (usually free of charge) before allowing use of the computers – so you might want to keep a passport or other form of ID handy.

Laundry

Self-service **launderettes** are hard to come by in Croatia, although most towns have a laundry (*praonica*) where you can leave a service wash.

Mail

Most **post offices** (*pošta* or *HPT*) are open Monday to Friday from 7 or 8am to 7 or 8pm, and Saturday 8am to 1 or 2pm. In villages and on islands, Monday to Friday 8am to 2pm is more common, though in big towns and resorts some offices open daily, sometimes staying open until 10pm.

Airmail (*zrakoplovom*) takes about three days to reach Britain, and eight to ten to reach North America; surface mail takes at least twice as long. **Stamps** (*marke*) can be bought either at the post office or at newsstands. If you're sending parcels home, don't seal the package until the post office staff have had a look at what's inside: customs duty is charged on the export of most things, although newsprint and books are exempt.

Maps

The biggest range of maps covering Croatia is by **Freytag & Berndt**, which produces a 1:600,000 *Slovenia, Croatia and Bosnia-Hercegovina* map, a 1:300,000 *Croatia* map, a 1:250,000 *Istria and northern Croatia* map and 1:000,000 regional maps of the Adriatic coast.

City and town plans are more difficult to come by, although **tourist offices** often give away (or sell quite cheaply) serviceable maps of their town or island. In addition, Freytag & Berndt publishes city plans of Zadar, Split and Dubrovnik. The best map of Zagreb is the 1:20,000 plan prepared by the **Geodetski zavod Slovenije** (Slovene Geodesic Institute), which is available in three versions: one published by a local firm in Zagreb, a second published by the Hungarian firm Cartographia and the third by Freytag & Berndt. All the above are available from shops in Croatia.

Money

Croatia's unit of currency is the **kuna** (Kn; the word *kuna*, meaning "marten", recalls the medieval period when taxes were paid in marten pelts), which is divided into 100 lipa. Coins come in denominations of 1, 5, 10, 20 and 50 lipa, and 1, 2 and 5 kuna; notes come in denominations of 5, 10, 20, 50, 100, 500 and 1000 kuna.

The best place to change money is at a **bank** (*banka*) or exchange bureau (*mjenjačnica*). Banks are generally open Monday to Friday 8am to 5pm, and Saturday 8am to 11am or noon. In smaller places they normally close for lunch on weekdays year round, and aren't open at all on Saturdays. **Exchange bureaux** are often found inside travel agencies (*putničke agencije*) and have more flexible hours, remaining open until 9 or 10pm seven days a week in summer if there are enough tourists around to justify it. The larger **post offices** also have exchange facilities, offering rates similar to those in banks. Exchange rates in hotels usually represent extremely poor value for money.

Travellers' cheques can be exchanged in almost all banks and exchange bureaux in Croatia but the transaction frequently takes ages. It's much easier (and perfectly safe) to withdraw cash from **ATMs**, found in all Croatian town centres and at most points of arrival in the country. **Credit cards** are accepted in most hotels and in the more expensive restaurants and shops, and can be used to get cash advances in banks.

EXCHANGE RATES

At the time of writing, the **exchange rate** was around 9Kn to £1, 7.5Kn to €1 and 5.75Kn to US$1.

Naturism

Naturism (denoted locally by the German acronym "FKK") has a long history on the Adriatic coast. There are self-contained naturist holiday villages in Istria (the biggest are just outside Poreč, Rovinj and Vrsar), and naturist campsites in Istria and the island of Krk. Throughout Croatia, you'll find isolated coves or stretches of beach where it is OK to be nude, providing it is at a discreet distance from the main family-oriented sections.

Opening hours

Shops in Croatia are usually open Monday to Friday from 8am to 8pm, and on Saturdays from 8am to 2 or 3pm, though we have listed exact

PUBLIC HOLIDAYS

Most shops and all banks are closed on the following public holidays:
January 1 New Year
January 6 Epiphany
March or April Easter Monday
May 1 Labour Day
June Corpus Christi
June 22 Day of the 1941 Anti-Fascist Uprising
June 25 Day of Croatian Statehood
August 5 National Thanksgiving Day
August 15 Assumption
October 8 Independence Day
November 1 All Saints' Day
December 25 & 26 Christmas

times throughout the Guide. City **supermarkets** often stay open late on Saturdays, and open on Sundays as well. On the coast, during summer, shops introduce a long afternoon break and stay open later in the evenings to compensate. **Office hours** are generally Monday to Friday 8am to 3 or 4pm.

Tourist offices, travel agents and tourist attractions often change their opening times as the year progresses, generally remaining open for longer during the summer season (usually June to September).

On the coast, **museums and galleries** are often open all day every day (sometimes with a long break in the afternoon) in July and August, and closed altogether in the depths of winter. At other times, things can be unpredictable, with attractions opening their doors when tourist traffic seems to justify it. In big cities and inland areas, museums and galleries are more likely to have regular opening times year-round, and are often closed on Mondays.

Churches in city centres and well-touristed areas usually stay open daily between 7am and 7pm or later, but many in smaller towns and villages only open their doors around Mass times. Churches or chapels that are known for being architecturally unique or that contain valuable frescoes may have set opening times and admission fees (in which case we've mentioned them in the Guide); otherwise you'll have to ask around to establish which of the locals has been nominated as holder of the key (*ključ*). **Monasteries** are often open from dawn to dusk to those who want to stroll around the cloister, although churches or art collections belonging to the monasteries conform to the opening patterns for museums and churches outlined above.

Phones

Croatian **phone booths** use magnetic cards (*telefonska kartica*), which you can pick up from post offices or newspaper kiosks. They're sold in denominations from fifteen up to one hundred units (*impulsa*). Generally speaking, a single unit will be enough for a local call, and the fifteen-unit card (costing around 15Kn) will be sufficient for making a few longer-distance calls within the country or a short international call. It's best to avoid making international calls from your **hotel room**: charges can be extortionate.

If you want to use your **mobile phone** abroad, check the likely call costs carefully and be aware of any charges for data roaming (your data roaming facility can in any case be switched off if you do not want to be liable for data charges). Bear in mind that you are likely to be charged extra for incoming calls when abroad. If you want to retrieve messages while you're away, you'll have to ask your provider for a new access code, as your home one is unlikely to work abroad.

Croatia's mobile phone operators (T-Com, VIP and Tele 2) all offer **pay-as-you-go** SIM cards that you can use during your stay. However, you'll first need to check that you have a phone that isn't automatically blocked by your home operator when you insert a foreign SIM card. It will cost you around 200Kn for the card (although a certain amount of this fee is in the form of prepayment for your future calls), after which you can purchase prepay top-ups in increments of 50Kn and upwards.

CALLING HOME FROM ABROAD

Note that the initial zero is omitted from the area code when dialling the UK, Ireland, Australia and New Zealand from abroad.

Australia international access code + 61
New Zealand international access code + 64
UK international access code + 44
US and Canada international access code + 1
Ireland international access code + 353
South Africa international access code + 27

Public toilets

Public toilets (*zahod* or *WC*) are rare outside bus or train stations, although every restaurant and café-bar will have one.

Smoking

Croatia is one of the few countries in Europe to introduce a total **smoking** ban (in May 2009), only to rescind it mere months later. At present, smoking is banned in restaurants, large cafés and the larger club-gig venues, but is permitted in cafés and bars that are smaller than 50m², and smoking zones in clubs.

Time

Croatia is one hour ahead of the UK, six hours ahead of US Eastern Standard Time, nine hours ahead of Pacific Standard Time, ten hours behind Australian Eastern Standard Time and twelve hours behind New Zealand. The clocks go back and forward by one hour in late October and late March, in line with other EU countries.

Tipping

Tips (*napojnice*) are not obligatory, and wait staff don't expect them if you've only had a cup of coffee or a sandwich. If you've had a round of drinks or a full meal, it's polite to round up the bill by ten percent or to the nearest convenient figure.

Tourist information

The best source of general information on Croatia is the **Croatian National Tourist Office** (Ⓦ croatia.hr). The tourist office can also supply brochures, accommodation details and maps of specific towns and resorts.

All towns and regions within Croatia have a tourist association (*turistička zajednica*), whose job it is to promote local tourism. Many of these maintain **tourist offices** (*turistički ured* or *turistički informativni centar*), although they vary a great deal in the services they offer. All can provide lists of accommodation or details of local room-letting agencies, but can't always book a room on your behalf. English is widely spoken, and staff in coastal resorts invariably speak German and Italian as well. Opening times vary according to the amount of tourist traffic. In July and August they might be open daily from 8am to 8pm or later, while in May, June and September, hours might be reduced to include an afternoon break or earlier closing times at weekends. Out of season, tourist offices on the coast tend to observe normal office hours (Mon–Fri 8am–3pm) or close altogether – although there's usually someone on hand to respond to emails and enquiries.

Travellers with disabilities

Many public places in Croatia are **wheelchair accessible**, especially in larger cities, though in general access to public transport and tourist sites still leaves a lot to be desired. There's a growing number of wheelchair-accessible **hotels**, though these tend to be in the more expensive price brackets and they are not spread evenly throughout the country. Tourist offices throughout Croatia will usually find out whether there are any suitable accommodation facilities in their region if you ring in advance, but be sure to double-check the information they give you – some tourist offices optimistically state that establishments have disabled facilities, when in fact they don't.

CONTACT

The Association of Organizations of Disabled People in Croatia (Zajednica saveza osoba s invaliditetom Hrvatske) Ⓣ 01 482 9394, Ⓦ soih.hr.

Travelling with children

Croatia is a family-oriented society and children are made welcome in hotels, restaurants and cafés, though this does not necessarily mean that **facilities** for children are widespread. Although some hotels, beaches and town centres will be equipped with play areas and parks, many will not. However, most Croatian beaches are full of other children – so finding playmates is not difficult. Families stay up quite late on the Adriatic – it is common to see children running around town squares and pavement cafés after 10 or 11pm. Baby food, disposable nappies, formula milk and other supplies are widely available in Croatia, although the choice of brands may not be as wide. Breastfeeding in public is becoming more common among the current generation of Croatian mums, though Croatia is still a conservative country and discretion is advised. Whether you come across baby-changing facilities or high chairs is very much a hit-and-miss affair.

Most Croatian **hotels** have three- and four-bed family rooms and suites, and each resort area will have a wide range of self-catering apartments of varying sizes. Most hotels will provide cots for babies and small children. There are no hard-and-fast rules regarding pricing policy in hotels and private accommodation, some apartment owners are very flexible and may provide an apartment with a child bed for the same price as a two-person studio; make it clear what you want when booking and see what is available. A lot of Adriatic towns have narrow stepped streets; so if you are travelling with a buggy, be sure to ask about ease of access.

Travelling by **public transport** in summer can be a hot and crowded affair so make sure you include plenty of liquid and other essentials in your hand luggage. On buses and trains, babies and toddlers travel for free providing they do not take up a seat of their own; children under 12 travel at half the adult fare. Folded pushchairs and buggies can be transported in the hold of the bus for a nominal luggage fee (7–10Kn). On ferries and catamarans, under 3s travel free, those aged 3–12 get a fifty percent discount.

Zagreb

1

Zagreb

Capital of an independent Croatia since 1991, Zagreb has served as the cultural and political focus of the nation since the Middle Ages. The city grew out of two medieval communities, Kaptol to the east and Gradec to the west, each sited on a hill and divided by a (long since dried up) river. Zagreb grew rapidly in the nineteenth century, and many of the city's buildings are well-preserved, peach-coloured monuments to the self-esteem of the Austro-Hungarian Empire. Nowadays, with a population reaching almost one million, the city is the boisterous capital of a self-confident young nation. A number of good museums and a varied and vibrant nightlife ensure that a few days here will be well spent.

Despite a fair sprinkling of Baroque and Art Nouveau buildings, **ZAGREB** is not the kind of city you fall in love with at first sight, and certainly can't compare with Dubrovnik (or even Split) in the glamour stakes. What the city does offer is a uniquely vivacious café life, a year-round programme of heavy-duty art exhibitions and at least one genuine cultural flagship in the shape of the recently opened **Museum of Contemporary Art**. The Croatian capital's growing reputation for arty fun also extends into its **nightlife**, with cutting-edge clubs, live gig venues and **summer festivals** that would put many a central European city to shame.

Just one word of advice: don't expect too much excitement in August, when locals head for the coast and the whole city seems to indulge in a month-long siesta.

Brief history

Despite evidence of Iron Age settlements on top of Gradec hill, the history of Zagreb doesn't really start until 1094, when Ladislas I of Hungary established a bishopric here in order to bring the northern Croatian lands under tighter Hungarian control. A large ecclesiastical community grew up around the cathedral and its girdle of episcopal buildings on **Kaptol** (which roughly translates as "cathedral chapter"), while the Hungarian crown retained a garrison opposite on **Gradec**. Following the Mongol incursions of 1240–42, King Bela IV declared Gradec a royal free town in order to attract settlers and regenerate urban life.

The communities of Kaptol and Gradec rarely got on – control of the watermills on the river dividing them was a constant source of enmity. The biggest outbreak of intercommunal fighting occurred in 1527, culminating in the sacking of Kaptol by the Habsburgs – who were now in control of Croatian lands. Henceforth the separate identities of Kaptol and Gradec began to disappear, and the name **Zagreb** (meaning, literally, "behind the hill" – a reference to the town's position at the foot of Mount Medvednica) entered popular usage as a collective name for both.

Under the Habsburgs

By the end of the sixteenth century the Ottoman Empire was in control of much of Croatia, reducing the country to a northern enclave with Zagreb at its centre. Despite

MUSEUM OF BROKEN RELATIONSHIPS

Highlights

❶ **Saturday on Cvjetni trg** Meeting for coffee before lunch on Saturday is the most important social event of the week for locals, who pack Cvjetni trg's cafés to overdose on caffeine and conversation. **See p.64**

❷ **Tkalčićeva** This pedestrianized strip of cafés and bars is the perfect venue for night-time promenading, people-watching or just posing. **See p.64**

❸ **Museum of Broken Relationships** Part museum, part art installation, this unique collection offers an irresistible insight into the turbulent world of love, loss and obsession. **See p.66**

❹ **The Lauba House** Housed in a reconditioned textile factory, this private art collection is a showcase for contemporary Croatian culture. **See p.78**

❺ **Museum of Contemporary Art** Zagreb was a key centre of avant-garde activity after World War II, a point dramatically proved by this ambitious new museum. **See p.79**

❻ **Mount Medvednica** The mountain ridge on Zagreb's doorstep is a paradise for woodland walkers. **See p.80**

❼ **Britanski trg market** This Sunday morning antiques and collectables fair is a social event as well as a shopping opportunity. **See p.92**

HIGHLIGHTS ARE MARKED ON THE MAPS ON PP.60–61 & P.77

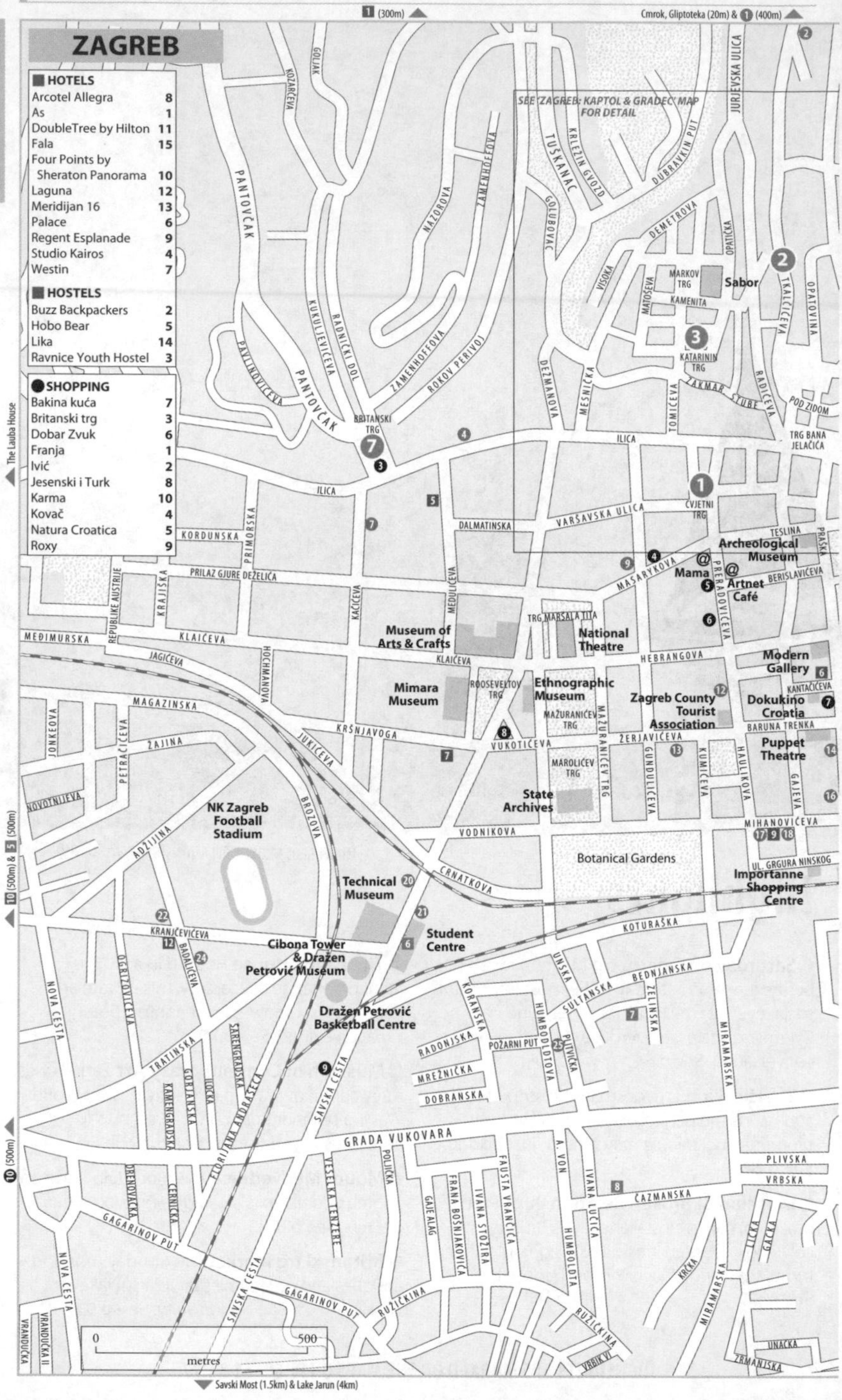

1

ZAGREB

HOTELS

Arcotel Allegra	8
As	1
DoubleTree by Hilton	11
Fala	15
Four Points by Sheraton Panorama	10
Laguna	12
Meridijan 16	13
Palace	6
Regent Esplanade	9
Studio Kairos	4
Westin	7

HOSTELS

Buzz Backpackers	2
Hobo Bear	5
Lika	14
Ravnice Youth Hostel	3

SHOPPING

Bakina kuća	7
Britanski trg	3
Dobar Zvuk	6
Franja	1
Ivić	2
Jesenski i Turk	8
Karma	10
Kovač	4
Natura Croatica	5
Roxy	9

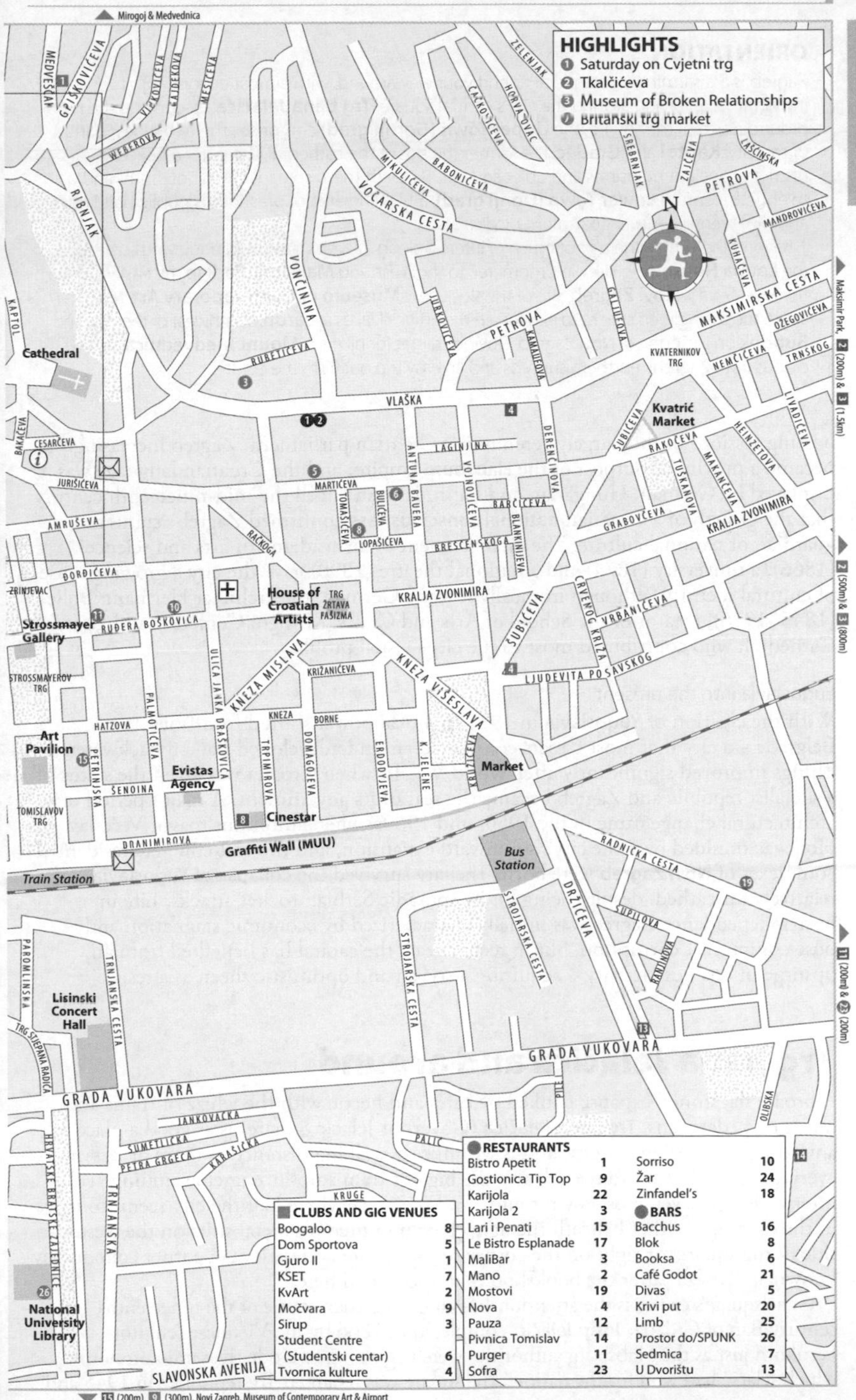

Mirogoj & Medvednica
HIGHLIGHTS
1 Saturday on Cvjetni trg
2 Tkalčićeva
3 Museum of Broken Relationships
4 Britanski trg market
Maksimir Park, 2 (200m) & 3 (1.5km)
2 (500m) & 3 (800m)
11 (200m) & 23 (200m)
15 (200m), 9 (300m), Novi Zagreb, Museum of Contemporary Art & Airport
Cathedral
Kvatrić Market
House of Croatian Artists
Strossmayer Gallery
Art Pavilion
Evistas Agency
Cinestar
Graffiti Wall (MUU)
Market
Bus Station
Train Station
Lisinski Concert Hall
National University Library
VLAŠKA
PETROVA
MAKSIMIRSKA CESTA
KRALJA ZVONIMIRA
KNEZA MISLAVA
KNEZA VIŠESLAVA
LJUDEVITA POSAVSKOG
GRADA VUKOVARA
SLAVONSKA AVENIJA
VOĆARSKA CESTA
RADNIČKA CESTA
STROJARSKA CESTA
TRNJANSKA CESTA
HRVATSKE BRATSKE ZAJEDNICE
CLUBS AND GIG VENUES
Boogaloo 8
Dom Sportova 5
Gjuro II 1
KSET 7
KvArt 2
Močvara 9
Sirup 3
Student Centre (Studentski centar) 6
Tvornica kulture 4
RESTAURANTS
Bistro Apetit 1
Gostionica Tip Top 9
Karijola 22
Karijola 2 3
Lari i Penati 15
Le Bistro Esplanade 17
MaliBar 3
Mano 2
Mostovi 19
Nova 4
Pauza 12
Pivnica Tomislav 14
Purger 11
Sofra 23
Sorriso 10
Žar 24
Zinfandel's 18
BARS
Bacchus 16
Blok 8
Booksa 6
Café Godot 21
Divas 5
Krivi put 20
Limb 25
Prostor do/SPUNK 26
Sedmica 7
U Dvorištu 13

ORIENTATION

Zagreb is a disarmingly easy place to find your way around, with almost everything of importance revolving around the city's central square, **Trg bana Jelačića**. Occupying the high ground north of the square, the **Upper Town (Gornji grad)** comprises the two oldest parts of the city, **Kaptol** and **Gradec**, the former the site of the cathedral, the latter a peaceful district of ancient mansions and quiet squares. Beneath them spreads the nineteenth- and twentieth-century **Lower Town (Donji grad)**, a bustling area of prestigious public buildings and nineteenth-century apartment blocks.

Beyond the centre, there's not much of interest along Zagreb's suburban boulevards save for the **Lauba House** art gallery in Črnomerec to the west, and **Maksimir Park** to the east. Across the River Sava is **Novi Zagreb**, site of the sleek new **Museum of Contemporary Art**. Maksimir apart, the main green spaces to aim for are the artificial lakes at **Jarun**, southwest of the city, and **Bundek** on the edge of Novi Zagreb. Obvious target for hikers is **Mount Medvednica**, served by bus from Zagreb's northern suburbs and an easy trip out from the centre.

hosting sessions of the (largely ceremonial) Croatian parliament, Zagreb increasingly became a provincial outpost of the **Habsburg Empire**, and the Croatian language was displaced by German, Hungarian and Latin. It wasn't until the mid-nineteenth century that the growth of a Croatian **national consciousness** confirmed Zagreb's status as guardian of national culture. The establishment of an academy of arts and sciences (1866), a university (1874) and a national theatre (1890) gave the city a growing sense of cultural identity, although ironically it was a German, the architect Hermann Bollé (1845–1926), creator of the School of Arts and Crafts, Mirogoj Cemetery and Zagreb Cathedral, who contributed most to the city's visual profile.

Yugoslavia into the present

With the creation of **Yugoslavia** in 1918, political power shifted from Vienna to Belgrade – a city that most Croats considered an underdeveloped Balkan backwater. Things improved significantly after World War II, when Croatia was given the status of a socialist republic and Zagreb became the seat of its government. A major period of architectural change came in the 1950s and 1960s, when ambitious mayor Većeslav Holjevac presided over the city's southward expansion, and the vast concrete residential complexes of **Novi Zagreb** were born. The city survived the **collapse of Yugoslavia** relatively unscathed, despite being hit by sporadic Serbian rocket attacks. Life in post-independence Zagreb was initially characterized by economic stagnation and post-communist corruption, but in recent years the capital has benefited from an upsurge in business activity – acquiring a stylish and optimistic sheen as a result.

Trg bana Jelačića and around

A broad, flagstoned expanse flanked by cafés and hectic with the whizz of trams and hurrying pedestrians, **Trg bana Jelačića** (Governor Jelačić Square) is as good a place as any to start exploring the city, and is within easy walking distance of more or less everything you'll want to see. It's also the biggest tram stop in Zagreb, standing at the intersection of seven cross-town routes, and the place where half the city seems to meet in the evening – either beneath the ugly clock mounted on metal stilts on the western side of the square, or right on the corner of the square and Gajeva (a corner colloquially known as "Krleža" after the bookshop that once stood here).

At the square's centre is the attention-hogging equestrian statue of the nineteenth-century Ban of Croatia, **Josip Jelačić**, completed in 1866 by the Viennese sculptor Fernkorn just as the Habsburg authorities were beginning to erode the semi-autonomy which Jelačić had won for the nation. The square was renamed Trg republike in 1945 and

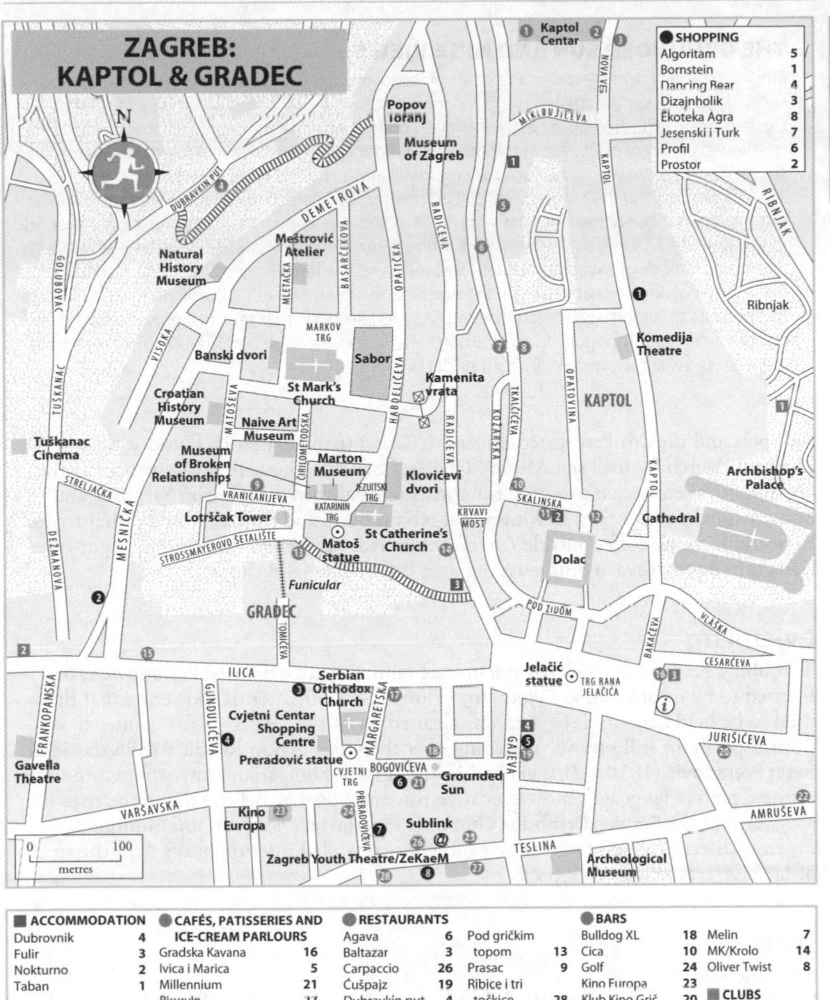

the statue – considered a potential rallying point for Croatian nationalism – was dismantled on the night of July 25, 1947. Its constituent parts were stored away in a basement until 1990, when it was restored to its rightful place – although the statue now faces in a different direction to that intended. Originally positioned with Jelačić's drawn sabre pointing north (a gesture of defiance to the Austro-Hungarian imperial order), it now points southwards, as if to emphasize the historic rupture between Croatia and her Balkan neighbours.

Gajeva and the pedestrian zone

South of the main square is the popular modern pedestrianized area around **Gajeva**, where the glass facade of the *Dubrovnik* hotel serves as a futuristic backdrop for passing

1

THE GROUNDED SUN AND NINE VIEWS

Presiding mutely over the pavement cafés of Bogovićeva is the **Grounded Sun** (Prizemljeno sunce), a bronze sphere created by sculptor Ivan Kožarić in 1971 and placed here in 1994. Despite being tarnished by the elements and covered with graffiti, it remains one of Zagreb's best-loved pieces of public art. In the mid-2000s conceptual artist Davor Preis decided to supply Kožarić's sun with an accompanying installation entitled **Nine Views**, with metal spheres symbolizing the nine planets placed throughout Zagreb at distances that are in exact proportion to those of the real solar system. Thus Mercury appears as a tiny metal ball attached to the wall of a building at Margaretska 3, while Venus (Trg bana Jelačića 3), Earth (Varšavska 9) and Mars (Tkalčićeva 25) appear equally insignificant. The remaining planets are much further out in areas of Zagreb that you wouldn't normally ever want to visit – culminating with Pluto, in a pedestrian underpass beneath the highway to Samobor. That said, tracing the solar system has become a highly popular form of urban safari – consult Zagreb tourist office or Preis's own website (W www.daworp.com) for further details.

shoppers and the drinkers seated outside *Charlie's* (named after its founder, the late Dinamo Zagreb football star Mirko "Charlie" Braun). This café is where most of the city's political elite seem to gather for conspiratorial chin-wagging on Saturday and Sunday lunchtimes – even in winter, Zagreb's movers and shakers would rather freeze to death drinking coffee outside *Charlie's* than risk not being seen. A sharp right here leads into **Bogovićeva**, a promenading area full of cafés and shops.

Cvjetni trg

Throbbing heart of Zagreb's pavement-café culture, pedestrianized **Preradovićev trg**, is referred to by most locals as **Cvjetni trg** (Flower Square), after the flower market that used to be held here until the area was cleaned up in the 1980s – a few sanitized florists' pavilions still survive. Watching over the scene is Ivan Rendić's 1895 statue of **Petar Preradović** (1818–72), a general in the Austro-Hungarian army who wrote some of the Croatian language's most evocative romantic poetry. Behind the statue rises the grey form of the **Serbian Orthodox Church** (Pravoslavna crkva), an unassuming nineteenth-century building whose candlelit, icon-filled interior, heavy with the smell of incense, is worth a quick peek.

Dolac

Mon–Sat 7am–3pm

Occupying a large terrace overlooking Trg bana Jelačića is **Dolac**, the city's principal market. This feast of fruit and vegetables and meat is held every morning, but is at its liveliest on Friday, when fresh fish arrives from the coast. Indoor market halls lie underneath the main outdoor section, with stalls selling all manner of bread, sausages, cured hams and cheeses.

Tkalčićeva

Arguably the prettiest single street in the city, pedestrianized **Tkalčićeva** preserves a neat ensemble of the one- and two-storey, steep-roofed nineteenth-century houses that have largely disappeared elsewhere. There's a smattering of boutiques and art galleries tucked into the street's low-ceilinged mansions, although most of these are now occupied by the youthful café-bars that have transformed Tkalčićeva into the city's prime area for drinking on warm summer evenings. In the first half of the twentieth century the whole area had a somewhat darker reputation, when **Kožarska**, the alleyway which runs parallel to Tkalčićeva to the west, served as the city's red-light district, "reeking of debauchery, adultery, crime, drunkenness, and promiscuity", in the words of diarist and novelist Miroslav Krleža. It was so popular with Hitler's soldiers in World War II that the city authorities had to put up signs in German banning military personnel from entering. Also leading off to the west of Tkalčićeva is **Krvavi most** ("Bloody Bridge" – a reminder of the often violent disputes between Gradec and Kaptol), a street that links up with Radićeva, offering a short cut up to Gradec.

Kaptol

Northeast of Trg bana Jelačića, the filigree spires of Zagreb's cathedral mark the edge of the district known as **Kaptol**, home to the city's Catholic institutions and still patrolled by pious citizens and nuns of various orders. The area consists of little more than one long street – initially called Kaptol, later becoming **Nova ves** in its northern reaches – and the cathedral itself, at its southern end, the district's only arresting feature.

Cathedral

Kaptol 31 • Mon–Sat 10am–5pm, Sun 1–5pm

Ringed by ivy-cloaked turrets, Zagreb's **cathedral** (katedrala) is almost wholly neo-Gothic, having been rebuilt by Viennese architects Friedrich von Schmidt and Hermann Bollé after a catastrophic earthquake in 1880. Most of the money and creative endeavour were invested in the two spires, the big architectural statement it was felt a growing city like Zagreb needed. The interior is high and bare – only four Renaissance choirstalls from the early sixteenth century and the faded remains of some medieval frescoes survive from before the quake. The modest main altar, bearing a copy of the statue of the Madonna and Child in the church at Maria Bistrica, stands in front of a glass casket holding an effigy of Archbishop Alojzije Stepinac, head of the Croatian Church during World War II and imprisoned by the communists immediately afterwards. Stepinac's grave, near the altar on the north wall of the church, is marked by a touching relief by Ivan Meštrović in which the archbishop kneels humbly before Christ. There's another statue by Fernkorn in front of the cathedral, depicting a richly gilded Madonna surrounded by four angels, which provides a beckoning sparkle as you approach Kaptol from the south.

Ribnjak

A small, shady park situated on the site of a former fishpond, the **Ribnjak** is overshadowed on one side by the crumbling remains of Kaptol's fortifications. One of the city's most charming open spaces, the park was reserved for Kaptol's priests until 1947, when the railings surrounding it were demolished by the same communist activists who put paid to the statue of Jelačić on Trg bana Jelačića.

Gradec

Funicular: daily 6.30am–9pm; every 10min; 5Kn each way

Gradec (or more colloquially "Grič") is the oldest and most atmospheric part of Zagreb, a leafy, tranquil area of tiny streets, small squares and Baroque palaces, whose mottled brown roofs peek out from the hill. The most leisurely approach is to take the **funicular** *(uspinjača)*, which ascends from Tomićeva, an alleyway about 200m west of Trg bana Jelačića; alternatively, wander up the gentle gradient of Radićeva towards the **Kamenita vrata**, or "stone gate", which originally formed the main eastern entrance to the town. Inside Kamenita vrata – actually more of a long curving tunnel than a gate

1

– lies one of Zagreb's most popular shrines, a simple sixteenth-century statue of the Virgin in a grille-covered niche. Miraculous powers have been attributed to the statue, largely on account of its surviving a fire in 1731 – a couple of benches inside the gate accommodate passing city folk eager to offer a quick prayer.

Klovićevi dvori

Jezuitski trg 4 • Tues–Sun 11am–7pm • Admission price varies according to what's on display • T 01 485 1926, W galerijaklovic.hr

Housed in a seventeenth-century former Jesuit monastery, **Klovićevi dvori** is one of the city's prime venues for major art exhibitions, frequently with a big-name international flavour, from Pompeii relics in 2011 to Degas sculptures in 2012. The galleried courtyard occasionally hosts summertime concerts.

St Catherine's Church

Katarinin trg • Daily 10am–1pm

Built for the Jesuits, **St Catherine's Church** (Crkva svete Katarine) contains one of the most delightful Baroque interiors in Croatia, with its lacework pattern of pink-and-white stucco whorls executed by Antonio Quadrio in the 1720s. Francesco Robba's delicate portrayal of the Jesuit order's founder, St Ignatius of Loyola, to the right of the main altar, is the outstanding piece of statuary, portraying the saint in a typically Baroque swoon of spiritual ecstasy.

Lotrščak Tower

Strossmayerovo šetalište 9 • May–Oct Tues–Sun 11am–8pm • 10Kn

Towering over the top station of Zagreb's funicular is **Lotrščak Tower** (Kula lotrščak or "Burglars' Tower"), from which a bell was once sounded every evening before the city gates were closed (to keep out burglars, hence the name). A tightly wound spiral staircase leads up to a small wooden terrace, with superb views of Zagreb's red-tiled roofs below. On the way up you'll pass the window through which a small cannon is fired every day at noon, a practice begun in 1877 to coordinate the city's bell-ringers. A story linking the cannon to a fifteenth-century Ottoman attack was subsequently invented by city fathers eager to provide Zagreb with an appealing urban legend.

Strossmayerovo šetalište

Running along the southern edge of the Gradec quarter, **Strossmayerovo šetalište** is a tree-lined promenade offering terrific views over the city. One of several benches along its length bears a seated statue of **Antun Gustav Matoš** (1873–1914), the modernist writer who frequently used Zagreb and its surroundings as the settings for his stories. Being photographed sitting next to Matoš has become an almost compulsory part of the Zagreb experience. Throughout the summer, the šetalište becomes the focus of Zagreb nightlife as the **Strossmartre** season of nightly open-air gigs, puppet shows and art happenings gets into gear (see box, p.91).

Museum of Broken Relationships

Ćirilometodska 2 • Daily: June–Sept 9am–10.30pm, Oct–May 9am–9pm • 25Kn • T 01 485 1021, W brokenships.com

For a voyage into the more tumescent recesses of the human psyche then there are few better starting points than Zagreb's **Museum of Broken Relationships** (Muzej prekinutih veza), the celebrated art installation that became a permanently grounded museum in 2010. It started out as an exhibit at the Zagreb Salon of 2006, at which co-creators Olinka Vištica and Dražen Grubišić (themselves a former item) displayed a collection of objects connected with all aspects of break-up, many of which were donated by friends with a story to tell. The exhibit struck an instant chord with the public, and became an international travelling exhibition, adding to its collection as more and more people donated meaningful mementoes.

Now located on the ground floor of Gradec's Kulmer Palace, it's a compelling and unique museum of wistful memory and raw emotion. Each of the exhibits is accompanied by a text explaining why it was so significant to the donor – some are touching, others quite kinky; and a few belong to the obsessive world of a David Lynch movie. The broken relationships in question aren't always what one expects; one member of the public donated the hands of his favourite mannequin, another an oil painting of a politician who failed to deliver. Among the most poignant exhibits is a comic book purchased after a particular break-up – because the ex-boyfriend in question had departed leaving nothing to be remembered by.

It is also one of the few Zagreb museums that has a genuinely cute café and a well-patronized shop: Bad Memory Eraser pencil rubbers are the big sellers.

The Marton Museum

Katarinin trg 2 • Tues–Sun 10am–6pm • 20Kn • ⓣ 01 483 8700, ⓦ muzej-marton.hr

Occupying the upstairs bits of the same Baroque palace that houses the Museum of Broken Relationships, the **Marton Museum** (Muzej Marton) is based on the applied-art collection of local businessman Veljko Marton. Having outgrown its previous home (the Marton Museum in Samobor; see p.111), the collection presents an entertaining jaunt through the history of glass and porcelain production, with Meissen tableware, Sèvres figurines and the Eastertide dinner plates of Russian Tsar Nicholas I jostling for attention. Frequent themed exhibitions add to the interest, while the building's creeky parquet floors and ancient-looking cylindrical stoves provide plenty of atmosphere.

The Naive Art Museum

Ćirilometodska 3 • Tues–Fri 10am–6pm, Sat & Sun 10am–1pm • 20Kn • ⓣ 01 485 1911, ⓦ hmnu.org

The **Naive Art Museum** (Muzej naivne umjetnosti) provides an excellent introduction to the work of Croatia's self-taught village painters, who created something of a sensation when first discovered by the mainstream art world of the 1930s. The work of Ivan Generalić (1914–92) from the east Croatian village of Hlebine dominates the first of the gallery's six rooms, his early watercolours of village life reflecting a Bruegelesque fascination with rural festivities. Subsequent rooms deal with later generations of naive painters, including Ivan Lacković-Croata's scenes of villages in winter, crowded with spindly, stylized trees and snow-laden houses; Emerik Feješ's kaleidoscopic cityscapes; and Ivan Rabuzin's meditative, almost abstract visions of rural harmony. The final room concentrates on Josip Generalić (son of Ivan), who painted like a comic-strip artist on acid, deserting rural themes in favour of subjects like war, actresses and religious cults.

Markov trg

At the centre of Gradec is **Markov trg** (St Mark's Square), a restrained square of golden-brown buildings which in many ways serves as Croatia's symbolic heart. Though it's not obvious from their modest facades, the buildings on the western side of the square include the so-called **Banski dvor** (Ban's Palace), originally the seat of the Habsburg-appointed governor and now the seat of Croatia's government, while those on the east include the **Sabor** (national parliament). Markov trg has always been an important focus of government ceremonial: rulers of Croatia were sworn in here from the mid-sixteenth century onwards, a tradition renewed by President Tuđman in the 1990s, while in 1573 peasant leader Matija Gubec was executed here in a parody of

1

such ceremonies – he was seated on a throne and "crowned" with a band of red-hot iron. Nowadays, you're unlikely to come across any signs of political activity aside from the occasional purr of a ministerial Mercedes or the furtive glances of sharp-suited security men.

St Mark's Church

Markov trg

The main focus of the St Mark's Square is the squat **St Mark's Church** (Crkva svetog Marka), a much-renovated structure whose multicoloured tiled roof displays the coats of arms of Zagreb and Croatia to the sky – and, it would seem from opening any book on Zagreb, dozens of photographers. The emblems adorning the Croatian coat of arms (the one on the left as you face it) symbolize the three areas which originally made up the medieval kingdom: north-central Croatia is represented by the red-and-white chequerboard known as the *šahovnica* – a state symbol since the Middle Ages; Dalmatia by three lions' heads; and Slavonia by a running beast (the *kuna*, or marten, Croatia's national animal) framed by two rivers – the Sava and Drava. The church itself is a homely Gothic building, originally constructed in the fourteenth century but since ravaged by earthquake, fire and nineteenth-century restorers, though some parts – including the south portal – are original. Inside, Jozo Kljaković's frescoes portray huge, muscle-bound Croatian kings caught in dramatic mid-gesture; Ivan Meštrović's *Crucifixion* is more sensitive, merging sympathetically with the rest of the church.

The Croatian History Museum

Matoševa 9 • Mon–Fri 10am–6pm, Sat & Sun 10am–1pm • 20Kn • T 01 485 1900, W hismus.hr

The **Croatian History Museum** (Hrvatski povijesni muzej), in one of the more crumbly of Gradec's Baroque mansions, houses seasonal history exhibitions which range in style from the absolutely unmissable to the bafflingly inconsequential. The museum is planning to move to the former tobacco factory on Klaićeva in the Lower Town, although it's a big project and completion is not expected any time soon.

Natural History Museum

Demetrova 1 • Tues, Wed & Fri 10am–5pm, Thurs 10am–8pm, Sat 10am–7pm, Sun 10am–1pm • 15Kn • T 01 485 1700, W hpm.hr

The **Natural History Museum** (Hrvatski prirodoslovni muzej) is remarkable as much for the style of the displays as for the exhibits themselves, with objects laid out in a succession of old-fashioned cabinets that haven't been significantly reorganized in more than half a century. The history of the world's fauna on the second floor is particularly atmospheric, with visitors proceeding through a narrow corridor lined with corals, skeletons and creatures in bottles. There's an impressive range of stuffed mammals at the end – although pride of place goes to the 8m-long basking shark caught in the north Adriatic in 1934. More modern exhibition galleries on the lower floors host regularly changing themed exhibitions.

The Meštrović Atelier

Mletačka 8 • Tues–Fri 10am–6pm, Sat & Sun 10am–2pm • 30Kn • T 01 485 1123, W mestrovic.hr

Occupying the house where Croatia's foremost twentieth-century sculptor, Ivan Meštrović (see box, p.296), lived between 1924 and 1942, the **Meštrović Atelier** is a delightful and intimate museum that you don't have to be a Meštrović fan to enjoy. Featuring wooden panelling and ceramic stoves ordered by the artist himself, the place still feels like a thoughtfully designed family abode rather than a reverential gallery. On display are sketches, photographs and small-scale studies for creations such as the giant

CLOCKWISE FROM TOP LEFT TKALČIĆEVA (P.64); ST MARK'S CHURCH ROOF; GILDED MADONNA STATUE (P.65) >

Grgur Ninski in Split and the *Crucifixion* in St Mark's Church, along with some lovely female statuettes in the small atrium.

The Museum of Zagreb

Opatička 20 • Tues–Fri 10am–6pm, Sat 10am–7pm, Sun 10am–2pm • 30Kn • T 01 485 1361, W mgz.hr

Telling the tale of Zagreb's development from medieval times to the present day, the **Museum of Zagreb** (Muzej grada Zagreba) is the most visually absorbing of the city's history museums. Approached through the courtyard of the former Convent of the Poor Clares, the museum occupies a complex of buildings tacked on to the thirteenth-century **Popov toranj** (Priests' Tower), which was built to provide the clerics of poorly defended Kaptol with a refuge in case of attack. Inside the museum, scale models of Zagreb through the ages reveal the changing face of the city, and there's a modest but well-chosen selection of weaponry, furnishings and costumes. Sacral art taken from local churches includes an expressive seventeenth-century sculptural ensemble depicting Jesus flanked by the apostles, which originally stood above the portal of Zagreb cathedral. Upstairs, political posters, photographs of political leaders and ideological slogans help to breathe life into the turbulent history of the twentieth century; one of the final rooms contains an unintentionally surreal display of the furniture destroyed by the JNA (Yugoslav People's Army) rocket attack on Gradec in October 1991, with smashed crockery and splintered furniture arranged as if part of some contemporary art exhibit.

The Gliptoteka

Medvedgradska 2 • Tues–Fri 11am–7pm, Sat & Sun 10am–2pm • 20Kn • T 01 468 6060

A collection of plaster copies of famous sculptures, the **Gliptoteka**, on the northern extension of Tkalčićeva, is far more interesting than it sounds – partly because of the atmospheric red-brick factory building in which it's housed. Things get under way with an impressive assemblage of replica *stećci* (medieval gravestones) from Bosnia-Hercegovina. Decorated with floral swirls, sun symbols and hunting scenes, they're a striking example of indigenous folk art. A collection of Croatian sculpture follows (comprising some originals among the copies), with twentieth-century greats Antun Augustinčić and Ivan Meštrović particularly well represented. The Gliptoteka also hosts fascinating seasonal architecture, design and photography exhibitions – the tourist office (see p.82) will tell you what's on.

Dubravkin put

Running round the northern end of Zagreb's Gradec quarter is an area of wooded knolls and dells that comes as a welcome and wholly unexpected surprise after so much historical architecture. **Dubravkin put** is a foot- and cycle path that runs north through the woodland zone, passing below the forest-shrouded Tuškanac open-air cinema (put to good use during the Fantastic Zagreb Film Festival; see p.91) before forging through a narrow vale surrounded by beech and spruce. After about twenty minutes on foot the path emerges into the open meadows of **Cmrok**, a public park in a V-shaped depression that's perfect for picnics, Frisbee games – and sledging if it snows in winter. From Cmrok you can either go back via the same route or descend to Gradec along leafy, suburban Jurjevska, passing upper-class villas and the outstanding *Bistro Apetit* restaurant (see p.87) along the way.

The Lower Town

South of the Upper Town, the modern **Lower Town** (Donji grad) is a bit of a sprawl, with grey office blocks and apartment buildings surrounding the occasional example of imposing Habsburg-era architecture. Breaking the urban uniformity is a series of interconnected garden squares, laid out from the 1870s onwards, which gives the downtown area a U-shaped succession of promenading areas and parks. Known as **Lenuci's Horseshoe** (Lenucijeva podkova) after Milan Lenuci, the city planner responsible for its layout, this was a deliberate attempt to give Zagreb a distinctive urban identity, providing it with public spaces bordered by the set-piece institutions – galleries, museums, academies and theatres – that it was thought every modern city should have. The horseshoe was never entirely finished, though, and it's unlikely you'll follow the full U-shaped itinerary intended by Lenuci. The first of the horseshoe's two main series of squares starts with Trg Nikole Šubića Zrinskog – usually referred to as **Zrinjevac** – which begins a block south of Trg bana Jelačića; to the west of Zrinjevac is the second line of squares, culminating with **Trg maršala Tita**. To the south are the **Botanical Gardens**, which were intended to provide the final green link between the two arms of the horseshoe, but didn't quite manage it: several characterless downtown blocks prevent it from joining Tomislavov trg to the east.

Zrinjevac

South of Trg bana Jelačića, the first section of Lenuci's Horseshoe, **Zrinjevac**, is a typical late nineteenth-century city park, featuring shady walks, a bandstand and a fountain which was designed by the ubiquitous Hermann Bollé and looks like a bizarre cross between a cake stand and a toadstool. Until 1873, when it was first laid out as a park, this area marked the southern boundary of the city: the muddy site of fairs and markets where peasants gathered to trade cows and horses.

The Archeological Museum

Zrinjevac 19 • Tues, Wed & Fri 10am–5pm, Thurs 10am–8pm, Sat & Sun 10am–1pm • 30Kn • T 01 487 3101, W amz.hr

The well-labelled three-floor collection of the **Archeological Museum** (Arheološki muzej) gets off to a colourful start with an impressive collection of Greek vases amassed by nineteenth-century Habsburg general Laval Nugent, before moving on to pottery and inscriptions recalling the Greek settlements on Croatia's Adriatic coast. The arrival of the Romans in the third century BC is illustrated by a dramatic display of military helmets, while the Roman theme continues with a third-century relief of the goddess Nemesis, portrayed here as a frowny-faced woman dismounting from her chariot. Serving as something of a trademark for the museum is the third-century Head of a Woman from the city of Salona (near present-day Split; see p.306), thought to be a portrait of the Empress Plautilla. The museum's other star exhibit is the **Vučedol Dove** (Vučedolska golubica), a three-legged zoomorphic pouring vessel unearthed at the Copper Age settlement at Vučedol, near Vukovar – and pictured on the 20Kn banknote. There are also two rooms of Egyptian mummies, mostly dating from the Ptolemaic period, one of which has a climate-controlled chamber all to itself. This last was found wrapped in a linen shroud (now displayed on the wall beside it) bearing ancient Etruscan writing – the longest known text in this as yet untranslated language.

The Modern Gallery

Hebrangova 1 • Tues–Fri 11am–7pm, Sat & Sun 11am–2pm • 30Kn • T 01 604 1040, W moderna-galerija.hr

An all-embracing collection of Croatian art from 1850 to the present day, the **Modern Gallery** (Moderna galerija) is a well-presented display that includes something for everybody. Highlights of the nineteenth-century section include Vlaho Bukovac's sensuous *Gundulić Imagining Osman*, in which Dubrovnik poet Ivan Gundulić is surrounded by cavorting nymphs; and the moody Symbolist paintings of contemporaries Bela Čikoš-Sesija and Mirko Rački. Socially committed twentieth-century artist Krsto Hegedušić is represented by canvases depicting life in the village of Hlebine in the 1930s, while the photographs of Tošo Dabac provide a visual urban safari through the Zagreb of the interwar years. A smattering of contemporary works serves as an appetizer for what's on display in the Contemporary Art Museum (see p.79) across the river. German-Croatian artist Dragutin Trumbetaš's mischievous depiction of Van Gogh engaged in oral sex (in room XXVIII) needs to be seen to be believed.

The Strossmayer Gallery of Old Masters

Zrinjevac 11 • Tues 10am–7pm, Wed–Fri 10am–4pm, Sat & Sun 10am–1pm • 20Kn • ⓣ 01 489 5117, ⓦ info.hazu.hr

Zagreb's foremost collection of old masters occupies the second floor of the Croatian Academy of Arts and Sciences, founded by **Juraj Strossmayer**, Bishop of Đakovo (see p.130), in 1866. Strossmayer's personal art collection forms the core of the gallery, which starts with two rooms of Renaissance Madonnas cradling chubby-cheeked babes. In the following room, a turbulent *Engagement of St Catherine* by Tintoretto stands next to a depiction of the same subject by fellow Venetian Veronese. Look out, too, for some early Flemish canvases by Joos van Cleve, the anonymous *Master of the Virgin among Virgins*, and French paintings by the likes of Fragonard and Poussin. Despite wearing what looks look a tea-cosy on her head, Jean Antoine Gros's *Madame Récamier* is arguably the finest nineteenth-century portrait in the collection. Finally, crouched in the lobby of the building is the **Baška Tablet** (Baščanska ploča), an eleventh-century inscription from the island of Krk bearing the oldest-known example of Glagolitic (see box, p.220), the archaic script used by the medieval Croatian Church.

The Art Pavilion

Tomislavov trg 22 • Mon–Sat 11am–7pm, Sun 10am–1pm • 20Kn; free on Mon • ⓣ 01 484 1070, ⓦ umjetnicki-paviljon.hr

Resplendent in the bright-yellow paint job beloved of Habsburg-era architects, the **Art Pavilion** (Umjetnički paviljon) hosts regular temporary art exhibitions in its gilded stucco and mock-marble interior. Built around a skeleton of cast-iron girders, the pavilion began life as the Croatian exhibition hall at the Budapest Millennium Exhibition of 1896 – it was taken down and re-erected in Zagreb soon afterwards.

The House of Croatian Artists (HDLU)

Trg Žrtava fašizma • Tues–Fri 11am–7pm, Sat & Sun 10am–2pm • Admission price varies depending on what's on • ⓣ 01 461 1818, ⓦ hdlu.hr

Dominating Trg Žrtava fašizma (Victims of Fascism Square), east of Zrinjevac, is the arrestingly doughnut-shaped **House of Croatian Artists** (Dom hrvatskih likovnih umjetnika), designed by the sculptor and architect Ivan Meštrović in the 1930s and arguably his best ever work. Initially intended as an exhibition pavilion dedicated to the young Yugoslav King Peter, it was converted into a mosque during World War II in an attempt to cultivate Bosnian Muslim support for the puppet regime installed by the Nazis. It's still colloquially referred to as the *džamija* (mosque), though its three minarets were demolished in 1947, after which it was press-ganged into use as a museum of the socialist revolution. Now belonging to the Croatian Artists' Union (HDLU), the boldly circular building is a wonderfully atmospheric venue in which to enjoy the top-notch contemporary art exhibitions held here.

Trg maršala Tita

Most appealing of Zagreb's squares is without doubt the grandiose **Trg maršala Tita** (Marshal Tito Square), dominated by the Croatian National Theatre. The square is one of the few spots in central Zagreb that still sticks to its communist-era name: Marshal Tito's World-War-II role in throwing foreign occupiers out of Istria and Dalmatia is unlikely to be forgotten by Croats, although the mass-murder of political opponents in the war's aftermath can't be struck from the historical record either. There is an on-off campaign to change the name of the square to something less divisive – it's likely that this dispute will run for some time.

Croatian National Theatre

Trg maršala Tita 15 • hnk.hr

Boasting a Neoclassical portal topped by a trumpet-blowing muse, the lemon-meringue-pie-coloured pile of the **Croatian National Theatre** (see p.91) was designed by Vienna-based architects Ferdinand Fellner and Hermann Helmer, responsible for building opera houses all over Europe from Augsburg to Odessa. It was opened by Habsburg Emperor Franz Josef in 1890, a vivacious statement of late nineteenth-century Croatia's growing cultural self-confidence. In front of the theatre, in a circular concrete pit, is Ivan Meštrović's tenderly erotic *Well of Life* (1905), a popular spot for students and tourists to lounge around.

The Museum of Arts and Crafts

Trg maršala Tita 10 • Tues, Wed, Fri & Sat 10am–7pm, Thurs 10am–10pm, Sun 10am–2pm • 20Kn • 01 488 2111, muo.hr

A long gabled building on the western side of Trg maršala Tita houses the **Museum of Arts and Crafts** (Muzej za umjetnost i obrt), a huge collection of furniture and textiles from the Middle Ages to the present day – anybody interested in the history of interiors will have a field day here. The interior is impressive in itself, with gilt lion heads gazing down from cast-iron balustrades above the central atrium.

First floor

The first floor kicks off with a fifteenth-century Virgin and Child altarpiece of Tyrolean origin, continues with a parade of furniture and porcelain through the ages, and culminates in a hall of **religious art** with restored wooden altarpieces from churches all over northern Croatia. Most striking is the seventeenth-century altar of St Mary from the village of Remetinec, northeast of Zagreb, showing a central Madonna and Child flanked by smaller panels in which a whole panoply of saints bend in a stylized swoon of spiritual grace.

Second floor

Objects on the second floor reflect Zagreb's status at the turn of the twentieth century as a prosperous outpost of Mitteleuropa, with locally produced **ceramics** from Zagreb's School of Applied Art (which has been nurturing innovative design ever since its foundation in 1882), as well as imported **furnishings** – notably Tiffany and Gallé glassware, and a plant-pot stand by doyen of the Viennese arts and crafts scene prior to World War I, Josef Hoffmann.

Third floor

The stairs leading up to the third floor are lined with examples of 1960s **poster art**, including several geometric designs produced by the Croatian abstract art pioneer Ivan Picelj. At the top lie an array of clocks, a lot of silverware and a collection of early twentieth-century **stained glass** produced by local firm Koch & Marinković. Among the last, look out for Vilko Gecan's *Life of the Woodcutter* (*Život drvosječe*) from 1924, five idealized panels illustrating the life cycle of the Croatian peasant, depicted here with the kind of reverence one would normally expect given to a church altarpiece.

The Mimara Museum

Rooseveltov trg 5 • Tues, Wed, Fri & Sat 10am–5pm, Thurs 10am–7pm, Sun 10am–2pm • 25Kn • 01 482 8100, mimara.hr

Housed in an elegant neo-Renaissance former high school, the **Mimara Museum** (Muzej Mimara) is the most controversial of Zagreb's art collections. It is made up of the

1

bequest of **Ante Topić Mimara** (1899–1987), a native of Dalmatia who grew rich abroad and presented his vast art collection to the nation. No one really knows how he amassed his wealth, how he came by so many prized objects, or indeed whether he was even the real Ante Topić Mimara – some maintain that he was an impostor who, in the chaos of a World War I battlefield, stole the identity tags of a fallen comrade. What's more, few people in the art community believe that all of Mimara's paintings were really painted by the masters to which they are attributed, which leaves the average visitor in the position of not really knowing what it is that they are looking at.

The good news is that there is a solid collection of applied art on the **lower floors**, with ancient glassware, Persian carpets and Ming vases decorated with bendy-bodied dragons. On the **first floor**, there is an extraordinary thirteenth-century enamelled crucifix from Limoges (room 16), and an exquisitely carved English ivory hunting horn from the 1300s (room 17). The **second floor** begins with an unintentionally ghoulish chamber containing Mimara's death-mask before embarking on a chronological trot through the history of European painting. It's here that the attributions should be taken with a pinch of salt: can Zagreb really boast a Rubens? Or a Rembrandt? The jury is still out.

The Ethnographic Museum

Mažuranićev trg 14 • Tues–Thurs 10am–6pm, Fri–Sun 10am–1pm • 10Kn • T 01 482 6220, W emz.hr

An old-fashioned collection housed in a badly lit building, the **Ethnographic Museum** (Etnografski muzej) nonetheless has its moments, and shouldn't be entirely crossed off your sightseeing list. Upstairs, the collection of costumes from every corner of Croatia is as complete as you'll find, displaying numerous examples of the embroidered aprons and tunics that are found throughout the country. Downstairs lies an engaging jumble of artefacts brought back from the South Pacific, Asia and Africa by intrepid Croatian explorers – most notably Mirko and Stjepan Seljan, who criss-crossed Africa and South America in the years before World War I.

The State Archives

Marulićev trg 21 • Guided tours Mon–Fri noon, 1pm & 2pm; 20Kn • T 01 480 1999

Zagreb's finest example of Art Nouveau architecture, the **State Archives** (Državni arhiv) building was designed by local architect Rudolf Lubynski in 1913 to serve as the University Library. Its pale sandstone exterior is covered with eccentric ornamental details, with reliefs by Robert Frangeš Mihanović just above head height and globe-wielding owls roosting at roof level. To appreciate the full splendour of the interior you should arrive in time for a **guided tour** of the former library reading rooms. The richly ornamented interiors feature stained glass, Art Nouveau desk lamps, ornate chandeliers and frescoes by Croatia's leading artists of the day – Vlaho Bukovac's *Evolution of Croatian Culture* in the main reading room shows the nation's greatest artists and poets queueing up to receive garlands from the goddess Athena.

The Botanical Gardens

Marulićev trg 9 • April–Oct Mon & Tues 9am–2.30pm, Wed–Sun 9am–7pm • Free

Pressed against the railway tracks at the southern end of the Lower Town are Zagreb's tranquil **Botanical Gardens** (Botanički vrt), where a colourful array of well-tended flowerbeds, rose gardens and rockeries fade into wilder areas of long grass and semi-forest. Despite being described as a "boring second-rate cemetery" by the novelist Miroslav Krleža, who used to sit here writing his diary during World War I, the place is nowadays an utterly charming island of city-centre tranquillity and relaxation – the perfect place to take some time out after a couple of hours' sightseeing.

The Museum of Street Art (MUU)/Branimirova wall

Branimirova • Ⓦ muu.com.hr

If you want to get some idea of the depth of Croatian graphic-art talent then the **concrete wall** that runs along the railway yards on **Branimirova** will tell you a lot more than any number of design magazines. The location has long been associated with public art, originally painted to mark the World Student Games of 1987 with designs made by the top artists of the day. By the late 1990s the designs had faded and a new generation of graffiti artists took over. In 2010 the wall became the first major project of Zagreb's **Museum of Street Art (MUU)**, who commissioned a range of street artists, graffiti writers and professional illustrators to redecorate all the panels. With over fifty artworks spread along almost half a kilometre of wall, there's a lot to enjoy. Stand-out pieces include street-artist OKO's face made up of a collage of entrails and offal, Pekmezmed's skeleton-headed skateboarders and Dunja Janković's green-and-red fish-in-space creature.

The Technical Museum

Savska cesta 18 **Museum** Tues–Fri 9am–5pm, Sat & Sun 9am–1pm • 15Kn **Planetarium** Tues–Fri 4pm, Sat noon • 15Kn extra **Tesla Laboratory Demos** Tues–Fri 3.30pm, Sat 11.30am • 15Kn extra • Ⓣ 01 484 4050, Ⓦ tehnicki-muzej.hr

One of the city's more entertaining collections, the **Technical Museum** (Tehnički muzej) begins with a set of historic fire engines, followed by a jumble of wooden watermills,

NIKOLA TESLA (1856–1943)

Born the son of a Serbian Orthodox priest in the village of Smiljan, just outside Gospić, **Nikola Tesla** went on to become the Leonardo da Vinci of the electronic age. He studied in Graz and Prague before working for telephone companies in Budapest and Paris, and in 1884 emigrated to the US where he found work with Thomas Edison – the pair allegedly fell out when Edison promised to reward Tesla with a US$50,000 bonus for improving his electricity generators, then failed to pay up.

After working for a time as a manual labourer, Tesla set up his own company and dedicated himself to generating and distributing electricity in the form of alternating current – a system which is now standard throughout the world. With financial support from American company Westinghouse, Tesla demonstrated his innovations at the Chicago World Fair in 1893, becoming an international celebrity in the process. In 1899 Tesla moved to Colorado Springs, where he built an enormous high-frequency current generator (the "Tesla Coil"), with which he hoped to transmit electric energy in huge waves around the earth. Photographs of Tesla's tall, wiry figure using the coil to produce vast electronic discharges helped turn the inventor into one of the iconic figures of modern science.

Tesla also pioneered the development of long-range radio-wave transmissions, but failed to demonstrate his innovations publicly and was scooped by Giuglielmo Marconi, who successfully sent wireless messages across the Atlantic in 1902. The US patent office credited Marconi as the inventor of radio – a decision overturned in Tesla's favour in 1943.

Official recognition was something that eluded Tesla throughout his career. In 1915 the Nobel committee considered awarding their science prize jointly to Tesla and Thomas Edison, but abruptly changed their minds on discovering that the pair were too vain to share it. Tesla's failure to capitalize on his inventions owed a lot to his secretive nature. His habit of announcing discoveries without providing any supporting evidence led many to see him as a crank. During his period at Colorado Springs, he claimed to have received signals from outer space, and in later life, he claimed at various times to be working on a death ray and an "egeodynamic oscillator", whose vibrations would be enough to destroy large buildings. On Tesla's death in 1943, the FBI confiscated some of the scientist's papers, prompting all kinds of speculation about the secret weapons that Tesla may or may not have been working on.

Tesla remains the subject of fascination for Croats and Serbs alike (indeed he is one of the few historical figures whose legacy they share), and Tesla-related museum displays in Zagreb, Belgrade and his home village of Smiljan are becoming ever more popular.

1 steam turbines and aircraft engines. A central hall holds buses, cars, trams and planes, as well as a World War II Italian submarine captured by the Partisans in 1943 and drafted into the Yugoslav navy under the name *Mališan* ("The Nipper"). Other attractions include models of spacecraft; a small **planetarium** with regular showings; and a section devoted to Croatian-born inventor **Nikola Tesla**, who pioneered the development of alternating current, radio transmission and electric lighting (to name but three of his obsessions; see box, p.75). There are daily demonstrations of Tesla's experiments – mildly boring science lectures which are well worth sitting through on account of the thunder-and-lightning finale.

The Student Centre

Savska cesta 25

Consisting of cinema, theatre, student canteen and a couple of bars, the **Student Centre** (Studentski centar) occupies the former pavilions of the interwar Zagreb Fairgrounds. The Centre's most iconic building is the **French Pavilion** (Francuski pavilijon), a barrel-shaped modernist masterpiece built in 1937 and currently the object of an expensive restoration programme – which initially involved being totally dismantled prior to a complete rebuilding. Once finished the pavilion will resume its former role as exhibition space and drama venue. Next to the pavilion, the **&TD Theatre** with adjoining bar and courtyard is a popular venue for drama, gigs and film festivals (see p.90).

The Dražen Petrović Museum

Trg Dražena Petrovića 3 • Mon–Fri 9am–5pm • 20Kn • ⓣ 01 484 3146, ⓦ drazenpetrovic.net

Honouring the Šibenik-born star who was considered basketball's answer to Mozart, the **Dražen Petrović Museum** (Muzej Dražen Petrović) occupies the ground floor of the cylindrical **Cibona Tower**, a 1980s office block whose highly reflective surface exudes a silvery, futuristic haughtiness. Best European player of his generation, Petrović (1964–93) began his career at home side Šibenka before leading Cibona to the European championships in 1985 and 1986. He subsequently played for Real Madrid and the New Jersey Nets before his career was cut short by a fatal car crash. The museum is warm and celebratory without being sentimental. Petrović's former team Cibona play immediately next door in the Dražen Petrović Basketball Centre.

Radnička cesta

Spearing southeast from the bus station, long, straight **Radnička cesta** is one of Zagreb's fastest developing new districts, with company HQs and fancy residential blocks rising above an inner-city area known previously for its factories and warehouses. It's not especially pretty, but few other areas of town provide such an immediate taste of how quickly the city is changing. Radnička is also a zone of growing leisure opportunities, with the Green Gold shopping centre offering luxury shops and smart cafés, and the nearby, brand-new *DoubleTree by Hilton* hotel holding out the promise of a future influx of well-heeled business guests. There are some good restaurants here too, notably the meat-eater's favourite *Mostovi* (see p.86) and the Bosnian-themed *Sofra* (see p.87).

The suburbs

Zagreb's sightseeing potential is largely exhausted once you've covered the compact centre, although there are a few worthwhile trips into the suburbs – all of which are easily accessible by tram or bus. **Maksimir**, **Jarun** and **Mirogoj cemetery** are the park-like expanses to aim for if you want a break from the downtown streets, while the **Sava**

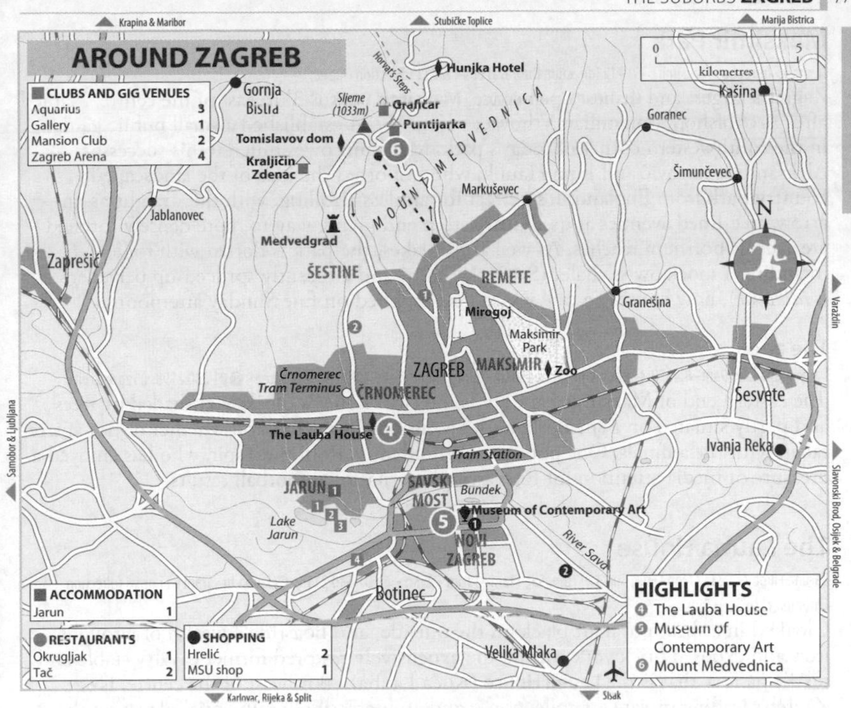

river embankment presents the ideal excuse for a long afternoon stroll. South of the river, the residential high-rise sprawl of **Novi Zagreb** is home to the city's coolest cultural attraction – the **Museum of Contemporary Art.**

Mirogoj

Bus #106 heads up to Mirogoj from Kaptol every 15min; otherwise, take tram #14 (direction Mihaljevac) from Trg bana Jelačića to Gupčeva Zvijezda, then walk the remaining 10min up to the cemetery via Mirogojska cesta

Ranged across a hillside just over 2km northeast of the centre, the main city cemetery of **Mirogoj** was laid out by Hermann Bollé in 1876. The main (western) entrance to the graveyard is in many ways his most impressive work: an ivy-covered, fortress-like wall topped by a row of greening cupolas. The cemetery serves all Zagreb's citizens regardless of faith, so alongside the Catholic gravestones you'll find Orthodox memorials bearing Cyrillic script, Muslim graves adorned with the crescent of Islam and socialist-era tombstones boasting the *petokraka*, or five-pointed star. Head round the back of the chapel just inside the main entrance to find the grave of independent Croatia's first president Franjo Tuđman, a black reflective-surfaced slab that draws its fair share of patriotic pilgrims.

The most evocative parts of this vast necropolis are the arcades running either side of the main entrance, containing work by some of Croatia's best late nineteenth-century sculptors, with rows of elegantly rendered memorials overlooked by spindly cast-iron lanterns. If you head right from the entrance, it's difficult to miss Ivan Rendić's grieving female figures atop the graves of Petar Preradović and Emanuel Priester; slightly farther on, Robert Frangeš Mihanović's extraordinary bleak relief of stooping bearded figures decorates the tomb of the Mayer family. Head left from the entrance to find the Miletić tomb, where Rudolf Valdec's fine *Angel of Death* is framed on either side by outstretched sculpted hands, into which descendants of the family still place roses.

Maksimir Park

Trams #5 (direction Maksimir), #7, #12 (direction Dubrava) or #4 & #11 (direction Dubec)

Zagreb's largest and lushest open space, **Maksimir Park** is 3km east of the centre. Named after Archbishop Maximilian Vrhovac, who in 1774 established a small public garden in the southwestern corner of today's park, Maksimir owes much to his successors Aleksandar Alagović and Juraj Haulik, who imported the idea of the landscaped country park from England. It's perfect for aimless strolling, with the straight-as-an-arrow, tree-lined avenues at its southwestern end giving way to more densely forested areas in its northern reaches. As well as five lakes, the park is dotted with follies, including a mock Swiss chalet (Švicarska kuća) and a recently spruced-up belvedere (*vidikovac*), now housing a café which gets mobbed on fine Sunday afternoons.

The zoo

Daily: May–Sept 9am–8pm; Oct–April 9am–4pm • 30Kn, children aged 7–14 20Kn, under 7s free • Ⓣ 01 230 2198, Ⓦ zgzoo.com

The eastern end of Maksimir Park holds the city's **zoo** (Zoološki vrt) shaded by trees and partly situated on a small island; it's a pleasant place to stroll whether or not you're taken with the animals. One popular zoo resident is Robi the Tapir, who has enjoyed a measure of media attention for forecasting international football results.

The Lauba House

Baruna Filipoviča 23a • Mon–Fri & Sun 3–11pm, Sat 11am–11pm • 25Kn • Ⓣ 01 630 2115, Ⓦ lauba.hr • Tram #11 or #6 (direction Črnomerec) to Sveti Duh

Cloaked in a sheath of matt black on the outside, and boasting a wealth of wrought iron and exposed brickwork within, the expensively restored former cavalry stable and textile factory that is the **Lauba House** (Kuća Lauba), 4km west of the centre, is Zagreb's leading private art collection – and an increasingly influential player on the contemporary arts scene. It's the brainchild of Tomislav Kličko (the name "lauba" is local dialect in Kličko's home village for a circle of tree branches), who systematically bought up the works of Croatia's leading contemporary artists at a time when few other individuals and institutions were making acquisitions. Unsurprisingly, Kličko ended up with the cream. Occupying centre stage in a regularly rotated collection are the figurative paintings of Lovro Artuković, light installations by Ivana Franke and the glitzy but disturbing sculptures and photographs of Kristian Kožul.

Kličko's company Filip Trade occupies the same building – and the Lauba House's idiosyncratic opening hours are partly based on the idea that the building is open for business during office hours, and open for art and leisure in the evening. The Lauba House's **café-bistro** (run by Lari i Penati; see p.86) provides ample reason to stick around.

The Sava Embankment

Built to prevent a repeat of the 1964 flood, the **Sava Embankment** (Savski nasip) runs along both sides of the River Sava for the whole length of the river's passage through Zagreb. With a foot- and cycle-path running along the top, it's here that locals come to stroll, ride bikes, get pulled along by dogs, or indulge in athletic bursts of exercise. Walking from the Bundek (see p.80) in the east to Lake Jarun (see opposite) in the west – crossing the river at **Most Slobode** – is a great way to spend an afternoon, and might feasibly be combined with a side-trip to the Museum of Contemporary Art (see opposite).

The busiest part of the Embankment is the stretch from Most Slobode to **Savski Most** (25min), which offers sweeping views of Zagreb's skyline on both sides of the river. The Kockica or **Cube**, originally built to serve as HQ of the Croatian League of Communists, is one of the cool slabs of modernist architecture you will pass on the way. Of the string of **sculptures** along this part of the embankment, Zvonimir Lončarić's *Putokaz* ("Signpost") is the most frequently photographed – it features a pair of brightly painted female legs pointing cheekily skyward. Looming to the west is the iconic cast-iron arch of the **railway bridge**, popularly known as "Hendrix Bridge" on account of the large-format graffiti on its western side.

From Savski Most you can catch a tram back to the centre or continue along the embankment to Lake Jarun (25min), enjoying views of the Zagreb Arena sports- and concert-hall on the opposite bank of the river. With Lake Jarun in sight you descend from the embankment just behind the *Aquarius* club (see p.89), which works as a café during the day and is the perfect place to take a breather.

Lake Jarun

Tram #17 from Trg bana Jelačića (direction Prečko) to the Staglišće or Jarun stops, either of which is a 10min walk north of the water's edge

On sunny days, city folk head out to **Jarun**, a 2km-long artificial lake encircled by footpaths and cycling tracks 6km southwest of the centre. Created to coincide with Zagreb's hosting of the 1987 World Student Games, it's an important venue for rowing competitions, with a large spectator stand at the western end, although most people come here simply to stroll or sunbathe. The best spot for the latter is **Malo jarunsko jezero** at Jarun's eastern end, a bay sheltered from the rest of the lake by a long thin island. Here you'll find a shingle beach backed by outdoor cafés, several of which remain open until the early hours. This is a good place from which to clamber up onto the dyke that runs along the banks of the River Sava, providing a good vantage point from which to survey the cityscape of Novi Zagreb beyond.

Novi Zagreb

Spread over the plain on the southern side of the River Sava, **Novi Zagreb** (New Zagreb) is a vast gridiron of housing projects and multi-lane highways, conceived by ambitious urban planners in the 1960s. The central part of the district is not that bad a place to live: swaths of park help to break up the architectural monotony, and each residential block has a clutch of bars and pizzerias in which to hang out. Outlying areas have far fewer facilities, however, and possess the aura of half-forgotten dormitory settlements on which the rest of Zagreb has turned its back.

The Museum of Contemporary Art

Avenija Dubrovnik 17 • Tues–Fri & Sun 11am–6pm, Sat 11am–8pm • 30Kn; first Wed of the month free • ⓣ 01 605 2700, ⓦ msu.hr • Tram #14 (destination Zapruđe) from Trg bana Jelačića to the Siget stop

Opened to the public in 2009, the **Museum of Contemporary Art** (Muzej suvremene umjetnosti) has quickly established itself as the leading art institution in the region. Taking the form of an angular wave on concrete stilts, the Igor Franić-designed building is a deliberate reference to the meandering motif developed by Croatian abstract artist Julije Knifer (1924–2004) and repeated – with minor variations – in almost all of his paintings. The interior is a bit of a meander too, with open-plan exhibition halls and a frequently rotated permanent collection that highlights home-grown movements without presenting them in chronological or thematic order. The whole thing demonstrates just how far at the front of the contemporary pack Croatian art always was, although it's a difficult story for first-time visitors to unravel.

Things you should look out for include the jazzy abstract paintings produced by Exat 51 (a group comprising Vlado Kristl, Ivan Picelj and Aleksandar Srnec) in the 1950s, which show how postwar Croatian artists escaped early from communist cultural dictates and established themselves firmly at the forefront of the avant-garde. Look out too for photos of it's-all-in-the-name-of-art streakers such as Tomislav Gotovac (1937–2010) and Vlasta Delimar (1956–), who either ran or rode naked through the centre of Zagreb on various occasions, putting Croatia on the international performance-art map in the process. Works by understated iconoclasts Goran Trbuljak,

Sanja Iveković and Mladen Stilinović reinforce Croatia's reputation for the art of the witty, ironic statement, while the museum's international collection takes in Mirosław Bałka's *Eyes of Purification* (a mysterious concrete shed outside the front entrance), as well as Carsten Holler's interactive toboggan tubes. A cinema, concert space and café provide additional reasons to visit.

The Bundek

1km walk north of the Museum of Contemporary Art, or take tram #6 (destination Sopot) to Most Mladosti then walk west along the Sava Embankment

Novi Zagreb has its own venue for outdoor recreation in the shape of the **Bundek**, a kidney-shaped lake surrounded by woodland and riverside meadow. Recently re-landscaped and bestowed with foot- and cycle-paths, it's an increasingly popular strolling and picnicking venue. There are large children's playparks at either side of the lake, and light-your-own-fire barbecue stations that are enormously popular with picnickers at weekends.

Mount Medvednica

The wooded slopes of **Mount Medvednica**, or "Bear Mountain", offer the easiest escape from the city, with the range's highest peak, **Sljeme** (1033m), easily accessible on foot or by road. The summit is densely forested and the views from the top are not as impressive as you might expect, but the walking is good and there's a limited amount of skiing in winter, when you can rent gear from shacks near the top.

ARRIVAL AND DEPARTURE — **MOUNT MEDVEDNICA**

By public transport Take tram #14 from Trg bana Jelačića to the Mihaljevac terminus, from where a bus (roughly hourly) ascends to Sljeme. The cable car (*žičara*) that used to run up to the summit is currently the subject of long-term renovation plans.

By car Driving, you can reach Sljeme by heading north out of central Zagreb along Ribnjak, and taking a well-signed right turn after about 3km – the hairpin ascent through forest is an exhilarating experience.

On foot Best way to enjoy Sljeme is to walk all the way up – indeed this is what swarms of locals do every weekend. The most popular route (2hr 30min–3hr) begins at the Zagreb suburb of Šestine (bus #102 from Mihaljevac or Britanski trg) and climbs via Medvedgrad (see below) and the Grafičar meadow and mountain hut before arriving at the summit. Red-and-white waymarkings will aid your ascent.

Medvedgrad

Commanding a spur of the mountain southwest of the Sljeme summit is the fortress of **Medvedgrad.** It was built in the mid-thirteenth century at the instigation of Pope Innocent IV in the wake of Tatar attacks, although its defensive capabilities were never really tested and it was abandoned in 1571. Partially reconstructed, the fortress has since the 1990s been home to the **Altar of the Homeland** (Oltar domovine), an eternal flame surrounded by stone blocks. You can roam the castle's ramparts, which enjoy panoramic views of Zagreb and the plain beyond, and there's a **restaurant** in a subterranean hall (closed Mon) serving traditional north Croatian favourites like *grah, štrukli* and *štrudl.*

Sljeme

However you arrive on **Sljeme**, its main point of reference is the **TV transmission tower**, built on the summit in 1980. The tower's top floor originally housed a restaurant and viewing terrace, but the lifts broke down after three months and it's been closed to the public ever since. A north-facing terrace near the foot of the tower provides good views of the low hills of the Zagorje, a rippling green landscape broken by red-roofed villages. Just west of here is the *Tomislavov Dom* hotel, home to a couple of cafés and a restaurant, below which you can pick up a trail to the medieval fortress of Medvedgrad (2hr; see opposite). Alternatively you can follow signs southwest from *Tomislavov Dom* to the *Grafičar* mountain hut, some twenty minutes away, where there's a café serving basic snacks.

Paths continue east along the ridge, emerging after about twenty minutes at the **Puntijarka** mountain refuge, a popular refreshment stop whose cafeteria serves excellent *grah* (bean soup) and grilled meats. Another twenty minutes along the ridge brings you to the *Hunjka* hotel, jumping-off point for a path that leads to **Horvat's Steps** (Horvatove stube), a northbound downhill trail comprising five hundred steps prepared by walking enthusiast Vladimir Horvat between 1946 and 1956. The trail provides a good taste of the stark limestone landscape that characterizes the northern face of the mountain. Follow the steps all the way down and you'll hit a trail that descends to the Zagorje village of Stubičke Toplice, a three-hour walk in total.

ARRIVAL AND DEPARTURE — ZAGREB

By plane Zagreb Pleso airport is situated around 10km southeast of the city and is connected with the bus station by half-hourly buses (30Kn; 40min) between 7.30am and 8pm; after that time buses run only to connect with Croatia Airlines flights. A taxi from the airport to the centre costs about 200–250Kn.

Domestic destinations Bol (April–Sept 1 or 2 weekly; 50min); Dubrovnik (April–Sept 3 daily, Oct–March 2 daily; 50min); Pula (1 daily; 50min); Split (April–Sept 4 daily, Oct–March 3 daily; 45min); Zadar (1 daily; 45min).

By train Zagreb's central train station (information on ⊤060 333 444, ⓦhznet.hr) is on Tomislavov trg, on the southern edge of the city centre, a 10min walk from Trg bana Jelačića.

Domestic destinations Osijek (4 daily; 4hr 15min); Rijeka (4 daily; 3hr 45min–4hr 20min); Split (2 daily; 5hr 30min–8hr); Zadar (2 daily; change at Knin; 6hr 30min–8hr).

International destinations Belgrade (4 daily; 6hr 30min); Graz (2 daily; 4hr); Ljubljana (6 daily; 2hr 20min); Maribor (2 daily; 2hr 30min); Salzburg (1 daily; 7hr); Sarajevo (1 daily; 10hr); Venice (2 daily; 7–8hr); Vienna (2 daily; 6hr 30min).

By bus The main bus station is about a 10min walk east of the train station at the junction of Branimirova and Držićeva. Tram #6 (destination Črnomerec) runs from here to Trg bana Jelačića, stopping at the train station on the way.

Domestic destinations Cres (2 daily; 6hr 30min); Dubrovnik (4 daily; 9–11hr); Korčula Town (1 daily; 13hr); Osijek (Mon–Sat 8 daily, Sun 6 daily; 5hr 30min); Pag Town (5 daily; 5hr); Plitvice (10 daily; 2hr 30min); Poreč (6 daily; 4hr–5hr 30min); Pula (10 daily; 4hr–6hr 30min); Rijeka (20 daily; 2hr 30min); Rovinj (6 daily; 4hr–5hr 40min); Split (20 daily; 5–9hr); Varaždin (12 daily; 2hr); Zadar (hourly; 3hr 30min–5hr).

International destinations Belgrade (5 daily; 6hr); Ljubljana (1 daily; 2hr 30min); Sarajevo (4 daily; 8hr 30min).

By car Free parking spaces in the city centre are hard to find, so it's best to head for one of the main garages, the handiest central ones being on Ilica and Langov trg (both 7Kn/hr).

GETTING AROUND

BY TRAM AND BUS

Zagreb's comprehensive network of trams and buses is run by ZET, the municipal transport authority (ⓦzet.hr). Trg bana Jelačića is the main hub of the system, of which maps are displayed at most tram stops. The network is divided into three concentric zones; all of Zagreb city falls within the central zone, so you'll only enter the outer two zones if making an out-of-town excursion.

Services Regular bus and tram services run from around 4.30am to 11.20pm, after which night trams come into operation. Night services operate different routes from their daytime counterparts and run at irregular intervals (usually every 40–50min), so knowing when and where to wait for them is very much a local art form.

Tickets Tickets are bought from newspaper kiosks throughout the city, or from the driver. Flat fare single-zone tickets are 12Kn from kiosks, or 15Kn from the driver; tickets for night services are 20Kn and 25Kn respectively. All kiosks also sell day tickets (*dnevne karte*; 40Kn), which can be used for unlimited travel within a single zone and are valid until 4am the following morning. All tickets are validated by punching them in the machines at the front end of the vehicle. A system of prepaid cards (30Kn for the card plus however much you want to prepay) is currently being introduced.

BY TAXI

For taxis, there's an initial charge of around 20Kn, after which it's 10Kn per kilometre; prices rise by twenty percent after midnight and on Sun. Taxis do not cruise the streets looking for fares: they are most easily found at ranks on Trg maršala Tita and on the corner of Teslina and Gajeva. To book, call Cammeo (⊤060 7100, ⓦtaxi-cammeo.net) or Ekotaxi (⊤1414, ⓦekotaxi.hr).

1

BY BIKE

Although the number of cycle lanes is increasing, central streets are far from bicycle-friendly. Local pedal-pushers tend to escape traffic-clogged roads by riding on the pavement – much to the annoyance of Zagreb's pedestrians.

INFORMATION

Tourist information centre (turistički informativni centar; TIC) Trg bana Jelačića 11 (June–Sept Mon–Fri 8am–8pm, Sat & Sun 9am–6pm; Oct–May Mon–Fri 8.30am–8pm, Sat 10am–5pm, Sun 10am–2pm; ⓣ01 481 4051 or ⓣ01 481 4052, ⓦzagreb-touristinfo.hr). Provides free city maps and the monthly booklet *Events and Performances*, an invaluable guide to theatre, classical music and gig schedules. The tourist office also sells the Zagreb Card (90Kn for 72hr), which entitles the bearer to free public transport, a fifty-percent discount on museum and gallery admissions and reductions in some theatres, discos and restaurants.

Zagreb County Tourist Association Preradovićeva 42 (Turistička zajednica zagrebačke županije; Mon–Fri 8am–4pm; ⓣ01 487 3665, ⓦtzzz.hr). The regional tourist association doesn't deal with Zagreb itself but is a mine of information on the surrounding countryside – invaluable if you're considering jaunts to Samobor (see p.109) or the Žumberak.

ACCOMMODATION

While Zagreb is well served with medium- and top-range **hotels**, budget choices are relatively thin on the ground and should be reserved well in advance. There is a growing number of backpacker **hostels**, many of which offer private double rooms as well as bunk beds in dorms. Zagreb tourist office has a list of locals offering private **rooms** or apartments in the city centre; a couple of dedicated agencies can also help (see p.84). There's no decent **campsite** in the city, but you can pitch a tent in the garden of *Ravnice Youth Hostel* (see p.84) for 60Kn per person.

ZAGREB STREET NAMES

The flexible nature of Croatian grammar means that there are often two ways of saying a **street name**, and the version you hear in the spoken language may not be the same one you see on street signs. Thus "Nikola Tesla Street" in the centre of Zagreb can be rendered as either ulica Nikole Tesle ("street of Nikola Tesla") or Teslina ulica ("Tesla's street"). The latter is more common in everyday speech and on maps, although the word ulica ("street") is usually dropped. Similarly, ulica Pavla Radića becomes Radićeva, and ulica Ivana Tkalčića becomes Tkalčićeva.

To complicate matters further, a couple of Zagreb's best-known squares have colloquial names that differ from their official ones. Trg Nikole Šubića Zrinskog usually goes under the name of Zrinjevac; and Trg Petra Preradovića is almost universally referred to as Cvjetni trg ("Flower Square"), because it has long been the venue of a florists' market.

VERSION SEEN ON STREET SIGNS	VERSION USED IN SPOKEN LANGUAGE AND ON MAPS
Trg svetog Marka	Markov trg
Trg Marka Marulića	Marulićev trg
Trg braće Mažuranića	Mažuranićev trg
Trg Petra Preradovića	Preradovićev trg/Cvjetni trg
Trg Josipa Jurja Strossmayera	Strossmayerov trg
Trg kralja Tomislava	Tomislavov trg
Trg Nikole Šubića Zrinskog	Zrinjevac
Ulica kneza Branimira	Branimirova
Ulica Ljudevita Gaja	Gajeva
Ulica Janka Draškovića	Draškovićeva
Ulica Andrije Hebranga	Hebrangova
Ulica Junije Palmotića	Palmotićeva
Ulica Pavla Radića	Radićeva
Ulica Augusta Šenoe	Šenoina
Ulica Nikole Tesle	Teslina
Ulica Ivana Tkalčića	Tkalčićeva

HOTELS AND B&B

CENTRAL ZAGREB

Arcotel Allegra Branimirova 29 ⓣ01 469 6000, ⓦarcotel.at; map pp.60–61. A perfect pied-à-terre for the design-conscious, with rooms featuring snazzy minimalist decor, large-screen TVs and proper bathtubs. The bed linen is decorated with pictures of Sigmund Freud, which may put a damper on your nocturnal activities. Guests have free use of gym and sauna. Handy for the train station and a 15min walk from the main square. 650Kn

DoubleTree by Hilton ul. grada Vukovara 269a ⓣ01 605 5999, ⓦdoubletree.hilton.com; map pp.60–61. New top-of-the-range hotel in the Radnička cesta district, with comfortable doubles, gym and spa centre, opened in autumn 2012. 800Kn

Dubrovnik Gajeva 1 ⓣ01 486 3555, ⓦhotel-dubrovnik.hr; map p.63. Dependable four-star comprising a 1920s main building overlooking Trg bana Jelačića, and an angular glass-and-steel annexe stretching along Gajeva to the south. Expect smart, pastel-coloured rooms (doubles have baths, singles come with showers); those in the older half of the hotel have rather dowdy furnishings but many have the compensation of main-square views. 870Kn

Fala 11. Trnjanske ledine 18 ⓣ01 611 1062, ⓦhotel-fala-zg.hr; map pp.60–61. Despite being next to a four-lane road, this small-scale family-run hotel has a peaceful, suburban backstreet feel. En-suite rooms are on the small side but are bright and pleasant, and the hallways are packed with houseplants. Wi-fi throughout. It's a 25min walk south of the centre; from the bus station, take tram #5 (destination Jarun) to the Lisinski stop. 500Kn

Laguna Kranjčevićeva 29 ⓣ01 304 7000, ⓦhotel-laguna.hr; map pp.60–61. Five-storey concrete affair opposite the NK Zagreb football stadium and a stone's throw from the Dražen Petrović Basketball Centre – which probably explains why it's so popular with visiting sports teams. Rooms are on the small side, but come with TV, bathtub and standard-issue socialist-era furniture. From the train station, tram #9 (direction Ljubljanica) to the Tehnički muzej stop. 580Kn

Meridijan 16 ul. grada Vukovara 241 ⓣ01 606 5200, ⓦmeridijan16.com; map pp.60–61. Attractively priced, medium-sized hotel a few steps south of the bus station, offering creamy-coloured rooms with laminated floors, a/c, flat-screen TV, WC/shower and a small desk. Buffet breakfast and secure car-parking space in the back yard complete the picture. Possible weekend reductions. 600Kn

Palace Strossmayerov trg 10 ⓣ01 489 9600, ⓦpalace.hr; map pp.60–61. Attractive turn-of-the-century pile between the train station and Trg bana Jelačića, preserving a few period fittings in the hallways and reception areas. Rooms are tidy, plush-carpeted affairs with a/c, minibar and bathtub. 730Kn

Regent Esplanade Mihanovićeva 1 ⓣ01 456 6666, ⓦregenthotels.com; map pp.60–61. Luxurious outpost of Mitteleuropa next to the train station, with marble-clad Art Deco lobby plus an opulent café and function rooms. The repro furniture in the rooms may be a bit over the top for some tastes, but the marble-floored bathrooms with big tubs represent a major plus. Good views of downtown Zagreb from north- and west-facing rooms. Breakfast is charged extra. 1200Kn

★ **Studio Kairos** Vlaška 92 ⓣ01 464 0680, ⓦstudio-kairos.com; map pp.60–61. Probably the only place in Zagreb that looks and feels like a B&B, *Kairos* (named after the Greek god of the fleeting moment) consists of four small but neat rooms with smart en-suite bathrooms, flat-screen TV, a/c and wi-fi. Most of the rooms are officially twins, but the slide-out, expandable beds will sleep three at a pinch. The kitchen/breakfast room is full of books about Zagreb. A 15min walk east of the main square, or trams #4, #7, #11 and #12 to the Petrova stop. 530Kn

Westin Kršnjavoga 1 ⓣ01 489 2000, ⓦwestin.com/zagreb; map pp.60–61. Formerly the *Zagreb Intercontinental*, this 335-room landmark is handily located close to the theatres and museums around Trg maršala Tita. All rooms come with bathtub, deep-mattressed beds piled high with pillows and tea- and coffee-making facilities. The indoor swimming pool is on the small side but has a lovely palm-court atmosphere. 1800Kn

THE SUBURBS

As Zelengaj 2a ⓣ01 460 9111, ⓦhotel-as.hr; map pp.60–61. Four-star comforts 2km northwest of the centre in the leafy suburb of Zelengaj, in a curvy-roofed contemporary building that blends rather well with its woodland surroundings. The roomy doubles offer classy nineteenth-century-style furnishings, TV, minibar and big bathtubs, and there's a top-notch, formal restaurant on site. You can walk down into the city through a belt of suburban forest. 980Kn

Four Points by Sheraton Panorama Trg Krešimira Čosića 9 ⓣ01 365 8333, ⓦfourpoints.com/zagreb; map pp.60–61. High-rise hotel 2km east of the centre, recently renovated to provide four-star levels of comfort. Rooms have warm colour schemes and most come with proper-sized bathtubs, and tea- and coffee-making facilities. North-facing rooms on the higher floors come with spellbinding views of the city. Take tram #9 (destination Ljubljanica) from the train station to Trešnjevački trg, then turn right onto Trakošćanska and after 5min you'll see the hotel looming up on your left. 1250Kn

Jarun Hrgovići 2 ⓣ01 369 1111, ⓦhotel-jarun-com; map p.77. Pleasant mid-price option that offers three-star comforts and friendly service at slightly cheaper rates than similar places in the centre. It's in a residential area just

1

north of Lake Jarun and the Sava Embankment, perfect for waterside walks. Tram #5 or #17 (direction Prečko) to Horvati. Weekend reductions. **600Kn**

HOSTELS

CENTRAL ZAGREB

Fulir Radićeva 3a ☎01 483 0882, mobile ☎098 193 0552, Ⓦfulir-hostel.com; map p.63. Cheery hostel in a galleried courtyard just off the main square. The six- to eight-bed dorms occupy the cosy attic, while there's a roomy kitchen and common-room area down below. Internet access is available for a few extra kuna. *Fulir* also rent out a two-person apartment with kitchenette in the same building. No credit cards. Dorms **150Kn**

Hobo Bear Medulićeva 4 ☎01 484 6636, Ⓦhobobearhostel.com; map pp.60–61. Cute and cosy hostel with a good location near Cvjetni trg. There are a couple of high-ceilinged bunk bed dorms, ranging in price according to size (up to 150Kn), and a brace of private doubles, with a basement common room with sofas and a well-stocked drinks fridge. Fully equipped kitchen, and wi-fi throughout. Dorms from **110Kn**, doubles **340Kn**

Nokturno Skalinska 2a ☎01 481 3325, Ⓦhostel .nokturno.hr; map p.63. Centrally located hostel squeezed between Dolac market and the Tkalčićeva strip, with sunny dorms, single rooms (no doubles), a common room, kitchen and downstairs pizzeria (see opposite). Free wi-fi. Dorms **130Kn**, singles **200Kn**

Taban Tkalčićeva 82 ☎01 553 3527, Ⓦbuzzbackpackers.com; map p.63. At the top of the Tkalčićeva café-bar strip and with a well-stocked ground-floor bar of its own, *Taban* will suit those who want to be at the heart of social life. It's also good for sleeping, however, with smartly furnished, well-isolated dorms and neat private doubles with TV. Wi-fi throughout. Dorms **150Kn**, doubles **500Kn**

THE SUBURBS

Buzz Backpackers Babukićeva 1b ☎01 232 0267, Ⓦbuzzbackpackers.com; map pp.60–61. Smart, comfortable hostel 2km east of the centre offering a good mix of bunk-bed dorms and private doubles, all with a/c. Small kitchen and common room, plus wi-fi access throughout. Trams #4 or #9 from the train station to Kvaternikov trg, or trams #5 or #7 from the bus station to Heinzelova. Dorms **140Kn**, doubles **450Kn**

Lika Pašmanska 17 ☎098 561 041, Ⓦhostel-lika.com; map pp.60–61. Friendly hostel with attentive hosts, located in a quiet street within walking distance of the bus station. Tidy dorms, clean WC and washing facilities, a common room with internet access and frequent barbecues in a shady garden. Take tram #6 (destination Sopot) to Slavonska, then follow the yellow feet painted on the ground. Dorms **120Kn**, doubles **40Kn**

Ravnice Youth Hostel 1. Ravnice 38d ☎01 233 2325, Ⓦravnice-youth-hostel.hr; map pp.60–61. Well-cared-for, easy-going and friendly hostel 4km east of the centre, in a pair of modern houses just behind Croatia's biggest confectionery factory. They offer bright, pastel-coloured bunk-bed rooms, plus a handful of doubles; there's also breakfast and a pair of kitchens, plus internet terminals in the common room, and you can also get your washing done for a nominal fee. Take either tram #4 (direction Dubec) from the train station, tram #7 (direction Dubrava) from the bus station, or trams #11 (direction Dubec) or #12 (direction Dubrava) from Trg bana Jelačića, and get off at Ravnice (the second stop after Maksimir soccer stadium). The hostel is well signposted, a 5min walk down 1. Ravnice. Dorms from **120Kn**, doubles **260Kn**

PRIVATE ROOMS

Evistas Šenoina 28 ☎01 483 9554, Ⓦevistas.hr. Private rooms (from 260Kn double) or apartments (from 360Kn) throughout the city.

★ **inZagreb** Remetinečka 13 ☎01 652 3201 or ☎091 652 3201, Ⓦinzagreb.com. Lovely apartments in good locations. Two- to three-person apartments start at 480Kn/night; four- to five-person apartments weigh in at around 670Kn/night. There are discounts for long-term stays. All apartments have wi-fi, fully equipped kitchen and a few basic supplies.

Never Stop/Nemoj stati Boškovićeva 7a ☎091 637 8111, Ⓦnest.hr. Agency offering well-kept apartments for long- or short-term stay.

EATING

Whatever your budget, there's no shortage of places to eat in Zagreb. While most **restaurants** concentrate on the Croatian repertoire of grilled meat and fish, there is a growing number of establishments offering modern European cuisine. Ethnic restaurants are still thin on the ground, but decent Italian pasta is widely available, and there's a surfeit of pizzerias around Trg bana Jelačića and Tkalčićeva. Some of the best restaurants are to be found in the northern suburbs – worth the trek out if you want to observe the local bigwigs at play. Note that quite a few restaurants are either closed or have limited opening hours on Sun, so always check the details given below before setting out. **Cafés** are absolutely everywhere in central Zagreb, and although most of them only serve drinks, there are several that also offer light meals, cakes and ice cream. For **snacks**, there's a good number of bakeries and sandwich bars in the central area, while picnic supplies can be purchased from the stalls of Dolac market, just above the main Trg bana Jelačića.

CAFÉS, PATISSERIES AND ICE-CREAM PARLOURS

Gradska Kavana Trg bana Jelačića 9 ⊕ 091 481 3007, ⓦ gradskakavana.hr; map p.63. Definitely worth visiting for the interior, a well-restored example of Art Deco, the "Town Café" is a bit ordinary when it comes to the coffee. Extravagant ice creams and cakes just about save its blushes. Mon–Sat 9am–11pm, Sun 9am–10pm.

Ivica i Marica Tkalčićeva 64 ⊕ 01 482 8999, ⓦ ivicaimarica.com; map p.63. This deservedly popular café and cake shop successfully mixes folksy traditions (wooden benches, waiting staff dressed in regional costume) with a thoroughly modern commitment to healthy living. All of their genuinely irresistible cakes are made from wholemeal flour and other natural ingredients. The *Međimurska gibanica* (layered cake from Međimurje incorporating cheesecake, apple and poppy seeds) is a masterpiece in itself. Mon–Sat 10am–11pm, Sun 1–10pm.

Millennium Bogovićeva bb ⊕ 01 481 0850, ⓦ slasticarnica-millennium.hr; map p.63. Swanky ice-cream parlour situated in the centre of Zagreb's principal pavement-café strip; as good a place as any to sit and observe promenading city-dwellers. Daily 8am–11pm.

Pingvin Teslina 7; map p.63. Courtyard kiosk with a few bar stools scattered outside, offering sandwiches (20–30Kn) with traditional Croatian ingredients such as *pršut* (home-cured ham) and *kulen* (spicy Slavonian salami). Mon–Sat 9am–3am, Sun 7pm–3am.

Slastičarna Vincek Ilica 18 ⊕ 01 483 3612, ⓦ vincek.com.hr; map p.63. A long-standing favourite of the sweet-toothed, *Vincek* offers some of the best ice cream in the city, alongside a hard-to-take-your-eyes-away selection of cakes and pastries. There's a takeaway counter at the front, if you fancy eating on your feet, and a sit-down area towards the back offering coffee and other hot drinks. Mon–Sat 8.30am–11pm.

★ **Torte i to** Kaptol Centar, Nova Ves 11 ⊕ 01 486 0691, ⓦ torte-i-to.hr; map p.63. Undisputed ruler of the cake scene at the time of writing, *Torte i to*'s tortes, cheesecakes and meringue pies will have you groggy with food-lust at first sight, and are well worth avoiding if you have any waistline issues. Daily 8am–11pm.

RESTAURANTS

KAPTOL, GRADEC, TRG BANA JELAČIĆA AND AROUND

Agava Tkalčićeva 39 ⊕ 01 482 9826, ⓦ restaurant-agava.hr; map p.63. Croatian restaurant offering a balance of Mediterranean pastas, central European meat dishes and Adriatic seafood, with turkey breast, Dalmatian *pašticada* and baked octopus featuring on an extensive menu. Outdoor seating provides a bird's-eye view of café life on Tkalčićeva. Mains around 90–110Kn. Daily 9am–midnight.

Baltazar Nova ves 4 ⊕ 01 466 6999, ⓦ restoran-baltazar.hr; map p.63. A 5min walk north of the cathedral along Kaptol, this is one of the best venues in the city for the standard northern Croatian repertoire of veal cutlets and pork fillets, all expertly grilled. There's a pleasant courtyard and service is attentive. *Baltazar*'s sister restaurant *Melchior* is in the same courtyard and does an equally good job with Adriatic fish – a kilo of heavenly scampi *buzara* (enough for two) will set you back 550Kn. Mon–Sat noon–midnight.

Carpaccio Teslina 14 ⊕ 01 482 2331, ⓦ ristorantecarpaccio.hr; map p.63. Across the board Italian-European fare, done with panache and care, good for a quick pasta or a more drawn-out Florentine steak, and prices are not discouraging. The city centre location is a big plus although there is no outdoor terrace. Mon–Sat 11am–midnight, Sun 11am–5pm.

Čušpajz Gajeva 9; map p.63. The term "soup kitchen" gets a whole new meaning from this new venture from Loredana Boban, wife of former football star Zvonimir. Delivering a quick lunch that is a great deal more than just fast food, *Čušpajz* cooks up three pots of soup a day (including at least one vegetarian option), offered at 35Kn per bowl – crusty rustic bread and salad nibbles included. Daily 11am–6pm.

Dubravkin put Dubravkin put 2 ⊕ 01 483 4975, ⓦ dubravkin-put.com; map p.63. This long-standing venue for quality seafood was given a lounge-bar makeover in 2010 but has lost nothing of its culinary prowess, serving up succulent fish in grilled, baked or stewed form. Dunked in a wooded vale round the back of Gradec hill, it has a lovely location. Mon–Sat 11am–midnight.

Kerempuh Kaptol 3 ⊕ 01 481 9000, ⓦ kerempuh.hr; map p.63. Often overlooked because it's hidden away behind the main fruit and vegetable market, this is one of the best places in town to gorge on traditional Croatian pork-based favourites. The cheap lunchtime dishes (50–70Kn) draw a regular stream of local office workers. Mon–Sat 7am–11pm, Sun 8am–4pm.

Mano Medvedgradska 2 ⊕ 01 466 9432, ⓦ mano.hr; map pp.60–61. Fine dining in a red-brick factory building (the rest of which is occupied by the Gliptoteka; see p.70), featuring excellent steaks, superb desserts and a wide-ranging (if expensive) wine list. On the posh side, but worth a splash-out providing you don't mind the background lounge music. Mains 100–150Kn. Mon–Sat noon–11pm.

Nokturno Skalinska 4 ⊕ 01 481 3394, ⓦ nokturno.hr; map p.63. In a side street just off Tkalčićeva, offering serviceable pizzas (from 50Kn) and sizeable salads (from 25Kn), with an outdoor terrace in one of Zagreb's most attractive alleyways. Daily 9am–midnight.

1

Pod gričkim topom Zakmardijeve stube 5 ⓣ01 483 3607, ⓦrestoran-pod-grickim-topom.hr; map p.63. Good Croatian food in a cosy restaurant on the steps leading down from Strossmayerovo šetalište to Trg bana Jelačića, with a nice garden terrace with great views of the Lower Town. Enjoy superb Croatian food from grilled fish to Dalmatian *pašticada* (beef stewed in prunes) and juicy steaks. Mains 90–140Kn. Mon–Sat 11am–midnight, Sun 11am–4pm.

Prasac Vranicanijeva 6 ⓣ01 485 1411 ⓦprasac.hr; map p.63. A tiny five-table restaurant in a corner of Gradec, the perfectly named "Piglet" serves up an imaginative and idiosyncratic mix of Croatian and Italian cuisine, with the menu changing daily according to what ingredients turned up at the market. Expect to pay upwards of 300Kn for a three-course meal. Mon–Sat noon–3pm & 7–11pm; closed for three weeks in Aug.

Ribice i tri točkice Preradovićeva 7/1 ⓣ01 563 5479, ⓦribiceitritockice.hr; map p.63. This is a good place to sample Adriatic cuisine without fear of having your wallet emptied afterwards, with traditional Dalmatian dishes (grilled squid, fried anchovies, fillets of hake and all manner of shells) served at village-tavern prices. With tables overlooked by the playful marine paintings of Vojo Radojčić, it's a fun place to eat too. Daily specials are chalked up on a board outside. Daily 9am–midnight.

★ **Takenoko** Kaptol Centar, Nova ves 17 ⓣ01 486 0530, ⓦtakenoko.hr; map p.63. If you like eating quality Asian food in design-conscious interiors then moodily minimalist *Takenoko*, in the Kaptol shopping centre, should do the trick. Most people come here for the excellent sushi although the menu also sweeps in steaks, teriyaki chicken, a broad range of wok-fried dishes and – fusion fans take note – wasabi-garnished lamb chops and Adriatic fish dressed with Asian spices. Mains around 150Kn. Mon–Sat noon–11.30pm, Sun noon–5pm.

Vinodol Teslina 10 ⓣ01 481 1427, ⓦvinodol-zg.hr; map p.63. Long-standing local favourite *Vinodol* offers a solid if unadventurous Croatian repertoire of meat and fish. Standards are reliable (they've been churning out the same meals for years) and the outdoor terrace in a semi-secluded courtyard is one of the city centre's biggest. Mains 70–100Kn. Daily 10am–midnight.

DONJI GRAD

Gostionica Tip Top Gundulićeva 18 ⓣ01 483 0349; map pp.60–61. Still popularly known by its former name of *Blato*, *Gostionica* has for years been a byword in tasty, affordable Dalmatian cooking, and has a loyal local clientele as a result. The interior is engagingly strange, with 1970s-vintage wood panelling and lampshades in the form of jellyfish. Lunchtime staples like *crni rižot* and *pašticada* might run out by evening, but there's plenty in the way of fish and seafood on the menu, all bearing a moderate price tag: *lignje* with boiled potatoes and *blitva* comes particularly recommended. Wash it all down with wines and spirits from the island of Korčula. Mon–Sat 7am–10pm.

Karijola/Karijola 2 Kranjčevićeva 16a ⓣ01 366 7044; Vlaška 63; map pp.60–61. Most satisfying of the pizzerias for the true pizza enthusiast, with thin-crust pies that look and feel authentic, topped with proper Italian-Mediterranean ingredients. The original branch is not exactly central, but handy for the Technical Museum and Student Centre, but as of summer 2012 there is a more central branch east of Gornji grad on Vlaška. Popular, so be prepared to queue. Daily noon–midnight.

★ **Lari i Penati** Petrinjska 42a ⓣ099 668 8101, ⓦlaripenati.hr; map pp.60–61. Deservedly popular deli-bistro serving up inexpensive but classy Adriatic/international food, with a menu of six or seven mains drawn up every day according to what's fresh. With only six tables and a handful of window-side stools inside, it's a cosy place that soon fills up. There's a small stretch of outdoor seating in summer. Mon–Fri 8am–8pm, Sat 11am–4.30pm.

Le Bistro Esplanade Mihanovićeva 1 ⓣ01 456 6611; map pp.60–61. Occupying a conservatory-like enclosure on the north side of the *Regent Esplanade*, *Le Bistro* is famous for serving up the best *štrukli* (baked or boiled pastries filled with cottage cheese; 65Kn) in the city, alongside French-influenced salads and quiches. Daily 8am–11pm.

★ **MaliBar** Vlaška 63; map pp.60–61. Homely and informal bistro brought to life by the Croatian/international cooking of well-known local food writer Ana Ugarković, *MaliBar* offers a choice of two or three main courses each day (usually one fish and one meat dish), with a longer list of light bites chalked up on the board above the bar. Mains might run out come the evening, when a convivial crowd come to drink Croatian wine and nibble their way through the tapas menu. Mon–Sat 10am–midnight.

Mostovi Radnička cesta 1 ⓣ01 619 2178, ⓦmostovi.hr; map pp.60–61. Bosnian-Hercegovinian restaurant that's enormously popular with the weekday lunching crowd, serving up delicious and generous portions of Balkan meat dishes – whether grilled, roast or stewed, its all done to near perfection. A takeaway section round the back sells traditional Bosnian pastries such as *buredžik* (with spicy minced beef), *pita od krumpira (*spicy potato pastry) or *pita od špinata* (crumbly white cheese and spinach pastry). Mon–Sat 9am–11pm.

Nova Ilica 72 ⓣ01 481 0059, ⓦbiovega.hr; map pp.60–61. A friendly, stylish and compact vegetarian restaurant in a cosy upstairs room, sharing the same building as Zagreb's premier health-food shop. Bean soups, salads, tofu stews and macrobiotic cakes, backed up by organic Croatian wines. Main dishes 40–60Kn, three-course menus from 90Kn. Mon–Sat noon–10pm.

★ **Pauza** Preradovićeva 34 ⓣ01 485 4598, ⓦrestaurant-pauza.com; map pp.60–61. Adriatic/Far Eastern fusion and lot more besides in one of Zagreb's more adventurous restaurants, offering wok-fried combinations of Adriatic fish and Asian spices, a range of pastas and salads, and rice dishes. Soups and dishes of the day will be chalked up on the blackboard. The sleek interior features comfy-benched booths and arty photo projections onto one of the walls. Mon–Fri 10am–11pm, Sat noon–5pm.

Pivnica Tomislav Tomislavov trg 18 ⓣ01 492 2255; map pp.60–61. This blast-from-the-past, brown-decorated beer cellar near the train station is unlikely to be your venue of choice for a romantic candlelit dinner. If you want cheap and filling portions of *grah*, *fileki* (tripe soup) or schnitzel with chips, however, then you need look no further. Mains 35–65Kn. Mon–Sat 7am–11pm, Sun 9am–9pm.

Purger Petrinjska 33 ⓣ01 481 0713; map pp.60–61. Don't be put off by the rather anonymous interior; this restaurant is a reliable source of inland Croatian cooking and moderately priced to boot. Staples like goulash or *grah* will sort you out at lunchtime, while more substantial dishes on the menu include just about every form of grilled meat and schnitzel you might wish for. Outdoor seating in the back yard. Main courses 80–100Kn. Mon–Sat 7am–11pm.

Sofra Radnička cesta 52 ⓣ01 411 1621, ⓦsofra.hr; map pp.60–61. Bosnian restaurant with pretty much every aspect of Bosnian cuisine well represented, from savoury pastries such as *krumpiruša* (potato pie) to *japrak* (stuffed vine leaves), grilled meats and lamb stews, with most meals safely under the 100Kn barrier. Located on the third floor of the Green Gold shopping centre – traditional Balkan furnishings, brass coffee pots and Bosnian music add the requisite amount of atmosphere. Mon–Sat 9am–midnight.

Sorriso Boškovićeva 11 ⓣ01 487 6392, ⓦsorriso.hr; map pp.60–61. Well-prepared, well-presented Italian food and a pretty good wine list too, in a moody, brick-lined subterranean space. Choose between mouthwatering risottos, own-recipe tortellini, seafood, lamb or duck. Mains in the region of 120Kn. Often closes for a month in summer. Mon–Sat 10am–midnight.

Žar Badalićeva 19 ⓣ01 382 0251; map pp.60–61. Simple but smart grill house right opposite the entrance to the *Laguna* hotel. The *gurmanska pljeskavica* (a large minced beef patty with chunks of bacon and cheese in the mix) will have you wondering how you ever put up with the culinary poverty of the western burger. Fill up on *pečeni grah* – oven-baked beans flavoured with paprika. Among the side orders, *kajmak* is a creamy cheese that goes perfectly with grilled meats. Mon–Sat 9am–11pm, Sun 11am–4pm.

Zinfandel's Mihanovićeva 1 ⓣ01 456 6666, ⓦregenthotels.com; map pp.60–61. Commanding a superb terrace on the eastern side of the *Regent Esplanade*, the elegantly furnished *Zinfandel's* offers arguably the best modern international cuisine in Zagreb and an extensive list of wines. Mains come with a 150–200Kn price tag. Daily 7am–11pm.

THE SUBURBS

★ **Bistro Apetit** Jurjevska 65A ⓣ01 467 7335, ⓦapetit.hr; map pp.60–61. For classic Adriatic fare with modern European pizzazz there are few better places than *Bistro Apetit*, a glass-fronted pavilion located in the leafy residential zone just north of Zagreb's Upper Town. The seasonal menu restricts itself to five or six seafood or meat main courses, all prepared and presented with creativity but without gimmicks. The wine list focuses on Croatia's best tipples, and the house desserts are divine. With a hedge and shrub-lined garden disturbed only by the thwack of rackets from a nearby tennis club, it's a delightful location. Sister restaurant *Apetit City*, in the centre at Obrtniški prolaz 7 (ⓣ01 481 1077) is also good, but doesn't quite have the same magic. Tues–Sun 9am–11pm.

Okrugljak Mlinovi 28 ⓣ01 467 4112, ⓦokrugljak.hr; map p.77. Traditional Croatian food in rustic surroundings, with wood-panelled booths indoors, plenty of seating outside and regular live music – popular tunes from classical to folk – on violin and piano. The menu includes calf knuckle, duck, game and other meat-heavy central European favourities, with mains exceeding the 100Kn mark. Tram #14 to the Mihaljevac terminus, followed by a 5min walk north. Daily 11am–midnight.

★ **Tač** Vrhovec 140 ⓣ01 377 6757, ⓦrestac.hr; map p.77. Occupying a house on a grassy knoll in the green northwestern suburbs, family-run *Tač* serves Istrian–central European fare in a supremely homely environment that features plenty of bare brick, bare wood and warm fabrics. The menu changes according to what's fresh and seasonal, and ranges from simple grills and stews to expansive platters of roast fowl and game. The family is famous for making their own pickles and preserves, and the desserts are irresistible. Tram #2, 6 or 11 to Slovenska, followed by bus #129B from Mandaličina. Daily noon–midnight.

DRINKING

There's a wealth of **café-bars** with outdoor seating in central Zagreb, especially in the pedestrianized section around Bogovićeva and Preradovićev trg. The other main strolling district is Tkalčićeva, just north of Trg bana Jelačića, which, with a watering hole every few metres, takes on the appearance of a vast outdoor bar on summer evenings. Saturday morning is the traditional time for meeting friends and lingering over a coffee, although downtown areas remain busy day and night, seven

1

days a week, if the weather is good enough for alfresco drinking. Things quieten down by mid-autumn, although the more inviting café-bars retain their clientele through the winter. Larger cafés may offer a range of pastries, ice creams and cakes, but the smaller establishments focus squarely on drinking – so don't expect to find much in the way of food.

KAPTOL, GRADEC, TRG BANA JELAČIĆA AND AROUND

Bulldog XL Bogovićeva 6 ⓣ 01 400 2072; map p.63. This elegant split-level bar and pavement café is one of the most popular meeting places in town, especially on Saturday mornings, when the whole of Zagreb seems to insist on sipping coffee here. The basement room hosts DJs and cover bands at weekends. Daily 9am–1am.

★ **Cica** cnr Tkalčićeva/Skalinska; map p.63. Arguably the most charming spot on Zagreb's most charming street, the cramped but cosy *Cica* features distressed second-hand furniture, domestic appliances and other bits of intriguing jumble – the interior is redesigned every year or so. The coffees and hot chocolates are first-rate, and there's an entire menu devoted to traditional Croatian *rakija* – with carob (*rogač*), honey (*medica*) and walnut (*orahovača*) flavours particularly recommended. Daily 8am–midnight.

Golf Preradovićeva 2; map p.63. If the pavement terrace of *Bulldog XL* (see above) attracts the dressier summer drinkers, the arty intelligentsia head for *Golf*. There's no logical reason why this particular stretch of outdoor tables is so popular with such a specific crowd – it just is. The indoor part of the café, located in a nearby courtyard, is quaint and cosy, with living-room furniture overlooked by all manner of golfing memorabilia. Mon–Wed 7am–11pm, Thurs–Sat 8am–midnight, Sun 1–11pm.

Kino Europa Varšavska 3 ⓣ 01 459 3691, ⓦ kinoeuropa.hr; map p.63. A lovely old interwar cinema that screens art movies and hosts the best of Zagreb's cinema festivals, the Europa also has a café that serves as a key meeting point for the city's art-and-culture tribes, especially in summer when the outdoor terrace fills up. There's a good choice of *rakijas* on the drinks menu, and retro discos in the foyer at weekends. Mon–Thurs 8am–11pm, Fri & Sat 8am–2am, Sun noon–10pm.

Klub Kino Grič Jurišićeva 6 ⓣ 01 483 4900; map p.63. The former lobby of this art cinema is now a smoky split-level bar filled regularly with students, young professionals and creative types. Directors' chairs and odd bits of celluloid memorabilia reinforce the cinema theme; DJs and art exhibitions spice up the weekends. Daily 8am–11.30pm.

Kolaž Amruševa 11 ⓣ 099 461 3112; map p.63. This semi-submerged box of a place is only a short stroll from the main square but seems to be in another world. The bare-brick interior, low-key lighting and odd quirky piece of art create the ideal ambience for a long night of alcohol-oiled conversation. Daily 9am–midnight.

Maraschino Margaretska 1 ⓣ 01 481 2612; map p.63. Comfy, relaxing and chic café-bar on the corner of Cvjetni trg. It's named after the cherry-based liqueur from the Adriatic city of Zadar, hence the collection of Zadar-themed photographs covering the walls. With DJs on summer weekends, it's standing-room-only on the terrace. Sun–Thurs 7am–1am, Fri & Sat 7am–4am.

Melin Kožarska 19 ⓣ 01 485 1166; map p.63. For years, the *Melin* has been attracting a wide-ranging crowd with its inexpensive drinks, postindustrial grunge decor and eclectic mix of sounds. A terrific alternative to some of the posier establishments nearby. Daily 5pm–1am.

MK/Krolo Radićeva 7; map p.63. Popularly known as *Krolo*, this classic 1970s-era café-bar has retained a unique local atmosphere, eschewing the frenzied makeovers that have taken hold elsewhere in the centre. With its semicircular bar and wooden fittings, it's a great period piece. Daily 7am–1am.

Oliver Twist Tkalčićeva 60 ⓣ 01 481 2206; map p.63. One of the prime places to see and be seen in a street that's full of bars, serving up a generous selection of local and imported beers in a two-level wood-panelled interior, with a big outdoor terrace. Daily 9am–3am.

DONJI GRAD

★ **Bacchus** Tomislavov trg 16 ⓣ 098 322 804; map pp.60–61. Hidden in a courtyard off the square in front of the train station, this tiny, semi-submerged pub filled with old books and vinyl records hosts jazz gigs in the winter and has a popular garden terrace in summer. Daily 10am–midnight.

Blok Tomašićeva 13; map pp.60–61. Tiny bar that looks like a welcoming padded cell, with soft green-cushioned benches, and the numbers of a slightly mad clock scattered across the chocolatey brown walls. Outdoor decking brings a touch of the lounge-bar to this otherwise quiet residential area. Mon–Sat 7am–11pm, Sun 8am–2pm.

Booksa Martićeva 14D ⓣ 01 461 6124, ⓦ booksa.hr; map pp.60–61. Literary café with a laid-back library atmosphere, good leaf teas and a regular programme of readings and talks – which might be in English, if the visiting scribblers are non-Croatian. Tues–Sun 11am–8pm.

Café Godot Savska cesta 23 ⓦ cafe-godot.com; map pp.60–61. A cosy and relaxing place, somewhere between a European café and an Irish pub in feel. Convenient place for a drink before attending concerts at the Student Centre, which is almost next door. Daily 8am–11pm.

Divas Martićeva 17 ⓣ 01 492 1295; map pp.60–61. A camp mash-up of boudoir, living room and Mediterranean patio, *Divas* is both an interior-design talking point and an excellent café, with good strong coffee cakes and a tempting choice of *rakija*. Mon–Sat 8am–11pm, Sun 8am–2pm.

Krivi put Savska cesta 14; map pp.60–61. Reopened in 2011 after being thrown out of its former home behind the Botanical Gardens, cult bar *Krivi put* ("Wrong Direction") still sucks in a huge cross-section of young, boisterous and edgily alternative types, with a smoke-saturated inner sanctum and a vast wooden-bench yard with space for hundreds. Bottled Velebitsko beer is the standard order. Daily 8am–1am.

Limb Plitvička 16 ⓣ 01 617 1683; map pp.60–61. Friendly neighbourhood bar that has become something of a cult destination owing to its Pop Art wall paintings of ladies of the night, eccentric choice of background CDs and late opening hours. Proximity to the *KSET* club (see p.90) ensures its popularity as the venue of choice for impromptu after-gig partying. Mon–Sat 9am–2am.

Prostor do/SPUNK Hrvatske bratske zajednice bb; map pp.60–61. Officially known as *Prostor do* but still known by many by its old name of *SPUNK* (named after a 1970s comic-strip magazine), this roomy bar is in the same building as the National University Library, and fills up with students and alternative types from the early evening onwards. Offbeat DJs, regular live bands, poster art on the walls and sci-fi murals by artist Igor Hofbauer provide four great reasons to visit. Handy for a pre-club drink if you're on the way to *Močvara* (see p.90). Mon–Thurs 7am–midnight, Fri & Sat 7am–2am, Sun 6pm–midnight.

Sedmica Kačićeva 7a ⓣ 01 484 6689; map pp.60–61. A bar so hidden away you imagine having to whisper "open sesame" at random keyholes – look out for the circular beer sign above the doorway. *Sedmica* is patronized by Zagreb's artists and bohemians, and has flyers for cultural events pinned to the entrance-hall walls. Erdinger and Fischer beers on tap, Leffe in bottles. The aphrodisiac *rakija od mirte* (misletoe brandy) is a popular order. Mon–Sat 7am–midnight, Sun 5pm–midnight.

U Dvorištu Žerjavićeva 7/2; map pp.60–61. A café-bar that also serves up a substantial cultural diet, the aptly named *U Dvorištu* ("In The Courtyard") hosts jazz gigs, poetry readings and art exhibitions, as well as functioning as a secluded and relaxing coffee-break corner during the day. Strong fair-trade coffee and a decent choice of draught beers. Mon–Sat 9am–11pm.

NIGHTLIFE AND ENTERTAINMENT

Zagreb offers the rich and varied diet of entertainment that you would expect from a metropolis of one million people. There's a regular diet of **classical music**, **theatre** and **club** culture throughout the year, and top international performers are increasingly drawn to the city's ever-expanding range of high-profile **festivals** (see box, p.91). Note that arts events tend to thin out in July and August, when there's more in the way of cultural activity on the coast. Extensive entertainment **listings** appear in the free monthly English-language pamphlet *Events and Performances*, available from the Zagreb tourist office (or on their website, ⓦ zagreb-touristinfo.hr).

CLUBS AND LIVE MUSIC

Zagreb is one of Central Europe's liveliest cities when it comes to DJ-driven club music and live alternative rock. Most activity takes place during the student year (roughly late Sept to late June), and many clubs take a summer break in July and August. Clubs are not necessarily open every night of the week, so check websites or ask around before heading out to the less central ones. Year-round gig listings are available on websites such as ⓦ last.fm and ⓦ muzika.hr. **Admission charges** for clubs and gigs range between 30Kn and 80Kn – more for big, one-off events.

CLUBS

Aquarius Aleja Matije Ljubeka bb, Jarun ⓦ aquarius.hr; map p.77. This waterfront pavilion at the eastern end of Lake Jarun, 4km southwest of the centre, is the city's main venue for electronic dance music – most of the big American house DJs have played here at least once over the last ten years. Expect commercial-ish house and techno on Fri and Sat, and more experimental stuff on Thurs and Sun. Big-name Croatian pop-rock stars perform on the outdoor terrace in summer. Tram #17 to Horvati. Wed–Sun 10pm till late; usually closed Mon & Tues unless live gigs are scheduled.

Boogaloo ul. grada Vukovara 68 ⓣ 01 631 3022, ⓦ boogaloo.hr; map pp.60–61. Sparsely decorated but roomy club occupying a former cultural centre and TV studio, a 10min walk south of the train station. They hold themed DJ nights aimed at the cooler end of dance culture, plus occasional gigs. Opening times depend on event.

Gallery Aleja Matije Ljubeka 7, Jarun ⓣ 099 444 2444, ⓦ gallery.hr; map p.77. Of the numerous places lining the northern shores of Lake Jarun this is one of the more worthwhile: a glass-and-timber pavilion serving expensive international beers and cocktails to a youngish feel-good crowd. Cultivates a loungey café vibe during the daytime, then turns into a frenetic pack-'em-in club on summer nights. Daily 10am till late.

Gjuro II Medveščak 2; map pp.60–61. Cult club just north of the centre, incorporating a long, narrow, bar area with a frequently packed dancefloor at the far end. Fills up with younger disco-pop fans on Fri and Sat, with a more discerning older crowd midweek. Closed Sun & Mon.

KSET Unska 3 ⓣ01 612 9758, ⓦkset.org; map pp.60–61. Small, intimate, student-run club and concert venue, concentrating on rock, jazz and experimental music. Notoriously difficult to find: from Savska cesta head east along Koturaška, turn right into Unska, then go straight over the crossroads and take the first dingy alley on the left. Daily usually 8pm until midnight, Sept–June only.

KvArt Heinzelova 66 ⓣ01 235 9273, ⓦfacebook.com/kvartzagreb; map pp.60–61. Gigs and DJ sessions in a former food-processing plant known as the Stara Klaonica (Old Slaughterhouse), some way east of the centre but still walkable from the Kvaternikov trg tram stop. Gritty but glam. Spring, early summer and autumn: Fri & Sat 10pm till late.

Močvara Jedinstvo factory, Trnjanski nasip bb ⓣ01 615 9668, ⓦmochvara.hr; map pp.60–61. Magnet for non-mainstream music fans, run by independent art cooperative URK in an old factory on the northern banks of the River Sava. Live gigs (by established foreign performers as well as Croatian indie bands) at least twice weekly, art-house film shows, theatre and club nights (anything from world music to 1970s funk) on other evenings. It's about 3km south of the centre: from the train station walk south towards the riverbank – once you get there, the club is away to your right. 8pm till late.

Mansion Club Jarunska obala bb ⓣ091 462 9464, ⓦmansion.hr; map p.77. One of the prime weekend drinking and dancing venues on the shores of Lake Jarun, attracting a steady stream of dressed-up kids and twentysomethings with a well-chosen mix of commercial dance music. Big-name DJs and live Croatian pop-rock acts occasionally perform on stage. Tram #17 to Jarun. April–Oct Fri & Sat 10pm till late.

Pepermint Ilica 24 ⓣ01 235 9172; map p.63. Look for the unmarked door in an archway (frequently given away by the queue of fashionistas) to find this first-floor bar and club. There's a small live stage and dancefloor, an amiable crush around the bar and a shimmy-friendly mixture of music from funk to soul. Daily 10am–4am.

Purgeraj Ribnjak 1 ⓣ01 482 9001, ⓦpurgeraj.hr; map p.63. In the park behind the cathedral, *Purgeraj* hosts either DJs or live music most nights of the week (predominantly rock, jazz or blues). Well worth visiting during the day when it serves as a mellow park-side café. Pick up the monthly schedule from the bar. Mon–Sat 10am–4pm.

Sirup Donje Svetice 40 ⓣ01 230 1695, ⓦsirupclub.com; map pp.60–61. A bit out of the way but important to keep in mind, *Sirup* goes for the kind of creative DJ culture that hovers above the boundaries of house, techno and hip-hop, with a bit of left-field experimentation thrown in. The crowd ranges from student and arty to up-for-a-party. It's a good 3km east of the centre: tram #13 to Donje Svetice followed by a taxi ride back. Fri & Sat 10pm till late.

Student Centre (Studentski centar) Savska cesta 25 ⓦsczg.hr; map pp.60–61. Rambling cultural centre incorporating several sit-down and standing-room-only venues, with frequent club nights and gigs (often featuring alternative acts of international stature). Look for posters or check the website. Closed July & Aug; times depend on event.

Tvornica kulture Ljudevita Posavskog 1 ⓣ01 562 1078, ⓦtvornicakulture.com; map pp.60–61. This is the best place to catch touring indie bands, mid-sized rock attractions and local up-and-coming talent. Based in a big former ballroom, it boasts two concert halls, the main one for big gigs and the smaller Mali Pogon for more intimate affairs. There's usually an after-gig DJ: check the schedule for details. 9pm till late.

VIP Jazz Club Trg bana Jelačića 9 ⓦvip-club.hr; map p.63. Live music and DJ club (often jazz, but not always) located in the fashionably matt-black basement of the *Gradska Kavana* café. Its central location makes it a popular place to drop in during the later stages of a city-centre bar crawl, but it's a bit too cool and thirtysomething to really get the party blood boiling. Tues–Sat 8pm till late.

BIG GIG VENUES

Dom Sportova Trg Krešimira Ćosića 1; map pp.60–61. Sports hall that also hosts big gigs (starting with the Rolling Stones in 1976), although its importance has been usurped in recent years by the Zagreb Arena (see below). Sometimes it is all-seating, sometimes you can stand in the pit, depending on the concert. Tram #3, #9, #12 (direction Ljubljanica) to Trešnjevački trg. See ⓦlast.fm for gig information.

Zagreb Arena Lanište, Novi Zagreb ⓦzagrebarena.hr; map p.77. This modern, 20,000-capacity sports arena is where the big names play – Sting, Beyoncé, Lady Gaga to name just three recent visitors. With no dancing in the aisles and little movement from one sector to another it's a very controlled experience – rock'n'roll it definitely ain't. Tram #14 (direction Zapruđe) to Savski gaj.

CLASSICAL MUSIC, DRAMA AND BALLET

Theatre and concert **tickets** are usually easy to come by, and tend to be about half the price of those in Western Europe. Performances, including opera, are almost invariably in Croatian, though there are productions by international groups during major festivals (see box opposite).

&TD Studentski Centar, Savska cesta 25 ⓣ01 459 3510, ⓦsczg.hr. This is the leading venue for leading contemporary drama and dance, with a repertoire based on the best in local directorial talent, frequently veering into the experimental. Box office Mon–Sat 11am–1pm, and 2hr prior to performances.

ZAGREB FESTIVALS

Zagreb's impressive menu of cultural events includes a range of **festivals** that attract prestigious international participants. Most of these have their own websites; otherwise, advance information can be obtained from the Zagreb tourist office.

Zagrebdox Late February/early March ⓦ zagrebdox.net. Impressive survey of international documentary films, with five days of screenings in venues across the city.

Festival of the European Short Story (Festival Evropske kratke priče) May ⓦ festival-price.profil.hr. Readings, panel discussions and drink-fuelled party evenings involving top authors from Croatia and abroad. Some readings are in English; others come with big-screen English translation.

Contemporary Dance Week (Tjedan suvremenog plesa) late May/early June ⓦ danceweekfestival.com. Varied, often challenging programme of modern choreography from around the globe, held in various venues across the city.

Cest is de best Late May/early June ⓦ kraljeviulice.com. Week-long festival of street performers augmented by a big range of live music, taking place on outdoor stages positioned throughout the city centre.

Animafest Late May/early June ⓦ animafest.hr. Zagreb was a major centre of animated film in the 1950s and Animafest helps to put the city back on the map, with a review of the year's best animation from Croatia and abroad.

Strossmartre (Ljeto na Strosu) Late May to early Sept ⓦ ljetonastrosu.com. Season of open-air concerts and events in Zagreb's Upper Town, with nightly happenings all summer long.

Dan D ("D Day") June ⓦ dan-d.info. Weekend-long design festival with stalls, shows and DJ events, held in the postindustrial splendour of the Stara Klaonica (Old Slaughterhouse).

Eurokaz Theatre Festival Late June ⓦ eurokaz.hr. Challenging avant-garde drama with an impressive roster of international guests.

In-music Late June ⓦ inmusicfestival.com. Three-day rock-and-pop fest on the shores of Lake Jarun with three stages, early-morning DJ tents and plenty of food and drink. Guests in recent years have included Kraftwerk, Franz Ferdinand, Arcade Fire and many more. Camping available.

Fantastic Zagreb Late June/early July ⓦ fantastic-zagreb.com. Fantasy, sci-fi, noir and cult trash cinema, celebrated with screenings in outdoor locations.

International Festival of Puppet Theatre (Međunarodni festival kazališta lutaka) late August ⓦ public.carnet.hr/pif-festival. A great chance to catch some of the best puppet productions from all over central and eastern Europe, with shows for both kids and adults.

World Theatre Festival (Festival svjetskog kazališta) mid-September ⓦ zagrebtheatrefestival.hr. Big names in international contemporary drama.

Perforations October ⓦ perforacije.org. Festival of experimental drama, contemporary dance and performance art that showcases pretty much everything that matters in the current Croatian board-treading scene.

Zagreb Film Festival October ⓦ zagrebfilmfestival.com. Initiated in 2003 and attracting outstanding documentaries and art movies from around the world.

Croatian National Theatre (Hrvatsko narodno kazalište; HNK) Trg maršala Tita 15 ⓣ 01 488 8415, ⓦ hnk.hr. Zagreb's cultural flagship, this sumptuous Neoclassical/neo-Baroque building provides the city's main venue for prestige classical drama, as well as opera and ballet. Box office Mon–Fri 10am–7.30pm, Sat 10am–1pm and 1hr 30min before performances.

Gavella Frankopanska 8 ⓣ 01 486 4616, ⓦ gavella.hr. Second only to the Croatian National Theatre in terms of prestige, this elegant, medium-sized auditorium hosts leading local and foreign theatre companies. Box office Mon–Sat 9.30am until performance time.

Vatroslav Lisinski Concert Hall (Koncertna dvorana Vatroslav Lisinski) Trg Stjepana Radića 4 ⓣ 01 612 1166, ⓦ lisinski.hr. Just south of the train station, this modern complex is Zagreb's main venue for serious music, with both the Zagreb Philharmonic and the Croatian Radio Symphony Orchestra performing regularly in the main auditorium, and chamber music in the small hall. Box office Mon–Fri 10am–8pm, Sat 9am–2pm.

Zagreb Puppet Theatre (Zagrebačko kazalište lutaka) Baruna Trenka 3 ⓣ 01 487 8445, ⓦ zkl.hr. Imaginatively designed puppets, wonderful stage sets and a repertoire strong in traditional fairytales. Performances start at noon or 6pm. Box office 1hr prior to performances.

Zagreb Youth Theatre (ZeKaeM) Teslina 7 01 487 2554, zekaem.hr. Top-quality work by leading (not youth, despite the name) theatre groups, with two modern auditoria bang in the city centre. Box office Mon–Fri 10am–8pm, Sat 10am–2pm, Sun 1hr prior to performances.

CINEMAS

Zagreb's cinemas show all the international releases you would expect; they're shown in the original language with Croatian subtitles.

Cinestar Branimirova 29 060 323 233, blitz-cinestar.hr. State-of-the-art if soulless multiplex, with plenty of drinking and snacking opportunities in the adjoining shopping mall.

Dokukino Croatia Katančićeva 3 01 481 3711, dokukino.net. Unique, tiny cinema with just 45 comfy armchairs; devoted to showing documentary films.

Europa Varšavska 3 01 482 9045, kinoeuropa.hr. Lovely old-style cinema with most of its 1920s furnishings still intact. International new-release films, with a bias towards European art movies. Most of the big festivals (Zagreb Film Festival, Animafest etc) have their main screenings here.

Tuškanac Tuškanac 1 01 484 8771, filmski-programi.hr. Repertory cinema putting on themed seasons and movie classics. Closed July & Aug.

SPECTATOR SPORTS

Football Traditionally the city's principal sporting preoccupation, football has fallen from grace in recent years with poor crowds watching a weak domestic league – which local team Dinamo Zagreb regularly win. Both Dinamo Zagreb (gnkdinamo.hr) and the Croatian national team play at the Maksimir stadium, Maksimirska 128 (tram #1 or #17 from Trg bana Jelačića or #9 from the train station to the Borongaj terminus). The season lasts from Sept to early May.

Ice hockey Significantly more excitement is generated by ice hockey, with local team Medveščak (medvescak.com), playing in the Central-European EBEL League, regularly packing out either Dom Sportova or the Zagreb Arena. The season climaxes in April.

Basketball Few other spectator sports attract sizeable crowds save basketball, with Zagreb's top teams Cibona (cibona.com) and Cedevita (kkcedevita.hr) playing at the Dražen Petrović Basketball Centre and the Dom Sportova respectively. The season lasts from Sept to May.

SHOPPING

You can find international brands aplenty in the brash suburban shopping malls girdling the city, but the real pleasure of retail culture in Zagreb lies in trawling the **markets**, with fresh food at Dolac (see p.64), bric-a-brac at Britanski trg (see below) and flea-junk at Hrelić (see below). In addition, the alleys and courtyards around Ilica, Radićeva and Tkalčićeva harbour all manner of craft stores, jewellery shops and kooky designer boutiques.

ANTIQUE AND FLEA MARKETS

Britanski trg map pp.60–61. Enjoyable weekly open-air market 1km west of the main square, featuring household bric-a-brac, old postcards, folksy textiles and the occasional genuine antique. Its central location and a decent choice of nearby cafés make this a popular spot with the locals. Two stops from Trg bana Jelačića on trams #6 and #11 (direction Črnomerec). Smaller markets specialize in books (Fri) and bric-a-brac (Sat). Main market Sun 8am–2pm.

Hrelić map p.77. Huge Sunday morning flea market occupying waste ground at the southeastern end of the city, offering row upon row of secondhand clothes, domestic knick-knacks, objets d'art and utter rubbish. Largely unshaded, so take a hat in summer. Tram #6 (direction Sopot) from Trg bana Jelačića to the Most mladosti stop (on the south side of Most mladosti bridge), followed by a 20min walk eastwards along the south bank of the river. Sun 7am–3pm.

ART AND DESIGN

Dizajnholik Ilica 11 01 410 0094, dizajnholik.hr; map p.63. Design store selling furniture, fabrics, light fittings and other household items, with a strong contemporary Croatian slant. Mon–Fri 11am–7pm, Sat 10.30am–2.30pm.

MSU Shop Avenija Dubrovnik 17, Novi Zagreb 01 605 2758, msu.hr; map p.77. The Museum of Contemporary Art shop sells the usual art cards, mugs and books, alongside rather more creative solutions to the souvenir quandary – ironic T-shirts, unusual stationery and handmade toys. Tues–Fri 11am–7pm, Sat 11am–8pm, Sun 11am–7pm.

Prostor Mesnička 5 01 484 6016, prostoreshop.com; map p.63. Clothes, bags, jewellery and other accessories by up-and-coming designers, hidden away in a courtyard off the street. Mon–Fri noon–8pm, Sat 10am–3pm.

BOOKS

Algoritam Gajeva 1 01 488 1555, algoritam.hr; map p.63. Large, up-to-date selection of foreign-language publications, including lots in English. International magazines are sold on the ground floor; books in the basement below. Mon–Fri 8.30am–9pm, Sat 8.30am–3pm.

Jesenski i Turk branches at Vukotinovićeva 4 ⓣ01 482 6233, map pp.60–61; Preradovićeva 5 ⓣ01 487 3458, map p.63; ⓦjesenski-turk.hr. Browser-friendly secondhand bookseller with a small selection of foreign-language paperbacks and plenty of large-format international art books. Mon–Fri 9am–8pm, Sat 10am–3pm.

Profil Bogovićeva 7 ⓣ01 487 7325; map p.63. Three-storey multimedia store with a decent selection of English-language fiction, tourist-oriented coffee-table titles and guidebooks. Mon–Sat 9am–9pm.

CDS AND RECORDS

Dancing Bear Gundulićeva 7 ⓣ01 483 0850, ⓦdancingbear.hr; map p.63. Wide range of both domestic and international releases in all genres. Mon–Fri 9am–8pm, Sat 9am–3pm.

Dobar Zvuk Preradovićeva 24 ⓣ01 485 4705; map pp.60–61. Secondhand store hidden away in a courtyard, much loved by vinyl junkies. Mon–Fri 10am–8pm, Sat 10am–3pm.

Karma Podgorska 3 ⓣ01 363 3685, ⓦkarmavinil.com; map pp.60–61. Treasure-trove of secondhand music on CD or vinyl, with all genres represented. Trams #3, #9 or #12 to Trešnjevački trg. Mon–Fri 9am–8pm, Sat 10am–3pm.

Kovač Masarykova 14 ⓣ01 487 2659; map pp.60–61. Another treasure-trove of old vinyl, secondhand CDs and a small selection of new and used clothes for those who like to wear black. They also sell tickets for gigs throughout town. Off the main street, in a courtyard. Mon–Fri 9am–7pm, Sat 9am–1pm.

Roxy Savska cesta 34 ⓦcdshop-roxy.com; map pp.60–61. Secondhand shop the size of a cupboard which still manages to fit in almost everything ever released in the former Yugoslavia, and much more besides. Mon–Fri 9am–7pm, Sat 9am–2pm.

FOOD AND DRINK

Bakina kuća Strossmayerov trg 7 ⓣ01 458 2525, ⓦbakina-kuca.hr; map pp.60–61. "Grannies House" offers a sumptuous range of upmarket alcoholic drinks, foodstuffs and fragrant herbs. Mon–Fri 8am–8pm, Sat 8am–2pm.

Bornstein Kaptol 19 ⓣ01 481 2361, ⓦbornstein.hr; map p.63. Upmarket wine shop selling domestic tipples with a strong Istrian slant. Mon–Fri 9am–7pm, Sat 9am–2pm.

Ekoteka Agra Teslina 11 ⓣ01 888 5534, ⓦekoteka-agra.hr; map p.63. Croatian specialities aplenty, with honeys, jams, chocolates and sweet-tooth nibbles well to the fore. Also a good place to pick up olive oil. Mon–Fri 8am–8pm, Sat 8am–3pm.

Franja Vlaška 62 ⓣ01 455 6391, ⓦfranja.hr; map pp.60–61. Coffee shop which also sells the kind of fancy food products that make perfect presents, including Croatian wine, *rakija*, olive oil and fig jam. Mon–Fri 7am–8pm, Sat 7am–5pm.

Ivić Vlaška 64 ⓣ01 461 7062; map pp.60–61. Fresh Dalmatian produce and plenty of bottled and tinned goodies from olives to truffles. Mon–Fri 8am–9pm, Sat 8am–3pm.

Natura Croatica Preradovićeva 8 ⓣ01 485 5076, ⓦnaturacroatica.com; map pp.60–61. Wine, *rakija*, olive oil and speciality biscuits. On the pricey side but very classy all the same. Mon–Fri 9am–9pm, Sat 9am–3pm.

DIRECTORY

Embassies and consulates Australia, 3rd floor, Kaptol Centar, Nova ves 11 ⓣ01 489 1200, ⓦcroatia.embassy.gov.au; Bosnia-Hercegovina, Torbarova 9 ⓣ01 468 3761; Canada, Prilaz Gjure Deželića 4 ⓣ01 488 1200; Ireland, contact the Irish Embassy in Ljubljana, Slovenia ⓣ00386 1 300 8970, ⓦirishembassy.si; Montenegro, Perkovićeva 2 ⓣ01 482 8348; Serbia, Pantovčak 245 ⓣ01 457 9067; UK, Ivana Lučića 4 ⓣ01 600 9100, ⓦukincroatia.fco.gov.uk; US, 10km south of the centre at Thomasa Jeffersona 2 ⓣ01 661 2200, ⓦzagreb.usembassy.gov.

Exchange There are exchange counters (*mjenjačnica*) at all banks, travel agents and post offices. Outside regular office hours, try the exchange counter at the bus station (24hr), or at the post office next to the train station at Branimirova 4 (24hr).

Hospitals The main casualty department is at Heinzelova 88 (ⓣ01 630 2911). The main children's hospital is at Klaićeva 16 (ⓣ01 460 0111). A private clinic with English-speaking doctors is Vallis Medica, Božidarevićeva 7 (ⓣ01 230 5444, ⓦmedicentar.hr).

Internet cafés Mama, Preradovićeva 18 ⓣ01 485 6400, ⓦmi2.hr; Sublink, Teslina 12 ⓣ01 481 9993, ⓦsublink.hr.

Laundry Service washes and dry-cleaning at Petecin, Kaptol 11 (Mon–Fri 8am–8pm, Sat 8am–2pm), and Doratex, Draškovićeva 31 (Mon–Fri 7am–7pm, Sat 8am–noon).

Left luggage At the bus station (daily 6am–10pm) and train station (24hr lockers).

Pharmacy cnr Trg bana Jelačića/Radićeva (24hr).

Phones National and international calls can be made from the metered booths at the post offices on Jurišićeva or Branimirova.

Post offices Jurišićeva 13 (Mon–Fri 7am–9pm, Sat 7.30am–2pm); Branimirova 4 (24hr).

Travel agents Atlas, Zrinjevac 17 ⓣ01 480 7300, ⓦatlas-croatia.com; STA Travel, Krvavi most 3 ⓣ01 488 6340, ⓦsta-zagreb.com.

Inland Croatia

PLITVICE LAKES NATIONAL PARK

Inland Croatia

2

The jumble of geographical regions that make up inland Croatia seem, on the face of it, to have little in common with one another. Historically, however, the Croats of the interior were united by a set of cultural influences very different from those that prevailed on the coast. After the collapse of the medieval Croatian kingdom in the early part of the twelfth century, inland Croatia fell under the sway of first Hungary, then the Habsburg Empire, increasingly adopting the culture and architecture of Central Europe. This heritage has left its mark: sturdy, pastel-coloured farmhouses dot the countryside, while churches sport onion domes and Gothic spires, providing a sharp contrast with the pale stone houses and Venetian-inspired campaniles of the coast.

The main appeal of inland Croatia lies in its contrasting landscapes. It's here that the mountain chains that run from the Alps down to the Adriatic meet the Pannonian plain, which stretches all the way from Zagreb to eastern Hungary. The **Zagorje** region, just north of Zagreb, resembles southern Austria with its knobbly hills and castles, while southwest of Zagreb are the captivating lakes and waterfalls of the **Plitvice Lakes.** Much less touristed but equally rewarding are the wetlands southeast of the capital, with the **Lonjsko polje Nature Park** offering a mixture of archaic timber-built villages and birdwatching opportunities. The eastern province of **Slavonia** features broad expanses of flat, chequered farmland only partially broken up by low green hills. Tucked away in the province's northeastern corner is the **Kopački rit Nature Park**, a wildlife-rich wonderland of reedy waterways and sunken forests. It's in these areas of natural beauty that **rural tourism** is taking off in a big way, with village B&Bs, folksy restaurants and well-signed cycling routes cropping up in the Zagorje, Plitvice, Lonjsko polje and Kopački rit. Vineyards and wine cellars are a growing feature of tourism too, especially around **Ilok** in the far southeast.

The region also has worthwhile urban centres, with several well-preserved Baroque towns in which something of the elegance of provincial Habsburg life has survived. The most attractive of these are **Varaždin**, northeast of Zagreb, and **Osijek**, a former fortress town in eastern Slavonia.

The Zagorje

Spread out between Zagreb and the Slovene border, the **Zagorje** is an area of chocolate-box enchantment: miniature wooded hills are crowned with the castles they seem designed for, and streams tumble through lush vineyards. At the top of almost every vineyard is a *klet*, a small, steep-roofed structure traditionally used for storing

TITO STATUE, KUMROVEC

Highlights

❶ **Kumrovec** Beautifully preserved Zagorje village which is also the birthplace of Croatia's most famous son, Josip Broz Tito. **See p.101**

❷ **Krapina Neanderthal Museum** The story of the Neanderthals – and indeed life on earth as a whole – comes vividly to life at this fabulous state-of-the-art museum. **See p.104**

❸ **Varaždin cemetery** The lovingly tended shrubs and hedgerows of this nineteenth-century necropolis will excite the amateur gardener in everyone. **See p.108**

❹ **Plitvice Lakes National Park** Breathtaking beauty spot offering a stunning profusion of forest-fringed lakes, waterfalls and rapids. **See p.114**

❺ **Lonjsko polje** A region of enchantingly archaic timber-built villages, frequented by storks and home to wild horses and spotty-hided pigs. **See p.116**

❻ **Tvrđa, Osijek** An atmospheric ensemble of Baroque buildings built by Habsburgs, now the centre of the city's nightlife. **See p.123**

❼ **Kopački rit** One of Central Europe's premier wetland areas, providing a natural habitat for herons, cormorants and birdwatchers. **See p.127**

❽ **Ilok** Medieval fortress town famous for its family-run wine cellars. **See p.133**

HIGHLIGHTS ARE MARKED ON THE MAP ON P.98

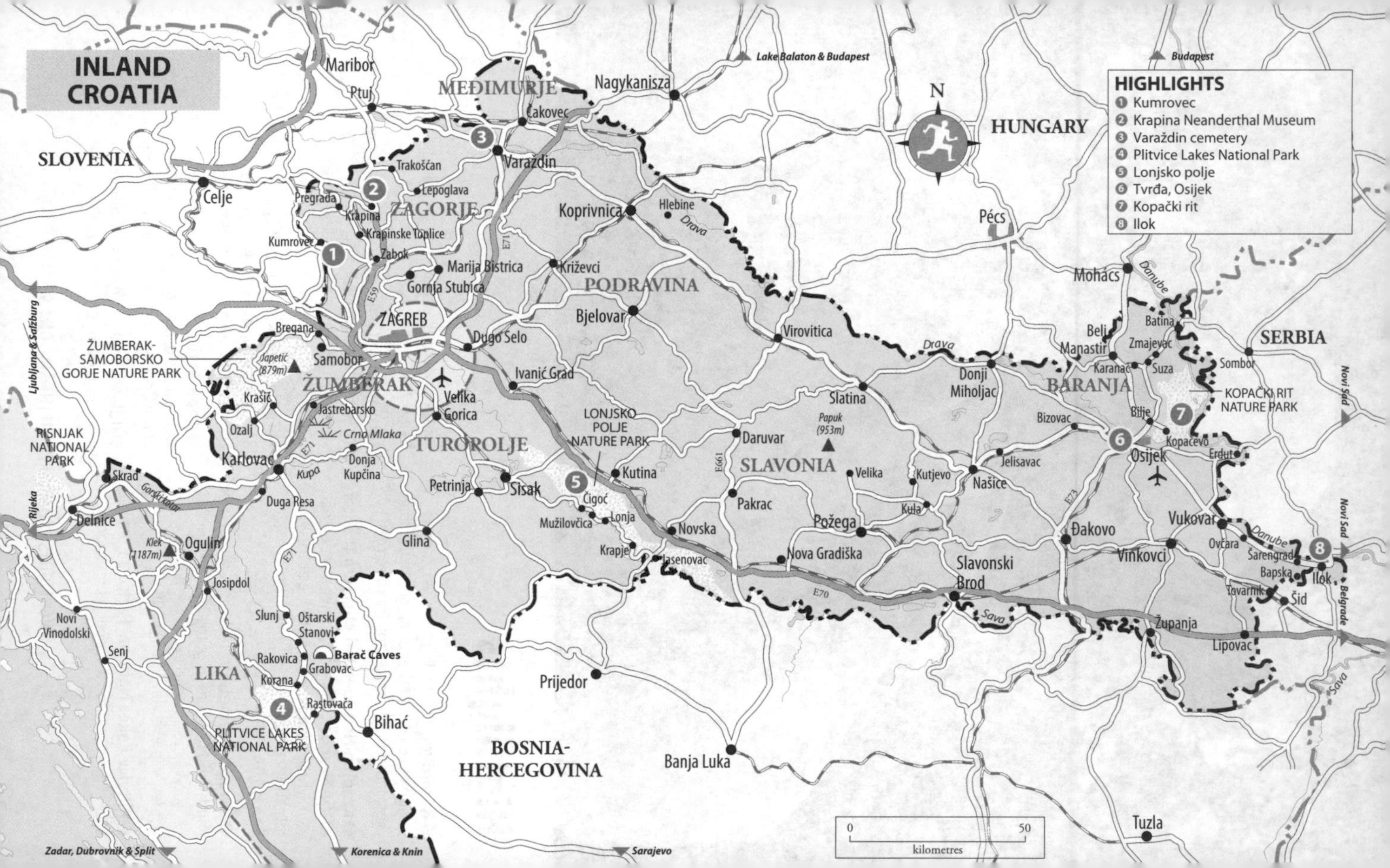
INLAND CROATIA
HIGHLIGHTS
1 Kumrovec
2 Krapina Neanderthal Museum
3 Varaždin cemetery
4 Plitvice Lakes National Park
5 Lonjsko polje
6 Tvrđa, Osijek
7 Kopački rit
8 Ilok
SLOVENIA
HUNGARY
SERBIA
BOSNIA-HERCEGOVINA
MEĐIMURJE
ZAGORJE
PODRAVINA
ŽUMBERAK
TUROPOLJE
SLAVONIA
BARANJA
LIKA
ZAGREB
Lake Balaton & Budapest
Budapest
Ljubljana & Salzburg
Rijeka
Zadar, Dubrovnik & Split
Korenica & Knin
Sarajevo
Novi Sad
Belgrade
Maribor
Ptuj
Celje
Nagykanisza
Čakovec
Varaždin
Trakošćan
Lepoglava
Pregrada
Krapina
Krapinske Toplice
Kumrovec
Zabok
Marija Bistrica
Gornja Stubica
Koprivnica
Hlebine
Drava
Križevci
Bjelovar
Virovitica
Pécs
Mohács
Danube
Beli Manastir
Batina
Zmajevac
Karanac
Suza
Sombor
KOPAČKI RIT NATURE PARK
Bilje
Kopačevo
Osijek
Erdut
Bizovac
Donji Miholjac
Slatina
Papuk (953m)
Daruvar
Velika
Kutjevo
Jelisavac
Našice
Kula
Pakrac
Požega
Nova Gradiška
Slavonski Brod
Sava
Đakovo
Vinkovci
Vukovar
Ovčara
Šarengrad
Ilok
Bapska
Tovarnik
Šid
Županja
Lipovac
Tuzla
Bregana
Samobor
ŽUMBERAK-SAMOBORSKO GORJE NATURE PARK
Japetić (879m)
Dugo Selo
Ivanić Grad
Velika Gorica
Jastrebarsko
Crna Mlaka
Krašić
Ozalj
Karlovac
Kupa
Donja Kupčina
Petrinja
Sisak
LONJSKO POLJE NATURE PARK
Kutina
Čigoć
Mužilovčica
Lonja
Krapje
Jasenovac
Novska
Glina
RISNJAK NATIONAL PARK
Skrad
Gorski kotar
Delnice
Duga Resa
Klek (1187m)
Ogulin
Josipdol
Novi Vinodolski
Senj
Slunj
Oštarski Stanovi
Barač Caves
Rakovica
Grabovac
Korana
Rastovača
PLITVICE LAKES NATIONAL PARK
Bihać
Prijedor
Banja Luka
E59
E71
E661
E70
E73
0
50
kilometres

FOOD AND DRINK IN INLAND CROATIA

Inland Croatian cuisine is invariably a waistline-enhancing affair, with generous helpings of pork, turkey, duck and freshwater fish forming the backbone of most menus. Signature dish of Zagorje and the northeast is **roast turkey** served with *mlinci*, sheets of pasta torn into misshapen scraps and covered with tasty juices from the bird.

Paprika is the main characteristic of Slavonia and the Baranja, where meat and fish is cauldron-stewed with generous helpings of the red spice. Carp, catfish and pike-perch from Sava and Drava rivers frequently end up in **fiš paprikaš**, the spicy, soupy mainstay of most restaurant menus around Osijek and in the southeast. Frequently served with tagliatelli-like noodles, *fiš perkelt* is a slightly reduced version of the same thing. The meat-eater's alternative to *fiš* is **čobanac**, a goulash-esque paprika-laden stew which is served up in vast tureens. Many Slavonian families keep a pig or two, traditionally slaughtered towards the end of November in the annual *kolinje*, or pig cull. The main pork-based delicacy is **kulen**, a rich, paprika-flavoured sausage served as a snack or hors d'oeuvre.

The **wines** of inland Croatia are an increasingly big deal, with excellent Graševina (Welschriesling) and Traminac (Gewurztraminer) on sale in the family-run wineries of Zmajevac (see p.128) and Ilok (see p.134).

2

wine (nowadays they're more often put to use as weekend cottages). Although the area is covered with a dense patchwork of villages, human beings seem outnumbered by the chickens, geese and turkeys that scavenge between the cornfields and vegetable plots. The museum village of **Kumrovec**, the Neanderthal Museum at **Krapina** and the castles at **Veliki Tabor** and **Trakošćan** are the main targets for visitors, although there are any number of Baroque churches and rural villages awaiting those who wish to explore further.

Most towns in the Zagorje have direct **bus** links with Zagreb, but you'll need your own transport if you want to explore the region in depth.

Marija Bistrica

Located below the northeastern spur of Mount Medvednica (see p.80) some 37km from Zagreb, **MARIJA BISTRICA** is home to the most important Marian shrine in Croatia. It's a popular destination for pilgrims year round, though things can get particularly crowded on August 15 (Assumption) and on the Sunday preceding St Margaret's Day (July 20), when the shrine is traditionally reserved for the city folk of Zagreb. The town itself is a small, rustic place onto which modern coach-party tourism has been rather unceremoniously grafted.

Pilgrimage Church of St Mary of Bistrica

Mon–Fri 7am–4pm, Sat & Sun 10am–3pm

Reconstructed on numerous occasions to accommodate ever-growing numbers of visitors, the **Pilgrimage Church of St Mary of Bistrica** (Hodočasnička crkva Marije Bistričke) dominates the hill on which Marija Bistrica is built. The current structure, put together between 1880 and 1884 by the architect of Zagreb cathedral, Hermann Bollé, is a remarkably eclectic and playful affair, its distinctive black-and-red chevroned steeple flanked by castellated red-brick turrets.

The principal object of popular veneration is the **Black Madonna**, a fifteenth-century statue of the Virgin set into the main altar. According to tradition, the statue was bricked into a church wall in 1650 to prevent it from falling into the hands of marauding Turks, and here it remained for 34 years until a miraculous beam of light revealed its hiding place. The story was spread by Bishop of Zagreb Martin Borković, who was eager to promote Marija Bistrica as a spiritual centre at a time when pilgrimages in general were being encouraged throughout the Habsburg lands – popular religion was seen as a useful way of getting the masses behind the

2

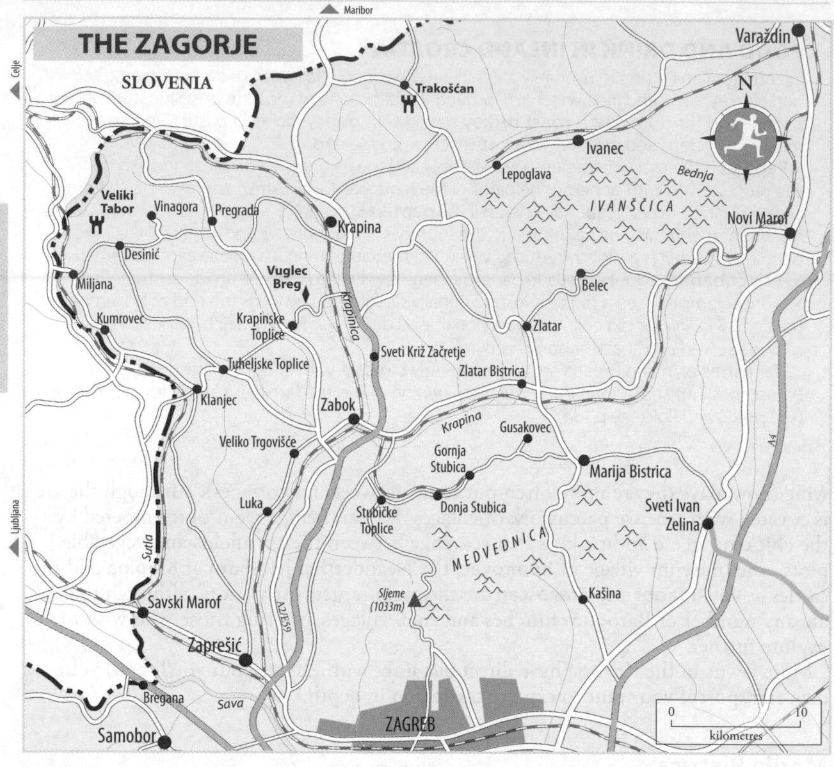

Catholic regime. The Madonna subsequently survived a fire in 1880 that destroyed almost everything else in the church, thereby adding to its aura.

ARRIVAL AND INFORMATION — MARIJA BISTRICA

By bus Marija Bistrica is served by numerous buses from Zagreb (Mon–Fri 12 daily, Sat 6 daily, Sun 4 daily; 1hr 15min) – the route follows a scenic road that crawls over the eastern shoulder of Mount Medvednica. Buses pick up and drop off on the main street immediately below the church, from where the pedestrianized Zagrebačka leads up to the pilgrimage church.

Tourist office Zagrebačka 66 (Tues–Fri 7am–3pm, May–Sept also Sat & Sun 8am–2pm; ⓣ049 468 380, ⓦinfo-marija-bistrica.hr).

ACCOMMODATION AND EATING

The tourist office can provide the addresses of a handful of local families offering private **rooms** (180Kn). Numerous cafés and bistros near Marija Bistrica's church serve the usual refreshments and snacks. On big pilgrimage days, several establishments along the main street offer grills and spit-roasts cooked on outdoor barbecues. Marija Bistrica is also famous for the large number of local **bakeries** churning out *licitari* and *medenjaci* (see box opposite); almost every shop in the town centre is overflowing with them.

Bluesun Hotel Kaj Zagrebačka bb ⓣ049 326 600, ⓦhotelkaj.hr. One of the Zagorje's best hotels for a cosy weekend break from the city, *Kaj* offers modern doubles with designer furnishings and a spa centre with beauty treatments and gym. The hotel restaurant mixes local Zagorje recipes with haute-cuisine panache. **860Kn**

Lojzekova hiža Gusakovec 116 ⓣ049 469 325, ⓦlojzekova-hiza.com. Inexpensive local food in a traditional farmhouse bordered by woods on one side and livestock-filled meadows on the other. Accommodation comes in the form of tiny but cosy en-suite attic rooms (including some with bunks for children). A 6km drive west of Marija Bistrica – follow signs to Stubičke Toplice and look for a signed right turn after 5km. B&B **250Kn**

GINGERBREAD HEARTS

One souvenir you'll come across again and again in the Zagorje is the *licitar*, the icing-covered pepper-flavoured biscuit that often takes the form of a big red heart (*licitarsko srce*; invariably translated as "**gingerbread heart**" even though there's rarely any ginger in them) and can sometimes assume enormous proportions. A popular holiday gift ever since the Middle Ages, the *licitar* is still considered an essential purchase for anyone visiting Marija Bistrica, where almost every bakery window displays gaudily decorated hearts, horses and other forms. *Licitari* are usually baked rock-hard and are supposed to be treasured as an ornament rather than eaten: sweet-toothed travellers may have better luck with the locally made *medenjaci*, melt-in-the-mouth biscuits made from honey dough.

Kumrovec

The village of **KUMROVEC**, 40km northwest of Zagreb, is renowned both as the best of Croatia's museum villages and as the birthplace of the father of communist Yugoslavia, **Josip Broz Tito** (see box, pp.102–103). The simple peasant house in which Tito was born was turned into a museum during his lifetime, while the surrounding properties were rebuilt and restored in the ensuing decades to provide a lasting example of an early twentieth-century Zagorje village. Those who remember Tito with affection (and there are plenty of them) still gather here on the weekend nearest May 25, which as Tito's "official birthday" was once marked with concerts and parades.

The museum complex

Daily: April–Sept 9am–7pm; Oct–March 9am–4pm • 20Kn • ⓣ 049 225 830, ⓦ mdc.hr/kumrovec

Set back from the main road behind a large car park, the "**Old Village**" **Museum** (Muzej "staro selo") consists of a collection of pastel-coloured houses and farmsteads ranged alongside a gurgling brook. Tito's birthplace, a few steps beyond the entrance, is marked by a trademark statue of the Marshal by Anton Augustinčić – blown up by right-wing hooligans on Boxing Day 2004, it has now been restored to its rightful place. Inside, lifelike re-creations of the 1890s rooms contain a restrained collection of photos and mementos, including the uniform worn by Tito while leading the Partisan struggle from the island of Vis in 1944.

The other buildings are each devoted to a particular rural craft, with displays of blacksmithery, basket-weaving and toy-making – the last featuring dainty, brightly painted carved wooden horses and other animals. One house is given over to a series of tableaux illustrating a traditional wedding feast, and is crowded with costumed mannequins and tables decked with imitation food. One recent addition to the museum is a house decorated with 1970s furniture, showing how lifestyles changed during the post-World War II period.

ARRIVAL AND DEPARTURE — KUMROVEC

By train and bus Getting to Kumrovec is easy enough, with commuter trains from Zagreb to Savski Marof (roughly every 30min; 35min) connecting with five daily Savski Marof–Kumrovec buses (the buses are run by Croatian Railways, so you can buy a through ticket). The buses terminate at the semi-derelict Kumrovec train station, a 20min walk north of the village itself.

ACCOMMODATION AND EATING

Pansion Zelenjak Risvica 1 ⓣ 049 550 747, ⓦ zelenjak.com. Set amid wooded riverside scenery 3km south of the village, *Zelenjak* is a good base from which to explore the area if you have your own transport, offering smart rooms with shower and TV. It also has a classy restaurant with a strong line in freshwater fish. **300Kn**

Stara Vura Josipa Broza 13 ⓣ 049 553 157, ⓦ staravura-kumrovec.hr. Situated 100m east of the museum complex in the new part of the village, this moderately priced but rather staid restaurant serves the full range of grilled pork, poultry and fish dishes. "Tito's Sunday Lunch" (170Kn) kicks off with a glass of whisky, centres on a six-meat mixed grill and winds up with a custard slice. Daily 6am–10pm.

2

JOSIP BROZ TITO (1892–1980)

Josip Broz was born on May 7, 1892, the seventh son of peasant smallholder Franjo Broz and his Slovene wife Marija Javeršek. After training as a blacksmith and metalworker, Josip Broz became an officer in the Austrian army in World War I, only to be captured by the Russians in 1915. Fired by the ideals of the Bolshevik revolution, he joined the Red Army and fought in the Russian Civil War before finally heading for home in 1920. Some believe that the man who came back to Croatia with a discernible Russian accent was a Soviet-trained impostor who had assumed the identity of the original Josip Broz – an appealing but unlikely tale. Whatever the truth, on his return Broz found himself in a turbulent Yugoslav state in which the Communist Party was soon outlawed, and it was his success in reinvigorating demoralized party cells that ensured his rise through the ranks.

Broz took the pseudonym **Tito** in 1934 upon entering the central committee of the Yugoslav Communist Party (he became leader in 1937). Nobody really knows why he chose the name: the most frequently touted explanation is that the nickname was bestowed on him by colleagues amused by his bossy manner – "*ti to!*" means "you [do] that!" in Croatian – although it's equally possible that he took it from the eighteenth-century Croat writer Tito Brezovacki.

Tito's finest hour came following the German invasion of Yugoslavia in 1941, when he managed to take control of the anti-fascist uprising, even though it wasn't initially inspired by the communists. Despite repeated (and often very successful) German counteroffensives, he somehow succeeded in keeping the core of his movement alive – through a mixture of luck, bloody-mindedness and sheer charisma rather than military genius. He also possessed a firm grasp of political theatre, promoting himself to the rank of marshal and donning suitably impressive uniforms whenever Allied emissaries were parachuted into Yugoslavia to meet him. The British and Americans lent him their full support from 1943 onwards, thereby condemning all other, non-communist factions in Yugoslavia to certain political extinction after the war.

Emerging as dictator of Yugoslavia in 1945, Tito showed no signs of being anything more than a loyal Stalinist until the Soviet leader tried to get rid of him in 1948. Tito's survival – subsequently presented to the world as "Tito's historic 'no' to Stalin" – rested on his innate ability to inspire loyalty among a tightly knit circle of former Partisans while isolating and

Veliki Tabor

Košnički Hum, Desinić • March & Oct Tues–Fri 9am–4pm, Sat & Sun 9am–5pm; April–Sept Tues–Fri 9am–5pm, Sat & Sun 9am–7pm; Nov–Feb Tues–Sun 9am–4pm • 20Kn • T 049 374 970, W velikitabor.com

Of all the Zagorje castles it is **Veliki Tabor**, 60km north of Zagreb, that lives up most to everybody's idea of what a medieval castle ought to look like, with imposing barrel-shaped bastions looking down on the road from a grassy hilltop. Built in the sixteenth century by the Rattkays, one of northern Croatia's most powerful landowning families, it consists of a pentagonal late-Gothic keep surrounded by a compact ring of semicircular towers. It once featured an outer loop of walls and towers, although only one of the bastions still survives. The castle's central courtyard received a thorough Renaissance makeover in the seventeenth century, wth the addition of three tiers of galleries.

A well-presented history **museum** occupies the castle keep, with a sequence of rooms filled with pikes, maces, knightly tombstones and other medieval oddments. Come here on a full moon and you may well hear the wailing ghost of **Veronika of Desinić**, a fifteenth-century local maiden who won the heart of young aristo Friedrich of Celje – ruining his father Count Hermann's plans of securing a better match. Local legend maintains that the Count had Veronika drowned as a witch, and her body was bricked into the walls of Veliki Tabor.

ARRIVAL AND DEPARTURE — VELIKI TABOR

By bus There are eight buses daily from Zagreb to the village of Desinić (1hr 40min), to the east of the castle, from where it's a 3km walk to the castle access road and a further 2km uphill to the site.

2

eliminating those who disagreed. Flushed with the prestige of having resisted Soviet pressure, he concentrated on affirming Yugoslavia's position on the world stage and increasingly left the nitty-gritty of running the country to others. Forming the **non-aligned movement** with Nehru, prime minister of India, and President Nasser of Egypt after 1955 provided a platform which allowed him to travel the world, giving Yugoslavia an international profile yet to be regained by any of its successor republics. In domestic affairs he contrived to present himself as the lofty arbiter who, far from being responsible for the frequent malfunctions of Yugoslav communism, emerged to bang heads together when things got out of control. Thus, his decision to bring an end to the Zagreb-based reform movement known as the Croatian Spring in 1971 was sold to the public as a Solomonic intervention to ensure social peace rather than the authoritarian exercise it really was.

A vain man who loved to wear fancy uniforms and medals, dyed his hair and used a sun lamp, Tito enthusiastically acquiesced to the **personality cult** constructed around him. May 25 was declared his official birthday and celebrated nationwide as "Dan mladosti" ("Day of Youth"), enhancing Tito's aura as the kindly father of a grateful people. He was also a bit of a ladies' man, marrying four times and switching partners with a speed that dismayed his more puritanical colleagues. Affection for Tito in Yugoslavia was widespread and genuine, if not universal. There's no doubt that Titoist communism was "softer" than its Soviet counterpart after 1948: many areas of society were relatively free from ideological control and, from the 1950s onwards, Yugoslavs were able to travel and work abroad.

For most Croats nowadays, Tito's legacy is ambiguous. Tito was fortunate enough to die before Yugoslavia's economy went seriously wrong in the 1980s, and for many he remains a symbol of the good old days when economic growth (paid for by soft Western loans) led to rising living standards and a consumer boom. However, the authority of the party – and Tito's leadership of it – was never to be questioned, and many dissenting voices ended up in prison as a result. Tito is also seen as the man responsible for the so-called **Way of the Cross** (Križni put) massacres of 1945 (when thousands of Croatian reservists were put to death by avenging Partisans), the repression of Croatia's Catholic Church, and the crackdown on the Croatian Spring. Despite keeping national aspirations on a tight leash, however, Tito's Yugoslavia ensured Croatian territorial continuity by establishing borders still in existence today. For this reason alone, many streets and squares in Croatia continue to bear Tito's name.

ACCOMMODATION AND EATING

Grešna Gorica Desinić ⓣ049 343 001, ⓦgresna-gorica.com. About 1km east of the castle, a well-signed turn-off leads up to this popular venue for long weekend lunches with a traditionally furnished dining room and splendid views of Veliki Tabor. It does a full range of Croatian cuisine, including Zagorje specialities such as *štrukli*, *purica z mlincima* (turkey with baked strips of pasta) and *srneći gulaš* (venison goulash). There's a small playground and a farmhouse zoo outside. Daily 11am–10pm.

Trsek Trnovec Desinički 23 ⓣ049 343 434, ⓦtrsek.hr. Hilltop farmstead near Desinić surrounded by vineyards, dishing up hearty traditional meals in a dining room hung with rustic knick-knacks. Cosy en-suite rooms are available if you want to stay. To get there, take the main road east out of Desinić and turn left when you see the sign. B&B **300Kn**

Krapina

Squeezed among lumpish, vine-covered hills, the busy little town of **KRAPINA**, 65km north of Zagreb, has been propelled into the premier league of Croatian tourism thanks to the newly built Neanderthal Museum, a boldly contemporary collection whose visitor-friendly mix of archeology, science and natural history draws coach-loads of visitors from all over the country. The museum commemorates so-called "Krapina Man" (*krapinski čovjek*), a type of Neanderthal who lived in caves hereabouts some thirty thousand years ago. The bones of these hominids were excavated by Dragutin Gorjanović Kramberger in 1899 on Hušnjakovo hill, a short walk west of the town centre on the far side of the River Krapinica.

Krapina Neanderthal Museum

Šetalište Vilibalda Sluge • Tues–Sun: March & Oct 9am–6pm; April–Sept 9am–7pm, Nov–Feb 9am–5pm • Adults 50Kn, children 25Kn, family ticket 100Kn • 049 371 491, mkn.mhz.hr

Ambitious, well designed and thought-provoking to boot, the **Krapina Neanderthal Museum** (Muzej Krapinskih Neandertalaca) is nothing short of a museum of life on earth. The bulding itself is well suited to the task, with a glass-walled atrium leading to a cylindrical structure built into the Hušnjakovo hillside – visitors ascend the cylinder by spiral pathway, confronting stages in the earth's development as they go. A light display reruns the Big Bang theory of the universe's creation, and life-sized models of mammals, monkeys and missing links illustrate how we got to where we are now: as a tour de force in evolutionary theory, the museum seems guaranteed to send creationists squealing for the exits. By far the most entertaining aspects of the museum are devoted to the Krapina Neanderthals themselves – a film featuring human actors in prosthetic masks re-creates a day in the life of a Neanderthal tribe, and the display culminates in a diorama featuring startlingly lifelike Neanderthal dummies.

Outside the musem, pathways leads up onto the wooded hillside towards the exact spot where Krambeger first excavated the bones, nowadays marked by life-sized statues of a Neanderthal family.

Church of St Mary of Jerusalem

Trški Vrh • Usually closed outside Mass times, but a local keyholder (check with the tourist office) will open up for you

Two kilometres east of town in the hillside suburb of Trški Vrh, the arcaded **Church of St Mary of Jerusalem** (Crkva svete Marije Jeruzalemske) has been a pilgrimage destination ever since the eighteenth century, when it was built to house the so-called Virgin of Jerusalem, a dainty statue of St Mary brought here from the Holy Land. Inside lies an exemplary riot of eighteenth-century religious fervour, with pinky-blue frescoes covering the ceiling and a series of five altarpieces – each bearing a dramatic tableau made up of three-dimensional carved wood figures.

ARRIVAL AND INFORMATION — KRAPINA

By train and bus Trains (8 daily; 2hr–2hr 30min; change at Zabok) and buses (10 daily; 1hr) from Zagreb arrive at Krapina's adjacent train and main bus stations, a 5min walk south of the town centre, although some bus services terminate at a new terminal 1km further south.

Tourist office Magistratska 11 (Mon–Fri 8am–3pm, Sat 8am–noon; 049 371 330, tzg-krapina.hr). The centrally located tourist office provides general formation on the Zagorje region.

ACCOMMODATION AND EATING

Gostionica pod Starim Krovovima Trg Ljudevita Gaja 15 049 370 536. Right on the main square, this is an informal place in which to tuck into a filling repertoire of grilled pork chops, schnitzels and freshwater fish. Above the restaurant (daily 6am–10pm) are a handful of bright, clean en-suite rooms with TV – the most atmospheric of which are the attic rooms, with sloping ceilings – and a couple of three- and four-bed rooms for families. **300Kn**

Vuglec Breg Škarićevo 151, Krapinske Toplice 049 345 015, vuglec-breg.hr. Seven kilometres southwest of Krapina on the hilly road to Krapinske Toplice, this ridge-top farmstead has become a major excursion destination, with a spacious restaurant serving up roast meats, roast turkey and old-fashioned dishes such as roast calf knuckle (*teleća koljenica*). The south-facing veranda offers views that stretch south as far as Mount Medvednica. They also have guest rooms spread across several rustic-looking buildings, featuring solid woody furnishings, smart bathrooms and wi-fi coverage. Mountain biking and pony riding are available to those who stay. B&B **500Kn**

Trakošćan castle

Trakošćan bb • Daily: April–Oct 9am–6pm, Nov–March 9am–5pm • 30Kn • 042 796 281, trakoscan.hr

Perched on a hilltop 20km northeast of Krapina, **Trakošćan castle** (Dvorac Trakošćan) is one of Croatia's most enduringly popular day-trip destinations, as the frequently full coach park amptly demonstrates. The sturdy thirteenth-century citadel was rebuilt in neo-Gothic style by Count Juraj Drašković in the 1850s, and Trakošćan's jaunty turrets and custard-coloured battlements are one of the most celebrated sights in the Zagorje region. With a well organized museum inside and a landscaped park with boating lake outside, you could easily spend a good half-day or longer here.

The **interior** is a tribute to the medieval tastes of its nineteenth-century owners, full of extravagantly pinnacled doorframes, elaborate woodcarving and monumental stone fireplaces. Hunting trophies, suits of armour and portraits of the Drašković family throughout the ages all add to the Gothic film-set effect. The first-floor Hunting Room (*lovačka dvorana*) boasts a rib-vaulted ceiling seemingly supported by stone lions and a ceramic oven decorated with sundry animal heads. In addition, there's a fascinating display of weaponry through the ages, and a big collection of aristocratic portraits on the upper floors.

ARRIVAL AND DEPARTURE — TRAKOŠĆAN CASTLE

By bus There are no direct buses to Trakošćan from Zagreb, although the eight daily services (fewer at weekends; 50min) from Varaždin ensure that you can just about tackle the castle as a long day-trip from the capital.

ACCOMMODATION AND EATING

Coning Trakošćan ⊕042 796 224, ⊛hotel-trakoscan.hr. Situated in meadows below the castle, this four-star hotel comes with spa facilities, gym and extensive grounds. The hotel restaurant concentrates on the hearty local meat and fowl repertoire. **850Kn**

Varaždin

Seventy kilometres northeast of Zagreb, **VARAŽDIN** is one of the best-preserved Baroque towns you are likely to find anywhere in Central Europe and is well worth a day-trip. An important military stronghold for successive Hungarian and Habsburg rulers in their struggle against Ottoman expansion, Varaždin grew fat on the profits of the Austrian–Turkish wars of the late 1600s and early 1700s, and many noble families built houses here. From 1765 to 1776 it was actually Croatia's capital, until a disastrous fire (allegedly started by a pipe-smoking local youth who fell over while chasing a pig) forced the relocation of the capital to Zagreb. Following the fire, life slowly returned to the town's opulent **Baroque palaces**, many of which remain resplendent in their original cream, ochre, pink and pale-blue colours. There's also a postcard-perfect **castle**, now home to northeastern Croatia's most worthwhile museum, and quite a few churches – all crammed within the compact old town. An additional reason to visit is provided by Varaždin's **graveyard**, famous throughout Croatia for its towering topiary and strollable park-like feel. A large student population ensures that modern Varaždin has a vivacious, youthful edge – the presence of an information technology faculty has made the town into one of the most prestigious places to study outside the capital. And Varaždin's one remaining claim to fame is the extraordinarily high incidence of **bicycle use** among its inhabitants, giving it the air of a prosperous provincial town in the Low Countries.

Franjevački trg

Really a broad street rather than a square, **Franjevački trg** is flanked by the mansions of wealthy merchants, their ostentatious arched portals surmounted by family crests and heavy stone balconies. Grabbing most of the attention is the cream-and-beige **Patačić Palace** (Palača Patačić), with Rococo mouldings writhing their way across its facade and a huge oriel window hovering above the corner of Franjevački trg and Gundulićeva. Now occupied by an Austrian bank, the palace was built for Franjo

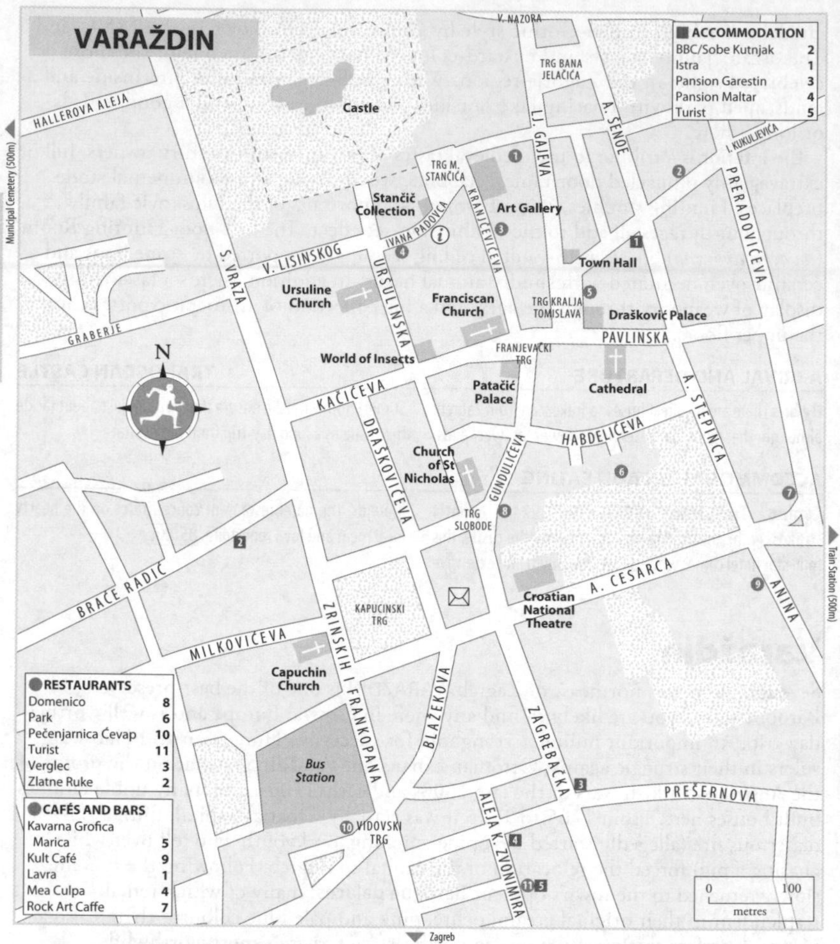

Patačić and his poetess wife, and became the centre of salon society in late eighteenth-century Varaždin.

Franciscan Church of St John the Baptist

Franjevački trg

On Franjevački trg's northern side is the seventeenth-century **Franciscan Church of St John the Baptist** (Crkva svetog Ivana Krstitelja), boasting a soaring belfry and an extravagantly gilded main altar. A scaled-down copy of Ivan Meštrović's *Grgur Ninski* statue, the original of which is in Split, stands outside.

World of Insects

Franjevački trg 6 • Tues–Fri 10am–5pm, Sat & Sun 10am–1pm • 20Kn • ⓣ 042 658 760, ⓦ gmv.hr

Housed in the Neoclassical **Herczer Palace**, the **World of Insects** (Svijet kukaca) features a display of more than 4500 insects based on the collection of local biologist Franjo Košćec, whose study is also re-created here. The exhibits are arranged thematically according to habitat – forest, meadow, riverbank and so on. Modern display cases and imaginative lighting lend the collection the character of a contemporary art installation.

Ursuline Church

Ursulinska

Dominating the narrow street of Ursulinska is the **Ursuline Church** (Ursulinska crkva), the recent recipient of a bright-pink makeover and whose soaring onion-topped tower is one of the most distinctive features of the Varaždin skyline. Inside is a pleasing array of both Gothic and Baroque fittings, with a late medieval sculpture of the Madonna and Child catching the eye to the left of the main altar, and an eighteenth-century organ above the entrance door encrusted with harp-twanging statuettes.

2

Trg kralja Tomislava and around

Varaždin's main square, **Trg kralja Tomislava** is surrounded by balustraded palaces and overlooked by the sky-rocketing clock tower of the sixteenth-century **town hall** (*vijećnica*). Arrive outside the town hall between 11am and noon on a Saturday and you'll witness the changing of the **town guard** (*građanska garda*); this ritual, enacted by volunteers clad in original nineteenth-century uniforms, is in memory of the (largely ceremonial) units that were a major source of civic pride during the Habsburg era.

Hugging the eastern side of the square is the coffee-coloured **Drašković Palace** (Palača Drašković), once home to the renowned eighteenth-century beauty Suzana Drašković. When her husband died in 1765, the viceroy of Croatia, Franjo Nadasdy, moved his entire court to Varaždin in order to be near her, turning the town into the de facto capital of Croatia in the process.

Cathedral

Pavlinska

Just off Varaždin's main square to the east, the **Church of the Ascension** (Crkva Marijinog Uznesenja) was originally built by the Jesuits in the 1640s. Now the town's cathedral, it stands on the cusp of the Baroque and Rococo eras, with most of the interior decorations, including the main altar, having been added in the 1730s. The plain, whitewashed interior provides the perfect setting for a no-holds-barred display of gilded statuary on the high altar and in the side chapels.

Art gallery

Trg Miljenka Stančića 3 • Tues–Fri 10am–5pm, Sat & Sun 10am–1pm • Price depends on what's on • ⓣ 042 214 172, ⓦ gmv.hr

Blessed with the kind of bright-orange exterior that looks like the funky imaginings of a 1970s-era designer, the seventeenth-century Palača Šermage conceals the town's **art gallery** (Galerija starih i novih majstora). The permanent collection ranges from Dutch still-lifes to early twentieth-century Croatian art, and the gallery's seasonal art and history exhibitions are always worth a look.

The Stančić Collection

Trg Miljenka Stančića • Tues–Sun 10am–1pm & 5–8pm • ⓣ 042 311 312, ⓦ gcv.hr

Occupying a plain corner house, the **Stančić Collection** (Zbirka Stančić) honours Varaždin-born painter Miljenko Stančić (1926–77) who painted local landscapes with a fantastical, surrealist twist. As a figurative artist whose highly individual work doesn't quite fit into the established chronologies of the art historians, Stančić is a fascinating one-off.

The castle

Museum: April–Sept: Tues–Sun 10am–6pm; Oct–March: Tues–Fri 10am–5pm, Sat & Sun 10am–1pm • 20Kn

A wooden drawbridge marks the approach to Varaždin **castle** (stari grad), an attractively turreted structure surrounded by grassy earthworks. Dating from the mid-1500s, when Varaždin was in danger of Ottoman attack, it was subsequently transformed into a stately residence by the Erdödy family, who lorded it over the region for several centuries. The balustraded courtyard has been beautifully restored, and the **museum** within contains an engrossing display of weaponry and furniture throughout the ages, much of it accompanied by English-language captions. Located at the end of a first-floor corridor are the **Chapel of St Lawrence** (Kapelica svetog Lovre), built by Toma Bakač Erdödy in thanks for his victory over the Ottomans at Sisak in 1593, and an adjoining circular sacristy, squeezed into a defensive tower.

The cemetery

Hallerova aleja • Daily: Feb 7am–6pm; March & Oct 7am–7pm; April & Sept 7am–8pm; May–Aug 7am–9pm; Nov–Jan 7am–5pm • Free

About 1km west of the castle, down Hallerova aleja, Varaždin's **municipal cemetery** (Gradsko groblje) is one of Croatia's greatest horticultural masterpieces. Begun in 1905, it was very much the life's work of park keeper Hermann Haller, a serious student of European graveyards who believed that cemeteries should be life-enhancing public parks rather than the sombre preserve of wreath-laying mourners. He accordingly planted row upon row of conifers, carefully sculpted into stately green pillars that towered over the graves themselves – thereby providing "quiet and harmonious hiding places" for the deceased, as Haller himself explained. In among the greenery are some outstanding grave memorials, notably **Robert Frangeš-Mihanović**'s 1906 Art Nouveau relief of Death, angels and grieving relatives atop the tomb of Vjekoslav and Emma Leitner – it's in the eastern end of the cemetery, and is marked as attraction no. 10 on the map at the main entrance.

The northern end of the cemetery (again, the map at the entrance will guide you) contains a memorial to the communist partisans of World War II, with a row of spindly pylons exemplifying the kind of bold abstract art that sadly doesn't often feature in public sculpture any more.

ARRIVAL AND INFORMATION — VARAŽDIN

By bus Varaždin's bus station is a 5min walk southwest of the town centre, reached by crossing Kapucinski trg.

Destinations Trakošćan (Mon–Fri 8 daily, Sat 4 daily, Sun 1 daily; 50min); Zagreb (12 daily; 2hr).

By train The train station is on the eastern fringes of the town centre at the far end of Kolodvorska.

Destinations Zagreb (4 daily; 2hr 20min).

Tourist office Padovčeva 3 (April–Oct Mon–Fri 8am–6pm, Sat 9am–1pm; Nov–March Mon–Fri 8am–4pm; T 042 210 987, W tourism-varazdin.hr). The friendly staff at the tourist office, near the castle, can provide advice and a free town map.

ACCOMMODATION

BBC/Sobe Kutnjak Braće Radić 7 T 042 210 671, E kutnjak@vz.hinet.hr. Four-room B&B (two singles, one double and one triple) located above the *BBC* café, just north of the bus station. Rooms come with WC/shower and TV. **400Kn**

Istra Ivana Kukuljevića 6 T 042 659 659, W istra-hotel.hr. Super-central hotel in a pre-World War I bulding, with a handful of well-equipped en suites above a café-restaurant. All feature sloping attic ceilings and skylight windows; the "superior" room on the corner of the building is well worth reserving in advance if you want space and cosiness at the same time. **800Kn**

Pansion Garestin Zagrebačka 34 T 042 214 314. Popular city-centre restaurant with ten rooms above, each featuring private facilities, a/c and TV. **420Kn**

Pansion Maltar Prešernova 1 T 042 311 100, W maltar.hr. A cosy, informal B&B, a 5min walk south of the main square. **480Kn**

Turist Aleja Kralja Zvonimira 1 T 042 395 395, W hotel-turist.hr. Centrally located, 100-room three-star, with comfortable en-suite rooms each with satellite TV. "Business class" rooms come with minibar and a bit more desk space. The international cuisine in the *Turist*'s restaurant is well above the usual standard of hotel food in inland Croatia. **820Kn**

EATING AND DRINKING

While fine **restaurants** are relatively thin on the ground in central Varaždin, there are plenty of places where you can get a satisfying inexpensive feed. As you would expect from a town with a large student population, there's no shortage of

FESTIVALS IN VARAŽDIN

Varaždin is at its liveliest during the **Špancirfest** (late Aug/early Sept; ⓦspancirfest.com), a week-long arts festival featuring street theatre, open-air rock, world music and jazz gigs, and carnivalesque costume parades. During the last two weeks of September the town's churches and palaces provide suitably ornate venues for the **Varaždin Baroque Evenings** (Varaždinske barokne večeri; ⓦvbv.hr), with international conductors and soloists performing a rich repertoire of early classical music.

2

central places to drink. The terrace **cafés** on Trg kralja Tomislava and Trg M. Stančića are the places to go on warm summer evenings; otherwise, head for one of the characterful indoor drinking dens listed below.

RESTAURANTS

Domenico Trg slobode 7 ⓣ042 212 017. The classiest of several central pizza outlets, occupying a wooden-beamed pavilion with views of the town park. Also offers a choice of moderately priced pasta dishes and a serviceable seafood risotto, with prices rarely exceeding the 40Kn mark. Daily 9am–11pm.

Park Habdelićeva 6 ⓣ042 211 498. Dependable range of typically central European veal- and pork-based dishes in a plain modern building, with mains clocking in at 80–90Kn. The outdoor terrace, jutting out into the town park, is a wonderful place to sit in summer. Daily 8am–11pm.

Pečenjarnica ćevap Vidovski trg 17 ⓣ042 312 674. The tastiest grilled-meat dishes in town, in an unpretentious sit-down snack bar just round the corner from the bus station. Mon–Sat 8am–11pm, Sun 11am–10pm.

Turist Aleja Kralja Zvonimira 1 ⓣ042 395 395, ⓦhotel-turist.hr. Hotel restaurant with an excellent menu of international and local fare, including some substantial and delicious pork and venison dishes. Mains 100Kn and above. Daily noon–11pm.

Verglec Kranjčevićeva 12 ⓣ042 211 131, ⓦgastrocom-ugostiteljstvo.com. Ideally located downtown, this pub-restaurant offers central European pork and veal fillets, and a large choice of pizzas. Frequently full of lunching locals, it's not too pricey, with mains starting at 60Kn. Mon–Sat 10am–10pm, Sun noon–7pm.

Zlatne Ruke Ivana Kukuljevića 13 ⓣ042 320 065, ⓦzlatneruke.com. Offering local food with a haute cuisine flourish, this is arguably the best restaurant in town for the traditional family-feast repertoire of freshwater fish, generous cuts of pork and veal, and roast fowl. As a basement restaurant painted almost entirely white, it's an enticing place. Daily 10am–11pm.

CAFÉS AND BARS

Kavarna Grofica Marica Trg Kralja Tomislava. Elegant main-square café with good coffee and excellent hot chocolate. Lovely desserts including own-brand chocolate cake and pralines. Daily 7am–10pm.

Kult Café Anina 2 ⓦwww.mmc-kult.com. Minimally decorated, mildly arty café-bar with a sporadic programme of small-scale concerts and DJ events. It's round the back of the Kult multimedia centre, basically a boutique cinema showing a mixture of mainstream and art movies. Mon–Thurs 7am–10pm, Fri & Sat 7am–1am, Sun 10am–9pm.

Lavra Gajeva 17. Snug, soothing cellar bar suitable for a daytime coffee or a longer evening drink. Stone-lined, barrel-vaulted interior, with outdoor seating in the yard. Sun–Thurs 9am–midnight, Fri & Sat till 2am.

Mea Culpa Ivana Padovca 5. Deep wicker armchairs, loungey decor and a fair-sized cocktail menu make this one of the most stylish watering holes in the centre. Sun–Thurs 8am–midnight, Fri & Sat til 2am.

Rock Art Caffe Petra Preradovićeva 24 ⓣ042 321 123, ⓦrock-art.hr. Roomy bar decorated with old guitars, album covers and the like. A big conservatory and plentiful outdoor seating make this a relaxing place to hang out whatever the time of day or night. Mon–Thurs 7am–midnight, Fri & Sat 7am–2am, Sun 9am–midnight.

ENTERTAINMENT

Croatian National Theatre (Hrvatsko narodno kazalište/HNK) Augusta Cesarca 1 ⓣ042 214 688, ⓦhnkvz.hr. The main venue for drama and classical concerts, in a fine nineteenth-century auditorium.

Samobor and around

Nestling beneath the eastern spur of the wooded Samobor hills around 25km west of Zagreb, **SAMOBOR** is every Croat's idea of what a provincial inland town should look like: a tidy, prosperous agglomeration of pastel-coloured houses, largely unsullied by

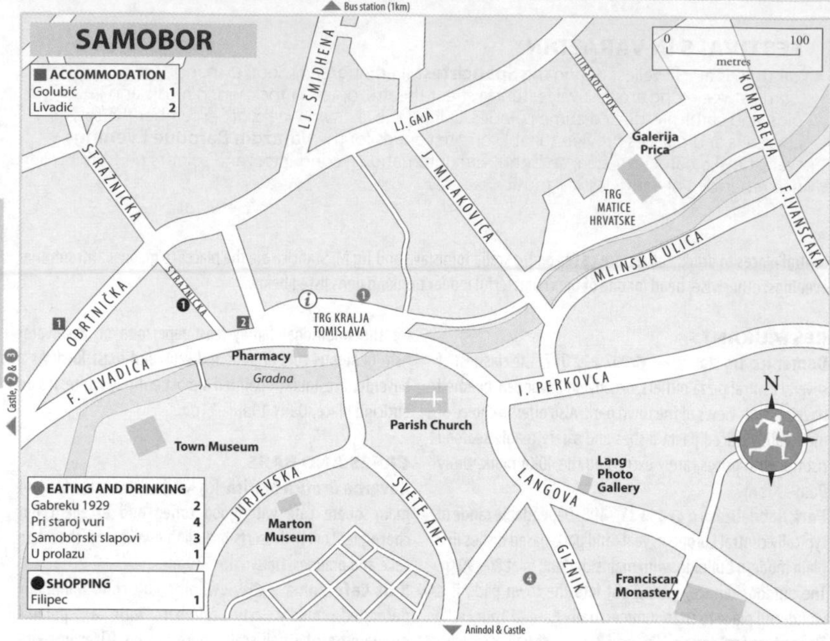

industry and modern architecture, and with an abundance of hilly woodland on the doorstep. Samobor rivalled Zagreb as a trade and craft centre in the Middle Ages, though it's nowadays very much a dormitory suburb of its big neighbour, attracting a smattering of day-trippers keen to explore the woods above the town or sample the local delicacy, **samoborska kremšnita**, a wobbly mass of vanilla custard squeezed between layers of flaky pastry. Other local goodies worth stocking up on include *samoborski bermet* (Samobor vermouth), a brownish, stomach-settling spirit that tastes like cough mixture, and the sharply flavoured *samoborska muštarda* (mustard).

Trg kralja Tomislava

The town centre revolves around the long, extended triangle of **Trg kralja Tomislava**, beside which flows the Gradna – a minor tributary of the Sava, and here more of a swollen brook than a river – spanned by a succession of slender bridges. Lined by sober, beige town houses and overlooked by a canary-yellow parish church, the square has a character that's overwhelmingly Baroque, which renders the Art Nouveau pharmacy at no. 11 all the more striking – note the haughty, starch-winged angels high up on the facade.

SAMOBOR CARNIVAL

One of the best times to be in Samobor is immediately preceding Lent, during the **Samobor carnival** (Samoborski fašnik; ⓦ fasnik.com). One of Croatia's best-known and most authentic festivals, it dates from the early 1820s and – apart from a short period in the wake of World War II, when it was suspended – has been a permanent fixture in the town calendar ever since. On the weekend before Shrove Tuesday floats rumble through the streets in lively parades and hedonistic locals run around in masks, creating an impromptu party atmosphere. On Shrove Tuesday itself, an effigy named Princ Fašnik ("prince of the carnival") is blamed for everything that has gone wrong over the previous twelve months and is ritually burned on the main square.

2

Marton Museum

Jurjevska 7 • Tues–Fri by arrangement, Sat & Sun 10am–1pm • 20Kn • ⓣ 01 332 6426, ⓦ muzej-marton.hr

The handsomely restored granary uphill from Samobor's main square, housing the **Marton Museum** (Muzey Marton), was the original home of the Marton collection of porcelain, glassware and furniture before the main body of the collection moved to Zagreb's Katarinin trg (see p.67). The collection is regularly rotated so that some of the pearls of the Marton hoard are still on display here in Samobor.

Lang Photo Gallery

Langova 15 • Mon–Fri by arrangement, Sat & Sun 11am–1pm & 4–7pm • ⓣ 01 336 2884, ⓦ fotogalerija-lang.com

Housed in what looks like a suburban garage, the **Lang Photo Gallery** (Fotogalerija Lang) is a small, privately owned space run by art historian Želimir Koščević, who lives nearby. Expect to see some of the best contemporary photography exhibitions in the country.

Galerija Prica

Trg Matice Hrvatske 3 • Tues–Thurs 9am–3pm, Fri 1–7pm, Sat & Sun 10am–1pm • 15Kn • ⓣ 01 336 0112, ⓦ pousamobor.hr

In a pleasant riverside park northeast of Samobor's main square, the second floor of the town's adult education centre provides a home for the **Galerija Prica**, which is devoted to the zestful, colour-charged canvases of local painter Zlatko Prica (1916–2003) and the significantly more sombre work of his photographer daughter Vesna (1947–96).

The Town Museum

F. Livadićeva 7 • Tues–Fri 9.30am–2pm, Sat 10am–1pm • 12Kn • ⓣ 01 336 1014, ⓦ samoborskimuzej.hr

Just off the western end of Samobor's main square, the **Town Museum** (Gradski muzej) is housed in **Livadićev dvor**, the nineteenth-century home of composer Ferdinand Wiesner (1799–1879), whose enthusiasm for the liberation of the Slavs from the Habsburg yoke led him to change his name to the more Croatian-sounding Ferdo Livadić. An important meeting place for the leaders of the Illyrian movement in the 1820s and 1830s, his home now contains a modest collection of furniture, ceramics and fusty portraits of local burghers. More interesting is the ethnographical section in an adjacent outbuilding, where a smattering of English-language texts help to tease significance out of the rough wooden agricultural implements on display.

Anindol

Uphill from Samobor's parish church, Svete Ane climbs past the town graveyard towards **Anindol**, a wooded hillside criss-crossed by paths. After about ten minutes, tracks lead off to the right towards the forest-bound **Chapel of St Anne** (Crkvica svete Ana), from where you can choose between a steep route uphill to the **Chapel of St George** (Crkvica sveti Jure) or a lateral path to Samobor's medieval **castle**. Both chapels are closed except for special Masses, and the castle is no more than an overgrown ruin, but the tranquillity of the surrounding woods makes a walk here worthwhile.

It was on Anindol that Josip Broz Tito (see p.102) organized the founding congress of the Croatian Communist Party on August 1, 1937, in an attempt to persuade the Croats that Yugoslav communists shared their nationalist aspirations. With communist organizations outlawed in the Yugoslavia of the time, the gathering had to be organized in secret. An annual hiking festival was used as a cover: with the whole area filling up with weekend visitors, party activists could infiltrate without arousing suspicion. Only sixteen communist agents actually made it to the "congress", and Tito was reduced to scratching the resolutions of the meeting on the back of a calendar with a penknife – or so the story goes.

2

HIKING IN THE SAMOBORSKO GORJE

Samobor is the obvious base for hiking trips into the **Samoborsko gorje**, a ravine-scarred upland region which rises abruptly to the west of town, and backs directly onto the hills of the Žumberak. Both ranges fall within the boundaries of the **Žumberak-Samoborsko gorje Nature Park** (Park prirode Žumberak-Samoborsko gorje; park-zumberak.hr), which begins 5km west of Samobor and stretches 30km farther southwest towards the town of Ozalj. An area of deep forest interspersed with subalpine meadows, the eastern end of the park is perfect for gentle uphill hikes, and is correspondingly busy with local families on summer weekends. The 1:50, 000 *Žumberak-Samoborsko gorje* **map** published by the Nature Park is a useful aid to exploration; Samobor tourist office or the Eco Centre at Slani Dol (see below) may have copies for sale.

VELIKI LIPOVEC TO JAPETIĆ

The best starting point for walks is **Šoićeva kuća**, a timbered cottage (closed Mon) serving refreshments at the western end of the village of **Veliki Lipovec**, which is 9km west of Samobor along the road passing the (signposted) *Samoborski slapovi* hotel and restaurant. Samobor–Lipovec **buses** ply this route eight to ten times daily. The most popular walk from *Šoićeva kuća* is the ascent of wooded **Japetić** (879m), the Samoborsko gorje's highest point (1hr 30min–2hr). Two hundred metres southwest of *Šoićeva kuća*, a road ascends steeply to the right, leading past cottages until the asphalt gives way first to gravel track, then to footpath. After a steady climb through the woods you reach a plateau, where fairly obvious signs direct you either to Japetić's summit, or to the Japetić mountain hut (weekends and holidays only) just to the south, which serves excellent *grah* and has good views of the Kupa valley to the southwest, with the forest-enclosed lakes of Črna Mlaka over to the left.

VELIKI LIPOVEC TO OŠTRC

An alternative hike from *Šoićeva kuća* leads to the 752-metre peak of **Oštrc**, ninety minutes' walk to the south. Directly opposite *Šoićeva kuća* a marked path heads uphill into the woods, passing through the ruins of the medieval Lipovec castle, continuing along a steep up-and-down path through the woods before eventually emerging onto the Preseka ridge, which runs above lush pastures. At the northeastern edge of the ridge lies Oštrc mountain hut (weekends only), serving good *grah* and simple cuts of meat. From here it takes only twenty minutes to reach the summit of Oštrc itself, where there are more fine views. From Oštrc you can either return to *Šoićeva kuća* the way you came, or follow a marked path to Japetić via a wooded saddle known as Velika vrata (the Oštrc–Japetić leg takes 1hr 30min), although the ascent of Japetić from Velika vrata is much steeper than the direct route from *Šoićeva kuća*.

SLANI DOL TO SOŠICE

An alternative access point to the hills is the ridge-top village of **Slani Dol**, 10km west of Samobor, reached by leaving town along the Veliki Lipovec road but forking right after about 3km instead of carrying on to *Šoićeva kuća*; the village is served by eleven **buses** daily from Samobor (fewer at weekends). Occupying the village's highest point is the **Eco Centre** (Eko centar; Mon–Fri 8am–4pm, Sat & Sun 9am–5pm; 01 332 7660), maintained by the Žumberak-Samoborsko gorje Nature Park and housing an informative display devoted to local flora and fauna – there's also a spectacular view of the surrounding vineyard-covered hills from the centre's forecourt. Slani Dol is also the start of a long-distance hiking trail known as **Queen Beech Way** (Put kraljice bukve), a two- to three-day trek that leads westward to **Sošice**, in the heart of the Žumberak hills. Recreational ramblers with limited time to spare can attempt the first leg, which ascends from Slani Dol through meadows and beech forest to the Sveti Bernard hut (1hr 30min), where there's a good view and the chance of refreshments at weekends.

ARRIVAL AND INFORMATION — SAMOBOR

By bus Samobor's bus station is on the main Zagreb–Bregana road 1km northwest of the main square. It is served by buses from Zagreb (18 daily; 25min) from both the main bus station and Črnomerec tram terminal (at the end of tram lines #2, #6 and #11).

Tourist office Trg kralja Tomislava 5 (Mon–Fri 8am–7pm, Sat 9am–5pm, Sun 10am–5pm; 01 336 0044, tz-samobor.hr). Hands out brochures, sells a town map and can help book accommodation.

ACCOMMODATION

Golubić Obrtnička 12 ☎01 336 0937. Family-run pension just behind the main square, offering a handful of unfussily decorated en-suite rooms with TV and fridge. The couple don't speak much English but they'll make you feel at home all the same. **250Kn**

★ **Livadić** Trg kralja Tomislava 1 ☎01 336 5850, ⓦhotel-livadic.hr. Medium-sized, friendly, family-run hotel in a 150-year-old house. All rooms are slightly different: some have parquet floors and retro-style furnishings, while others come with modern designer fittings. All have reasonably sized TVs and bathrooms, but if you want a full-size bathtub you'll have to ask for one of the atmospheric attic suites. The *Livadić*'s café offers superb *kremšnite* alongside a cholesterol-raising range of other home-baked desserts. **470Kn**

2

EATING AND DRINKING

CAFÉ

U prolazu Trg kralja Tomislava 5 ☎01 336 3704. The best cafés in which to linger over coffee and cake are those on the main square, among which, despite its rather plain interior, *U prolazu* is traditionally held to offer the best *samoborske kremšnite* in town (though regular patrons of the *Livadić* hotel may beg to differ; see above). Simply watching the creamy cubes wobble as the serving personnel lift them out of the counter-side chiller cabinet is an experience of almost erotic proportions. Daily 7am–11pm.

RESTAURANTS

★ **Gabreku 1929** Starogradska 46 ☎01 336 0722, ⓦgabrek.hr. Unassuming from the outside, *Gabreku* is justly famous for gut-busting portions of north Croatian food, with highlights including sausages with sauerkraut, roast veal with potatoes and old-fashioned favourites such as grilled calves' brains. Many people come here just for the *juha od vrganja* (mushroom soup). There's a pleasant courtyard at the back. Mains from 70Kn. Tues–Sun noon–midnight; closed Aug.

Pri staroj vuri Giznik 2 ☎01 336 0548, ⓦpri-staroj-vuri.hr. Located on a suburban street just above the parish church, this folksy spot with wood-panelled rooms, old clocks and checked tablecloths specializes in traditional north Croatian cuts of meat. It's one of the best places in the region to tuck into local specialities such as *lungić* (lean pork fillet) and *pačja prsa* (breast of duck). Mains in the 90–110Kn region. Mon & Wed–Sat noon–11pm, Sun noon–6pm; closed Tues.

Samoborski slapovi Hamor 16 ☎01 338 4061. Three kilometres northwest of town on the Lipovec road but worth the excursion, this hotel restaurant dishes up excellent trout and other freshwater fish from their own pond, with prices hovering around 70Kn per portion. Daily 7am–midnight.

SHOPPING

Filipec Stražnička 1a ☎01 336 4835, ⓦbermetfilipec.hr. Well-known local delicatessen firm selling *bermet* and *muštarda* from a hole-in-the-wall shop next to a cellar where both specialities are made. If there's nobody there, ring the bell. Usually daily 11am–8pm.

Slunj

Perched on a hilltop on the old Zagreb–Split road, the small town of **SLUNJ** hovers above the confluence of the Korana and Slunjčica rivers, with the rushing waters of the latter dropping into the Korana gorge through a series of small waterfalls and burbling rapids. In times past this natural power source led to the development of a riverside watermilling settlement known as **Rastoke**, where several traditional millers' buildings still survive – solid structures with stone lower floors and timber upper storeys. It's a delightful area for a stroll, with wooden bridges crossing gurgling torrents of channelled water, although many of Rastoke's most picturesque spots are on privately owned land. Otherwise there are excellent views of the gorge from the path above the north bank of the Korana, visible when entering the town by road from the north.

Pod Rastočkim Krovom

Rastoke 25b • Mon–Thurs 9am–9pm, Fri–Sun 9am–10pm • 25Kn • ☎047 801 460, ⓦslunj-rastoke.com

Best view of the cataracts is from the garden of **Pod Rastočkim Krovom**, a restaurant and B&B (see p.114) which allows members of the public to stroll around it's grassy garden (for a fee). It's an undeniably beautiful spot, with a waterside meadow offering great views of the cataracts. You can also inspect traditional water-driven technology, such as a flour mill and carpet-washing mill.

ARRIVAL AND INFORMATION — SLUNJ

By bus Buses on the Zagreb–Plitvice route pass through Slunj, stopping on the main square 800m uphill from Rastoke.

Destinations Plitvice (9 daily; 30min); Zagreb (9 daily; 2hr).

Tourist office Braće Radića 7 (Mon–Fri 8am–3pm; ⓣ 047 777 630, ⓦ tz-slunj.hr).

ACCOMMODATION AND EATING

The helpful tourist office can point you in the direction of private **rooms** (150Kn) in Slunj and outlying villages.

Petro Rastoke 29 ⓣ 047 777 709, ⓦ petro-rastoke.com. This cute waterside cabin in the Rastoke quarter has a large outdoor terrace with tables set out underneath rush parasols and a central pool full of trout. You can dine on grilled trout and pike-perch – count on paying around 150Kn for a big, two-fish portion. Daily 9am–11pm.

Pod Rastočkim Krovom Rastoke 25b ⓣ 047 801 460, ⓦ slunj-rastoke.com. A cluster of original buildings within earshot of Rastoke's rushing waters, offering en-suite rooms with hardwood floors and traditional furnishings. The restaurant (10am–9pm) offers a broad selection of dishes in the freshwater fish and central European schnitzel line. **300Kn**

Plitvice Lakes National Park and around

Daily: April, May, Sept & Oct 8am–6pm; June–Aug 7am–8pm; Nov–March 9am–4pm • April–Oct 110Kn, children 55Kn; rest of year adults 80Kn, children 40Kn; under 7s free • ⓣ 053 751 001, ⓦ np-plitvicka-jezera.hr

Forty kilometres south of Slunj, the **Plitvice Lakes National Park** (Nacionalni park plitvička jezera) is the country's biggest single natural attraction, and with some justification. The eight-kilometre string of sixteen lakes, hemmed in by densely forested hills, presents some of the most eye-catching scenery in mainland Croatia, with water rushing down from the upper lakes via a sequence of waterfalls and cataracts. This unique landscape was created by the movement of travertine, calcium-rich material picked up by the river and then deposited downstream – a process which, when repeated over the course of several millennia, produced a terraced sequence of barriers behind which lakes formed. Nowadays these lakes – a bewitching turquoise when seen from a distance – teem with fish and watersnakes, while herons frequent the shores of the quieter, northern part of the system, and deer, bears, wolves and wild boar throng the wooded heights above.

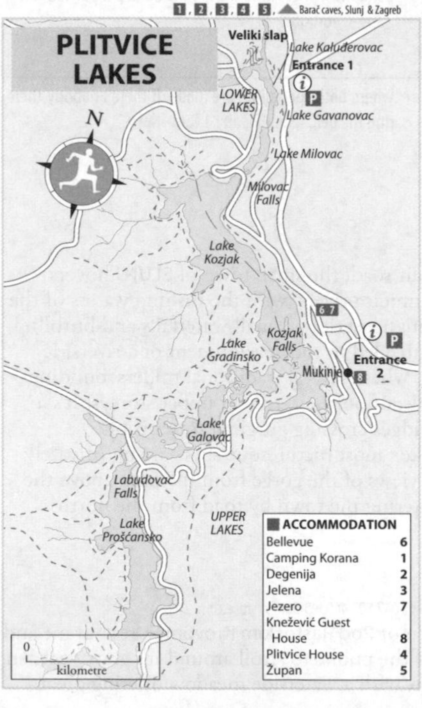

The park is remarkably well organized: paths are easy to follow, regular shuttle buses and boats ferry visitors to major trailheads, and English-speaking staff are on hand with advice at the park's two major entry points. All this ensures

that you can see a great deal in a short space of time, although keen walkers could easily spend a day or two exploring the whole area.

The park can be entered from two points on the main Zagreb Split road: **Entrance 1** (Ulaz jedan) is at the northern (lower) end of the lake system, while **Entrance 2** (Ulaz dva) is 2.5km further south.

2

Entrance 1

Entrance 1, situated at the point where the lake waters flow off into the Korana gorge, is ten minutes' walk away from **Veliki slap** (literally "the big waterfall") – with a drop of some 78m, it is the park's single most dramatic feature. Paths lead to the foot of the waterfall, passing alongside the top of the smaller **Sastavci** fall, which empties into the cliff-lined Korana gorge. From Veliki slap you can proceed south on foot towards the lower group of cataracts, where wooden walkways traverse the foaming waters. Beyond lies **Kozjak**, the largest of Plitvice's lakes. Enthusiastically croaking frogs provide an enjoyable soundtrack from spring to autumn, while shoals of fish can be observed moving through the crystal-clear waters. By sticking to the western side of Kozjak, you'll eventually emerge at the northern terminus of the **shuttle ferry** service (included in entrance ticket), which will take you south towards Entrance 2. Otherwise you can walk to Entrance 2 along the eastern bank of Kozjak, or take the bus from the road just above the lakeside path.

Entrance 2

Entrance 2 is the best jumping-off point for the biggest group of cataracts, where waters from the highest of the Plitvice Lakes, **Prošćansko**, tumble down into a succession of smaller pools and tarns before reaching Kozjak lower down. The tumbling waters emit an impressively thunderous roar when you get up close, throwing off a refreshing blanket of mist. Exploring this part of the system can easily absorb at least half a day; to save time, you can take the **shuttle bus** (cost included in entrance ticket) to the southernmost stop (Labudovac) and take a stroll around the upper cataracts from there. **Labudovac** is also the jumping off point for woodland walks that cross the rolling hills west of the lakes – clearly displayed maps at the shuttle-bus terminal will allow you to choose a suitable itinerary.

The Barač caves

April & Oct Fri–Sun 10am–4pm; May, June & Sept daily 10am–6pm; July & Aug daily 9am–7pm • Tours (40min) every 45min–1hr • 50Kn • ⓣ 047 782 007, ⓦ baraceve-spilje.hr • No public transport

Some 10km north of Plitvice's Entrance 1, a well-signed road leads east from the village of Rakovica through rolling countryside to the **Barač caves** (Baračeve špilje), a trio of caverns in a wooded valley. The highest of the three is open to visitors, a short walk up the hillside. With only about 200m of the system accessible to the public, Barač hardly qualifies as a speleological must-see, but the guided tour contains plenty to enjoy. Soon past the cave entrance, guides delight in pointing out a three hundred-year-old pile of bat scat before proceeding to the so-called Hall of Elephants' Feet – although "hall of the dangling phallus" would perhaps be a more accurate description if the stocky, bell-ended forms of the stalagmites are anything to go by. Beyond here is the Hall of Lost Souls (Dvorana izgubljenih duša), a yawning fissure with stalagmite-studded roof.

ARRIVAL AND INFORMATION — PLITVICE LAKES NATIONAL PARK AND AROUND

By bus Getting to Plitvice is straightforward: many (but not all) buses from Zagreb to Split or Zadar pass along the main road that fringes the park to the east, dropping passengers off at both entrances. Moving on can be a tricky business: there's not always any timetable information at the roadside bus shelters, and many bus drivers fail to stop unless you jump out into the road and gesticulate.

By car There are big car parks at both Entrance 1 and Entrance 2 (7Kn/hr or 70Kn/day).

Information offices Offices at Entrance 1 (April–June & Sept 9am–5pm; July & Aug 8am–8pm; Oct–March 9am–4pm) and Entrance 2 (April–June & Sept 9am–5pm; July & Aug 8am–7pm) offer a wealth of advice, but are short on printed information and maps of the park.

ACCOMMODATION

2

There's a cluster of national park-owned **hotels** near Entrance 2, of which the *Jezero* (see below) is the least bland. A better choice are the family-run **guesthouses** in nearby villages, notably Mukinje near Entrance 2, and Selište Drežničko and Grabovac some 6–8km north of Entrance 1. Inter-city buses pick up and drop off in these places too, but owing to the paucity of on-the-spot timetable information, you can't rely on them to shuttle you in and out of the park once you've arrived.

HOTELS AND GUESTHOUSES

IN AND AROUND THE PARK

Bellevue Plitvička Jezera bb ☎053 751 015, Ⓦnp-plitvicka-jezera.hr. Acceptable but unexciting en-suite rooms in a park-owned hotel, conveniently placed just inside Entrance 2. 560Kn

Jezero Plitvička Jezera bb ☎053 751 015, Ⓦnp-plitvicka-jezera.hr. Looking like an oversized alpine chalet, *Jezero* is the best of the park-owned establishments near Entrance 2 – a resort-hotel which has all amenities from tennis courts to hairdressing salon. 890Kn

Knežević Guest House Mukinje 57 ☎053 774 081 or ☎098 168 7576, Ⓦknezevic.hr. Modern ten-room guesthouse built in traditional farmhouse style and very handy for the park – it's a short walk from Entrance 2. Breakfast available on request. 350Kn

NORTH OF THE PARK

Degenija Selište Drežničko bb ☎047 782 060 or ☎098 365 458, Ⓦrestoran-degenija.hr. Neat and cosy doubles above a busy restaurant 6km north of Entrance 1, with roomy triples in a house nearby. The restaurant serves up workmanlike schnitzel-and-chips fare alongside reasonable pizzas. 380Kn

Jelena Selište Drežničko 65A ☎047 782 043 or ☎091 580 0388, Ⓦhousejelena.hostel.com. Family house signed just off the main road 6km north of the park, roughly opposite the *Korana* campsite. Cosy en-suite doubles with a small TV. Breakfast included. 350Kn

Plitvice House Grabovac 199 ☎047 784 276. Balconied chalet-style house, just off the main road 8km north of Entrance 1, with eight rooms – some with shared facilities, some en suite. Bikes for hire. Breakfast optional for a few extra kuna. 300Kn

Župan Rakovica 35, Rakovica ☎047 784 057 or ☎098 168 8165, Ⓦsobe-zupan.com. Family house 10km north of Entrance 1, offering snug, modern en suites, plus a communal kitchen, snooker room and a nice big garden. 300Kn

CAMPSITE

Camping Korana ☎053 751 015, Ⓦnp-plitvicka-jezera.hr. Located on the main road about 7km north of Entrance 1, this is the closest campsite to the park. It's a large and well-organized place with bungalows (from 300Kn), a restaurant and a supermarket. 70Kn per person, pitches from 25Kn

EATING

Both entrances have **snack bars** offering a range of drinks and hot food (although the menus don't extend much further than fries, sausages and grilled meats). Look out for local women selling home-made **cheese** (the mild yellow *škripavac*) along the roadside. It's usually sold in large circular pieces weighing over a kilo, but you can ask for a half (*polovina*) or quarter (*četvrtina*) if you don't think you can manage a whole one.

The Lonjsko polje

Ⓦpp-lonjsko-polje.hr

Just over an hour's drive southeast of Zagreb lies a particularly beautiful stretch of seasonally flooded wetland known as the **Lonjsko polje**, an enchanting area of ancient timber houses, rustic lifestyles and – most famously of all – nesting storks. Marking the Lonjsko polje's southern end, the town of **Jasenovac** was the site of a notorious concentration camp in World War II and is now home to a dignified memorial park.

Lonjsko polje can be treated as a day-trip from Zagreb if you have your own transport, although the bucolic **B&Bs** of the region provide sufficient inducement to

FROM TOP TRAKOSCAN CASTLE (P.104); WOODEN HOUSE IN THE LONJSKO POLJE; VARAŽDIN (P.105) >

linger. However you approach the region, you'll find yourself on a badly surfaced road which winds its way along the banks of the River Sava, passing through a sequence of single-street villages characterized by their chicken-choked yards and the kind of tumbledown, timber-built houses that seem to have jumped straight out of an illustrated book of fairy stories. The polje's dyke-top roads are perfect for cyclists, and many of the B&Bs rent out **bikes**.

The polje (which literally means "field") is at its wettest in spring and autumn, when the tributaries of the River Sava habitually break their banks and the area is colonized by spoonbills, herons and storks. The area's oak forests and pastures are also home to the Posavlje horse (Posavski konj), a stocky, semi-wild breed, and the spotty-hided Turopolje pig (Turopoljska svinja), which lives off acorns. The villages of the polje contain more in the way of nineteenth-century wooden architecture than any other region of Croatia, and are protected – alongside the flora and fauna – by the **Lonjsko polje Nature Park** (Park prirode Lonjsko polje).

ARRIVAL AND DEPARTURE — THE LONJSKO POLJE

By bus There are hourly buses from Zagreb (1hr 10min) to the town of Sisak. From there, four daily buses go to Čigoć, 30km southeast of Sisak (45min), of which two carry on to the village of Lonja (another 20min), calling at Mužilovčica (28km from Sisak) on the way.

By car Leave the Zagreb–Belgrade Autocesta at the Popovača exit, head towards Sisak, and turn left after 15km when you see a sign reading "Lonja".

Čigoć

The village of **ČIGOĆ** is a world-renowned migrating stop for white storks, which head here every spring (usually arriving late March or early April) ready to feast on the polje's abundant supply of insects, fish and frogs, and nest on chimneys and telegraph poles throughout the village. You stand a good chance of seeing baby storks during the hatching season, which falls in late April or May. According to tradition, the storks leave Čigoć for the wintering grounds of southern Africa (an eight- to twelve-week journey) on St Bartholomew's Day (August 24), although a handful of creatures stay in the village all year, their migratory instincts weakened by food handouts by soft-hearted locals.

Most of the houses in Čigoć are traditional two-storey structures with shingle roofs, overhanging eaves and a main entrance on the first floor, reached by a covered outside staircase known as a *ganjak*; many also have elaborately carved porches or balconies.

Čigoć Tourist Association

Čigoć 29 • Daily whenever the family is in residence • 5Kn • ⓣ 044 715 321

Located in an old house on Čigoć's main street, the **Čigoć Tourist Association** (Turistička družba Čigoć) is really a small private museum, consisting of an upstairs room crammed with traditional textiles and colourful embroidery.

Ethnographical collection

Čigoć 34 • Daily whenever the family is in residence • 10Kn

Four doors away from the Čigoć Tourist Association, the Sučić family's **ethnographical collection** (Etnografska zbirka Sučić) features more of the same, plus a rickety barn filled with just about every outmoded agricultural implement that Mr Sučić could lay his hands on.

INFORMATION — ČIGOĆ

Park information Čigoć 26 (daily 8am–4pm; ⓣ 044 715 115). Midway through the village, the park information point sells tickets (20Kn) to the park on an honour-based system (many people simply drive through), along with a map (25Kn). They can also advise on trails leading east from Čigoć, and the other villages, out into the countryside, parts of which might be under water depending on the time of year.

ACCOMMODATION AND EATING

Iža na trem Čigoć 57 ⓣ 044 715 167, ⓦ iza-na-trem.hr. Traditional timber house with a huge rose bush trailing up the side. Inside are a brace of doubles and one four-person apartment with kitchenette, all featuring wooden floors and ceilings. **260Kn**

Tradicije Čigoć Čigoć 7a ⓣ 044 715 124 or ⓣ 099 264 4555, ⓦ tradicije-cigoc.hr. Restored wooden house dating from 1820 and retaining a typical woody aroma. The cosy rooms feature rustic-looking wooden beds, traditional textiles and modern bathrooms, and there's camping available in the meadow (with WC facilities in an artfully converted former pigsty) and bicycles for rent. The café-restaurant downstairs serves freshwater fish and generous cuts of meat. **260Kn**

2

Mužilovčica

Beyond Čigoć lies a succession of villages similar in appearance but without as many storks. First you come to **MUŽILOVČICA**, which sits beside a beautiful curve of the river frequently choked with lilies and reeds. A dirt road at the southern end of Mužilovčica leads northeast to the so-called **Retencisko polje**, an area of pastureland bordered by dykes which becomes a huge lake in the wake of rainy periods, attracting numerous species of waterfowl.

ACCOMMODATION AND EATING — MUŽILOVČICA

Ravlić Mužilovčica 72 ⓣ 044 710 151 or ⓣ 091 530 1199, ⓦ obitelj-ravlic.hr. This beautifully renovated farmstead is almost an ethnographic museum in its own right, featuring traditional wooden furnishings and hand-embroidered textiles – although the en-suite rooms also come with modern TVs and bathroom facilities. Food and drink are available although the menu might be limited to what's in stock. There are also horses for riding in the stables out the back. **250Kn**

Ustilonja Lonja 8 ⓣ 044 710 621 or ⓣ 098 227 609, ⓦ ustilonja.hr. Some 5km east of Mužilovčica in the similarly river-hugging village of Lonja, this is a good choice for those who want rustic accommodation with modern comforts, where antique furnishings and traditional ceramic stoves rub shoulders with contemporary fittings. Catering can be arranged for groups. **375Kn**

Krapje

One of the most spectacular of the Lonjsko polje's strung-out, tumbledown villages is **KRAPJE**, whose wooden houses sit in a neat row, spaced at regular intervals – the orderly result of strict regulations introduced by the Habsburgs to control house building in the settlements of the Military Frontier, the defensive cordon developed by the Habsburg Empire and organized along military lines. There is a small private **museum** in the shape of Etno-Kuća Palaić, containing agricultural and domestic knick-knacks in a traditional timber house dating from 1912 – call in at the *Palaić* farmstead (see below; leave a donation) at the northern end of the village to get the key. A path from the park information office (see below) leads to the ornithological reserve of **Krapje Djol**, which serves as an important nesting ground for spoonbills.

INFORMATION — KRAPJE

Park information Krapje 16 (ⓣ 044 672 080; April–Oct Mon–Fri 9am–4pm).

ACCOMMODATION AND EATING

Eko Etno Selo Strug Plesmo 26, Krapje ⓣ 044 611 212, ⓦ ekoetno-selo-strug.hr. Located 3km northeast of Krapje (and well signed), this is a collection of new-build bungalows containing a mixture of original and reproduction rustic furniture. The retro theme-park look of the place won't suit everyone, but the restaurant (with veranda overlooking a fish pond) is a reliable source of freshwater fish dishes. **400Kn**

Palaić Krapje 167 ⓣ 044 540 921 or ⓣ 091 566 4921, ⓦ sg-palaic.com. Two doubles in a traditional house with old furniture and wooden floorboards, and a two-person studio with kitchenette in a renovated grain store out the back. You can rent the whole house for 500Kn. **200kn**

Jasenovac

Fifteen kilometres east of Krapje and 10km south of the Novska exit of the Autocesta highway, **JASENOVAC** is the site of a notorious World War II **concentration camp** that stretches alongside the main road into town from the Novska direction. Established in autumn 1941, this was the largest in an archipelago of camps stretching from Krapje in the north to Stara Gradiška in the south. It was here that the pro-Nazi puppet state, the NDH (Nezavisna Država Hrvatska or "Independent State of Croatia"), incarcerated Serbs, Jews, Gypsies and anti-fascist Croats and set them to work producing bricks and metal chains. Unproductive or unwanted prisoners were murdered in cold blood, while overwork, malnourishment and a succession of cold winters took their toll on countless thousands of others. When Jasenovac was finally wound up in April 1945, the Ustaše attempted to murder the remaining inmates, six hundred of whom staged a mass breakout – a total of 91 got away. Ever since World War II Jasenovac has been a bone of contention with competing historians, with Serbian nationalists inflating the number of victims in order to draw attention to Ustaše-sponsored genocide, while some of their Croatian counterparts have minimized the importance of Jasenovac in order to sweep memories of the Ustaše period under the carpet. Outside observers nowadays consider 70,000 to be a fair estimate of the numbers killed here, of which around 40,000 were Serb and at least 14,000 were Gypsies. The camp was razed in the late 1940s and turned into a **memorial park** (spomen-park) two decades later.

The rest of Jasenovac still bears the scars of a more recent war: the centre of town was cleared of Croats in 1991, and its church dynamited. The local Serbs suffered a similar fate when the Croats returned in May 1995.

The museum

Braće Radića 147 • Tues–Fri 9am–5pm, Sat & Sun 10am–4pm • Free • T 044 672 319, W jusp-jasenovac.hr

The **museum**, at the park entrance, tells the story of the camp through a poignant mixture of original photographs and filmed interviews with survivors, although it is not arranged chronologically and is difficult for a first-time visitor to make sense of. East of the museum the former camp (now a meadow) is dominated by a striking modern **sculpture** described as a "melancholy lotus" by its creator, Serbian architect and politician Bogdan Bogdanović (who, as the liberal mayor of Belgrade in the 1980s, was purged by Slobodan Milošević's hardliners). The path towards the lotus passes a restored stretch of railway where a cattle-truck train (on which inmates were delivered to the camp) is permanently parked.

ARRIVAL AND INFORMATION — JASENOVAC

By train There are only three trains a day from Zagreb to Jasenovac, and they take almost two and a half hours to get here, so it's better to come by car if at all possible.

Tourist office Trg Kralja Petra Svačića 19 (Mon–Fri 7.30am–3.30pm; T 044 672 490, E tz_opcine _jasenovac@inet.hr).

EATING

★ **Gostiona kod Ribiča** Vladimira Nazora 24 T 044 672 066. This unpretentious small-town restaurant hung with fishing trophies is arguably the best place in the region to tackle the local freshwater fish, with carp, catfish and pike-perch (prices depend on the size of the fish; expect to pay about 160Kn/kg) cooked simply in the pan or on the grill. They also do a fine *fiš paprikaš* with pasta noodles (50Kn). Mon–Sat 8am–10pm, Sun 11am–6pm.

Slavonia

Stretching from the Lonjsko polje to the Danube, which forms Croatia's border with Serbia, the rich agricultural plain of **Slavonia** has an unjust reputation as the most scenically tedious region of the country. All that most visitors ever see of it is the view from the Autocesta – the highway originally built to link Zagreb with Belgrade, and still the main route into the eastern corner of the country – as it forges across unbroken flatlands. However the region does have its attractions, not least a distinctive and often captivating rural landscape, characterized in summer by a seemingly endless carpet of corn and sunflowers, with vineyards on the low hills to the north.

Slavonia's main urban centre is **Osijek**, a former Austrian fortress town which retains a dash of Habsburg-era elegance. It's around Osijek that the best of Slavonia's scenery lies, a patchwork of greens and yellows dotted with dusty, half-forgotten villages, where latticed wooden sheds groan under the weight of corncobs and, in the autumn, strings of red paprikas hang outside to dry. Just north of Osijek, the **Kopački rit Nature Park**, with its abundant birdlife, is Croatia's most intriguing wetland area, while in the far southeast the siege-scarred town of **Vukovar** is slowly regaining its provincial Baroque charm. Elsewhere in Slavonia there's a relative dearth of urban sights, save in the pleasant provincial towns of **Našice** and **Đakovo**.

Osijek

Tucked into the far northeastern corner of Slavonia, 30km from the Hungarian border and just 20km west of the Serbian province of Vojvodina, **OSIJEK** is the undisputed capital of the region. An easy-going, park-filled city hugging the banks of the River Drava, Osijek has a relaxed spaciousness – owing in large part to its being spread out across three quite separate town centres. The oldest of these, **Tvrđa**, retains the air of a living museum; originally a Roman strongpoint, it was subsequently fortified by the Ottomans and then finally rebuilt in Baroque style by the Austrians, who kicked the Turks out in 1687. The Austrians were also responsible for the construction of **Gornji grad** (Upper Town – so called because it's upriver from Tvrđa), the nineteenth-century area which still exudes a degree of *fin-de-siècle* refinement and now serves as the administrative heart of the modern city. At the eastern end of town, **Donji grad** (Lower Town) is a relatively quiet residential district, developed at around the same time as Gornji grad in order to accommodate economic migrants from the surrounding plains.

After the fall of Vukovar in November 1991, the Yugoslav People's Army and Serb irregulars laid siege to Osijek and subjected the town to a nine-month bombardment. Osijek survived, but the sense of economic stagnation that followed the conflict is only just beginning to lift.

Osijek has enough in the way of sightseeing and nightlife to detain you for a day or two, and the city's proximity to the Kopački rit Nature Park (see p.127) provides the perfect excuse to lengthen your stay.

Parish Church of St Peter and Paul

Trg Ante Starčevića

At the centre of Osijek's Gornji grad, the triangular Trg Ante Starčevića is dominated by the rocketing 90m spire of the town's red-brick, neo-Gothic **Parish Church of St Peter and Paul** (Župna crkva svetog Petra i Pavla). Commissioned in the 1890s by the energetic bishop of Đakovo, Josip Juraj Strossmayer, the church is filled from floor to ceiling with bible-story frescoes by leading twentieth-century painter Mirko Rački, all executed in engagingly simple and colourful style.

Along Europska avenija

Connecting Osijek's Gornji grad with the Tvrđa district is the broad, tree-lined sweep of **Europska avenija**, site of the most spectacular group of **Art Nouveau** houses in Croatia. Commissioned by rich local lawyers and merchants in the years before World War I, each is richly decorated with reliefs of caryatids, nymphs, herculean hero figures and other motifs typical of the period. For a more modernist take on pre-World War I architecture, nip down Stjepana Radića to the **Urania cinema** (built in 1912), on Šetalište V. Hengija 1, where you'll encounter a monumental, grill-like facade that brings to mind the open jaws of an enormous whale.

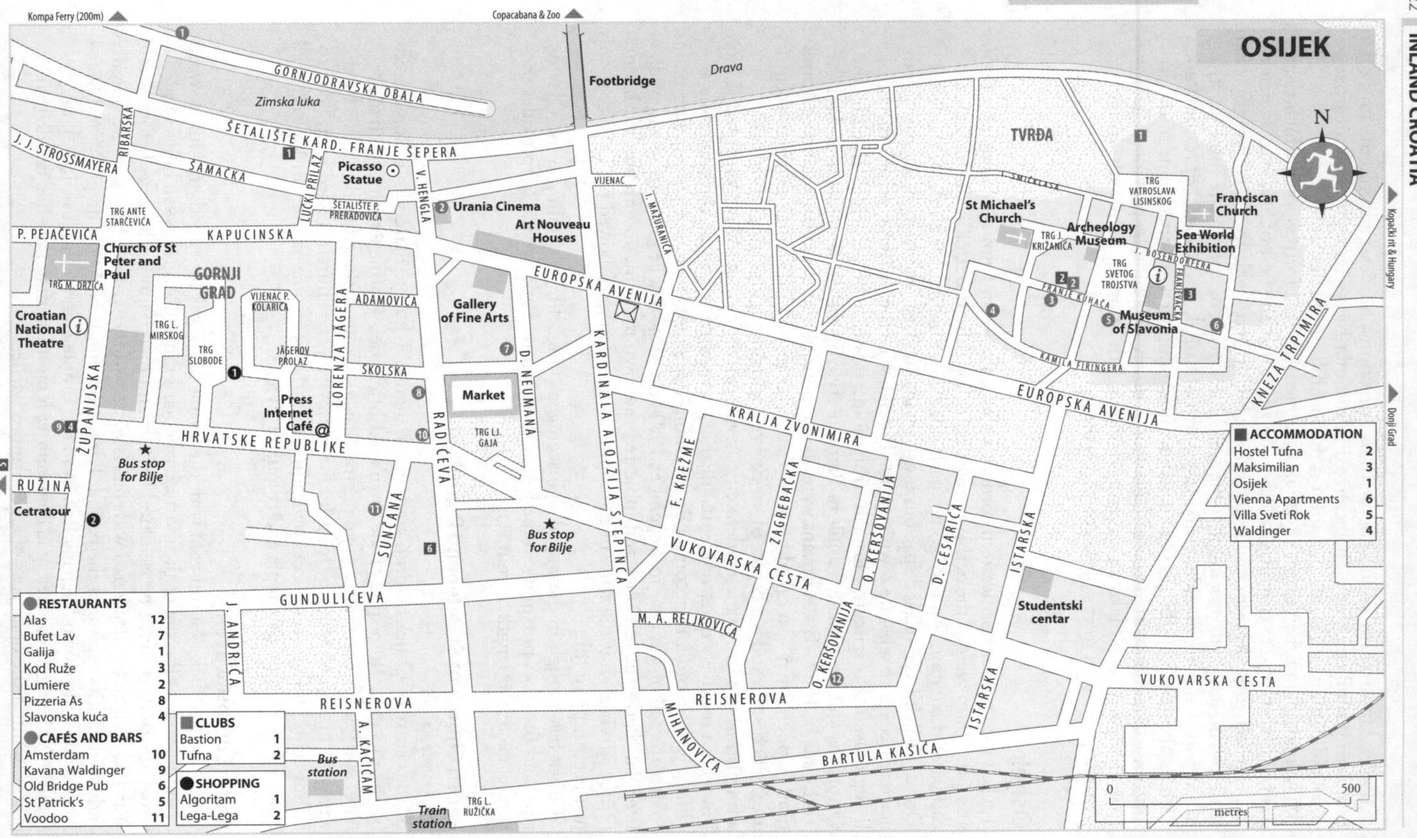
OSIJEK
N
Kompa Ferry (200m)
Copacabana & Zoo
Kopački rit & Hungary
Donji Grad
5
Drava
Zimska luka
Footbridge
GORNJODRAVSKA OBALA
ŠETALIŠTE KARD. FRANJE ŠEPERA
J. J. STROSSMAYERA
RIBARSKA
ŠAMAČKA
LUČKI PRILAZ
Picasso Statue
ŠETALIŠTE P. PRERADOVIĆA
V. HENGLA
Urania Cinema
Art Nouveau Houses
VIJENAC
I. MAŽURANIĆA
TVRĐA
I. SMIČIKLASA
St Michael's Church
TRG J. KRIŽANIĆA
Archeology Museum
TRG VATROSLAVA LISINSKOG
Franciscan Church
Sea World Exhibition
J. BOSENDORFERA
TRG SVETOG TROJSTVA
FRANJE KUHAČA
FRANJEVAČKA
Museum of Slavonia
KAMILA FIRINGERA
KNEZA TRPIMIRA
EUROPSKA AVENIJA
TRG ANTE STARČEVIĆA
P. PEJAČEVIĆA
KAPUCINSKA
Church of St Peter and Paul
TRG M. DRŽIĆA
GORNJI GRAD
Croatian National Theatre
VIJENAC P. KOLARIĆA
TRG L. MIRSKOG
TRG SLOBODE
JÄGEROV PROLAZ
LORENZA JÄGERA
ADAMOVIĆA
ŠKOLSKA
Gallery of Fine Arts
Market
TRG LJ. GAJA
D. NEUMANA
KARDINALA ALOJZIJA STEPINCA
Press Internet Café
ŽUPANIJSKA
HRVATSKE REPUBLIKE
RADIĆEVA
Bus stop for Bilje
RUŽINA
Cetratour
SUNČANA
Bus stop for Bilje
KRALJA ZVONIMIRA
F. KREŽME
ZAGREBAČKA
O. KERSOVANIJA
D. CESARIĆA
ISTARSKA
VUKOVARSKA CESTA
Studentski centar
GUNDULIĆEVA
J. ANDRIĆA
M. A. RELJKOVIĆA
REISNEROVA
MIHANOVIĆA
BARTULA KAŠIĆA
A. KAČIĆAM
Bus station
Train station
TRG L. RUŽIČKA
ACCOMMODATION
Hostel Tufna 2
Maksimilian 3
Osijek 1
Vienna Apartments 6
Villa Sveti Rok 5
Waldinger 4
RESTAURANTS
Alas 12
Bufet Lav 7
Galija 1
Kod Ruže 3
Lumiere 2
Pizzeria As 8
Slavonska kuća 4
CAFÉS AND BARS
Amsterdam 10
Kavana Waldinger 9
Old Bridge Pub 6
St Patrick's 5
Voodoo 11
CLUBS
Bastion 1
Tufna 2
SHOPPING
Algoritam 1
Lega-Lega 2
0
500
metres

The Gallery of Fine Arts

Europska avenija 9 • Tues, Wed & Fri 10am–6pm, Thurs 10am–8pm, Sat & Sun 10am–1pm • 10Kn • ⓣ 031 251 280, ⓦ gluo.hr

The **Gallery of Fine Arts** (Galerija likovnih umjetnosti) houses an eye-catching collection of works by local Slavonian painters, and a regular programme of international contemporary exhibitions. Adolf Waldinger's nineteenth-century Slavonian landscape paintings are the pride and joy of the permanent collection, although it's the colourful, sensuous pictures by Croatian twentieth-century painters that exert the real fascination here.

Tvrđa

2

Tram #1 from Trg Ante Starčevića or walk along Europska avenija or Šetalište Kardinala Franje Šepera, the broad path along the Drava

Two kilometres east from Gornji grad lies the Baroque quarter known as **Trvđa** (literally "citadel"), a collection of military and administrative buildings thrown up by the Austrians after the destruction of the earlier Ottoman castle. Tvrđa's grid of cobbled streets zeros in on **Trg svetog Trojstva**, a broad expanse bearing a **plague column**, built in 1729 with funds donated by the local fortress commander's wife to give thanks for deliverance from a devasting outbreak of plague which is thought to have killed a third of Osijek's population. The square is surrounded by former Habsburg military buildings, many of which are now occupied by high schools or university faculties – the local cafés are filled with coffee-swilling students on weekdays.

Museum of Slavonia

Trg svetog Trojstva 6 • Tues–Fri 8am–2pm, Sat & Sun 10am–1pm • 15Kn • ⓣ 031 250 730, ⓦ mso.hr

Occupying the high-ceilinged, parquet-floored rooms of the eighteenth-century former magistrate's office on the southeast corner of Trg svetog Trojstva, the **Museum of Slavonia** (Muzej slavonije) hosts temporary themed exhibitions on local history. The tourist office will have details of what's on.

The Archeological Museum

Trg svetog Trojstva 2 • Tues, Wed & Fri 10am–3pm, Thurs 10am–3pm & 5–8pm, Sat & Sun 10am–1pm • 10Kn • ⓣ 031 232 132, ⓦ arheoloskimuzejosijek.hr

Diagonally opposite on the northwestern corner of Trg svetog Trojstva is the former **guard house** (glavna traža), a quaint Baroque building with ground-level arcades and an attractively leaning watchtower. Inside, the **Archeological Museum** (Arheološki muzej) displays a well-labelled collection of Neolithic pottery, dark-age jewellery and medieval kitchenware. The glass-roofed atrium harbours sculptural fragments recovered from Roman Mursa, Osijek's distant forerunner – look out for the exquisitely carved gravestone portraying a satyr derobing a nymph.

The churches

Off Trg svetog Trojstva to the west, the double onion-dome frontage of the former Jesuit **St Michael's Church** (Crkva svetog Mihovila) lords it over a knot of narrow alleys, although it's relatively bare inside save for an ornate cherub-encrusted pulpit. A few steps northeast of Trg svetog Trojstva, on Lisinskog, the eighteenth-century **Franciscan church** (Franjevačka crkva) features a much-venerated Gothic statue of the Virgin and Child on the high altar.

Sea World Exhibition

Svodovi bb • Tues, Wed & Fri 10am–4pm, Thurs 10am–8pm, Sat & Sun 10am–1pm • 20Kn • ⓣ 031 322 907, ⓦ gloria-maris.hr

Occupying the arched chamber of one of Tvrđa's old military buildings, the **Sea World Exhibition** (Izložba morskog svijeta) is the private initiative of a lifelong marine biology enthusiast and diver, whose personal collection of shells and preserved creatures forms a colourful and well-presented display. With fish, sea-snails, coral, vicious-looking water snakes and other creatures from all over the world, it's a fascinating ensemble. The owner will want to give you a guided tour, so it's best to devote a certain amount of time to your visit.

The riverfront

Alleys descend from Tvrđa towards the riverfront, where you can follow Šetalište Kardinala Franje Šepera back towards Gornji grad, passing a pedestrian bridge which crosses the Drava towards ritzy-sounding **Copacabana** on the opposite bank – a grassy bathing area with an open-air pool, a waterslide and a couple of cafés. Back on the south side of the river, the Šetalište arrives eventually at the **Zimska luka** (winter harbour), a dock for small pleasure craft protected by a breakwater from the strong currents of the Drava, and another popular spot for lounging around in cafés. Sitting grinning on a pillar at the eastern end of Zimska luka's café strip is Ivan Sabolić's more or less lifesize statue of Picasso, placed here in celebration of the 100th anniversary of the artist's birth.

The kompa

Departures on demand • April–Oct 9am–8pm, Nov–March 9am–6pm • 10Kn

Two hundred metres upstream from the Zimska luka is the southern terminal of an archaic passenger ferry known as the **kompa**. Basically a wooden raft, it drifts from one bank of the Drava to the other, propelled by the river current and held on course by a metal chain.

Osijek Zoo

Daily 9am–7pm • 20Kn • ⓣ 031 285 234, ⓦ zoo-osijek.hr

On the north bank of the Drava, near the terminus for the *kompa*, the grassy expanse of **Osijek Zoo** (Zoološki vrt) features a modest collection of exotic animals and birds. Among the stars are Croatia's only giraffes, Edgar and Johan, who made all the local newspapers when acquired from a Czech zoo in 2012. From the zoo you can walk east along the northern bank of the river towards the pedestrian bridge and Copacabana beach.

ARRIVAL AND DEPARTURE — OSIJEK

By air The airport (currently served from Zagreb, Split and Frankfurt-Hahn) is 20km southeast of town at Klisa (ⓣ 031 514 440, ⓦ osijek-airport.hr).

By train Osijek's train station is on Trg L. Ružička, on the south side of the town centre. From here it's a 10min walk – first up Radićeva, then left into Kapucinska – to reach Trg Ante Starčevića, the heart of Gornji grad; alternatively, travel three stops on tram #2.

Destination Zagreb (4 daily; 4hr 45min).

By bus The bus station is 100m west of the train station.

Destinations Batina (6 daily; 1hr 10min); Bilje (every 30min; 10min); Đakovo (Mon–Sat hourly, Sun 8 daily; 45min); Ilok (6 daily; 1hr 50min); Vinkovci (Mon–Sat hourly, Sun 5 daily; 1hr); Vukovar (Mon–Sat hourly, Sun 8 daily; 45min); Zagreb (6 daily; 4hr–5hr 30min).

INFORMATION AND TOURS

Tourist offices Županijska 2, a few doors up from the church of St Peter and Paul (Mon–Fri 7am–4pm, Sat 8am–noon; ⓣ 031 203 755, ⓦ tzosijek.hr); Trg svetog Trojstva 5, Tvrđa (Mon–Fri 9am–4pm, Sat 8am–1pm; ⓣ 031 210 120).

Tours Cetratour, at Ružina 16 (ⓣ 031 372 920, ⓦ cetratour.hr), organizes bike and canoe expeditions to the Kopački rit Nature Park.

GETTING AROUND

By tram Osijek has two tram lines: tram #2 operates a circular route between the train and bus stations and Trg Ante Starčevića, while tram #1 runs from west to east linking Gornji grad, Tvrđa and Donji grad. Single-journey tickets cost 12Kn and are bought from the driver.

By taxi There are ranks outside the train station; otherwise ring ⓣ 031 200 100.

ACCOMMODATION

There's an improving choice of accommodation in Osijek, and a handful of **B&B** options in the village of **Bilje**, a 10min bus ride to the north (see p.127).

Hostel Tufna Franje Kuhača 10/1 ⓣ 031 215 020, ⓦ tufna.com.hr. First-floor hostel in the heart of the Tvrđa district with a pair of dorms with a/c, and a TV lounge with retro 1970s touches. Free internet, and a small but well-equipped kitchen. Washing can be done for a few kuna extra. Dorms 110Kn

★ **Maksimilian** Franjevačka 12 ⓣ 031 497 567, ⓦ maksimilian.hr. Charming seven-room pension on the first floor of an old Tvrđa building, with a mix of old and new furnishings – some rooms feature old sewing machines and a bundle of 1930s-vintage fashion magazines. Breakfast included, and there's a big lounge-cum-kitchen with all-day tea and coffee. Free wi-fi. 450Kn

Osijek Šamačka 4 ⓣ 031 230 333, ⓦ hotelosijek.hr. A concrete lump on the Drava waterfront, the *Osijek* has been renovated to four-star standard, and the quality of service is everything you would expect from the price. The north-facing rooms have superb views of the river. 780Kn

★ **Vienna Apartments** Radićeva 26A ⓣ 031 214 026, ⓦ vienna-smjestaj.com. Friendly mini-hotel located in a quiet courtyard a 10min walk from the bus and train stations. The rooms are small but thoughtfully designed, with electric kettle for tea and coffee as well as flat-screen TV, wi-fi and pristine modern bathrooms. No breakfast, but there are plenty of cafés and bakeries along Radićeva. 435Kn

Villa Sveti Rok Svetog roka 13 ⓣ 031 310 490, ⓔ villa.sveti.rok@os.t-com.hr. Seven-room pension offering four-star hotel comforts, 1km west of the city centre. Rooms come with a/c, minibar, TV and state-of-the-art showers full of water-spewing nozzles. Free wi-fi. 780Kn

Waldinger Županijska 8 ⓣ 031 250 450, ⓦ waldinger.hr. Peaceful, sixteen-room four-star housed in a nineteenth-century building. High-ceilinged, tastefully furnished rooms come with TV, desk space and bathtub. The three-star annexe in the back yard is billed as a "pension" and offers simply furnished en suites overlooking a neat patch of garden. Main building 950Kn, pension 500Kn

EATING

Good **restaurants** are sprinkled rather sparingly through the city. Once you locate them, however, you'll find the range of fish dishes and paprika-flavoured stews generally excellent. There are plenty of good-value **snack** possibilities on the way into town from the bus and train stations, with a string of plainly decorated bistro-type places offering grilled food and pizzas.

RESTAURANTS

★ **Alas** Reisnerova 12a ⓣ 031 213 032. One of the best places in the city for sampling freshwater fish – either fried in breadcrumbs or stewed in traditional Slavonian, paprika-laden style. The speciality of the house is *perkelt od soma* (big chunks of catfish swimming in spicy goulashy soup), usually served with delicious home-made noodles. Prices are moderate too, with mains costing around 60–70Kn. Mon–Sat 11am–9pm, Sun 11am–5pm.

Bufet Lav Trg Ljudevita Gaja 5. If you want good home cooking and don't mind a few rough edges, then this basic but friendly place near the market will sort you out with a filling bowl of *grah*, *čobanac* or *fiš paprikaš* – a great place for a quick, cheap lunch. Mon–Sat 5am–10pm, Sun 5am–3pm.

Galija Gornjodravska obala ⓣ 031 283 500, ⓦ galija.co. Decent pizzas, pasta dishes and salads on a boat moored just round the corner from the Zimska luka. Floor-to-ceiling windows make this a great spot from which to observe life on the riverbank. Prices are moderate. Daily 9am–10pm.

Kod Ruže Franje Kuhača 25a ⓣ 031 206 066, ⓦ omnia-osijek.hr. This smartish, folk-themed restaurant with a traditional Slavonian menu is a bit of a tourist trap, but the Tvrđa location, pleasant back courtyard and frequent live music ensure that it shouldn't be discounted completely. Prices are slightly higher than in the other local-cuisine places. Mon–Sat 10am–11pm, Sun 11am–4pm.

Lumiere Šetalište Kardinala Franje Šepera 8 ⓣ 031 201 088, ⓦ lumiere.hr. Right next to the cinema, this sleek and snazzy restaurant opts for Croatian cuisine with an Italian twist: there are pasta dishes galore, classic dishes such as veal or chicken Genovese, and also the option of Adriatic or freshwater fish. With mains in the 60–90Kn range, it's not likely to be a wallet-emptying experience. Mon–Sat 11am–11pm.

Pizzeria As Radićeva 16 ⓣ 031 212 500. Generous thin-crust pizzas with a reasonably authentic range of Italian toppings (and a tempting 35–45Kn price tag), served in a comfortable and relaxing brick cellar. Also offers decent pasta and risotto. Mon–Sat 9am–11pm, Sun 11am–11pm.

★ **Slavonska kuća** Kamila Firingera 26 ⓣ 031 369 955, ⓦ slavonskakuca.com. Small and intimate restaurant with checked cloths on the tables and fishing nets hanging from the roof. Choose between freshwater fish fried in batter (50Kn) or huge bowls of *fiš perkelt* and *fiš paprikaš* (serving two; 100Kn). Daily 9am–11pm.

DRINKING AND NIGHTLIFE

The biggest concentration of **drinking venues** is on and around Trg svetog Trojstva in Tvrđa. It's also worth checking out the Zimska luka, with its string of summer-only cafés below the *Osijek* hotel, and the stretch of Radićeva between Hrvatske republike and Gundulićeva, where there's an enjoyable café-bar every 20m or so. Places in Gornji grad tend to close at 11pm; in Tvrđa opening hours are somewhat more elastic.

2

CAFÉS AND BARS

Amsterdam Radićeva 18. Cramped but civilized subterranean bar with a laid-back clientele, classic rock soundtrack and an appetizing range of bottled beers. Daily 7am–11pm.

Kavana Waldinger Županijska 8 ⓣ031 250 450, ⓦwaldinger.hr. Delectable cakes and ice cream in an elegant café in the *Waldinger* hotel (see p.125). Daily 8am–11pm.

Old Bridge Pub Franje Kuhača 4 ⓣ031 211 611, ⓦoldbridgepub.com. Roomy drinking palace with a pub-style space on the ground floor, lounge-bar furnishings in the attic above, and a stone-lined cellar below. The Croatian, German and Irish beers on tap attract a mixed clientele ranging from suits to students. Reasonably priced menu of pub food. Sun–Thurs 9am–midnight, Fri & Sat 9am–2am.

St Patrick's Trg svetog Trojstva ⓣ031 205 202, ⓦst-patricks-pub.hr. Most enjoyable of the Tvrđa café-bars, with a large outdoor terrace (mobbed on warm weekend nights) facing the best of Osijek's Baroque buildings, and a comfy interior featuring – for some perverse reason – a shrine to Chelsea so-called football club. Mainstream Irish beers on tap, as well as the locally brewed Osiječko pivo. Sun–Thurs 8am–midnight, Fri & Sat till 2am.

Voodoo Sunčana 8. Initially named *Voodoo*, then renamed *S.Co.Bar*, then re-named *Voodoo* again, this studenty, alternative meeting place is something of an Osijek institution. The beer garden at the back is the place to be in spring and summer. Upstairs, Pop Art frescoes line the walls, and there are cool sounds and a friendly vibe. Mon–Sat 8am–midnight, Sun 8am–11pm.

CLUBS

Bastion Trg Vatroslava Lisinskog bb ⓣ099 705 5859. The aptly named *Bastion* occupies one of Tvrđa's defensive towers, with an outdoor terrace occupying a stretch of the ramparts and great views across the river. Thurs–Sat 9pm–4am.

Tufna Franje Kuhaća 10 ⓣ031 215 020, ⓦtufna.com.hr. Bar-cum-club beneath the *Tufna* hostel, with DJ-driven party nights at weekends. The club interior is an eccentric one-off, a Baroque arched space whose walls are covered with crazy tiling, album covers and pages torn from old magazines. Thurs–Sat 10pm–4am.

ENTERTAINMENT

Croatian National Theatre (Hrvatsko narodno kazalište) Županijska 9 ⓣ031 220 700, ⓦhnk-osijek.hr. The main venue for classical music and theatre.

Urania V. Hengla 1 ⓣ031 211 560, ⓦkinematografi-osijek.hr. Old-style single-screen cinema in the heart of town, showing art movies and mainstream films. Usually closed in Aug.

SHOPPING

The Sajam **antiques fair** (*antikviteta*) on Trg sveta Trojstva takes place monthly on the first Saturday of each month (9am–3pm).

Algoritam Trg Slobode 7 ⓣ031 214 310, ⓦalgoritam.hr. English-language paperbacks and guidebooks. Mon–Fri 8am–8pm, Sat 8am–2pm.

Lega-Lega Županijska 25 ⓣ031 494 104, ⓦlega-lega.com. Taking its name from Osijek word *Lega* (local slang for "What's up dude?"), this local design team produces groovy T-shirts (artfully packed in what look like milk cartons) and a range of stationery. If you want a 100 percent Croatian souvenir which is well designed and has character, you need look no further. Mon–Fri 9am–6pm, Sat 9am–2pm.

DIRECTORY

Internet Press Internet Café, L. Jägera 24 (daily 8am–11pm).

Pharmacy Ljekarna Centar, Trg A. Starčevića 7 (Mon–Sat 7am–8pm, Sun 8am–2pm; night counter open 8pm–7am – ring the bell for service).

Post and telephone The main post office is on the corner of Europska avenija and Kardinala Stepinca (Mon–Sat 7.30am–7pm).

The Baranja

North of Osijek, the main road to Hungary forges through the pastel-coloured villages and corn-rich fields of the **Baranja**, a fertile extension of the Slavonian plain which fills the triangle formed by the Drava to the west, the Danube to the east and the low hills of southern Hungary to the north. Despite having spent the years from 1991 to 1998 first under Serbian occupation, then UN control, Baranja is getting back to normal life with remarkable speed. The tourist potential of its wine-growing areas, natural wetlands and rustic settlements is yet to be fully exploited, making it ripe for discovery. The main attraction of the region is the **Kopački rit Nature Park**, although it possesses enough in the way of picturesque villages and wine cellars to justify a more extensive trip. Featuring largely flat terrain and well-signed cycling routes, the region is perfect for touring **by bike**, though sights are of a disparate nature and to explore further afield you really need a car.

Bilje

Eight kilometres out of Osijek the road passes through the village of **Bilje**, main gateway to the Kopački rit Nature Park and home to a sizeable stock of **B&B accommodation**. There are cafés and shops grouped around Bilje's main T-junction.

ARRIVAL AND INFORMATION — BILJE

By bus Bilje is served by half-hourly buses from Osijek from either Hrvatske republike or Trg Ljudevita Gaja.

Tourist office Kralja Zvonimira 10, next to the post office just south of the bus stop (T 031 751 480, W tzo-bilje.hr).

Bikes can be hired from the *Crvendać* and *Mazur* B&Bs (see below) for 70Kn/day.

ACCOMMODATION AND EATING

★ **Crvendać** Biljske satnije ZNG RH 5 T 031 750 264 and T 091 551 5711, W crvendac.com. Cosy house offering eight newly furnished rooms sleeping from two to four, most with quirky red colour schemes. Some are en suite; all come with a/c and TV. Check out the beautifully embroidered costumes in the breakfast room. Free wi-fi. **300Kn**

★ **Kod Varge** Kralja Zvonimira 37A T 031 750 031, W kod-varge.hr. Unpretentious but undeniably excellent restaurant at the southern end of the village. There's a lot in the meat and freshwater fish line on the menu, but it would be a shame to come to *Varge* without asking about its most celebrated dish: a delicious *fiš paprikaš* with noodles for around 55Kn. Daily 9am–10pm.

★ **Mazur** Kneza Branimira 2 T 031 750 294 or T 098 897 649, W mazur.hr. A couple of doubles and a triple, each featuring attic ceilings, a small TV and old-fashioned furnishings assembled by the antique-collecting owners. Some en suite, others sharing facilities in the hallway. **300Kn**

Kopački rit Nature Park

May–Sept 30Kn; Oct–April 10Kn • T 031 285 370, W kopacki-rit.com

Stretching east of Bilje, the **Kopački rit Nature Park** (Park prirode Kopački rit) covers an area of marsh and partly sunken forest just north of the point where the fast-flowing River Drava pours into the Danube, forcing the slower Danube waters to back up and flood the plain. The resulting wetland is inundated from spring through to early autumn, when fish come here to spawn and wading birds congregate to feed off them. At this time you'll also see cormorants, grey herons and, if you're lucky, black storks, which nest in the oak forests north of Bilje. Autumn sees the area fill up with migrating ducks and geese, while the surrounding woodland provides a year-round home for deer and wild boar. Some of the fields and country lanes surrounding the park are yet to be cleared of **mines** – anyone walking or driving through the area should stick to the roads, and remain on the lookout for local "mine" signs.

The main route into the park is along the dyke-top road that heads north from the visitor centre and runs past commercial fish ponds before eventually arriving at the magisterial sunken forest of **Lake Sakadaš**, where wading birds stalk their prey among a tangle of white willows. North of here, tracks continue through **Tikveš**, an area of oak forest where you stand a good chance of spotting wild pigs and deer. Josip Broz Tito used the fine villa of **Dvorac Tikveš** as a hunting lodge; it was neglected during the Serb occupation (when most of the furnishings disappeared), but you can still see the balcony where Tito and guests waited, rifle in hand, while servants drove forest beasts out onto the lawn in front of them. Some of the outbuildings are being transformed into an international ecology centre, and the villa itself is earmarked for luxury hotel development.

Kopačevo

Before leaving the area it's worth taking a look at the village of **Kopačevo** itself, immediately east of the visitor centre. Home to a mixed Croatian–Hungarian population, it contains some of the best traditional architecture in eastern Slavonia, with the kind of houses you'll see all over the Hungarian plain, southeastern Croatia and the Serbian Vojvodina, laid end-on to the road, with long verandas facing in onto secluded courtyards.

2

ARRIVAL AND INFORMATION — KOPAČKI RIT NATURE PARK

Access to the park To get to Kopački rit from Bilje, head east from the main T-junction along the road to Kneževi vinogradi. After about 500m, take the right fork to Kopačevo. At the entrance to Kopačevo village, a left turn to Tikveš brings you to the visitor centre. Individual tourists can then drive, cycle or walk into the park – the most interesting bits of wetland around Lake Sakadaš are 2–3km away. The ideal way to get there is to hire a bike in Bilje (see p.127); otherwise the walk will take you 40–50min.

Visitor centre The visitor centre (Prijemni centar) serves as the main entrance to the park. It sells tickets, rents out bikes (10Kn/hr), offers advice on how to explore the park and doles out English-language leaflets and a map.

GETTING AROUND

Boat trips Hour-long boat trips (tickets from the visitor centre; 80Kn), navigating some of the wildfowl-rich waterways that can't be accessed by car or on foot, set out from Lake Sakadaš. There are usually about three boat trips a day at weekends, fewer on weekdays – ring the park in advance to make sure you don't miss out.

EATING

Kormoran Kopački rit ⓣ 031 753 099, ⓦ belje.hr. On the road towards Tikveš, this is a good place to sample the local carp, which is toasted on the end of a stick beside an open fire. Daily 11am–10pm.

Zelena Žaba Ribarska 3, Kopačevo ⓣ 031 752 212. Small and cosy café-restaurant in the centre of Kopačevo village, famous for its frogs' legs and *fiš perkelt* (Hungarian fish casserole). Daily 10am–10pm.

Karanac

There's plenty more to see in the Baranja beyond Kopački rit. Twenty-five kilometres north of Bilje, the Baranja's main market centre, Beli Manastir, is an unexciting little place, and you'd be better off heading for smaller villages like **KARANAC**, 8km east of Beli, where you'll see streets lined with traditional one-storey farmhouses, their south-facing verandas draped with drying paprikas and other vegetables.

ACCOMMODATION AND EATING — KARANAC

Baranjska kuća Kolodvorska 99 ⓣ 031 720 180, ⓦ baranjska-kuca.com. An atmospheric restaurant with plenty of exposed brick and timbers, serving up roast meats, chicken *paprikaš* and local cauldron-bubbling mainstays such as *čobanac* and *fiš*. There's a good chance of live Roma music at weekends. Mon–Thurs 11am–10pm, Fri & Sat 11am–1am, Sun 11am–5pm.

Sklepić Kolodvorska 58 ⓣ 031 720 271 and ⓣ 098 739 159, ⓦ sklepic.hr. This beautifully restored nineteenth-century farmstead on Karanac's main street features traditionally furnished rooms (including embroidered pillowcases and tablecloths) alongside reassuringly modern bathrooms. 380Kn

Zmajevac and around

Northeast of Beli Manastir, the monotony of the Slavonian–Baranjan plain is broken by the **Banska kosa**, a ridge of sandy hills covered with vineyards. The most interesting of the settlements here is the long, straggling village of **ZMAJEVAC**, whose wine cellars, cut into the southern slopes of the Banska kosa, are increasingly noted for their Graševina, Riesling and other whites. Most of the cellars occupy man-made caverns on the hilly north side of the village: should you wish to down a glass or even buy a few bottles, several cellars are open to the public and are signed from the main road.

EATING **ZMAJEVAC AND AROUND**

★ **Kovač Čarda** Maršala Tita 215, Suza ⊕031 733 101. Located at the eastern end of Suza, the Hungarian speaking village immediately west of Zmajevac, this is one of the best places on the Pannonian plain to eat *fiš paprikaš*, and displays framed competition-winning certificates aplenty on the wood-panelled walls of the dining room. Portions (two-person being the minimum) are served in a big metal pot and feature rough-cut hunks of either catfish on its own or catfish with carp and pike perch – the latter is supposed to be the classic recipe. The paprika content can be varied according to taste – you can choose between mild, medium or hot. Expect a 50min cooking time and eat with care – there will be bones. Daily 10am–11pm.

2

Batina

The easternmost extremity of the Banska kosa, overlooking the River Danube at the frontier town of **BATINA**, provides a suitably dramatic perch for one of Croatia's most imposing **communist-era memorials**. Taking the form of a monumental female statue brandishing a five-pointed star, it was built to commemorate the Soviet Red Army, who crossed the river here in November 1944 in the face of fierce German resistance. It's an outstanding example of ideological sculpture, and well worth visiting for the views you get from its concrete plinth, with the wooded shores of the Danube down below, and the Serbian province of Vojvodina stretching out on the opposite bank.

Našice

Fifty kilometres west of Osijek, the small town of **NAŠICE** sits on the shoulder of one of Slavonia's few genuinely hilly regions, where lush green tobacco plantations jostle up against vineyards and cornfields. Našice is a typical Slavonian one-street settlement, with all its principal buildings laid out in a single strip.

Našice Regional Museum

Pejačevićev trg 5 • Mon & Fri 8am–3pm, Tues–Thurs 8am–6pm, Sat 9am–noon • 12Kn • ⊕031 613 414, ⓦmdc.hr/nasice

Dwarfing the other buildings along Našice's main street is the former palace of the Pejačević family, built in the early nineteenth century in fanciful neo-Renaissance style and now sporting an eye-catching ochre paint job. Inside, an elegant double staircase sweeps you up to the **Našice Regional Museum** (Zavičajni muzej Našice), which celebrates Croatia's first female composer Dora Pejačević (1885–1923) with a room full of family photographs and mementos – a CD selection of Pejačević's compositions usually plays in the background while you browse. There's also a room full of works by local-born sculptor Hinko Juhn (1891–1940), and a ravishing display of traditional embroidery.

Behind the palace, the tree-filled **Pejačević park** descends towards a small serpentine-shaped lake.

ARRIVAL AND DEPARTURE **NAŠICE**

By bus Buses on the Osijek–Požega route (5 daily; 1hr) stop at Našice bus station (1km northeast of the centre) before continuing to the main street, where they pick up and drop off outside the museum.

ACCOMMODATION AND EATING

Hotel Park Pejačevićev trg 4 ⊕031 613 822, ⓦhotel-park.hr. Virtually next door to the palace, this is a comfortable if unexciting three-star. The hotel's restaurant serves up solid meat-and-two-vegetable fare in a vast impersonal dining room. 500Kn

Đakovo

The neat and tidy plains town of **ĐAKOVO**, 60km south of Osijek, is dominated by the skyline-hogging, 84m-high twin towers of its neo-Gothic, red-brick cathedral. The

ĐAKOVAČKI VEZOVI FOLK FESTIVAL

Đakovo is the scene of one of Croatia's most important **festivals** of authentic folk culture, **Đakovački vezovi** (literally "Đakovo embroidery"; early July), which features a weekend-long series of song and dance performances by folkloric societies from all over Croatia. Performances take over the town park from mid-morning till mid-evening, after which there"s usually some sort of live music and revelry in the town centre.

2

town's other main claim to fame is the Lippizaner stud farm, home to a sizeable community of the famously handsome white horses. Đakovo is worth a day-trip from Osijek but probably doesn't merit a longer stay.

Cathedral

Strossmayerov trg • Daily 7am–noon & 3–7pm

Constructed between 1862 and 1882 by the Viennese Gothic-Revival architect Baron Frederick Schmidt, **Đakovo Cathedral** (Đakovačka katedrala) was commissioned by Bishop Josip Juraj Strossmayer, who used Đakovo as a base from which to promote a south Slav cultural renaissance, promoting native-language book production and facilitating contacts between Croatian and Serbian intellectuals. The cathedral exterior is jazzed up with all kinds of intriguing details, from the beehive-like cones standing guard on either side of the entrance, to the pinnacled cupola which rises above the main transept. Inside, walls and ceilings are decorated with uplifting biblical scenes, painted in the style of the Nazarenes (German contemporaries of the Pre-Raphaelites) by the father-and-son team of Alexander and Ljudevit Seitz.

Lippizaner stud farm

Augusta Šenoe 47 • Office open Mon–Fri 7am–3pm, Sat 9am–1pm • 20Kn; the ticket office is just inside the stud farm's entrance • ⓣ 031 813 286, ⓦ ergela-djakovo.hr

Ten minutes' walk from the centre (follow Matije Gupca eastwards from the cathedral), the **Lippizaner stud farm** (Državna ergela Đakovo) is another legacy of the Strossmayer period, and still enjoys a Europe-wide reputation for rearing and training the famous white horses. The stud farm frequently puts on shows for coach parties, and individual visitors can take a peek at the stables.

ARRIVAL AND INFORMATION — ĐAKOVO

By train The train station is 1km east of the centre at the far end of Kralja Tomislava.

Destinations Osijek (2 daily; 35min); Zagreb (1 daily; 3hr 25min).

By bus the bus station is a 5min walk east of the cathedral along Splitska.

Destinations Osijek (Mon–Sat hourly, Sun 8 daily; 45min); Zagreb (Mon–Sat 6 daily, Sun 4 daily; 4hr 30min).

Tourist office Kralja Tomislava 3 (Mon–Fri 8am–3pm, Sat 8am–noon; ⓣ 031 812 319, ⓦ tz-djakovo.hr). Has free town maps, but you may not always find an English speaker there.

EATING

Gradski podrum Ivana Pavla II 9 ⓣ 031 813 199, ⓦ gradski-podrum-djakovo.com. Restaurant on the pedestrianized strip north of the cathedral, offering a broad range of meat-and-potatoes main dishes and inexpensive lunches chalked up on a board – usually including the local favourite *čobanac*. Daily 7am–11pm.

Vukovar and around

Set amidst wheat and cornfields on the west bank of the Danube, **VUKOVAR** was until 1991 the most prosperous town in Croatia, with a quaint Baroque centre, a successful manufacturing industry based around the Borovo tyre and footwear factory, and an urban culture that was lively, open and tolerant. However, the town's proximity to the Serbian border and ethnically mixed population (of whom 44 percent were Croat and

THE SIEGE OF VUKOVAR

Inter-ethnic tension flared in Vukovar at the dawn of the Croat–Serb conflict in April 1991, when barricades went up between the Croatian-controlled town centre and the Serb-dominated suburbs. The firing of a rocket at the Serb district of **Borovo Selo** by Croat extremists was a calculated attempt to raise the stakes. Croatian policemen patrolling Borovo Selo were shot at by Serbian snipers on May 1, and when a busload of their colleagues entered the suburb the following day, they were met by an ambush in which twelve of them lost their lives. The JNA (Yugoslav People's Army) moved in, ostensibly to keep the two sides apart, digging into positions that were to serve them well with the breakout of all-out war in the autumn.

On September 14, 1991, the Croatian National Guard surrounded the JNA barracks in town. Serb irregulars in the outlying areas, supported by the JNA, responded by launching an attack. Croatian refugees fled the suburbs, crowding into the centre. Aided by the fact that many of the outlying villages were ethnically Serb, the JNA swiftly encircled the town, making it all but impossible to leave (the only route out was through sniper-prone cornfields), and subjecting the population to increasingly heavy shelling. By the beginning of October the people of Vukovar were living in bomb shelters and subsisting on meagre rations of food and water, their plight worsened by the seeming inactivity of the government in Zagreb. Some of the town's defenders suspected that Vukovar was being deliberately sacrificed in order to win international sympathy for the Croatian cause. Vukovar finally fell on November 18, with most of the inhabitants fleeing back to the town hospital or making a run for it across the fields to the west. Of those who fell into Yugoslav hands, the women and children were usually separated from the men – many of the latter simply disappeared.

The worst atrocities took place after Yugoslav forces reached the **hospital**, which they proceeded to evacuate before the agreed arrival of Red Cross supervisors. Those captured here were bundled into trucks and driven away to be murdered, finishing up in a mass grave near the village of **Ovčara**, 6km southeast (see p.132). About two thousand Croatian soldiers and civilians died in the defence of Vukovar, and those listed as missing still run into the hundreds. The fact that Vukovar held out for so long turned the town into an emotionally powerful symbol of Croatian resistance, and also put paid to the JNA as an effective army of conquest.

37 percent Serb) conspired to place Vukovar at the sharp end of the Croat–Serb conflict. The resulting **siege** and capture of the town by the Yugoslav People's Army and Serbian irregulars killed hundreds of civilians, left the centre of town in ruins, and did untold emotional damage to those lucky enough to escape (see box above). In January 1998 Vukovar was returned to Croatia as part of the Erdut Accord, though Croats driven away seven years earlier were initially slow to return, either because their homes were still in ruins or because the local economy wasn't yet strong enough to provide sufficient jobs. There are currently about 18,000 Croats and 9000 Serbs living in Vukovar – about two-thirds of the original population – although social contact between the two communities is virtually nonexistent. Today, the town is a strange mixture of ruined buildings, restored facades and glitzy post-1995 shopping centres.

Borovo

Entering Vukovar by road from the north, you'll pass through the suburb of **Borovo**, built as a model workers' settlement by Czech shoe manufacturer Bata in the 1930s. With a huge red-brick factory at its centre, and smaller red-brick housing units scattered among the surrounding pine trees, it's an enduring – if somewhat under-appreciated – monument to interwar urban planning.

The Old Town

Vukovar's **Old Town** sits just inland from the confluence of the Vuka and Danube rivers. There are many fine eighteenth- and nineteenth-century buildings here, many of which are still undergoing long-term restoration after shell damage in the 1991–95 war.

Facing the river Vuka is the **Radnički Dom** ("House of the Workers"), where the Yugoslav Socialist Party met to transform itself into the Yugoslav Communist Party in June 1920, only to be banned by the government five months later. Beyond lies the town's main street, Stjepana Radića, lined with late Baroque buildings with arcaded lower storeys. On high ground to the southeast stands the eighteenth-century **Franciscan monastery** (Franjevački samostan), faithfully reconstructed after almost total destruction, while beyond the monastery the ice-cream-cone-shaped **water tower** thrusts skywards, still displaying dramatic signs of shell damage.

Town Museum

Dvorac Eltz Županisjka 2

Just north of Vukovar's Old Town is the **Eltz Palace** (Dvorac Eltz), an imposing aristocratic seat built for a local landowning family in the early eighteenth century. Badly damaged in the siege, the palace is home to the **Town Museum** (Gradski muzej), whose collections were expropriated by the Serbs in 1991. An agreement to return them was signed in 2001, and the palace is currently undergoing long-term restoration in preparation for a grand reopening some time in the future.

Vukovar General Hospital

Županijska 37 • Mon–Fri 9am–3pm • Free • ⓣ 032 452 002

During the siege of Vukovar the town's **General Hospital** (Opća bolnica), a twenty-minute walk north of the town centre, was deliberately targeted by enemy shelling, and wards were moved into the hospital basement to avoid casualties. A section of the basement is now a **memorial centre.** A shell hole has been left unrepaired in one section of the roof, and a re-creation of one of the makeshift wards contains beds and equipment crammed together, and dummy-like sculptures symbolizing the patients.

Ovčara Memorial Site

Daily 10am–5pm • Free • ⓣ 032 512 345 • Ovčara is 6km east of Vukovar on the road to Ilok

One of the most notorious single massacres of the Croat–Serb conflict occurred just after the fall of Vukovar on November 21, when 261 people (mostly wounded defenders and civilians but also including some hospital staff) were taken to storehouses belonging to a collective farm at **Ovčara** outside the town and shot. The storehouse where most of the victims were held is now a memorial centre, a grim grey space that is deliberately poorly illuminated in commemoration of the fact that the murders took place at night. Star-shaped lights in the ceiling symbolize the victims, while shell cases are installed in the floor. Pictures of those who died are mounted on the wall, and display cases nearby contain personal effects found in Ovčara's mass grave.

ARRIVAL AND INFORMATION — VUKOVAR AND AROUND

By bus The bus station lies opposite the main market, a 5min walk from the Old Town.

Destinations Ilok (6 daily; 50min); Osijek (Mon–Sat hourly, Sun 8 daily; 45min); Zagreb (4 daily; 5hr–5hr 30min).

International destination Novi Sad (3 daily; 2hr 15min).

Tourist office Strossmayerova 15, on the way to the Eltz Palace (Mon–Fri 7am–3pm; ⓣ 032 442 889, ⓦ turizamvukovar.hr).

ACCOMMODATION AND EATING

Hotel Lav Strossmayerova 18 ⓣ 032 445 100, ⓦ hotel-lav.hr. Just outside the town centre and near the river, the four-star *Lav* provides plush rooms with warm colour schemes, a/c, desk space and minibar. The restaurant offers a meat-heavy menu of central European favourites – such as *perkelt od soma* served with cheesy noodles, and fine cuts of meat and poultry – in smart surroundings. **900Kn**

Vrške Parobrodarska 3 ⓣ 032 441 788, ⓦ restoran-vrske.hr. On a small islet behind the *Lav* hotel, *Vrške* dishes up cutlets of breaded catfish and carp on a pleasantly tree-shaded terrace facing the water. **Sun–Thurs 11am–11pm, Fri & Sat till midnight.**

Ilok

Long considered the kind of provincial town you race through en route to the Serbian border, Danube-hugging **ILOK** is fast emerging as one of eastern Croatia's most compelling destinations. With **wine cellars** galore grouped around an imposing hilltop castle, it certainly promises enough to keep you occupied for a day or two. The town can also boast a great choice of affordable accommodation, making it a far better base for exploring the region than Vukovar. With the bridge to the Serbian side of the Danube only 2km downstream, it is also a good jumping-off point for Novi Sad and Belgrade.

Ilok Fortress

Much of modern Ilok huddles around the **fortress** (tvrđava), its ruddy walls dominating a ridge overlooking the Danube. It owes its present shape to Nikola Iločki (1415–77), the local power baron who turned the town into a major strategic point in Europe's defences against the Ottoman Turks. Occupied by the Ottomans in 1526, Ilok became a Habsburg possession in 1688 when it was presented to the Pope's nephew Livio Odescalchi, who built a fine Baroque palace (now the Ilok Museum; see below) inside the walls.

The fortress walls and towers are in a good state of preservation and can be admired by walking through the park that runs around its western and southern side. Inside the fortress walls are a collection of old and not-so-old buildings, including a restored granary earmarked as a future exhibition centre and tourist office.

Franciscan Church

Trg sv. Ivana Kapistrana

Although architecturally undistinguished, the **Franciscan Church** (Franjevačka crkva) at the southern end of the fortress precinct is famous for being the last resting place of St John of Capistrano (Ivan Kapistran), the militant Italian friar who fought against the Ottomans at the battle of Belgrade in 1456, dying at Ilok later the same year. Nikola Iločki energetically promoted the warrior-priest's posthumous fame, and Capistrano became the centre of a local cult long before his official canonization in 1690. At the last visit, both Capistrano and Nikola Iločki's tombstones were stacked by the door and wrapped in black polythene sheeting because the church didn't quite know where to display them.

Ilok Museum

Šetalište Mladena Barbarića 5 • Tues–Thurs 9am–3pm; Fri 9am–6pm, Sat 11am–6pm • 20Kn • ⓣ 032 827 410, ⓦ mgi.hr

Occupying the superbly restored Odescalchi Palace, **Ilok Museum** (Muzej grada Iloka) is one of the most visually attractive collections in the country, with a display

CROSSING INTO SERBIA

Crossing from eastern Croatia **into Serbia** shouldn't present too many problems. At the time of writing, citizens of EU countries, Australia, Canada, New Zealand and the United States are allowed to enter Serbia on production of a valid passport. Citizens of other countries should check current visa regulations before setting out.

The main road crossing points are at **Lipovac**, on the Županja–Sremska Mitrovica stretch of the Autocesta, **Tovarnik** on the Vinkovci–Šid road, **Ilok** on the Vukovar–Novi Sad road, **Erdut** on the Osijek–Novi Sad road and **Batina** on the Beli Manastir–Sombor road. Crossing the border can be an unpredictable process, with Serbian border guards subjecting travellers they don't like the look of to thorough searches, while waving others straight through.

There's an increasing number of public transport links between the two countries, with five daily **trains** and several daily buses between Zagreb and Belgrade. If you're heading for Novi Sad, capital of the Serbian Vojvodina, then make your way to Vukovar or Ilok and catch one of the four daily buses from there.

that ranges from Neolithic pots to sepia photographs of nineteenth-century town life. The section documenting the 1991–95 war is one of the most immediate – the town was evacuated en masse in 1991 to prevent its destruction in a siege, and the inhabitants didn't return until 1998. And do not overlook the ethnographic section in the timber-beamed attic, a colourful explosion of embroidery and textiles, including the kinky pink costumes worn by married women from the ethnic Slovak village of Gložani.

2

Iločki podrumi

Dr Franje Tuđmana 72 • Daily 10am–10pm • ⓣ 032 590 003, ⓦ ilocki-podrumi.hr

Located beside the entrance to Ilok fortress, **Iločki podrumi** is one of Croatia's biggest wineries, producing on average over 4.5 million litres of wine a year. Dry white Graševina (also known as Welschriesling) represents the bulk of their output, although it is the slightly sweeter Traminac (aka Gewürztraminer, brought from Austria by the Odescalchi family in 1710) that enjoys widespread renown. Wines can be sampled in the wood-panelled tasting room, and there is of course a variety of bottles for sale. Groups (and individuals if a member of staff is available) will be shown around the fifteenth-century cellars, where oak barrels are kept at a constant temperature of 10–12°C. With the bulk of Iločki podrumi's production moved to a modern winery on the outskirts of town, the cellars are nowadays used for archiving vintage wines, including some spectacularly dusty bottles of 1947 Traminac – 11,000 of which were ordered by the British court to celebrate the coronation of Elizabeth II.

ARRIVAL AND INFORMATION — ILOK

By bus Buses pass along Ilok's main street, stopping opposite the fortress and down the hill below the fortress. Destinations Osijek (6 daily; 1hr 50min); Vukovar (6 daily; 50min); Zagreb (1 daily; 5hr 35min).

International destination Novi Sad (3 daily; 1hr 30min).

Tourist office Trg Nikole Iločkog 2 (Mon–Fri 8am–3pm; ⓣ 032 590 020, ⓦ turizamilok.hr).

ACCOMMODATION AND EATING

★ **Dunav** Julija Benešića 62 ⓣ 032 596 500, ⓦ hoteldunavilok.com. Appealing medium-sized hotel on the Danube riverfront, with neat three-star rooms with TV and internet access. The hotel restaurant (daily 8am–11pm) serves local *smuđ* (pike-perch) and *som* (catfish) done in different ways, and a prize-winning *fiš paprikaš* (the minimum order is for a two-person portion), with diners seated in a collection of gazebo-like structures beside the riverbank. 500Kn

Hostel Cinema Julija Benešića 42 ⓣ 032 591 159, ⓦ cinema.com.hr. Converted cinema building containing a mix of six- and twelve-bed dorms with wooden floors and high ceilings, together with cosy four-bed rooms in the attic with skylight windows. On the ground floor of the building there is a checked-tablecloth pizzeria, and a café-bar wallpapered with pages from 1970s pop-culture

ILOK WINE CELLARS

Although Iločki podrumi (see above) is the most famous of Ilok's **wine producers**, it is the large number of independent wineries that give the town its flavour. These are by and large family businesses, selling wines directly to visitors to their cellars. Visitors are welcome (you can taste wines by the glass and might also be offered cheese-and-ham nibbles), although a prior phone call is advisable to ensure that someone is at home.

★ **Buhač** Hercegovačka 1 ⓣ 032 593 100 and ⓣ 098 933 3995. One of the up-and-coming boutique producers in Ilok, producing good Graševinas and Chardonnays, as well as a highly regarded Merlot.

Knezović Matije Gupca 101 ⓣ 032 593 257. Friendly family house with cellar and tasting room, offering Chardonnay and red Frankovka (Blaufränkisch) alongside the usual Graševina.

Stipetić Radićeva 16 ⓣ 032 591 068. A family winery with a two hundred-year tradition right in the centre of Ilok, with cellars built into the hillside. Known for good-quality Graševina and Rhine Riesling.

magazines. The original cinema auditorium is now a nightclub (Fri & Sat only). Dorms from **120Kn**

Pansion Masarini Radićeva 4 ⓣ032 590 050 and ⓣ098 164 6855. Friendly pension in a restored barn featuring five doubles and a triple, decorated in pastel pinks and greens and with plenty of original timber features. Breakfast is served at the *Pod starim krovovima* restaurant on the opposite side of the street. **420Kn**

Srijemska kuća Matije Gupca 89 ⓣ032 593 064 and ⓣ098 718 612, ⓦsrijemska-kuca.com.hr. A 10min walk from the centre in a street lined with traditional houses, this old farmstead in a balustraded courtyard offers en-suite rooms (two doubles and one triple) with plush carpets, exposed brickwork and wooden beams. The whole house is available for rent for those travelling as a group. B&B **300Kn**

★ **Villa Iva** Radićeva 23 ⓣ032 591 011, ⓦvilla-iva-ilok.com. Thirteen en-suite rooms ranged around a flower-bedecked courtyard, each with TV, fridge and stencil-painted wall designs. *Villa Iva*'s restaurant (daily 9am–11pm) serves up the usual freshwater fish and grilled meats – house specialities include pasta with catfish in white sauce, and *šnenokle* (a delicious creamy dessert that looks like whipped custard). B&B **300Kn**

2

Istria

AMPHITHEATRE, PULA

Istria

A large, triangular peninsula pointing down into the northern Adriatic, Istria (in Croatian, "Istra") represents Croatian tourism at its most developed. In recent decades the region's proximity to Western Europe has ensured an annual influx of sun-seeking package tourists, with Italians, Germans, Austrians and what seems like the entire population of Slovenia flocking to the mega-hotel developments that dot the coastline. Istrian beaches – often rocky areas that have been concreted over to provide sunbathers with a level surface on which to sprawl – lack the appeal of the out-of-the-way coves that you'll find on the Dalmatian islands, yet the hotel complexes and rambling campsites have done little to detract from the essential charm of the Istrian coast, with its compact towns of alley-hugging houses grouped around spear-belfried churches. Meanwhile, inland Istria is an area of rare and disarming beauty, characterized by medieval hilltop settlements and stone-built villages.

Istria's cultural legacy is a complex affair. Historically, Italians lived in the towns while Croats occupied the rural areas. Despite post-World War II expulsions, there's still a fair-sized Italian community, and Italian is very much the peninsula's second language.

With its amphitheatre and other Roman relics, the port of **Pula**, at the southern tip of the peninsula, is Istria's largest city and a rewarding place to spend a couple of days; many of Istria's most interesting spots are only a short bus ride away. On the western side of the Istrian peninsula are pretty resort towns like **Rovinj** and **Novigrad**, with their cobbled piazzas, shuttered houses and back alleys laden with laundry. Poised midway between the two, **Poreč** is much more of a package destination, but offers bundles of Mediterranean charm if you visit out of season. Inland Istria couldn't be more different – historic hilltop towns like **Motovun**, **Grožnjan**, **Oprtalj** and **Hum** look like leftovers from another century, half-abandoned accretions of ancient stone poised high above rich green pastures and forests.

ARRIVAL AND DEPARTURE — ISTRIA

By bus Regular buses connect Pula, Rovinj and Poreč with Zagreb; otherwise, the city of Rijeka, in the Kvarner Gulf (see p.186) is the most convenient gateway to the region.

By car Approaching from Rijeka by road gives you a choice of two routes: either along the coast or through the Učka Tunnel (30Kn/vehicle) which burrows its way through Mount Učka before emerging to breathtaking views of the Istrian hills on the other side.

Getting around Istria's coastal resorts are well connected by bus, but public transport inland is meagre – so you'll probably need a car to "do" the hill towns in any style.

Some history

Istria gets its name from the **Histri**, an Illyrian tribe that ruled the region before succumbing to the **Romans** in the second century BC. The invaders left a profound

MOSAIC, BASILICA OF EUPHRASIUS, POREČ

Highlights

❶ **Pula amphitheatre** The Romans built things to last, and this two thousand-year-old monument is still the dominating feature of Pula's landscape. **See p.142**

❷ **Brijuni islands** An idyllic offshore paradise that once served as President Tito's personal holiday resort. **See p.152**

❸ **Rovinj** Italianate, chic and bustling – the pick of the west coast resorts. **See p.156**

❹ **The Basilica of Euphrasius, Poreč** A venerable sixth-century structure whose Byzantine-influenced mosaics are as good as any around the Mediterranean. **See p.163**

❺ **Our Lady on the Rocks, Beram** Incandescent paintings by medieval masters light up this village chapel in inland Istria's rustic heartland. **See p.171**

❻ **Grožnjan** Rich in historical resonances, the mellow hill town of Grožnjan seems a world away from the heavily touristed coast. **See p.176**

❼ **Truffles in the Buzet region** The most celebrated of Istria's gastronomic delights, this smelly fungus deserves to be tasted at least once. **See box, p.178**

HIGHLIGHTS ARE MARKED ON THE MAP ON P.140

mark on the area, building farms and villas, and turning Pula into a major urban centre. **Slav tribes** began settling the peninsula from the seventh century onwards, driving the original Romanized inhabitants of the peninsula towards the coastal towns or into the hills.

Venetians and Habsburgs

Coastal and inland Istria began to follow divergent courses as the Middle Ages progressed. The coastal towns adopted **Venetian suzerainty** from the thirteenth century onwards, while the rest of the peninsula came under **Habsburg control**. The fall of Venice in 1797 left the Austrians in charge of the whole of Istria. They confirmed Italian as the official local language, even though Croats outnumbered

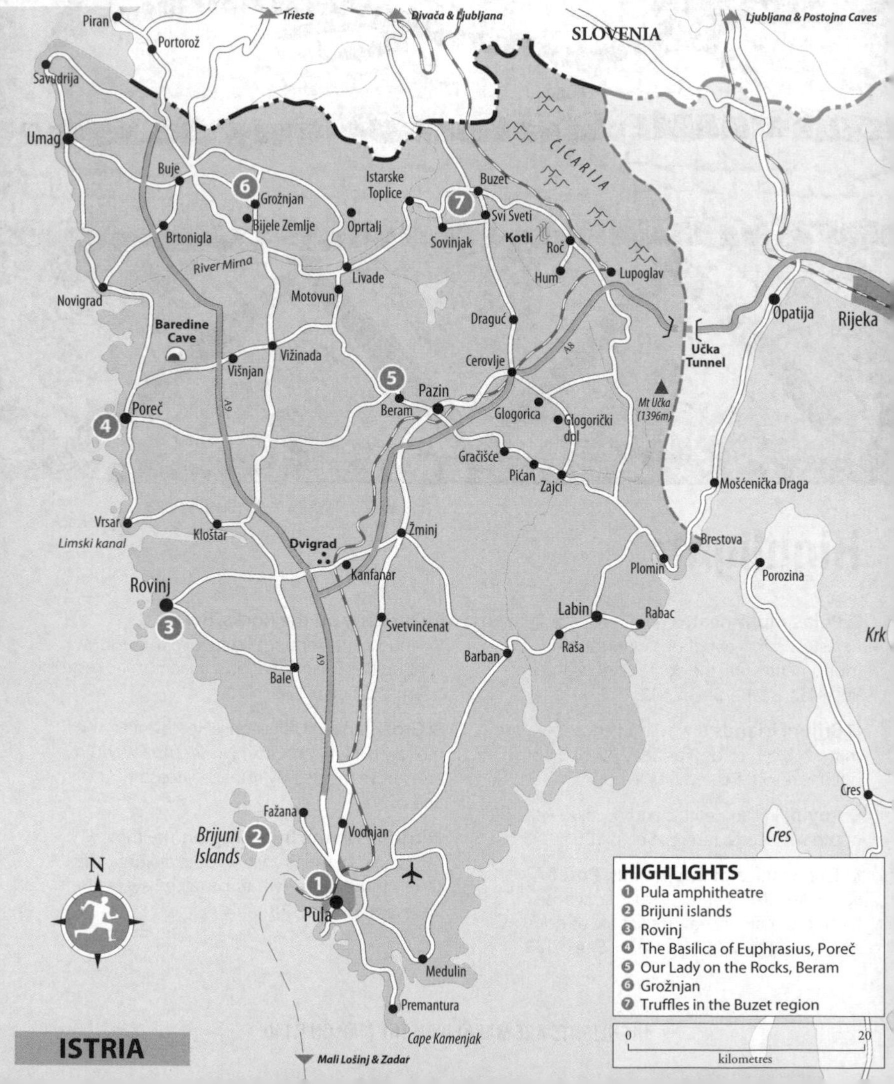

Italians by more than two to one. Istria received a degree of autonomy in 1861, but only the property-owning classes were allowed to vote, thereby excluding many Croats and perpetuating the Italian-speaking community's domination of Istrian politics.

Croatians and Italians

Austrian rule ended in 1918, when **Italy** – already promised Istria by Britain as an inducement to enter World War I – occupied the whole peninsula. Following Mussolini's rise to power in October 1922, the Croatian language was banished from public life, and Slav surnames were changed into their Italian equivalents. During World War II, however, opposition to fascism united Italians and Croats alike, and Tito's Partisan movement in Istria was a genuinely multinational affair, although this didn't prevent outbreaks of inter-ethnic violence. The atrocities committed against Croats during the Fascist period were avenged indiscriminately by the Partisans, and the *foibe* of Istria – limestone pits into which bodies were thrown – still evoke painful memories for Italians to this day.

After 1945 Istria became the subject of bitter wrangling between Yugoslavia and Italy, with the Yugoslavs ultimately being awarded the whole of the peninsula. Despite promising all nationalities full rights after 1945, the Yugoslav authorities actively pressured Istria's Italians into leaving, and the region suffered serious **depopulation** as thousands fled. In response, the Yugoslav government encouraged emigration to Istria from the rest of the country, and today there are a fair number of Serbs, Macedonians, Albanians and Bosnians in Istria, many of whom were attracted to the coast by the **tourist industry**, which took off in the 1960s and has never looked back.

Istria today

Geographically distant from the main flashpoints of the Serb-Croat conflict, Istria entered the twenty-first century more cosmopolitan, more prosperous and more self-confident than any other region of the country. With locals tending to regard Zagreb as the centre of a tax-hungry state, Istrian particularism is a major political force, with the **Istrian Democratic Party** (Istarska demokratska stranka, or IDS) consistently winning the lion's share of the local vote.

FOOD AND DRINK IN ISTRIA

The Istrian peninsula is a cornucopia of culinary riches, with the **seafood** of the coast melding with the hearty meat-based fare of Central Europe. Whether you're looking for a haute-cuisine restaurant or an informal village inn, culinary standards are high and ingredients first class. Regional delicacies include oysters (*oštrige*) from the Limski kanal, and cured ham (*pršut*), wild asparagus (*šparoga*) and truffles (*tartufi*; see box, p.178) from the hills inland. Istrian **meats**, such as *kobasice* (succulent, fatty sausages) and *ombolo* (smoked pork loin), are often cooked on the *kamin* or open hearth. *Fuži* (pasta twists) and *njoki* (gnocchi) are very much local staples, and are often freshly made by hand in the more traditional country inns. Istrian **olive oil**, as elsewhere in Croatia, is largely produced by individual farmers or regional cooperatives, ensuring a high degree of quality and recognizably individual flavours.

Best known of Istria's **wines** is the crisp white Malvazija that is produced all over the peninsula; mass-market brands like De Mar are perfectly palatable, although family winery Radovan and the craft winemaker Clai offer more in terms of quality. The slightly acidic but eminently drinkable Teran is a characterful indigenous red. A typical Istrian **spirit** is *biska*, the aphrodisiac mistletoe brandy associated with the region around Buzet (see p.176) and Hum (see p.179). One Istrian concoction you should definitely try at least once is *supa*, an earthenware jug of red wine mulled with sugar, olive oil and pepper, served with a slice of toast for dipping purposes.

One consequence of Istria's newfound sense of identity has been a reassessment of its often traumatic relationship with Italy, and a positive new attitude towards its cultural and linguistic ties with that country. Bilingual road signs and public notices have gone up all over the place, and the region's Italian-language schools – increasingly popular with cosmopolitan Croatian parents – are enjoying a new lease of life.

Pula

Once the Austro-Hungarian Empire's chief naval base, **PULA** (in Italian, Pola) is an engaging combination of working port and brash Riviera town. The Romans put the city firmly on the map when they arrived in 177 BC, bequeathing it an impressive **amphitheatre** whose well-preserved remains are the city's single greatest attraction, though it's just one of an easily accessible cluster of **classical** and **medieval** sights in the city centre. Pula is also Istria's commercial heart and transport hub, and the rough-and-ready atmosphere of the crane-ringed **harbour** makes a refreshing contrast to the seaside towns and tourist complexes farther along the coast. The city also possesses the peninsula's sole airport, so you're unlikely to visit the region without passing through at least once. Central Pula doesn't boast much of a seafront, but there's a lengthy stretch of rocky **beach** about 3km south of the city centre, leading to the hotel complex on the **Verudela peninsula**, which was built in the 1980s to accommodate package-holidaying Brits.

According to legend, Pula was founded by the Colchians, who pursued the Argonauts here after the latter had stolen the Golden Fleece. The prosaic truth is that the city began life as a minor Illyrian settlement, and there's not much evidence of a significant town here until 177 BC, when the Romans arrived and transformed Pula into an important commercial centre endowed with all the imperial trimmings – temples, theatres and triumphal arches – appropriate to its status.

The amphitheatre

Istarska • Daily: April 8am–8pm; May, June & mid-Aug to Sept 8am–9pm; July to mid-Aug 8am–midnight; Oct 9am–7pm; Nov–March 9am–5pm • 40Kn • Ⓦ ami-pula.hr

The chief reminder of Pula's Roman heritage is the immense **amphitheatre** (Amfiteatar or arena), just north of the centre, a huge grey skein of connecting arches whose silhouette dominates the city skyline. Built towards the end of the first century BC, it's the sixth largest surviving Roman amphitheatre in the world, with space for 22,000 spectators, although why such a capacious theatre was built in a small Roman town of only five thousand inhabitants has never been properly explained.

The outer shell is remarkably complete, although only a small part of the seating remains anything like intact; the interior tiers and galleries were quarried long ago by locals, who used the stone to build their own houses. It is, in fact, lucky that the amphitheatre survives here at all: overcome by enthusiasm for Classical antiquities, the sixteenth-century Venetian authorities planned to dismantle the whole lot and reassemble it piece by piece in their own city; they were dissuaded by the Pula-born patrician Gabriele Emo, whose gallant stand is remembered by a plaque on one of the amphitheatre's remaining towers. Once inside, you can explore some of the cavernous rooms underneath, which would have been used for keeping wild animals and Christians before they met their deaths. They're now given over to a display devoted to Roman-era wine production in Istria, with an atmospherically lit collection of olive presses and crusty amphorae.

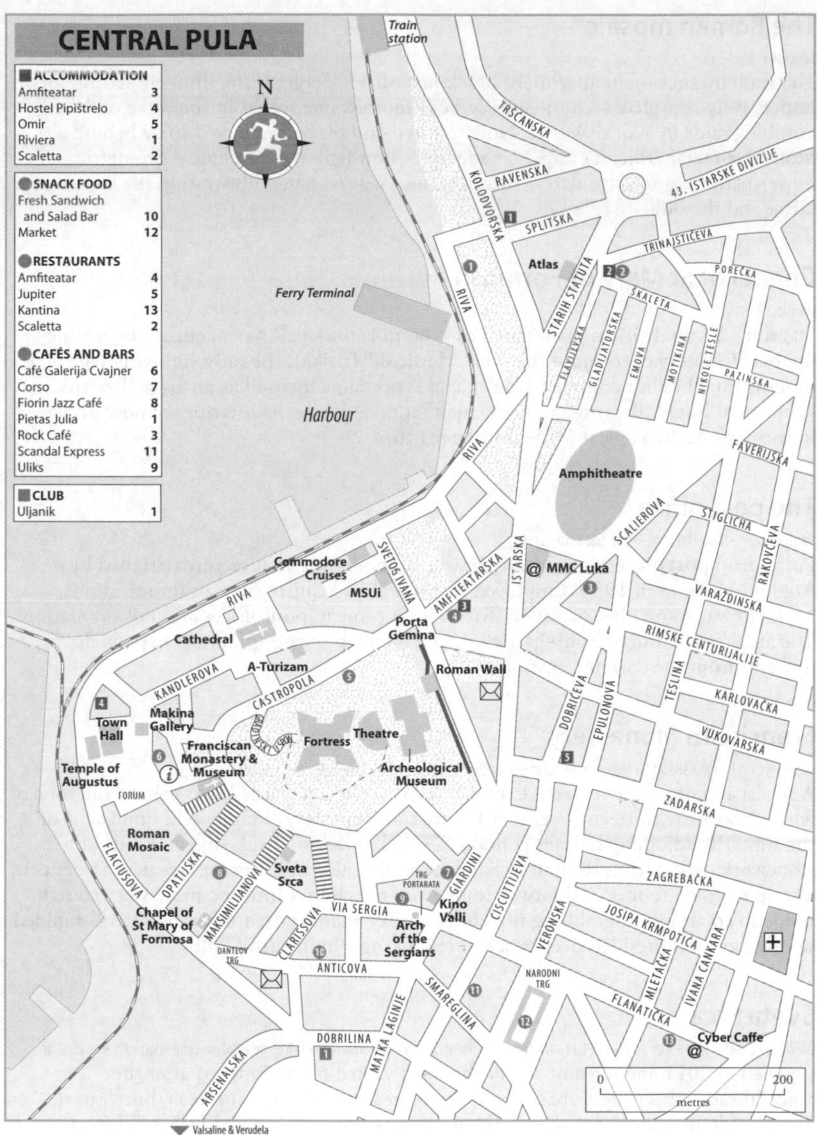

The Arch of the Sergians

Via Sergia

Also known as Zlatna vrata, or the Golden Gate, the **Arch of the Sergians** is a self-glorifying monument built by one Salvia Postuma Sergia in 30 BC. The west face of the arch is the more interesting, with reliefs of winged victories framing an inscription extolling the virtues of the Sergia family – one of whom (probably Salvia's husband) commanded a legion at the Battle of Actium in 31 BC. The arch leads to the pedestrianized **Via Sergia** , which heads into the historic heart of Pula, running beneath a pyramidal hill.

The Roman mosaic

Opatijska

The rear entrance of an apartment block just off Via Sergia is the unlikely setting for an impressively complete second-century floor **mosaic**, uncovered in the wake of Allied bombing raids in World War II. Now restored and on permanent display behind a protective metal grille, it's largely made up of non-figurative designs – geometric flower-patterns and meanders – surrounding a central panel illustrating the legend of Dirce and the bull.

Chapel of St Mary of Formosa

Flaciusova

Standing demurely in an open patch of ground is the small sixth-century Byzantine **Chapel of St Mary of Formosa** (Crkvica Marije od Trstika), the only surviving part of a monumental basilica complex. The chapel is occasionally used as an art gallery in summer, although the mosaic fragments that once graced its interior are now displayed in the city's Archeological Museum (see p.146).

The post office

Danteov trg 4 • Mon–Fri 8am–9pm, Sat 8am–3pm

Pula's main **post office** is a celebrated piece of modernist architecture designed by Angiolo Mazzoni in 1933. Employed by the Italian Ministry of Communications, Mazzoni was something of a specialist when it came to post offices and railway stations. The architect's Futurist leanings are evinced by the staircase spiralling awesomely upwards from the dark red vestibule.

Franciscan Monastery

Uspon svetog Franje Asiškog 9 • Museum mid-June to mid-Sept daily 10am–1pm & 4–7pm • 10Kn

A succession of stepped streets ascend from Via Sergia towards Pula's central hill, one of which passes the thirteenth-century **Franciscan Monastery** (Franjevački samostan) on the way. The adjoining cloister contains a small **museum**, displaying all kinds of stonework dating from Roman to late medieval times, and Roman mosaic fragments in a couple of side rooms. A doorway leads from the cloister into the monastery **church**, home to an attention-grabbing fifteenth-century altarpiece featuring two tiers of gilded saintly figurines presided over by a severe-looking Virgin with Child.

Sveta Srca

De Villeov uspon • Tues–Sun: June–Sept 11am–2pm & 5–9pm; Oct–May 11am–7pm • Prices depend on exhibition • ⓦ ami-pula.hr

Opened in 2011 and already one of the most visited places in town after the amphitheatre, this gallery space occupies the recently restored former Church of the Hearts of Jesus and Mary – hence the name **Sveta Srca** or "Sacred Hearts". It's an outstanding example of how an early twentieth-century church can be spectacularly modernized, with creamy-coloured surfaces, atmospheric lighting and shiny metal railings adding up to an altogether sublime exhibition hall. Run by the Archeological Museum, it hosts a wide variety of exhibitions from local history to contemporary art – the Pula tourist office (see p.148) can tell you what's on.

The Forum

Via Sergia finishes up at the ancient Roman **Forum**, nowadays the old quarter's pedestrianized main square. The building on the square's northern end began life as a

JAMES JOYCE IN PULA

In October 1904 the 22-year-old **James Joyce** eloped from Ireland to mainland Europe with his girlfriend (and future wife) Nora Barnacle. He sought work with the Berlitz English-language schools in Zürich and Trieste, but the organization found him a post in Pula instead, where he was paid £2 for a sixteen-hour week teaching Austro-Hungarian naval officers (one of whom was Miklos Horthy, ruler of Hungary between the wars). Despite their straitened circumstances, the couple enjoyed this first taste of domestic life – although Joyce viewed Pula as a provincial backwater, and, eager to get away at the first opportunity, accepted a job in Trieste six months later.

Though Joyce had a productive time in Pula, writing much of what subsequently became *Portrait of the Artist as a Young Man*, the city made next to no impact on his literary imagination. In letters home he described it as "a back-of-God-speed place – a naval Siberia", adding that "Istria is a long boring place wedged into the Adriatic, peopled by ignorant Slavs who wear red caps and colossal breeches."

There are few places in modern Pula that boast Joycean associations: the *Café Miramar*, where Joyce went every day to read the newspapers, was until recently a furniture store; there are current plans to turn the building into a luxury hotel. You can always, however, enjoy a drink in the café-bar *Uliks* ("Ulysses" in Croatian), situated on the ground floor of the apartment block which once housed the language school (see p.151); the terrace boasts a life-size bronze sculpture of the artist himself sitting on one of the chairs, and there's a small glass cabinet containing Joyce memorabilia inside.

Temple of Diana before being modified and rebuilt as the **Town Hall** (Gradska vijećnica) in the thirteenth century – a Renaissance arcade was added later.

The Temple of Augustus

Forum • Mid-June to mid-Sept Mon–Fri 9am–8pm, Sat & Sun 9am–3pm • 10Kn

On the northwestern corner of Pula's forum is the **Temple of Augustus** (Augustov hram), built between 2 BC and 14 AD to celebrate the cult of the emperor and one of the finest Roman temples outside Italy, with an imposing facade of high Corinthian columns. Inside, there's a permanent exhibition of the best of Pula's Roman finds, including the sculpted torso of a Roman centurion found in the amphitheatre, and a figure of a slave kneeling at the sandalled feet (more or less all that's left) of his master.

Makina Gallery

Kapitolinski trg 1 • Tues–Sun 6–9pm • Free

Round the back of Pula's Town Hall, at the beginning of Kandlerova, the **Makina Gallery** (Galerija Makina) is one of Croatia's best photography galleries, with year-round displays of both local and international work. A major show is usually timed to coincide with the Pula Film Festival (see p.150).

The cathedral

Kandlerova • Daily 7am–noon & 4–6pm

Pula's simple and spacious **Cathedral of St Mary** (Katedrala svete Marije) offers a compendium of styles, with a dignified Renaissance facade concealing a Romanesque modification of a sixth-century basilica, itself built on the foundations of a Roman temple. There's a great deal of interest inside: the stately pillars running either side of the nave are topped by ornately carved sixth-century capitals, while fragments of original floor mosaic can still be made out just in front of the high altar. The altar itself consists of a third-century marble sarcophagus that's said to have once contained the remains of the eleventh-century Hungarian King Solomon.

The fortress

Museum: Gradinski uspon 6 • June–Sept daily 8am–5pm; Oct–May by appointment • 10Kn • ⓣ 052 211 566, ⓦ pmi.hr

Occupying the mossy seventeenth-century **fortress** (*kaštel*), built by the Venetians in the form of a four-pointed star, the **Historical and Maritime Museum of Istria** (Povijesni i pomorski muzej Istre) is a sparse and uninformative collection that is worth visiting for the setting rather than the exhibits themselves. Forget the seafaring memorabilia and scale models of ships, and ramble instead around the fortress's ramparts, which provide commanding views of Pula and its environs. You can see the cranes of the Uljanik shipyard clustered over to the west, and the spire of Vodnjan church, a distant but discernible presence 12km away to the north.

The Archeological Museum

Carrarina 3 • May–Sept Mon–Sat 9am–8pm, Sun 10am–3pm; Oct–April Mon–Fri 9am–2pm • 20Kn • ⓦ ami-pula.hr

3

The greater part of Pula's movable Roman relics have finished up in the rather old-fashioned **Archeological Museum** (Arheološki muzej), with room upon room of unimaginatively displayed ceramics, brooches and oil lamps; English-language labelling helps to ease your progress from one display case to the next. Highlights include the Roman gravestones arranged in the hallways and stairwells, many of which feature sensitive portraits of the deceased, and the pre-Roman artefacts from the Illyrian settlement of Nesactium – especially the enigmatic, squiggle-embellished tombstones, one of which takes the form of a man riding a horse, upon whose flanks an image of a fertility goddess has been carved. Just by the museum is the Roman **Porta Gemina**, smaller and plainer than the Arch of the Sergians, whose two arches give it its name: the Twin Gate.

MSUi (Istrian Contemporary Art Museum)

Svetog Ivana 1 • June–Sept Mon–Fri 11am–2pm & 5–9pm; Oct–May Tues–Fri 11am–7pm • 10Kn • ⓦ 052 423 205

Occupying the atmospherically grotty factory floors of a former printing house, the embryonic **MSUi**, or **Istrian Contemporary Art Museum** (Muzej suvremene umjetnosti Istre), isn't really a museum yet and doesn't have a permanent collection on display. However, it does host frequently excellent exhibitions by Croatian and foreign artists. Granted a ten-year lease on its current home in 2010, the MSUi plans to move to a purpose-built space in central Pula before the decade is out.

South of the centre

Immediately **south of Pula**, the city's dusty high-rise suburbs suddenly give way to a series of rocky promontories and forest-fringed inlets, culminating, 6km away, in the Verudela peninsula. The best **beaches** are at Verudela, although the rocky shores of Valkane and Valsaline are also popular with the locals.

Valkane and Valsaline bays

Bus #4 from Trg republike

The nearest beach to the city centre is **Valkane** bay, some 2km southwest of the downtown area. A stylish seaside rendezvous in the interwar years, it nowadays has a grubby, unkempt look about it, and it's far better to head left along the **Lungomare**, the road running southeast along the coast towards **Valsaline** bay, passing a succession of broad rock slabs which provide perfect spots for bathing.

Fort Bourguignon

Mon 7–9pm, Tues–Fri & Sun 11am–1pm & 7–9pm, Sat 11am–1pm • 10Kn

Heading uphill near the *Hotel Splendid*, just beyond Valsaline, brings you to a gravel track which leads to **Fort Bourguignon**, an enormous doughnut-shaped lump of stone built in 1861–66 and named after an Austrian admiral. Visitors can wander the galleries and peruse a display documenting the eleven other forts built around the city by the Habsburgs, who turned Pula into an impregnable fortress in the process.

Verudela peninsula

Bus #2a and 3a from Giardini

Site of most of Pula's large hotels, the wooded **Verudela peninsula** is bordered to the east by the lovely **Verudski kanal** inlet, home to Pula's marina. The southern extremity of the peninsula, **Punta Verudela**, is home to a couple of good shingle beaches, of which the Havajka, on the west side of the peninsula behind the *Park* hotel, and the Ambrela,

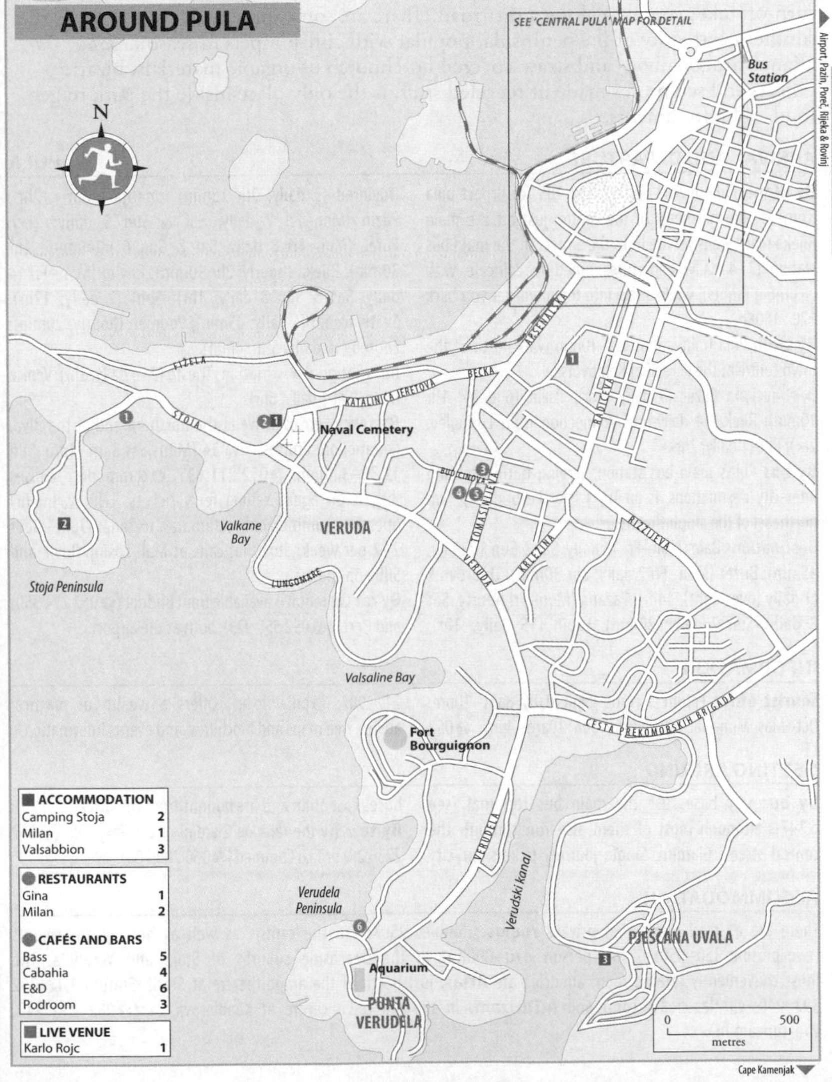

northwest of the *Brioni* hotel, are the most popular. The beaches are deluged with vacationing city folk during the summer, and remain a popular strolling area throughout the year.

South of Pula: Cape Kamenjak

Free for hikers and cyclists; 30Kn per car • kamenjak.hr • No public transport

Some of the most spectacular **beaches** in the Pula region can be found on **Cape Kamenjak** (Kamenjak rt), a bleak, scrub-covered finger of land some 13km beyond the city limits at the southernmost tip of the Istrian peninsula. The whole of the peninsula is protected as a **Nature Park**, and boasts a variety of secluded coves and beaches. They're reachable by the main road from Pula to Premantura, from where a marked turn-off takes you 3km along a dirt road. There are some quite high cliffs towards the southern extremity of the peninsula, popular with cliff-jumpers in season. *Safari Bar*, a fantastical bamboo- and straw-covered hotchpotch of organic materials, bizarre objects and sculptures made of recycled stuff, is the only place inside the park to get food and refreshments.

ARRIVAL AND DEPARTURE — PULA

By plane Pula airport (052 530 105, airport-pula.com) is 5km northeast of the centre, just off the main Rijeka road. A bus service links the airport to the main bus station (3–4 daily; departures timed to coincide with incoming flights), while a taxi into town will set you back 120–150Kn.

By train Pula train station is a 10min walk north of the town centre at the far end of Kolodvorska.

Destinations Buzet (3 daily; 2hr); Pazin (6 daily; 1hr 10min); Rijeka (4 daily, bus connection from Lupoglav; 2hr); Roč (1 daily; 2hr).

By bus Pula's main bus station, serving both local and inter-city destinations, is on Trg 1 Istarske brigade, 1km northeast of the amphitheatre.

Destinations Bale (Mon–Fri 16 daily, Sat & Sun 10 daily; 45min); Buzet (Mon–Fri 2 daily; 2hr 30min); Dubrovnik (1 daily [overnight]; 14hr); Fažana (Mon–Fri hourly, Sat 8 daily, Sun 7 daily; 30min); Labin (15 daily; 1hr); Novigrad (3 daily; 2hr 15min); Opatija (hourly; 2hr); Pazin (Mon–Fri 7 daily, Sat & Sun 5 daily; 1hr); Poreč (Mon–Fri 8 daily, Sat & Sun 6 minimum; 1hr 30min); Rijeka (hourly; 2hr 30min); Rovinj (Mon–Fri 14 daily, Sat & Sun 8 daily; 1hr); Split (2 daily; 12hr); Svetvinčenat (5 daily; 45min); Vodnjan (hourly; 20min); Zagreb (16 daily; 5hr 30min).

International destinations Trieste (2–4 daily; 3hr); Venice (Mon–Sat 1 daily; 6hr).

By ferry Ferries arrive at the northern end of the Riva. Commodore Cruises, Riva 14 (Mon–Sat 8am–4pm, Sun 12.30–3.30pm; 052 211 631, commodore-cruises.hr), is an agent selling ferry tickets. LNP (lnp.hr) operate a summer-only catamaran to Zadar (June–Sept 2–7 per week; 5hr) that calls at Mali Lošinj, Ilovik and Silba on the way.

By car Car rental is available from Budget (052 224 350) and Hertz (052 550 923), both at the airport.

INFORMATION

Tourist office Forum 3 (June–Sept daily 8am–10pm; Oct–May Mon–Sat 9am–7pm, Sun 10am–4pm; 052 212 987, pulainfo.hr). Offers a wealth of practical advice, free maps and brochures, and events information.

GETTING AROUND

By bus City buses use the main bus terminal (see p.147), although most of them also run through the central street, Giardini. Single-journey tickets for city buses cost 10Kn and are bought from the driver.

By taxi Try the rank on Giardini or call Taxi Pula (052 223 228) or Taxi Cammeo (060 700 700).

ACCOMMODATION

There are a small number of private **rooms** (doubles 250Kn) in the centre, as well as holiday apartments (two-person 350–450Kn, four-person 470–600Kn) in the beachside suburbs of Stoja and Verudela. The most conveniently located room agencies are **Atlas**, just north of the amphitheatre at Starih Statuta 1 (052 393 040, atlas-croatia.com) and **A-Turizam**, in the old town centre at Kandlerova 24 (052 212 212, a-turizam.hr).

HOTELS AND B&BS

CENTRAL PULA

★ **Amfiteatar** Amfiteatarska 6 ⊕052 375 600, ⊕hotelamfiteatar.com; map p.143. Comfortable, affordable and central, the medium-sized *Amfiteatar* occupies a renovated nineteenth-century building, with rooms decorated in cool greys with contemporary furnishings. The top-floor rooms with porthole windows and sloping attic ceilings are particularly cosy. The ground-floor restaurant (see below) is one of Pula's best. 670Kn

Omir Dobrićeva 6 ⊕052 218 186, ⊕hotel-omir.com; map p.143. Small, friendly but rather plain hotel with serviceable en-suite singles, doubles and triples, slightly uphill from Giardini, off Zadarska. 450Kn

Riviera Splitska 1 ⊕052 211 166, ⊕arenaturist.hr; map p.143. Probably the best-known building in Pula after the amphitheatre, the once-grand *Riviera* is Istria's finest example of Habsburg-era architecture when viewed from the outside – but the interior is drab save for a few ornate touches in the dining room, and the en-suite rooms are rather dowdy. In July and Aug it's overpriced for what it is, but quite reasonable at other times. 600Kn

★ **Scaletta** Flavijevska 26 ⊕052 541 599, ⊕hotel-scaletta.com; map p.143. Small and cosy family-run hotel offering pastel-coloured en suites with TV and minibar. Some of the rooms are on the small side, but friendly staff make up for any rough edges. Needless to say, it fills up quickly. 640Kn

OUT FROM THE CENTRE

Milan Stoja 4 ⊕052 300 200, ⊕milan1967.hr; map p.147. Family-run hotel in a suburban setting 2km west of the centre. Rooms are en suite and come with TV, minibar and a/c. One of Pula's best restaurants (see p.150) is on the ground floor, so splashing out a few extra kuna on half board is well worth considering. Bus #1 from Giardini. 850Kn

Valsabbion Pješčana uvala IX/26 ⊕052 218 033, ⊕valsabbion.hr; map p.147. Modern family-run B&B, featuring fully equipped rooms decked out in bold colours, a top-floor fitness studio and a small pool. Bus #27 from Giardini. 750Kn

HOSTEL AND CAMPSITE

Camping Stoja Stoja 37 ⊕052 387 144, ⊕arenacamps.com; map p.147. The nearest site to central Pula, with a wooded rocky peninsula all to itself some 3km southwest of town in the suburb of Stoja. The surroundings are idyllic, but it can get noisy and dirty at the height of summer. Bus #1 from Giardini stops outside the entrance. April–Oct. 50Kn per person, pitches from 40Kn

★ **Hostel Pipištrelo** Flaciusova 6 ⊕052 393 568, ⊕hostel-pipistrelo.com; map p.143. Opened in summer 2011, "The Bat" is exactly what central Pula needed, an imaginatively designed hostel that is backpacker-friendly but which also offers a couple of en-suite doubles for the comfort conscious. The nicely restored building is decked out in bold greens, yellows and salmon-pinks, with Pop Art adorning the walls of several rooms, each of which has a/c, TV and evocative views of shipyard cranes. The top floor quad has comic-strip-style panels to which guests can add their own drawings and comments. There's a small kitchen on the ground floor, a social area next to the reception and several shelves of books that are available for exchange. Wi-fi throughout. Dorms 135kn, rooms 400kn

3

EATING AND DRINKING

There's a good supply of serviceable **restaurants** in the centre of Pula, and several outstanding eating places in the suburbs. For snacks and supplies, the covered **market** and the surrounding cafés on Narodni trg, about 100m east of the Arch of the Sergians, are the best place for buying provisions or picking up sandwiches and pastries. Although the alfresco cafés around the Forum and along Flanatička provide plenty of opportunities for daytime **drinking**, central Pula doesn't really lend itself to a night-time bar-crawl. Most of the hostelries popular with Puležani are spread throughout the city, and you'll have to be prepared to venture beyond the tourist-trodden areas in order to enjoy the city at its best.

SNACK FOOD

Fresh Sandwich and Salad Bar Anticova 5 ⊕091 722 7712; map p.143. Something of a godsend in this land of fatty-pastry bakeries and pizza-slice outlets, *Fresh* serves up inexpensive and wholesome sandwiches, salads and usually something sweet – be it banana bread or carrot cake. A soup of the day is usually on offer – check the board beside the counter. Eat in or takeaway. Mon–Fri 8.30am–4.30pm.

Market Narodni trg; map p.143. Fresh-food shopping in a lovely cast-iron pavilion. Look out for deli products on the top floor, including pasta, cheeses, *pršut* and sausage. Mon–Sat 7am–2pm.

RESTAURANTS

★ **Amfiteatar** Amfiteatarska 6 ⊕052 375 600, ⊕hotelamfiteatar.com; map p.143. Mere steps away from the amphitheatre, *Amfiteatar* offers Mediterranean food that's imaginative, attractive and eminently affordable at the same time. The decor is minimalist, with matt blacks and bold textiles. Look out for daily menus (one fish, one meat, one vegetarian) chalked up on the back wall. Daily 11am–10pm.

Gina Stoja 23 ⊕052 387 943; map p.147. Three kilometres west of the centre in the suburb of Stoja, this charming family-run place offers the standard Adriatic repertoire of shellfish, grilled white fish and breaded squid

– all of which is exceedingly well executed and reasonably priced to boot. Wooden ceiling beams and slightly distressed furniture create a relaxing semi-rustic atmosphere. Bus #1 from Giardini. Daily 11am–11pm.

Jupiter Castropola 42 ⓣ052 214 333; map p.143. Homely pizzeria halfway up Pula's central hill, with a comfortable wooden-bench interior and a small outdoor terrace. The food is dependable and represents good value for money, with regular pizzas weighing in at 35-45Kn, "jumbo" family-sized pies 80Kn. They also do the grilled-meat repertoire rather well. Mon–Fri 10am–11pm, Sat noon–11pm, Sun 1–11pm.

Kantina Flanatička 18 ⓣ052 214 054, ⓦkantina-pula.com; map p.143. Central lounge-bar-cum-restaurant just beyond the city market, set in a stylishly furnished stone-clad cellar. The menu sticks to the tried-and-tested grilled fish and steaks offering you'll find elsewhere, but quality and presentation are a cut above the average. Big salads and meatless pasta dishes provide vegetarians with something to get their teeth into. Coffee, toasted sandwiches and cakes are on offer in the upstairs café-bar. Mon–Sat 7am–11pm.

3

Milan Stoja 4 ⓣ052 300 200, ⓦmilan1967.hr; map p.147. A family-run restaurant in a modern suburban pavilion just opposite the Naval Cemetery, offering good seafood (especially the shellfish) and high-class service at above-average prices. The three-course or five-course tasting menus (350–550Kn), each served with appropriate wine for each course, are worth splashing out on. Steaks and baked-fish mains come in at around 140–150Kn. The cake trolley is well worth waiting for. Bus #1 from Giardini. Daily 11am–11pm.

Scaletta Flavijevska 26 ⓣ052 541 599, ⓦhotel-scaletta.com; map p.143. A swish, expensive, intimate place attached to the hotel of the same name (see p.149), with top-quality seafood and meat dishes – try the sea bass in saffron sauce, or the steak with asparagus (both 90Kn). Daily noon–2.30pm & 6–11pm.

CAFÉS AND BARS

Bass Širolina 3, Veruda ⓣ052 211 993, ⓦbass.hr; map p.147. Animated night-time drinking haunt in a warren of cosy chambers, their walls decorated with characters from the *Alan Ford* comic strip. There's a large, partly covered, conservatory-style terrace, and a cubbyhole with internet terminals. Daily 8am–midnight.

Cabahia Širolina 4, Veruda; map p.147. Large café-bar with a cute and homely bar area and a huge covered terrace that looks a bit like a wild-west saloon crossed with a stable. It's on the same street as *Bass* (see above) and just round the corner from *Podroom* (see opposite), making it an essential stop-off on any Veruda bar crawl. Daily 8am–midnight.

Café Galerija Cvajner Forum 2 ⓣ052 216 502, ⓦcvajner.com; map p.143. The prime people-watching venue on the main square, next to the tourist office. Comfy sofas and contemporary art exhibits dominate inside. Daily 8am–11pm.

Corso Giardini 3; map p.143. One of the better city-centre cafés if it's coffee, cakes and ice cream you're after. Lots of outdoor seating on the busy Giardini. Mon–Sat 7am–11pm.

E&D Verudela 22 ⓣ052 213 404, ⓦeanddlounge.com; map p.147. If this roomy place has a lounge-bar feel on the inside, then it's a garden bar on the outside, with clipped lawns, shrubs, a water feature and views towards the open sea. It's a perfect coffee-break venue if you happen to be on the Verudela peninsula in the daytime, and in the evening you can plough your way through the cocktail menu. Bus #2A to the end of the line. Daily 8am–2am.

Fiorin Jazz Café Via Sergia 24 ⓣ052 212 322; map p.143. Characterful café with snug benches overlooked by a jumble of reproduction posters and adverts, with some old radios and clocks perched on high shelves. Known for its good coffee and jazz theme – which explains both the background music and the choice of album covers hanging near the door. Daily 6am–9pm; opens later if there is a jazz gig.

Pietas Julia Riva 24 ⓣ091 181 1911; map p.143. This magnet for weekend hedonists is just west of the amphitheatre. Choose between the standing-room-only bar area, the open-plan pizza restaurant or the lounge-style terrace, from where you can gaze out towards a

PULA FILM FESTIVAL

Ever since 1953 the amphitheatre has hosted the **Pula Film Festival** (late July/early Aug; ⓦpulafilmfestival.hr), which traditionally premieres the year's crop of domestic feature films. Back in the days when the Yugoslav film industry produced several big-budget features a year, the Pula Film Festival was a major international glam-fest which attracted big-name stars – along with guest-of-honour President Tito, who revelled in the opportunity to be photographed next to actresses like Gina Lollobrigida, Elizabeth Taylor and Sophia Loren. Now that Croatia only produces a handful of (largely low-budget) films a year the festival has lost some of its former sheen, although the amphitheatre makes the perfect backdrop to what is still a great social occasion. The festival usually runs over two weeks, with an international programme of films (shown in the Kino Valli and open-air Kaštel cinema) preceding the Croatian programme in the amphitheatre itself.

typical Pula landscape of palm trees and shipyard cranes. Daily 8am–2am.

Podroom Budicinova 16 (cnr Tomasinijeva) ☎098 255 193; map p.147. Lounge around on designer banquettes in Pula's funkiest interior, or mingle with a fun-seeking crowd on the outdoor terrace. Handily situated round the corner from *Bass*. Thurs–Sat 9am–2am, Sun–Wed 9am–midnight.

Rock Café Scalierova 8 ☎052 210 975, ⓦmyspace.com/rockcaffepula; map p.143. A spacious place with a stage for live music, alcoves decorated with rock-star murals and a lot of fancy wood carving adorning the main bar and the wall panelling. Regular gigs feature predominantly local cover bands, when a broad cross-section of Pula youth crowd in. Daily 8am–midnight.

Scandal Express Ciscuttijeva 15; map p.143. Cosy, narrow and inviting, this is home from home to a mixed crew of students, artysomethings and local professionals. Mon–Fri 7am–midnight, Sat 7am–2pm & 6pm–midnight, Sun 6pm–midnight.

Uliks Trg Portarata 1 ☎052 219 158; map p.143. Right beside the Arch of the Sergians, *Uliks* is something of a Pula classic, comprising plush chairs and fitted benches in a space that's simply brimming with brass nautical instruments, naval swords and century-old sepia photos. It's located on the ground floor of a building where James Joyce once taught English, and there's a small and somewhat token display of Joyce memorabilia in a glass case opposite the bar – although the jumble of antique objects on display elsewhere in the café does more than enough to evoke the pre-World War I Pula that Joyce must have known. Mon–Sat 7am–10pm.

3

NIGHTLIFE AND ENTERTAINMENT

Pula's **amphitheatre** hosts large-scale opera and pop performances in the summer, often featuring major international stars – check the tourist office for schedule details.

CLUBS AND LIVE VENUES

Karlo Rojc Gajeva 3 ⓦrojcnet.pula.org; map p.147. A huge former barracks occupied by cultural organizations and NGOs, in which alternative gigs, theatre events and other cultural happenings occasionally take place. It's located just off Radićeva, a 10min walk south of the centre. Opening times vary according to event.

Uljanik Dobrilina 2 ☎098 285 969, ⓦclubuljanik.hr; map p.143. Long-standing club hosting DJ nights (anything from commercial techno to alternative rock) throughout the year, as well as live gigs on a big open-air terrace in summer – posters in town will provide an idea of what's on. 10pm till late (depending on event).

CINEMA

Kino Valli Giardini 1 ☎052 213 808, ⓦkinovalli.net. Traditional, non-multiplex cinema in the city centre screening a mix of Hollywood new releases and art films. The cinema café is a good place for a pre-show meet-up.

DIRECTORY

Banks and exchange Zagrebačka banka, M. Laginje 1 (Mon–Fri 7.30am–7pm, Sat 7.30am–noon), has an ATM outside. The exchange bureau on Giardini has longer opening hours (Mon–Sat 7am–8pm, Sun 8am–1pm).

Hospital Gradska Bolnica, Zagrebačka 30 ☎052 376 500.

Internet access Cyber Caffe, Flanatička 14; MMC Luka, Istarska 30.

Left luggage At the bus station on Trg 1 Istarske brigade (daily 5am–10.30pm).

Post office The main post office is at Danteov trg 4 (daily 8am–9pm), and there's a smaller branch just south of the amphitheatre at Istarska 7 (Mon–Sat 8am–3pm).

Pharmacy Ljekarna centar, Giardini 15 (24hr).

Police Trg republike 2 ☎92.

The west coast

Istria's **west coast** represents the peninsula at its most developed. In itself it's attractive enough, with fields of rich red soil and pinewoods sloping gently down to the sea, but a succession of purpose-built resorts has all but swallowed up the shoreline. Inland, the coastal strip fades imperceptibly into conifer-studded heathland and fields bounded by dry-stone walls and dotted with *kažuni*, the characteristic stone huts with conical roofs traditionally used by Istrian shepherds for shelter when overnighting with their flocks. **Rovinj** is Istria's best-preserved old Venetian port; farther north, beyond the picturesque hilltop village of **Vrsar** and the **Limski kanal**, spreads the large resort of **Poreč** – package-holiday-land writ large, although it does boast the peninsula's finest ecclesiastical attraction in the shape of the mosaic-filled Basilica of St Euphrasius.

The Brijuni islands

North of Pula lie the **Brijuni** (in Italian, Brioni), a small archipelago of fourteen islands that became famous as the private retreat of Tito before being accorded **national park** status and opened to tourists in 1983 – visitors are still only allowed on two of the islands, **Veli Brijun** – the biggest island and main tourist draw – and **Mali Brijun**, home to an Austrian fortress (see p.154), and travel here remains strictly controlled.

You can visit the Brijuni on an **organized day-trip** (4hr) – which involves a tour of Veli Brijun by tourist train followed by free time at the Veli Brijun hotel settlement – or book into one of the hotels themselves, in which case you'll have freedom to stroll around parts of the island unsupervised.

The obvious gateway to the islands is the small fishing village of **FAŽANA**, 8km northwest of Pula.

Veli Brijun

3

After a fifteen-minute crossing of the Brijuni channel, excursion craft from Fažana arrive at Kupelweiser's hotel complex on **Veli Brijun**'s eastern shore. From here a **miniature train** with an English-speaking guide heads north through the golf course (see p.154) towards a **safari park** at the northern tip of the island. This was originally stocked with beasts given to Tito as presents by world statesmen, and you can see zebras, antelopes and indigenous long-horned cattle (*boškarin*) from the Istrian interior.

THE PRESIDENTIAL PLAYGROUND

Although the islands were a popular rural retreat for wealthy Romans, the Brijunis' history as an offshore paradise really began in 1893, when they were bought by Austrian industrialist **Paul Kupelweiser**. Kupelweiser, whose aim was to turn the islands into a luxury resort patronized by the cream of Europe's aristocracy, brought in Nobel Prize-winning bacteriologist Robert Koch, who rid the Brijunis of malaria by pouring petroleum on the swamps. Smart hotels and villas were built on Veli Brijun, and the Mediterranean scrub was cleared to make way for landscaped parks. The Brijunis' heyday was in the period immediately before World War I: Archduke Franz Ferdinand and Kaiser Wilhelm II both stayed on the islands, and struggling English-language teacher James Joyce came here to celebrate his 23rd birthday on February 2, 1905.

Following World War I, the development of Brijuni as a golf- and polo-playing resort helped preserve the islands' reputation as a key venue for aristocratic fun and games. Running costs proved high however, and Kupelweiser's son Karl committed suicide here in 1930 when it became clear that this elite paradise would never turn a profit.

After World War II, **Tito** decided to make Veli Brijun one of his official bases, planting much of the island's subtropical vegetation and commissioning a residence (the White Villa, or "Bijela Vila") in which he was able to dazzle visiting heads of state with his hospitality. It was here that Tito, Nehru and Nasser signed the Brioni Declaration in 1956, which paved the way for the creation of the **Non-Aligned Movement**, which nowadays consists of 118 nations (but none of the republics of the former Yugoslavia). Far away from prying eyes, the islands were the perfect spot from which to conduct secret diplomacy – Yugoslav-sponsored terrorist Abu Nidal was a house guest in 1978.

Tito himself resided in an ultra-secluded villa on the islet of **Vanga**, just off the western coast of Veli Brijun. He contrived to spend as much time here as possible, conducting government business when not busy hunting in his private game reserve or pottering about in his gardens and orchards (tangerines from which were traditionally sent to children's homes throughout Yugoslavia as a New Year's gift). International stars attending the Pula Film Festival (see box, p.150) stayed here as Tito's personal guests, bestowing his regime with a veneer of showbiz glamour.

After Tito's death in 1980 the islands were retained as an official residence, and a decade later became the favoured summer destination of President Tuđman. Tuđman's rank ineptitude as a world statesman ensured that no foreign leader ever came to visit him here, and with successive presidents declining to make use of the islands, it looks like the Brijuni have lost their mythical status in Croatian politics.

The train continues along the western side of the island to the **White Villa** (see box opposite) and other official residences, including the **Villa Jadranka**, where guests have included Queen Elizabeth II and Gina Lollobrigida, and stops at the southwestern corner of the island to allow exploration of a ruined **Byzantine fortress**; the fortress's stark grey walls make a bleak contrast to the green paradise it was built to defend. The train then returns to the hotel complex via the scant remains of a first-century-BC **Roman villa** at Veriga bay.

At the end of the tour, day-trippers are free to explore an additional group of sights beside the hotel complex before returning to the mainland. Most prominent of these is a fifteenth-century **Gothic church**, restored by Kupelweiser prior to World War I and ceremonially reopened by ill-fated Archduke Franz Ferdinand.

Tito on Brijuni

Daily: May & Oct 8am–6pm; June & Sept 8am–7pm; July & Aug 8am–8pm; opens for excursion boats only at other times of year • Free with excursion ticket

Near to the Veli Brijuni hotel complex is an exhibition hall entitled **Tito on Brijuni** (Tito na Brijunima). It starts with a display of the animals given to Tito as presents and stuffed after their deaths, including four seven-week-old giraffes poisoned by salmonella soon after their arrival from Africa. Upstairs is a fascinating exhibition of photos documenting Tito's various personae: one moment a man of the people talking to Fažana fisherfolk; the next, a sharp-suited dandy sharing jokes with Elizabeth Taylor and Richard Burton, who played the part of Tito in the epic war film *Sutjeska* in 1970. Another photograph shows Tito taking Ho Chi Minh for a spin in a motorboat, both men sporting raffish panama hats – an experience which the Vietnamese leader appears to be enjoying somewhat less than the Marshal.

Across the lawn from the exhibition building, a large cage serves as the summer residence of one of Tito's favourite pets, **Koki the parrot**. Koki still likes to chirrup the banal phrases learnt from its erstwhile master, and it's strange to think that the voice of the Yugoslav leader still lives on via the beak of this snowy-feathered beast.

ARRIVAL AND DEPARTURE — THE BRIJUNI ISLANDS

By ferry There are about eight excursions daily from Fažana (accessible on bus #18 from Pula) from May to mid-Oct and one daily the rest of the year (Jan–March, Nov & Dec 125Kn; April, May & Oct 170Kn; June & Sept 200Kn; July & Aug 210Kn). Tickets are sold at the Brijuni National Park office (see below) on the Fažana quayside. These day-trips are frequently overbooked in summer, when it's a good idea to ring in advance. Excursions are also offered by travel agents in Rovinj and Poreč, but note that the trips to Brijuni offered by boats in Pula and Rovinj harbours usually sail around the islands and are unlikely to take you anywhere near the national park.

INFORMATION

Tourist office Riva 2, Fažana (May & Sept Mon–Fri 8am–3pm, June–Aug daily 8am–10pm; ☎ 052 383 727, ⓦ infofazana.hr). Provides local information, maps and brochures.

National Park office Riva bb, Fažana (June & Sept daily 8am–8pm, July & Aug daily 8am–10pm, Oct–April Mon–Sat 8am–3pm; ☎ 052 525 882, ⓦ www.brijuni.hr). The Brijuni National Park office sells tickets for day-trips to Veli Brijun, and can arrange transport to the hotels.

GETTING AROUND

If you are staying on the island, the best way to get around is to hire a **golf cart** (500Kn for 5hr) or **bicycle** (100Kn per day) from the sports centre just along from the *Neptun-Istra* hotel.

ACCOMMODATION AND EATING

FAŽANA

Stefani Trade at Župni trg 3, Fažana (mid-June to mid-Sept daily 8.30am–11pm; ☎ 052 521 910, ⓦ fazana-brijuni.com) rents out **apartments** (two-person studios from 375Kn, four-person apartments from 520Kn).

VELI BRIJUN

Brijuni National Park operate a couple of **hotels** and a

handful of luxury **apartments** on Veli Brijun. Food and drink is available from the **café-restaurants** of the hotels.

APARTMENTS

If you want a real taste of luxury then consider staying in one of the island's stylish historic **villas** (booked through the National Park office in Fažana), located in secluded coastal spots towards the southern end of Veli Brijun: there's the eight-person *Primorka* (15,000Kn per day), the four-person *Dubravka* (8000Kn per day), or the five-person *Lovorka* (10,300Kn per day). It's the *Lovorka* that has most in the way of an aristocratic pedigree, having served as the summer home of the polo-playing party animal that was the Duke of Spoleto between the two world wars.

HOTEL

Neptun-Istra ⓣ 052 525 807. A historic institution that has seen its fair share of interwar aristocracy, communist bigwigs and Pula-bound movie folk, the *Neptun-Istra* still has bags of atmosphere although it is not by any means a sleek or contemporary hotel. The frumpy but adequate rooms come with TV, minibar and bath, and the Brijuni setting is unique. **1530Kn**

ENTERTAINMENT

Theatre Ulysses Mali Brijun ⓦ ulysses.hr. Throughout July and Aug a former Austrian fortress on Mali Brijun becomes the home of Theatre Ulysses, which brings together the cream of Croatian acting talent to perform the classics on an open-air stage. Tickets are available from the National Park office in Fažana, from where a boat service ferries theatregoers to and from the stage.

3

SPORTS

Golf ⓣ 052 525 883 or enquire at *Neptun-Istra* hotel. There's a 22-hole golf course just north of the hotels, designed along ecological lines in order to reduce the amount of watering and pesticides required for its upkeep. The fairways are nibbled by deer rather than mown, and the greens are made from compacted sand. You can rent golf gear and pay green fees at the sports centre.

Vodnjan

Eleven kilometres north of Pula lies the historic town of **VODNJAN** (Dignano), its warren of weather-beaten alleys gathered tightly around a main square.

St Blaise's Church

June–Sept Mon–Sat 9am–7pm & Sun 2–7pm; Oct–May open only when the priest is around • 35Kn, 38Kn including the Collection of Sacral Art

Sporting the highest campanile in Istria, the eighteenth-century **St Blaise's Church** (Crkva svetog Blaža) is famous for housing the **Vodnjan mummies** – the desiccated bodies of various saints. Kept behind a burgundy-coloured curtain to the rear of the main altar, the mummies originally belonged to the Church of San Lorenzo in Venice, and were brought to Vodnjan in 1818 after the monastic order that originally looked after them had been dissolved. Three complete and well-preserved bodies are laid out in glass cases, with a range of smaller relics in a series of containers above – one of which holds a twisted brown form reputed to be the torso and arm of St Sebastian. The most revered of the bodies is that of Leon Bembo the Blessed, a twelfth-century Venetian cleric and diplomat who gave up worldly pleasures for the monastic life, developing a reputation as a faith healer and sage. Beside him lie St Nikoloza of Koper (with a still-fresh-looking garland of flowers round her head) and St Ivan Olini of Venice, both renowned medieval healers – popular belief maintains that there's a link between the saints' healing powers and the subsequent failure of their bodies to decompose.

Collection of Sacral Art

June–Sept Mon–Sat 9am–7pm, Sun 2–7pm; Oct–May open only when the priest is around • 10Kn, 38Kn with the mummies

The **Collection of Sacral Art** (Zbirka sakralne umjetnosti) in the sacristy of St Blaise's Church has innumerable smaller relics, including one glass jar that is claimed to contain the lower jaw and tongue of St Mary of Egypt, a sixth-century Alexandrian courtesan who converted to Christianity and thereafter opted for a life of asceticism in the desert. The star exhibit is Paolo Veneziano's early fourteenth-century polyptych of St Bembo the Blessed, with scenes showing Bembo exercising his healing powers, and pilgrims paying homage to Bembo's miraculously preserved body.

ARRIVAL AND INFORMATION — VODNJAN

By bus Pula–Vodnjan services #22 and #41, as well as inter-city buses from Pula to Pazin, Rovinj and Poreč, pick up and drop off on the western edge of town, a short walk from the main square, Narodni trg.

Tourist office Narodni trg 3 (May–Sept daily 8am–noon & 5–8pm; Oct–April Mon–Fri 8am–3pm, ⓣ 052 511 700, ⓦ vodnjandignano.com).

EATING

Vodnjanka Istarska 22 ⓣ 052 511 435. This restaurant on the edge of town on the main Pula–Pazin road has an interior that looks like a cross between a nineteenth-century barn and a kooky art gallery. It serves up some of the best in local cuisine, including spicy Istrian sausages and divine pasta dishes. **Feb–May & Oct–Dec Mon–Sat 11am–11pm; June–Sept daily 11am–midnight; closed Jan.**

Bale

BALE (Valle), 10km north of Vodnjan, occupies a hilltop site typical of the peninsula, with houses built in a defensive circle. Unlike some of the depopulated hill towns inland, it's a lively little community with an equal mix of Croats and Italians.

Soardo-Bembo Palace and around

The most arresting edifice in Bale is the **Soardo-Bembo Palace** (Palača Soardo-Bembo), a fifteenth-century Venetian Gothic building with an elegant balcony built into its towered facade. It's currently being restored and will probably house a local history museum at some point in the future.

Beside the palace, an arch topped by a Venetian lion leads into the **old town**, which amounts to little more than a circular alleyway lined with rough stone buildings.

St Elizabeth's Church

Lapidarium mid-June to mid-Sept daily 9am–1pm & 5–8pm; 10Kn

St Elizabeth's Church (Crkva svete Elizabete) is a largely neo-Baroque building that preserves a Romanesque campanile and fragments from earlier sixth- and eighth-century churches in the crypt. It also houses a **lapidarium** in the basement (entrance round the back), with a small collection of ancient stones found in churches around Bale.

Bale Sports Hall

Domenico Cernecca 3

Tucked away behind the blue facade of an old village school just off Bale's main T-junction is an enigmatic slate-grey building that looks like a cross between an ancient barn and something dreamt up by Le Corbusier. It is in fact Bale's new **sports hall**, a building that takes its cue from Istria's traditional dry-stone construction techniques and which has won awards (including first prize for sports buildings in the Barcelona World Festival of Architecture 2009) for its Zagreb-based architects 3LHD.

ARRIVAL AND INFORMATION — BALE

By bus Pula–Rovinj buses stop just below the entrance to the old town.

Tourist office Rovinjska 1 (mid-June to Aug daily 8am–2pm & 3–9pm; ⓣ 052 824 391, ⓦ bale-valle.hr).

ACCOMMODATION AND EATING

A limited number of private **rooms** (doubles from 250Kn) are available from **Amfora**, La Musa 3 (ⓣ 052 841 773, ⓦ amfora-turist.hr), although they disappear fast in summer.

★ **Kamene Priče** Kaštel 57 ⊕052 824 235, mobile 091 525 3383, ⊛kameneprice.com. Four two- to three-person studio apartments in a medieval stone house just above the Soardo-Bembo Palace – you'll need to reserve well in advance. Wonderful fresh food is served in their ground-floor *konoba*, and they also organize the Minute Jazz Festival in late July/early Aug, which features five days of top-quality performance in an intimate atmosphere. Mid-April to mid-Oct. Studios from **450Kn**

Rovinj

Delicately poised between medieval port and upmarket tourist resort, **ROVINJ** (Rovigno) has managed to preserve its character better than anywhere else along the Istrian coast. Spacious Venetian-style houses and elegant piazzas lend an overridingly Italian air to the town, and the harbour is a likeable mix of fishing boats and swanky yachts. Rovinj is also the most Italian town on this coast: there's an Italian high school, the language is widely spoken, and street signs are bilingual.

3

Rovinj's urban core is situated on what was formerly an island. The strait separating it from the coast was filled in during the mid-eighteenth century, after which the town expanded onto the mainland, until then the site of a separate settlement of Croat farmers. Initially, the urban Italian culture of Rovigno assimilated that of the mainland Slavs, until industrial development in the late nineteenth century encouraged a wave of economic migrants, tipping the demographic scales in the Croats' favour. Playing a leading role in this was the Rovinj **tobacco factory**, founded in 1872 – the firm still produces the bulk of Croatia's cigarettes, although production was moved inland to Kanfanar in 2007. The demon weed remains a driving force in the local economy, with the tobacco factory investing heavily in Rovinj's tourist industry.

Rovinj's other claim to fame is the **artists** who have gravitated here since the 1950s and whose studios fill the streets of the Old Town. On the second Sunday of August the main street, Grisia, is taken over by an open-air display in which anyone can take part, providing they register their works at the town museum on the morning of the show.

The Old Town

Rovinj's most famous street is **Grisia**, the narrow pedestrianized alleyway that passes through a cute Baroque archway before climbing steeply through the heart of the **Old Town**. It's here that Rovinj's most atmospheric streets can be found – narrow, cobbled alleyways packed with craft shops and galleries, overlooked by the thin, thrusting **chimneys** that have become something of a Rovinj trademark. Traditionally, pressure on housing forced married sons to set up home in a spare room of their parents' house, and before long every house in town accommodated several families, each with its own hearth and chimney.

St Euphemia's Church

May–Sept daily 10am–6.30pm; Oct–April open for mass only

Presiding over the summit of Rovinj's peninsula is the eighteenth-century **St Euphemia's Church** (Crkva svete Eufemije), whose 58-metre-high tower – said to be modelled on that of St Mark's in Venice – dominates Rovinj from the top of its stumpy peninsula. Topping the tower is a statue of St Euphemia, a Christian from Chalcedon in Asia Minor who was martyred during the reign of Diocletian – she was supposedly thrown to the lions in the Constantinople hippodrome after having survived various other tortures, symbolized by the wheel which leans against her flanks. The church itself is a roomy three-aisled basilica with a Baroque altarpiece at the end of each aisle. The altar of St Euphemia is the one furthest to the right, behind which is a small sanctuary containing Euphemia's sixth-century sarcophagus. A bare stone box, it was brought to Rovinj in 800 AD to keep it safe from the Iconoclasts, who were in the process of smashing up all the relics they could find in Constantinople.

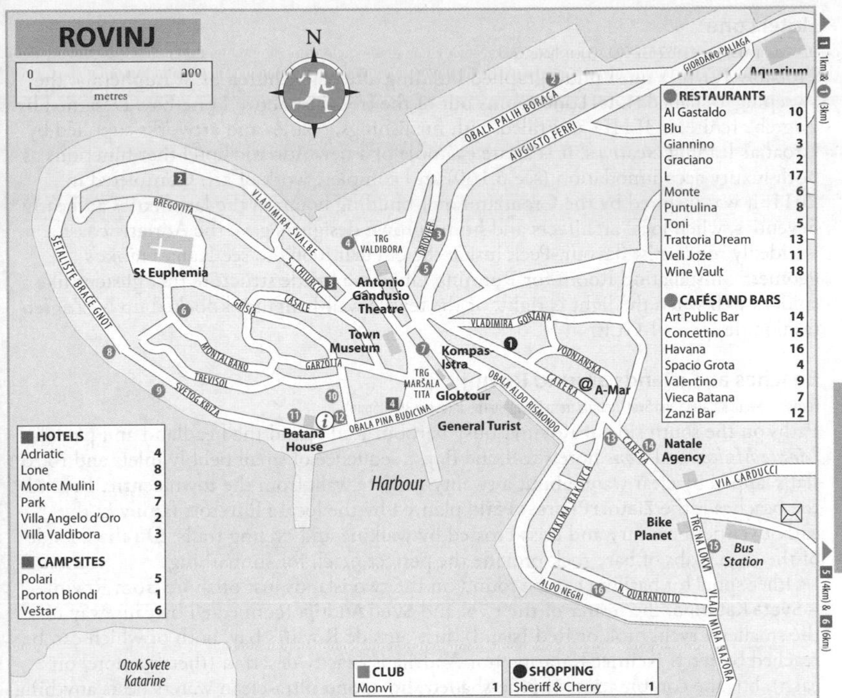

Town Museum

Trg maršala Tita 11 • June–Sept Tues–Fri 10am–2pm & 6–10pm, Sat & Sun 10am–2pm & 7–10pm; Oct–May Tues–Sat 10am–1pm • 15Kn • muzej-rovinj.hr

The **Town Museum** (Zavičajni muzej Rovinj) has archeological oddments, model ships and antique furniture, although it's the wide-ranging art collection that stands out. Highlight among the numerous Madonna and Childs is Leandro Bassano's vibrant *Madonna with Child, St John and the Angels* (early seventeenth century), while an anonymous Venetian *Toilet of Venus* features the kind of peach-like buttocks that you may find difficult to tear yourself away from. Contemporary artists get a look in too, with an annually changing display of those who have stayed and worked in the town.

The Batana House

Obala Pina Budicina 2 • Jan & Feb by appointment; March–May & Oct–Dec Tues–Sun 10am–1pm & 3–5pm; June–Sept daily 10am–3pm & 6–10pm • 10Kn • 052 812 593, batana.org

On the southern side of the peninsula, **Batana House** (Kuća o batani) honours the tiny, flat-bottomed fishing boats in which Rovinj fishermen used to ply their trade. Featuring old photographs, videos and artfully arranged fishing tackle, it's a visually arresting display.

Aquarium

Giordano Paliaga 5 • Daily: April, May & Oct 10am–4pm; June–Sept 9am–8pm • 40Kn • 052 804 712

Dominating the waterfront on the northern side of Rovinj is the Marine Biological Institute, home to an **aquarium** dating back to 1891 – it's one of the oldest in Europe – and featuring tanks of Adriatic marine life and flora.

Hotel Lone

Luje Adamovića 31 • ⓣ 052 632 000, ⓦ lonehotel.com

Probably Rovinj's most photographed building after the Church of St Euphemia, the sweeping Y-shaped **Hotel Lone** looms out of the trees just above Lone Bay. Designed by Zagreb architects 3LHD and filled with furnishings, textiles and artworks supplied by Croatia's leading creatives, it is a rare example of a new Adriatic hotel that functions as both luxury accommodation (see p.160) and complete work of art. Completed in 2011, it was inspired by the Croatian hotel-building boom of the late Sixties and early Seventies, when local architects and home-grown designers gave the Adriatic coast a decidedly modernist flavour. Peek inside the circular lobby to see Ivana Franke's geometric installation Room for Running Ghosts, a brittle structure that glistens like a spider's web when the light is right, or the textile wall-hangings knocked up by Zagreb fashion designers I-GLE.

Beaches and islands around Rovinj

3

Ferries to Sveta Katarina and Sveti Andrija from Rovinj harbour (every 30–45min)

Paths on the south side of Rovinj's busy harbour lead round the headland and past the *Monte Mulini* and *Lone* hotels to Lone Bay, a sequence of small pebbly inlets and rocky slabs lapped by clear water about a twenty-minute walk from the town centre. Behind the beaches is the **Zlatni rt Forest Park**, planted by the local Hütterott family in the early twentieth century and criss-crossed by walking and cycling trails. On the far side of the cape, slabs of bare rock provide the perfect perch for sunbathing.

Other spots for bathing can be found on the two islands just offshore from Rovinj – **Sveta Katarina**, the nearer of the two, and **Sveti Andrija** (connected by causeway to the smaller Crveni otok or Red Island), just outside Rovinj's bay, both of which can be reached by ferry. Neither Katarina nor Andrija is exactly deserted (there's a hotel on each), but the combination of pine-shaded shores and ultra-clean waters beats anything else the coast around Rovinj has to offer.

ARRIVAL AND DEPARTURE — ROVINJ

By bus Rovinj's bus station is set back from the seafront, a 5min walk from the Old Town.

Destinations Bale (Mon–Fri 16 daily, Sat & Sun 10 daily; 15min); Buje (2 daily; 1hr 30min); Buzet (1 daily; 2hr 15min); Dubrovnik (1 daily; 16hr); Kanfanar (Mon–Fri 8 daily, Sat & Sun 3 daily; 20min); Labin (5 daily; 2hr); Novigrad (3 daily; 1hr 30min); Pazin (Mon–Fri 5 daily, Sat 1 daily; 1hr); Poreč (Mon–Fri 7 daily, Sat & Sun 4 daily; 1hr); Pula (Mon–Fri 16 daily, Sat & Sun 10 daily; 1hr); Rijeka (6 daily; 2–3hr); Split (1 daily; 11hr); Vrsar (4 daily; 30min); Zagreb (7 daily; 4–7hr).

International destinations Koper (Mon–Sat 1 daily; 2hr 20min); Trieste (Mon–Sat 1 daily; 3hr); Venice (Mon–Sat 1 daily; 5hr).

By catamaran During high season, Venezia Lines run a weekly catamaran service from Rovinj to Trieste (mid-June to mid-Sept 1 per week; 2hr 15min) and Venice (April 1 per week, mid-May to mid-June 3 per week, mid-June to Aug 6 per week; 3hr 30min) from the harbour on the north side of the peninsula.

INFORMATION AND TOURS

Tourist office Obala Pina Budičina 12, just off Trg maršala Tita (mid-June to mid-Sept daily 8am–9pm; mid-Sept to mid-June Mon–Sat 8am–3pm; ⓣ 052 811 566, ⓦ tzgrovinj.hr). The tourist office should be able to provide a free city map and a map of biking trails around town, as well as an English-language information booklet.

Tours Kompas-Istra, Trg maršala Tita 5 (ⓣ 052 813 187, ⓦ kompas-istra.hr), and GeneralTurist, Trg maršala Tita 2 (ⓣ 052 811 402, ⓔ generalturist@generalturist.com), offer heaps of day-trips, including a fish picnic to the Limski kanal (4hr; 250Kn), an all-day excursion to Plitvice (500Kn) and a day-trip to Brijuni (300Kn).

Internet A-Mar, Via Carera 26 (May–Sept Mon–Sat 9am–7pm, Sun 10am–1pm; Oct–April Mon–Fri 9am–5pm).

GETTING AROUND

By bike Bikes and scooters can be rented from Bike Planet on Trg na Lokvi opposite the bus station (daily 8am–noon & 5–8pm; ⓣ 052 811 161) from 70Kn/240Kn/day respectively.

CLOCKWISE FROM TOP LEFT ST EUPHEMIA'S CHURCH (P.156); MARKET, TRG VALDIBORA (P.162); OPEN-AIR CAFÉ, ROVINJ >

ACCOMMODATION

There's a smattering of private **rooms** (doubles from 230Kn) and **apartments** (two-person studios from 385Kn, four-person apartments from 520Kn) in the Old Town, although most are in the more modern areas. They can be booked through numerous agencies (usually open daily 8am–10pm in July and Aug, but may take an afternoon break in the shoulder season); try **Natale**, opposite the bus station at Via Carducci 4 (Mon–Sat 7.30am–9.30pm, Sun 8am–5pm; T 052 813 365, W rovinj.com); or **Globtour**, at Obala A. Rismondo 2 (T 052 814 130, W globtour-turizam.hr). Some private-room hosts offer breakfast for an additional 30–40Kn per person – ask when making a booking. With so many well-appointed private rooms and apartments, Rovinj's mainstream **package hotels** are not worth the price unless you go upmarket – luckily, a number of places rise above the crowd.

HOTELS

Adriatic Obala Pina Budičina 2 T 052 803 510, W maistra.hr. Venerable establishment right on the harbour, offering en-suite rooms with a/c, phone and TV. Most are comfortable, although all are beginning to show their age and there are several poky rooms with backyard views. With only 27 rooms it has an intimate, almost genteel feel – so book very, very early. 1130Kn

3

Lone Luje Adamovića 31 T 052 632 000, W lonehotel.com. Opened in 2011 to a (for once fully deserved) fanfare of publicity, *Lone* is an art-and-design hotel that looks good, feels luxurious and delivers quality on every level without ever being over the top. It has a spa centre, indoor pool, café-bars and three restaurants (one of which, *L*, is a gourmet destination in its own right; see opposite). And it's within walking distance of both the beaches and the town centre, so it never feels like a self-contained resort. 2120Kn

Monte Mulini A. Smareglia T 052 636 000, W montemulinihotel.com. Right next to the *Lone*, but in totally different style, *Monte Mulini* looks like a pile of interlocking glass and concrete boxes. Rooms are smart and comfortable. The basement spa centre is decked out in ultra-camp style (half the things in it are painted gold or silver), although guests can use the more relaxingly chocolatey spa centre of the *Lone* if they wish. Art-spotters should note that the *Monte Mulini*'s *Mediterraneo* restaurant is decorated with dauby paintings by Boris Bućan; the *Wine Vault* (see opposite) goes for a more rustic approach. 3150Kn

Park Ronjgova T 052 808 000, W maistra.hr. This is a prim and proper three-star in a fairly uninspiring building 10min walk south of the town centre. However, the north-facing rooms offer the best views in Rovinj, with the Old Town and its church filling the horizon. 1460Kn

Villa Angelo d'Oro Vladimira Švalbe 38–42 T 052 840 502, W rovinj.at. Superbly restored town house on the north side of the peninsula. The luxurious rooms are decorated with antique furnishings, and there's a charming rooftop terrace, a sauna and a solarium. Open April–Sept. 1690Kn

Villa Valdibora S. Chiurco 8 T 052 845 040, W valdibora.com. Luxury apartments in a seventeenth-century stone house, with repro furniture and beautiful fabrics. Two-person apartments 1875Kn, four-person apartments 2600Kn

CAMPSITES

Polari Polari bb T 052 801 501, W campingrovinjvrsar.com. Spacious campsite with its own beach, shops, swimming pool and a section reserved for naturists, 4km south of town. 72Kn per person, pitches from 130Kn

Porton Biondi Aleja Porton Biondi 1 T 052 813 557, W portonbiondi.hr. Nearest site to central Rovinj, occupying a roomy, pine-shaded location right by the sea 1km north of town. 42Kn per person, tent and vehicle 76Kn

Veštar Veštar bb T 052 803 700, W campingrovinjvrsar.com. Big, well-appointed site in its own secluded bay 6km south of Rovinj. 75Kn per person, pitches from 150Kn

EATING AND DRINKING

There are more seafood **restaurants** in Rovinj than you can shake a stick at, some of which have an Istria-wide reputation for good food. Many of the harbourfront establishments however are bland, overtouristed and worth avoiding, although one or two of them have inexpensive fish specials chalked up on boards outside, and you can munch your way through serviceable pizzas almost everywhere. The open-air **market** on Trg Valdibora is a great place to pick up fresh fruit and vegetables. Rovinj's harbour area is full of places where you can enjoy a daytime coffee and ice cream. In the evening, head for the knot of convivial **bars** on and around Joakima Rakovca, just behind the seafront, where stools and tables are stuffed into narrow pedestrian alleyways.

RESTAURANTS

Al Gastaldo Iza kasarne 14 T 052 814 109. A smart but cosy establishment decked out in domestic knick-knacks, with outside tables crammed into a narrow alleyway festooned with potted plants. A good place for seafood pastas (100kn) and fresh-fish mains (140–150Kn). No credit cards. Daily 11am–3pm & 6–11pm.

★ **Blu** Val di Lesso 9 T 052 811 265, W blu.hr. Shoreside restaurant 3km north of town that gets top marks from the local food critics for its mixture of haute cuisine and Istrian tradition. The menu changes according to what is seasonally available, but expect exquisite seafood to play a major role. As much care goes into the desserts as the main courses, and there's a wide-ranging wine list too. Mains 200Kn and up. Daily 10am–midnight; closed Nov–Feb.

★ **Giannino** A. Ferri 38 ⊕ 052 813 402. One of the best places in town for lobster, grilled shellfish and fish, although there's plenty in the pasta line if you're looking for a cheaper, lighter meal. The quirky-but-chic interior is filled with paintings and ceramics, while outdoors there are tables scattered across a cobbled street sheltered from breezes. Grilled fresh fish will set you back 120–150Kn per portion, although you can get a pan-fried fillet for around 80Kn. Mon 6–10pm, Tues–Sun 11am–3pm & 6–11pm; closed mid-Nov to Feb.

★ **Graciano** Obala palih boraca 4 ⊕ 052 811 515, ⊕ graciano.hr. Popular quayside pavilion which combines high standards with bearable prices – a pan-fried fillet of fish will set you back 70–80Kn, while the fish platter for two weighs in at 200Kn. The partially covered rooftop terrace is particularly good for watching sunsets. Daily 11am–3.30pm & 6–11pm.

★ **L** Hotel Lone, Luje Adamovića 31 ⊕ 052 632 000, ⊕ lonehotel.com. Classiest of the *Lone* hotel's three restaurants, located on the lowest, seaside-facing level of the building and decked out in sombre designer tones – eating on the park-side outdoor terrace is more fun than sitting inside. Pretty much everything on the menu is an exercise in fusion of one sort or another – mixing seafood with central European flavours, or Mediterranean ingredients with Far Eastern spices – all beautifully prepared and presented. Daily 10am–midnight.

★ **Monte** Montalbano 75 ⊕ 052 830 203, ⊕ monte .hr. Right below St Euphemia's Church, this is a fine restaurant that blends nouvelle cuisine with local seafood. It's a good place to splash out on shellfish and lobster, and there is an extensive wine list. The excellent baked fish with potatoes (for two) weighs in at 400kn. Daily noon–2.30pm & 7–11.30pm; closed Nov–Feb.

Puntulina Sv. Križa 38 ⊕ 052 813 186. Shore-hugging restaurant with a colourful interior and a menu concentrating almost exclusively on quality seafood – with the odd pasta-with-truffles dish thrown in. You can also perch on steps above the shore and order a glass of wine or a cocktail. Daily except Wed 11am–2pm & 6–11pm.

Toni Driovier 3 ⊕ 052 815 303. Cosy place with a growing gastronomic reputation, located down a narrow side-street with tables crammed into a homely dining room. Good for shellfish served with freshly made pasta, and a knockout squid stew (*brudet od sipe*). Prices are moderate. Daily except Wed noon–3pm & 6–10.30pm.

Trattoria Dream Joakima Rakovca 18 ⊕ 052 830 613, ⊕ dream.hr. If you tire of grilled fish and seafood then *Dream* might be just the ticket, with an international menu of meaty mains, moderately priced pastas, risottos, healthy salads and a range of desserts that go beyond the usual pancake and ice cream fare. Mains 75–100Kn. Daily noon–10pm.

Veli Jože Sv. Križa 1 ⊕ 052 816 337, ⊕ velijoze.net. The over-designed interior looks like a nautical junk shop, but the food is solid, with excellent fish dishes, steaks and pasta. Main courses are in the 100–150Kn range. Daily 11am–midnight; closed Jan & Feb.

★ **Wine Vault** Hotel Monte Mulino, A. Smareglie bb ⊕ 052 636 017, ⊕ montemulinihotel.com. Headed up by leading chef Tomislav Gretić, the *Wine Vault* provides Adriatic seafood with French finesse, backed up by a head-spinning selection of quality Istrian wines. The menu changes seasonally and is limited to a handful of well-chosen mains (with a couple of seafood choices jostling for attention alongside lamb and fowl). As for the desserts: if death by chocolate mousse was ever your chosen way to end it all, the *Wine Vault* would be the perfect place to plan your exit. Mains 110–190Kn. Daily 10am–midnight.

3

CAFÉS AND BARS

Art Public Bar Carera 88. Head through the passageway and into the back yard to locate this dark and welcoming Irish-themed drinking den, catering for a mixed bag of youngsters downing shots and older drinkers enjoying draught Guinness and Kilkenny. There's a small outdoor terrace, and live music on Thurs. Daily 11am–midnight.

Concettino Na Lokvi 7 ⊕ 052 434 668, ⊕ concettino.hr. Right by the bus station, this neat and tidy bakery-cum-café offers freshly baked loaves, free wi-fi and a big choice of nibbles, from breakfast pastries to sandwiches, pizza slices, fruit tarts and chocolate cheesecake. Try the apricot *crostata* (11Kn). *Concettino* takes orders too, should you need a festive cake in a hurry. Daily 7am–10pm.

Havana Aldo Negri bb. Sea-facing terrace with giant straw parasols, comfy bamboo chairs, pricey designer cocktails and Cuban cigars for sale. Daily noon–1am.

Spacio Grota Trg Valdibora. Standing-room-only bar,

ROVINJ FESTIVALS

Key annual events include the **Avantgarde Jazz Festival**, a season of international jazz concerts that takes place in spaces throughout the town from late May to late July (⊕ avantgardejazzfestival.com); and **Rovinj Photo Days**, Croatia's biggest photography event featuring exhibitions and workshops in June (⊕ photodays-rovinj.com).

right by the market, serving local wine from the barrel (a glass of the house red will set you back 6Kn), and selling good-quality bottles of Malvazija from Istrian vineyards for 75-160Kn. Daily 7am–6pm.

Valentino Sv. Križa ⓣ 052 830 683, ⓦ valentino-rovinj.com. Rather pretentious wine and cocktail place which nevertheless benefits from its unique position, with cushioned seating right on the rocks. Daily 6pm–2am.

Viecia Batana Trg maršala Tita. Roomy town-centre café patronized by locals and tourists alike, serving reliably strong coffee and a solid choice of cakes. Daily 7am–1am.

Zanzi Bar Sv. Križa ⓣ 052 813 206. A loggia filled with comfy zebra-print sofas, this place is good for daytime coffee, even better for night-time cocktails and lounge-bar ambience. Daily 8am–1am.

NIGHTLIFE AND ENTERTAINMENT

CLUB

Monvi Luja Adamovića bb ⓣ 052 545 117, ⓦ monvicenter.com. Located up behind the *Lone* and *Monte Mulini* hotels, *Monvi* features numerous bar areas decorated in different styles and a dance floor that draws both big-name international DJs and live Croatian pop-rock acts. Late May to early Oct 11pm–5am.

THEATRE

Antonio Gandusio Theatre Trg Valdibora ⓣ 052 811 588. The pre-World War I theatre retains many of its original furnishings and is a great place to catch contemporary films as well as alternative rock and jazz gigs.

3

SHOPPING

Rovinj's colourful daily **market** is a good place to buy fruit, veg and fresh fish; although the honey, olive oil and wine sold at the touristy stalls towards the back of the market is of dubious origin and quality.

Sheriff & Cherry Carera 6 ⓣ 052 842 310. Cutting-edge fashion and accessories from the Rovinj-based Sheriff & Cherry label and other Croatian independent designers. May–Sept Mon–Fri 10am–1pm & 4.30–7pm, Sat 10am–1pm; Oct–April Mon–Fri 9am–5pm.

The Limski kanal

North of Rovinj, the main coastal route detours inland around the **Limski kanal**, a turquoise fjord – or more accurately a ria – lined with thick woods rising sheer on either side, which cuts a deep green wedge into the Istrian mainland. In Roman times this marked the boundary between the Poreč and Pula regions – "Lim" is derived from *limes*, a Latin word meaning "border" or "limit" – but it later became a favourite shelter of pirates, who used it as a base from which to attack the Venetians. An appealing local legend associates the *kanal* with pirate and adventurer **Captain Morgan**, who liked it so much he decided to settle down here with his crew, founding the village of **Mrgani** (which still exists 5km inland from the *kanal*) in the process.

Mussels and oysters are cultivated here, and can be sampled along with other fresh fish, in the heavily touristed *Viking* and *Fjord* restaurants.

Vrsar and around

Occupying high ground near the mouth of the Limski kanal is **VRSAR**, a picturesque hilltop village curled tightly around a campanile-topped summit. It's a beautifully preserved, tranquil place, a labyrinth of steep narrow alleyways, leafy patios and blue-shuttered stone houses. Giacomo Casanova visited twice in the late eighteenth century, mentioning the place fondly in his memoirs, and relatively little has changed since then.

Church of St Martin

Campanile: June–Sept daily 8.30am–7pm; 10Kn

Crowning the hill is the nineteenth-century **Church of St Martin** (Crkva svetog Martina) with its recently added **campanile**, offering a wonderful panorama of the coast from its summit.

Dušan Džamonja Sculpture Park

Tues–Sun 9–11am & 6–9pm • Free • ⓦ dusan-dzamonja.com

Twenty minutes' walk north of town, along the main road to Poreč, the grassy **Dušan Džamonja Sculpture Park** (Park skulptura) honours one of Croatia's greatest postwar artists with an extensive open-air display, right next to the villa where the artist spent his summers. Džamonja (1928–2009) was an unabashed modernist, and the shiny aluminium eggs and enigmatic lumps of browned steel on display here will appeal to anyone whose tastes tend towards the abstract.

Koversada

A kilometre south of town on the coast is one of the world's largest naturist colonies, **Koversada.** Established in 1960, this was the first of the Adriatic's naturist communities, and is nowadays a self-contained mini-city where up to fifteen thousand residents can dress as nature intended on a 24-hour basis.

ARRIVAL AND INFORMATION — VRSAR AND AROUND

By bus Buses from Poreč stop at the bottom of central Vrsar's hill, a short walk from the marina.

By car Take the side road that leaves the Rovinj–Poreč route near the village of Kloštar to get down to the Vrsar and northern side of the inlet.

By boat Numerous excursions to the *kanal*, often including a fish picnic or a lunch stop en route, are advertised on the quaysides of Rovinj, Vrsar and Poreč; expect to pay around 250–300Kn for the trip.

Tourist office Rade Končara 56 (June–Sept daily 8am–6pm; ⓣ 052 441 187, ⓦ infovrsar.com). The small tourist office, uphill off the main square, provides local information.

EATING

Konoba Bare Kamenarija 4, Funtana ⓣ 052 445 193, ⓦ konoba-bare.hr. Just north of town on the road to Poreč, *Konoba Bare* serves risottos and pastas with Istrian ingredients such as truffles and asparagus, together with fish, lamb and veal baked *pod čripnjon* (under an ash-covered lid). Mon, Tues & Thurs 5–11pm, Fri, Sat & Sun 11am–11pm; closed Wed.

Trošt Obala maršala Tita 1a ⓣ 052 445 197, ⓦ restoran-trost.hr. Located on the second floor of the marina reception building, *Trošt* serves some of the best seafood in the region on a terrace with views over the marina. Excellent for shrimp, lobster and octopus. Daily 10am–midnight.

Poreč and around

How you react to **POREČ** (Parenzo) may well depend on what time of year you arrive. From May to late September, Istria's largest tourist resort can seem positively engulfed by mass-market tourism; outside this period it can be just as charming as any other well-kept former fishing port. Happily, Poreč's gargantuan hotel complexes are mainly concentrated in vast tourist settlements like **Plava Laguna** and **Zelena Laguna** to the south, and the town's labyrinthine core of stone houses – ice-cream parlours and tacky souvenir shops notwithstanding – remains relatively unspoiled. Main points in Poreč's favour are the Romanesque **Basilica of Euphrasius**, Istria's one must-see ecclesiastical attraction, and the town's transport links, which make it a convenient base from which to visit the rest of the Istrian peninsula.

The Basilica of Euphrasius

Eufrazijeva • Daily 7.30am–8pm • Free

Poreč's star turn is the **Basilica of Euphrasius** (Eufrazijeva basilika), situated in the centre of the town just off Eufrazijeva. Decorated with incandescent mosaics, this sixth-century Byzantine basilica created by Bishop Euphrasius around 535 is the central component of a complex that includes the bishop's palace, atrium, baptistry and campanile. Entry is through the **atrium**, an arcaded courtyard whose walls incorporate ancient bits of masonry, although it was heavily restored in the last century.

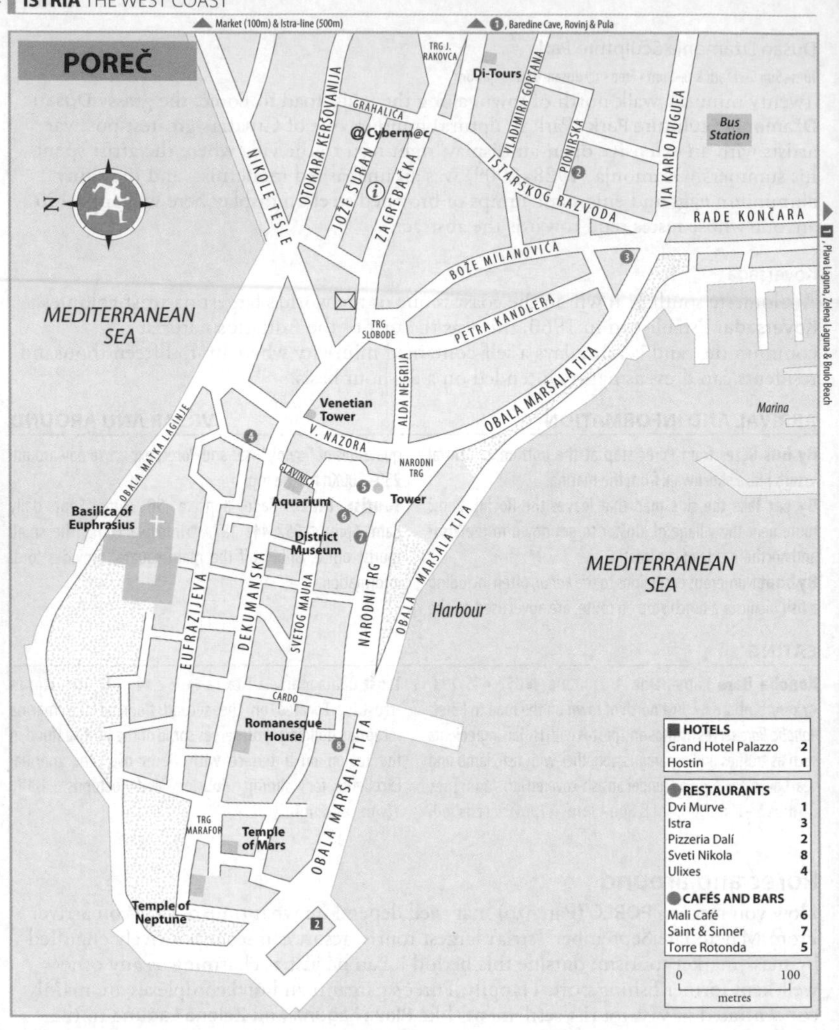

The basilica was the last in a series of late Roman and early Byzantine churches built on this spot, the remains of which are still in evidence. Surviving stonework from the first, the **Oratory of St Maur** (named after the saint who is said to have lived in a house on the site), can be seen on the north side of the basilica. This was a secret place of worship when Christianity was still an underground religion, and fragments of mosaic show the sign of the fish, a clandestine Christian symbol of the time. Inside the basilica, the mosaic floor of a later, less secretive church has been carefully revealed through gaps in the existing floor. The present-day basilica is a rather bare structure: everything focuses on the apse, with its superb, late thirteenth-century ciborium and, behind this, the **mosaics**, with Byzantine solemnity quite different from the geometric late Roman designs. They're studded with semiprecious gems, encrusted with mother-of-pearl and punctuated throughout by Euphrasius's personal monogram – he was, it's said, a notoriously vain man. The central part of the composition shows the Virgin enthroned with Child, flanked by St Maur, a worldly looking Euphrasius holding a model of his church and, next to him, his brother.

The baptistry and Bishops' Palace

Both daily 10am–7pm • 10Kn (same ticket)

On the opposite side of the atrium, the octagonal **baptistry** (baptisterijum) is bare inside save for the entrance to the campanile, which you can ascend for views of Poreč's red-brown roof tiles. On the north side of the atrium is the **Bishop's Palace**, a seventeenth-century building harbouring a fascinating selection of mosaic fragments that once adorned the basilica floor, and an exquisite collection of Gothic altarpieces and Baroque statuary.

Dekumanska

Once you've seen the basilica, the most interesting of Poreč's buildings are ranged along **Dekumanska**, the pedestrian-only street that runs through the centre of the old town. Just off its eastern end stands a **Venetian tower** from 1448, now used as a venue for art exhibitions, while towards the western end the so-called **Romanesque House** (Romanička kuća) is a distinctive thirteenth-century building with an unusual projecting wooden balcony. Just beyond here, **Trg Marafor** occupies the site of the Roman forum and contains the scant remains of **temples** to Mars and Neptune.

3

Aquarium Poreč

Glavinića 4 • Daily: May & Oct 10am–8pm; June–Sept 9am–10pm; Nov–April 10am–4pm • 40Kn • ⓦ istra360.com

Just off Dekumanska, **Aquarium Poreč** is billed as one of Istria's major attractions but is really rather modest, consisting of a short fish-tank-lined corridor leading to a gift shop. It's a colourful place nevertheless, and gives you a chance to study living examples of the creatures you might be eating later in the evening.

District Museum

Dekumanska 9 • May–Sept daily 9am–noon & 6–10pm; Oct–April Mon–Fri 10am–1pm • 10Kn • ⓣ 052 431 585, ⓦ muzejporec.hr

The **District Museum** (Zavičajni muzej) is housed in the handsome, Baroque Sinčić palace. A fine collection of Roman tombstones includes one relief of a patrician standing underneath an olive tree – Istrian olives were famed throughout Italy during antiquity. Upstairs, rooms are decorated with portraits of the family of Rinaldi Carli – Venetian ambassador to Constantinople in the late 1600s – dressed in Ottoman garb.

Poreč beaches

Boats to Sveti Nikola run every 15–30min; 30Kn

The **beaches** around the old town are generally crowded, and it's better to take a boat from the harbour to the island of **Sveti Nikola**, though this too gets busy with sunbathers from its pricey *Fortuna* hotel. Alternatively, staying on the mainland, walk south beyond the marina, where pathways head along a rocky coastline shaded by gnarled pines to reach several rocky coves; you'll eventually end up at **Zelena Laguna**, where there are concreted bathing areas.

The Baredine Cave

Daily: April & Oct 10.30am–3.30pm; May, June & Sept 10am–5pm; July & Aug 9.30am–6pm • 45Kn • ⓦ istra.com/baredine • No public transport

One of the most popular excursions from Poreč is to the **Baredine Cave** (Jama Baredine), a series of limestone caverns 7km northeast of town just off the road to Višnjan – it's well signed if you're driving. During a forty-minute tour, guides will lead you through five exquisite chambers of dangling stalactites and limestone curtains, and will also delight in telling you the legend of thirteenth-century lovers Gabriel and Milka, who got lost down here and died looking for each other. You'll also get to see a couple of captive specimens of the *Proteus anguineus*, a kind of salamander which is indigenous to the karst caves of Croatia and Slovenia, and looks like a pale-bodied worm with legs.

ARRIVAL AND DEPARTURE — POREČ

By bus Poreč's bus station is just north of the town centre, behind the marina, from where it's a 5min walk to the tourist office.

Destinations Buje (Mon–Sat 3 daily, Sun 2 daily; 1hr); Buzet (Mon–Fri 2 daily, Sat & Sun 1 daily; 1hr 30min); Lanterna (June–Sept; 5 daily; 30min); Novigrad (8 daily; 20min); Opatija (4 daily; 3hr 30min); Pazin (Mon–Fri 10 daily, Sat & Sun 3 daily; 45min); Pula (Mon–Fri 8 daily, Sat & Sun 6 minimum; 1hr 30min); Rijeka (12 daily; 2hr); Rovinj (Mon–Fri 7 daily, Sat & Sun 4 daily; 1hr); Vrsar (Mon–Fri 12 daily, Sat & Sun 6 daily; 15min); Zagreb (7 daily; 5hr); Zelena Laguna (9 daily; 15min).

International destinations Koper (1 daily; 2hr 30min); Ljubljana (2 daily; 3hr); Munich (2 per week; 10hr); Piran (1 daily; 2hr); Portorož (1 daily; 1hr 50min); Trieste (Mon–Fri 2 daily; 2hr).

By catamaran In the summer, Venezia Lines runs a weekly catamaran service from Poreč to Trieste (mid-June to mid-Sept 1 per week; 1hr 15min) and Venice (April 1 per week, May–June 3 per week, July & Aug 4 per week; 2hr 30min); tickets can be bought at most travel agencies.

INFORMATION

3

Tourist office Zagrebačka 8 (May–Oct daily 8am–10pm; Nov–April Mon–Fri 8am–3pm; ☎ 052 451 293, Ⓦ istria-porec.com). The tourist office should be able to give you a free map and brochures.

Internet You can surf the net at Cyberm@c, M. Grahalića 1 (Mon–Fri 10am–3.30pm & 4.30–6pm, Sat 10am–2pm).

GETTING AROUND

To Plava Laguna and Zelena Laguna The main tourist complexes can be reached by bus from the bus station (9 daily), by hourly ferry from the dock on the maršala Tita promenade or, in summer, by the tourist train (every 30min) which runs from outside the *Hostin* hotel, right by the city beach.

By bikes and scooter Bikes and scooters can be rented from any number of outlets along the seafront; try Contigo on Rade Končara 5, between the *Poreč* and *Hostin* hotels, where scooters go from 200Kn per day and bikes from 80Kn.

By boat Brulo Beach, a 15min walk along the coastal path beyond the *Hostin* hotel, is the place to rent pedal boats, rowing boats and canoes.

ACCOMMODATION

Several agencies in the streets just north of the tourist office offer **rooms** (from 250Kn) and **apartments** (two-person studios from 375Kn, three- and four-person apartments 580Kn), most of which are in the modern suburbs which fringe the old town; two of the best firms are **Di-Tours**, Prvomajska 2 (☎ 052 432 100, Ⓦ di-tours.hr), and **Istra-line**, Partizanska 4 (☎ 052 427 062, Ⓦ istraline.com). Stays of less than four nights are usually subject to a thirty percent surcharge. Poreč sports a quite amazing number of **hotels**, both in the town itself and in the surrounding tourist villages; most are overpriced identikit package hotels that you'd expect to find in a heavily touristed place like this.

HOTELS

Grand Hotel Palazzo Obala maršala Tita 24 ☎ 052 858 800, Ⓦ hotel-palazzo.hr. *Belle-époque* waterside hotel lovingly renovated, and (with the addition of a modern extension) now serving as a quality modern establishment with super-sleek furnishings and attention-to-detail service. **1500Kn**

Hostin Rade Končara 4 ☎ 052 408 800, Ⓦ hostin.hr. Comfortable three-star, right across from the city beach and surrounded by fragrant pine forest. The spacious en suites all have balconies (ask for a forest view, as some overlook a car park), a/c and TV. The outdoor terrace is a great place for a leisurely breakfast, and there's a swimming pool with jacuzzi, a sauna and a fitness centre. **980Kn**

EATING AND DRINKING

Despite the bland pizzerias spreading plague-like throughout central Poreč, there's still a sprinkling of decent places to **eat** in the old town. The **drinking** scene remains remarkably old fashioned, with a visit to one of the innumerable *slastičarnice* for ice cream and coffee providing the main source of after-dinner entertainment. There's less in the way of cafés and bars, and the town can appear disastrously dead by the end of August, when the high-spending peak-season crowd is replaced by visitors of more modest means.

RESTAURANTS

★ **Dvi Murve** Grožnjanska 17, Vranići ☎ 052 434 115, Ⓦ dvimurve.hr. Located 3km north of the old town (150Kn in a taxi), this is one of the most acclaimed restaurants on this stretch of the coast. Deliciously prepared, top-quality seafood is served on a spacious terrace; try the octopus carpaccio, squid ink-stained black spaghetti with scampi or fish in wine sauce, and for dessert their chocolate mousse is a must. Reservations essential. Daily noon–11.30pm; closed Jan.

Istra Bože Milanovića 30 ⓣ 052 434 636. Traditional Istrian fare including top-of-the-range seafood and meaty alternatives such as *svinjski but* (roast pork in a rich sauce). Look out for inexpensive lunchtime favourites such as *maneštra*. It's a good idea to reserve on summer weekends. Daily 10am–midnight.

Pizzeria Dalí Istarskog razvoda 11 ⓣ 052 452 666. Good-quality oven-baked pizza, salads and pasta dishes just off Zagrebačka. Daily 10am–midnight.

★ **Sveti Nikola** Obala maršala Tita 23 ⓣ 052 423 018, ⓦ svnikola.com. Award-winning seafood restaurant serving up superb risottos, excellent seafood pasta and fillets of Adriatic fish in a range of innovative sauces. The decor looks a bit straight-laced but the atmosphere is laid back and informal. Daily 11am–1am.

Ulixes Dekumanska 2 ⓣ 052 451 132. Good local food, either in a stone-clad interior stacked with rustic implements, or on an outdoor terrace in a walled garden. There are several imaginative variations on the usual fish and shellfish themes, and the service is welcoming and friendly. Daily noon–midnight.

CAFÉS AND BARS

Mali Café Narodni trg ⓣ 091 443 3222. Relaxing place near the seafront with comfy leather chairs and a good cross-section of local drinkers. Mon–Thurs 7am–midnight, Fri & Sat 7am–2am, Sun 9am–10pm.

Saint & Sinner Obala maršala Tita 12 ⓣ 099 221 1811, ⓦ saint-sinner.net. Minimalist black-and-white colour scheme and loungey furniture mark this out as something of a magnet for the young and trendy. A good place for coffee-sipping in the daytime; a DJ-driven party vibe takes over in the evenings. Daily 10am–4am.

Torre Rotonda Narodni trg 3A ⓣ 098 255 731, ⓦ torrerotonda.com. Housed in a medieval tower, this is an atmospheric spot with snug seating inside the tower wall and a panoramic terrace on top. Daily 10am–1am.

3

Novigrad

Reached by regular bus, **NOVIGRAD** (Cittanova), 18km north of Poreč, is a pleasant peninsula-bound place centred around a Venetian-style church, although it has lost most of its old buildings apart from a few toothy sections of town wall. Novigrad's privately run hotels have more character than the packagey accommodation in Poreč, and the atmosphere is more laid-back all round – this is one place on the west coast where you can safely wander the streets without being stampeded to death by herds of ice-cream-wielding promenaders.

For **bathing**, the stretch of rock-and-concrete beach on the south side of town is outshone by the wonderful stretch of coastline to the north, where the rocky reefs backed by woods are more attractive and less crowded.

Church of St Pelagius

Veliki trg

At the tip of the peninsula, the parish **Church of St Pelagius** (Crkva svetog Pelagija) was the seat of a bishop until the mid-nineteenth century, and still boasts a few luxuriant Baroque furnishings – notably the balustraded altar supporting a parade of porky cherubs. The crypt in which the bones of St Pelagius are kept is usually locked, but a grilled window provides glimpses of a vaulted eleventh-century ceiling supported by a cluster of stout columns.

Lapidarium

Veliki trg 8a • Daily: June–Sept 10am–1pm & 6–10pm; Oct–May 10am–1pm & 5–7pm • 10Kn • ⓣ 052 726 582, ⓦ muzej-lapidarium.hr

If there was a league table for outstanding small museums of the world, then Novigrad's **Lapidarium** would surely end up somewhere in the top ten. Designed by Rijeka-based architects Randić and Turato, the innovative structure consists of two black-box exhibition spaces enclosed within a glass pavilion. The exhibits feature some fabulous examples of stone carving taken from Novigrad's medieval churches, featuring not just the *plutej* (the plaited pattern for which the Croatian Romanesque is famous) but also floral patterns, rosettes and swooning cypresses. Note the animated gryphons adorning one stone tablet (no. 11 on the museum plan) and the relief of a peacock that has become the museum's visual calling card. Mugs, cards and well-designed stationery are on sale at the ticket desk.

Gallerion

Mlinska 1 • Tues–Sun 7–11pm • 20Kn • ⓦ kuk-marine-museum.com

The **Gallerion** celebrates Novigrad's maritime history with an entertaining display of nautical bric-a-brac and Habsburg-era naval uniforms. The collection's strongest point is the fantastic array of model ships, from eighteenth-century wind-powered frigates to the World War I dreadnoughts of the Austro-Hungarian navy.

ARRIVAL AND INFORMATION — NOVIGRAD

By bus Novigrad's bus station is 500m inland from the town centre.

Destinations Buje (3 daily; 45min); Buzet (2 daily; 2hr 15min); Poreč (7 daily; 30min); Pula (4 daily; 2hr 15min); Rijeka (4 daily; 4hr 30min); Rovinj (3 daily; 1hr 30min); Zagreb (4 daily; 5hr 30min).

International destinations Koper (1 daily; 2hr); Trieste (Mon–Fri 2 daily; 2hr).

Tourist office Porporella 1 (May to mid-June & mid-Sept to end Sept daily 8am–8pm; mid-June to mid-Sept daily 8am–9pm; Oct–April Mon–Sat 8am–3pm; ⓣ 052 757 075, ⓦ novigrad-cittanova.hr). The helpful tourist office is located at the entrance to the old town.

3

ACCOMMODATION

There are plenty of private **rooms** (180Kn) and **apartments** (two-person studios 400Kn, three- to four-person apartments 500–550Kn) in and around the centre: two accommodation agencies worth trying are **Festino**, in the bus station building (ⓣ 052 758 614, ⓦ festino.hr), and **Rakam**, between the bus station and the centre at Gradska Vrata 45 (ⓣ 052 757 047, ⓦ rakam-trade.hr).

HOTELS

Cittar Venecijanski prolaz bb ⓣ 052 757 737, ⓦ cittar.hr. Mid-sized hotel incorporating part of the old town wall in its facade, offering tastefully furnished rooms with wooden floors, TV, minibar, a/c and en-suite bath. **1020Kn**

Maestral Tere ⓣ 052 858 630, ⓦ laguna-novigrad.hr. A sweeping flying-V of concrete that accommodates hundreds of holidaymakers in summer, the *Maestral* is well worth considering out of season, when you have the seawater-fed pool, spa facilities and huge gym almost to yourself, and the whole place has the feel of a health retreat. Overall, facilities are four-star, although the Liliput-sized proportions of some of the rooms can be a bit of an issue. **1150Kn**

Santa Marija Gradska Vrata 37 ⓣ 052 757 444, ⓦ santa-marija.hr. Fifteen-room pension just outside of the old town, with neat modern rooms and a smart first-floor restaurant. **700Kn**

Torci 18 Torci 34 ⓣ 052 757 799, ⓦ torci18.hr. Old-town pension behind the sea wall, offering prim en-suite rooms with TV and a/c grouped around a central courtyard with a restaurant. **525Kn**

CAMPSITE

Sirena Tere ⓣ 052 858 690, ⓦ laguna-novigrad.hr. A big woodland campsite right by the beach, an easy walk along the shore southeast of town. **60Kn** per person, pitches from **55Kn**

EATING AND DRINKING

Novigrad is one of the best places to eat in western Istria, offering first-rate seafood and some interesting culinary combinations. Prices are on the high side, but are usually worth it.

čok Sv. Antuna 2 ⓣ 052 757 643. Family-run establishment just off the harbour offering traditional Adriatic seafood freshened up with tricks borrowed from French and other Mediterranean cuisines. It's a cosy place indoors, with six or seven tables set out in a living room-style space and well-chosen paintings crowding the walls. The service can sometimes seem a bit take-it-or-leave-it, but the food is generally excellent. Don't be surprised if you see hungry gourmet travellers nosing around outside at 5.55pm waiting for *čok* to open. Daily except Wed noon–3pm & 6–11pm.

Damir i Ornella Zidine 5 ⓣ 052 758 134, ⓦ damirornella.com. Something of a cult place hereabouts, serving up unique, sushi-influenced raw-fish recipes alongside divine pastas and risottos. Booking essential. April–Sept Tues–Sat noon–3pm & 6.30–11pm.

Pepenero Porporela bb ⓣ 052 757 706, ⓦ pepenero.hr. For outstanding creative cuisine with more than a dash of pretentiousness, *Pepenero* is probably without equal in Istria. The experience kicks off with a *couvert* (40Kn) consisting of delectable savoury balls mounted on stalks.

After this you can choose between the à-la-carte menu (probably the safer option in terms of quality and value), or the 5- or 7-course tasting menus that take you through just about everything in *Pepenero*'s culinary armoury (such as vegetables smoked inside a glass box, and fillets of fish served on top of a rock). Reservations essential. Daily 6.30–11pm.

Mandrač Mandrač 6 ⓣ052 757 120. Harbourside restaurant dishing up quality seafood including grilled scallops (*jakopove kapice*) and pasta with lobster (*jastog*). Daily noon–3pm & 6–11pm; closed Dec–Feb.

Vitriol Ribarnička 6 ⓦvitriolcaffebar.com. Mellow café-bar on the seafront offering tea, coffee and chocolate cake during the daytime and cocktails, speciality Belgian beers and sunsets come the evening. The interior is gently camp, with gold-painted walls and silky-to-the-touch tablecloths. Free wi-fi. Daily 8am–1am.

Brtonigla

Located 8km inland from Novigrad on the road to Buje, **Brtonigla** (Verteneglio) is on the face of it a rather ordinary Istrian village, its huddle of grey-brown houses grouped around an anonymous-looking church. However it's at the centre of the kind of agriculturally rich area in which many of Istria's fabled gastronomic riches are concentrated – wine, olives, vegetables and muscular horned cattle to name but a few. Perhaps because of this Brtonigla has become famous for its **restaurants**, which regularly make it into the best-of lists compiled by the Croatian media.

3

EATING

Konoba Astarea Ronkova 6 ⓣ052 774 384, ⓦkonoba-astarea-brtonigla.com. Fish or lamb with potatoes baked under a *čripnja* (a metal lid covered with embers) is the house speciality, although their grilled steaks and seafood are also highly rated. Sometimes you are given a menu, sometimes the owner tours the tables to see who wants what. Daily 11am–midnight.

Morgan Bracanija 1 ⓣ052 774 520, ⓦkonoba-morgan.eu. In the hamlet of Bracanija 2km northeast of Brtonigla, just off the road to Buje, *Morgan* concentrates on doing traditional things very well: home-made pasta and local meats (chicken, rabbit or wild boar) roast under a metal lid. Daily noon–10pm.

San Rocco Srednja 2 ⓣ052 725 000, ⓦsan-rocco.hr. *San Rocco* offers impeccably prepared and served game, fish and truffle dishes. There is a seasonally changing choice of five-course set menus, priced at 400–600Kn – slightly higher than average, but well worth it. Daily 12.30–10pm.

San Rocco Vinoteka-Konoba Bunarska 2 ⓣ052 774 704, ⓦsan-rocco.hr. Wine shop and top-notch pizzeria belonging to *San Rocco* in the centre of the village. Daily 1pm–midnight; closed in Jan.

Inland Istria

You don't need to travel away from the sea for long before the hotels and flash apartments give way to rustic villages of heavy grey-brown stone, many of them perched high on hillsides, a legacy of the times when a settlement's defensive position was more important than its access to cultivable land. The landscape is varied, with fields and vineyards squeezed between pine forests, orchards of oranges and olive groves. It's especially attractive in autumn, when the hillsides turn a dappled green and auburn, and the hill villages appear to hover eerily above the early morning mists.

Istria's hilltop settlements owe their appearance to the region's borderland status. Occupied since Neolithic times, they were fortified and refortified by successive generations, serving as strongholds on the shifting frontier between Venice and Hungary, or Christendom and the Ottoman Turks. They suffered serious depopulation in the last century, first as local Italians emigrated in the 1940s and 1950s, then as the rush for jobs on the coast began in the 1960s. Empty houses in these half-abandoned towns have been offered to painters, sculptors and musicians in an attempt to keep life going on the hilltops and stimulate tourism at the same time – hence the reinvention of **Motovun** and **Grožnjan** in particular as cultural centres.

GETTING AROUND

INLAND ISTRIA

By bus Pazin is the hub of the local bus network, with services to Motovun, Buzet and coastal towns like Rovinj and Poreč.

By train The train line from Pula to Buzet (and on into Slovenia) stops at Pazin before passing close to Roč, although a certain amount of walking is required to get to the latter.

Pazin

Unassuming **PAZIN**, which lies in a fertile bowl bang in the middle of the Istrian peninsula, is an unlikely regional capital. A relatively unindustrialized provincial town, it was chosen following World War II by Yugoslavia's new rulers, who were eager to establish an Istrian administration far away from the Italianate coastal towns – the choice of Pazin was a deliberate slap in the face for cosmopolitan Pula. Although fairly bland compared to Istria's other inland towns, Pazin does boast a couple of attractions, most notably its medieval castle and the limestone gorge below, and it's also a useful base from which to visit the renowned frescoes in the nearby church at Beram (see opposite).

3

The castle museums

Trg Istarskog razvoda 1275 1 • Castle and museums: mid-June to mid-Sept Tues–Sun 10am–6pm; mid-Sept to mid-June Tues–Thurs 10am–3pm, Fri noon–5pm, Sat & Sun 11am–5pm • 15Kn • T 052 622 220, W emi.hr

Pazin's prime architectural landmark is the **castle** (*kaštel*), a stern ninth-century structure remodelled many times since. Nowadays it is home to two institutions which effectively form one single (and enjoyably extensive) museum; the **Istrian Ethnographic Museum** (Etnografski muzej Istre) and the **Pazin Museum** (Muzej grada Pazina). Together they offer a fine collection of traditional Istrian costumes housed in atmospheric medieval galleries, along with a wide-ranging display of rural handicrafts and a mock-up of a kitchen featuring the traditional Istrian *kamin* (hearth), a fire laid on an open brick platform around which the cooking pots were arranged.

St Nicholas's Church

Eufrazijeva

Apart from the castle, Pazin's most distinguished historical building is **St Nicholas's Church** (Crkva svetog Nikole), a thirteenth-century structure whose sanctuary vaulting is filled with late fifteenth-century frescoes. Most of these show Old Testament scenes, although there's a fine depiction of a sword-wielding St Michael in the central panel.

Pazin Gorge

Educational trail April–Oct 10am–7pm; 30Kn

Pazin's castle overhangs the **gorge** of the River Fojba below, where a huge abyss sucks water into an underground waterway which resurfaces towards the coast. This chasm was supposed to have prompted Dante's description of the gateway to Hell in his *Inferno*, and inspired Jules Verne to propel one of his characters – Matthias Sandorf from the eponymous book, published in 1885 – over the side of the castle and into the pit. In the book, Sandorf manages to swim along the subterranean river until he reaches the coast – a feat probably destined to remain forever in the realms of fiction. Verne himself never came to Pazin, contenting himself with the pictures of the castle posted to him by the mayor.

JULES VERNE CLUB

Jules Verne's use of Pazin as a location in his novel *Matthias Sandorf* (see above) has prompted locals to form the **Jules Verne Club**, which publishes a newsletter and organizes various events, including the annual Jules Verne Days in late June (details from the tourist office). You can become a member by "donating a book or any other cultural material connected to Jules Verne for the club collection". More information can be found on W ice.hr/davors-members.htm.

Beginning on the road just below the castle, a self-guided educational **trail** (poučna staza) leads down into the gorge, providing close-up views of its limestone cliffs before zigzagging its way up the slope on the opposite side of the river – all in all about a forty-minute walk.

ARRIVAL AND INFORMATION — PAZIN

By train Pazin's train station is a 10min walk uphill from the centre.

Destinations Buzet (3 daily; 45min); Hum (4 daily; 20min); Pula (6 daily; 1hr); Roč (2 daily; 35min).

By bus Pazin's bus station is a 5min walk uphill from the centre.

Destinations Buzet (Mon–Fri 1 daily; 1hr 10min); Labin (1 daily; 1hr 10min); Motovun (Mon–Fri 2 daily; 45min); Poreč (Mon–Fri 10 daily, Sat & Sun 3 daily; 45min); Pula (Mon–Sat 8 daily, Sun 4 daily; 1hr); Rijeka (6 daily; 1hr); Rovinj (Mon–Fri 5 daily, Sat & Sun 1 daily; 40min); Zagreb (6 daily; 3hr 30min).

Tourist office Franine i Jurine 14 (June–Sept Mon–Fri 9am–7pm, Sat & Sun 10am–1pm; Oct–May Mon–Fri 9am–3pm, Sat 10am–1pm; T 052 622 460, W tzpazin.hr). The tourist office, just short of the castle, provides town plans, maps of biking and hiking trails and information on central Istria.

EATING

Pod Lipom Trg Pod Lipom 2a T 052 622 022. A 5min walk east of St Nicholas's Church, along Muntriljska and behind the town bowling court, is this traditional restaurant. Aka *Poli Nina*, it's popular with locals, serving cheap lunch dishes like *maneštra* (chunky soup) and *fuži* (fat scrolls of pasta stuffed with cheese, mushrooms and other goodies) that are chalked up on a board, and a regular menu of more substantial meaty fare. Daily 8am–10pm.

Beram

BERAM, 6km west of Pazin just off the road to Poreč and Motovun, is an unspoilt hilltop village with moss-covered stone walls and some of the finest sacred art in the region.

Chapel of Our Lady on the Rocks

The key (*ključ*) to the chapel is kept by the Šestan family at Beram 38 (in the centre of the village behind the parish church); call ahead on T 052 622 903 or ask at the tourist office in Pazin to ensure that there's someone waiting in Beram for you • Free, but it's polite to give a small sum of money to the keyholder

One kilometre northeast of the village is the **Chapel of Our Lady on the Rocks** (Crkvica svete Marije na škriljinah), a diminutive Gothic church with a set of frescoes dating from 1475, signed by local artist Vincent of Kastav. Of the many well-executed New Testament scenes that cover the chapel interior, two large **frescoes** stand out. The marvellous, 8m-long equestrian pageant of the *Adoration of the Kings* reveals a wealth of fine detail – distant ships, mountains, churches and wildlife – strongly reminiscent of early Flemish painting, while on the west wall a *Dance of Death* is illustrated with macabre clarity against a blood-red background: skeletons clasp scythes and blow trumpets, weaving in and out of a Chaucerian procession of citizens led by the pope. A rich merchant brings up the rear, greedily clinging to his possessions while indicating the money with which he hopes to buy his freedom.

Dvigrad

Southwest of Pazin, the main road and rail routes to Pula forge across a mixed landscape of woodland, cornfields and Mediterranean scrub. After 20km the road enters **Kanfanar**, a frumpy little town founded in the seventeenth century by refugees from nearby **DVIGRAD**, a walled city suddenly abandoned by citizens demoralized by outbreaks of plague and raids by pirates. A cluster of moody grey ruins surrounded by farmland and forest, Dvigrad is an atmospheric place, with its huge crown of jagged battlements guarded by two massive towers. A path curls round one side of the battlements, passes through a ruined gate and leads into the ancient city, its rough paving stones now overgrown with weeds. At its northern end looms the shell of a twelfth-century basilica, the **Church of St Sofia** (Crkva svete Sofije). The road on the western side of the fortress zigzags up the hillside, affording impressive views back towards the dramatic ruins.

ARRIVAL AND DEPARTURE **DVIGRAD**

By car To reach Dvigrad, head west out of Kanfanar along the road to Rovinj and turn right onto a well-signed minor road leading downhill to the ruins. There are no buses.

Svetvinčenat

The tiny town of **SVETVINČENAT** (known in local dialect as "Savičenta"), 5km southeast of Kanfanar, lies just off the main Pula-bound road and rail routes, but is well worth a detour if you're a fan of well-proportioned Mediterranean town squares. Svetvinčenat's is certainly among the most attractive in Istria, watched over by the trefoil Renaissance facade of the **Church of the Assumption** (Crkva navještenja), which harbours several Mannerist altar paintings by sixteenth-century Venetians. Off to the left, the **castle** of the Grimani family, which dates back to the thirteenth century, sports a spacious courtyard (claimed to be the site of a witch burning in 1632, of a village woman who supposedly had a love affair with one of the Grimani family) where summer concerts are held, and a pair of grizzled-looking towers. An eighteenth-century town hall and loggia complete the ensemble.

Gračišće

The fortified settlement of **GRAČIŠĆE** , 6km southeast of Pazin, is the most interesting of a succession of quiet hill villages en route towards Labin, its main gate leading through to a knot of atmospheric alleys, stone houses and churches. On the other side of the village, the terrace behind the Baroque parish church provides terrific views of the surrounding countryside, with the western flanks of **Mount Učka** presiding over a landscape of sandy hills and mixed evergreen and deciduous forest.

Church of St Mary-on-the-Square

Just inside the town's main gate is the porticoed **Church of St Mary-on-the-Square** (Crkva svete Marije na placu), whose fifteenth-century frescoes are usually visible through grilled windows even when the door is locked. The centrepiece is a stunning *Adoration*, in which mounted figures in medieval garb are greeted by a radiant Madonna and Child.

Solomon Palace

The impressive Venetian-style building behind the Church of St Mary-on-the-Square is the **Solomon Palace**, sporting a trio of Gothic windows. It originally served as the summer palace of the bishops of Pićan, a now insignificant village 3km down the road which was an important ecclesiastical centre in the Middle Ages.

St Simeon's hiking tail

The **St Simeon's hiking trail** (10km), which starts just outside the town walls, takes you on a three-hour wander around the countryside, passing through quaint villages and fields of wild asparagus and strawberries.

ACCOMMODATION AND EATING **GRAČIŠĆE**

Konoba Marino Gračišće 75 ☎ 052 687 081. Owned by the same people as the *Poli Luce* B&B, this wooden-bench *konoba* dishes up excellent Istrian food including *maneštra*, pasta, game dishes and tender chops of smoked pork loin. Daily except Wed 2–10pm.

Poli Luce ☎ 052 687 081. A delightful B&B just inside Gračišće's town gate, set in a restored stone house and offering three comfortable en suites with tasteful rustic furniture. **400Kn**

Motovun

Fifteen kilometres northwest of Pazin is perhaps the most famous of the Istrian hill towns, **MOTOVUN** (Montona), an attractive clump of medieval houses straddling a green wooded hill, high above a patchwork of wheatfields and vineyards. Like so many towns in Istria, Motovun was predominantly Italian-speaking until the 1940s (when racing driver Mario Andretti was born here), after which most of the inhabitants left for Italy. The problem of depopulation was partly solved by turning Motovun into an artists' colony – the godfather of Croatian naive art, Krsto Hegedušić, was one of the first painters to move here in the 1960s, and several studios and craft shops open their doors to tourists over the summer.

St Stephen's Church

Trg Andrea Antico

Occupying Motovun's main square, Trg Andrea Antico, is the Renaissance **St Stephen's Church** (Crkva svetog Stjepana), topped by a campanile whose crenellated top looks like a row of jagged teeth. Above the main altar, the eighteenth-century Venetian painting of the *Last Supper* is full of touching detail – note the dog under the table waiting for scraps.

Town battlements

At the far end of the main square, a path leads to a promenade around the town **battlements**, made up of two concentric walls with a tiny moat (nowadays dry) in between. From here there are fantastic views over the Mirna valley and surrounding countryside, which produces some of the finest Istrian wines – Teran and Malvazija are among the better known.

ARRIVAL AND DEPARTURE — MOTOVUN

By bus Buses to Motovun from Pazin and from Pula to Buzet pick up and drop off in Kanal (where there's also a large car park), a 25min walk from the old town.

ACCOMMODATION

Bella Vista Gradiziol 1 ⓣ 052 681 724, ⓦ apartmani-motovun.com. A lovingly restored stone house featuring a homely trio of two- to four-person apartments, each with a/c, TV and kitchenette. **550Kn**

Kaštel Trg Andrea Antico 7 ⓣ 052 681 607, ⓦ hotel-kastel-motovun.hr. Right on the main square, the *Kaštel* occupies a building of medieval origins but offers thoroughly modern en-suite rooms with TV, wi-fi and a generous buffet breakfast. **730Kn**

House of Gold Gradiziol 46 ⓣ 052 681 816, ⓦ motovunaccommodation.com. Near the top of the hill just down from the town gates, this B&B has a clutch of kooky but swish rooms, featuring lots of white surfaces with black and red details. **500Kn**

Motovun House Barbacan 4 ⓣ 091 200 2582, ⓦ motovunhouse.com. A tall, thin, four-storey building on an alley that spirals its way up the hill, *Motovun House* has three double rooms that can be rented separately or on a whole-house basis. **500Kn**

THE MOTOVUN FILM FESTIVAL

All accommodation in Motovun and central Istria is likely to be booked solid during the **Motovun Film Festival** (ⓦ motovunfilmfestival.com), which usually straddles a long weekend at the end of July or beginning of August. Since its inception in 1999 the festival has established itself as Croatia's premier cinematic event, with feature films (European art-house movies for the most part) premiered on an open-air screen in the main town square. A healthy mixture of Croatian and international actors and directors attend, and awards in the shape of an aeroplane propeller are presented for the best films. Featuring a minimum of segregation between stars and public, the festival is also one of the key social events of the summer, with thousands of celebrants ascending Motovun's hill – most are here to enjoy the 24-hour party atmosphere as much as the films. Box offices at the entrance to the old town sell tickets to the screenings.

EATING AND DRINKING

Konoba Barbacan Barbacan 1 ⓣ052 681 791. Right outside the entrance to the old town, this tiny – and pricey – restaurant serves up beautifully presented Istrian dishes with a *nouvelle cuisine* twist, with truffles served in all shapes and forms. Daily except Tues 12.30–3.30pm & 6.30–9.30pm.

Montona Gallery Trg Josefa Ressela 1 ⓣ052 681 754. Situated between the two main town gates, *Montona Gallery* has outdoor tables hugging a much envied parapet-side position with panoramic views of the surrounding hills. Ice cream cups from 20Kn, pizza and a full range of alcoholic drinks are on offer. Daily 8am–11pm.

Pod Voltom Trg Josefa Ressela 6 ⓣ052 681 923. Inside the walls of the upper town gate, *Pod Voltom* offers pasta, game dishes and steaks flavoured with truffles. Daily except Wed noon–10pm.

Zigante Livade 7 ⓣ052 664 302, ⓦrestaurantzigante.com. Two kilometres north of Motovun on the far side of the main crossroads, *Zigante* offers an upmarket take on the whole truffle experience, with truffle-garnished steak, rabbit and duck dishes accompanied by the best local wines and served up by attentive waiting staff in a refined, starched-napkin environment. Daily noon–10pm.

SHOPPING

3

Art in Situ Gradiziol 15 ⓣ095 560 7660. T-shirts, pillowcases and shoulder bags screen-printed with cute and quirky graphics. Daily 10am–6pm.

Zigante Gradiziol 8 ⓣ052 681 668, ⓦzigantetartufi.com. Fresh truffles, truffle sauces and truffle-flavoured oils from a local outfit famous for its truffle products. Daily 11am–6pm.

Oprtalj

Straddling a grassy ridge high above the Mirna Valley, **OPRTALJ** (Portole) was, like Motovun, off the map for many years, half of its houses in ruins and tufts of grass growing from the walls of the rest. In recent years, however, it's undergone a rebirth; old houses are being renovated, new restaurants are opening and more and more visitors are finding out about the place. Both the fifteenth-century **St Mary's Church** (Crkva svete Marije) in the village centre, and the sixteenth-century **Chapel of St Rock** (Crkvica svetog Roka) at the entrance to town have some interesting fresco fragments you can glimpse through the windows; otherwise the nicest way to spend your time here is simply to wander.

EATING

Loggia Matka Laginje bb ⓣ091 555 7028. Cheese-and-*pršut* snacks, or more substantial meals of Istrian sausage and smoked pork chop, served up in a cool stone tavern or on outdoor tables set out on the town loggia. Daily 10am–8pm.

THE PARENZANA HIKING AND CYCLING TRAIL

Completed in 1902 but only operational until 1935, the **Parenzana** (derived from Parenzo, the Italian name for Poreč) was a 130km-long narrow-gauge railway line that linked the port of Trieste with the growing tourist destination of Poreč. It followed a meandering course across the Istrian countryside, with skilfully engineered embankments and viaducts negotiating the peninsula's notoriously up-and-down terrain. The process of converting the former track into a **foot- and cycle-path** was begun in 2006, with a highly scenic 60km section of the railway ("Parenzana I") in central Istria receiving most of the initial attention. Tunnels and bridges along the route were restored and made safe for visitors. A second phase ("Parenzana II"), revitalizing the stretch from Vižinada, 10km southwest of Motovun, to Poreč, was completed in 2012.

The most breathtaking sections of the Parenzana are those connecting Buje, Grožnjan, Livade, Motovun and Vižinada. Gradients are reasonably smooth, and seasoned cyclists will be able to cover a lot of ground in the space of a day's riding; walkers should limit themselves to one stage at a time.

Free maps of the Parenzana are available from tourist offices in inland Istria; and more **information** is available on ⓦparenzana.net.

Grožnjan

North of Motovun on the other side of the Mirna valley, **Grožnjan** (Grisignana) is an ancient hill village that was severely depopulated during the Italian exodus after World War II and given a new lease of life in the 1970s when many of its properties were offered to artists and musicians as studios. There's also a summer school for young musicians, many of whom take part in outdoor concerts organized as part of the **Grožnjan Musical Summer** (Grožnjansko glazbeno ljeto; hgm.hr), which takes place every August. Indeed high summer is the best time to come, when most of the artists are in residence and a smattering of galleries open their doors. Outside this time, Grožnjan can be exceedingly quiet, but it's an undeniably attractive spot, with its jumble of shuttered houses made from honey-brown stone, covered in creeping plants. The town's **battlements** command superb views of the surrounding countryside, with Motovun perched on its hilltop to the southeast, and the ridge of Mount Učka dominating the horizon beyond it.

3

Church of St Vitus and St Modestus and around

Overlooking the town is the **Church of St Vitus and St Modestus** (Crkva svetog Vida i Modesta), a largely unadorned eighteenth-century affair which harbours a much older pair of exuberantly carved choirstalls. The main altar painting showing martyrs Vitus and Modestus being thrown to a collection of romping felines is something of a kitsch classic, painted by local artist Ermenegildo de Troy in 1914.

Slightly downhill from here, the graceful arches of a Renaissance **loggia** form one side of a tiny, gently sloping square, which looks out on what used to be the main town gate.

ARRIVAL AND INFORMATION — GROŽNJAN

By bus Unless you have your own transport, Grožnjan is difficult to get to: catching a Buzet–Buje bus as far as the hamlet of Bijele Zemlje, then walking uphill to Grožnjan via a signed minor road (3km), is your best bet.

Tourist office U. Gorjan 3 (May–Sept Mon 9am–12.30pm, Tues–Sun 9am–12.30pm & 4–7pm; 052 776 131, istria-groznjan.com). The seasonal tourist office, inside the town hall, can help find private accommodation.

ACCOMMODATION

Černac V. Gortana 5 052 776 122 and 091 528 8253. On a narrow Old Town street, the Černac family offers a clutch of rustically decorated en-suite doubles and three-person apartments, some with cooking facilities. They also sell home-made olive oil, wine and *rakija*. **300Kn**

Pintur Mate Gorjana 5 052 776 397 and 098 586 188. Three simple en-suite rooms (two doubles and one single) above a restaurant, in a traditional stone house bang in the centre of town. **300Kn**

EATING AND DRINKING

Bastia 1 Svibnja 052 776 370. Village-centre restaurant with an attractive outdoor terrace in a tiny square. The menu is pretty wide-ranging, embracing everything from specifically Istrian dishes to a Croatia-wide repertoire of grilled meats and steaks. Daily noon–10pm.

Café Vero Trg Cornera 3 091 551 7209. This is a chic place for a drink, its terrace offering expansive views down the valley. You can snack on toasted sandwiches too. Daily 8am–midnight.

★ **Kaya Energy Bar & Design** Vincent iz Kastva 2. A wine-and-much-more-besides bar in a nook of the town walls, with a well-chosen list of local tipples, exquisite cakes and cheese-platter nibbles. There is outdoor seating beneath a large tree on the town ramparts, or in a walled enclosure downstairs. The interior involves cool cushions, fantastic lighting features and a design shop selling handcrafted jewellery and domestic fittings. Daily 9am–11pm.

Buzet and around

The second-largest town in the Istrian interior is **BUZET**, whose original old hilltop settlement quietly decays on the heights above the River Mirna while the bulk of the population lives in the new town below. Though it's not as pretty as Motovun or Grožnjan, Buzet has good accommodation, good food and is an excellent base from which to explore the region. The town's importance as a truffle-hunting centre is celebrated by the **Buzetska Subotina festival** ("Buzet Saturday"; usually the second weekend of September), when an enormous truffle omelette is cooked on the main square and shared out among thousands of visitors, and local pop-rock bands play on a pair of outdoor stages in the town centre – the tourist office will have details.

Reached by a winding road or a step flight of stairs, old Buzet's cobbled streets seem a world away from the largely concrete new quarter down on the valley floor. The remaining ramparts of Buzet's medieval fortifications provide expansive views, with the Mirna valley below and the imposing grey ridge of the **Ćićarija** to the east.

Regional Museum

Rašporskih kapetana 8 • Mon–Fri 9am–3pm • 15Kn

Standing on one of the old quarter's tiny squares, the **Regional Museum** (Zavičajni muzej) has a small collection of Roman gravestones and a display of folk costumes. It's particularly strong on the functional wool and hemp garments worn by the hardy villagers of the Ćićarija.

The Mirna valley: walks and cycle rides

The tourist office can provide the relevant charts and leaflets

Buzet is the ideal starting point for several rustic walks and cycle rides, with a sequence of well-marked, well-mapped trails in and around the verdant **Mirna valley**. Most popular of the hiking routes is the **Mirna River Trail** (Put Mirne), a 12km route that begins just outside the *Mostovi* restaurant in Buzet and takes in the water features of Kotli (see p.180) before ascending to the odd little town of Hum (see p.179). Other options include the **Vela Peć Trail** (6km) that goes from Buzet towards the Mirna canyon and passes two waterfalls (Vela and Mala peć) before returning to town; and its longer extension, the **Trail of the Seven Waterfalls** (Staza 7 slapova; 15km) that combines elements of all the above.

Cyclists can attempt a Buzet–Hum route that follows much of the Mirna River Trail (see above), or take up the challenge of the **Tartufina**, a gruelling 35km mountain-bike trail that heads up into the hills around Sovinjak (p.181).

ARRIVAL AND INFORMATION — BUZET AND AROUND

By bus Buses arrive at the eastern end of the new town.
Destinations Motovun (Mon–Fri 1 daily; 45min); Pazin (Mon–Fri 1 daily; 1hr 10min); Poreč (Mon–Fri 2 daily, Sat & Sun 1 daily; 2hr); Pula (Mon–Fri 2 daily, Sat & Sun 1 daily; 2hr 30min); Rijeka (Mon–Sat 3 daily; 1hr 10min)

By train The train station can be found 2km uphill to the northeast.
Destinations Pula (4 daily; 2hr).

Tourist office Vladimira Gortana 7 (Mon–Fri 8am–3pm, Sat 9am–2pm; ⊕052 662 343, ⓦtz-buzet.hr). Located just outside the old town next to the *Vela Vrata* hotel, the tourist office offers a wealth of sightseeing, hiking and biking information.

ACCOMMODATION

The tourist office (see above) has information on private **rooms** (doubles from 170Kn), most of which are in out-of-town farmhouses.

HOTELS AND B&BS

Fontana Trg fontana 1 ⊕052 662 615, ⓦhotelfontanabuzet.com. This rather angular concrete building dating from the 1980s contains newly renovated en-suite rooms decked out in warm furnishings. **480Kn**

★ **Vela Vrata** Vladimira Gortana 2 ⊕052 494 750, ⓦvelavrata.net. A restored old-town mansion harbouring comfortable and wonderfully soothing accommodation, with bright spacious rooms, modern bathrooms, big pillows and mildly kitschy (but never overpowering) furnishings. Wi-fi throughout, and a splendid restaurant (see p.178). **740Kn**

Volte Kozari 16 ⊕052 665 210, ⓦvolte.hr. A handful of homely rooms (three with en-suite facilities, two with shared) in a modern family house surrounded by wooded hills, 5km out of Buzet on the Cerovlje road. There's an excellent restaurant (closed Tues) on site. **320Kn**

TRUFFLES: ISTRIA'S CULINARY GOLD

The woods around Motovun and Buzet are one of Europe's prime hunting grounds for the **truffle** (*tartuf*), a subterranean fungus whose delicate taste – part nutty, part mushroomy, part sweaty sock – have made it a highly prized delicacy among the foodie fraternity. Truffles, which look like small tubers, tend to overpower whatever other ingredients they're mixed with, and so are used very sparingly in cooking – either grated over a freshly cooked dish, or used in a sauce to give a defining flavour.

The truffle-hunting season begins in late September and carries on through the autumn, with locals and their specially trained dogs heading off into the Istrian fog to sniff out the fungus. During this period most of the region's **restaurants** will have at least one truffle-based recipe on the menu, even if only a simple truffle-and-pasta dish or a truffle *fritaja* (omelette). Truffle dishes offered outside this period will most probably use preserved (rather than fresh) truffles – definitely worth trying, but not quite as mouthwatering as the just-unearthed variety.

To mark the start of the season, **Truffle Days** (Dani Tartufa) are organized in various places in the Motovun/Buzet region from mid-September until early November; these might involve truffle-tasting events, live music or just lots of good-natured drinking. Best known of these fungus-fixated fiestas is the **Buzetska Subotina** ("Buzet Saturday"), when an enormous truffle omelette is fried up on the main square and then scoffed by an army of hungry celebrants (see p.177).

3

EATING

When it comes to eating you are spoilt for choice, with a handful of good restaurants in town, and *Toklarija* and *Vrh* in the hills above (see p.181).

Paladin Naselje Franječići 25 ⊕052 662 061. Just northeast of the new town in the village suburb of Naselje Franječići, this homely place serves up excellent pasta dishes garnished with seasonal goodies (such as asparagus, mushrooms and the ubiquitous truffle) alongside local sausages and pork chops. Mon–Sat 9am–9pm.

Stara Oštarija Petra Flega 5 ⊕052 694 003, ⊕stara-ostarija.com.hr. Old-town restaurant dishing up pasta dishes and steaks (most with the option of truffle-flavoured sauces). An enclosed terrace gives good views of modern Buzet down below. Mon & Wed–Fri noon–5pm, Sat & Sun noon–11pm.

Vela Vrata Vladimira Gortana 2 ⊕052 494 750, ⊕velavrata.net. A relaxing terrace just outside the old town gates makes this hotel restaurant a good place to unwind over quality food or a glass of local wine. The seasonally changing menu usually has at least one main course each from the fish, meat and poultry fields, alongside a lively choice of imaginative starters and soups. If you have time and cash to spare, order the five- or six-course tasting menu (300–400Kn). Daily noon–9.30pm.

SHOPPING

Zigante Trg fontana ⊕052 663 340, ⊕zigantetartufi.com. You can buy truffles and truffle-based products throughout the year in this specialist shop.

Roč and around

Framed against the backdrop of the rocky Ćićarija ridge, the dainty village of **ROČ**, about 10km east of Buzet, sits behind sixteenth-century walls so low that the place looks more like a child's sandcastle than an erstwhile medieval strongpoint. Roč has a strong **folk music** tradition, with performing skills passed down from one generation to the next, and almost the entire population is involved in some capacity or other with the local folk music society, **Istarski željezničar** ("Istrian railwayman"), which has a brass section, male and female choirs and an accordion band. The locals use an archaic, push-button accordion known as the Triestina, which is rarely found outside Istria and northeastern Italy. Best time to hear it in action is during the **International Accordion Festival** (Z armoniku v Roč) over the second weekend in May: the tourist office in Buzet will have details.

With their neat rows of sturdy farmhouses, the narrow lanes of Roč provide a wonderful environment in which to savour the rustic atmosphere of eastern Istria.

There's a small display of **Roman tombstones** inside the arch of the main gate into town, and the Romanesque **St Barthol's Church** (Crkva svetog Bartula) in the centre, an ancient, barn-like structure lurking behind an enormous chestnut tree and sporting an unusually asymmetrical bell tower.

Raspadalica

Follow signs to the village of Nugla, pass through it, and keep going for about 3km

If you've got your own transport, you can follow the road leading northwest out of Roc to get up onto the summit of the Ćićarija ridge. Crossing heathland covered in conifers and subalpine meadows, the road ends up at **Raspadalica**, a local beauty spot that serves as an ideal launch pad for local hang-gliding enthusiasts, and offers fine views to everyone else – there's a superb panorama of the Mirna valley, with the hill town of Motovun in the distance.

ARRIVAL AND DEPARTURE — ROČ AND AROUND

By bus Buzet–Rijeka buses will drop you off at the Roč turn-off 500m from the village.

By train The train station (on the Pula–Buzet line) is about 1.5km east of the village.

ACCOMMODATION AND EATING

Drago Cerovac Roč 58 ⓣ 052 666 481. A handful of small, simply furnished rooms with WC and shower in the hallway – the owner also rents bikes (100Kn/hr). Breakfast included. 300Kn

Ročka konoba Roč 14 ⓣ 052 666 451. This checked-tablecloth tavern in the centre of the village is a good place for asparagus and truffles in season, as well as the regular repertoire of *fritaje* omelettes, *ombolo* (smoked pork chops, cooked on the hearth), *kobasice* and home-made *fuži* pasta. Summer Tues–Sun noon–10pm; winter Sat & Sun only (same times).

3

Hum and around

Heaped up on a hill surrounded by grasslands and forest, **HUM** is the self-proclaimed "smallest town in the world", since it has preserved all the attributes – walls, gate, church, campanile – that a town is supposed to possess, despite its population having dwindled to a current total of just fourteen. Originally fortified by the Franks in the eleventh century, Hum was a relatively prosperous place in the Middle Ages, and it still looks quite imposing as you pass through a town gate topped by a castellated bell tower. Beyond, the oversized, neo-Baroque **Church of the Blessed Virgin Mary** (Crkva blažene djevice Marije), built in 1802 as the last gasp of urban development in a shrinking town, lords it over a settlement which now amounts to two one-metre-wide streets paved with grassed-over cobbles and lined by chunky grey-brown farmhouses.

Gallery Museum

April–Oct daily 11am–9pm • Free

Squatting beside the northernmost of Hum's two streets is the **Gallery Museum** (Galerija muzej), really just a gift shop but an entertaining one nevertheless, offering Glagolitic characters modelled from clay or wood, locally made *biska (*mistletoe brandy), and a small ethnographic display of agricultural implements.

Chapel of St Hieronymous

The key for the chapel is available from *Humska Konoba* (see p.180)

Just outside the town walls, the Romanesque cemetery **Chapel of St Hieronymous** (Crkvica svetog Jeronima) preserves a number of twelfth-century frescoes that display a melding of Romanesque and Byzantine styles. As usual, the life of Jesus provides the subject matter: there's a fine *Annunciation* spanning the arch above the altar, together with a *Crucifixion*, *Pietà* and *Deposition* on the walls.

Glagolitic Alley

The 7km-long minor road that connects Hum with Roč is known as the **Glagolitic Alley** (Aleja glagoljaša) after a series of roadside sculptures celebrating the Glagolitic alphabet (see box, p.220). An archaic Slavonic script developed in the early Middle Ages, Glagolitic was used by Istrian priests right up until the nineteenth century. Positioned every kilometre or so, the sculptures mostly take the form of Glagolitic characters – seductively decorative forms that look like a cross between Cyrillic and Klingon.

ARRIVAL AND DEPARTURE — HUM AND AROUND

By car Take the minor road (the so-called "Glagolitic Alley") from Roč.

On foot/by bike Pick up a map from Buzet tourist office and take the Put Mirne (Mirna Valley Trail; 12km).

ACCOMMODATION AND EATING

Humska Konoba Hum 2 ⓣ 052 660 005. Right outside the town gate, this is a well-touristed *konoba* that keeps things simple and does them rather well. Choose between pasta with truffles (95Kn), *ombolo* pork chop (50Kn) or succulent sausages (35Km), with optional side portions of bacon-flavoured sauerkraut (12Kn). As the only *konoba* in town, with a stone veranda boasting sweeping valley views, it attracts everyone from individual diners to school parties – so expect a crowd in summer. Tues–Sun 11am–10pm.

Nela Grabar Hum 12 ⓣ 052 660 004 and ⓜ 091 575 7408. Family house within Hum's walls offering a couple of cosy doubles with shared facilities, and one self-catering apartment – the tourist office in Buzet (see p.177) will act as an intermediary if you can't get through to an English speaker. **180Kn**

3

Kotli

The half-abandoned hamlet of **KOTLI**, 2km northwest of Hum, has become something of a cult destination among summer bathers. It's here that the young River Mirna tumbles through a series of small bowls carved out of the local limestone, creating a sequence of shallow, gurgling **pools** that some have compared to an open-air jacuzzi – although low water levels often leave visitors wondering what all the fuss is about. Whether you're in swimming mood or not, it's a fine spot for a riverside ramble. On the far side of the river, Kotli itself is a moody clump of farmhouses and barns, half-hidden by runaway vegetation.

ARRIVAL AND DEPARTURE — KOTLI

By car Kotli is reached by a minor road that leaves the Glagolitic Alley (see above) midway between Roč and Hum.

On foot The hamlet can also be reached on foot from Buzet (2hr). The footpath starts on the south side of town, on the far side of the bridge over the River Mirna – the Buzet tourist office will give you directions.

EATING

Kotlić Kotli 3 ⓜ 099 351 7077. One of Kotli's old farm buildings has been refurbished and turned into this café-restaurant, which serves up excellent *maneštra* and other local staples on a shady terrace. May–Oct Tues–Sun noon–8pm.

The Buzet uplands

One of the most scenic routes heading out of Buzet is the one that climbs southwards to the hamlet of **Svi Sveti** (actually more of a road junction than a place), then follows a mountain ridge towards Cerovlje on the Pazin–Rijeka road. With the Mirna valley to the east and the Butoniga basin way down to the west, the ridge offers some of the best views of inland Istria's undulating landscape, with pudding-basin hills rising up above a patchwork of forests, vineyards and pumpkin patches. To see this landscape at its best, consider a detour to **Sovinjak** (on a side road that loops towards Istarske Toplice), after which you can return to Svi Sveti and rejoin the southbound route to Cerovlje, calling in at **Draguć**.

Sovinjak

With its corral of ochre-and-brown houses drawn tightly around a dumpy-looking church, the hilltop village of **SOVINJAK**, 6km west of Svi Sveti, is an undeniably beautiful spot, its grassy ramparts looking out over the bottle-green woodland of the Mirna valley.

Dragući

Some 10km south of Svi Sveti en route to Cerovlje, **DRAGUĆ** is a ridge-top village stranded among cornfields above the Mirna basin. Its fourteenth-century **Chapel of St Rock** (Crkvica svetog Roka) contains frescoes similar to those in Beram, although slightly less well preserved – to get in, ask for the key (*ključ*) in the village square. There's a large *Journey of the Magi* on the left as you enter, with an *Annunciation* above it, and a *Martyrdom of St Sebastian* and *Flight into Egypt* on the right, all rendered in vivid greens and browns.

EATING **THE BUZET UPLANDS**

SOVINJAK

★ **Toklarija** Sovinjsko Polje 11 ⓣ 052 663 031. Two kilometres east of Sovinjak in the hamlet of Sovinjsko Polje, this is one of the nicest places to eat in Istria if not the whole country. An atmospheric, intimate restaurant housed in a venerable stone building with an oil press in the front room, it's famous for home-made pasta and seasonal local products – asparagus in spring, mushrooms and truffles in autumn – none of which comes cheap. Reservations compulsory. Daily except Tues 1–10pm.

★ **Vrh** Vrh ⓣ 052 667 123. South of Sovinjak in the village of Vrh, this is a worthy alternative to the *Toklarija*, which serves up some of the best home-made *fuži* anywhere in Istria, alongside plenty of pork and game dishes and some extraordinary herbal *rakijas* (*kopriva* – or nettle – being one particular favourite). Tues–Sun 1–10pm.

DRAGUĆ

Bufet Zora Dragući 7 ⓣ 052 665 105. A snug, wood-panelled village inn hung with domestic and agricultural implements, *Zora* confines itself to simple country fare, with *pršut*, local cheeses and *fritaja* omelettes forming the backbone of the menu. Benches outside on the main square make this a fine place to wind down. Tues–Sun 11am–6pm.

The east coast

Compared with the tourist complexes of the west, Istria's **east coast** is a relatively quiet area with few obvious attractions. East of Pula, the main road to Rijeka heads inland, remaining at a discreet distance from the shoreline for the next 50km.

Raša

Thirty kilometres out of Pula the road passes through **RAŠA**, built by the Italians as a model coal-mining town in 1937. Alongside neat rows of workers' houses, Raša also boasts a fine example of Mussolini-era architecture in **St Barbara's Church** (Crkva svete Barbare) – Barbara being the patron saint of miners. It's an austere but graceful structure featuring a campanile in the shape of a pithead, and a curving facade representing an upturned coal barrow.

Labin

Five kilometres beyond Raša, **LABIN** is divided into two parts, with an original medieval town crowning the hill above and a twentieth-century suburb, **Podlabin**, sprawling across the plain below. Labin was for many years Croatia's coal-mining capital, and earned itself a place in working-class history in 1921, when striking miners declared the "Labin Republic" before being pacified by the Italian authorities. There's precious little sign of mining heritage nowadays apart from the one remaining pithead in

Podlabin, which still bears the word "Tito" proudly spelt out in wrought-iron letters. Subsidence caused by mining led to Labin's Old Town being partially abandoned in the 1980s, although the subsequent decline of the coal industry, coupled with a thoroughgoing restoration programme, encouraged people to return. The offer of cheap studio space encouraged artists to move to old Labin, and several ateliers open their doors from April through to October. It's consequently one of the more attractive of Istria's hill towns – all the more so for its proximity to the beach at **Rabac**, only forty minutes' walk downhill.

The Old Town

Labin's hilltop **Old Town** is a warren of steep alleys threading their way between houses attractively decked out in ochres and pinks. At the highest point of the Old Town there is a **viewing terrace** providing superb views of the coast, with Rabac in the foreground and the mountainous shape of Cres beyond.

Church of the Birth of the Blessed Virgin Mary

1. Maja

Presiding over the Old Town's stepped main street is the **Church of the Birth of the Blessed Virgin Mary** (Crkva rođenja blažene djevice Marije). On its facade, a fourteenth-century rose window is upstaged by a seventeenth-century Venetian lion, and by a bust of patrician Antonio Bollari, who defended the town against Uskok pirates.

Town Museum

1. Maja 6 • Mon–Sat 10am–1pm & 6–8pm, Sun 10am–1pm • 15Kn • ⓣ 052 852 477

The burgundy Batiala-Lazarini Palace now holds the **Town Museum** (Gradski muzej), with a small collection of Roman tombstones and a display of local costumes, including examples of the enormous woollen scarves worn by local women to cushion the load of water pitchers and other heavy burdens. There's also a small but atmospheric re-creation of a coal mine, which involves donning a (totally unnecessary) hard hat and embarking on a stooping walk between pit props.

Municipal Art Gallery

1. Maja 5 • Mon–Fri 10am–2pm & 6–8pm, Sat 10am–1pm • Free • ⓣ 052 852 123

Directly opposite the Town Museum, the **Municipal Art Gallery** (Gradska galerija) is the venue for interesting themed exhibitions during the summer.

Alvona Art Gallery

G. Martinuzzi 16 • Mid-June to mid-Sept daily 10am–noon & 6–9pm; mid-Sept to mid-June Mon–Fri 10am–1pm • Free • ⓦ galerija-alvona.hr

Situated in the former Chapel of Our Lady of Carmel (Crkvica Gospe od Karmene), the **Alvona Art Gallery** (Galerija Alvona) hosts high-profile contemporary displays with a strong regional flavour.

Rabac

Buses run every 2hr from the main bus station in Podlabin (via Titov trg in Labin); alternatively it's a 40min walk from Labin – head along the Rabac road, then taking the path that leads into the woods just behind the Porta Tours tourist agency on the edge of town

Squeezed into a narrow bay on the coast, the resort village of **RABAC** was initially developed by the Italians in the interwar years as a workers' holiday settlement, though nowadays has an almost totally modern appearance, its hillsides covered in apartment blocks. There's a reasonable shingle beach on the northern side of the bay, and the usual string of so-so bars and restaurants along the harbour.

ARRIVAL AND INFORMATION

LABIN

By bus Pula–Rijeka buses stop at the bus station in Podlabin, from where it's a 15min walk uphill to the main square, Titov trg.

Tourist office Aldo Negri 20 (mid-May to mid-Oct Mon–Sat 8am–9pm, Sun 10am–1pm & 6–9pm; mid-Oct to mid-May Mon–Fri 7am–3pm; ⓣ052 855 560, ⓦrabac-labin.com), plus a summer only information point on Titov trg (June Sept Mon–Fri 8am–8pm, Sat & Sun 5–8pm). Can provide sundry brochures covering Labin and Rabac.

ACCOMMODATION

Kompas Rabac-Labin, Slobode bb, Rabac (ⓣ052 856 599) provides two-person **studios** (360Kn) and four-person **apartments** (from 480Kn) in and around Rabac.

Camp Oliva Rabac ⓣ052 884 150, ⓦmaslinica-rabac.com. Right on the beach and backed by attractive woodland, and an olive grove from which the camp gets its name. Open May–Sept. **60Kn** per person, pitches from **60Kn**

EATING AND DRINKING

For **drinking and nightlife**, there's a sprinkling of café-bars either on or just off Titov trg.

Due Fratelli Montozi 6 ⓣ052 853 577, ⓦdue-fratelli.com. About 2km out of town on the road to Rabac, this restaurant offers top-notch fresh fish, which is served either grilled or oven-baked. Reservations advised at weekends. Tues–Sun noon–midnight.

Kvarner Šetalište San Marco ⓣ052 851 337, ⓦkvarnerlabin.com. Just off the square below the town gate, *Kvarner* offers a more tourist-oriented menu of grilled fish and steaks, although the outdoor terrace comes with good views towards the sea. Mon–Sat 9am–11pm, Sun noon–11pm.

Velo Kafe Titov trg 12 ⓣ052 852 745. *Velo Kafe* fulfils the role of main-square café and prime lunching spot with considerable aplomb, and has a list of Istrian soups and pasta dishes chalked up on a board outside. It's famous for its cakes, and you should never leave without trying dessert. Daily 11am–11pm.

ENTERTAINMENT

The **Labin Art Republika festival** in July and August features open-air performances, concerts and cultural events in the Old Town every Thursday and Friday evening. Details from the tourist office.

Lamparna Rudarska 1, Podlabin ⓣ052 857 041, ⓦlabinary.org. Cultural centre in the former pithead which organizes gigs, raves, theatre and art exhibitions, and has a bar and internet café.

3

HOTEL
BELLEVUE

The Kvarner Gulf

PALACE-BELLEVUE HOTEL, OPATIJA

The Kvarner Gulf

Squeezed between the Istrian peninsula to the north and Dalmatia to the south, the Kvarner Gulf brings together many of the Croatian coast's most enticing features: grizzled coastal hills and mountains, an archipelago of ochre-grey islands and fishing villages with narrow alleys and gardens groaning under the weight of subtropical plants. The Kvarner island of Rab boasts sandy beaches of almost Caribbean proportions, and the range of rocky and pebbly coves on offer elsewhere will have Adriatic-beach enthusiasts scouring their brains in search of superlatives.

4

Croatia's largest port and centre of the Kvarner's transport network, **Rijeka** is a prosperous and cultured city brimming with hedonistic energy and a busy gateway to the **islands** that crowd the gulf to the south. Of these, **Krk** is the most accessible, connected to the mainland by a road bridge just half an hour's drive from Rijeka; the islands farther out – **Lošinj**, **Rab** and **Cres** – are only accessible by ferry and have a correspondingly rural, laid-back feel. Each has its fair share of historic towns, along with some gorgeous coves and **beaches** – especially the sandy ones at Baška on Krk and Lopar on Rab. Although lush and green on their western flanks, islands like Rab and **Pag** are hauntingly bare when seen from the mainland, the result of deforestation during the Venetian period, when local timber was used to feed the shipyards of Venice; the fierce northeasterly wind known as the bura (see box, p.223) has prevented anything from growing there again.

Back on the mainland, the Habsburg-era villas of **Opatija** and **Lovran** preserve an evocative flavour of the *belle époque*. The southern part of the Kvarner coastline is dominated by the stark and majestic **Velebit** mountains, a huge chain that comprises both the Northern Velebit and Paklenica national parks at opposite ends of the range.

Getting around the region is straightforward: Rijeka is the hub of the transport system, with buses along the coast and ferries to the islands.

Rijeka

Rows of cumbrous cranes front the soaring apartment blocks of **RIJEKA** (pronounced "Ree-acre"), a down-to-earth city that mixes industrial grit with a Mediterranean sense of *joie de vivre*. It is the northern Adriatic's only true metropolis, harbouring a reasonable number of attractions and an appealing urban buzz; the hilltop suburb of **Trsat**, home to a famous pilgrimage church, is particularly attractive. Accommodation

PAKLENICA NATIONAL PARK

Highlights

❶ **Eating in Volosko** This cute former fishing village boasts some of the finest seafood restaurants in the country. **See p.201**

❷ **Lovran** An Italianate, green-shuttered coastal town scattered with Habsburg-era villas. **See p.202**

❸ **Cres** One of the more unspoiled Kvarner Gulf islands, its ancient villages hovering above a craggy, uncrowded coast. **See p.204**

❹ **Veli Lošinj** An attractive little port with a warren of pastel-coloured houses strung tightly around a boat-filled harbour. **See p.212**

❺ **Northern Velebit National Park** Highland hiking paradise offering spectacular views of the coast, rustic villages and close encounters of the brown-bear kind. **See p.223**

❻ **Paklenica National Park** Staggeringly beautiful mountain landscape comprising an enticing mixture of karst wilderness, deciduous forests and fir-clad slopes. **See p.225**

❼ **Rab Town** Peninsula-hugging medieval town famous for its skyscraping church belfries. **See p.228**

❽ **Lopar Peninsula**, **Rab** Truly sandy beaches in Croatia are few and far between, but this scrub-covered peninsula is studded with them. **See p.235**

HIGHLIGHTS ARE MARKED ON THE MAP ON P.188

in town is limited to a handful of hotels, however, and if you want to stay in the area it may be better to aim for the Opatija Riviera to the west, an area amply served by Rijeka's municipal bus network. Much of Rijeka was rebuilt after World War II, though a fair number of nineteenth-century buildings remain, many of them in solid ranks along the **Riva**.

Brief history

Although Trsat is an ancient hilltop site once occupied by both the Illyrians and the Romans, the port below didn't really begin to develop until the thirteenth century, when it was known – in the language of whichever power controlled it – as St Vitus-on-the-River, a name subsequently shortened to the rather blunt "River" – which is what Rijeka (and its Italian version, "Fiume") actually means. From 1466 the city belonged to the Habsburgs, but was awarded to Hungary in 1868 when the Habsburg Empire was divided up into Austrian and Hungarian halves.

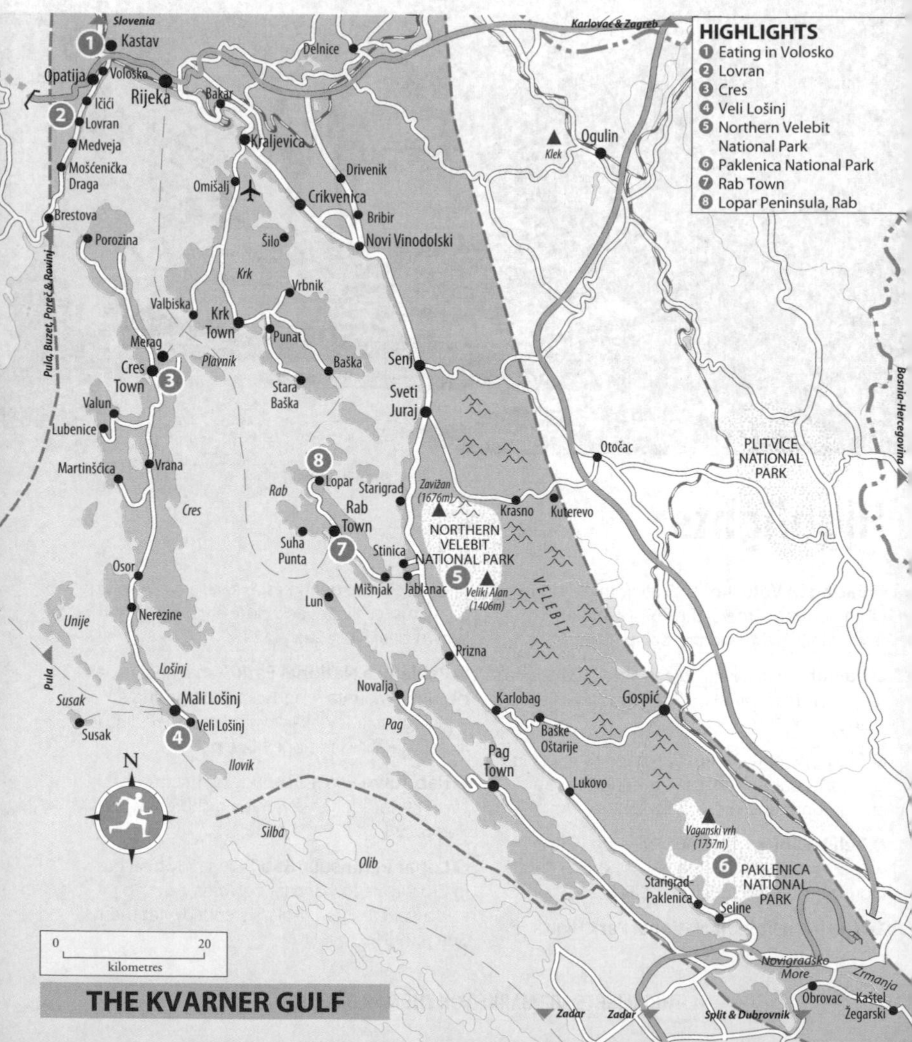

FOOD AND DRINK IN THE KVARNER GULF

Seafood in the Kvarner is as good as anywhere in Croatia, although the Gulf is famous above all for its **scampi**, which thrive in this part of the Adriatic due to the sea's uniquely sandy bottom. Kvarner scampi can be prepared in a number of ways although the classic recipe is *škampi na buzaru*, served in a garlic and wine sauce. The scampi are invariably served whole and unpeeled – you are supposed to prize them open with your fingers and suck out the white flesh.

Prime among the island-based specialities is **Pag cheese**, a hard and piquant affair that is best eaten as a nibble-and-savour starter. A regional staple found on the island of Krk and on the nearby mainland too is *šurlice*, long, thin tubes of **pasta** dough, traditionally eaten *sa gulašom* (with goulash) or *sa žgvacetom* (with lamb stew). Visitors to Rab should not leave without sampling **rabska torta**, the marzipan-filled pastry sold in local patisseries, while most famous of the region's **wines** is Vrbnička Žlahtina, an excellent white from Vrbnik on Krk's east coast.

Some of Croatia's best **restaurants** are in the Rijeka–Volosko–Opatija strip (see p.201), with establishments like *Bevanda* (Opatija), *Plavi Podrum* and *Le Mandrać* (both Volosko) frequently topping local culinary surveys.

Rijeka under Hungarian rule was a booming city with a multinational population – the centre was predominantly Italian-speaking, while the suburbs were increasingly Croat – and both Italians and Croatians laid claim to the city when it came up for grabs at the end of World War I. The Allies had promised Rijeka to the infant Kingdom of Serbs, Croats and Slovenes (subsequently Yugoslavia), prompting a coup by Italian soldier-poet **Gabriele d'Annunzio** (see box, p.191) – who marched into Rijeka unopposed and established a proto-fascist regime. D'Annunzio soon fell, leaving Rijeka to be gobbled up by Mussolini's Italy.

Rijeka was returned to Yugoslavia after World War II, when most of the Italian population was induced to leave. In the years that followed, its shipbuilding industry flourished, and the city acquired its high-rise suburbs. Nowadays shipbuilding is in decline, and Rijeka's rich stock of port-side workshops and warehouses has become the subject of (as yet unrealized) urban regeneration schemes.

Jadranski trg

Just inland from Rijeka's seafront Riva, fountain-splashed **Jadranski trg** serves as the western entrance to Rijeka's pedestrianized city centre. Looming above it is one surviving symbol of interwar Italian architecture, the russet-coloured **Veliki neboder** (literally "big skyscraper"), a boldly functional office block whose grid-like facade looks like a monumental CD rack – and has unsurprisingly earned the building the nickname of *ormar-ladičnjak* or "chest of drawers". On the south side of the square look out for the towering neo-Renaissance **Jadrolinija building**, originally built for the Adria shipping company in 1897 and sporting allegorical statues symbolizing the continents.

The Korzo

Running east from Jadranski trg, the pedestrianized **Korzo** is Rijeka's main shopping area and the focus of most of its bustling streetlife. Marking the western end of the Korzo is **The Walker** (Hodač), a confidently striding statue courtesy of leading contemporary sculptor Ivan Kozarić (1921–), placed here in 2010 and already something of an urban trademark. The main landmark along the Korzo is the **City Tower** (Gradski toranj), a medieval gateway with Baroque additions. Known locally as "Pod uriloj" (after the Italian word for clock, *orologio*), it has a relief on its street-facing side bearing the Habsburg double-headed eagle surmounted by busts of Austrian emperors Leopold I (on the left) and Charles VI (on the right). It was the latter's decision to declare Rijeka a free port in 1717 that kick-started the city's economic growth.

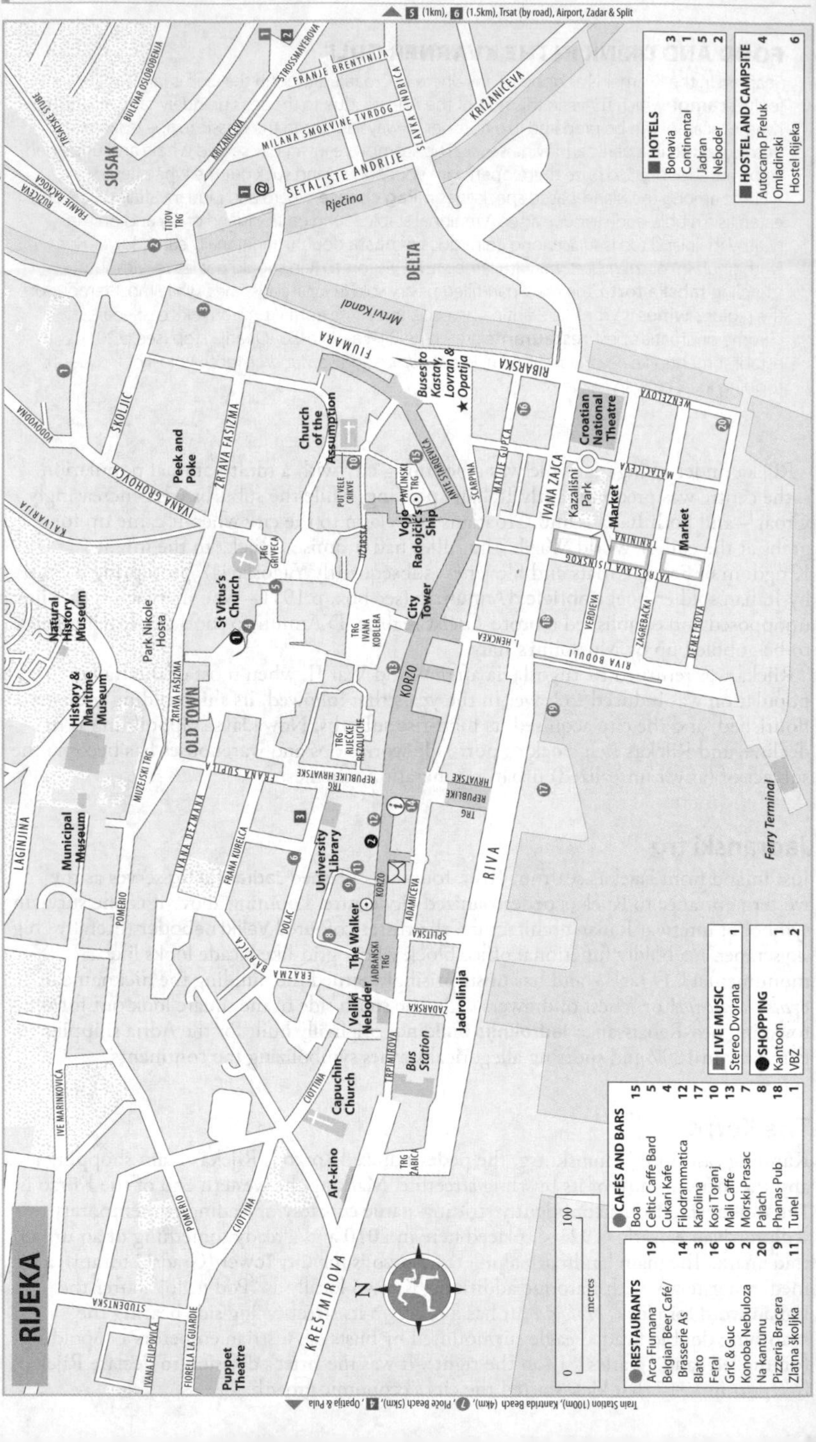

RIJEKA

Zagreb ▲ Trsat (on foot) ▲

▲ 5 (1km), 6 (1.5km), Trsat (by road), Airport, Zadar & Split

▲ Train Station (100m), Kantrida Beach (4km), 7, Ploče Beach (5km), 4, Opatija & Pula

RESTAURANTS	
Arca Fiumana	19
Belgian Beer Café/ Brasserie As	14
Blato	3
Feral	16
Gric & Guc	6
Konoba Nebuloza	2
Na kantunu	20
Pizzeria Bracera	9
Zlatna školjka	11

CAFÉS AND BARS	
Boa	15
Celtic Caffe Bard	5
Cukari Kafe	4
Filodrammatica	12
Karolina	17
Kosi Toranj	10
Mali Caffe	13
Morski Prasac	7
Palach	8
Phanas Pub	18
Tunel	1

LIVE MUSIC	
Stereo Dvorana	1

SHOPPING	
Kantoon	1
VBZ	2

HOTELS	
Bonavia	3
Continental	1
Jadran	5
Neboder	2

HOSTEL AND CAMPSITE	
Autocamp Preluk	4
Omladinski Hostel Rijeka	6

0 — 100 metres

GABRIELE D'ANNUNZIO IN RIJEKA

Following World War I, Italy's failure to win territories in the eastern Adriatic provoked profound feelings of national frustration. Italian army officers calculated that an attack on Rijeka would be enormously popular with the Italian public, and chose flamboyant poet, orator and decorated war hero **Gabriele d'Annunzio** (1863–1938) to lead the enterprise.

D'Annunzio marched into Rijeka on September 12, 1919, at the head of 297 volunteers – whose numbers were soon swelled by patriotic adventurers. He immediately declared Italy's annexation of Rijeka, a deed that the Italian government in Rome, suspicious of the radical d'Annunzio, disowned. By September 1920, d'Annunzio – who now styled himself "Il Commandante" – had established Rijeka as an independent state entitled the **Reggenza del Carnaro**, or "Regency of the Kvarner", which he hoped to use as a base from which to topple the Italian government and establish a dictatorship. The enterprise attracted all kinds of ex-soldiers and political idealists from Italy and beyond. D'Annunzio's court was copiously provisioned with both cocaine and courtesans, providing these adventurous souls with added inducements to stick around.

Under d'Annunzio, political life in Rijeka became an experiment in totalitarian theory from which fellow Italian nationalist Benito Mussolini was to borrow freely. D'Annunzio's main innovation was the establishment of a **corporate state**, ostensibly based on the Italian medieval guild system, in which electoral democracy was suspended and replaced by nine "corporations" – each corresponding to a different group of professions – by which the populace could be organized and controlled. The Regency was also a proving ground for fascism's love of spectacle, with d'Annunzio mounting bombastic parades and carefully choreographed mass meetings.

Pressured by the Western allies to bring d'Annunzio to heel, Italian forces began a **bombardment of the city** on Christmas Eve, 1920. D'Annunzio surrendered four days later, finally leaving town on January 18, thereby ending one of twentieth-century history's more bizarre episodes.

4

The Old Town

The gate beneath the City Tower gives access to the **Old Town** (Stari grad), a rather hopeful description for an area of scruffy squares and glass-fronted department stores.

St Vitus's Church

Trg Grivica

At the top of the sloping Trg Grivica stands **St Vitus's Church** (Crkva svetog Vida), surmounted by a rotunda built in 1638 in imitation of Santa Maria della Salute in Venice. Look out for the Gothic **crucifix** above the high altar: in 1296, the story goes, a gambler was losing at cards outside the church and ran inside in a rage, flinging stones at this crucifix, which began to bleed. The ground beneath the man's feet promptly opened up and swallowed him completely, except for one hand. The faithful claim that one of the stones he threw is still embedded in the side of the wooden Christ.

Church of the Assumption

Užarska

Dominating a small piazza at the eastern end of the Old Town is the **Church of the Assumption** (Crkva Uznesenja), which boasts a beautiful Baroque interior and a fourteenth-century bell tower which leans ever so slightly to the north – earning it the title of **Kosi toranj** or "slanting tower".

Vojo Radojčić's Ship

Pavlinski trg

A broad rectangle packed with cafés, Pavlinski trg is the site of one of Rijeka's most easily identifiable monuments, a cast-iron **sculpture** of a tubby-looking ship designed by local artist Vojo Radojčić (1930–). A well-known painter of jolly maritime scenes, Radojčić's distinctive motifs are visible throughout the city, from the local tourist office brochures to the menu cards at the *Bracera* pizzeria (see p.196). Intended as a tribute to the Rijeka shipbuilding industry, the ship sculpture is backed by a huge Radojčić mural, covering the wall of an apartment block and brightening up the square significantly as a result.

Peek and Poke

Ivana Grahovca 2 • Open intermittently; call to check • 20Kn • ⓣ 091 780 5709, ⓦ peekpoke.hr

Although it never seems to keep regular working hours, **Peek and Poke** is one Rijeka attraction that you should at least try to visit. Founded by local computer freaks, it is basically a museum of information technology containing scores of calculators, gaming consoles and PCs. As well as some obvious landmarks in consumer history (a Sinclair Spectrum here; an early Nintendo console there), the collection also contains some of the less-remembered landmarks in home computer design, notably the Galeb and Orao PCs made by Croatian company PEL in the 1980s.

The Gubernatorial Palace and around

Muzejski trg 1 • **History and Maritime Museum** Mid-June to mid-Sept Tues–Fri 9am–8pm, Sat 9am–1pm; mid-Sept to mid-June Tues–Fri 9am–1pm • 10Kn • ⓣ 051 213 578, ⓦ ppmhp.hr

4

Uphill from the Old Town looms the late nineteenth-century **Gubernatorial Palace** (Guvernerova palača), whose marvellously over-the-top state rooms now provide a sumptuous setting for the **History and Maritime Museum** (Povijesni i pomorski muzej). It was here that Gabriele d'Annunzio installed himself for his short period of power, until shelling by the Italian battleship *Andrea Doria* on Boxing Day, 1920 persuaded him to leave. Its huge echoing rooms hold costumes, period portraits and weaponry, while the model ships on the ground floor include replicas of the huge tankers formerly made by the local 3 Maj shipyard.

Lapidarium

Outside the Maritime Museum but still within the palace grounds, a **lapidarium** displays tombstones throughout the ages and a curious sculptural ensemble known as **Adamić's Witnesses** (Adamićevi svjedoci) – a row of ugly stone heads commissioned by eighteenth-century merchant Simon Adamić in order to ridicule the fourteen locals who had accused him (unjustly, as the Habsburg courts ultimately decided) of stealing a hoard of recently discovered treasure.

The Municipal Museum

Muzejski trg 1/1 • Mon–Fri 10am–1pm & 4–8pm, Sat 10am–1pm • 20Kn, free on Mon • ⓣ 051 336 711, ⓦ muzej-rijeka.hr

Inside the grounds of the Gubernatorial Palace, just behind Adamić's Witnesses, a modern concrete structure holds the **Municipal Museum** (Muzej grada Rijeke). There is no permanent collection, but the changing exhibitions relating to local history are frequently absorbing.

Natural History Museum

Lorenzov prolaz 1 • Mon–Sat 9am–7pm, Sun 9am–3pm • 10Kn • ⓦ prirodoslovni.com

Behind the Gubernatorial Palace to the northeast, the **Natural History Museum** (Prirodoslovni muzej) has beautifully presented displays on geology and marine life, including some ferocious-looking stuffed sharks, and a soothingly atmospheric subterranean aquarium. Shrubs and herbs typical of the Kvarner region sprout from the museum's fragrant garden.

The University Library

Dolac 1 • **Museum of Contemporary and Modern Art** Tues–Sat 10am–1pm & 5–8pm • Prices vary • ⓦ mmsu.hr **Glagolitic Exhibition** Mon & Thurs 2–9pm; Tues, Wed & Fri 9am–2pm; for entry ask at the library information office on the floor above • 10Kn

Rijeka's rather unassuming-looking **University Library** (Sveučilišna knjižnica) is home to two gallery attractions, beginning with the **Museum of Modern and Contemporary Art** (Muzej moderne i suvremene umjetnosti) on the top floor. The permanent collection is currently in storage (plans for the relocation of the gallery are pending), although the changing exhibitions featuring leading artists from Croatia and abroad are usually well worth attending.

A couple of floors down, the **Glagolitic Exhibition** (Izložba glagoljice) tells the history of the archaic script common to the Kvarner region in the Middle Ages (see box, p.220). It's a visually attractive display, marred only by the lack of English-language labelling.

The Capuchin Church

Trg Žabica

Opposite Rijeka's main bus station rises the neo-Gothic bulk of the **Capuchin Church** (Kapucinska crkva), sporting a russet-and-cream striped facade and an attention-grabbing double stairway. Begun in 1904, the project ran out of money within a decade and the cash-strapped Capuchins called on Slovene faith healer **Johanca of Vodice** to help raise funds. Johanca's customary performance consisted of falling into a spiritual trance and appearing to sweat blood – an effect achieved by squeezing a pouch of calf's blood hidden beneath her cloak. Johanca was ultimately imprisoned for fraud, her name subsequently entering the Slovene language as a byword for charlatanism. Construction of the Capuchin Church meanwhile stumbled on, reaching completion in 1929.

Trsat

Bus #1 or #1a from Fiumara or the Riva, or walk (see below)

Occupying a bluff high above the city, **Trsat** is famous as the site of a pilgrimage church, a medieval fortress and its splendid views of the Kvarner Gulf. According to legend, it was the place where the House of the Virgin Mary and Joseph rested for three years during its miraculous flight from the infidel in Nazareth to Loreto in Italy, where it was set down in December 1294. The **Church of Our Lady of Trsat** (Crkva gospe trsatske) supposedly marks the spot where the house rested. Although you can zip up to Trsat on the bus, it can alse be reached on foot via the **Trsatske Stube**, a stairway of 538 steps beginning on the north side of Titov trg. The stairway was built in 1531 at the bidding of Uskok commander Petar Kružić, but was almost completely rebuilt in 1824 – the more devout pilgrims sometimes scale Kružić's steps on their knees.

THE RIJEKA CARNIVAL

On the last Sunday before Shrove Tuesday, Rijeka plays host to the biggest **carnival** celebrations in Croatia, culminating in a spectacular parade. Much of the parade centres on carnival floats and fancy-dress costumes, although there is one authentic older element in the shape of the **zvončari**, young men clad in animal skins who ring enormous cow bells to drive away evil spirits. Many of the villages in the hills north of Rijeka have their own groups of *zvončari*, a tradition which has survived since pre-Christian times. The Rijeka parade, which normally culminates with a large party of *zvončari* strutting their stuff, usually kicks off at around 1pm and takes around five hours to complete. Afterwards, participants and spectators alike troop off to the Riva, where there's an enormous marquee, in which drinking and dancing continue into the early hours.

Up at the top, the pilgrimage church features an altar with an icon of the Virgin, sent here by Pope Urban V in 1367. The altar is surrounded by necklaces and other trinkets hung there by grateful pilgrims, who are required to walk round it three times. At the side of the church is a **Franciscan monastery** whose chapel of votive gifts (Kapela zavjetnih darova) is plastered with pictures and tapestries left by those whose prayers have been answered; the numerous enthusiastic paintings depicting events such as shipwrecks and car crashes, in which the Virgin is supposed to have intervened, are particularly striking.

Trsat Castle

Zrinskoga 6 • Daily: April–June, Sept & Oct 9am–5pm; July & Aug 9am–8pm; Nov–March 9am–3pm • Free

The turrets and parapets of Trsat's ivy-clad **Castle** (Trsatska gradina) provide excellent views of Rijeka, with the islands of Cres and Lošinj in the distance. Parts of the castle date back to Roman times, when it was an important way-station on the trade routes linking the Adriatic with the Pannonian plain, but the fortress assumed its current shape in the thirteenth century, when it became a stronghold of the Frankopans of Krk. The castle was taken over in 1826 by Laval Nugent, the Irish-Austrian general who commanded Habsburg forces during the Napoleonic wars. He made several Neoclassical additions to the place, including the family mausoleum in the shape of a Doric temple that dominates the central courtyard – the mausoleum occasionally serves as a gallery of contemporary art. The castle hosts open-air theatre, dance performances and concerts, and has a seasonal café.

4

Kantrida Beach

Bus #1 or #32 to Kantrida football stadium

Nowhere conjours up Rijeka's is-it-the-beauty-or-is-it-the-beast split personality more than **Kantrida beach**, 4km east of the centre, which offers views of Mount Učka on one side and the cranes of the 3 Maj shipyard on the other. Located behind the Kantrida football stadium, it's a simple pebbly affair that's always been popular with local families but has remained well off the radar of foreign visitors. The *Morski Prasac* beach bar (see p.196) is something of a cult summer destination for the Rijeka alternative crowd.

Ploče Beach

Bus#1 or #32 to Kantrida swimming complex

Situated below the Kantrida swimming complex, 5km west of the centre, **Ploče** is one of the best organized urban beaches in the northern Adriatic, with a broad bay of shallow pebble backed by play areas, and with good views of the Opatija Riviera across the gulf. There's a beach bar and a pizzeria at the back of the beach.

ARRIVAL AND INFORMATION — RIJEKA

By plane Rijeka's airport (T 051 842 040, W rijeka-airport.hr) is 25km south of town on the island of Krk; flights are met by a minibus to Rijeka's main bus station (40min; 30Kn). A taxi into the centre will set you back 300Kn.

Destination Zagreb (3 per week; 35min).

By train Rijeka's train station lies a few hundred metres west of the city centre on Krešimirova.

Destination Zagreb (3 daily; 4hr).

International destination Ljubljana (2 daily; 2hr 30min).

By bus The main bus station, handling all inter-city buses, is right in the centre at Trg Žabica (information T 060 302 010). Local buses from Kastav, Opatija and Lovran terminate on Jelačićev trg on the east side of the city centre.

Destinations Cres (4 daily; 2hr 30min); Dubrovnik (Mon–Sat 4 daily, Sun 3 daily; 12–13hr); Kastav (every 30min; 30min); Krk Town (hourly; 1hr 30min); Lovran (every 30min; 45min); Mali Lošinj (4 daily; 3hr 30min–4hr); Opatija (every 30min; 30min); Pag (Mon–Sat 1 daily; 3hr 45min); Rab Town (July & Aug 3 daily, Sept–June 2 daily; 3hr); Senj (12 daily; 1hr 30min); Split (12 daily; 8–9hr); Starigrad-Paklenica (12 daily; 3hr 35min); Zadar (12 daily; 4hr 40min–5hr); Zagreb (hourly; 2hr 30min–4hr).

International destinations Ljubljana (2 daily; 2hr 30min); Sarajevo (5 per week; 16hr); Trieste (6 daily; 2hr 30min).

By boat Ferries and catamarans dock at the passenger terminal on the south side of Rijeka harbour. Ferry and

catamaran tickets can be bought at Jadrolinija in the passenger terminal (Mon, Wed, Fri & Sun 7am–8pm; Tues, Thurs & Sat 7am–6pm; ☎ 051 211 444, Ⓦ jadrolinija.hr).
Ferries to: Dubrovnik (June–Sept 2 per week; 20hr); Hvar (June–Sept 2 per week; 12–14hr); Korčula (June–Sept 2 per week; 18hr); Split (June–Sept 2 per week; 10–12hr); Zadar (June–Sept 2 per week; 6hr).
Catamarans to: Cres (1 daily; 1hr 20min); Mali Lošinj (1 daily; 3hr 20min–3hr 50min); Novalja (1 daily; 2hr 30min); Rab (1 daily; 1hr 45min); Susak (6 per week; 2hr 40min–3hr 10min).
Tourist office Korzo 33 (mid-June to mid-Sept Mon–Sat 8am–8pm, Sun 8am–2pm; mid-Sept to mid-June Mon–Fri 8am–8pm, Sat 8am–2pm; ☎ 051 335 882, Ⓦ www.tz-rijeka.hr). The tourist office has town plans and a wealth of information on the Kvarner region.

GETTING AROUND

By bus Municipal bus tickets can be bought from newspaper kiosks (valid for two journeys) or from the driver (valid for one). Fares are calculated according to a zonal system: most city destinations, including Trsat, fall within zone 1 (10Kn from the driver; 16Kn from a kiosk); Opatija is in zone 3 (16Kn/26Kn), and Lovran lies in zone 4 (21Kn/30Kn).
By taxi Both the train and bus stations have ranks outside; alternatively call ☎ 051 335 138 or 051 332 893.

ACCOMMODATION

Rijeka's choice of **accommodation** is modest, and there are very few private **rooms** in the town itself (the tourist office can provide you with a list of phone numbers). There is plenty of choice a short bus ride away in Opatija and Lovran.

HOTELS

Bonavia Dolac 4 ☎ 051 357 100, Ⓦ bonavia.hr. Fully renovated four star hotel bang in the centre of town, with the standards of service that you'd expect at this level. Rooms feature plush carpets, swish bathrooms, TV, minibar and a/c. **1050Kn**
Continental Šetalište Andrije Kačića Miošića 1 ☎ 051 372 008, Ⓦ jadran-hoteli.hr. Conveniently central three-star, but a bit old-fashioned and gloomy in parts. The en-suite rooms with TV were renovated in 2008 and are reasonably cheery. **660Kn**
Jadran Šetalište XIII divizije 46 ☎ 051 216 600, Ⓦ jadran-hoteli.hr. On the shore 2km east of the centre, this minimalist grey box of a building is one of Rijeka's best examples of modernist architecture from the pre-World War I days. Rooms come with creamy colour schemes, Scandinavian-style furnishings, TV and a/c – some have bathtubs, but others only come with shower. The (more expensive) south-facing rooms have marvellous views across the water to the island of Cres. Bus #2 (direction Pećine) from the train station or from the Riva. **840Kn**
Neboder Strossmayerova 1 ☎ 051 373 538, Ⓦ jadran-hoteli.hr. If you want to sleep in a modernist landmark then stay in the *Neboder* ("Skyscraper"), an eight-storey sliver of reinforced concrete thrown up in the 1930s, when it was the former Yugoslavia's most futuristic-looking building. Within easy walking distance of downtown, it offers small but neat en suites with modern furnishings and TV – insist on a south-facing room for a tiny balcony and a fantastic view of the city. **580Kn**

HOSTEL AND CAMPSITE

Autocamp Preluk ☎ 051 623 500, Ⓦ autocamp-preluk.com. Located on the cusp of the Kvarner Gulf 8km north of town, this is a waterfront site that becomes a bit of a squeeze in summer. Bus #32 (from Jelačićev trg or from opposite the train station) passes the entrance. **50Kn** per person, pitches from **30Kn**
Omladinski Hostel Rijeka Šetalište XIII divizije 23 ☎ 051 406 420, Ⓦ hfhs.hr. Attractive interwar villa converted into a youth hostel, featuring bright, clean rooms with linoleum floors and pine beds. Rooms range in size from doubles to six-bed dorms; some come with en-suite WC and shower, others share facilities in the hallway. There's plenty of common-room space, and the price includes breakfast. Doubles **320Kn**, dorms **150Kn**

EATING AND DRINKING

Rijeka has a reasonable cross-section of good **restaurants**, and there are plenty more opportunities for a slap-up meal in nearby Opatija (see p.201). There are plenty of **snack** and sandwich joints along the Korzo, and a bustling fruit and veg **market** just beyond the eastern end of the Riva. For daytime drinking, the pavement **cafés** lining the Korzo or those girdling the church in Trsat are the places to hang out.

RESTAURANTS

Arca Fiumana Gat Karoline riječke bb ☎ 051 319 084. Moored beside the Riva, this former ferryboat is a pleasant place to tuck into grilled fish, scampi and *šurlice*. Daily 11am–11pm.
Belgian Beer Café/Brasserie As Trg republike Hrvatske 2 ☎ 051 212 345. Multipurpose eating, coffee-sipping and beer-guzzling venue, conveniently located midway between the Riva and the main shopping streets. An all-embracing menu includes vegetarian pasta dishes

4

as well as steak-and-chips pub food. The wood-panelled interior helps to create a welcoming brasserie atmosphere, and the handful of bottled Belgian beers on offer just about justifies the name. Daily 7am–1am.

Blato Titov trg 8c ⓣ051 336 970, ⓦblato1902.hr. Unpretentious, cosy *konoba* with a simple menu of daily specials scratched on a blackboard, usually covering everything from mushroom omelettes to juicy steaks, with a lot of reasonably priced seafood too. Good place to fill up on staples such as Dalmatian *pašticada* or *pržene lignje* (fried squid). Mon–Fri 7am–10pm, Sat 7am–8pm.

Feral Matije Gupca 5b ⓣ051 212 274, ⓦkonoba-feral.com. Semi-formal seafood restaurant with high standards and higher-than-average prices – it's one of the best places in the region to eat *jakopske kapice* (scallops) and other shellfish. The brick-lined rooms have the feel of a cosy cellar. Mon–Fri 10am–10pm, Sat 11am–6pm.

Gric & Guc Dolac 8 ⓣ051 319 043. With a name that might loosely be translated as "Nibble and Glug", this part-restaurant part-beer hall aims to provide good food and drink in comfortable surroundings at a reasonable price. Order from the menu or ask the waiter about daily specials; *šurlice* with goulash, fillets of hake and *fažol* crop up regularly. Main courses rarely top the 55Kn mark. Mon–Fri 6am–midnight, Sat till 1am; closed Sun.

4

Konoba Nebuloza Titov trg 2b ⓣ051 372 294, ⓦkonobanebuloza.com. Local food in a smart but homely setting, with a chequered-tablecloth dining room overlooking the River Riječina. Dishes include Krk-made *šurlice* with seafood or goulash, inexpensive fried fish fillets and hearty sausage-and-sauerkraut dishes. Mon–Fri 10am–11pm, Sat noon–11pm.

Na kantunu Demetrova 2 ⓣ051 313 271. In a workaday grid of streets behind the market, this is a popular buffet serving up solid, satisfying and cheap seafood to an appreciative crowd of local port and office workers. Expect mackerel, sardines and other forms of *plava riba* (oily fish), as well as *oslić* (hake), shellfish and risottos. Mon–Sat 8am–10pm.

Pizzeria Bracera Kružna 12 ⓣ051 322 498, ⓦpizzeria-bracera.com.hr. Located in an alleyway just off the Korzo, this is the best of the central pizzerias, with a range of well-presented thin-crust pies alongside pasta dishes and salads. Place mats and menus feature cute maritime designs courtesy of local artist Vojo Radojčić (see p.191). Tends to fill up at lunchtimes, so arrive early or be prepared to wait. Daily 11am–11pm.

Zlatna školjka Kružna 12a ⓣ051 213 782, ⓦzlatna-skoljka.hr. Charming little seafood restaurant just off the Korzo, with an interior stuffed with nautical bric-a-brac. Plenty of shrimp and squid dishes (including an excellent and not too expensive *crni rižot*, as well as the full range of fish. Mon–Sat 11am–11pm.

CAFÉS AND BARS

Boa Ante Starčevića 8 ⓣ091 339 9339. A place to see and be seen, this hip bar with lots of glass and black-and-white designer furniture has music blasting until the wee hours at weekends. The two pavement terraces shaded by giant parasols are pleasant for a daytime drink. Sun–Wed 8am–11pm, Thurs–Sat 8am–3am.

★ **Celtic Caffe Bard** Trg Grivica 68 ⓣ051 215 235, ⓦcaffebard.com. Cosy, laid-back and intimate café-bar opposite St Vitus's Church, serving international beers to an older crowd. With only a handful of tables outside, people perch on nearby walls and steps on summer evenings. Mon–Sat 8am–midnight.

★ **Cukari Kafe** Trg Jurje Klovića 4 ⓣ099 583 8276. With white chairs, white tables and even white fur above the bar, this looks a bit like the dream sequence from a 1960s movie. Good coffee, own-brand biscuits and soothing background music make it a laid-back choice for a daytime break; bottled Belgian beers bring in discerning drinkers come the evening. Mon–Wed 7am–midnight, Thurs & Fri till 2am, Sat 8am–2am.

Filodrammatica Korzo 28. Fulcrum of the city's social life for generations (a rabble-rousing Benito Mussolini addressed crowds here in 1919), *Filodrammatica* has been through numerous reincarnations, most recently serving as a branch of the Hemingway cocktail-bar chain before reverting to its more traditional role as city-centre café (although this time it comes with bookshop attached). The lounge-bar decor of the Hemingway era still remains; juices, breakfasts, brunches and a range of fancy drinks keep the quality up. Daily 7am–11pm.

Karolina Gat Karoline riječke bb ⓣ051 330 909. This glass box by the quayside comes into its own in the summer months, when café tables, DJ decks and a crowd of fun-seeking locals explode out onto the surrounding flagstones. Bigger than usual choice of international spirits, and quality wines by the glass. Sun–Wed 7am–2am, Thur–Sat till 5am.

Kosi Toranj Put Vele crikve 1 ⓣ051 336 214. Loungey café-bar equipped with purple sofas and floor-to-ceiling windows, catering for style-conscious coffee-guzzlers during the day and fans of DJ culture in the evening. Mon–Sat 8am–midnight, Sun 3–11pm.

Mali Caffe Korso 18 ⓣ051 335 606. With good strong coffee and energy-lifting loud music, this is a good place for a daytime refuelling or a pre-bar crawl drink. It's also the ideal vantage point from which to observe the ebb and flow of humans on the Korso. Mon–Sat 7am–11pm, Sun 9am–11pm.

Morski Prasac Kantrida bb. Cult beach bar behind the football stadium comprising four turquoise wooden tables – and a lot of pebble beach. Impromptu live music and DJ events in the summer. Summer only Sun–Thurs 9am–midnight, Fri & Sat till 2am.

Palach Kružna 6. For lovers of guitar music and graffiti aesthetics there are few better places than *Palach*, hidden away in a spray-paint splattered alleyway behind the Korzo. It has been the nerve centre of Rijeka's alternative scene since 1968, when it was named (rather provocatively for the times) after the Czech anti-communist martyr Jan Palach. It comprises an art gallery, a roomy bar area scattered with distressed wooden tables and a space for live gigs and club nights. Mon–Wed 9am–midnight, Thurs 9am–2am, Fri & Sat 9am–3am, Sun 5pm–midnight.

Phanas Pub Ivana Zajca 9 ⓣ 051 312 377, ⓦ phanas.hr. Wood-panelled pub-like bar that's a popular social hub in winter, when Rijeka's beau monde arrives to peruse the cocktail list and wiggle their body parts to pop-rock-disco background beats. Sun–Wed 7am–1am, Thurs–Sat till 5am.

Tunel Školjić 12 ⓣ 051 327 116. A railway arch (hence the "tunnel" in the title) converted into one of Rijeka's coolest bars, with a regular diet of jazz, blues, funk and rock on record or live, weekly jam sessions included. Mon–Thurs 9am–midnight, Fri 9am–2am, Sat 5pm–2am.

NIGHTLIFE AND ENTERTAINMENT

Rijeka prides itself on its **live music** traditions, with regular gigs at *Palach* and *Tunel* (see above), a concert programme at *Stereo Dvorana* (see below) and one of the key **summer festivals** in the shape of Hartera (see box below).

LIVE MUSIC

Stereo Dvorana Strossmayerova 1 ⓦ zabava.hr. Medium-sized concert venue located right behind the *Neboder* hotel, hosting live rock, jazz and DJ-driven club nights. The event season usually lasts from Oct to June.

Puppet Theatre (Gradsko kazalište lutaka) B. Polića 6 ⓣ 051 325 688, ⓦ gkl-rijeka.hr. The leading puppet theatre in this part of Croatia, with enchanting shows for children taking place on Thurs and Fri at 6pm, Sat at 11am.

THEATRE

Croatian National Theatre (Hrvatsko narodno kazalište) Trg Ivana Zajca ⓣ 051 337 114, ⓦ hnk-zajc.hr. Splendid nineteenth-century theatre with plush seats, now accommodating opera, ballet, orchestral concerts and drama.

CINEMA

Art-kino Croatia Krešimirova 2 ⓣ 051 323 261, ⓦ art-kino.org. Old-school single-screen cinema near the bus station, specializing in the more intelligent Hollywood movies and European art films. Closed July & Aug.

4

SHOPPING

Kantoon pod Kaštelom 5 ⓣ 051 215 040, ⓦ kantoonshop.com. Small boutique selling the kind of imaginative and well-designed accessories (bags, shoes, scarves etc) that you just don't get at the regular souvenir shops. Most products come courtesy of small-scale designers and eco-friendly producers. Mon–Fri 9am–1pm & 3–8pm, Sat 9am–2pm.

VBZ Korzo 32 ⓣ 051 324 015, ⓦ vbz.hr. Large bookshop with a good choice of local titles and English-language paperbacks. Mon–Sat 9am–10pm.

DIRECTORY

Exchange Erste banka is at Jadranski trg 3a, with ATMs outside.

Hospital Krešimirova 42 (ⓣ 051 658 111), on the north side of the road, just west of the train station.

Internet There is a public wi-fi zone in the central area of town around the Korzo.

RIJEKA FESTIVALS

For three days in mid-June a former paper factory in the steep-sided gorge of the River Rječina becomes the scene of **Hartera** (ⓦ hartera.com), one of Central Europe's most intriguing rock festivals. Live music and DJ sets take place in a variety of postindustrial spaces, with the decoration of the stark halls of the factory taking a different theme each year. There's a good mixture of top international names and local acts, and with capacity limited to around three thousand people the festival has an intimate, boutique feel. Check the website for deals on tent accommodation in the Hartera camp, and cut-price offers on hotels in Opatija.

Other major festivals to look out for include **Rijeka Summer Nights** (Riječke ljetne noći; July; ⓦ rijeckeljetnenoci.com), involving classical music, drama and dance in both indoor and outdoor venues throughout the city; and **Summer in the Castle** (Ljeto na gradini; Aug–Sept; information from the tourist office or on ⓦ bascinskiglasi.hr), a series of open-air theatre performances, film screenings and pop-rock concerts in the courtyard of Trsat castle.

Left luggage There's a *garderoba* at the bus station (daily 5.30am–10.30pm).

Pharmacy Jadranski trg 1 (24hr).

Post office The most central post office is halfway down the Korzo at no.13 (Mon–Fri 7am–9pm, Sat 7am–2pm); there's a 24hr branch beyond the train station at Krešimirova 7.

The Opatija Riviera

Just to the west of Rijeka, the **Opatija Riviera** (Opatijska rivijera) is a twenty-kilometre stretch of sedate seaside resorts lining the western side of the Kvarner Gulf. Protected from strong winds by the ridge of **Mount Učka**, this stretch of coast became the favoured retreat of tubercular Viennese fleeing the central European winter. At the centre of the Riviera is the town of **Opatija**, whose nineteenth-century popularity made it the Austro-Hungarian Empire's answer to the Côte d'Azur. The Habsburg ambience survives in some attractive *fin-de-siècle* architecture, the best of which is in the dainty town of **Lovran**, just southwest of Opatija. There's an abundance of good accommodation throughout the Riviera, although private rooms and pensions tend to be cheaper in Lovran than in Opatija.

ARRIVAL AND DEPARTURE — THE OPATIJA RIVIERA

By bus The main Rijeka–Pula road cuts right through the Riviera. From Rijeka, bus #32 (daily 4.30am–10.30pm from Jelačićev trg; every 20–30min) travels via Opatija to terminate in either Lovran or Mošćenička Draga, the latter just south of Medveja. If you're approaching from Pula, most Rijeka-bound buses will drop you off in Lovran or Opatija.

4

Kastav

The best view of the Opatija Riviera is from the village of **KASTAV**, a worthwhile side-trip 10km northwest of Rijeka on the karst ridge overlooking the gulf. A windswept knot of cobbled alleyways hemmed in by scraps of surviving fortification, Kastav is strong on atmosphere but short of real sights. Head first for **St Helena's Church** (Crkva svete Jelene), from whose terrace there's an expansive panorama of the Gulf. On the other, landward side of the village is the **Crekvina**, the stark remains of an enormous church begun by the Jesuits but never finished. Given the village as a fief by the Habsburgs, the Jesuits proved unpopular masters, greedy for taxes. One of their civilian administrators, Frano Morelli, was drowned in a well on the main square in 1666 – a crime that was committed en masse by the villagers and therefore proved unpunishable.

ARRIVAL AND INFORMATION — KASTAV

By bus Kastav is easily accessible from either Rijeka (bus #18) or Opatija (bus #37), but there may not be any information on return services when you get here, so check schedules before setting out if you can.

Tourist office Trg Matke Laginje 5, beside the old town gate (Mon–Fri 7am–3pm; ⓣ 051 691 425, ⓦ kastav-touristinfo.hr).

EATING

★ **Kukuriku** Kastav 120 ⓣ 051 691 519, ⓦ kukuriku.hr. One of the most celebrated restaurants in the Kvarner Gulf offers an upmarket take on Istrian-Mediterranean cuisine, with fine seafood and game featuring on a menu that changes every day – guests are invited to choose a three-or-more-course set meal and suitable wines will be selected to go with it. Prices are high and – unless money is no object – you should check what you are paying for as you order, though the experience is likely to be worth the outlay. Reservations advisable. Daily noon–midnight.

Opatija

Longest established of the Kvarner Gulf resorts, **OPATIJA** is very much the grande dame of Croatian tourism. It was the kind of town that sucked in celebrities from all over Europe during the *belle époque*, an era that lives on in Opatija's fine Austro-Hungarian buildings and neatly clipped parks. The resort continues to be patronized by central Europeans of a certain age (there are times when you can walk the length of the seafront without seeing anyone under 45), although recent years have seen an influx of younger holidaymakers from Russia, Ukraine and further east. Opatija's proximity to Rijeka ensures a regular influx of weekend trippers throughout the year, when the town's famous shoreline promenade can be jammed with strollers. Top-quality **seafood restaurants** have taken off in a big way in Opatija, especially in the fishing-village suburb of Volosko, turning the town into a major target for gastro-pilgrims.

The town is a long thin hillside settlement straddling along the base of Mount Učka. At its centre is the **Slatina beach**, a concrete lido surrounded by cafés and souvenir stalls. The main street, **Maršala Tita**, runs past some grand examples of *fin-de-siècle* architecture, although the seaside promenade of Šetalište Franza Jozefa offers a far better way of exploring.

Brief history

Opatija was little more than a fishing village until the arrival in 1844 of Rijeka businessman **Iginio Scarpa**, who built the opulent Villa Angiolina as a holiday home for his family and aristocratic Habsburg friends. In 1882 the villa was bought by **Friedrich Schüller**, head of Austria's Southern Railways; having just built the line from Ljubljana to Rijeka, he decided to promote Opatija as a mass holiday destination and the town's first hotels (including the *Kvarner*, *Krönprinzessin Stephanie* – today's *Imperial* – and *Palace-Bellevue*) soon followed. Opatija quickly developed a Europe-wide reputation: Franz Josef of Austria met Kaiser Wilhelm II of Germany here in 1894, while playwright Anton Chekhov holidayed at the *Kvarner* in the same year. A decade later Isadora Duncan installed herself in a villa behind the *Krönprinzessin Stephanie* and was inspired by the palm tree outside her window to create one of her best-known dance movements – "that light fluttering of the arms, hands and fingers which has been so much abused by my imitators".

4

Šetalište Franza Josefa

One of the Adriatic's most scenic strolls, the tree-shaded promenade of **Šetalište Franza Josefa** runs along the rocky seafront all the way to the old fishing village of Volosko (2km to the north) and the sedate resort of Lovran (6km to the south). Working its way around bays, beaches and promontories, passing *belle-époque* mansions and modern hotels on the way, it offers any number of perspectives on the changing Kvarner scene.

Park Angiolina

Museum of Tourism Villa Angiolina • Tues–Sun 9am–1pm & 5–8pm • Free • ⓣ 051 603 636 **Juraj Šporer Art Pavilion** Times and prices depend on what's on

Set back slightly from the seafront lie the exotic shrubs and palms of the **Park Angiolina**, where the custard-coloured **Villa Angiolina** presides over neatly trowelled flowerbeds. Built by Iginio Scarpa in 1844 to serve as both holiday house and venue for upscale parties, its opulent pseudo-Grecian interior now holds the **Museum of Tourism** (Muzej turizma) – a highly enjoyable assemblage of old postcards, holiday brochures and beachware. On the western edge of the park is the oldest and grandest of Opatija's hotels, the *Kvarner*, whose facade, complete with trumpet-blowing cherubs and bare-chested Titans, looks more like a provincial opera house than a hotel. Immediately west of the hotel, the **Juraj Šporer Art Pavilion** (Umjetnički pavilion Juraj Šporer) hosts contemporary art exhibitions in an attractive colonnaded building that once served as a seafront patisserie.

Volosko

Offering a complete contrast to Opatija are the steep, narrow alleyways and shuttered houses of **Volosko**, once a separate village but now swallowed up by Opatija's suburban sprawl, an easy twenty minutes' walk northeast along the coastal promenade. It's an atmospheric place for a short wander, with its whitewashed buildings arranged into a kasbah-like maze of streets, and a small fishing fleet in its tiny *mandrać* (inner harbour).

Beaches

Opatija's main beach, **Slatina**, is the biggest letdown in the Adriatic, a cemented-over lido opposite the bus station. Five minutes walk further northeast, the beach in front of Angiolina Park is a better proposition; a broad shallow bay with a sandy sea floor. Otherwise, it's better to walk 3km south to **Ičići**, where there's a pebbly beach popular with families and backed by volleyball courts.

ARRIVAL AND DEPARTURE — OPATIJA

By bus Opatija's bus station occupies a small square just off the waterfront.

Destinations Kastav (Mon–Fri 9 daily, Sat 5 daily, Sun 2 daily; 20min); Lovran (every 30min; 15min); Rijeka (every 30min; 30min).

INFORMATION AND TOURS

Tourist office Maršala Tita 128 (April–Sept Mon–Sat 8am–9pm, Sun 3–8pm; Oct–March Mon–Fri 8am–3pm, Sat 8am–2pm; ☎ 051 271 310, 🌐 opatija-tourism.hr). The tourist office is well stocked with town maps and brochures; they also sell a map of hiking and biking trails on Mount Učka (20Kn).

Tours Katarina Line (see below) organize tours and small-boat cruises.

ACCOMMODATION

4

Accommodation in Opatija can be expensive unless you opt for the private **rooms** (200Kn) and **apartments** (two-person studios 380Kn, four-person apartments 500–650Kn). The website 🌐 opatijaholiday.com is a reliable resource for rooms and apartments, as is **Katarina Line**, Maršala Tita 75/1 (☎ 051 603 400, 🌐 katarina-line.hr), who also offer them elsewhere in Kvarner.

HOTELS

Ambassador Feliksa Peršića 5 ☎ 051 743 333, 🌐 liburnia.hr. Built in the 1960s to serve as a modernist riposte to the Habsburg-era buildings elsewhere in town, this brutish grey box of a hotel is all comfort and light when seen from the inside. All rooms have good views and the on-site facilities are excellent, with indoor swimming pool and a very well-equipped gym-cum-spa-centre in the basement. **1200Kn**

Kvarner-Amalia P. Tomašića 1–4 ☎ 051 271 233, 🌐 liburnia.hr. This is the grandest of the pre-1914 hotels and still boasts bags of atmosphere, even though it's beginning to look decidedly frumpy in comparison to some of the more modern developments. Along with comfy rooms and old-world furnishings, it has a superb position right on the waterfront, with its own stretch of private beach, plus indoor and outdoor pools. The adjacent *Amalia* has slightly cheaper and simpler rooms. **850Kn**

Miramar I. Kaline 11 ☎ 051 280 000, 🌐 hotel-miramar.info. Opulent, Austrian-run hotel occupying nineteenth-century buildings that overlook the seaside path midway between Opatija and Volosko. Also boasts a state-of-the-art spa, beauty and wellness centre; if you want to swan around like a latter-day Habsburg while having papaya mousse rubbed into your chest, then this is undoubtedly the place to do it. **1150Kn**

Palace-Bellevue Maršala Tita 144–146 ☎ 051 271 811, 🌐 liburnia.hr. Cheapest of the Habsburg-era places, whose lobby and bar areas still convey a whiff of *fin-de-siècle* voluptuousness. The en-suite rooms have been recently renovated, but remain simple and affordable. **780Kn**

Villa Ariston Maršala Tita 179 ☎ 051 271 379, 🌐 villa-ariston.hr. Small-scale hotel occupying an elegantly restored villa designed by Viennese architect Karl Seidl in Opatija's pre-World War I heyday. Most doubles are in the attic and come with atmospheric sloping roofs, as well as attached baths, TV, a/c and minibar. **830Kn**

EATING AND DRINKING

Provided you stay well away from the bland fare served up in hotel restaurants, Opatija is an excellent place in which to sample Adriatic seafood at its best – some of the town's **restaurants** are truly outstanding. Most of the historic **cafés** along Maršala Tita have had all trace of the *belle époque* ripped out of them, although there are plenty of places to enjoy coffee and cake. The harbour, 1km northeast of the bus station, is the prime evening **drinking** area, where a forest of chairs, tables and parasol stands spreads out from a cluster of flash cafés and cocktail bars.

RESTAURANTS

Amfora Črnikovica 4, Volosko ⓣ051 701 222, ⓦrestaurant-amfora.com. Succulent fresh fish in a pricey restaurant at the northern end of Volosko, its dining room overlooking a rocky, wave-battered cove. Try the fish platter (*riblji pladanj*), which usually features the grilled catch of the day garnished with the odd squid and shrimp. Daily noon–midnight.

Bevanda-Lido Zert 8 ⓣ051 493 888, ⓦbevanda.hr. Superior-quality seafood served up by attentive, liveried staff in a Neoclassical pavilion near Opatija's harbour. Good for fresh lobster, but there's also an extensive list of Croatian wines, plus the biggest choice of desserts in town. Daily noon–midnight.

★ **Le Mandrać** Obala F. Supila 10, Volosko ⓣ051 701 357, ⓦlemandrac.com. *Le Mandrać*'s stridently modern-looking glass-enclosed front porch is a fitting introduction to the cuisine itself: a stylish take on Adriatic seafood prepared with a modern European slant. Daily three-course menus (150Kn) show off some of the more innovative dishes, although the five-course tasting menu (490Kn) is the way to go if you are in the mood for gastronomic overload. Daily noon–midnight.

Pečenjarnica Gusto Maršala Tita 220 ⓣ051 631 169. The perfect antidote to the fancy world of central Opatija is this family-run grill 2km southwest of the centre, with six tables on a small terrace above the street. There's not much on the menu apart from calamari, anchovies, *pljeskavice* and *čevapčići*, none of which are likely to break the 35Kn barrier. Daily 9am–midnight.

★ **Plavi Podrum** Obala F. Supila 12, Volosko ⓣ051 701 223, ⓦplavipodrum.com. An award-winning establishment right on Volosko's harbour, renowned for its expertly prepared seafood and masterfully composed wine list – manager Danijela Kramarić is a leading sommelier. Kvarner scampi is a major feature of the menu, which can here be sampled in numerous different sauces, while fillets of fish (150–180Kn) are also served up in several exciting combinations of sauce and spice. Reservations are advisable – although the harbour-facing terrace is quite roomy and it's frequently possible to walk in on weekdays. Daily noon–midnight.

★ **Tramerka** Andrije Mohorovičića 15, Volosko ⓣ051 701 707. Located on a narrow alley just up the steps behind *Plavi Podrum* (see above), *Tramerka* has a trio of wooden benches sitting outside a cool, dark, cave-like interior. It's a

4

HIKING ON MOUNT UČKA

Dominating the skyline above Opatija and Lovran is the long, forest-covered ridge of the **Učka massif**, which divides the Kvarner region from central Istria and is protected as a Nature Park (ⓦpp-ucka.hr). It is accessible by road from Rijeka via a route running over the northern shoulder of the mountain, which passes a turn-off to the 1396-metre summit of **Vojak** on the way. Rather than driving to Vojak, however, the best way to enjoy Učka's wooded slopes is to walk. Paths are well marked, and the *Učka* **map** (25Kn), available from the tourist offices in Opatija and Lovran, is an invaluable guide.

Lovran is the starting point for the most direct **hiking route** up the mountain – the ascent takes around three and a half hours. A flight of rough-hewn steps begins immediately behind Lovran's old centre, leading to the small Romanesque Chapel of St Rock on the edge of the village of **Liganj**. Join the road into Liganj for a couple of hundred metres, before heading uphill to the right through the hamlets of **Dindići** and **Ivulići** – semi-abandoned clusters of farmhouses and moss-covered dry-stone walls. From Ivulići it's a steady two-hour ascent through oak and beech forest before you emerge onto a grassy saddle where an expansive panorama of inland Istria suddenly opens up, revealing the knobbly green and brown forms of the peninsula's central hills; the peak of Vojak is another twenty minutes' walk to the right. At the top, there's an observation tower, TV mast and splendid views of Rijeka and the spindly form of Cres beyond. An **alternative ascent**, which takes about fifty minutes longer, starts just behind the *Medveja* campsite (see p.204) and ascends to the village of **Lovranska Draga** before climbing steeply up a wooded ravine to join the main path from Lovran.

From Vojak, a path descends north to **Poklon** (1hr), where you meet up with the old Rijeka–Istria road. There's a terrace offering another view of the Kvarner Gulf here. On Sundays, **bus #34** from Opatija climbs as far as Poklon once a day, making this a good starting point from which to tackle Vojak if time is short. From Poklon, you can work your way southeast back to Lovran (roughly a 2hr walk) by a downhill path which ultimately joins the main route you came up on.

RESTAURANT

Dopolavoro Učka 9 ⓣ051 299 641, ⓦdopolavoro.hr. A fine restaurant 1km west of Poklon, offering top-notch Istrian cuisine and game dishes such as venison, pheasant, bear and boar. Daily noon–11pm.

very good place to indulge in the best fresh fish (360Kn/kg); the owner will advise on what the boat has brought in that morning), although seafood pastas and risottos also come highly recommended. Daily 1pm–midnight.

Villa Ariston Maršala Tita 179 ⊕051 271 379, ⊛villa-ariston.hr. Top-of-the-range seafood, plus pork and chicken in rich sauces, and a long wine list. You can sit either inside, in what looks like a nineteenth-century French drawing room, or outside in the palm-packed garden. Can be entered from either Maršala Tita or the seafront promenade. Daily noon–11pm.

CAFÉS AND BARS

Choco Bar Maršala Tita 94 ⊕051 603 562, ⊛raschocobar.com. Run by Zagreb-based chocolate manufacturer Kraš, this is something of a temple to the brown stuff, with a menu of sweet and gloopy drinks that runs to several pages. Excellent desserts, and boxed-up chocolates for sale. Daily 8am–10pm.

Grand Café Viktora Cara Emina 6. Modern café done out in *belle-époque* style, offering good, strong coffee and a superb array of cakes and pastries. The handmade chocolates, sold loose by weight as well as in presentation boxes, are likely to prove addictive. Daily 7am–11pm.

Hemingway Zert bb. This roomy glass-fronted building on a stretch of the seafront well supplied with bars is a bit like a funky conservatory, with loungey chairs, DJ-driven sounds and a long menu of designer cocktails. Sandwiches and salads are served up during the daytime, and there's an Italian themed restaurant on the top floor. Sadly, there are next to no mementoes connected to the bearded scribbler in the title however. Daily noon–2am.

Monokini Maršala Tita 96. Marginally more arty and alternative than *Hemingway* and its neighbours, *Monokini* attracts the hip crowd with its monthly art shows, postindustrial decor and soul-funk soundtrack. Daily 9am–2am.

Lovran

4

LOVRAN is an Italianate, green-shuttered little town with a small harbour, fringed by palatial *belle époque* villas sporting curly wrought-iron balustrades. Uphill from the harbour is an old quarter of vine-shaded alleys which converge on the fourteenth-century **St George's Church** (Crkva svetog Jurja); the frescoes behind the main altar, which date from 1479, are reminiscent in style of the wall paintings at Beram and other Istrian churches. Opposite the church, the **House of St George** bears an eighteenth-century relief of the saint slaying a dragon above the doorway; it's become something of a town trademark.

Villa Gianna

Maršala Tita 23

Habsburg-era villas are scattered all over Lovran. Some of the best are concentrated northeast of the centre along Maršala Tita, where you can hardly miss the Secessionist **Villa Gianna**, a mauve-pink confection built in 1904 by local architect Attilio Maguolo. It's embellished with ornate Corinthian columns and winged dragons clutching shields inscribed with the initials IP, a reference to the original owner, Iginio Persich.

Beaches around Lovran

Ičići, 2km north of Lovran, is currently main contender for the title of best family beach, with a shallow pebbly bay backed by beach volleyball courts and cafés. The larger shingle beach at **Medveja**, 3km south of Lovran, is no longer the relaxed and welcoming place it used to be, with the *Hemingway* beach bar renting out divan-like sun loungers and jet skis to an aspirational cocktail-sipping crowd.

ARRIVAL AND INFORMATION — LOVRAN

By bus Buses pick up and drop off on Lovran's main street, where most of what you need is located.

Destinations Liganj (11 daily; 15min); Lovranska Draga (11 daily; 20min); Rijeka (every 30min; 45min).

By foot It's an easy hour's walk to the town along the coastal promenade south from Opatija, following a rocky shore punctuated by two pebbly coves at Ičići and Ika.

Tourist office Trg slobode 1 (June–Sept Mon–Sat 8am–9pm, Sun 8am–1pm; Oct–May Mon–Sat 8am–3pm; ⊕051 291 740, ⊛tz-lovran.hr). The helpful tourist office dispenses free town plans, bus timetables and hiking info.

FROM TOP LEFT KVARNER HOTEL, OPATIJA (P.199); LOVRAN; WATERFRONT, CRES TOWN (P.205) >

ARN
PEPSI

LOVRAN CHESTNUT FESTIVAL

The Lovran area is famous for its chestnut trees, which were originally imported from Japan in the seventeenth century. They are harvested in mid-autumn, an event celebrated by the **Marunada Chestnut Festival** (call the tourist office for details), which takes place over three weekends in October: the first two weekends see festivities in hill villages above town, while the final weekend takes place in Lovran itself. The festival is used as an excuse for making a wide variety of cakes flavoured with chestnut purée, which are sold in all the local cafés.

ACCOMMODATION

Plentiful private **rooms** (200Kn) and **apartments** (studios 350Kn, four-person apartments from 450Kn) are available from a couple of central agencies (usually open June–Sept 8am–8pm, Oct–May Mon–Fri 9am–3pm): **Hill**, Trg slobode 15 (T 051 293 700, W hill-lovran.com), and **dmc Lovrana 1873**, Stari Grad 1 (T 051 294 910, E lovrana@lovranske-vile.com).

HOTELS AND B&B

Villa Astra Viktora Cara Emina 11 T 051 294 604, W lovranske-vile.com. Lovran's most exclusive hotel, this beautifully restored four-star villa, surrounded by lush subtropical plants, sports six tastefully decorated en-suite rooms, a gourmet restaurant and a lovely outdoor terrace with a heated pool. 2400Kn

4

Villa Stanger 26 Divizije 2 T 051 291 403, E dragan.stanger@hep.hr. Cosy bed and breakfast in a modern, three-storey house a stone's throw from the centre uphill from Maršala Tita. Rooms are en suite with tiny balconies. The owners speak Italian and German. 350Kn

CAMPSITES

Autocamp Opatija Ičići T 051 704 387, W rivijera-opatija.hr. A pleasant, wooded site on a terraced hillside about a 5min walk above the main coastal road, 2km north of Lovran. 40Kn per person, pitches from 31Kn

Camping Medveja Medveja bb T 051 291 191, W liburnia.hr. A well-appointed and spacious campsite attractively tucked into a steep-sided valley, with a supermarket and grill restaurant on site. Medveja beach (see p.202) is right opposite. 60Kn per person, pitches from 50Kn

EATING AND DRINKING

Guc Lučica. If there was a competition for the most evocatively situated Adriatic café-bar then *Guc* would be a strong contender, with candlelit tables spread out on the water's edge among upturned boats. Good choice of shots and cocktails. Daily 9am–2am.

Knezgrad Trg slobode 12 T 051 291 838. Quality meat and fish dishes at moderate prices; there are often cheap lunchtime menus chalked up on a board outside. Terrace tables face onto a park with well-kept flowerbeds and palms. Daily 11am–11pm.

Kvarner Maršala Tita 65 T 051 291 118, W restoran-kvarner-lovran.hr. Excellent fresh seafood, slightly pricier than at *Knezgrad*, overlooking the harbour. Daily 10am–midnight.

★ **Najade** Maršala Tita 69 T 051 291 866. Family-run seafood restaurant of long-standing good reputation, with a big outdoor terrace overlooking the bit of the shore where Lovran's small boats are moored. Freshly caught fish (360–380Kn/kg); the squid stuffed with *pršut* and cheese (90Kn) is exceptional. Daily 11am–midnight.

Wine Bar Loza Stari Grad 5 T 051 490 777. Generous choice of quality Croatian wines, plenty of which are available by the glass, with a handful of tables scattered across an Old Town alleyway. A choice of Mediterranean nibbles is chalked up on a board daily. Daily 10am–midnight.

Cres and Lošinj

The westernmost of the Kvarner islands, **CRES** and **LOŠINJ** (really a single island divided by an artificial channel), together make up a narrow sliver of land which begins just south of the Istrian coast and extends most of the way across the Kvarner Gulf. Allegedly the place where Jason and the Argonauts fled with the Golden Fleece, the islands were originally known as the Absyrtides; according to legend, Medea killed her brother Absyrtus here and threw his remains into the sea, where two of his limbs became Cres and Lošinj.

Despite its proximity to the mainland, Cres (pronounced "tsress") is by far the wilder and more unspoiled of the two islands, boasting a couple of attractively weatherbeaten old settlements in **Osor** and **Cres Town**, as well as numerous villages and coves in which modern-day mass tourism has yet to make an impact. The island marks the transition between the lush green vegetation of northern Croatia and the bare karst of the Adriatic, with the deciduous forest and overgrown hedgerows of northern Cres – the so-called **Tramuntana** – giving way to the increasingly barren sheep-pastures of the south.

Lošinj (pronounced "losheen") is smaller and more touristed than Cres, with a thick, woolly tree cover that comes as a relief after the obdurate grey-greenness of southern Cres. The island's main town, **Mali Lošinj**, is a magnet for holiday-makers from Central Europe, though even here you'll find a charming old town and port relatively unsullied by concrete mega-developments. Its near-neighbour **Veli Lošinj**, which lies within walking distance, is smaller and offers more in terms of fishing-village charm – although it too can get crowded in August.

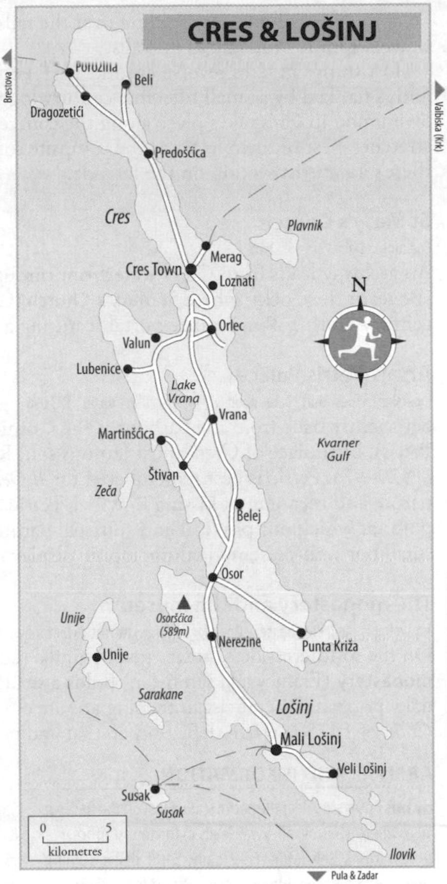

ARRIVAL AND DEPARTURE

CRES AND LOŠINJ

By ferry Ferries run hourly from Brestova, just south down the Istrian coast from Opatija, to Porozina in northern Cres, and every 90min from Valbiska on Krk to Merag on Cres.

By catamaran There's a daily catamaran service between Rijeka and Mali Lošinj, stopping in Cres Town and on Susak. From Istria or Dalmatia, each of the two ferries weekly that run between Pula and Zadar call at Mali Lošinj.

Cres Town to: Mali Lošinj (1 daily; 2hr–2hr 30min); Rijeka (1 daily; 1hr 20min); Susak (6 per week; 1hr 30min–1hr 50min).

By bus Most buses plying the Rijeka–Cres–Lošinj route use the Brestova ferry crossing, although at least one bus daily goes via Valbiska on Krk.

By car If you're driving, bear in mind that both ferry services attract lengthy queues on summer weekends, so it's best to arrive early or bring a good book.

GETTING AROUND

Although buses run daily up and down the main road along the island's hilly central spine, to properly explore some of the smaller places on Cres – such as Beli, Valun and Lubenice – you'll need either plenty of time and good walking shoes, or your own transport.

Cres Town

Strung around a small harbour, **CRES TOWN** has the attractively crumpled look of so many of the towns on this coast: tiny alleys lead nowhere, minuscule courtyards shelter an abundance of greenery spilling over the rails of balconies, while mauve and pink flowers sprout from cracks in walls.

Most things in Cres revolve around **Trg F. Petrića**, which opens out onto the harbour and is flanked by a small fifteenth-century loggia and a sixteenth-century clock tower. **Swimming** in Cres takes place along the concreted Lungomare promenade, which stretches west of town as far as the campsite some 1.5km away in the suburb of Melin; there's a naturist section on the far side.

St Mary's Church

Pod urom • Daily 9am–6.30pm

An archway leads from Cres's waterfront through to a square known as **Pod urom** (Beneath the clock), where **St Mary's Church** (Crkva svete Marije) boasts a fifteenth-century Gothic–Renaissance portal featuring a fine relief of the Virgin and Child.

Arsan-Petris Palace

Ribarska 7 • Tues–Sun 10am–noon & 7–9pm • 20Kn • ⓣ 051 573 096

Set slightly back from the harbour is the Gothic **Arsan-Petris Palace** (Palača Arsan-Petris), birthplace of Cres's most famous son, Renaissance philosopher Frane Petrić (1529–97). Petrić is best remembered for *Il Delfino* ("The Dolphin"), a treatise on the nature and meaning of kissing in which Petrić opines, "the moment of the kiss is the point at which our physical and spiritual natures meet and become one". There is a small but well-presented ethnographic display inside.

4

The monastery and the museum

Trg svetog Frane 6 • **Monastery** Open for Sun mass **Museum** by appointment • 5Kn • ⓣ 051 571 217

On the southern side of town, just behind a rather ugly shipyard area, the **Franciscan monastery** (Franjevački samostan) holds a shaded cloister and a small **museum**, in which flaky portraits of Franciscan theologians are outshone by Andrea de Murano's *Virgin and Child* of 1475, a warm depiction of a fat and mischievous Jesus with dove in hand.

ARRIVAL AND INFORMATION — CRES TOWN

By bus Buses stop near the petrol station just off the harbour area, where a narrow alleyway leads to the tourist office.

Destinations Beli (Mon–Fri 2 daily, Sat 1 daily; 30min); Lubenice (5 weekly; 40min); Mali Lošinj (Mon–Fri 6 daily, Sat & Sun 4 daily; 1hr 45min); Osor (Mon–Fri 6 daily, Sat & Sun 4 daily; 45min); Rijeka (4 daily; 2hr 30min); Valun (5 weekly; 20min); Veli Lošinj (Mon–Fri 6 daily, Sat & Sun 4 daily; 2hr); Zagreb (2 daily; 5hr 30min).

INFORMATION AND ACTIVITIES

Tourist office Cons 10 (June–Sept Mon–Sat 8am–8pm, Sun 9am–1pm; Oct–May Mon–Fri 8am–3pm; ⓣ 051 571 535, ⓦ tzg-cres.hr). Has a respectable stock of English-language brochures and can tell you just about everything you need to know about the island.

Diving *Camp Kovačine* (see below) has its own diving school; introductory dives start at 290Kn.

GETTING AROUND

By bike/scooter Bikes (80Kn/day) and scooters (200Kn/day) can be rented from the Šumice kiosk in front of the *Hotel Kimen*, on the waterfront 1km northwest of Cres Town.

ACCOMMODATION

Rooms (from 220Kn) and **apartments** (from 350Kn, four-person apartments 450–550Kn) in the old town and in the suburb of Melin, 1km to the west, are available either from the **Croatia Travel Agency**, next door to the tourist office (daily 8am–8pm; ⓣ 051 573 053, ⓦ cres-travel.com), or the **Cresanka Turist Biro**, round the corner on the harbour (daily 8am–8pm; ⓣ 051 571 161, ⓦ cresanka.hr).

Camp Kovačine Melin I ⓣ 051 573 150, ⓦ camp-kovacine.com. A well-equipped site with a terraced seaside area shaded by trees. It has a diving school (see above), and a large naturist section on the far side. **90Kn** per person, pitches **80Kn**

EATING AND DRINKING

CRES

Belona Šetalište 23 Travnja 24 ⓣ 051 571 203. Uncomplicated and inexpensive restaurant with a mainstream menu of risottos, seafood pastas and grilled fish fillets. The street-side terrace just outside the old town is a pleasant place to spend the evening. March–Nov daily 9am–10pm.

Riva Riva creskih kapetana 13 ⓣ 051 571 107. Right on the harbourfront, *Riva* is a great place to try top-quality grilled fish such as *orada* (gilthead) and *škrpina* (groper). April–Oct daily noon–11pm.

OUT OF TOWN

Bukaleta Loznati bb ⓣ 051 571 606. Cres is famous for its lamb (*janjetina*), and *Bukaleta*, 5km south of town just off the Lošinj road in the village of Loznati, is one of the best places to sample it. Specialities include *njoki* with lamb goulash, grilled lamb, oven-baked lamb – and lamb tripe for the unsqueamish. Sheep's cheese and home-baked bread provide the extra detail. April–Sept daily noon–midnight.

Beli

Huddled atop a knobbly hill high above the channel dividing Cres from Krk, the village of **BELI** is an impressive agglomeration of ancient stone houses, many of them now left uninhabited as locals move away in search of work. It's gloriously rustic and peaceful, and there's a small shingle cove below the village at the end of a steep road.

Caput Insulae Ecology Centre

Beli 4 • Daily: April & Oct 9am–6pm, May & Sept 9am–7pm, June–Aug 9am–8pm • 50Kn • ⓣ 051 840 525, ⓦ supovi.hr • The centre is located at the end of a stony road to the left as you enter the village

Beli is home to the **Caput Insulae Ecology Centre** (Eko-centar Caput Insulae), established in the mid-1980s to monitor and protect the community of **griffon vultures** indigenous to Cres (see box below). The centre has an exhibition on the vultures, with photographs and English-language text, and a small aviary in the back garden where sick vultures are often kept before being returned to the wild. They can also provide directions for the centre's **ecology paths** (*eko-staze*), three circular hiking trails which start here and lead through the forest, passing through a mixed area of pasture, forest, abandoned villages and *gradine* (the small, walled-off areas of cultivable land typical to Croatia's limestone areas) on the way. The most interesting of the trails is the 7km red path that takes you past twenty open-air sculptures by Ljubo de Karina, inscribed with Glagolitic script and poems by local poet Andro Vid Mihičić. The vultures themselves regularly scour the sparsely inhabited northern extremities of Cres in search of food – there's quite a good chance of spotting one, but don't count on it.

THE GRIFFON VULTURES OF CRES

The white-headed **griffon vulture** (*bijeloglavi sup*) formerly lived all over the Kvarner region, coexisting with a local sheep-farming economy that guaranteed the carrion-eating birds a constant supply of food. With the decline of sheep-rearing in the twentieth century, vulture numbers fell dramatically and communities of the birds are nowadays only found on the northeast coast of Cres and in a few isolated spots on Krk and the mainland. When conservationists first came to the area in the mid-1980s there were 24 pairs of vultures on the island; that number has now risen to about seventy.

Fully grown griffon vultures have a wingspan of 2.5m, live for up to sixty years and can spot a sheep carcass from a distance of 6km. Their nesting area in the cliffs south of Beli is protected by law: it's forbidden to sail within 50m of the cliffs, as young birds may fall out of their nests if startled. The vultures nest in December and produce one egg per pair, the young bird staying with its parents until August, when it begins a five-year roving period – which could take it to other vulture colonies in the Balkans or Near East – before returning to the island to breed. The main threats to the vultures are telephone wires, electricity power lines and contact with man-made poisons, such as the bait left out for vermin; the vulture population of Plavnik, an uninhabited island off the east coast of Cres, disappeared completely after the food chain had become contaminated in this way.

4

ARRIVAL AND DEPARTURE **BELI**

By bus There are two daily buses from Cres to Beli (Mon–Fri).

By car Some 13km north of Cres Town a minor road forks right off the main road, passing through half-deserted hamlets and oak and chestnut forests en route to Beli.

EATING

Gostionica Beli Beli 6 ⓣ 051 840 515. A cosy place decorated with farm tools and serving up a wide range of fish and meat dishes – including local roast lamb. It is also a good place for a drink. **April to mid-Oct daily 8am–midnight.**

Valun

In the sparsely populated western side of the island, **VALUN** is a tiny fishing village with colourful houses crowding round its harbour, a quiet shingle beach and ultra-clear waters. It's very popular with weekending Italians, but remains more or less free from development.

ARRIVAL AND DEPARTURE **VALUN**

By bus Valun is only served by one bus a day from Cres (Mon–Fri only), so unless you come here by car you're more or less compelled to stick around here for a while.

By car Some 8km south of Cres Town, turn off along a minor road towards the west of the island; after 5km a side road descends to Valun.

ACCOMMODATION AND EATING

Cresanka tourist agency in Cres Town (see p.206) can organize **rooms** (from 200Kn/double).

4

Camping Zdovice Valun bb ⓣ 051 571 161. A very attractive small site 100m east of the harbour, right on the beach. Facilities are simple, but the location is superb. May–Sept. Pitch included in per-person price: **110Kn**

Konoba Toš Juna Valun bb ⓣ 051 525 084. This *konoba* has a terrace on the harbourfront and is a good place to try the local *škampi* (shrimps) and *creška janjetina* (Cres lamb). **March–Oct daily 10am–midnight.**

Lubenice

Accessed by a narrow road 5km southwest from Valun, **LUBENICE** is a windswept village occupying a ridge high above the shore. Almost medieval in appearance, it's like a more extreme version of Beli – a depopulated cluster of half-ruined stone houses and a dwindling permanent population of around twenty. The square at the entrance to the village boasts an invigorating view of the rugged western coast, with a pair of idyllic, secluded pebbly coves far below; they're only accessible by boat or via a very steep and tiring path.

The village hosts alfresco classical music concerts on the main square as part of **Lubenice Music Nights** (Lubeničke glazbene večeri) every Friday evening in July and August; tickets (including transport) are usually handled by one of the tourist agencies back in Cres Town – enquire at the tourist office for details.

ARRIVAL AND DEPARTURE **LUBENICE**

By bus There are only two daily buses (Mon–Fri only) from Cres Town to Lubenice, so you'll need a car to explore thoroughly.

Osor

Set beside the narrow strait which divides Cres from Lošinj, **OSOR** is an erstwhile cathedral town which has shrunk to the size of a hamlet. It's the oldest settlement on either island, a prosperous Roman city which some historians believe once had a population of fifteen thousand, although a couple of thousand seems more realistic. Osor's regional importance survived into the medieval era, thanks in part to the reputation of eleventh-century holy man (and later saint) Gaudentius, who established the now-ruined monastery of St Peter here and turned Osor into a centre of Glagolitic manuscript production. Gaudentius died in Rome but his remains miraculously returned to Osor in a seaborne wooden chest; they're now kept on the high altar of Osor's former cathedral.

Osor nowadays is a small village with a permanent population of around seventy. The cobbled kernel of the village stands just above the **Kavuada**, the narrow channel – just 11m wide – which divides Cres and Lošinj. Dug either by the Romans or their Illyrian predecessors, it's now spanned by a swing bridge that opens at 9am and 5pm every day to let boats through.

Church of the Assumption

Presiding over a funnel-shaped main square is the **Church of the Assumption** (Crkva Uznesenja) – originally a cathedral – which was completed in 1497 and boasts an elegant trefoil facade in smooth, pale stone. The **Osor Evenings** (Osorske večeri), a festival of chamber music, has been staging performances in the church in July and August for the last thirty years – the tourist office in Mali Lošinj (see p.211) will have schedules and details.

Archeological Museum

Easter to mid-June & mid-Sept to Oct Tues–Sat 10am–2pm, Mid-June to mid-Sept Tues–Sat 10am–1pm & 7–10pm; Nov & Dec Tues–Sun 10am–1pm • 10Kn • ⓣ 051 233 892, ⓦ muzej.losinj.hr

The small **Archeological Museum** (Arheološki muzej) in the Venetian town hall has Roman relics and a model of medieval Osor enclosed by extensive town walls, stretches of which survive in much reduced form.

Bishop's Palace

Just off Osor's main square, a narrow street runs past the fifteenth-century **Bishop's Palace**, now a sporadically open lapidarium harbouring bits of masonry from Osor's many churches, several of which are covered with the *plutej*, a plait-like design characteristic of Croatian medieval art. The most imposing item on display is the **bishop's throne**, a composite work made from Romanesque stone fragments taken from the cathedral graveyard – the backrest is embellished with a fine carving of two birds hovering above a lion-like beast.

4

Franciscan Monastery

Ten minutes' walk north of the main square, past the graveyard, lies Bijar Bay, where a small beach is overlooked by the ruins of the thirteenth-century **Franciscan monastery**, another important centre of Glagolitic culture in its day.

ARRIVAL AND DEPARTURE — OSOR

By bus All Cres-Mali Lošinj services (Mon–Fri 6 daily, Sat & Sun 4 daily) pass through Osor.

ACCOMMODATION AND EATING

Camping Bijar Osor bb ⓣ 051 237 147, ⓦ camp-bijar.com. Well-appointed campsite enjoying a shady seafront position on the northern side of town. Late April to Sept. 60Kn per person, pitches from 30Kn

Konoba Bonifačić Osor 64 ⓣ 051 237 413. This well-respected local restaurant offers a wide range of local seafood, Cres specialities like *janjeći žgvacet* (lamb stew) and a beautiful garden setting. Daily 10am–11pm.

Mali Lošinj

Straggling along either side of a deep bay, **MALI LOŠINJ** is as charming an Adriatic port as you'll find, with slender cypresses and spiky green palms poking up between rows of colour-washed houses. It has been a tourist resort since the turn of the twentieth century, when local Ambroz Haračić supervised the reforestation of the Čikat peninsula just west of town, and promoted the place as a winter health retreat for consumptive central Europeans. It's now a popular family-oriented package destination, although most of the hotels have been kept well out of the way on the Čikat peninsula, together with an enormous campsite and the island's most crowded beaches.

THE APOXYOMENOS

One thing that you can't fail to notice adorning brochures and posters throughout Lošinj is the handsome form of the **Apoxyomenos** (Apoksiomen in Croatian), a first-century BC Graeco-Roman statue of a naked athlete cleaning himself after training – the ancient Greek term *apoxyomenos* might be loosely translated as "the man scraping himself off". Lost in an ancient shipwreck, the statue was discovered on the seabed near Lošinj in 1996 and quickly became a European sensation, exhibited in Florence and Paris as well as throughout Croatia itself. A permanent home for the much-travelled scraping man is currently under construction in a nineteenth-century palace on the Mali Lošinj harbourfront, where the statue will be displayed in a special climate-controlled chamber designed by Rijeka architects Randić and Turato.

Most life in Mali Lošinj revolves around the quayside **Riva lošinjskih kapetana**, where rows of potted cacti and subtropical plants line a harbourfront overrun in summer with souvenir stalls and café tables. The Riva's southern end opens out into the triangular open space of Trg Republike Hrvatske, from where **Braće Vidulića**, the main street, runs inland through the oldest part of town.

Lošinj Museum

Vladimira Gortana 35 • Jan–March call ⓣ 051 231 173 and they'll open the museum for you; April to mid-June Tues–Sat 10am–1pm & 6–8pm; mid-June to mid-Sept daily 10am–1pm & 7–10pm; mid-Sept to Oct Tues–Fri 10am–1pm & 6–8pm, Sat 10am–1pm; Nov & Dec Tues–Fri 10am–1pm & 5–7pm, Sat 10am–1pm • 20Kn • ⓣ 051 233 892, ⓦ muzej.losinj.hr

4

Just behind the harbourfront, a nineteenth-century mansion known as the Fritzy Palace houses the **Lošinj Museum** (Lošinjski muzej), home to two private art collections. First up is that of art critic and poet Andro Vid Mihičić, which concentrates on Croatian twentieth-century works, notably the mottled cityscapes of Paris-trained Emanuel Vidović. The second collection, that of Giuseppe Piperata – a Lošinj doctor who emigrated to Italy in 1945 but was prevented from taking his most valuable paintings with him – inclines more towards the Baroque. Highlights include Francesco Solimena's lively *Meeting with Rebecca*, and Francesco Fontebasso's mid-eighteenth-century *Female Portrait*, portraying an anonymous ruby-lipped beauty.

The Upper Town

The upper, older part of Mali Lošinj, reached via the stepped narrow streets ascending from the Riva, is a quiet maze of stone houses that seems a world away from the tourist industry down below. Presiding serenely over the scene is the **Parish Church of the Nativity** with its Venetian-style belfry. Behind the church, steps lead to the **Kaštel**, a seventeenth-century fortification with largely intact stone walls and bastions. Once used as an outdoor concert venue, it is currently fenced-off and empty.

Čikat Bay

Mali Lošinj's main beach area is around **Čikat Bay**, 3km west of town, where a coastal path runs past a succession of concreted bathing areas, rocky beaches and a couple of stretches of pebble. It's a laid-back area, good for strolling whatever the season, with Habsburg holiday villas sheltering among wind-bent tamarisks and pines, and cafés and shacks renting out snorkelling gear and surfboards along the more popular stretches.

Valeškura Bay

One of the best ways to to avoid the package-holiday crowds is to head for the coastal path from Mali Lošinj to Veli Lošinj, which winds its way around **Valeškura Bay**. It's a long, sinuous stretch of rocky coast devoid of bars or sun-loungers, perfect for finding a slab of stone to lay your towel on. The path ultimately arrives at Mali Lošinj's *Punta* hotel, which has a largely rock-and-concrete beach.

ARRIVAL AND INFORMATION

MALI LOŠINJ

By bus Buses from Rijeka and Cres stop at the northern end of Mali Lošinj's harbour.

Destinations Cres Town (Mon–Fri 6 daily, Sat & Sun 4 daily; 1hr 45min); Osor (Mon–Fri 6 daily, Sat & Sun 4 daily; 45min); Rijeka (4 daily; 3hr 30min–4hr); Zagreb (2 daily; 6hr 30min).

By ferry Ferries from Pula and Zadar stop at the northern end of Mali Lošinj's harbour. Jadrolinija, Lošinjskih brodograditelja 22 (☎ 051 231 765, ⓦ jadrolinija.hr), and Lošinjska Plovidba, Riva lošinjskih kapetana 8 (☎ 051 231 077, ⓦ losinjplov.hr), sell ferry tickets for Susak (among other nearby islands) as well as for Pula, Zadar, Rijeka and Novalja.

Destinations Pula (mid-June to mid-Sept 2 per week, mid-Sept to mid-June 1 per week; 3hr 35min); Susak (1 daily; 1hr); Zadar (mid-June to mid-Sept 2 per week; 7hr).

By catamaran Catamarans stop at the northern end of Mali Lošinj's harbour.

Destinations Cres (1 daily; 2hr–2hr 30min); Rijeka (1 daily; 3hr 20min–3hr 50min); Susak (6 per week; 1hr 10min); Zadar (July & Aug 2 per week; 3hr 15min).

Tourist office Riva lošinjskih kapetana 29 (mid-June to mid-Sept Mon–Sat 8am–8pm, Sun 9am–1pm; mid-Sept to mid-June Mon–Fri 8am–3pm; ☎ 051 231 884, ⓦ tz-malilosinj.hr). Has bundles of free brochures and local maps, including one covering foot- and bike paths all over the island.

TOURS AND ACTIVITIES

Island tours Private boats moored in Mali Lošinj harbour offer half-day excursions to Susak (120Kn and upwards) or panoramic island tours (160–200Kn, with lunch included).

Mountain bikes and windsurf boards can be rented (both about 70Kn/hr) on the seafront promenade in Čikat, in front of the *Bellevue* hotel.

Diving The scuba-diving centre in Čikat (☎ 051 233 900, ⓦ diver.hr) rents out gear and offers crash courses from 375Kn.

ACCOMMODATION

There's a wealth of accommodation in town. Numerous agencies offer private **rooms** (250Kn) and **apartments** (two-person studios from 350Kn, four-person apartments from 510Kn): most helpful is the ★ **Cappelli agency** (☎ 051 231 582, ⓦ cappelli-tourist.hr), on the main road at the northern entrance to town at Kadin bb.

4

HOTELS

Apoksiomen Riva lošinjskih kapetana 1 ☎ 051 520 820, ⓦ apoksiomen.com. The most stylish place in town, with a prime location right on the Riva, swish four-star rooms with marble-tiled bathrooms, wonderful sea vistas and original artwork on display. There's also a pleasant café on the ground floor. April–Oct. **1000Kn**

Mare Mare Riva lošinjskih kapetana 36 ☎ 051 232 010, ⓦ mare-mare.com. Boutique B&B with neat little doubles decked out in warm reds and oranges with a few rustic design touches and featuring swanky modern bathrooms. Common balcony with outdoor jacuzzi. Guests have free use of bikes. **850Kn**

Villa Favorita Sunčana Uvala ☎ 051 520 640, ⓦ villafavorita.hr. A renovated Habsburg-era mansion on the Čikat side of town surrounded by nicely landscaped gardens. The hotel has an outdoor pool, a sauna and massage room, and offers eight spacious en suites with a/c, TV, minibar and internet access. **1200Kn**

CAMPSITE

Autocamp Čikat Čikat bb ☎ 051 231 708, ⓦ camp-cikat.com. At the northwestern end of Čikat, a 30min walk from the town centre, this vast campsite occupies a wooded site with good access to the beaches. Open April to mid-Oct. **60Kn** per person, pitches from **30Kn**

EATING, DRINKING AND ENTERTAINMENT

There's a (not particularly cheap) fruit and veg **market** just uphill from the harbourfront on Braće Vidulića, and a fish market (Mon–Sat mornings only) on Trg Republike Hrvatske. **Drinking** and nightlife is a relatively tame, family-oriented affair, with cafés along the Riva putting more effort into their ice creams than their cocktail menus.

RESTAURANTS

Artatore Artatore 132 ☎ 051 232 932, ⓦ restaurant-artatore.hr. Fine dining in a bay-side settlement 7km north of town, just off the road to Cres. It's an elegantly furnished establishment renowned for its fresh seafood, home-baked bread and baked lamb – ring in advance if you want to order the latter. Lengthy list of top Croatian wines. Daily 10am–midnight.

Konoba Corrado Sv. Marije 1 ☎ 051 232 487. Walled garden shaded by vine-trellises, just off the eastern end of Braće Vidulića, with a smallish menu of fresh fish (both grilled and baked), as well as fresh scallops (*jakopove kapice*) and other shellfish. House specialities, including octopus or lamb baked *ispod peke* (under a charcoal-covered bell), should be ordered at least a day in advance. Extensive list of Istrian and Dalmatian wines. April–Oct daily 11am–11pm.

Lanterna Sveti Martin 71 ⓣ 051 233 625. Romantically situated on a small harbour beside a ruined boathouse, a 15min walk east of the town centre, this is a good place to admire the sunset and tuck into excellent, not-too-pricey Adriatic food. There's a good mix of fish, shellfish, risottos and grilled cuts of meat. Roast Cres lamb is also on the menu, but has to be ordered 24hr in advance. Mon–Sat 10am–11pm.

Silvana Lošinjskih pomoraca 2 ⓣ 052 232 591, ⓦ silvana.hr. In a suburban area 1km east of the town centre this restaurant doesn't offer that much in the way of a view, but the food is first class. Fish and shellfish are among the best in town, while traditional meat dishes like roast lamb (*pečena janjetina*) and gnocchi with lamb stew (*janjeći žgvacet*) add variety to the menu. Impeccable service, and an interesting list of Croatian wines. March–Oct daily noon–10pm.

BARS

Katakomba del Conte Giovanni 1. In an alleyway just off the harbour, this is a wonderfully rustic-looking bar with a bare stone interior and a couple of wooden benches (the rest is standing room only). Live rock and jazz at the weekends – although goodness knows how they manage to squeeze the musicians onto the tiny stage. Daily 10am–1pm & 7pm–2am.

Mystic Bar brace Vidulića 40. Plain to look at but pretty raucous on weekend evenings, this is where a large proportion of Lošinj's party crowd end up come the wee hours. Themed events and DJs throughout the summer. 7am–3am.

Veli Lošinj

Despite the name (*veli* means "big", *mali* "little"), **VELI LOŠINJ** is actually a smaller, quieter version of Mali Lošinj, a warren of pastel-coloured houses strung tightly around a tiny natural harbour. It's a forty-minute walk from the centre of Mali Lošinj along a scenic shoreline path via Valeškura Bay (see p.210).

4

St Anthony's Church

You can't miss the hangar-like Baroque **St Anthony's Church** (Crkva svetog Antuna), which contains a fine tempera-on-wood *Madonna with Saints* (above a side door on the left as you enter) painted by Bartolomeo Vivarini in 1475. Originally commissioned by the Venetian senate, the painting was paraded around Venice every year on the anniversary of the Battle of Lepanto to celebrate the famous naval victory over the Ottomans, until being bought by a Lošinj family shortly after the fall of the Venetian Republic.

Lošinj Marine Education Center

Kaštel 24 • Daily: April, May & Oct 9am–2pm; June–Sept 9am–noon & 5–10pm; Nov–March 10am–noon • 30Kn • ⓣ 051 604 666, ⓦ blue-world.org

The **Lošinj Marine Education Center** has a small but very informative and entertaining display on Adriatic marine life, the main focus being the group of 120 or so bottlenose dolphins that frequent the waters around Lošinj and Cres. There's a thirty-minute documentary film with English subtitles, touch-screen computer info – and a kiddies' corner complete with instructions on how to annoy your parents by honking like a sea-turtle. You can also pick up information on how to support local conservation initiatives, most notably by adopting one of the dolphins for 150Kn a year – see the website for more details.

The Tower Museum-Gallery

Museum Tues–Sun: mid-April to mid-June & mid-Sept to Oct 10am–1pm; mid-June to mid-Sept 10am–1pm & 4–10pm • 10Kn • ⓣ 051 236 594, ⓦ muzej.losinj.hr

Just behind the harbour, a narrow alleyway leads to a crenellated **tower** (kula), built in 1455 to discourage raids by the Uskoks of Senj (see box, p.222). It now houses the small **Tower Museum-Gallery** (Galerija Kula), which houses changing displays related to the history of the island.

ACCOMMODATION **VELI LOŠINJ**

Rooms (200Kn) and **apartments** (studios from 330Kn, four-person apartments from 520Kn) are available from **Turist**, Obala Maršala Tita 17 (ⓣ 051 236 256, ⓦ island-losinj.com).

★ **Pjacal** Kaštel 3 ⓣ 051 236 244, ⓦ pjacal.hr. On a backstreet behind the harbour is a seven-room B&B run by a Croatian–German family offering neat little en-suite rooms decked out in whites and blues and a buffet breakfast in a beautiful back garden filled with herbs and pot plants. **500Kn**

Vila Tamaris Obala maršala Tita 35 ⓣ 051 867 900, ⓦ tamarishotels.com. Harbourside building containing swanky en suites with tiled floors, flat-screen TVs and small but smart bathrooms. Most have views of the port, and there's an attractive breakfast terrace in an inner courtyard. **800Kn**

EATING AND DRINKING

There's the usual chain of cafés around the harbour, and a sprinkling of good **restaurants** – a fair few of which are in Rovenska, a self-contained cove at the eastern end of town.

★ **Bora Bar** Rovenska 3 ⓣ 051 867 544, ⓦ borabar.com. Right on Rovenska harbour, *Bora Bar* dishes up delicious handmade pasta and gnocchi dishes in a range of imaginative sauces, with Istrian truffles featuring heavily as a keynote flavour. Risottos and fresh fish (either grilled or oven-baked) also feature on the menu, alongside a quality choice of Croatian wines. The home-baked bread is well worth the 10Kn *couvert*. Tables and chairs painted in a mixture of pastelly blues, greens and yellows set the right tone of Mediterranean charm. Easter–Nov daily 10am–11pm.

Mol Rovenska 1 ⓣ 051 236 008. *Mol* is more staid in style than its neighbour the *Bora Bar*, but can always be counted on for excellent seafood and outstanding lobster. March–Oct daily 9am–11pm.

Ribarska koliba Obala Maršala Tita 1a ⓣ 051 236 235. Family-run restaurant beneath Veli Lošinj's church, right by the water, serving up succulent fresh seafood – fish fillet of the day is sometimes chalked up on a board outside. Cres lamb is frequently on the menu, but not every day. April to mid-Oct daily 9am–midnight.

4

Susak

About 9km west of Mali Lošinj by sea, **SUSAK** is arguably the most compelling of the smaller Kvarner islands. Its sandy composition gives it an appearance quite different from the rocky terrain of the other Adriatic islands, with ochre-coloured cliffs covered in ferns, wild fennel and soaring bamboo-like grasses. Criss-crossed by footpaths, it's a blissfully easy island to explore, and the sandy **beaches** are superb.

Susak's isolation has produced a distinctive way of life: islanders still speak their own dialect and have retained many customs, including a local costume which consists of gaudy green-and-yellow skirts worn with even brighter pink tights. Postcards and guidebooks would have you believe you'll see this all the time, although hardly anyone ever wears it nowadays. The island's industry, fish canning, has long since died out, and many islanders emigrated to the Americas in the early twentieth century (hence the sizeable Susak community in Hoboken, New Jersey). The remaining population relies on money sent back by relatives to supplement income from sales of, among other things, Susak's **wines** – the red *pleskunac*, and *trojišćina*, an intriguing, dry rosé.

Susak celebrates its **annual feast-day** on July 30, when hundreds of émigrés return to the island for a day of folk music, eating and drinking – don't expect to find any accommodation on or around the island on this date.

Susak village

The island's only settlement (and arrival point for ferries) sits on a broad sandy bay. Narrow streets climb up from the seafront to the oldest part of Susak village, which grew up around an eleventh-century Benedictine monastery. The only surviving part of the monastery is **St Nicholas's Church** (Crkva svetog Nikole), inside which there's a large wooden twelfth-century crucifix known by the locals as *Veli Buoh* – the "Great God".

Susak beaches

Susak's main beach, **Spiaza**, is a huge crescent of smooth grey-brown sand stretching away east from the harbour. The bay is very shallow – you need to wade out for about half a kilometre before the sea is deep enough to swim in. Similarly sandy is **Bok bay** further east; it tends to be slightly less crowded because you have to walk round a rocky headland to get there. Unlike family-oriented Spiaza, Bok is the kind of beach where nude bathing will not raise any eyebrows. There are numerous other (frequently pebbly or stony) coves around the island, although you will need time to explore the island's network of sandy tracks to find one that suits.

ARRIVAL AND DEPARTURE — SUSAK

By ferry Day-trips to Susak from Mali Lošinj are possible, providing you study the ferry timetables carefully. A daily Jadrolinija ferry from Mali Lošinj does the rounds of the local islands including Susak, and the daily Mali Lošinj–Rijeka catamaran also calls at Susak. There are also excursions to Susak in private boats (from around 100Kn per person), leaving from Mali Lošinj's Riva.

ACCOMMODATION AND EATING

There's a limited number of private **rooms** (200kn) on Susak but they're usually reserved months in advance – the tourist office in Mali Lošinj can give you a list of telephone numbers (they're also posted on the Ⓦ tz-malilosinj.hr website), but won't make bookings on your behalf. Accommodation listings are also posted on Ⓦ otok-susak.org.

Konoba Barbara Susak village Ⓣ 051 239 012. You can tuck into grilled squid and freshly caught fish at this small wooden-bench *konoba*, tucked into an alleyway behind St Nicholas's Church. Susak rosé is on the wine list. Daily 9am–midnight.

4

Krk

Joined to the mainland by a dramatically arcing bridge, **KRK** (pronounced "Kirk", with a strongly rolled *r*) is the Adriatic's largest island and also its most developed, a result of its proximity to Rijeka, whose airport is situated on the island. The main settlements are **Krk Town**, a historic little place with scraps of city wall surrounding a compact old centre; and **Baška**, a fishing village-cum-tourist resort with a spectacular sandy beach. Both of the above are heavily touristed, although there are plenty of quieter, quirkier places to explore – notably the wine-making centre **Vrbnik.**

ARRIVAL AND DEPARTURE — KRK

By plane Rijeka airport (see p.194) is on Krk island, 2km west of the road bridge to the mainland. If travelling to places on Krk you will need a taxi.

By bus Regular buses run from Rijeka to Krk Town (1hr 30min).

By ferry Krk's main ferry port is Valbiska on the island's northwestern coast; from here services run to and from Lopar on Rab (June–Sept 4 daily; 1hr 30min; Ⓦ lnp.hr), and Merag on Cres (12 daily; 30min; Ⓦ jadrolinija.hr).

Krk Town

The island's main centre, **KRK TOWN**, centres on a small, partly walled city crisscrossed by narrow cobbled streets. Krk's main **bathing** area lies to the east of town, where a sequence of small rocky coves provides a variety of atmospheric perches. There's a naturist beach about twenty minutes' walk east, by the *Politin* campsite.

Trg bana Jelačića and around

The main fulcrum of the town is **Trg bana Jelačića**, a large open space just outside the town walls to the west, looking out onto a busy little harbour. Watching over the southeastern corner of Trg bana Jelačića is a hexagonal **guard tower** of thirteenth-century vintage which, like many of Krk's buildings, makes much use of Roman-era masonry. A Roman gravestone is positioned halfway up one wall of the tower, carved-relief portraits of the deceased peering down on passers-by as if casually observing street life through an open window.

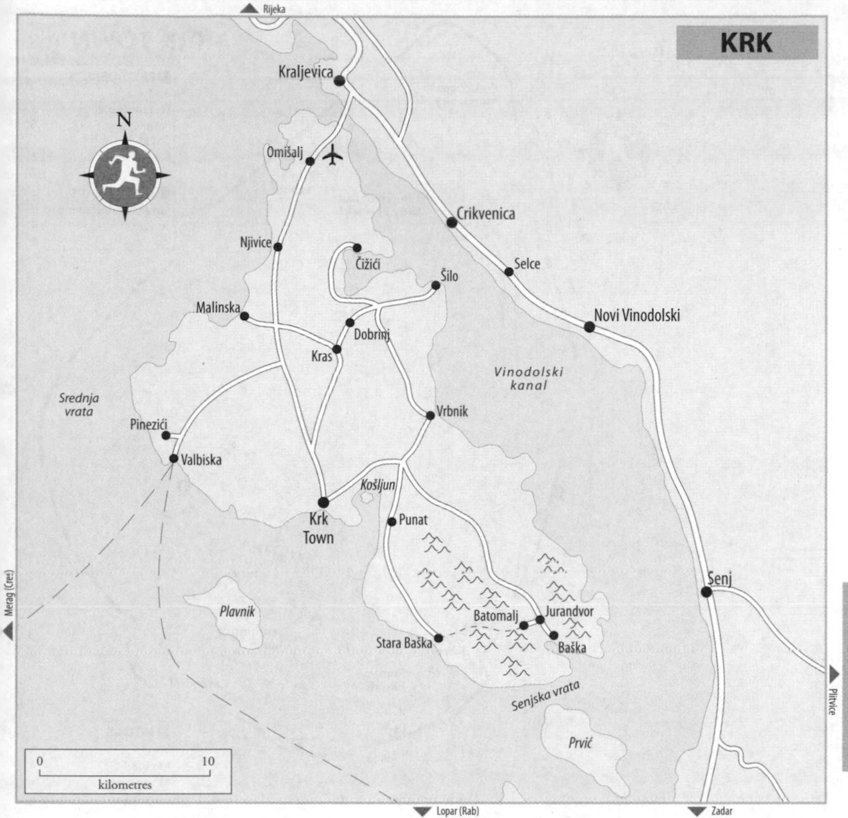

4

An opening on the eastern side of the square leads through to **Vela placa**, a smaller public space overlooked by another medieval guard tower, this time sporting a rare sixteenth-century 24-hour clock (noon is at the top, midnight at the bottom).

J.J. Strossmayera

Heading roughly east from Vela placa is the old town's main thoroughfare, **J.J. Strossmayera**, a two-metre-wide alleyway that becomes virtually impassable on summer nights, when the entire tourist population of the island seems to choose it as the venue for their evening *corso*.

Roman Mosaic

Ribarska • Daily 8.30am–2pm & 6pm–midnight • 7Kn

Café Bar Mate at Ribarska 7 is the entry point to one of Krk's most charming attractions, the **Roman Mosaic** (Rimski mozaik). Discovered under the floor of a private house adjacent to the café, the third-century fragment boasts colourful scenes of sea beasts, including a fish-tailed humanoid playing a flute.

Cathedral of the Assumption

Daily 9.30am–1pm

The Romanesque **Cathedral of the Assumption** (Katedrala Uznesenja) is a three-aisled basilica built in 1188 on the site of a fifth-century church (and, before that, a Roman bath complex) incorporating pillars taken from a range of Roman buildings. There are

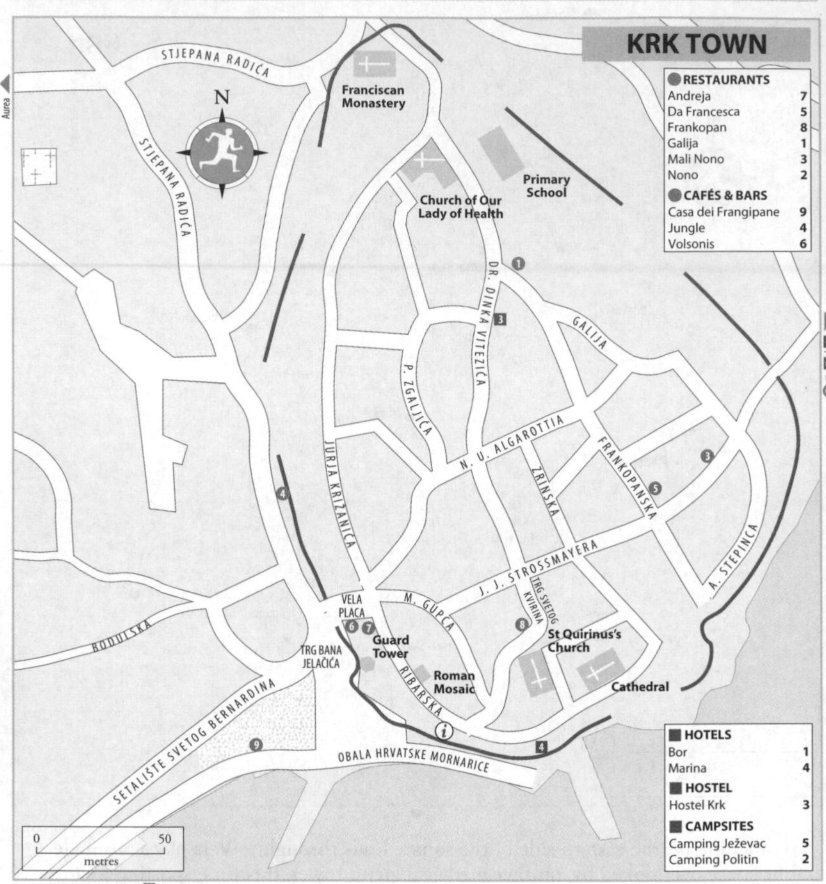

two rows of ten columns fashioned in a variety of designs and materials – limestone, marble and red granite – with their capitals decorated with intricate floral patterns and scenes of birds eating fish. Among the altar paintings, look out for a sixteenth-century *Deposition* by Giovanni Antonio da Pordenone, and a largish *Battle of Lepanto* by A. Vicenti, showing the Madonna and Pope Pius V watching approvingly over victorious Venetian forces.

St Quirinus's Church

Treasury: April to mid-Oct daily 9.30am–1pm • 7Kn

Built alongside the cathedral, from which it is separated by a narrow passageway, **St Quirinus's Church** (Crkva svetog Kvirina) is another Romanesque structure, whose campanile sports an onion dome topped by a trumpet-blowing angel. The campanile's lower storey is now a **Treasury** (Riznica) housing numerous artworks amassed by the bishops of Krk, most famously the *Madonna in Glory*, a silver-plated altarpiece made in 1477 by Venetian workshops for the last Duke of Krk, Ivan VII. It's a – literally – dazzling piece of craftsmanship, with central panels showing reliefs of the coronation of the Virgin and side panels depicting various saints.

Krk Primary School

Krk is quite unusual among well-preserved Adriatic towns in that it also accommodates the odd bit of contemporary architecture within its medieval city walls. Winning plaudits among modern architecture critics is the **Primary School** (Osnovna škola) designed by Rijeka architects Randić & Turato, whose double-v shaped facade follows the contours of the Old Town's hillside. A similarly geometric sports hall, courtesy of the same architects, is currently taking shape next door.

ARRIVAL AND INFORMATION — KRK TOWN

By plane Rijeka airport is 20km away at the northern end of Krk island. There's no public transport to and from the airport; a taxi into Krk Town will cost 150–180Kn.

By bus Buses from Zagreb and Rijeka arrive at the bus station on the harbourfront, a 2min walk west of Trg bana Jelačića.

Destinations Baška (9 daily; 50min); Punat (9 daily; 15min); Rijeka (hourly; 1hr 30min); Vrbnik (Mon–Fri 2 daily; 30min); Zagreb (2 daily; 5hr).

By car For car hire, Aurea agency (see below) have a fleet of Renaults.

Tourist office Obala hrvatske mornarice bb (June–Sept Mon–Fri 8am–3pm, Sat 8am–1pm, Sun 8am–noon; Oct–May Mon–Fri 8am–3pm; T 051 221 414, W tz-krk.hr). The tourist office has free town plans, a map of hiking paths on the Prniba peninsula just east of town, and information on cultural events.

ACCOMMODATION

Private **rooms** (250Kn) and **apartments** (studios 375Kn, four-person apartments 500–600Kn) are available from innumerable agencies around town, with only tiny variations in price from one to the next: most convenient are **Autotrans** (Mon–Sat 8am–9pm, Sun 9am–1pm & 3–9pm; T 051 222 661, W autotrans-turizam.com), in the bus station building; and **Aurea**, at the northern entrance to town at Vršanska 26L – you'll see it on the right as you enter Krk from the Rijeka direction (May–Sept daily 8am–8pm; Oct–April Mon–Fri 8am–3pm, Sat 8am–1pm; T 051 221 777, W aurea-krk.hr).

HOTELS

Bor Šetalište Dražica 5 T 051 220 200, W hotelbor.hr. Squeezed between large package hotels a 10min walk east of town, this small private hotel is the best value in Krk, offering eighteen spacious en-suite doubles with TV; sea-facing rooms are only slightly more expensive. **800Kn**

Marina Obala hrvatske mornarice 8 T 051 221 128, W hotelikrk.hr. Dating from the 1920s, this comfortable four-star is slap-bang on the seafront. With only ten rooms – all of which have sea views – it has a boutique feel. Open May–Oct. **1100Kn**

HOSTEL

Hostel Krk D. Vitezića 32 T 051 220 212, W hostel-krk.hr. Perfectly situated in a quiet corner of the Old Town, the hostel occupies the restored building of the island's first-ever hotel. The shaded patio hosts a restaurant serving some unusual dishes such as ostrich goulash as well as good-quality mainstays. The rooms (five doubles, three triples, seven quads and two six-beds) are neat and tidy, and guests can use a washing machine and rent bikes for 75Kn per day. Rates include breakfast; other meals available at extra cost. **150Kn** per person

CAMPSITES

Camping Ježevac Plavnička bb T 051 221 081, E camping@valamar.com. A large site set on partly wooded, sloping terrain right on the beach, a 10min walk south of the bus station. Camping spots range from simple tent spaces to "comfort" pitches with own water tap (150Kn). **60Kn** per person, plus pitches from **75Kn**

Camping Politin Narodnog preporoda bb T 051 221 351, E camping@valamar.com. An exclusively naturist site on the eastern side of town just beyond the *Koralj* hotel, with well-tended pitches (with or without electricity), good facilities and supermarket. **60Kn** per person, plus pitches (without electricity) from **75Kn**

EATING AND DRINKING

There are plenty of good restaurants serving fresh fish as well as traditional Krk recipes, although they all fill up fast on summer evenings. There are also plenty of busy **cafés** on the waterfront.

RESTAURANTS

Andreja Vela placa 6 T 051 220 166, W adrijan-krk.hr. In summer this cosy subterranean *konoba* gets a bit too touristy, but year-round it's one of the best places to sample local favourites such as *šurlice sa gulašem* (home-made pasta with goulash; 55Kn). There's a tiny outdoor terrace squeezed into a courtyard round the back. Daily 11am–11pm.

Da Francesca Frankopanska 4 T 051 520 344. With a nice courtyard, substantial salads in the 40–50Kn range, and pastas and risottos clocking in at 50–60Kn, *Da*

Francesca is a good place for a Mediterranean lunch. Daily noon–11pm.

Frankopan Trg svetog Kvirina 1 ⊕051 221 437. Just inland from the waterfront restaurants, *Frankopan* serves up top-of-the-range fish, shellfish and lobster in a slightly more formal atmosphere, with a restful terrace facing the cathedral. Jan–Oct daily noon–11pm.

Galija Frankopanska 38 ⊕051 221 250, ⊛galijakrk.com. Popular pizzeria with a big choice of pizzas in the 50–60Kn range, served up in a cool, dark, timber-beamed interior. Daily 11am–11pm, summer till 2am.

Mali Nono J.J. Strossmayera 39 ⊕051 221 995. Old Town branch of *Nono* (see below) occupying a cosy stone-clad room packed with wooden tables – there's a small terrace in the alley outside. Staples include *šurlice* with seafood (60–70Kn) and grilled fillets of fish. Daily 10am–10pm.

Nono Krčkih iseljenika 8 ⊕051 222 221. Just east of the Old Town, this is the best place for authentic Krk recipes, augmenting the customary seafood with roast lamb, *šurlice* and other regional favourites – although the mock-rustic interior comes across as trashy rather than traditional. April–Oct daily 11am–midnight.

CAFÉS AND BARS

Casa dei Frangipane Šetalište sv. Bernardina bb ⊕099 702 2727. Fancy café-bar with crimson-cushioned sofas and a harbourside terrace, offering all kinds of coffee, pots of leaf tea and a decent array of cakes. A popular spot for cocktails in the evening. Daily 7am–2am.

Jungle Stjepana Radića bb ⊛junglekrk.com. A pavement café with loungey furniture out front, and a trendy disco bar with roof terrace at the back. Daily 9am–5am.

Volsonis Vela placa ⊕051 880 249, ⊛volsonis.hr. Cocktail bar and gallery set in an underground vault with its own small collection of archeological finds. There's an outdoor terrace on the other side of the city walls. Daily 7am–2am.

Punat and around

4

The village of **PUNAT**, 7km east of Krk Town, is set on the tranquil, enclosed bay of Puntarska draga. A largely modern place made up of souvenir stalls, apartment blocks and a massive marina just to the north of town, it's not the most evocative town on the island. However, there's a promising sequence of gravel **beaches** to the south, which quickly fade into quieter, rockier stretches of coast.

Košljun: Franciscan monastery

Monastery and museum Mon–Sat 9.30am–6pm, Sun 10.30am–12.30pm • 20Kn • Taxi-boat 30Kn return

The main reason to come to Punat is to take a taxi-boat across the bay to the islet of **Košljun**, about 800m offshore, where there is a **Franciscan monastery** (Franjevački samostan) founded by monks settled here by the Frankopans in 1447. From Košljun's jetty, a path leads up to the **monastery church**, which has a lofty, wood-beamed interior. Look out for the 1532 polyptych by Girolamo da Santacroce on the high altar, showing scenes from the life of the Virgin. Stretching across the arch above the altar is a large and dignified *Last Judgement*, executed in 1654 by E. Ughetto, whose swirling panoramas of heaven, hell and purgatory provide a contrast with the simpler but no less harrowing *Stations of the Cross* by the twentieth-century Expressionist Ivo Dulčić. There are some rather more off-the-wall exhibits in the cloister outside, like a one-eyed sheep in a glass case and a two-headed lamb in a bottle. The adjoining **museum** has an interesting mishmash of stuff, including some ancient typewriters and gramophones and a display of local costumes. Outside, a confusing array of paths leads through the wilderness of the monastery gardens, although Košljun is so small that it's difficult to get really lost.

ARRIVAL AND DEPARTURE — PUNAT AND AROUND

By bus Punat is served by hourly buses from Krk Town.

Stara Baška

STARA BAŠKA, 12km south of Punat, is a tiny place clinging to a narrow coastal strip beneath the sage-covered slopes of the 482-metre Veli Hlam – this would be the most beautiful spot on the island if it weren't for the unsightly holiday homes. There are several small stretches of shingle **beach**, the best of which is in Oprna Bay 2km north of the village, visible from the road as you descend from the Punat direction.

ARRIVAL AND DEPARTURE — STARA BAŠKA

There are only two weekly **buses** from Krk Town to Stara Baška, so you might be better off renting a **car** to get here – unless you want to walk over the hills from Batomalj (see box below), near Baška, a minor road heads south from Punat.

ACCOMMODATION AND EATING

The **Zala** agency, at Stara Baška 80 in the centre of the village (**T** 051 844 755, **W** zala.hr), has a range of studios and family-sized apartments.

Camp Škrila **T** 051 844 678, **W** skrila.hr. Campsite idyllically located on the shoreline at Stara Baška's northern end. 52Kn per person, 40Kn per pitch

Nadia Stara Baška 253 **T** 051 844 663, **W** nadia.hr. The best place to eat in the village, with fresh local fish like *škarpina* (groper) and *kovač* (John Dory) pricey but worth it. It also has bright en-suite rooms with TV. Open Easter–Oct. 400Kn

Baška and around

Lying at the island's southern end, **BAŠKA** is set in a wide bay ringed by stark mountains. At the heart of a rapidly modernizing town lies the kind of fishing village that wouldn't look out of place in Brittany or Cornwall, a tangle of crooked alleyways and colourful houses perched on a steep slope facing the sea. Baška's star attraction, however, is its two-kilometre stretch of **beach**, a mixture of sand and fine shingle that from a distance looks like a long crescent of demerara sugar – not that you'll be able to appreciate this in July and August, however, when its entire surface is covered with parasols, beach towels and pink-hued north Europeans contentedly roasting themselves in the sun. Despite the crowds, it's undoubtedly one of the best beaches in the Adriatic, and the view – embracing the bare offshore island of **Prvić** and the Velebit mountains in the background – is dramatic whatever the time of year. In season, taxi-boats shuttle bathers to and from the shingle coves of Prvić, or to the succession of bays east of Baška – of which long, shallow **Vela Luka** is the most alluring.

Aquarium

Na Vodici 2 • May–Sept daily 9am–noon & 5–8pm • 20Kn • **T** 098 211 630, **W** akvarij-baska.com.hr

Rainy-day attractions in Baška are few and far between, although this privately owned **Aquarium** with a modest display of Adriatic fish and shellfish, displayed in attractively illuminated tanks, is an option.

Jurandvor: St Lucy's Church

Jurandvor • Daily 10am–3pm & 5–9pm • 10Kn

Twenty minutes' walk inland from Baška (back along the main road to Krk), **St Lucy's Church** (Crkva svete Lucije) in the village of **JURANDVOR** is the site of one of Croatian archeology's most important discoveries: the inscription known as the **Baška tablet** (Bašćanska ploča). Recording a gift to the church from the eleventh-century King Zvonimir, the tablet is the first mention of a Croatian king in the Croatian language and the oldest surviving text in the Glagolitic script (see box, p.220). The original tablet is now in the Croatian Academy in Zagreb (see p.72), but there's a replica inside the church, and most places on the island seem to have sprouted copies.

BAŠKA TO STARA BAŠKA ON FOOT

It's a three-hour walk across the mountains from **Baška** to **Stara Baška**. West from Jurandvor, a twenty-minute inland from Baška (see above), a minor road leads to the hillside village of Batomalj, 1km away, the starting point for the path. The walk then rises steeply before skirting the 482-metre peak of Veli Hlam – it's well maintained and marked in either direction, although the going can be very tough in wind, rain or hot sun. You will need to avail yourself of the invaluable hiking map provided free by Baška tourist office (see p.220) before setting out.

4

THE GLAGOLITIC SCRIPT

The origins of Glagolitic go back to ninth-century monks **Cyril and Methodius**, who were chosen by the Byzantine emperor to convert the Slavs to Christianity. In order to translate the Gospels into the Slav tongue, Cyril and Methodius developed a new alphabet better suited to its sounds than either Latin or Greek. They began their missionary work with a trip to Moravia in 863, collecting a group of followers who then brought the script to the Adriatic seaboard – where it was adopted by Croatian priests.

The script, which came to be known as **Glagolitic** (because so many manuscripts began with the words "*U ono vrijeme glagolja Isus…*" or "And then Jesus said…") is an extremely decorative 38-letter alphabet which borrowed some shapes from Greek, Armenian and Georgian, but which also contained much that was original. Other disciples of Cyril and Methodius made their way to Bulgaria, where they produced a modified version of the script, called **Cyrillic** in recognition of one of their mentors, versions of which are still in use today throughout Eastern Europe.

Despite the Roman Catholic church's preference for the Roman script, Glagolitic proved surprisingly enduring on the Adriatic coast. In inland Istria the script remained in use until 1818, when it was banned by the Austrian authorities. The growth of Croatian nationalism occasioned a Glagolitic revival in the late nineteenth century, but the universal dissemination of the Roman alphabet through mass education had by this stage condemned Glagolitic to obscurity.

There is, however, currently something of a **Glagolitic revival** going on in coastal Croatia, although this is less to do with its everyday usefulness than its visual appeal – the characters look great on souvenir mugs and T-shirts. Aesthetic considerations aside, the number of Croats who could write their name in Glagolitic remains very small indeed.

4

BAŠKA AND AROUND

ARRIVAL AND INFORMATION

By bus Buses (frequent from Krk Town) terminate at a gravelly car park, from where it's a 5min walk downhill to the town's main T-junction.

Tourist office Kralja Zvonimira 114 (July & Aug Mon–Sat 7am–9pm, Sun 8am–noon; Sept–June Mon–Fri 8am–3pm; ☎051 856 817, tz-baska.hr). The tourist office has a generous supply of brochures and town maps.

ACTIVITIES

Diving Squatina Diving, at the far end of the beach at Zarok 88a (April–Sept; ☎051 856 034, squatinadiving.com), offer plenty of two- and four-day courses, plus excursions to local wrecks for the more experienced.

ACCOMMODATION

Private **rooms** (250Kn) and **apartments** (studios 375Kn, four-person apartments 420–550Kn) are available from two agencies right beside the T-junction: **Primaturist**, Zvonimirova 98 (July & Aug daily 8am–10pm; ☎051 856 132, primaturist.hr), and next-door **Guliver**, also at Zvonimirova 98 (July & Aug daily 9am–10pm; ☎051 856 004, pdm-guliver.hr).

Atrium Residence Emila Geistlicha 39 ☎051 656 111, hotelibaska.hr. Best equipped of Baška's package joints, this is a stylish four-star with spacious en suites, an indoor swimming pool and a "wellness" centre offering massage, solarium, facials and other vanity treats. **1100Kn**

Bunculuka ☎051 856 806, hotelibaska.hr. At the eastern side of Baška, discreetly tucked into the next bay along, this is a naturist campsite with its own stretch of pebble beach **70Kn** per person, **150Kn** per pitch.

Camping Zablaće Emila Geistlicha bb ☎051 856 909, hotelibaska.hr. An enormous, largely shadeless campsite which runs for about 1km along the southern end of Baška's beach. **60Kn** per person **120Kn** per pitch.

EATING AND DRINKING

Cafés and restaurants are in plentiful supply along the seafront or in the alleyways just inland.

RESTAURANTS

Cicibela Emila Geistlicha bb ☎051 856 013, cicibela.hr. A smart, glass-fronted restaurant on the beachside promenade, offering excellently prepared seafood (try the sea bass in white wine sauce, 95Kn), and a respectable range of steaks, plus a full range of pizzas to keep the kids happy. April–Oct daily 10am–midnight.

Franica Ribarska 39 ☎051 860 023, franica.hr. Homely place at the eastern end of the harbour, with an interior stuffed with nautical bits and pieces, and a sheltered terrace overlooking the port. The traditional menu takes in local-made pasta with *žgvacet* (lamb goulash), roast lamb with potatoes, baked octopus and the usual grilled fish. Mains 60–100Kn. April to mid-Oct daily 11am–11pm.

Konoba Placa Gorinka 2 ⓣ 091 533 1258. Unpretentious and lively tavern on the pedestrianized alley running parallel to the harbourfront, serving cheap and potent local wines and a good choice of *rakijas* – accompanied by cold cuts of meat and cheese. May–Sept daily 6pm–midnight.

Vrbnik

Perched on a 50m-high sea cliff and arguably the most dramatically situated of Krk's towns is **VRBNIK**, a hive of narrow cobbled alleys which occasionally part to reveal views of Crikvenica and Novi Vinodolski across the water. The alleys are paved with stones of different shapes, sizes and colours, creating patterns that you can gawp at for ages. Below the Old Town to the north, Vrbnik's small but divine **beach** is set in a shallow inlet, with a pebbly strand bordered by rocks and cliffs.

Vrbnik is primarily known for its highly regarded Žlahtina wine, which originates in the vineyards that cover the **Vrbničko polje** plain just west of town. The dry white is served in numerous local wine cellars, and unmarked bottles of the stuff are sold by local families from outdoor stalls.

ARRIVAL AND INFORMATION — VRBNIK

By bus Buses from Rijeka and Krk Town terminate on an unshaded bus park a 10min walk downhill from the Old Town.

Tourist office Placa vrbničkog statuta 4 (Easter–Oct Mon–Fri 8am–3pm, Sat & Sun 8am–1pm; ⓣ 051 857 479, ⓦ vrbnik.hr). The tourist office gives out local information and brochures.

Bikes Bikes can be rented from the Mare agency (see below) for 70Kn/day.

ACCOMMODATION AND EATING

The Mare agency in the Old Town at Pojana 4 (Mon–Sat 8am–8pm, Sun 9am-4pm; ⓣ 051 604 400, ⓦ mare-vrbnik.com) can book private **rooms** (200Kn) and **apartments** (studios 300Kn, four-person apartments 450Kn).

Gospoja Frankopanska 1 ⓣ 051 857 142, ⓦ gospoja.hr. Just above the main beach and with great views of the mainland from its terrace, *Gospoja* serves excellent local food, including fine seafood risottos and *šurlice* with asparagus, alongside good Žlahtina wine. April–Nov daily noon–6pm.

Nada Glavača 22 ⓣ 051 857 065, ⓦ nada-vrbnik.hr. Located at the sea-facing tip of the town, *Nada* is a good seafood restaurant with a scenic terrace upstairs and an evocatively fusty cellar hung with hams downstairs, where you can try the family's wine accompanied by local cheese and *pršut*. It is popular with coach parties but there is usually space to squeeze in. Mid-March to Nov daily 11am–11pm.

Senj

Heading southeast from Rijeka takes you along one of the most exhilarating stretches of the Adriatic coast, with rocky highlands hovering above deeply indented bays, and bewitchingly stark grey-brown islands looming across the water. Long-standing beach resorts such as Crikvenica and Novi Vinodolski are pleasant enough to merit a brief stopoff, but insufficiently compelling to justify an overnight stay. **Senj**, a somewhat gritty little town of twisting alleyways, boasts an imposing fortress and is also a good base from which to explore the Sjeverni Velebit National Park.

The main focus of the town is **Pavlinski trg**, the harbourfront square, dotted with café tables, behind which lies a warren of alleyways and smaller piazzas.

Nehaj Fortress

Daily: May, June , Sept & Oct 10am–6pm; July & Aug 10am–9pm • 15Kn

Senj's prime attraction is the **Nehaj Fortress**, which looks over the town from a rubble-covered peak south of the harbour – "Nehaj" means "fear not" or "heedless".

4

THE USKOKS

"May God preserve us from the hands of Senj." So ran a popular Venetian saying, inspired by the warrior community known as the **Uskoks**, who in 1537 made Senj their home and used it as a base from which to attack Adriatic shipping.

The Uskoks started out as refugees from the Ottoman conquest of Bosnia, who gravitated towards the Adriatic and organized themselves into military groups in order to repel further Ottoman encroachment. Klis fortress (see p.307) was a major centre of Uskok activity until it fell to the Ottomans in 1537 – they subsequently withdrew to Austrian-controlled Senj, from where they mounted further resistance. Although regarded as a useful component in the Habsburg Empire's defences, the Uskoks were consistently underpaid, forcing them to turn to piracy in order to survive. Harassing Adriatic shipping from their 15m-long rowing boats, they considered anything Ottoman a legitimate target, which in practice meant attacking the (usually Venetian) ships on which Ottoman goods were transported. The Austrians turned a blind eye, regarding Uskok piracy as a convenient way of challenging Venetian dominance of the Adriatic.

All this ultimately proved too much for the Venetians, who began a propaganda campaign accusing the Uskoks of eating the raw hearts of their enemies. In 1615 the Venetians provoked the so-called **Uskok War** with Austria in an attempt to bring an end to the problem. The Uskoks gave a good account of themselves until their Austrian protectors withdrew their support, and eager to make peace with Venice undertook to resettle the Uskoks inland. Senj was occupied by the Austrian navy, and the Uskoks left for new homes in Otočac, just to the southeast, or in the Žumberak hills north of Karlovac.

It was constructed in 1558 under the auspices of Uskok commander Ivan Lenković, who obtained building materials by demolishing all the churches and monasteries that lay outside the town walls and so couldn't be defended against the Ottomans. Inside are three floors of exhibits illustrating the history of the Uskoks, featuring weaponry, costumes and excellent English-language commentary. The view from the battlements justifies the climb, with the convoluted street plan of central Senj spread out immediately below, and the pale, parched flanks of Krk across the water.

ARRIVAL AND INFORMATION — SENJ

By bus Hourly buses pound their way down the Rijeka–Zadar–Split coastal route, stopping on the waterfront close to the main square.

Tourist office Stara cesta 2 (July & Aug daily 8am–8pm; rest of year Mon–Fri 8am–3pm; ☎ 053 881 068, ⓦ tz-senj.hr). The tourist office, about 200m north of the main square along the seafront, will help out with basic information and might have a free town map.

EATING

Gostionica Jablan Senjska Draga 19 ☎ 053 764 022, ⓦ gostionica-jablan.com. Around 6km inland from Senj on the road that ascends towards the Vratnik pass and the Zagreb–Split autocesta, *Jablan* is a fine place to tuck in to spit-roast lamb, frequently served in big hunks on the bone and priced by weight. The interior is on the plain and functional side, but there's a nice terrace outside. Daily 8am–11pm.

Martina Vukasovića 23 ☎ 053 881 638. One kilometre northwest of the centre on the main coastal road, *Martina* offers a range of grilled meat, fish and shellfish on an outdoor terrace looking towards the sandy-coloured eastern shores of Krk. Daily 8am–10pm.

The Velebit

South from Senj, the Magistrala picks its way beneath the rocky slopes of the **Velebit**, the mountain chain which follows the coast for some 100km. A stark, grey, unbroken wall, the Velebit is a forbidding sight when seen from the coast, although there are patches of green pasture and forest just below its string of summits. Two areas, **Northern Velebit** and **Paklenica**, have been designated as national parks. Offering some of the most exhilarating hiking in southeastern Europe, the Velebit can also be a dangerous place for the unprepared. Weather can be very unpredictable – it may seem sunny on the coast below, but a storm might be raging on the mountain once you reach a certain altitude. Avoid hiking alone, pick up weather forecasts from the relevant national park offices, and announce your arrival in advance if you're planning to stay at any mountain shelters.

Northern Velebit National Park

Much of the northern Velebit comes under the protection of the **Velebit National Park** (Nacijonalni park Sjeverni Velebit). Best starting point for excursions is **Zavižan**, the peak at the northern end of the park where there is a car park and a mountain hut. Travelling between the park and the Zagreb–Split autocesta will take you through the logging village of **Krasno** and the bear sanctuary at **Kuterevo**. Although just outside the boundaries of the park, one of the Northern Velebit's most breathtaking features is Zavratnica cove, on the coast near the pretty harbour of **Jablanac**.

Zavižan and around

Easily reached from the nearby road's-end car park, smooth-topped **Zavižan** (1676m) is the principal peak of the northern Velebit and offers fantastic views of the Kvarner Gulf and its islands. Below the peak is the highest meteorological station in Croatia, which also functions as a mountain hut (see p.225) and serves basic refreshments. A ten-minute walk south of the car park is the **Velebit Botanical Garden** (Velebitski botanički vrt), with a circular trail leading round a meadow planted with herbs and flowers typical of these highlands.

The Premužić Trail

Just south of the Velebit Botanical Garden is the start of the **Premužić Trail**, a 57km-long path mapped out by lifelong Velebit enthusiast Ante Premužić in the 1930s. Working its way from one side of the Velebit's central ridge to the other, the trail provides a superb taste of the mountain's varied geography, with lush deciduous woodland alternating with pine forests and arid rocky wastes. The trail was deliberately engineered to provide easy walking with gentle gradients – although the surface is stony and proper hiking boots are required. The easiest way to tackle it as a day-trip is to walk from Zavižan to *Rossijeva Koliba*, an unmanned mountain refuge to the south (2hr 20min). From here you can return to Zavižan, or follow a trail downhill that meets the main coastal road near Starigrad, midway between Senj and Jablanac.

Jablanac and around

Jumping-off point for both Zavratnica cove and the walking trail to Veliki Alan, the cute harbour village of **JABLANAC** is a short drive downhill from the main coastal road. Jablanac itself is worth a quick stroll; the main ferry port for Rab until 2012 (when a new harbour was opened at nearby Stinica), Jablanac is now a peaceful and altogether pretty little place, with stone houses arranged around a horseshoe-shaped harbour.

THE BURA

One of the Kvarner Gulf's most famous natural phenomena is the **bura**. A cold, dry northeasterly, it blows across the central European plain and gets bottled up behind the Adriatic mountains, escaping through the passes at places like Senj, where it is claimed to be at its worst. It's said that you can tell the bura is coming when a streak of white cloud forms atop the Velebit. At its strongest, it can overturn cars and capsize boats. When it's blowing, ferry crossings between the mainland and the islands are often suspended, and the road bridge to Krk as well as the road to Starigrad-Paklenica will either be off limits to high-sided vehicles, or closed altogether.

4

Zavratnica Cove

For an outstanding example of the Adriatic coast at it most jaw-droppingly dramatic then look no further than **Zavratnica cove**, a fifteen-minute walk southeast from Jablanac. This sheer-sided sea inlet cuts into the lower slopes of the northern Velebit massif, roughly opposite the island of Rab. With a footpath running along Zavratnica's shore and a small beach at its eastern end, it's an easily accessible place in which to lie back and admire the scenery.

Jablanac to Veliki Alan

Jablanac is the starting point of one of the Northern Velebit's most popular hiking trails, which ascends steeply towards the **Veliki Alan** mountain pass. The marked path starts at the *Dr Miroslav Hirtz* mountain hut in Jablanac, and leads through the hamlet of **Donji Baričevići** all the way to *Alan* mountain hut (1305m). From here, you can enjoy splendid views of the sea below with the islands of Rab and Pag in the distance. If you've come up this way, you can then walk another ten minutes up from the hut to meet the Premužić Trail (see p.223) at 1379m.

Krasno

Just outside the Northern Velebit National Park, the sleepy village of **KRASNO** lies on the road that links Sveti Juraj with the Otočac junction of the Zagreb–Split autocesta. It is also the site of the park's visitor centre (see opposite).

4

Forestry Museum

Krasno bb • T 053 851 116

Krasno still supports an active logging industry and the village's **Forestry Museum** (Muzej šumarstva) provides an intriguing overview of life in the shadow of the Velebit. Before World War II, foothill villages like Krasno supported a much larger population; local workers would fell trees with handsaws before transporting the trunks down to the coast on horseback.

Church of the Holy Mother of God

Perched on a hill at the eastern end of the village is the whitewashed **Church of the Holy Mother of God** (Crkva majke božje krasnarske), focus of a popular pilgrimage cult ever since local shepherds experienced a divine vision. Non-believers can enjoy the views of Krasno, lying in a green pastoral bowl between wooded hills.

Kuterevo: Velebit Bear Sanctuary

Pod crikvom 103 • Open daylight hours April–Oct • T 053 799 222, W kuterevo-medvjedi.com.hr

Draped over green hills midway between the Northern Velebit National Park and the Zagreb-Split autocesta, the village of **KUTEREVO** is an increasingly popular destination among Croatian school parties and other nature-friendly trippers, thanks to the **Velebit Bear Sanctuary** (Velebitsko utočište za medvjede), established in 2002. The sanctuary cares for sick and orphaned cubs who couldn't survive in the wild, although they do have to spend their entire lives in some form of captivity once they've experienced long-term human intervention – they can't be reintroduced to their natural habitat. An enclosure near the entrance to the sanctuary acts as a "nursery" for young bears who require close nurturing; they are subsequently released into a much larger compound at the back of the sanctuary when they become more independent.

ARRIVAL AND INFORMATION — NORTHERN VELEBIT NATIONAL PARK

By car To get to Zavižan take the tortuously twisting mountain road from the village of Sveti Juraj, 5km south of Senj, and then turn onto the part-asphalt, part-gravel road to Babić Siča, where there is a national park barrier and a hut selling tickets (3-day ticket 45Kn). There is no public transport to the park.

National Park office Krasno (July & Aug daily 8am–8pm; rest of year Mon–Fri 8am–3pm; ⓣ053 665 380, ⓦnp-sjeverni-velebit.hr). The National Park visitor centre can sell you hiking maps and entrance tickets.

ACCOMMODATION

Butina Kuterevo 21a ⓣ053 799 607 and ⓣ099 200 9321, ⓦbutina-kuterevo.com.hr. Family-run B&B with cute home-style rooms located above a rustically decorated restaurant guarded by friendly looking bears (in wooden-sculpture form). Rooms feature fresh-smelling pine floorboards and pine cupboards. A studio apartment and a double come with en-suite facilities; two more doubles share a bathroom in the hallway. **250Kn**

Forestry House (Šumarska kuća) Krasno bb ⓣ053 851 116. Comfortable en-suite double rooms run by the Krasno Forestry Museum (see opposite), in a restful rustic environment. **300Kn**

Zavižan Mountain Hut ⓣ053 614 200. One double, one quad and two large dorms in the weather station just below Zavižan Peak. The host is a mine of information and simple food and drink is available on request. Open all year round. **80Kn** per person

Paklenica National Park

The southern end of the Velebit massif culminates in a flourish of tortured limestone formations above the straggling seaside town of **Starigrad-Paklenica**. It constitutes the obvious base for the **Paklenica National Park** (Nacionalni Park Paklenica), the most accessible hiking area in the southern Velebit. At the centre of the park are two limestone gorges, **Velika Paklenica** and, 5km to the south, **Mala Paklenica** (literally, Big Paklenica and Small Paklenica), which run down towards the sea, towered over by four-hundred-metre-high cliffs. Velika Paklenica is a major tourist destination busy with hikers and rock-climbing enthusiasts from spring through to autumn, while Mala Paklenica has deliberately been left undeveloped in order to protect its status as a (relatively) untouched wilderness – paths are not well maintained and you'll need good maps (available from local shops and the national park office in Starigrad) if you want to explore.

4

Starigrad-Paklenica and Seline

With its long line of holiday apartments running either side of the main coastal road, **STARIGRAD-PAKLENICA** isn't the most immediately attractive of towns along the Adriatic coast. However, it's full of hikers eager to launch themselves on the stark grey heights towering above town to the northeast, and also figures as a fairly attractive beach resort. Focal point is the high-rise *Hotel Alan* in the centre of Starigrad. From here an attractive shingle **beach** stretches southwards, culminating in a broad cape overlooked by a ruined medieval tower. At its southern end, Starigrad runs imperceptibly into the next town along, **SELINE**, site of the curving, pebbly Pisak beach.

ARRIVAL AND DEPARTURE — STARIGRAD AND SELINE

By bus Most coastal buses plying the Rijeka–Zadar route run through Starigrad, stopping near the *Hotel Alan* (handiest for the national park) or at the northern end of the village, where there's a small harbour.

Destinations Rijeka (12 daily; 3hr 30min); Zadar (hourly; 1hr–1hr 20min).

INFORMATION

Tourist office Trg Tome Marašovića 1 (May–Sept Mon–Sat 8am–8pm, Sun 8am–noon & 3–8pm; Oct–April Mon–Sat 8am–1pm; ⓣ023 369 255, ⓦrivijera-paklenica.hr). The tourist office, opposite the bus stop at the northern end of Starigrad, is where you can pick up leaflets about the park and advice on what to see.

National Park office Dr F. Tuđmana 14a, Starigrad (Mon–Fri 8am–3pm, Sat & Sun 8am–noon & 5–8pm; ⓣ023 369 202, ⓦpaklenica.hr). A visit to the National Park office is essential if you're planning trips into the mountains – they sell detailed hiking maps, can advise on weather conditions and book rooms in the *Paklenica* mountain hut in Velika Paklenica.

ACCOMMODATION AND EATING

Koma Maras, in the shopping mall in front of the high-rise *Hotel Alan* at F. Tuđmana 14 (daily 9am–1.30pm & 5.30–9pm; ⓣ 023 359 206, ⓦ koma-maras.hr), will find rooms or **apartments** in Starigrad or Seline. Camping isn't allowed in the park itself, but there's an abundance of **campsites** in Starigrad (see below). All the hotels listed below have good **restaurants** offering the usual repertoire of seafood risottos and fresh fish; there's also a string of inexpensive grills along the main road through Starigrad, and stores in which to stock up on provisions.

HOTELS

STARIGRAD

Rajna Franje Tuđmana 105 ⓣ 023 359 121, ⓦ hotel-rajna.com. Medium-sized place on the main highway, sporting ten standard en-suite rooms with TV and a/c in the main building, and rustic-style accommodation in restored stone cottages slightly inland. The nearest hotel to the park entrance, thus popular with trekkers. The owner organizes 4WD trips into the Velebit mountains. **340Kn**

Vicko Jose Dokoze 20 ⓣ 023 369 304, ⓦ hotel-vicko.hr. Swanky, intimate family hotel on the main highway, just up from the tourist office and about 1.5km north of the main park entrance, featuring neat rooms with TV and a/c. The quality of the hotel restaurant is such that it's worth paying an extra 115Kn for half board. **830Kn**

SELINE

Croatia Put Jaza bb ⓣ 023 369 190, ⓦ pansion-croatia.com. Medium-sized family-run hotel at the northern end of Seline, on a nice stretch of beach, offering a couple of cosy en-suite doubles and several two- or four-person apartments. They also rent out a two-bedroom stone house in Marasovići (whole house 900Kn/day), near the entrance to the National Park. **325Kn**

Marija Seline 8 ⓣ 023 656 102, ⓦ pansion-marija.com. Right on the shore near Pisak beach, with a neat collection of two- to five-person apartments, each with kitchenette and small balcony, and there's a café-restaurant with seating on the water's edge. **330Kn**

CAMPSITE

Kamp Nacionalni Park ⓣ 023 369 202. A large, well-tended site right next to the Paklenica National Park office, occupying a pleasantly shingly stretch of beach. Mid-March to mid-Nov. **40Kn** per person, pitches from **30Kn**

4

Velika Paklenica

Tickets 30Kn, or 40Kn including entry to the Manita Peć cave

The entrance to the **Velika Paklenica gorge** is about 2km inland from Starigrad, reached by a road which heads east just south of the *Hotel Alan*; there's no public transport along this route. After you pass through the half-abandoned, stone village of Marasovići, there's a **ticket booth** where you pay an entrance fee and receive a basic free map, if you haven't already picked one up from the National Park office in Starigrad (see p.225). You can park here, or at a second car park 2km further on inside the park.

Paklenica Mill to the underground tunnels

Just beyond the ticket booth, the roadside **Paklenica Mill** (Paklenički mlin; mid-June to mid-Sept daily 8am–7pm; fee included in park ticket) contains a small ethnographic display and, if there's enough water in the local stream, a working demonstration of how these water-driven corn-grinding mills actually worked. Beyond the mill, the gorge begins to narrow in earnest, with dramatic rock outcrops towering above a boulder-strewn riverbed. After about twenty minutes of moderate ascent, the path passes a sequence of **underground tunnels** (*bunkeri*) built by the former Yugoslav Army to serve as a high-security bomb shelter for state officials. They're currently being renovated and should soon hold a display devoted to the flora and fauna of the park.

Anića kuk to Vidakov kuk

Another 45 minutes' walk up the main trail, a well-signposted side-path heads right to **Anića kuk**, a craggy peak lying a steep climb to the south. Beyond here, the main path levels out for a while, passing through elm and beech forest – surprisingly lush after the arid Mediterranean scrub of the coast below. After another fifteen minutes, a second side-path ascends steeply to the left. A strenuous forty-minute walk up here

here will bring you to the **Manita peć cave** (10am–1pm: April Sat only; May Wed & Sat only; June & Oct Mon, Wed & Sat; July–Sept daily; supplementary ticket required 20Kn), a complex of stalactite packed caverns about 500m long. From here you can either turn back the way you came, or head on (the path leads from the left of the cave as you emerge) up some fairly steep and none-too-easy slopes to **Vidakov kuk** (1hr 30min), an 800m-high peak that gives fine views over the coast and islands.

Lugarnica hut to Vaganski vrh

Back on the main path, it's about twenty minutes to the **Lugarnica hut**, where you can get food and drink (April, May & Oct weekends only June–Sept daily 10.30am–4.30pm), and a further thirty minutes to the *Paklenica* mountain hut, the starting point for assaults on the major peaks above. The most prominent of these is **Vaganski vrh**, which at 1757m above sea level is the southern Velebit's highest peak. The views from the top are spectacular, but you'll need to be reasonably fit, have a good map and make an early start if you're going to attempt the hike up.

The Educational Trail and Mala Paklenica

The ticket booth at the entrance to Velika Paklenica is the start for an **Education Trail** (Poučna staza), an easy-going walk that leads through the hamlets and farms at the foot of the mountains to the mouth of the **Mala Paklenica**, fifty minutes' walk to the south. The trail runs through a typical cross-section of Adriatic environments, with infertile rock-strewn heath alternating with olive groves, vegetable plots and sheep pastures. Mala Paklenica itself is a beautifully rugged canyon, with a boulder-strewn trail at the bottom that's a bit of a scramble. To return to civilization, take the asphalt path from the mouth of Mala Paklenica to Seline (25min).

4

Zrmanja Gorge

Contact the tourist office in Starigrad or any of the hotels for details of trips • Around 250Kn per person, including lunch

Tourist agencies in Starigrad advertise boat and rafting trips through the **Zrmanja Gorge**, a narrow canyon that empties into a broad lagoon known as the Novigradsko more ("Sea of Novigrad"), just south of the Paklenica National Park. It is one of the most remarkable karst formations in the country, its sheer sides rising as high as 200m. Raft trips on the upper stretches of the Zrmanja begin at Kaštel Žegarski, 25km upriver from the Novigradsko more, and finish at Muškovci, a further 10km downstream.

Rab

South of Krk and east of Cres, mainland-hugging **RAB** is the smallest but arguably the most beautiful of the main Kvarner Gulf islands. Its eastern side is rocky and harsh, rising to a stony grey spine that supports little more than a few goats, but the western side is lush and green, with a sharply indented coast and some beautiful coves. Medieval **Rab Town** is the island's highlight, while the **Lopar peninsula** at the northern end of the island possesses some of the sandiest beaches in the country.

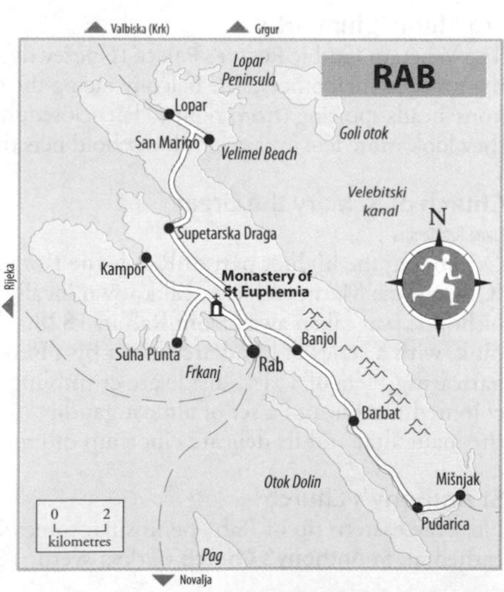

ARRIVAL AND DEPARTURE RAB

By ferry A car ferry runs from Stinica on the mainland to Mišnjak on the island's southern tip. You can also hop over to Rab by ferry from Valbiska on Krk to Lopar, though bear in mind that this leaves you a good 10km from Rab Town and buses don't always connect with the ferry arrivals.

By catamaran There's a daily catamaran service from Rijeka via Rab to Novalja on Pag.

Rab to: Novalja (1 daily; 45min); Rijeka (1 daily; 1hr 45min).

By bus The two daily (three in summer) Rijeka–Rab buses use the Stinica-Mišnjak ferry, finishing up in Rab Town.

Rab Town

A perfectly preserved, late medieval Adriatic settlement squeezed onto a slender peninsula, **RAB TOWN** is famous for the quartet of Romanesque campaniles that run along its Old Town's central ridge. It's a genuinely lovely place: a tiny grey-and-ochre city, enlivened with splashes of green palm, huddles of leaning junipers and sprigs of olive-coloured cacti which push their way up between balconied palaces. The population today is only a third of what it was in Rab's fourteenth-century heyday, although it's swelled significantly by the influx of summer visitors, who create a lively holiday atmosphere without overly compromising the town's medieval character.

The Old Town divides into two parts: **Kaldanac**, the oldest quarter, at the end of the peninsula, and **Varoš**, which dates from between the fifteenth and seventeenth centuries. Together they make up a compact and easily explored grid of alleyways traversed by three parallel thoroughfares: Donja (Lower), Srednja (Middle) and Gornja (Upper) ulice.

4

Trg svetog Kristofora

Rab's Old Town is entered from **Trg svetog Kristofora** (St Christopher's Square), a broad open space overlooked by the jutting bastion of the **Gagliardi Tower** (Tvrđava Galijarda), built by the Venetians in the fifteenth century to defend the landward approaches to the town.

St Nicholas's Church

About five minutes' walk east of Trg svetog Kristofora, **Srednja ulica** opens out into a small piazza mostly taken up by a dinky Venetian loggia and, tucked away in the corner, the tiny Gothic **St Nicholas's Church** (Crkva svetog Nikole), which nowadays hosts a sporadically open art gallery.

Trg Municipium Arbe

The Venetian Gothic **Rector's Palace** (Knežev dvor), on **Trg Municipium Arbe**, now houses the town council offices. The balcony facing the square is supported by three sculpted lions' heads sporting (from right to left) closed, half-open and wide-open jaws – although they look more like overweight household pets than fearsome beasts of the savanna.

Church of St Mary the Great

Ivana Rabljanina

Occupying the highest part of Rab is the Romanesque **Church of St Mary the Great** (Crkva svete Marije Velike), still known locally as the Katedrala even though the bishopric was taken away from Rab in 1828. The west front is striped pale grey and pink, with a series of blind arches cut by a Renaissance doorway that supports a harrowing Pietà of 1514. Inside are crumbling, brown walls flecked with agate-coloured marble and a set of almost gaudily carved chestnut choirstalls, dominated by the main altar and its delicate ciborium of grey marble.

St Anthony's Church

Near the eastern tip of Rab's peninsula, somewhat in the shadow of the nearby cathedral, **St Anthony's Church** (Crkva svetog Antuna) preserves its original rib-vaulted

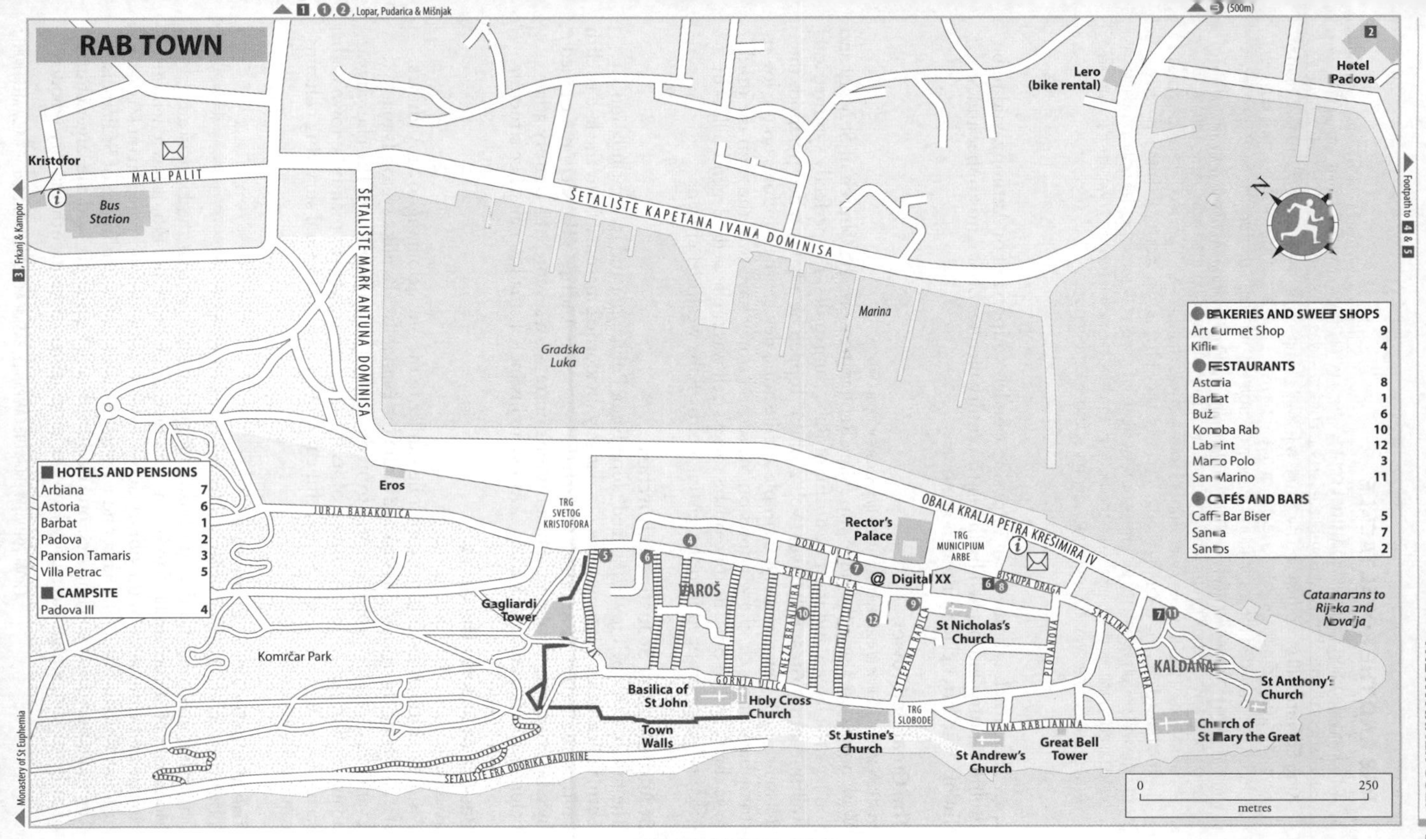
RAB TOWN
1, 1, 2, Lopar, Pudarica & Mišnjak
3 (500m)
3, Frkanj & Kampor
Footpath to 4 & 5
Monastery of St Euphemia
Kristofor
MALI PALIT
Bus Station
ŠETALIŠTE KAPETANA IVANA DOMINISA
ŠETALIŠTE MARK ANTUNA DOMINISA
Lero (bike rental)
Hotel Padova
Gradska Luka
Marina
Eros
JURJA BARAKOVIĆA
TRG SVETOG KRISTOFORA
OBALA KRALJA PETRA KREŠIMIRA IV
Rector's Palace
TRG MUNICIPIUM ARBE
DONJA ULICA
SREDNJA ULICA
GORNJA ULICA
KNEZA BRANIMIRA
STJEPANA RADIĆA
BISKUPA DRAGA
PIOVANOVA
SKALINE A. TESTENA
IVANA RABLJANINA
TRG SLOBODE
@ Digital XX
VAROŠ
KALDANA
Gagliardi Tower
Komrčar Park
Basilica of St John
Holy Cross Church
Town Walls
St Justine's Church
St Nicholas's Church
St Andrew's Church
Great Bell Tower
Church of St Mary the Great
St Anthony's Church
Catamarans to Rijeka and Novalja
ŠETALIŠTE FRA ODORIKA BADURINE
HOTELS AND PENSIONS
Arbiana 7
Astoria 6
Barbat 1
Padova 2
Pansion Tamaris 3
Villa Petrac 5
CAMPSITE
Padova III 4
BAKERIES AND SWEET SHOPS
Art Gourmet Shop 9
Kifla 4
RESTAURANTS
Astoria 8
Barbat 1
Buž 6
Konoba Rab 10
Labirint 12
Marco Polo 3
San Marino 11
CAFÉS AND BARS
Caffe Bar Biser 5
Sanda 7
Santos 2
N
0 250
metres

4

RAB AND THE ROYAL TACKLE

Rab's long-standing status as a **naturist** centre – the Frkanj peninsula just west of town was established as one of the first naturist resorts in Europe – was popularized by the visit of British **King Edward VIII** (accompanied by future wife Wallis Simpson) in the summer of 1936. Whether Edward actually got the royal tackle out or not remains the subject of much conjecture, but his stay on Rab provided the inspiration for a recent Croatian musical, *Kralj je gol* (literally "The King is Naked", although in colloquial Croatian it means much the same thing as the expression "The Emperor's New Clothes"). After visiting Rab, Edward and Wallis continued down the Adriatic aboard a luxury yacht packed with sundry toffs and royal hangers-on. Pursued by Europe's press, the trip turned into the celebrity media-fest of its day, with thousands of locals lining the streets to ogle the couple when they came ashore at Šibenik, Split and Dubrovnik. The only journalists who failed to follow the cruise were the British – the idea that their monarch was romancing an American divorcee was too mind-bogglingly scandalous to report.

apse. The church is home to an imposing wooden sculpture of St Anthony, said to be twelfth century and flanked by fifteenth-century pictures of St Christopher and St Tudor – the latter clad in Roman armour.

The Great Bell Tower

Ivana Rabljanina • Mid-June to mid-Sept daily 10am–1pm & 7.30–9.30pm • 5Kn

4

Walk northwest along the ridge-top Ivana Rabljanina from the Church of St Mary and you pass the largest and most beautiful of Rab's campaniles, the perfectly symmetrical twelfth-century **Great Bell Tower** (Veli zvonik). Topped by a balustraded pyramid, the 25-metre-high tower employs a simple architectural device: the windows on the lower storey have one arch, the windows on the second storey have two, those on the third have three, and so on. The tone of the tower's bell was mellowed – legend tells – by gold and silver dropped into the casting pot by Rab's wealthier citizens.

St Andrew's and St Justine's churches

The first of three bell towers spaced along Ivana Rabljanina and its continuation, **Gornja ulica**, is a utilitarian piece of relatively unadorned masonry from the late twelfth century attached to **St Andrew's Church** (Crkva svetog Andrije). The second – capped by a bulbous spire reminiscent of a bishop's mitre – is a seventeenth-century affair belonging to **St Justine's Church** (Crkva svete Justine), a small Renaissance structure.

Basilica of St John the Great

Gornja ulica

A simple thirteenth-century campanile similar to the one belonging to St Andrew's stands beside the ruined **Basilica of St John the Evangelist** (Bazilika svetog Ivana Evanđeliste), which probably dates from the sixth or seventh century. The church was abandoned in the 1830s and much of its masonry taken away to mend the town's other sacred buildings, although the graceful curve of its apse and several surviving columns can still be admired.

The Monastery of St Euphemia

June & Sept Mon–Sat 9am–noon & 3–5pm; July & Aug daily 10am–noon & 4–6pm • 10Kn

Thirty minutes' walk northwest of town along the seaside path is the Franciscan **Monastery of St Euphemia** (Samostan svete Eufemije). Built in 1446, it has a delicate cloister and a museum in the library above, which contains illuminated manuscripts, a headless Roman figure of Diana and a fifteenth-century wooden image of St Francis. The monastery has two churches: one dedicated to St Euphemia, and the larger church of St Bernardin, which has a gory late-Gothic crucifix, a seventeenth-century wooden

FROM TOP VIEW FROM THE CAMPANILE, BASILICA OF ST JOHN THE GREAT; RAB WATERFRONT >

ceiling decorated with scenes from the life of St Francis, and a polyptych painted by the Vivarini brothers in 1458, showing a Madonna and Child flanked by two tiers of saints.

Šetalište Fra Odorika Badurine

Šetalište Fra Odorika Badurine, the waterside walkway on the west side of town (reached via steps from the fragrant, shady Komrčar Park), is actually one of the best urban "beaches" in Croatia – it doesn't amount to much save for a concrete strand, but the water is super-clear, and there are plenty of trees to provide shade if you're not in the mood to be grilled senseless.

The Frkanj peninsula

There are some attractive shingle beaches east of town beyond the *Padova* hotel, but far more popular is the **Frkanj peninsula**, 1km west of the town as the crow flies. The peninsula boasts numerous rocky coves backed by deep green forest, and there's a large naturist area on the far side. You can reach the peninsula from the harbour by taxi-boat or by walking the 3km from the tourist complex of **Suha Punta**, at the end of a side road that leaves the Rab–Kampor route just beyond the Monastery of St Euphemia.

ARRIVAL AND DEPARTURE — RAB TOWN

4

By bus Rab's bus station is in the modern shopping centre just northeast of the Old Town, a 5min walk from Trg svetog Kristofora.

Destinations Kampor (Mon–Sat 7 daily, Sun 1 daily; 15min); Lopar (Mon–Sat 11 daily, Sun 9 daily; 30min); Rijeka (July & Aug 3 daily, Sept–June 2 daily; 3hr); Senj (July & Aug 3 daily, Sept–June 2 daily; 2hr); Zagreb (July & Aug 4 daily, Sept–June 3 daily; 6hr).

By catamaran Catamarans operating the Rijeka–Rab–Novalja route dock at the eastern tip of the Old Town.

INFORMATION

Tourist offices There are two tourist offices, the main one on the central square, Trg Municipium Arbe 8 (June–Sept daily 8am–10pm; Oct–May Mon–Fri 8am–3pm; ⊤ 051 771 111, ⓦ tzg-rab.hr), and a seasonal one behind the bus station on Mali Palit (June–Sept daily 8am–10pm).

Internet Trg Municipium Arbe is a free wi-fi zone (enquire at the tourist office about the password); otherwise you can surf the net at Internet Digital XX on Srednja ulica (daily 10am–2pm & 6pm–midnight; 30Kn/hr).

GETTING AROUND

Bikes can be rented from Eros (see below), or from Lero, on the other side of the harbour at Banjol 117a (Daily 8am–noon & 6–8pm, ⊤ 051 771 048). Expect to pay around 80Kn/day.

ACCOMMODATION

There are numerous agencies in town offering **rooms** (250Kn) and **apartments** (studios 375Kn, four-person apartments 420–550Kn), either in the Old Town or in the modern suburbs to the northeast: ★ **Kristofor**, just behind the bus station at Mali Palit bb (⊤ 051 725 543, ⓦ kristofor.hr) is very accommodating and will try to find you something that suits – several hosts on their books offer bed-and-breakfast deals. Eros, on the harbourfront between the bus station and Old Town (⊤ 051 724 688, ⓦ rab-novalja.com), is a reliable alternative.

HOTELS AND PENSIONS

Arbiana Obala kralja Petra Krešimira IV ⊤ 051 775 900, ⓦ arbianahotel.com. Located in an ornate pre-World War II villa near the tip of the peninsula, this is the place to luxuriate in high-ceilinged, fully equipped rooms, some of which have balconies overlooking the harbour. 1290Kn

Astoria Trg Municipium Arbe ⊤ 051 774 844, ⓦ astoria-rab.com. Renaissance palace in the heart of the Old Town, offering a handful of well-equipped apartments with kitchenette, plush furnishings and exposed brickwork. 900Kn

Barbat Barbat ⊤ 051 721 858, ⓦ hotel-barbat.com. Thirteen sea-facing rooms in a lovely shoreside villa, 6km out of town on the road to the Mišnjak ferry terminal. It's an eminently comfortable and relaxing spot, decked out in warm colours, with stained glass and paintings in the hallways, and a quiet beach and the coastal path are at your disposal. Half board only, but the top-class restaurant makes it worth the expense. Open March–Oct. 900Kn

Padova Banjol 322 ⊤ 051 724 544, ⓦ imperial.hr. On the opposite side of the bay from the Old Town and featuring comfortable three-star rooms and a number of larger four-star rooms with bathtubs, a/c, minibar, TV and balconies – so you're likely to get a good view of Rab's belfried skyline. There's also a new wellness centre with outdoor and indoor pools, sauna and solarium. **940Kn**

Pansion Tamaris Palit 285 ⓣ051 724 925, ⓦtamaris-rab.com. Family-run fourteen-room pension situated a 10min walk west of town in Palit, a suburban area of seaside villas. Neat en-suite rooms feature laminated floors, relaxing ochre colours, a/c, a small TV and wi-fi coverage. A tidy garden runs down to the seaside path and a small-boat harbour. **700Kn**

Villa Petrac Banjol ⓣ051 771 088, ⓦvillapetrac.com. Sitting on a promontory just east of the *Padova III* campsite (a 20min walk or short taxi-boat ride from the centre), *Petrac* offers bright and modern studio apartments and big, open-plan family-sized apartments all with TV, kitchenette and free wi-fi. The ground-floor restaurant has great views back towards the Old Town, and half board (an extra 150Kn per person) is worth considering. **850Kn**

CAMPSITE

Padova III Banjol bb ⓣ051 667 788, ⓦcamping.imperial.hr. The nearest campsite to town is this large and well-equipped place about 2km away in the resort suburb of Banjol; to get there, simply follow the sea path on the eastern side of the harbour. The site is right beside a shingle beach, although it's only partially shaded and gets very crowded in season. **60Kn** per person, pitches from **120Kn**

EATING AND DRINKING

There are plenty of good seafood **restaurants** in the Old Town, and although some are quite stylish they remain affordable. **Cafés and ice-cream parlours** abound in the Old Town, and at night the main Trg Municipium Arbe takes on the appearance of a huge outdoor bar, with chairs and tables covering the flagstones.

BAKERIES AND SWEET SHOPS

Art Gurmet Shop Srednja 1. The main outlet for local confectioners Vilma (see box below), who produce *rabska torta* in various sizes, as well as biscuits, chocolates and mouthwatering chocolate mousse. Daily 8am–11pm.

Kiflić Srednja 26 ⓦkiflic.hr. A good source of fresh bread, pastries and muffins, which also sells its own particularly succulent version of local delicacy *rabska torta*, with a marzipan-rich soft centre. Daily 6.30am–10pm.

RESTAURANTS

Astoria Trg Municipium Arbe 7 ⓣ051 774 844, ⓦastoria-rab.com. Smart, chic seafood restaurant attached to the hotel of the same name, with a splendid first-floor terrace looking over the main square. The fish comes grilled, baked or cooked in traditional sauces – try the monkfish (*grdobina*) in white-wine sauce. There's an impressive list of classy Croatian wines, and the mousse-type concoctions on the dessert menu make a nice change from the pancakes and ice cream on offer elsewhere. A little on the pricey side if you order à la carte, although the three-course set menus (chalked up daily; 140Kn) are well worth investigating. Reserve at weekends. April–Sept daily noon–3pm & 6–11pm.

★ **Barbat** Barbat ⓣ051 721 858, ⓦhotel-barbat.com. Highly regarded restaurant of the *Barbat* hotel 6km out of town (see opposite), serving up first-rate seafood in a smart dining room with exposed brickwork and a wall-hugging aquarium. There's also plenty of outdoor seating in a lovely garden. Daily 8am–midnight; closed Nov.

Buža Ugalje bb. Sit-down snack bar in a narrow alley just off Trg svetog Kristofora, with excellent toasted sandwiches in the 18–25Kn range and a decent menu of cocktails come the evening. Daily 9am–2pm & 6pm–2am.

Konoba Rab Kneza Branimira 3 ⓣ051 725 666. Cosy split-level place with folksy touches – the fishing nets and dried herbs hanging from the thick stone walls make it feel like a cross between a boathouse and granny's cottage. The menu features a good range of seafood and traditional meat dishes such as *teleća koljenica* (calf knuckle); local speciality *janjetina pod peku* (pieces of lamb cooked in an ember-covered pot) has to be ordered a day in advance. Mid-Feb to Oct daily 10am–2pm & 5–11pm.

★ **Labirint** Srednja 9 ⓣ051 771 145. Delicious scampi, squid and fish dishes served in a split-level collection of dining rooms and open terraces. You could do worse than try the "fish in the style of a Rab housewife", which is catch of the day baked with white wine, garlic and herbs (400Kn/kg; minimum of two people required); or the St Christopher seafood platter for two (290Kn), which includes a taste of everything. Good service and an extensive choice of Croatian wines. Daily 11.30am–2pm & 5.30pm–midnight.

RABSKA TORTA

Widely available in local shops and cafes, Rab's deliciously sweet **rabska torta** ("Rab cake") is really more of a pie than a cake, consisting of marzipan wrapped in sugary dough that is part pastry, part biscuit. Vilma (ⓦrabskatorta.com) and *Kiflić* (see above) are the main local producers and their recipes are rather different – thereby providing you with a perfect excuse to try them both.

4

THE RAPSKA FJERA

Rab's biggest annual event is the **Rapska fjera festival**, a three-day gala comprising St James's Day (July 25), St Anne's Day (July 26) and St Christopher's Day (July 27). Taking a traditional fourteenth-century holiday as its cue, the town literally reverts to the Middle Ages – six hundred participants don home-made costumes to re-create the olden times with games, dances, traditional cooking and other cultural events. Street stalls, processions, knightly tournaments and crossbow competitions are the cornerstones of the programme, and with thousands of visitors pouring into town to celebrate, there's no more invigorating time to be on the island.

4

★ **Marco Polo** Banjol 486 ⓣ051 725 846, ⓦmarcopolo-rab.com. A 20min walk from the Old Town in suburban streets above the *Padova III* campsite, serving up superb steaks and seafood. If the idea of a whole fresh fish seems a bit too much, opt for a grilled fillet of *zubatac* (dentex) for around 90Kn. Eat on the terrace surrounded by trees, or in the smart exposed-brick interior. Daily noon–2pm & 6–11pm.

San Marino Obala kralja Petra Krešimira IV ⓣ051 775 900, ⓦarbianahotel.com. The restaurant of the *Arbiana* hotel (see p.232) stretches invitingly across a shady courtyard, its terrace rubbing up against a cute triangle of Old Town park. Classier than the Adriatic average but not quite haute cuisine, *San Marino* offers some excellent seafood risottos, individual fish fillets (priced at around 90Kn each rather than by weight), and a good choice of desserts. Daily 6–11pm.

CAFÉS AND BARS

Caffe Bar Biser Srednja 21 ⓣ051 724 497. This is probably the longest-standing coffee-and-cakes venue in town; a good place for croissants and ice cream during the daytime, with a tree-shaded terrace strategically placed at the western end of the Old Town's main street. Daily 7am–midnight.

Sanda Donja ⓣ051 725 764. One of several café-bars in a narrow alleyway just off Trg Municipium Arbe, with an abstract art interior and an attractively priced cocktail menu. Daily 9am–2am.

Santos Pudarica Bay ⓦsanantonio-club.com. Nine kilometres out of town just off the road to the Mišnjak ferry terminal on party-central Pudarica Bay, this daytime beach bar becomes a kicking club at night, when it offers some of the best DJ-driven partying in this Adriatic corner. Beware that the *Santos* season is short. Usually late June to early Sept.

Kampor

KAMPOR, 6km from Rab Town, is a small, scattered village with a deep swath of shallow sandy beach. About 1km inland from Kampor, back along the road to Rab, lies the **Graveyard of the Victims of Fascism** (Groblje žrtava fašizma), a site commemorating the concentration camp established here by the Italian occupiers in 1942. It's referred to locally as the "Slovene Cemetery" owing to the large numbers of Slovenes who were imprisoned and died here, although it housed a wide range of Partisans, Jews and political undesirables, rounded up in the Italian-controlled portions of Slovenia and Croatia. Most of the internees were crowded together in flimsy tents and starved of food and drink – it is estimated that 4500 died in the winter of 1942–43. After the collapse of Italy in September 1943, most of the able-bodied survivors joined Tito's Partisans, who were briefly in control of the island before the arrival of a German garrison. The site is a dignified and restful place, with long lines of graves – one for every four people who died – surrounded by well-tended lawns, trees and shrubs.

ARRIVAL AND DEPARTURE — KAMPOR

By bus There are seven buses from Mon to Sat from Rab Town to Kampor, with one service on Sun (15min).

The Lopar peninsula

The road that climbs out of Rab to the north makes its way down the island's broad central valley. After passing the sprawling settlement of Supetarska Draga, the main road reaches a T-junction at the neck of the Lopar peninsula. The left turn leads to the village of **LOPAR**, a handful of houses spread around a muddy bay. The right turn leads to **San Marino**, 1km south.

San Marino

SAN MARINO is a largely modern village which nevertheless lays claim to being the birthplace of St Marin, a fourth-century stonemason who fled persecution by crossing the seas to Italy, founding the town that subsequently became the republic of San Marino.

Veli Mel Beach

San Marino stretches around a vast expanse of sand known as **Veli mel** (*mel* being an archaic word for "beach", although it's also referred to hereabouts as Rajska plaža – "Paradise Beach" – or simply "Copacabana"), backed by cafés and restaurants and packed with families from June to September. The bay on which Veli mel is situated is unusually shallow, and you can paddle almost all the way to an islet about 1km offshore.

There's a sequence of smaller, progressively less crowded sandy beaches beyond the headlands to the north, beginning with **Livačina Bay**, followed by the predominantly naturist **Kaštelina Bay** slightly further up.

4

Northern Lopar beaches

Taxi boat 40–50Kn return from the tourist port at the northeastern corner of Veli mel

If the crowded atmosphere of Veli mel isn't to your taste, there is a sequence of wilder, uncommercialized sandy beaches lining the heavily indented northern shore of the Lopar peninsula. Best-known of these is **Sahara**, a broad shallow bay reserved for naturists, although there are equally inviting stretches of sand squeezed into the bays on either side. Attitudes to clothing are fairly relaxed wherever you are, and the views of the mainland are fantastic. The northern Lopar beaches can be reached either by taxi-boat from Veli mel, or by following the tracks that lead out of San Marino to the north, crossing a sandy heath covered by prickly evergreens – the walk takes over half an hour and is unshaded, so take plenty of liquid.

GOLI OTOK

Immediately to the east of the Lopar peninsula is **Goli otok** (Bare Island), a hummock of arid rock that was used to imprison communists who remained loyal to the Soviet Union after Stalin's break with Tito in 1948. Over a period of five years in the late 1940s and early 1950s, a total of fifteen thousand alleged Stalinists were "re-educated" on Goli otok through forced labour in the island's quarry. Few of the prisoners were guilty of seriously plotting against the regime; the majority were minor figures who had simply spoken out against Tito in private and been betrayed by a colleague or friend. Inmates were subjected to a harsh regime of beatings and torture; recalcitrant prisoners had their heads immersed in buckets of human excrement, while those who confessed their ideological errors were recruited to torture the others.

As ideological tensions lessened in the mid-1950s, Goli was used to incarcerate common criminals, and the prison regime was softened. Sent here as an army deserter, Romany singing legend Šaban Bajramović (1936–2008) played in goal for the prison football team and performed in the prison orchestra, going on to become a pan-Yugoslav musical superstar after his release. Goli otok's role in the anti-Stalinist purges was not officially admitted until the 1980s, by which time Tito – on whose personal initiative the camp had been established – was already dead.

ARRIVAL AND INFORMATION — THE LOPAR PENINSULA

By bus There are nine buses daily from Rab to Lopar, all of which pass the beach at San Marino.

Tourist office At the T-junction between Lopar and San Marino (June–Sept daily 7.30am–9pm; ☎051 775 508, 🌐lopar.com)

Pag

Seen from the mainland, **PAG** is a desolate pumice-stone of an island that looks as if it could barely support any form of life. Around eight thousand people live here, looking after three times as many sheep, who scour the stony slopes in search of edible plant life. Much of their diet comes from sage, which covers the eastern side of the island with a grey-green carpet. The two main settlements are **Pag Town**, with an attractive historic centre, and **Novalja**, a bland modern settlement whose beach-based nightlife has earned it the title the "Croatian Ibiza". Tourism apart, the island's main industry is the production of **salt**, with saltpans stretching out along the island's central valley.

ARRIVAL AND DEPARTURE — PAG

By ferry Approaching Pag from the north, there's an hourly ferry from Prizna, on the mainland 3km below the Magistrala, to Žigljen, 5km north of Novalja (hourly; 20min).

By bus Novalja and Pag can be reached by bus from Rijeka (Mon–Sat 1 daily) or from Zadar in Dalmatia (roughly 4 daily).

By car The island's southern end is connected to the mainland via the Pag Bridge (Paški most), about 26km north of the Posedarje exit of the Zagreb–Split highway.

4

Pag Town

Today's **PAG TOWN** is essentially a fifteenth-century settlement built 3km to the south of its original site – which was torched by troops from Zadar in 1395 in an attempt to win control of the salt trade. The Venetians stepped in to re-establish order, hiring the architect Juraj Dalmatinac (see box, p.269) to build a new island capital from scratch, creating the present town with its tight grid of streets and well-proportioned Renaissance churches. A seafront promenade and pebbly stretches of beach provide the finishing touches to what is a pleasant and relaxing holiday town.

Salt-panning aside, Pag's main traditional activity is **lace-making**, a craft that for the moment remains refreshingly uncommercialized. Small pieces are sold from doorways by the lacemakers themselves, many of whom wear the dark, full-skirted local costume that seems to have endured here longer than anywhere else on the Adriatic.

Trg kralja Petra Krešimira IV

Flanking the town's central square, **Trg kralja Petra Krešimira IV**, are two of architect Juraj Dalmatinac's original buildings: the **Rector's Palace** (Knežev dvor), currently in the throes of long-term restoration, and the **parish church** (Župna crkva), on the other side of the square; the rose window on the church facade echoes the patterns found in Pag lace. Inside, lean stone columns sport capitals bearing a variety of carved beasts, including griffins, and dolphins drinking from cups.

PAG CHEESE

Pag's main culinary claim to fame is a hard, piquant **sheep's cheese** (*paški sir*), which has a taste somewhere between mature cheddar and Parmesan; you'll find it in supermarkets all over the country. The distinctive taste is due to the method of preparation – the cheeses are rubbed with a mixture of olive oil and ash before being left to mature – and the diet of the sheep, which includes many wild herbs (notably the ubiquitous sage) flavoured by salt picked up from the sea by the wind and deposited on vegetation across the island.

Skrivanat

Zvonimirova heads west from the main square towards the one surviving bastion of Pag's (largely dismantled) fortifications, topped by the curious-looking lookout tower known as the **Skrivanat**, which has an asymmetrical gate-like arch cut through the middle.

The beach

A causeway-like strip of land connects central Pag with its suburbs on the western side of Pag Bay, where you'll also find the town's main pebble **beach**. Behind it lies the Lokunjica, a muddy lagoon, and the saltpans, which stretch south for 6km.

Stari grad

Three kilometres from Pag on the west bank of the saltpans is **Stari grad** (Old Town), the original town which was abandoned in the 1440s. There are a few ruined buildings here, including the cloister of a Franciscan monastery, and a church dating from 1392 with a fine Gothic relief of the Virgin above the portal. A statue of the Virgin inside the Old Town church is taken in procession to the new parish church on August 15 (Assumption) each year, where it's kept until September 8 (Birth of the Virgin).

ARRIVAL AND INFORMATION — PAG TOWN

By bus Buses stop at a car park on the northern edge of town.
Destinations Novalja (Mon–Fri 6 daily, Sat 2 daily, Sun 1 daily; 35min); Rijeka (Mon–Sat 1 daily; 3hr 45min); Split (1 daily; 4hr); Zadar (Mon–Fri 4 daily, Sat 2 daily, Sun 1 daily; 1hr 15min); Zagreb (Mon–Sat 1 daily; 5hr 30min).

Tourist office Trg kralja Petra Krešimira IV (May 8am–3pm & 6–9pm; June–Sept daily 8am–10pm; Oct–April Mon–Fri 8am–3pm; ⓣ 023 611 301, ⓦ tzgpag.hr. The tourist office gives out a wealth of brochures and a map of hiking and biking trails around the island.

4

ACCOMMODATION

Rooms (from 200Kn) and **apartments** (studios from 330Kn, four-person apartments 450–550Kn) are available from **Perla**, on the main road into town at bana Jelačića 21 (ⓣ 023 600 003, ⓦ perla-pag.hr), and **Mediteran** (ⓣ 023 611 238, ⓦ mediteranpag.com), behind the bus stop at Golija 41.

HOTELS AND PENSIONS

Pagus Ante Starčevića 1 ⓣ 023 492 050, ⓦ hotel-pagus.hr. Smart and swish four-star right on the seafront with spacious en-suite rooms and its own stretch of pebble beach. Additional facilities include on-site gym and beauty treatments, and small indoor and outdoor pools. Half board is only a few kuna more expensive than the bed-and-breakfast price. April–Oct. From **1100Kn**

Pension Jerko Prosika 29 ⓣ 023 611 162, ⓦ pension-jerko.com. Family-run pension right by the beach offering neat en suites and lovely food in the downstairs restaurant. April–Oct. Half board only. **700Kn**

Tamaris Križevačka bb ⓣ 023 612 277. Small family-run hotel just uphill from the town centre, offering neat en-suite rooms with TV, and quality food in the downstairs restaurant. May–Sept. **850Kn**

Tony Dubrovačka 39 ⓣ 023 611 370, ⓦ hotel-tony.com. Medium-sized, family-run hotel 2km west of town on the northern side of Pag's bay. The en-suite rooms are simply decorated, but the location is relaxing, and there's a secluded stretch of pebble beach at the bottom of the garden. Food in the restaurant is excellent so it's well worth paying an extra 40–50Kn for half board. April–Oct. **650Kn**

PAG'S CARNIVALS

Pag Town is the venue for two **carnivals**, the first an authentic local event immediately before Lent, the second on the last Saturday in July, a re-enactment of the first for the benefit of tourists. Both feature parades and a good deal of folk music and traditional dancing, and the pre-lenten carnival culminates with the burning of the effigy known as Marko, whose ritual death is claimed to rid the community of all the bad things that have happened over the previous year. Both carnivals traditionally featured performances of *Paška robinja* (*Slave Girl of Pag*), a play of Renaissance origins concerning a captive of the Turks who is purchased and freed by a good Christian knight. Made up of rhyming couplets delivered in a monotone, it's nowadays considered too boring for the average audience, and is no longer performed every year.

CAMPSITE

Šimuni Šimuni bb ⊕023 697 441, ⓦcamping-simuni.hr. On the island's western shore, 8km from Pag Town on the road to Novalja, this large site incorporates shops, restaurants, a windsurfing school and a handsome stretch of shingle beach; Pag–Novalja buses will drop you near the site's access road. Open all year round. 80Kn per person, pitches from 120Kn

EATING AND DRINKING

There are numerous **café-bars** on the main square and along the waterfront, and several places serving traditional food.

Konoba Bile Jurija Dalmatinca 35 ⊕023 611 127. Just up from Pag's parish church, this homely tavern dispenses local wine from barrels and serves up an accompanying array of cheeses, smoked hams and anchovies. Daily 7.30pm–midnight.

Konoba Bodulo van Grada 19 ⊕023 611 989. Just northwest of the Old Town near the Skrivanat tower, family-run *Bodulo* serves fresh fish and shellfish in a vine-shaded courtyard with wooden benches and stone walls. May–Oct daily noon–midnight.

★ **Na Tale** S. Radića 2 ⊕023 611 194. Located at the end of Pag's seafront this is arguably the best restaurant in town, where you can dine on mussels, squid and fish (including succulent white fish in wine-and-herb sauces) in a relaxing courtyard shaded by trees. Daily 8am–11pm; closed Jan.

Novalja and around

4

NOVALJA, 20km north of Pag Town, is the island's main resort, much more developed and crowded than Pag Town, and famous as *the* 24-hour party destination for young Croatians. Just in case you think that life in Novalja is a non-stop disco, however, be aware that most of the nightlife is based on the beaches of Zrće and Katarelac, a good 2–3km away from the centre, and that the beach-party season is largely limited to July and August – outside these times, Novalja is just as charming and relaxing as anywhere else on the Adriatic. At the south side of town is a curving gravel beach, from where a stony path leads south to the much larger, pebbly **Straško beach**.

The Italian Hole

Kralja Zvonimira 27 • June–Sept Mon–Sat 9am–1pm & 6–10pm, Sun 6–10pm • 15Kn • ⊕053 661 160, ⓦmuzej.novalja.hr

Originally a Roman settlement dating from around the first century AD, Novalja preserves a few ancient remains, including an underground **water conduit** (*vodovod*; also known by locals as the *Talijanova buža* or "Italian Hole"). This can be entered from the basement of the **Town Museum** (Gradski muzej), clearly signposted just north of the seafront. The museum features a small ethnological display, traditional wine-making equipment and, the star exhibit, a bunch of encrusted amphorae from a shipwrecked Roman merchant ship.

Zrće and Katarelac beaches

Minivans shuttle party-goers back and forth between Zrće and the Cocomo bar on Novalja's seafront (hourly until midnight)

Some 2km south of Novalja on the road to Pag Town, a side road descends to the east-facing **Zrće beach**, a vast, gravelly expanse with a view of the pale ochre hills of eastern Pag and the greenish Velebit mountains beyond. In summer, a string of alfresco **DJ bars** set themselves up here, turning the area into a dance-till-dawn paradise for clubbers (see opposite). Food and drink is served round the clock, so you can just about spend 24 hours partying and chilling on the beach if you want to.

Southeast of Zrće on the same sea inlet, **Katarelac beach** – dubbed Bura Bura Beach by promoters – is emerging as a destination for the slightly more mature party animals (see opposite).

ARRIVAL AND INFORMATION — NOVALJA AND AROUND

By bus Novalja's bus station is on the southern outskirts of town, a 15min walk from the seafront.

Destinations Pag Town (Mon–Sat 7 daily, Sun 2 daily; 35min); Rijeka (Mon–Sat 2 daily, Sun 1 daily; 3hr); Split (1 daily; 4hr 30min); Zadar (3 daily; 1hr 30min); Zagreb (7 daily; 5hr).

By catamaran Services run to Rab (1 daily; 45min) and Rijeka (1 daily; 2hr 30min).

Tourist office Šetalište hrvatskih mornara 1, on the seafront (May, June & Sept daily 8am–1pm & 4–6pm; July & Aug daily 7am–10pm; Oct–April Mon–Fri 8am–3pm; ⓣ 053 661 404, ⓦ tz-novalja.hr).

ACCOMMODATION AND EATING

Rooms (200Kn) and **apartments** (two-person studios 375Kn, four-person apartments 500–550Kn) are available from **Aurora Travel**, midway between the bus station and the centre at Slatinska bb (ⓣ 053 663 493, ⓦ aurora-travel.hr), who may be able to fix you up with a host who provides bed and breakfast.

Boškinac Novaljsko Polje ⓣ 053 663 500, ⓦ boskinac.com. One kilometre north of town in Novaljsko Polje and surrounded by vineyards and olive groves, *Boškinac* offers eleven spacious doubles or suites, each with exquisite Mediterranean-inspired decor. The restaurant (open to non-guests, but you must reserve) dishes out top-notch island specialities prepared with home-grown ingredients, washed down with *Boškinac*'s own-label wines. Restaurant open noon–11pm. **1000Kn**

Camping Straško Straško Beach ⓣ 053 661 226, ⓦ turno.hr. This site on the waterfront southwest of town is like a small town in its own right, with shops, bars and spaces for four thousand campers – a third of which are reserved for naturists. **70Kn** per person, pitches from **160Kn**

Steffani Skopljanska 20 ⓣ 053 661 697. Restaurant opposite Novalja's tourist office that cooks up a superlative range of fish and shellfish (try the two-person seafood platter for 320Kn), alongside excellent pastas and risottos. Daily noon–11pm.

NIGHTLIFE

Zagreb-based establishments like *Papaya* (ⓦ papaya.com.hr) and *Aquarius* (ⓦ aquarius.hr) decamp to **Zrće beach** for the holiday season, although it's local outfit *Kalypso* (ⓦ kalypso.com.hr) that has been on the beach the longest – and has developed a cult following in the process. All three organize live concerts and DJ-driven party nights – often featuring DJs of international repute – from late June through to late August. On **Katarelac beach**, bars like *Noa* (ⓦ noa-beach.com), situated on an offshore circular pontoon, and *Pepermint*, a branch of the Zagreb club (see p.90; ⓦ pepermint.hr), pump out a mixture of soul, funk, Latin and chill-out music.

4

Northern Dalmatia

KORNATI NATIONAL PARK

5

Northern Dalmatia

Compact and easily explored, northern Dalmatia presents a greater concentration of the highlights of Adriatic travel than almost any other part of Croatia. Along the coast are beautifully preserved medieval towns poised above some of the clearest waters in Europe, while offshore are myriad islands adorned with ancient stone villages and enticing coves. The region increasingly serves both as a focus for the party crowd and as a get-away-from-it-all destination, with a burgeoning roster of festivals dovetailing neatly with stirring scenery and soothing beaches.

The main urban centre of northern Dalmatia is **Zadar**, an animated jumble of Roman, Venetian and modern styles that presents as good an introduction as any to Dalmatia's mixed-up history. It's within day-trip distance of the medieval Croatian centre of **Nin**, and is also the main ferry port for the unassuming northern Dalmatian islands of **Silba**, **Olib** and **Dugi otok**, where you'll find peaceful villages, laid-back beaches, and a level of tourism that has not yet become an industry.

The next major town south of Zadar is **Šibenik**, with a quiet historic centre and a spectacular fifteenth-century cathedral, and the most convenient base from which to visit the tumbling waterfalls of the **Krka National Park**. The main natural attraction in this part of Dalmatia is the **Kornati archipelago**, a collection of captivatingly bare and uninhabited islands accessed from the coastline-hugging, easy-going island of **Murter**. Joining Murter to the mainland is the swing-bridge at **Tisno**, a small town that's become the main venue for the summer-long cycle of festivals run by the Garden organization.

Dalmatia's long history of Roman, then Venetian cultural penetration (for a history of the region, see the box, pp.246–247) has left its mark on a region where children still call adult males *barba* ("beard" – Italian slang for "uncle") and respected gents go under the name of *šjor* (the local version of *signore*), but modern Dalmatia's identity is difficult to pin down. People from northern Croatia will tell you that life is lived at a much slower pace in Dalmatia, whose inhabitants are joshingly referred to as *tovari* ("donkeys") by their compatriots, though the briefest of visits to bustling regional centres like Zadar will be enough to persuade you that these clichés are somewhat wide of the mark. The Dalmatians themselves will tell you that life is to be enjoyed and should not be hurried – which is why food, wine, music and café life are accorded so much quality time.

GETTING AROUND — NORTHERN DALMATIA

By bus Frequent buses run up and down the main coastal road, the Jadranska Magistrala, or Adriatic Highway.

By car The Zagreb–Split toll motorway runs several kilometres inland of Zadar and Šibenik, but can still be a quick way of getting from north to south.

By ferry Just about every inhabited island is connected by some kind of regular local ferry or catamaran, with Zadar serving as the main passenger port. Ferries also ply the Zadar–Ancona route in summer.

ŠIBENIK CATHEDRAL

Highlights

❶ **The Sea Organ, Zadar** A wave-powered musical instrument that also serves as vantage point from which to observe the sunset, the Sea Organ will soon lull you into a state of Adriatic bliss. **See p.249**

❷ **Silba** Arcadian car-free island at the north of the Zadar archipelago, with a stunning coastline and a picturesque main village. **See p.259**

❸ **Telašćica Nature Park** Compact natural wonderland comprising rugged coastline, dramatic sea cliffs and a tangle of offshore islands. **See p.262**

❹ **Murter** Covered with olive groves and dotted with picturesque small ports, Murter is perfect for the independent tourist. **See p.263**

❺ **Kornati National Park** This stark chain of sparsely inhabited islands is a deservedly popular target for boat trips. **See p.265**

❻ **Šibenik Cathedral** A unique engineering marvel that straddles both late Gothic and early Renaissance, this is a fitting centrepiece to the historic town of Šibenik. **See p.268**

❼ **Terraneo Festival** The major summer meet-up for Croatia's alternative tribes, offering international performers and a friendly vibe. **See p.272**

❽ **Krka National Park** Tumbling waterfalls, gurgling rapids and arid canyons characterize Dalmatia's most-visited natural attraction. **See p.276**

HIGHLIGHTS ARE MARKED ON THE MAP ON P.244

FOOD AND DRINK IN NORTHERN DALMATIA

As elsewhere in the Adriatic fresh **seafood** dominates the northern Dalmatian menu, although the broad maquis-covered plateaus just inland provide plenty in the way of lamb and game. The practice of **roasting meats** and bulky seafood dishes such as octopus *ispod peke* (slow-cooked under an ember-covered metal lid) is widespread – you should definitely try a *peka*-style at least once, though note that they require several hours of preparation and restaurants usually require advance notice. **Lamb and suckling pig** roasted on a spit is another regional favourite, and roadside restaurants will frequently have a carcass revolving slowly over an open fire in the front yard.

Nowhere is the blend of maritime and inland cuisine better developed than in **Skradin**, the small town that stands at the entrance to the Krka National Park. Here, the plenteous shellfish and oysters of the Krka estuary are consumed alongside the freshwater fish and eels of the river's upper reaches. Dishes found in Skradin and nowhere else include *Skradinski rižot*, a meat-based risotto that was (traditionally at least) slow-cooked for days prior to important feasts; and *Skradinska torta*, a cake composed of finely crushed nuts and syrup.

Vineyards run along the coast and new ones are being planted all the time. Best known of the local **wines** is Babić, a fruitily drinkable red; it is closely associated with Primošten (where arguably the best Babić is grown), although it's found all along the Šibenik coast.

Zadar

The ancient capital of Dalmatia, **ZADAR** is one of the runaway success stories of the Croatian Adriatic, combining ancient and medieval heritage with a bustling café life, a vibrant bar scene and the kind of go-ahead architectural projects (such as the *Sea Organ* and the *Greeting to the Sun*) that give the seafront the appearance of a contemporary art installation.

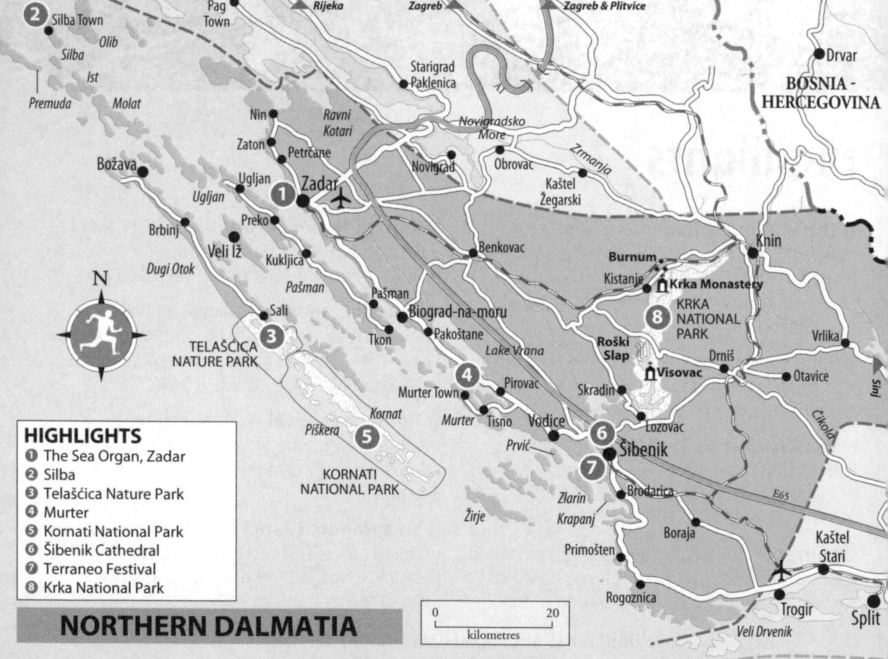

ZADAR ORIENTATION

Zadar has a compact centre crowded onto a thumb of land jutting northwest into the sea. Much of the town centre consists of narrow medieval streets, squares and leafy courtyards, barred to motor traffic. The two sides of the peninsula are quite different in feel: the **northern waterfront**, lined by a surviving section of city wall, is busy with the hustle of ferry traffic, while the **southern side**, along Obala kralja Petra Krešimira IV, has the air of a relaxing Riviera-town promenade, with ravishing views of the offshore islands and two compelling outdoor art installations in the shape of the *Sea Organ* and the *Greeting to the Sun*. On the eastern side of the peninsula lies the **Jazine**, the sheltered harbour, beyond which lie the modern parts of town, uneventful save for a snazzy yacht club and a few marinas. Four kilometres northwest of town, the resort area of **Borik** (also known as Puntamika) is home to hotels and beaches – it can be reached via a lazy waterside walk or short ride on local bus #5 or #8.

Zadar was bombed no fewer than 72 times by the Allies during World War II, and it lacks the museum-like quality of so many Adriatic towns, displaying instead a pleasant muddle of architectural styles, where lone Corinthian columns stand alongside rectangular 1950s blocks, and Romanesque churches are jostled by glass-fronted café-bars. With a population of around 75,000, the city boasts an international airport and is also the main ferry port for northern Dalmatia, and Zadar's growing popularity with visitors ensures that the central streets are swarming with life from June to September. Outside that time, the city's invigorating café culture is left very much to the locals.

Brief history

Long held by the Venetians (who called it Zara), Zadar was for centuries an Italian-speaking city, and its university, established by Dominican monks in 1396, claims to be the oldest in Croatia. Ceded to Italy in 1921 under the terms of the Treaty of Rapallo, the town became part of Tito's Yugoslavia in 1947 – when most Italian families were expelled. Postwar reconstruction resulted in something of an architectural mish-mash, and further damage was meted out in 1991, when the JNA (Yugoslav People's Army), supported by Serbian irregulars, came close to capturing the city. Despite the UN-sponsored ceasefires of 1992, Zadar remained exposed to Serbian artillery attack right up until 1995, when the Croatian offensives finally drove them back.

After spending the 1990s in the economic doldrums Zadar became an important focus for investment from around 2000 onwards, when bars and clubs mushroomed and the city's airport became a major entry point for tourists visiting the middle Adriatic.

The Forum

The collective name for a series of interlocking squares that forms Zadar's centre, the **Forum** is the site of the original Roman marketplace – although little original now remains save for a surviving pillar of a colonnade which was once the size of a football pitch.

St Donat's Church

Trg svete Stošije • May–Sept daily 9am–10pm • 10Kn • ⓣ 023 250 516, ⓦ amzd.hr

Much of the original stone from the Forum found its way into the ninth-century **St Donat's Church** (Crkva svetog Donata), a hulking cylinder of stone built – according to tradition – by St Donat himself, an Irishman who was bishop here for a time. It's an impressive example of Byzantine architecture, resembling the Basilica of San Vitale in Ravenna and Charlemagne's Palatinate Chapel in Aachen. The cavernous, bare interior has a pleasing simplicity: a high-ceilinged space with a gallery held up by six chunky supports and two Corinthian columns. It was deconsecrated in 1797, subsequently

5

A BRIEF HISTORY OF DALMATIA

As the part of Croatia most exposed to influences from elsewhere in the Mediterranean, Dalmatia has had a distinct role in the country's development, dating back to its colonization by Greeks and Romans. It was the **Romans** who first gave Dalmatia its name, probably inspired by the Illyrian word *delmat*, meaning a proud, brave man. Based in cities like **Jadera** (Zadar) and **Salona** (Solin, near Split), the Romans nurtured a Latinate urban culture which survived largely unaffected by the fall of the Roman Empire, and was soon reorganized into the Byzantine Province of Dalmatia. The Avar-Slav invasion of 614 destroyed Salona, although a new settlement founded by the fleeing Roman-Illyrian citizenry would eventually become Dalmatia's largest city, Split. The Byzantines retained control of the coastal strip but increasingly left the hinterland to the **Croats**, who arrived here soon after the Avars.

By the eleventh century Dalmatia had become part of the Hungaro-Croatian kingdom and an increasing number of Croats moved into Dalmatia's towns. In 1409 Hungaro-Croatian king Ladislas of Naples sold Dalmatia to Venice, opening up Dalmatia to Renaissance culture. However, the urban elite of fifteenth-century Dalmatia clearly saw themselves as Croats, and were keen to develop the local language as a medium fit for their patriotic aspirations. Prime movers were **Marko Marulić** of Split, whose *Judita* ("Judith") of 1521 was the first ever epic tale "composed in Croatian verse", as its own title page proclaimed; and **Petar Zoranić** of Zadar, whose novel *Planine* ("Mountains") of 1569 contains a scene in which the nymph Hrvatica (literally "Croatian girl") bemoans the lack of Dalmatians who show pride in their own language.

Venetian political control went largely unchallenged, however, because of the growing threat of the **Ottoman Turks**. Ottoman control of the Balkan interior had a serious impact on the make-up of the Dalmatian population, Slavs from Bosnia and beyond fleeing to the coast and its immediate hinterland. Many of those who settled the inland parts of Dalmatia belonged to the Orthodox faith, and were increasingly identified as Serbs when national consciousness became an issue.

The collapse of the Venetian Republic in 1797 was followed by a brief Austrian interregnum until, in 1808, **Napoleon** incorporated Dalmatia into his **Illyrian Provinces**, an artificial

serving as a military storehouse and museum, and is now an empty but captivating architectural space. It serves as an atmospheric concert venue during the **St Donat Music Evenings** (Glazbene večeri u svetog Donatu) in July and August.

The Archeological Museum

Trg Opatice Čike 1 • Jan–March Mon–Sat 9am–2pm; April, May & Oct–Dec Mon–Sat 9am–3pm; June–Sept daily 9am–9pm • 15Kn • ⓣ 023 250 516, ⓦ amzd.hr

Opposite St Donat's Church is a modern concrete building housing the **Archeological Museum** (Arheološki muzej), which kicks off with a larger-than-life first-century statue of a bare-chested Emperor Augustus watching over the ticket desk. The rest of the collection is displayed in chronological order with richly decorated Neolithic vessels on the top floor, and finds from the Liburnian, Roman and medieval Croatian periods arranged as you descend. Highlights include several examples of the characteristic Liburnian gravestone or *cipus*, a tapering bollard-like affair crowned with carved leaf shapes, rather like a fat stalk of asparagus; and beautiful stone reliefs from medieval Croatian churches featuring angels, griffins and peacocks.

St Mary's Church

Trg Opatice Čike

On the same side of the Forum as the Archeological Museum, **St Mary's Church** (Crkva svete Marije) dates from 1066 and includes some salvaged Roman and medieval pillars in the nave, though its trefoil Renaissance frontage was added in the sixteenth century, and the interior was given a thorough refurbishment in the eighteenth, when the rippling stucco balconies of the gallery were added. The Romanesque bell tower next door is the oldest in Dalmatia, having been built in 1105.

amalgam of Adriatic territories with its capital at Ljubljana. The French played an important role in Dalmatia's development, building roads, promoting trade and opening up the region to modern ideas. There's little evidence that the French were popular, however: their decision to close the monasteries offended local Catholic feeling, and they also dragged Dalmatia into wars with the Austrians and the British, who occupied Vis in 1811.

After 1815, Dalmatia was incorporated into the Habsburg Empire and Italian was made the official language. After the fall of the Habsburgs in 1918, Dalmatia was claimed by both Italy and the new Kingdom of Serbs, Croats and Slovenes (subsequently Yugoslavia). Yugoslavia received the lion's share, but fear of **Italian irredentism** remained strong, especially after Mussolini came to power in 1922. The Italian occupation of Dalmatia between 1941 and 1943 only served to worsen relations between the two communities, and at the war's end most remaining Italians fled.

The advent of socialism in 1945 failed to staunch major **emigration** to the New World and Australasia. After World War II, the traditional olive-growing and fishing economy of the Adriatic islands and villages was neglected in favour of heavy industry, producing a degree of rural depopulation which has only partly been ameliorated by the growth of tourism. The arrival of package tourists in the 1960s brought prosperity to the locals, while urban-dwellers from inland cities like Zagreb and Belgrade increasingly aspired to **vikendice** ("weekend houses") on the coast, changing the profile of the village population and turning the Adriatic into a vast recreation area serving the whole of Yugoslavia.

During the **break-up of Yugoslavia**, Dalmatia suffered as much as anywhere else in Croatia. Serbian forces secured control of the hinterland areas around Knin and Benkovac but never quite reached the sea. Coastal hotels soon filled with refugees, however, and the tourist industry wound down owing to lack of custom. With the resumption of peace, tourists were quick to return to their former stomping grounds. Completion of the **Zagreb–Split motorway** (Autocesta Zagreb–Split) in 2004 placed the coast within easy driving distance of Central Europe, turning Dalmatia into one of the continent's most cosmopolitan summer playgrounds.

The Church Art Exhibition

Trg Opatice Čike 1 • Mon–Sat 10am–1pm, Sun 10am–noon • 20Kn • ⓣ 023 250 496

The **convent** adjacent to St Mary's Church houses the **Permanent Exhibition of Church Art** (Stalna izložba crkvene umjetnosti), more commonly referred to as the **Gold and Silver of Zadar** (Zlato i srebro Zadra). A storehouse of church treasures that is very much the pride of the city, it's a fabulous museum, subtly arranged, beautifully lit and just small enough to be manageable in a single visit. The first floor has numerous reliquaries, including an extraordinary thirteenth-century reliquary for the shoulder blade of St Mark, which resembles a small grand piano mounted on three clawed legs. Some very diverse iconic representations of the Madonna and Child include a Paolo Veneziano work from the 1350s, in which the rigidity of sacred painting is softened with a touch of naturalistic portraiture. On the second floor there's a large fifteenth-century gang of apostles carved in wood by the Venetian Matej Moronzon in 1426, and an early six-part polyptych by Vittore Carpaccio, one panel of which features a much-reproduced picture of a youthful, tousle-haired St Martin of Tours lending his cloak to a beggar.

Cathedral of St Anastasia

Trg svete Stošije • Daily Mass at 7pm

On the northwestern side of the Forum, the twelfth- and-thirteenth-century **Cathedral of St Anastasia** (Katedrala svete Stošije) is a perfect example of the late Romanesque style, with an arcaded west front reminiscent of the churches of Tuscany. Around the door frame stretches a frieze of twisting acanthus leaves, from which various beasts emerge – look for the rodent and bird fighting over a bunch of grapes – while to either side hang figures of four apostles, engagingly primitive pieces of stonework which were probably taken from the facade of an earlier church on this site.

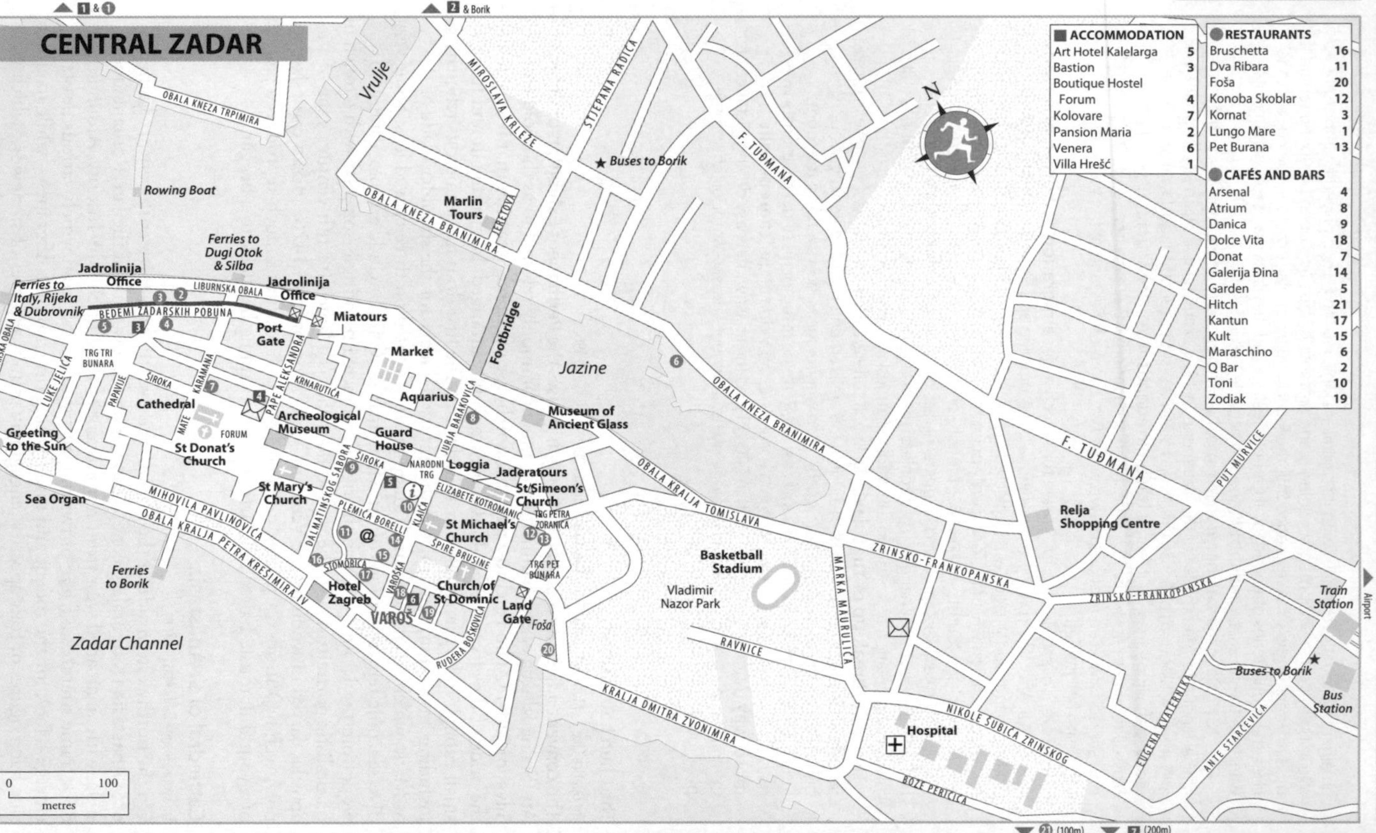
CENTRAL ZADAR
1 & 1
2 & Borik
ACCOMMODATION
Art Hotel Kalelarga 5
Bastion 3
Boutique Hostel Forum 4
Kolovare 7
Pansion Maria 2
Venera 6
Villa Hrešć 1
RESTAURANTS
Bruschetta 16
Dva Ribara 11
Foša 20
Konoba Skoblar 12
Kornat 3
Lungo Mare 1
Pet Burana 13
CAFÉS AND BARS
Arsenal 4
Atrium 8
Danica 9
Dolce Vita 18
Donat 7
Galerija Đina 14
Garden 5
Hitch 21
Kantun 17
Kult 15
Maraschino 6
Q Bar 2
Toni 10
Zodiak 19
N
Vrulje
OBALA KNEZA TRPIMIRA
MIROSLAVA KRLEŽE
STJEPANA RADIĆA
Buses to Borik
F. TUĐMANA
Rowing Boat
Marlin Tours
JERETOVA
OBALA KNEZA BRANIMIRA
Ferries to Dugi Otok & Silba
Jadrolinija Office
Ferries to Italy, Rijeka & Dubrovnik
LIBURNSKA OBALA
BEDEMI ZADARSKIH POBUNA
Miatours
Port Gate
Footbridge
Jazine
Market
ISTARSKA OBALA
TRG TRI BUNARA
LUKE JELIĆA
PAPAVIJE
ŠIROKA
KARAMANA
PAPE ALEKSANDRA
KRNARUTIĆA
Aquarius
JURJA BARAKOVIĆA
Cathedral
MATE
FORUM
Archeological Museum
Museum of Ancient Glass
Greeting to the Sun
St Donat's Church
Guard House
NARODNI TRG
Loggia
Jaderatours
Sea Organ
St Mary's Church
DALMATINSKOG SABORA
ELIZABETE KOTROMANIĆ
St Simeon's Church
MIHOVILA PAVLINOVIĆA
OBALA KRALJA PETRA KREŠIMIRA IV
PLEMIĆA BORELLI
KLAIĆA
St Michael's Church
TRG PETRA ZORANIĆA
SPIRE BRUSINE
STOMORICA
VAROŠKA
TRG PET BUNARA
Hotel Zagreb
Church of St Dominic
Land Gate
Foša
VAROŠ
RUDERA BOŠKOVIĆA
Ferries to Borik
Zadar Channel
OBALA KRALJA TOMISLAVA
Basketball Stadium
Vladimir Nazor Park
MARKA MARULIĆA
RAVNICE
KRALJA DMITRA ZVONIMIRA
Relja Shopping Centre
ZRINSKO-FRANKOPANSKA
PUT MURVICE
Hospital
NIKOLE ŠUBIĆA ZRINSKOG
BOŽE PERIČIĆA
EUGENA KVATERNIKA
ANTE STARČEVIĆA
Train Station
Bus Station
Airport
0 100 metres
21 (100m)
7 (200m)

The cathedral's high **interior** focuses on a Gothic ciborium of 1332, its deftly chiselled columns enclosing a ninth-century altar engraved with fat crosses and palms. The side altar at the end of the left-hand aisle is surmounted by a plain marble casket holding the bones of St Anastasia, made – as the workmanlike inscription records – in the time of Bishop Donat in the ninth century. The cult of Anastasia probably came to Zadar from Aquileia in northern Italy, where she was honoured as a saintly Roman woman who performed many miracles.

Campanile

April–Oct daily 9.30am–1pm & 5–8pm • 10Kn

You can climb up the cathedral's 56-metre **campanile** for sweeping vistas of Zadar's rooftops and the islands in the distance. The campanile was only finished in the 1890s by the English writer and architect T.G. Jackson; if you've been to Rab you may find it familiar – he modelled it on the cathedral bell tower there.

Along the seafront

West of the cathedral, alleys emerge out onto the seafront boulevard of **Obala kralja Petra Krešimira IV**, where there's a fine view across the water to the hilly island of Ugljan. The palm-lined seafront path attracts a steady stream of strollers.

The Sea Organ

Obala kralja Petra Krešimira IV

Most visitors ultimately gravitate towards the so-called **Sea Organ** (Morske orgulje) on the peninsula's southwestern shoulder. Designed by local architect Nikola Bašić and completed in 2005, the organ consists of a broad stone stairway descending towards the sea. Wave action pushes air through a series of underwater pipes and up through niches cut into the steps, producing a selection of mellow musical notes. The organ is at its best when the sea is choppy, but even during calm periods the tranquil tones of the organ will be sufficient to lull you into a meditative state.

Greeting to the Sun

Obala kralja Petra Krešimira IV

Two hundred metres further on towards the tip of the peninsula is another of Bašić's innovative set-pieces, **Greeting to the Sun** (Pozdrav suncu). Intended as a companion to the *Sea Organ*, it consists of a huge disk paved with light-sensitive tiles, which accumulate solar power during the daytime and radiate a seemingly random sequence of coloured lights at night. It's absolutely hypnotic and enormously popular with tourists of all ages, who can spend hours here basking in the *Greeting*'s mood-enhancing glow.

Hotel Zagreb

Obala kralja Petra Krešimira IV

One of the major landmarks of Zadar's coastal promenade, **Hotel Zagreb** was built in 1902 and long served as the top address in town. Closed in the wake of the 1991–95 war, the city's most desirable piece of real estate is still awaiting renovation. An adjacent signboard bears a large-format portrait of one of the hotel's erstwhile guests, **Alfred Hitchcock**. The mercurial suspense-meister was entranced by Zadar when on holiday here in 1964, famously describing the local sunset as "the most beautiful in the world".

Around the Port Gate

Zadar's ferry dock is overlooked by an impressively intact length of **city wall**, one of the few surviving stretches of a defensive system completed in 1570, just in time to save Zadar from a two-year Ottoman siege. Cutting through the wall in an elegant arch is

5

the **Port Gate** (Lučka vrata), a Roman triumphal arch, later topped with a relief of St Chrysogonus, the city's protector, on horseback.

The market

Pod bedemom • Mornings only

Filling a long rectangular square pressed up against the landward side of Zadar's city walls is one of the Adriatic's most animated daily **markets** (*pijaca*). Here you'll find all manner of fruit and vegetables brought in daily from the surrounding countryside, while traders in an adjacent hall sell freshly caught fish. The kiosks selling freshly baked bread, cheeses and cured meats are an ideal source of picnic-ready supplies.

The Museum of Ancient Glass

Poljana Zemaljskog odbora 1 • June–Sept daily 9am–9pm, Oct–May Mon–Sat 9am–4pm • 30Kn • Ⓣ 023 363 831, Ⓦ mas-zadar.hr

Although it may sound a bit too specialized for any but the most committed of museum surfers, Zadar's **Museum of Ancient Glass** (Muzej antičkog stakla) is a visual tour de force, displaying beautifully presented Roman-era vessels from archeological sites all over the region. The building itself is controversial, fusing a nineteenth-century villa with a contemporary glass-and-chrome pavilion that looks much better inside than out. The collection moves from dainty Roman perfume bottles (few of which would look out of place in a designer store of the present day) to a spectacular room full of globe-shaped glass cremation urns, discovered during the building of the Relja shopping centre on the other side of the Jazine. If you're interested in glass-blowing and how the ancient Romans did it, then the ten-minute English-language film on show on the ground floor (ask at the ticket desk) is an excellent introduction. The replica glassware in the museum shop makes for some tasteful souvenirs.

Narodni trg

At the centre of Zadar's Old Town is **Narodni trg**, which took over from the Forum as the main focus of civic activity in the Middle Ages. It's overlooked by the **Guard House** (Gradska straža), a single-storey building with a soaring square clock tower, built in 1562. The niche to the left of the entrance houses a fine bust of the Venetian governor G.G. Zane from 1608, sporting stylized furrowed brows and a veritable carpet of a beard.

Town Loggia

Narodni trg • Daily 9am–8pm • 5Kn • Ⓦ nmz.hr

Immediately opposite the Guard House, the **Town Loggia** (Gradska loža) has been enclosed in plate glass and transformed into an art gallery. On show is predominantly contemporary stuff, with local artists well represented.

St Simeon's Church

Trg Petra Zoranića

If Zadar's rich medieval heritage had one central focus then it would be **St Simeon's Church** (Crkva svetog Šimuna), an outwardly simple edifice that serves as the revered shrine of St Simeon, one of Zadar's patron saints and a contemporary of Christ – he is believed to have held the baby Jesus in the Temple. Simeon's bones are housed in a silver-gilt **reliquary** that sits on the high altar, held aloft by two Baroque angels cast from captured Turkish cannons. Ordered by Queen Elizabeth of Hungary in 1377, the reliquary was fashioned from 250kg of silver by a team of local artisans working under a Milanese silversmith. The story goes that Elizabeth so wanted a piece of the saint's body that she broke off a finger and hid it in her bosom, where it immediately began to decompose and fill with maggots

FROM TOP GREETING TO THE SUN (P.249); LAND GATE AND HARBOUR (P.252) >

5

– a process only reversed when she returned the finger to its rightful place. The creation of the reliquary was her way of atoning for the theft, though it also had a political dimension: her patronage of the cult of St Simeon increased the local popularity of her husband, King Louis of Anjou, and dented the appeal of Venice. Reliefs on the reliquary portray the discovery of St Simeon's body in a monastery on the outskirts of Zadar, and Louis of Anjou's triumphant entry into the city following an eighteen-month Venetian siege. The reliquary is opened every year on the feast of St Simeon (Oct 8).

Land Gate

Dramatically marking the southeastern entrance to Zadar's Old Town is the **Land Gate** (Kopnena vrata), a triumphal arch topped by a row of eight cattle skulls – thought to be a death symbol intended to ward off would-be invaders – and a monumental winged lion of St Mark; tellingly, this symbol of Venetian power dwarfs the civic emblem – another relief of St Chrysogonus on horseback – immediately below it. On the far side of the Land Gate lies the **Foša**, a narrow channel which once fed Zadar's moat and is now a small harbour crowded with pleasure boats.

The Varoš quarter

Arguably the most evocative section of Zadar's Old Town is the **Varoš quarter**, which takes up the southeastern corner of the peninsula. It's here that the alleyways seem narrower and more atmospheric than elsewhere, lined with the kind of café-bars that pull in their fair share of caffeine-refuelling students during the day (Zadar University is just round the corner), and more dedicated drinkers on weekend nights.

St Michael's Church

On the corner of Špire Brušine and M. Klaića, the main portal of **St Michael's Church** (Crkva svetog Mihovila) is topped by an animated fourteenth-century relief of St Michael spearing a demon, flanked by Zadar's ubiquitous patrons, Anastasia and Chrysogonus. Peering out from the facade higher up are three fish-eyed male heads, the remains of a crudely carved late Roman gravestone.

ARRIVAL AND DEPARTURE — ZADAR

By plane Zadar airport (ⓦ zadar-airport.hr) is 12km southeast of town at Zemunik. There are about eight buses per day (6.45am–10.25pm; 25Kn) between the airport and the ferry port. A taxi will cost 150–200Kn.

Destinations Zagreb (April–Sept 2 daily, Oct–March 1 daily; 30min).

By train Zadar's train station lies about 1km east of the town centre, a 15min walk or a quick hop on municipal bus #1 or #4. Buses #5 and #8 go from the station to Borik.

Destinations Knin (3 daily; 2hr 10min); Zagreb (2 daily, with change at Knin; 6hr 20min–9hr).

By bus Zadar's bus station is next to the train station.

Destinations Dubrovnik (7 daily; 8hr); Murter (1 daily; 1hr 20min); Nin (Mon–Fri every 50min, Sat 12 daily, Sun 10 daily; 30min); Novalja (2 daily; 1hr 40min); Pag (Mon–Fri 5 daily, Sat & Sun 2 daily; 1hr); Plitvice Lakes (5 daily; 3hr); Pula (3 daily; 7hr); Rijeka (12 daily; 4hr 40min–5hr); Šibenik (hourly; 1hr 30min); Split (hourly; 3hr 30min); Trogir (hourly; 2hr 30min); Zagreb (20 daily; 3–5hr).

International destinations Belgrade (1 daily; 11hr); Ljubljana (1 daily; 8hr); Sarajevo (1 daily; 11hr).

By ferry and catamaran Ferries and catamarans arrive at the quays lining Liburnska obala, from where the town centre is a 5min walk uphill. Tickets for most services are available from Jadrolinija, Liburnska obala 7 (ⓣ 023 254 800, ⓦ jadrolinija.hr), though for the Zadar–Silba–Olib and Zadar–Mali Lošinj–Pula catamarans they're sold by Miatours, Vrata sv Krševana (ⓣ 023 254 300, ⓦ miatours.hr).

Ferry destinations Mali Lošinj (6 weekly; 5hr); Preko (hourly; 30min); Sali (1 daily; 1hr 30min); Silba (1 daily; 2hr 20min–4hr 20min); Zaglav (2 daily; 1hr 45min).

International ferry destinations Ancona (3–6 weekly; 6–8hr; most services overnight).

Catamaran destinations Božava (mid-June to mid-Sept 8 weekly; 1hr 15min); Mali Lošinj (June–Sept 2–5 weekly; 2hr 25min); Olib (1 daily; 1hr 45min); Pula (June–Sept 2–5 weekly; 4hr 5min); Sali (2 daily; 45min); Silba (1 daily; 1hr 30min).

By car For car rental, Hertz is at Zadar airport 1 (ⓣ 023 348 400); Dollar/Thrifty, Bože Peričića 14 (ⓣ 023 315 733).

INFORMATION AND TOURS

Tourist office Cnr Narodni trg/Miho Klaića (June & Sept daily 8am–8pm; July & Aug daily 8am–midnight; Oct–May Mon–Fri 8am–3pm; ☎023 316 166, @tzzadar.hr). The tourist office has helpful multilingual staff and a wealth of free brochures and maps.

Tours and excursions GeneralTurist, Obala kneza Branimira 1 (☎023 318 997, @generalturist.hr), organizes local excursions, including trips to the Kornati Islands. Tours of Telašćica Bay and the Kornati islands (260–300Kn per person) are offered by excursion boats lining the quay beside the footbridge.

GETTING AROUND

By bus For local bus rides, pay the driver (10Kn flat fare) or buy a ticket in advance, valid for two journeys, from newspaper and tobacco kiosks (16Kn). The seaside suburb of Borik is accessible by bus #5 or #8 (every 20–30min) from the train and bus stations or from Miroslava Krleže just northeast of the centre.

By boat Zadar's most enjoyable form of public transport is the rowing boat (*barkajol*; 5Kn) that operates between Liburnska obala in the town centre and Obala kneza Trpimira across the water to the north.

By taxi Try the ranks on Liburnska obala (☎023 251 400); otherwise ring Taxi Lulić (☎023 494 494) or Taxi Denis (☎091 262 2621).

ACCOMMODATION

There's a smattering of private **rooms** in the Old Town and plenty of **apartments** (two-person apartments 375Kn, four-person apartments from 450Kn) in the coastal suburbs to the west, although they're speedily snapped up in summer. Friendliest of the accommodation agencies is ★ **Marlin Tours**, across the footbridge from the ferry port at Jeretova 3 (☎023 305 920, ✉marlin-tours@zd.t-com.hr); and **Jaderatours**, in the Old Town on Elizabete Kotromanić (☎023 250 350, @jaderatours.hr). **Hotels** in central Zadar are in short supply, but there's plenty of choice in nearby suburbs.

HOTELS AND PENSIONS

CENTRAL ZADAR

Art Hotel Kalelarga Majke Margarite 3 ☎023 233 000, @arthotel-kalelarga.com; map p.248. Beautifully restored late medieval house right in the centre of town, with ten individually decorated en suites decorated in soothing fawn and cream tones. **1250Kn**

Bastion Bedemi zadarskih pobuna 13 ☎023 494 950, @hotel-bastion.hr; map p.248. As the name suggests, this cute 27-room hotel is pressed up against the town's medieval fortifications, bang in the centre of the Old Town. Rooms feature lush fabrics, crisp modern bathrooms and wi-fi. **1050Kn**

Kolovare Bože Peričića 14 ☎023 203 200, @hotel-kolovare.com; map p.248. Plush business-class accommodation a 5min walk south of the bus and train stations, in a 200-room concrete structure built around a swimming pool. Close to the (rock-and-concrete) Kolovare beach. **1100Kn**

Venera Šime Ljubića 4a ☎023 214 098, @hotel-venera-zd.hr; map p.248. The only pension-style place (really an accommodation agency with twelve rooms above the office), situated in the heart of the Varoš, central Zadar's most atmospheric quarter. Rooms are minuscule but neat and comfortable, and come with en-suite shower. **500Kn**

OUTSIDE THE CENTRE

★ **Art Hotel Villa Ines** Augusta Šenoe 17 ☎091 730 005; map p.254. Homely B&B run by a Croatian-Australian whose own artwork covers the walls, offering en-suite doubles with a mix of furnishings. There's a flower-filled garden with a dinky swimming pool. Midway between the centre and Borik on the #5 and #8 bus route. **700Kn**

Club Funimation Borik Majstora Radovana 7, Borik ☎023 206 100, @falkensteiner.com; map p.254. A seafront holiday complex set in well-tended gardens and boasting a long pebble beach. It's run by an Austrian hotel group and offers reliable four-star comforts plus swimming pools, family-friendly activities and a spa centre. **1200Kn**

Mediteran Matije Gupca 19 ☎023 337 500, @hotelmediteran-zd.hr; map p.254. Small private hotel northeast of the beach at Borik. All rooms come with balcony, en-suite shower and TV; some of the more expensive ones have a/c and minibar. Take the boat, or hop on bus #5 or #8 to *Camping Borik* and walk 5min uphill. **720Kn**

Niko Obala kneza Domagoja 9 ☎023 337 880, @hotel-niko.hr; map p.254. Small, swish, private hotel across the seafront just west of Borik, above the top-notch restaurant of the same name (see p.255). Spacious rooms have plush furnishings, a/c, TV and minibar, and many sport balconies providing lovely vistas of Zadar's Old Town. **950Kn**

Pansion Maria Put Petrića 24 ☎023 334 244, @pansionmaria.hr; map p.248. Family-run B&B in a suburban street midway between the centre and Puntamika. Doubles and triples are smallish but

5

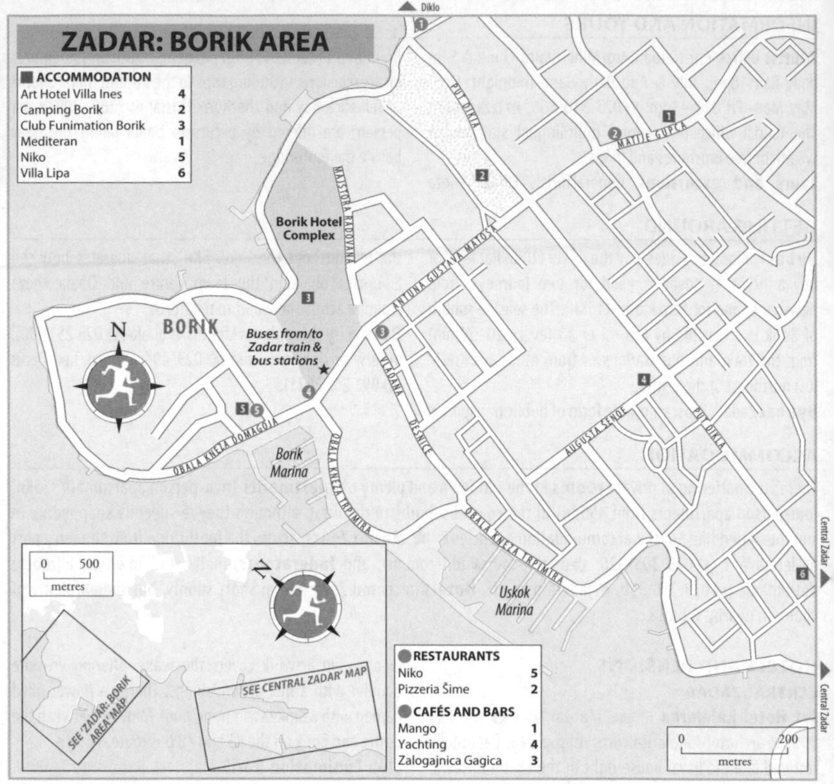

comfortable, with en-suite WC/shower and (in some cases) TV and a tiny balcony. Some rooms come with bright-white colour schemes, others are stuffed with old-fashioned furniture and china ornaments. Breakfast is in a covered patio in the garden. Midway between the centre and accessible on bus #5 or #8. 500Kn

Villa Hrešć Obala kneza Trpimira 28 ⊕023 337 570, ⊕villa-hresc.hr; map p.248. Lovingly restored villa on the coastal promenade, midway between the Old Town and Borik, with bright, fully equipped doubles or self-catering apartments in a relaxed, well-looked-after ambience. There's even a small open-air pool. 1350Kn

Villa Lipa Put Dikla 13 ⊕098 638 727, ⊕villa-lipa.com; map above. Five two- to four-person apartments in a modern building with relaxing beige-coloured rooms and a nice garden. Midway between Borik and the centre (take bus #5 or #8). Four-person apartments from 900Kn. Two-person studios 700Kn

HOSTEL AND CAMPSITE

Boutique Hostel Forum Široka 20 ⊕023 253 031, ⊕hostelforumzadar.com; map p.248. Designer hostel decked out by the team responsible for *Goli & Bosi* in Split, offering a mixture of dorm rooms and hotel-standard private doubles (the latter at 740Kn with breakfast). Free wi-fi and a fully equipped kitchen are yours to use. 180Kn

Camping Borik Majstora Radovana, Borik ⊕023 206 559, ⊕campingborik.com; map above. Next to the hotel complex of the same name in Borik, 4km northwest of town (bus #5 or #8 from the train and bus stations), this is a large, tidy site, shaded by a variety of deciduous and coniferous trees. 50Kn per person, pitches from 70Kn

EATING AND DRINKING

There is a decent and varied sprinkling of **restaurants** throughout both the Old Town and the Borik area. For **snacks** and **picnics**, the daily market just inside the Old Town walls off Jurja Barakovića is the place to get fruit, vegetables, local cheeses and home-cured hams. For **drinking**, the central strip from Narodni trg to the Forum is well supplied with terrace cafés and ice-cream parlours, while many of the more atmospheric café-bars are crammed into the narrow alleys of the **Varoš** quarter. Be sure to try a shot of **maraschino**, the potent cherry liqueur that's been produced in Zadar since the sixteenth century.

RESTAURANTS

CENTRAL ZADAR

Bruschetta Mihovila Pavlinovića 12 ⊕023 312 915, ⊕bruschetta.hr; map p.248. *Bruschetta* has quickly developed a solid local reputation for turning out a wide range of recipes reasonably well – some maintain that it's the best pizza-and-pasta restaurant in the city, while others sing the praises of its Adriatic seafood. Pastas and risottos are in the 45–75Kn range, meat and fish mains about twice as much. Daily 11am–11pm.

Dva Ribara Borelli 7 ⊕023 213 445; map p.248. Conveniently placed city-centre eatery with minimalist interior full of matt-black furnishings and straight lines. There's a wide-ranging meat and fish menu, but *Dva Ribara* is particularly known for its pizzas, which keep the locals coming in droves. Daily 10am–midnight.

Foša Kralja Zvonimira 2 ⊕023 314 421, ⊕fosa.hr; map p.248. A long-standing reputation for quality seafood has made *Foša* into something of a destination restaurant, with fresh fish and shellfish served up in a chic, renovated former gatehouse, or on a harbourside terrace with views of bobbing boats. Daily noon–midnight.

★ **Konoba Skoblar** Trg Petra Zoranića ⊕023 213 236; map p.248. Serving up the broad gamut of Dalmatian food at prices that won't lead to tears, *Skoblar* continues to draw in locals eager for *marende* (elevenses) or a more expansive mid-afternoon lunch. Daily specials are chalked up on a board outside the door; anything featuring the house's freshly made gnocchi will be divine. Daily 10am–11pm.

★ **Kornat** Liburnska obala 6 ⊕023 254 501, ⊕restaurant-kornat.com; map p.248. Harbourside restaurant at the quiet end of Zadar's main ferry dock, offering superior seafood in a moderately formal atmosphere (the waiting staff wear ties, but this doesn't mean that you have to). The grilled fresh fish is first class and the breadth of recipes quite impressive (check out the sea bass in scampi sauce, or monkfish cooked in white wine). There's a generous selection of quality Croatian wines. Daily noon–1am.

★ **Lungo Mare** Obala kneza Trpimira 23 ⊕023 331 533, ⊕lungo-mare.com; map p.248. On the seafront promenade midway between the Old Town and Borik, this is a popular choice with Zadar folk who are after decent food in a relaxed setting. Seating is on a large terrace shaded by trees and there's a large selection of fresh fish and shellfish and a decent list of Croatian wines. Daily 11am–11pm.

Pet Bunara Trg pet bunara ⊕023 224 010, ⊕petbunara.hr; map p.248. Churning out tasty and trustworthy pizzas alongside refined Adriatic-Mediterranean cuisine that makes best use of local ingredients, the "Five Wells" is truly a restaurant for all occasions – and comes well recommended by locals. Daily 8am–1am.

OUTSIDE THE CENTRE

★ **Niko** Obala kneza Domagoja 9 ⊕023 337 888, ⊕hotel-niko.hr; map opposite. Upmarket seafood restaurant hidden away in an anonymous street just off the seafront west of Borik. They serve superbly prepared fish and shellfish and a wonderful tiramisu – it's the kind of place where Zadar people go for a special meal. Daily noon–midnight.

Pizzeria Šime Matije Gupca 15 ⊕023 334 848; map opposite. Monster-sized terrace restaurant uphill from Borik, known for its filling, reasonably authentic thin-crust pizzas (40–45Kn) and zippy service. Can get packed out in July and Aug. Daily noon–midnight.

CAFÉS AND BARS

CENTRAL ZADAR

Arsenal Trg tri bunara 1 ⊕023 253 833, ⊕arsenalzadar.com; map p.248. Housed in the former Venetian navy's storehouse, this huge barn of a place is filled with lounge-bar furniture, and also has clothes boutiques and gallery spaces off to either side. A great place for drinks and cocktails, it also has free wi-fi and an extensive range of food, taking in pizzas, Croatian hams and cheeses, and a choice of breakfast menus. Frequent live rock, jazz and DJ events, when there's an entrance fee. Note that it may close in winter except for specific events. Sun–Thurs 8am–midnight; Fri & Sat 8am–2am.

Atrium Jurja Barakovića 6 ⊕023 315 938; map p.248. Popular daytime coffee-sipping venue on the way to the footbridge from the Old Town, featuring a relaxing inner courtyard, a pavement terrace outside, good coffee and delicious French-style pastries. Daily 7am–midnight.

Danica Široka bb ⊕023 211 016; map p.248. Café and cake shop opposite the theatre, with the biggest range of sweets and pastries in the city. Daily 7am–midnight.

Dolce Vita Matice Dalmatinske 6 ⊕091 553 9727; map p.248. Convivial drinking den decorated in dark browns and reds, with murals of DJs spinning vinyl records on the walls. It's a reliable source of good coffee during the daytime, and a lively place for guzzling and conversing at night– as long as you like r'n'b or hip-hop played loudish. Daily 9am–11pm, till 1.30am on summer weekends.

Donat Trg sv. Stošje ⊕023 250 829, ⊕donatice.hr; map p.248. The best of Zadar's ice-cream parlours, with outdoor seating right by the cathedral and a full range of nonalcoholic drinks. Both this and the café next door (*Lloyds*) are popular vantage points from which to observe the ebb and flow of the evening *korzo*. Daily 7am–midnight.

Galerija Đina Varoška 2; map p.248. Chic and comfy café with tiny wooden tables in the shape of artist's palettes in one of the tightest-packed alleyways of the Varoš quarter – savour the distinctive Zadar experience of listening to music simultaneously pumped out by three or four cafés. Daily 7am–1am.

5

★ **Garden** Bedemi zadarskih pobuna ⓣ 023 364 739, ⓦ thegardenzadar.com; map p.248. This open-air garden bar occupying a stretch of the city walls was founded by UB40's drummer and tour manager in 2004 and quickly became something of a Croatian institution, establishing a hip summer lounge-bar recipe that has been much imitated elsewhere. You can relax on sofas, sprawl on mattresses looking out to port, or perch beside the central water-feature. Slightly more expensive than other places in town, but not punishingly so. DJ-driven club nights at weekends, when there may be an entrance charge. April–Oct daily 11am–2am.

Hitch Kolovare bb ⓣ 095 914 5620, ⓦ hitch-bar.com; map p.248. With a partially covered terrace jutting out into the Adriatic with views across the straits to the island of Ugljan, this is one of Zadar's best bets for sunset cocktail-sipping and after-sundown clubbing. The interior consists of a roomy pavilion with loungey seating, a DJ booth and a pumping sound system that is put through its paces at weekends. Daily 7am–5am.

Kantun Stomorica 5; map p.248. Beautifully minimalistic little bar with black-and-white floor tiles, blood-red walls and a bar that cuts diagonally into the main space like the prow of a ship. The music policy is strictly alternative/indie/heavy, which more or less dictates the kind of young local you will find drinking in here. Mon–Sat 7am till late.

Kult Stomorica; map p.248. An eternally popular hang-out in the Varoš quarter, *Kult* offers the best terrace in the Old Town by a long chalk, with lots of outdoor seating in an attractively tatty residential courtyard. Additional attractions include an alfresco cocktail bar, and occasional live gigs laid on in high summer. Wooden reliefs featuring weird characters from the Glagolitic alphabet help to add mystique to an otherwise straightforward café-bar interior. Daily 8am–1am.

Maraschino Obala kneza Branimira 6 ⓣ 023 224 093, ⓦ maraschinobar.hr; map p.248. Chic café-bar with an expansive terrace overlooking the Jazine harbour. Becomes party central after midnight, when most of the Old Town bars begin to close and nocturnal revellers flow across the footbridge in search of loud DJ music, cocktails and youthful glamour. Daily June–Sept 7am–3am, Oct–May 7am–11pm.

Q Bar Liburnska obala 10 ⓣ 023 251 716; map p.248. This large and popular pub (formerly known as "Maya") features a club-like interior complete with dancefloor and sound system, and a terrace looking towards the harbour. DJs and live pop-rock acts liven up the weekends, and proximity to both *Arsenal* and *Garden* ensure its place on any Zadar nightlife crawl. Daily 7am–3am.

Toni Klaića ⓣ 023 316 847; map p.248. Tiny but enduringly popular café-bar occupying a key junction on the route into the Varoš quarter, attracting a slightly older crowd than *Galerija Đina* or *Kult*. Daily 7am–1am.

★ **Zodiak** Šimuna Ljubavca 2; map p.248. A long-standing Varoš favourite, with a poky but cosy interior and outdoor wooden-bench seating. The eclectic range of non-pop music on the CD system attracts everyone from old rockers to dreadlock-wearing alternative types. Daily 8am–midnight.

OUTSIDE THE CENTRE

Mango Krešimirova obala, Diklo; map p.254. North of the *Borik* campsite, with lounge-bar furnishings on the sea-facing terrace. A good place for watching sunsets and sipping moderately priced cocktails. Daily 8am–4am.

Yachting Antuna Gustava Matoša bb; map p.254. Right by the Borik bus stop and with an outdoor terrace facing Borik marina, *Yachting* is somewhat functional but nonetheless an enjoyable cross between café, cocktail lounge and raucous DJ bar. Within easy strolling distance of *Mango* (see above) and *Gagica* (see below). Daily 8am–2am.

Zalogajnica Gagica Antuna Gustava Matoša bb ⓣ 023 332 220; map p.254. Opposite the entrance to the Borik complex, this cult Zadar snack bar (famed for its mouth-watering *ćevapi* and *pljeskasvice*) was always popular with the locals as *the* place in Borik to stop off for a drink. It has now morphed into a fully-fledged café-bar with loungey furniture and a terrace, attracting a lively cross-section of Zadar folk. Daily 7am–4am.

FESTIVALS IN ZADAR

The most internationally prestigious of Zadar's summer arts festivals is the **St Donat's Musical Evenings** (Glazbene večeri u sv. Donatu; early July to early August; ⓦ donat-festival.com), featuring solo and chamber music performers from around the world making the most of the excellent acoustics at St Donat's Church. Running more or less concurrently is the **Zadar Theatrical Summer** (Zadarsko kazališno ljeto; late June to early August), with theatre and dance groups from all over the country – imaginative use of the city's historic spaces (venues include the Church of St Dominic and various courtyards) makes for some striking visual entertainment. More accessible for non-Croatian audiences is **Zadar Dreams** (Zadar snova; July or August; ⓦ zadarsnova.hr), a festival of alternative theatre, performance art and music held in Old Town churches and squares.

SPORT

Basketball The local basketball team, Zadar, is one of the major forces in the Croatian game and a source of local pride. The futuristic, flying-saucer-like Višnjik sports hall (ⓦ visnjik.hr), east of the Old Town at Splitska bb, is a great place to catch a game (usually on Sat from Sept to April).

DIRECTORY

Hospital Just east of the centre, opposite the *Kolovare* hotel, at Bože Peričića 5 (ⓣ 023 315 677).

Internet access HG spot, Stomorica 8 (daily 7am–midnight).

Left luggage At the bus station (Mon–Sat 9am–10pm, Sun 5–10pm).

Pharmacy Donat, just off Široka at Braće Vranjana 14, and Centar, at Jurja Barakovića 6, both have 24hr counters.

Post office/telephones The main branch is at Kralja S Držislava 1 (Mon–Fri 7.30am–9pm, Sat 7.30am–8pm).

Nin

About 15km north of Zadar, the small town of **NIN** is one of the few places in Croatia where it's really worth bringing a bucket and spade: whereas elsewhere in Dalmatia long sandy beaches only exist in the fertile imaginations of tourism propagandists, here they are very real – and are rarely swamped by skin-cooking sunbathers.

Nin is also an important historical centre boasting medieval churches and surviving town walls. Much of its medieval wealth came from the salt trade, and glittering saltpans can still be seen stretching east of town. The residence of the early Croatian kings and a major see of their bishops from 879, Nin fell under Venetian rule in the fifteenth century and was soon threatened by Ottoman advances, until in 1646 the Venetians evacuated the town and then shelled it from the sea, after which it slipped quietly into obscurity.

The town is built on a small island connected to the mainland by two bridges: Gornji most and Donji most ("upper bridge" and "lower bridge"). Donji most is your most likely starting point, across which lies a medieval gateway which leads through to **Branimirova**, the main thoroughfare, and a delightful mesh of pedestrianized streets.

St Anselm's Church

Branimirova

Halfway up Nin's main street stands the plain-looking **St Anselm's Church** (Crkva svetog Anzelma), an eighteenth-century structure dedicated to a first-century martyr believed to be the town's first bishop. Inside, a small chapel to the right of the main altar holds a fifteenth-century statue of the Madonna of Zečevo, which commemorates an apparition of the Virgin on a nearby island. A copy of the statue (the original is too fragile) is borne in a procession of boats to Zečevo on May 5, the anniversary of the vision.

The treasury

Branimirova • June to mid-Sept Mon–Sat 9am–noon & 6–9pm • 10Kn

Next door to St Anselm's Church, its **treasury** (riznica) houses an extraordinary collection of gold- and silver-plated reliquaries, beginning with a ninth-century chest of Carolingian origin containing the shoulder blade of St Anselm, and decorated with reliefs of sts Marcela, Ambrozius and (on the extreme left with hands raised) Anselm himself. Fourteenth-century Zadar goldsmiths produced the nearby reliquary for Anselm's arm, as well as skull reliquaries for Anselm and Marcela – their lids are embossed with angels and griffins. The treasury's collection of St Anselm's body parts is rounded off by a dainty casket in the shape of a foot.

The Archeological Museum

Trg Kraljevac 8 • Mon–Sat: June–Aug 9am–10pm; Sept–May 9am–1pm • 10Kn • T 023 264 210

At the top of Nin's main street, the **Archeological Museum** (Arheološki muzej) houses a small but attractively presented collection, kicking off with an ancient Liburnian *peka* (a cooking pot on top of which embers are piled) which looks identical to those still in use in Dalmatian kitchens today. The imported ceramics dredged up from Liburnian wrecks in Zaton harbour, to the south, include a wealth of north Italian tableware and a dog-faced ornamental jug from Asia Minor. One room is devoted to a reconstructed eleventh-century ship rescued by marine archeologists from shallow waters nearby. This easily manoeuvrable, 8m-long vessel could have been used either for fishing or fighting, and could easily be pulled up onto land or hidden in small bays.

The Church of the Holy Cross

Enquire at the tourist office for opening times

Squatting in a grassy space just east of Branimirova, the small, cruciform **Church of the Holy Cross** (Crkva svetog Križa) is the oldest church in the country, with an inscription on the lintel referring to Župan (Count) Godezav dated 800 AD. A simple whitewashed structure with high, Romanesque windows and a solid dome, its bare but beautifully proportioned interior is usually open in summer.

St Nicholas's Church

Two kilometres southeast of Nin on the Zadar road stands the tiny **Church of St Nicholas** (Crkva svetog Nikole), an eleventh-century structure surrounded by slender Scots pines. It was built on an ancient burial mound and later fortified by the Turks – the resulting crenellations give it the appearance of an oversized chess piece. The interior is almost always locked, but it's an impressive site nevertheless, with a fine view to the worn shape of Nin and the silver-grey ridge of the Velebit mountains in the distance.

The beaches

A short walk north of town is the narrow 1km-long **Ždrijac spit**, which curves banana-like to almost enclose Nin's quiet bay. From its eastern tip you can wade or swim to the eastern extremity of the long, luxuriant **Kraljičina plaža** (Queen's Beach), which can also be reached by walking from the town centre – follow the waterside path from the landward side of Donji most, passing a small boat harbour before ascending to meet a small crossroads, where you carry straight on for about twenty minutes, passing *Camping Ninska Laguna* on the way. The beach is genuinely sandy and relatively uncommercialized save for a brace of beach bars. Whichever part of the beach you end up on, there's a spectacular view of the Velebit mountains across the water. Don't be alarmed if you catch sight of fellow bathers smearing themselves in sludge: the reedy area behind Kraljičina plaža is rich in **peloid mud**, particularly effective in easing rheumatic and muscular complaints.

ARRIVAL AND INFORMATION — NIN

By bus Regular buses from Zadar (approximately every hour; 30min) drop passengers at a road junction at the western, mainland side of town.

Tourist office Trg braće Radića 3 (June–Aug Mon–Fri 8am–8pm, Sun 8am–1pm; Sept–May Mon–Fri 8am–3pm; T 023 264 280, W nin.hr). The tourist office, beside Donji most, can advise on local sights and public transport.

ACCOMMODATION

The tourist office can give you addresses of private **rooms** (from 200Kn/double) and **apartments** (two-person apartments from 275Kn, four-person apartments from 460Kn); otherwise they can be booked through the **Lotos** agency in Sukošan, near Zadar (T 023 394 636, W lotos-croatia.com).

Autocamp Dišpet Put Ždrijaca bb ⓣ098 304 1651. A short walk north of town and near the sandy Ždrijac spit, this is a good base for sightseeing and swimming. April to mid-Oct. 70Kn per person, 40Kn per pitch

Camping Ninska Laguna Put Blata 10 ⓣ023 264 265, ⓦninskalaguna.hr. On the way to Kraljičina plaža, this is an orderly little place with a reasonable amount of shade, although it tends to get cramped in season. April to mid-Oct. 75Kn per person, 40Kn per pitch

EATING

Konoba Dalmacija Zrinsko-Frankopanska 2 ⓣ023 264 163, ⓦkonobadalmacijanin.hr. Located between the Old Town and the bus stop, this friendly *konoba* offers the best in the grilled-fish line and has decent pizzas too. Daily 9am–11pm.

Perin Dvor Hrvatskog sabora 1 ⓣ023 264 307. Just inside the Lower Town Gate, *Perin Dvor* has good home cooking with the accent on steaks and grilled fish, served in a nice garden. Daily 9am–11pm.

The Zadar archipelago

The small, often bare islands of northern Dalmatia – sometimes called the **Zadar archipelago** – see much less in the way of mass tourism than those in the south, and their unspoilt, largely rural nature provides them with bags of off-the-beaten-track allure. The northern end of the archipelago is full of semi-abandoned islands boasting beautiful bays and lush inland scenery, although few other than **Silba** possess significant tourist facilities. Silba's near-neighbour **Olib** is worth considering as a day-trip if not necessarily a lengthy stay. Densely inhabited Ugljan, directly opposite Zadar, is almost a suburb of the city, and it is the long and barren **Dugi otok**, on the far side of Ugljan, that offers most in the way of stunning scenery. It is here that you will find the beautiful **Telašćica Bay** – the archipelago's most celebrated natural beauty spot.

Silba

For connoisseurs of soothingly unspoilt islands with no traffic and no hotels, kidney-shaped **Silba** is as perfect as they come. Not only are there no cars on the island, an unofficial ban on bicycles from mid-July to late August serves to preserve the island's pedestrian pace. Strolling along maquis-lined country lanes in search of wild beaches is the only adrenalin sport you are likely to encounter here.

Eight kilometres in length and only 1km wide at its narrowest point, Silba probably gets its name from the Latin word *silva* (wood) and is still covered with trees (notably *crnika* or Mediterranean black oak), giving it an atmosphere quite different from that of its scrub-covered neighbours. The island's one settlement, **Silba Town**, has an air of relaxed luxury, its palm-shaded stone houses and their walled gardens serving as reminders of the island's erstwhile commercial wealth, when sailing ships from Silba dominated the carrying trade between Dalmatia and Venice – only to be put out of business by the steam-powered vessels of the nineteenth century. During the 1970s Silba attracted a significant slice of both Croatia and Slovenia's post-hippy, pre-punk intelligentsia, who camped wild on the southern part of the island. Nowadays a permanent population of about three hundred is swelled tenfold in summer, when weekenders from Zadar and independent travellers from all over Croatia come to enjoy the island's uniquely relaxing rural atmosphere.

Silba Town

Silba Town straddles the island's narrowest point, its narrow streets sloping down towards two bays. The one on the western side of town contains the **ferry dock** and has some splendid sections of pebble **beach** – great places from which to observe the sun setting over the open sea. Rising over the middle of the town is the **Marinić Tower**, a lookout post with a spiral staircase running up the outside, supposedly built by a sea captain for the beautiful daughter of a woman who jilted him when a young man. Near

5

the town church is an open-air **sculpture park** devoted to Marija Ujević Galetović (1933–), famous for her expressive human and half-human forms – notably the cat-headed woman who dominates the collection here.

The bay that marks the east of Silba Town is home to a **harbour** for small boats and yachts, and **Šotorišće Beach**, a broad, shallow bay with a sandy sea floor and a summer-only café-bar. Paths and gravel roads lead all over the island towards a multitude of other bays and beaches. One of the most popular is **Dobre Vode**, a majestic sweep of rock and pebble some fifty minutes' walk south of the village.

ARRIVAL AND INFORMATION — SILBA

By boat Silba is a midpoint stop-off on Jadrolinija's Zadar–Mali Lošinj ferry (2 weekly), and the more frequent Zadar–Olib catamaran (daily) operated by Miatours, Vrata sv Krševana bb, Zadar (T 023 254 300, W miatours.hr).

Tourist office In the centre of the village near the church (June–Aug daily 8am–3pm & 6–10pm; T 023 370 010, W tzsilba.hr).

ACCOMMODATION AND EATING

The tourist office (see above) posts a list of private **rooms** (180Kn) and **apartments** (two-person apartments 350Kn, four-person apartments from 420Kn) on their website and may help you make contact with the owners if you can't find an English speaker. The season is short on Silba and many private-room hosts may not be in residence outside the peak July/August period.

★ **Fregadon** Silba bb T 023 370 104, W pansion-silba.com. Offering pleasant rooms, friendly owners and a soothing garden setting, this modern house is almost in the boutique category. Right in the middle of Silba Town, it consists of three double rooms and a four-person attic apartment, each equipped with a/c, fridge, electric kettle and – attic apartment excepted – a large terrace. Breakfast and an evening meal are offered in the downstairs garden restaurant. Open April–Oct. Half board **580Kn**

Konoba Mul Silba bb T 023 370 351, W silbakonobamul.com. Towards the eastern side of Silba Town, *Mul* serves up freshly caught seafood in a stone chamber decorated with fishing nets and other nautical knick-knacks, or on a terrace with swaying wicker lamps. Seafood risottos, mixed-fish kebabs and grilled or baked fish (380Kn/kg) all come recommended. May–Sept daily 3–11pm.

Olib

With a catamaran operating daily between Silba and Zadar it's possible to fit one of the other islands of the northern archipelago into a trip of one day or longer. One of the most rewarding of these is **Olib**, another small, car-free place offering unspoilt nature and an unhurried pace of life. In the twentieth century it was traditional for Olib families to emigrate to New Jersey, and you will encounter older locals speaking English with a pronounced North American drawl. A handful of local families offer accommodation, so it's feasible to stay here if you plan in advance, although most people limit themselves to a day on the beach.

Olib's main settlement is much more of a scattered rural village than a compact town, with long distances between family houses and only a church belfry to tell you where the centre might be. Beside the **church** is an impressively rugged latemedieval tower, built to provide refuge from raiding pirates. Beyond the church, a signed path leads to **Slatinica Bay**, some fifteen minutes' walk between dry-stone-walled olive groves, where you will find a broad crescent of shingle and a shallow, sandy-floored bay.

ARRIVAL AND DEPARTURE — OLIB

By boat Olib is the starting point of the Zadar–Olib catamaran line. In addition, Jadrolinija's Zadar–Mali Lošinj ferry calls in twice a week.

EATING

Konoba Bočvica Olib bb T 098 161 7689. Right on the seafront, a short distance from the ferry dock, this summer-only *konoba* serves lobster and crab on a sea-facing terrace, and also runs a café-bar a few steps away. Daily 11am–11pm.

Dugi otok

Some 43km long and at no point more than 4.5km wide, **Dugi otok** (Long Island) is the largest and arguably the most beautiful of the Zadar archipelago islands. Fewer than two thousand people live here, and parts of the island are very remote – some settlements are accessible only by sea, and the fresh water supply can be limited. It boasts a wilder and more dramatic landscape than any of its neighbours, with sheer cliffs on its western side and a rugged, indented coastline.

Dugi otok's main attraction is **Telašćica Nature Park**, which is best approached from the island's main settlement, **Sali**, although the quiet villages and headlands of the northern part of the island are also worth a visit. It's also a possible base from which to visit the Kornati archipelago, with boat captains in Sali offering trips, though the archipelago is more usually approached from Murter (see p.263).

ARRIVAL AND DEPARTURE — DUGI OTOK

By boat Catamarans run from Zadar to Sali (3 daily; 1hr), and there is a car ferry from Zadar to Brbinj (2–3 daily; 2hr) near the northern end of Dugi otok. There are few buses linking the two ports.

GETTING AROUND

By car You'll need a car if you want to explore the island's single north–south road, with its spectacular views of the rest of the Zadar archipelago to the east. If you're driving, note that the island's only petrol station is just north of Sali in Zaglav.

ACCOMMODATION

There are no campsites on the island, and private **rooms** and **apartments** should be booked in advance if you're planning to come here in peak season.

Northern Dugi otok

Despite **BRBINJ**'s importance as a ferry port there's nothing much here (apart from a tiny seasonal tourist office; see below) Hop straight onto one of the buses which head north to **BOŽAVA**, a small fishing village of 150 inhabitants, with an attractive harbour and a path leading east round the headland to a rocky coast overlooked by swooning trees.

Driving northwest out of Božava on the road to the village of Soline, you get a good view of the north of the island as it finishes in a flourish of bays and peninsulas. To get to one of the island's best beaches, follow the road up the westernmost of these peninsulas, **Veli rat**, then take a left turn onto an unmarked gravel track about 3km out of Božava and proceed about 1km through fragrant forest (drivers will have to park about halfway down). At the end of the path you'll come to **Sakarun**, a 500m-long bar of pebbles with a sandy fringe and a shallow sandy sea-floor perfect for paddling. As you carry on up Veli rat, the road terminates beside a stumpy, ochre lighthouse, built in 1849 by the Austrians, who painted it with egg whites. It is now a popular spot for bathing, with an attractively rocky coastline stretching away on both sides.

ARRIVAL AND INFORMATION — NORTHERN DUGI OTOK

By bus Buses run from Brbinj to Božava (1–2 daily; 25min).

Tourist office At the northern end of the harbour, Božava (July & Aug daily 8am–9pm; ⊤ 023 377 607, ⓦ dugiotok.hr).

ACCOMMODATION

Božava's tourist office can help you locate private **rooms** (doubles from 180Kn) and **apartments** (two-person apartments from 270Kn, four-person apartments from 400Kn).

Božava ⊤ 023 291 291, ⓦ hoteli-bozava.hr. The *Božava* hotel complex, set among fragrant pines west of the harbour and with its own rocky beach, sports three sections: the tastefully refurbished three-star *Agava* offers apartments with balconies, a/c and TV; the three-star *Lavanda* has pleasant en-suite rooms with the best sea

5

views and an outside swimming pool; while the four-star *Maximi* has thicker carpets, flat-screen TVs and swish modern bathrooms. Open late April to end Oct. *Agava* 1200Kn; *Lavanda* 1200Kn; *Maximi* 1380Kn

Sali and around

The island's largest village and the centre of a prosperous fishing industry, **SALI** is a quiet place, though the smattering of cafés round the harbour provide the requisite air of Mediterranean vivacity on warm summer nights. A great time to be in Sali is the first weekend in August, when the Saljske užance **festival** takes place, with outdoor concerts, feasting and performances of *tovareća muzika* ("donkey music" – so called because it's a tuneless racket that sounds like braying), which features the locals raucously blowing horns.

INFORMATION — SALI AND AROUND

Tourist office (July & Aug daily 8am–9pm; Sept–May Mon–Fri 8am–3pm; T 023 377 094, W dugiotok.hr). The tourist office, on the western side of the harbour, is well supplied with local info.

ACCOMMODATION

Rooms (doubles from 200Kn) and **apartments** (two-person apartments from 330Kn, four-person apartments from 420Kn) can be booked through **Adamo** (T 099 518 2929, W adamo.hr), in the same building as the tourist office, or **Kartolina** a little further beyond (T 023 377 191, W kartolina-turist.com).

★ **Pansion Roko** Zaglav 28 T 023 377 182 or T 098 627 133, W pansion-roko.hr. Five kilometres northwest of Sali, the lovely bay-hugging hamlet of Zaglav is home to *Pansion Roko*, which offers small but neat en-suite rooms with laminated floors, TV and teeny balconies. It's well worth paying the extra 100Kn or so for half board: the fresh fish and shellfish in the downstairs restaurant are among the best on the island. Doubles with breakfast 360Kn

Sali Sali bb T 023 377 049, W hotel-sali.hr. Over the hill from the harbour in the next bay to the north of Sali, Sašćica, this hotel boasts a magnificent position right above an azure, pine-tree-shaded bay, its four pavilions offering pleasant en-suite rooms with balconies, a/c and TV. There is also a diving centre and bike rental (100Kn/day). 630Kn

EATING AND DRINKING

Konoba kod Sipe Sali 174 T 023 377 137. Traditional *konoba* uphill from the harbour, with fresh fish, squid and lobster served up in an unpretentious village-tavern environment. Daily noon–10pm.

Maritimo Sali bb. Next to the catamaran dock, *Maritimo* café-bar is very much a social institution, where people come to watch comings and goings during the daytime or drink late into the evenings. Daily 6am–1am.

Telašćica Nature Park

It's about 3km from Sali to the northern edge of **Telašćica Bay** (W telascica.hr), a 7km channel overlooked by smooth hills and indented with numerous smaller bays which run down to the tangle of islands at the northern end of the Kornati archipelago. The flora along the shoreline marks the transition from the green vegetation of the Zadar archipelago to the bare wilderness of the Kornati – banks of deep forest slope down towards the western shore of the bay, where maquis-covered offshore islands rise like grey-brown cones from the water – and the whole place has been designated a **nature park**.

From the car park (see below) it's a twenty-minute walk to **Uvala mira** (Bay of Peace) at the park's centre. There's a bar and **restaurant** here, and a path that leads, after five minutes' walk up a wooded hillside, to a stretch of ruddy clifftop looking out towards the open sea. Five minutes south of the restaurant lies **Jezero mira**, a saltwater lake cut off from the sea by a narrow barrier of rock at the lake's southernmost end. The rock is a favourite with naturists, while the lake itself is popular swimming territory. The excessively salty water of the lake is several degrees warmer than the sea in summer, and has therapeutic fango mud in its southeastern corner.

ARRIVAL AND DEPARTURE — TELAŠĆICA

By car To get to Telašćica Bay from Sali, take the signposted minor road that heads west from the Sali–Božava route about 1.5km out of town. You'll finish up at a car park and barrier (no cars beyond this point).

On foot/by bike It's possible to walk (2hr) or cycle from Sali – the initial stretch along asphalt road is pretty boring, but once you turn off onto the Telašćica-bound side road the Mediterranean landscape of olive groves, tumbledown stone walls and turquoise sea inlets is truly wonderful.

Murter

One of northern Dalmatia's most pleasantly laid-back islands is **Murter**, just off the main coastal highway and joined to the mainland by a small bridge at the channel-hugging settlement of **Tisno**. Main settlement **Murter Town** is the main base for boat trips to the Kornati National Park (see p.265) and is an enjoyable place in its own right, a quaint settlement of stone houses that soon fills up with tourists in July and August. There is only a handful of hotels on the island, and Murter is an excellent destination for independent travellers looking for private accommodation and campsites.

ARRIVAL AND DEPARTURE — MURTER

By bus The most convenient way to arrive is with the local Šibenik–Vodice–Murter bus service (Mon–Fri 8 daily; Sat & Sun 6 daily).

By car Take the Murter-bound turn off the main coastal Magistrala mid-way between Pirovac and Vodice.

Tisno

Murter is connected to the mainland by the bridge at **Tisno**, a pleasant chain of shoreside buildings running along either side of the channel dividing the island from terra firma; the bridge at Tisno's centre swings open twice a day (at 9am and 5pm) to allow yachts to pass through. An excellent place for shoreline strolls, and with good bay-hugging beaches within walking distance of the centre, Tisno is also famous as the site of the summer-long programme of **festivals** put on by the Garden organization, which took up residence in a bay on the mainland side east of Tisno in 2012 and looks set to stay for several years to come (see box below).

ARRIVAL AND INFORMATION — TISNO

By bus Šibenik–Murter buses pick up and drop off on the landward side of Tisno's bridge.

Tourist office Istočna gomilica 1a (July–Sept daily 8am–9pm; Oct–June Mon–Fri 8am–2pm; ⓣ 022 438 604, ⓦ tz-tisno.hr). A good source of info a few steps away from the bus stop.

ACCOMMODATION

Nik Ive, Vodopije 1 (ⓣ 022 438 909, ⓦ nik.hr) is a seasonally open agency (out of season you can contact the main branch in Šibenik; see p.270), with plenty of **studio apartments** (from 350Kn).

GARDEN TISNO

Tisno owes its exalted position on the Adriatic party map to the DJ-driven, dance-oriented festivals that come under the umbrella of the Zadar-based **Garden** organization, which spent six years organizing hugely successful events at Petrčane until moving here in 2012. Based at the former *Hostin* campsite and bungalow settlement overlooking Rastovac Bay, the Garden site has its own beach and is sufficiently far away from central Tisno to allow the partying to continue into the early hours. The festival season kicks off with **Garden Festival** in early July (ⓦ thegardenfestival.eu); **Electric Elephant** (ⓦ electricelephant.co.uk), **Soundwave** (ⓦ soundwavecroatia.com) and **Stop Making Sense** (ⓦ stopmakingsense.eu) follow soon afterwards, with additional weekend events filling up the calendar throughout the summer. With accommodation for about seven hundred campers and a festival-going capacity of around three thousand, Tisno offers an especially intimate festival experience – tickets for all events should be booked online well in advance.

5

Camping Jezera Uvala Lovišća ☎022 439 600, ⓦwww.jezera-kornati.hr. Just out of Tisno on the road to Murter Town, opposite the turn-off for the village of Jezera, this is a large site with restaurants, shops and bungalows occupying a succession of hillside terraces above a crescent-shaped pebble beach. There is a reasonable amount of shade, and a coastal path to Tisno. Šibenik–Murter buses pick up and drop off at the entrance. 70Kn per person, pitches from 40Kn

Murter Town

An attractive huddle of stone houses on the western side of the island, **MURTER TOWN** was traditionally home to the fishermen and sheep-farmers who owned land on the Kornati islands and spent most of their time sailing in Kornati waters. The settlement's seafront is still characterized by the untidy jumble of boathouses and jetties that jut out from each household – this is one Adriatic town that does not have a continuous, strollable Riva. However Murter's alleyways are as atmospheric as they come, and the oldest part of town – grouped up on a hill 1km inland from the modern centre – is well worth the climb. The sea around Murter is crystal clear, the surrounding countryside is unspoiled, and there is a relative lack of package hotels – giving the place a relaxed, independent-traveller vibe.

Beaches

There are pleasant if unexciting family-oriented **beaches** (mostly concrete and gravel) at Zdrače at the eastern end of town and Hramina at the west. More attractive is the pebbly affair at **Slanica Bay**, fifteen minutes' walk farther west – there's rarely enough room to swing a bikini here on summer weekends, but it's an enchanting place from which to watch the sun set over the Kornati once the crowds have thinned. Taking the coastal path south from Slanica leads you past several rocky bathing areas before arriving at **Čigrađa Bay** (20min), which is as attractive as Slanica but much less crowded.

ARRIVAL AND INFORMATION — MURTER TOWN

By bus Buses from Šibenik (see p.266) terminate on the seafront just east of Murter's main square.

Tourist office Trg Rudina (mid-May to June daily 8am–2pm & 6–9pm; July & Aug daily 8am–10pm; Sept to mid-May Mon–Fri 8am–3pm; ☎022 434 995, ⓦtzo-murter.hr). Doles out free town plans, and advises on which agents are offering the best trips to the islands.

Kornati National Park office Butina 2 (Mon–Fri 8am–3pm; ☎022 435 740, ⓦkornati.hr). They give out park information, and sell maps and diving and fishing permits.

TOURS AND ACTIVITIES

Day-trips to the Kornati Trips are advertised by almost all the travel agents in Murter: among the longest established are Coronata, Trg Rudina bb (☎022 435 933, ⓦcoronata.hr); Eseker, just off Trg Rudina on the seafront (☎022 435 669, ⓦesekertours.hr); and KornatTurist on Trg Rudina (☎022 435 855 and ☎091 254 9227, ⓦkornatturist.hr).

Vehicle rental Eseker (see above) is the place to rent small boats (from 230Kn/day), scooters (230Kn/day upwards) and bikes (60Kn/day).

Diving Diving in the Kornati can be organized through Aquanaut, Luke 57 (☎022 434 988, ⓦdivingmurter.com), and Najada, Put Jersan 17 (☎022 435 630, ⓦnajada.com).

ACCOMMODATION

Rooms (doubles 250Kn) and **apartments** (two-person apartments 340Kn, four-person apartments 450–550Kn) are available from the Coronata bureau and KornatTurist (see above).

Camping Slanica Podvrške bb ☎022 434 205, ⓦmurter-slanica.hr. Running along the edge of Slanica Bay and occupying rocky-surfaced sloping woodland, this is a good base for the beach. May–Sept. 40Kn per person, 35Kn per pitch

Colentum Slanica bb ☎022 431 100, ⓦhotel-colentum.com. This box-like hotel overlooking Slanica Bay offers smart en suites, most of which have balconies facing the beach, and an outdoor pool. Open mid-April to mid-Oct. 1200Kn

EATING AND DRINKING

Eating in Murter is a hit-and-miss affair – usually a hit as far as the food goes, frequently a miss when it comes to the service. As far as **drinking** is concerned, both the main square and neighbouring alleyways have their fair share of cafés and lounge-bars.

RESTAURANTS

Boba Butina 22 ⓣ098 948 5272. Looking like a cross between a stylish modern living room and a gastro-pub, *Boba* breaks ranks with the nautical decor on display almost everywhere else in northern Dalmatia. The food is quality Adriatic fare, with fresh fish and shellfish cooked on an open hearth, alongside good risottos and pasta dishes. March–Dec daily noon–midnight.

Čigrađa Čigrađa Bay ⓣ022 435 704. Three kilometres southwest of town (slightly longer if you take the picturesque coastal path from Slanica Bay), *Čigrađa* enjoys a magnificent pine-shaded beach-side setting – perfect for watching the sun set. Tuck in to the usual array of seafood, washed down with a broad range of Dalmatian wines. Mid-May to Sept daily 10am–midnight.

Fabro Hrokešina bb ⓣ022 434 561, ⓦrestoran-fabro.hr. Fine seafood and steaks in a bright, modern interior or on an outdoor terrace spread across a small jetty. Not quite up to the standards of *Tic Tac* in the culinary department (see below) but the service is a bit more conscientious. Mains in the 100–130Kn bracket. March–Nov daily noon–midnight.

★ **Tic Tac** Hrokešina 5 ⓣ022 435 230, ⓦtictac-murter.com. Something of a Murter legend, *Tic Tac* is arguably the best place on the island to enjoy local seafood with a modern European twist. Fish (grilled, baked or stewed in a variety of sauces) is the trademark; the steaks (from 120Kn) are also excellent. The checked-tablecloth interior is cute and cosy, and there is plenty of seating in an arched alleyway or out on the quay. Does get busy in season. March–Dec daily noon–11pm.

BARS

Lantana Čigrađa bb. Cult alfresco bar on Čigrađa Bay (30min walk southwest of the square) with tables and chairs strewn across sloping ground above the shore. Frequent gigs and DJ nights pull in a varied crowd, and pizzas and sandwiches are served into the bargain. Mid-May to mid-Oct noon till late.

Reful Sabuni 11. *Reful* is Dalmatian dialect for a sudden gust of wind (in the meteorological sense), and this purple-decorated venue is indeed a welcome blast of fresh air, pumping out rock and world music on the sound system and hosting impromptu gigs on its tiny stage. There's also a snooker table and a small sea-facing terrace. Stays open all year and has a loyal local following. Daily: mid-June to mid-Sept 7am–2am; mid-Sept to mid-June 7am–midnight.

The Kornati islands

Scattered like pebbles to the west of Murter lie the ninety or so islands of the **Kornati archipelago**, grouped around the 35km-long island of Kornat. A national park since 1980, the Kornati archipelago comprises a distinctively harsh and bare environment, almost devoid of life. The islands range in colour from stony white to pale ochre, mottled with patches of pale green sage. They were once covered in forest until it was burned down to make pasture for sheep, who proceeded to eat everything in sight. The dry-stone walls used to pen them in are still visible, although the sheep themselves – save for a few wild descendants – are no more.

The islands were originally owned by the nobles of Zadar, who allowed the peasants of Murter to raise flocks and grow olives on them in return for a share in the cheese and oil thus produced. When the Zadar nobility fell on hard times in the nineteenth century, the islands were sold to the Murterians – and their descendants, the Kurnatari, remain owners of most of the Kornati to this day. Despite the number of stone cottages scattered over the islands (Vruje, on **Kornat**, is the biggest single settlement with fifty houses), most Kurnatari actually live in Murter nowadays – returning to the islands for a few months in the summer, when they come to relax, fish, or take advantage of the growing opportunities offered by tourism. The popularity of the Kornati with the international **yachting** fraternity is having a profound impact on the archipelago's development, with shoreline restaurants serving top-quality seafood springing up in every available cove. There's a fully equipped yachting marina on the island of **Piškera**, on the western side of the archipelago, and an even bigger one on the island of **Žut**,

5

which lies just outside the park boundaries to the east. With clear waters and relatively untouched ecology, the Kornati can also be a spectacular place for **scuba diving**.

ARRIVAL AND DEPARTURE — THE KORNATI ISLANDS

Day-trips Unless you have access to a boat, the easiest way of seeing the Kornati is to go on one of the day-trips arranged by one of the travel agents in Murter (see p.264). Travel agencies in Sali (p.262) and Zadar (p.253) also offer similar trips, although they are slightly further away from the islands and travel time is longer. Wherever you start, excursions are likely to set off around 8 or 9am and return at 5 or 6pm, weaving in and out of the islands on the western side of the archipelago, stopping a couple of times so that you can stretch your legs, swim and consume some of the local food and drink. Prices start at around 275Kn per person if you're travelling from Murter, 300Kn if you're approaching from Sali or Zadar, and include the national park entrance fee, and probably lunch with wine too.

On your own boat If you're approaching the islands in your own boat, look out for the rubber dinghies operated by national park wardens, which cruise the area selling entrance tickets (from 250Kn per boat, depending on size).

INFORMATION AND ACTIVITIES

Kornati National Park office Butina 2, Murter (T 022 435 740, W kornati.hr; see p.264).

Diving Permits for diving in the park, which can be arranged with outfits in Murter (see p.264), cost 100Kn per person, in addition to the entrance fee.

ACCOMMODATION

Staying in one of the island's stone cottages is popular with visitors who want a period of complete peace and quiet, although accommodation is scarce and needs to be booked well in advance.

Apartments KornatTurist in Murter (see p.264) provide apartments but prefer lengthy stays (seven days preferred) because of the logistics involved. Prices are around 3500–3900Kn per week for a two-person apartment, or 5000–5700Kn per week for a four-person apartment, including return boat transfer. Small boats can be rented through the agencies for about 700Kn per week.

Catering Once you're there provisions will be delivered to you by boat twice a week; if you've chosen one of the islands with a marina or restaurant you'll also be able to eat out.

Šibenik

Very much the surprise package of middle Dalmatia, **ŠIBENIK** offers the blend of Mediterranean architecture, island beaches and festival culture that better publicized cities like Split and Dubrovnik have long regarded their exclusive preserve. The city's maze-like medieval centre is as evocative as any on the Adriatic, and the cathedral is one of the finest architectural monuments in southeastern Europe. Islands Zlarin and Prvić (both easy day-trips by ferry) are among Dalmatia's most enchanting offshore destinations, and the fabulous waterfalls of the Krka National Park (see p.276) lie just inland. To cap things off, the arrival of the annual **Terraneo rock festival**, initiated in August 2011 (see box, p.272) has bestowed the city with a newfound aura of urban cool – a status enhanced by the fact that the Garden Tisno (see box, p.263) is only a short bus ride away. Šibenik's only drawback is the relative dearth of accommodation; rooms and apartments are in short supply in the city itself, although there are plenty in Brodarica 7km to the south.

Šibenik began life as an eleventh-century Croatian fortress, falling under Venetians in the fifteenth century, when it became an important strongpoint in their struggles against the Ottomans. Relics of this era, notably the huge decaying **fortresses** that hover above the town centre, are well worth exploring.

Clinging to the side of a hill, Šibenik's ancient centre is a steep tangle of alleys, steps and arches bisected by two main arteries, **Zagrebačka** and **Kralja Tomislava** (the latter popularly known as Kalelarga), which run northwest from the main square, **Poljana**.

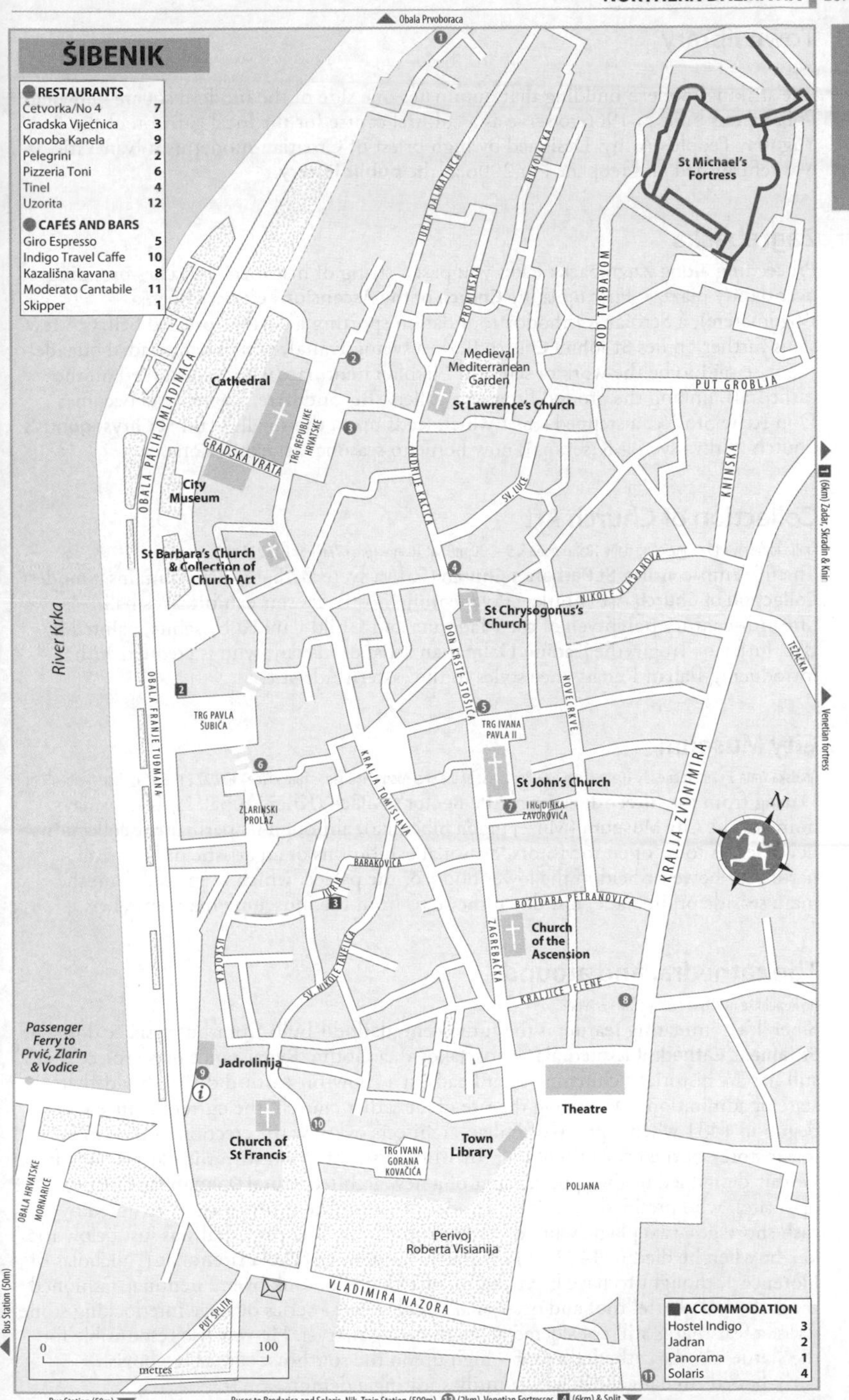
ŠIBENIK
RESTAURANTS
Četvorka/No 4 7
Gradska Viječnica 3
Konoba Kanela 9
Pelegrini 2
Pizzeria Toni 6
Tinel 4
Uzorita 12
CAFÉS AND BARS
Giro Espresso 5
Indigo Travel Caffe 10
Kazališna kavana 8
Moderato Cantabile 11
Skipper 1
ACCOMMODATION
Hostel Indigo 3
Jadran 2
Panorama 1
Solaris 4
Obala Prvoboraca
St Michael's Fortress
Medieval Mediterranean Garden
Cathedral
St Lawrence's Church
City Museum
St Barbara's Church & Collection of Church Art
St Chrysogonus's Church
St John's Church
Church of the Ascension
Jadrolinija
Theatre
Church of St Francis
Town Library
Perivoj Roberta Visianija
POLJANA
River Krka
Passenger Ferry to Prvić, Zlarin & Vodice
JURJA DALMATINCA
BUKOVAČKA
PROMINSKA
POD TVRĐAVOM
PUT GROBLJA
OBALA PALIH OMLADINACA
TRG REPUBLIKE HRVATSKE
GRADSKA VRATA
ANDRIJE KAČIĆA
SV. LUCE
KNINSKA
NIKOLE VLADANOVA
DON KRSTE STOŠIĆA
NOVE CRKVE
TEŽAČKA
OBALA FRANJE TUĐMANA
TRG PAVLA ŠUBIĆA
TRG IVANA PAVLA II
KRALJA TOMISLAVA
KRALJA ZVONIMIRA
ZLARINSKI PROLAZ
TRG DINKA ZAVOROVIĆA
BARAKOVIĆA
JURJA
BOŽIDARA PETRANOVIĆA
USKOČKA
SV. NIKOLE JAVELIĆA
ZAGREBAČKA
KRALJICE JELENE
TRG IVANA GORANA KOVAČIĆA
OBALA HRVATSKE MORNARICE
VLADIMIRA NAZORA
PUT SPLITA
N
(6km) Zadar, Skradin & Knin
Venetian fortress
Bus Station (50m)
0
100
metres
Buses to Brodarica and Solaris, Nik, Train Station (500m), 12 (2km), Venetian Fortresses, 4 (6km) & Split

Town library

Poljana

The striking modern building that dominates one side of the modern square known as Poljana was built in 1966 to serve as a cultural centre for the local garrison of the Yugoslav People's Army. Designed by high priest of Croatian modernism Ivan Vitić, it was refurbished and reopened in 2006 as the **public library**.

Zagrebačka

Proceeding along Zagrebačka takes you past a string of historical churches presiding over dainty piazzas. First up is the **Church of the Ascension** (Crkva Uspenja Bogomatere), a Serbian-Orthodox foundation sporting a curious orielled belfry. A few steps further on lies **St John's Church** (Crkva svetog Ivana), with a balustraded outside staircase said to be the work of sculptor Nikola Firentinac (who also worked on the cathedral), linking the ground floor to a gallery. Beyond here, Zagrebačka becomes Don Krste Stošića, a stepped street which leads up to the small, plain **St Chrysogonus's Church** (Crkva svetog Krševana), now home to seasonal art exhibitions.

Collection of Church Art

Kralja Tomislava 19 • June–Aug daily 10am–noon & 5–7.30pm, Sat 10am–1pm • 7Kn • 022 214 899

The fifteenth-century **St Barbara's Church** (Crkva svete Barbare) now contains a modest **Collection of Church Art** (Zbirka crkvene umjetnosti). Its star exhibit is a small fifteenth-century polyptych of the Madonna and Child flanked by saints, painted by Blaž Jurjev of Trogir, the leading Dalmatian artist of his day, who is credited with introducing Italian Renaissance styles to the eastern Adriatic.

City Museum

Gradska Vrata 3 • Summer daily 10am–1pm & 6–8pm; rest of the year Mon–Fri 10am–1pm • Free • 022 213 880, muzej-sibenik.hr

Dating from the fifteenth century, the **Rector's Palace** (Kneževa palača) is nowadays home to the **City Museum** (Muzej grada Šibenika), although its permanent collection never seems to be open to visitors. Seasonal exhibitions of an artistic or historical nature are however held in the lower floors of the palace, which is entered from the main seaside promenade, just down the steps from the museum's main entrance.

The cathedral and around

Trg Republike Hrvatske • Daily 9am–7.30pm

Šibenik's dominating feature is the tumescent, daffodil-bulb-from-outer-space dome of **St James's Cathedral** (Katedrala svetog Jakova), a Gothic Renaissance masterpiece that still has art historians clutching their heads in a "how-on-earth-did-they-build-that?" state of admiration. Occupying the site of an earlier church, the current edifice was begun in 1431 when a group of Italian architects oversaw the erection of the Gothic lower storey of the present building. In 1441, dissatisfaction with the old-fashioned Gothic design led to the appointment of a new architect, **Juraj Dalmatinac** (see box opposite), who presided over three decades of intermittent progress, interrupted by cash shortages, two plagues and one catastrophic fire. The cathedral was just below roof height when he died in 1473 and his Italian apprentice **Nikola Firentinac** ("Nicholas of Florence"), thought to have been a pupil of Donatello, took over. Firentinac fashioned the cathedral's barrel roof and octagonal cupola from a series of huge interlocking stone slabs, a feat that is still considered an engineering marvel. He was also responsible for the statues on the cathedral's roof – high up on the southeast corner is a boyish, curly-haired Archangel Michael jauntily spearing a demon.

JURAJ DALMATINAC

Juraj Dalmatinac (George the Dalmatian; c.1400–73) was the most prolific stonemason of the Dalmatian Renaissance, but little is known of the man save for the works he left behind. Born in Zadar some time around 1400, he learnt his trade in Venice, setting up a workshop there which made his reputation as a mason. The Šibenik authorities engaged him to work on the cathedral in 1441, paying him 150 golden ducats a year as well as covering his family's moving expenses and providing free housing.

When work on the cathedral stalled, Dalmatinac picked up commissions elsewhere, notably the **sarcophagus of St Anastasius** in Split cathedral (see p.290), and the main facade of Ancona cathedral. In 1464 he replaced Michelozzo Michelozzi as the chief fortification engineer in Dubrovnik, finishing off the finest of the system's many bastions, the **Minčeta Fortress** (see p.393). Following working visits to Urbino and possibly Siena, he returned to Šibenik, where he died in 1473, the cathedral still unfinished.

Dalmatinac's great skill was to blend the intricate stoneworking techniques of the Gothic period with the realism and humanism of Renaissance sculpture. His stylistic innovations were carried over to the next generation by his pupils **Andrija Aleši** and **Nikola Firentinac**, who were involved in the completion of Šibenik cathedral before going on to produce their own masterpieces in Trogir.

Entry to the cathedral is by the **north door**, framed by arches braided with the swirling arabesques that led to Dalmatinac's style being dubbed "floral Gothic". Inside, the cathedral is a harmonious blend of Gothic and Renaissance styles; the sheer space and light of the east end draw the eye towards the soft grey Dalmatian stone of the raised sanctuary. Follow the stairs down from the southern apse to the **baptistry** (Krstionica), Dalmatinac's masterpiece. It's an astonishing piece of work, a cubbyhole of Gothic carving, with four scallop-shell niches rising from each side to form a vaulted roof, beneath which cherubs playfully scamper.

The frieze of stone heads

Outside the cathedral, around the exterior of the three apses, Dalmatinac carved a unique **frieze** of 71 stone heads, apparently portraits of those who refused to contribute to the cost of the cathedral and a vivid cross-section of sixteenth-century society. On the north apse, beneath two angels with a scroll, he inscribed his claim to the work with the words *hoc opus cuvarum fecit magister Georgius Mathei Dalmaticus* – "These apses have been made by Juraj Dalmatinac, son of Mate."

Medieval Mediterranean Garden of St Lawrence's Monastery

Strme srube 1 • April–Oct daily 8am–11pm; Nov–March by arrangement only • 15Kn • ⓣ 022 212 515, ⓦ spg.hr • To reach it, climb the staircase in the northeastern corner of Trg Republike Hrvatske and continue to ascend the stepped alleyways at the top

Laid out in 2007, the **Medieval Mediterranean Garden of St Lawrence's Monastery** (Srednjovjekovni samostanski mediteranski vrt sv Lovre) spreads across a terrace right behind the monastery's belfry. Intended to re-create the shape and content of a typical medieval monastery garden, it contains all the plants and herbs once thought necessary for a sound mind and body, arranged in four large beds neatly divided by box hedge. With a smart modern café at the garden's edge, it's a supremely tranquil spot to take a breather.

St Michael's Fortress

Somewhere at the northeastern end of Šibenik's Old Town the tangle of alleyways opens out to reveal a broad staircase that ascends towards **St Michael's Fortress** (Kaštel svetog Mihovila) on the top of the hill. Constructed by the Venetians to keep Šibenik safe from the Ottomans, the fortress was built on the ruins of the earlier Croatian

5

citadel. Nowadays there's not much inside except for rubble, although the ramparts afford a panorama of the Old Town (including a clear view of the cathedral's roof), Šibenik Bay beyond, and the endless green ripple of offshore islands in the background. From the fortress, what remains of Šibenik's **city walls** plunge downhill to meet the sea, forming the Old Town's northern boundary.

The Venetian Fortresses

The views from St Michael's Fortress are good, but they are not quite as fabulous as those from the jutting grey bastions of the two **Venetian fortresses** occupying the high ground immediately east of Šibenik's Old Town. **Šubićevac Fortress** (Tvrđava Šubićevac) and **St John's Fortress** (Tvrđava svetog Ivana) were both built in the mid-sixteenth century to hold back a sequence of ever more dangerous Ottoman offensives. Best way to explore them is to head uphill from central Šibenik along 29 listopada 1918 to the suburb of Šubićevac, where an asphalt path leads up to Šubićevac Fortress, clearly visible up to your left. A crumbling relic covered in graffiti, Šubićevac is still an evocative spot. From here a path continues north along an ascending ridge to the much larger St John's Fortress, which is in a better state of preservation and offers superb views of the coast from its ramparts.

ARRIVAL AND INFORMATION — ŠIBENIK

By bus Šibenik's bus station is right on the waterfront at Obala Hrvatske mornarice, with a left-luggage office in the ticket hall (daily 7am–10pm).

Destinations Dubrovnik (10 daily; 6hr); Knin (8 daily; 1hr 20min); Murter (Mon–Fri 8 daily, Sat & Sun 6 daily; 1hr 10min); Skradin (Mon–Fri 6 daily, Sat & Sun 2 daily; 45min); Split (hourly; 2hr); Trogir (hourly; 1hr 30min); Zadar (hourly; 1hr 30min), Zagreb (15 daily; 6hr 30min).

By train The train station, for what it's worth (trains run from here only to the inland town of Knin, where there are infrequent connections to Split or Zagreb), is a 15min walk south of the centre.

Destinations Knin (4 daily; 2hr); Zagreb (1 daily with change at Knin; 7hr 30min).

By ferry There are four daily departures (two on Sun) to the islands of Zlarin and Prvić. Tickets can be bought from the Jadrolinija office on the waterfront at Obala Franje Tuđmana 7 (Mon–Fri 5.30am–9.15pm, Sat & Sun 7.30–11am & 5–10.30pm; ☎ 022 213 468).

Destinations Prvić Luka (Mon–Sat 4 daily, Sun 2; 45min); Šepurine (Mon–Sat 4 daily, Sun 2; 55min); Zlarin (Mon–Sat 4 daily, Sun 2; 30min).

Tourist office Obala Franje Tuđmana 5, on the seafront (May to mid-Sept daily 8am–11pm; mid-Sept to April Mon–Fri 8am–3pm; ☎ 022 212 075, ⓦ sibenik-tourism.hr). A relatively helpful source of information on the whole Šibenik area, and gives out brochures and a free city map.

ACCOMMODATION

With only one functioning **hotel** in the centre, and only a handful in suburban areas, accommodation in Šibenik is pretty limited. **Nik**, a 5min walk southeast of the centre at Ante Šupuka 5 (☎ 022 338 550, ⓦ nik.hr), will sort out private **rooms** (300Kn) and **apartments** (for two people 370Kn, for four people from 440Kn) in Šibenik or in Brodarica, 7km south of town (see p.273) and linked to Šibenik by urban bus.

HOTELS

Jadran Obala Franje Tuđmana 52 ☎ 022 242 000, ⓦ rivijera.hr. Five-storey box offering nondescript but perfectly adequate en-suite rooms with TV. Right on the Riva, a 5min walk away from everything you might want to see. **750Kn**

Panorama Šibenski most 1 ☎ 022 213 398, ⓦ hotel-panorama.hr. Six kilometres north of town beside the main road, this may seem a bit isolated, but it does have its compensations, squatting amid olive groves next to a dizzyingly high bridge across the Šibenik channel. The hotel itself is basically a grey cube containing neat balconied rooms; a café, restaurant and gym are on site. **750Kn**

Solaris ☎ 022 361 007, ⓦ solaris.hr. Bland holiday development 6km south of the centre, boasting a clutch of four-star hotels (*Ivan*, *Andrija*, *Ivan*, *Jakov* and *Niko*), and girdled by undistinguished beaches. An indoor swimming-pool complex and wellness centre is shared by all the hotels. Otherwise, the resort is a bit too self-contained and there are no interesting walks in the vicinity: hourly buses to Šibenik represent the only form of escape. Mid-April to mid-Oct. **1050Kn**

FROM TOP SKRADINKSI BUK, KRKA NATIONAL PARK (P.277); TERRANEO FESTIVAL (BOX, P.272) >

5

HOSTEL

Hostel Indigo Jurja Barakovića 3 ⓣ 022 200 159 and ⓣ 091 337 3744, ⓦ hostel-indigo.com. A tall, narrow four-storey house right in the wiggly-alley maze that is central Šibenik, *Indigo* offers neat bunk-bed quads in earthy beige colours with a/c. All rooms have sea-facing views and the top-floor terrace comes with a panorama of old Šibenik's red-tiled roofs. Wi-fi throughout. Optional breakfast in the *Indigo Travel Caffe* (see opposite). Beds from **120Kn**

EATING AND DRINKING

Šibenik has plenty of good **restaurants** in and around the Old Town, while for those who want to buy fresh fruit and veg, there's a **market** just uphill from the bus station. For **drinking**, there's a stretch of youth-oriented café-bars on the seafront just north of the *Jadran* hotel, and a handful of more charming places in and around the Old Town.

RESTAURANTS

Četvorka/No 4 Trg Dinka Zavorovića 4 ⓣ 022 217 517. Chic little place with a cosy café-bar on one level and a small dining area on the floor above. Good pasta dishes and steaks, and outdoor seating on a tiny Baroque square. Daily noon–11pm.

Gradska Vijećnica Trg Republike Hrvatske 1 ⓣ 022 213 605. Smart and stylish restaurant occupying the arcaded front of the former town hall, with excellent views of the cathedral. Good pastas and salads, and lavish main courses utilizing the best of the local seafood. Daily 8am–midnight.

Konoba Kanela Obala Franje Tuđmana 5 ⓣ 022 214 986. Decent place on the seafront specializing in fish and seafood (and the only establishment on the Riva brave enough to hang a sign outside reading "No pizzas here"). Pleasant terrace, cosy interior and moderate prices. Daily 8am–11pm.

★ **Pelegrini** Jurja Dalmatinca 1 ⓣ 022 213 701, ⓦ pelegrini.hr. Chic restaurant and wine bar in a restored medieval building just above the cathedral, with a highly individual range of traditional and Adriatic/world fusion fare. Look out for imaginative pasta dishes (70–80Kn), classic white-fish dishes in various sauces (100–140Kn) and top-notch shellfish and lobster. April–Oct daily noon–midnight; Nov–March Thurs–Sat noon–midnight, Sun noon–6pm.

Pizzeria Toni Zlarinski Prolaz 1. In a passageway next to Trg Pavla Šubića, this place has a lovely outdoor terrace by an ancient church. The interior is covered in pop-culture memorabilia celebrating – among other things – local basketball legend Dražen Petrović and quality crooner Arsen Dedić, and the kitchen dishes up cheap tasty pizza, pasta, sandwiches and *palačinke* (crêpes). It doubles as a popular beer hall at night. Daily 8am–midnight.

Tinel Trg pučkih kapetana 1 ⓣ 022 331 815. Occupying a dainty tree-shaded terrace opposite the Church of St Chrysogonus, this restaurant serves up simple lunches like *fažol sa kobasicom* (beans with sausage), mid-priced staples like wine goulash and *pašticada*, and classy fish dishes. April–Oct Mon–Sat 10am–4pm & 6.30–11pm, Sun 6.30–11pm.

★ **Uzorita** Bana Josipa Jelačića 58 ⓣ 022 213 660, ⓦ uzorita.com. Nestling in an old stone building between concrete residential blocks just north of the football stadium (an easy 20min walk from the centre if you head up 29. listopada 1918 and keep going), *Uzorita* (an old-fashioned word that means "most esteemed") mixes sleek modern furnishings with down-on-the-farm design features to create a chic but homely feel. Fresh fish, squid and locally farmed shellfish are the house specialities, although chop-and-chips fans are also well catered for. Mains 90–150Kn. Daily noon-midnight.

CAFÉS AND BARS

Giro Espresso Zagrebačka 2 ⓣ 022 310 166, ⓦ giroespresso.com. Something of a temple to the cult of the brown bean, this chic café full of bold whites and reds is

FESTIVALS IN ŠIBENIK

Many of the festivals up and down the Adriatic coast are actually package holidays in disguise, catering for Brits and other northwestern Europeans who simply want a long party weekend with a Mediterranean backdrop. **Terraneo** (ⓦ terraneofestival.com), held in August, on the other hand is the real McCoy, a genuinely international music festival that locals actually go to in large numbers. Held in the former JNA barracks midway between the city centre and the *Solaris* resort, it features three days of music from the best international indie/alternative names, and a range of after-gig DJ events. On-site camping is available.

Straddling a fortnight in late June/early July, the **International Children's Festival** (Međunarodni dječji festival; ⓦ mdf-sibenik.com), frequently turns out to be great fun for all ages, incorporating street entertainers, musical theatre and high-quality puppet performances – as well as singing-and-dancing troupes of children from all over Croatia.

by far the best place to start your day if a well-made macchiato or cappuccino is what gets your engine going. Leaf teas and free wi-fi are also on the menu. Mon–Sat 7am–11pm, Sun 8am–2pm.

Indigo Travel Caffe Biskupa Fosca 11 ⓣ 022 200 217. A cosy café that consists of an odd-shaped pentagonal room with not more than four tables – although there's plenty of room on the awning-covered terrace that stretches out into the alley. In summer breakfast cereals and toast are on the menu – this is where guests at the *Hostel Indigo* (see opposite) start the day. Free wi-fi. Mon–Sat 9am–10pm.

Kazališna kavana Kralja Zvonimira bb. Small, chic place with a coffee-and-cream colour scheme and a small outdoor terrace. The name means "theatre café" – appropriately enough, it's just behind the municipal theatre, and the walls are plastered with photos of board-treading actors old and new. Daily 6am–11pm.

Moderato Cantabile Stjepana Radića 1 ⓣ 022 213 647. Popular daytime coffee-drinking and newspaper-reading venue with a big, bright interior and large outdoor terrace. Named after a popular song penned by Šibenik-born crooner (and Croatian national treasure) Arsen Dedić. Mon–Sat 7am–11pm, Sun 7am–10pm.

Skipper Obala prvoboraca 12. One of the more alluring places in a line of waterfront bars, with an interior that's perfect for an intimate drink and a terrace shaded by palm fronds. A good choice of cocktails and bottled beers. Sun–Thurs 8am–1am; Fri & Sat till 2am.

Krapanj

Lying three hundred metres across the water from the mainland south of Šibenik, **Krapanj** has the minor distinction of being the smallest inhabited island in the Adriatic. It is reached by ferry shuttle from **BRODARICA**, an undistinguished village which stretches along the shore for some 3km. Ferries arrive at a sleepy harbour backed by an enjoyable warren of grey-brown houses. Diving for sponges used to be the main occupation on Krapanj, although there's not much evidence of this now, save for a couple of shops on the harbour selling spongy souvenirs. Krapanj fills up with Croatian weekenders in July and August, when there's a fair number of sunbathers sprawled out on either side of the quay – the rest of the time women clad in traditional black widows' weeds outnumber other residents four to one.

Franciscan monastery

Museum June–Sept Mon–Sat 9am–noon & 5–7pm • 15Kn

The one bona fide attraction is the fifteenth-century **Franciscan monastery** (Franjevački samostan), ten minutes' walk north of the harbour, where a **museum** contains a couple of Renaissance paintings. Next door to the monastery is Krapanj's **cemetery**, containing several memorials commemorating sponge-diving families – look out for carved reliefs of diving suits, diving helmets and other symbols of the island's main source of income.

ARRIVAL AND DEPARTURE — KRAPANJ

By ferry From Brodarica, a ferry crosses to Krapanj every hour. Buses to Brodarica run every hour from the bus stop beside Šibenik market.

ACCOMMODATION AND EATING

BRODARICA

Pansion Zlatna Ribica Krapanjskih Spužvara 46 ⓣ 022 350 300, ⓦ zlatna-ribica.hr. Down on the Brodarica seafront, near the jetty for the Krapanj ferry, this top-notch restaurant is famous for its superbly grilled fish – it's probably one of the best places to eat seafood in the Šibenik region and not overly expensive, so advance reservations are recommended. The same family have a pension behind the restaurant, which offers cosy a/c rooms with TV. Restaurant daily noon–11pm. Pension **550Kn**

KRAPANJ

Spongiola Obala I 58 ⓣ 022 348 900, ⓦ spongiola.com. Small-scale boutique hotel right on Krapanj's mainland-facing waterfront, offering fully equipped, hardwood-floored en suites in various shapes and sizes. There's a museum of sponge-diving, complete with antiquated diving suits, in the hotel basement. Sauna, gym and small pool are also on site. Open April–Oct. **700Kn**

5

Zlarin and Prvić

Your best bet for bathing opportunities in the Šibenik area is to head for the nearby islands of **Zlarin** and **Prvić**, where you stand a good chance of finding a secluded bit of rocky shoreline and crystal-clear water. There's no mass tourism on the islands, and no cars – merely a succession of orderly and neat little villages kept alive by a trickle of independent tourists and weekending Croatians.

The ferry trip from Šibenik is a treat in itself, with the boat ploughing its way through **St Anthony's Channel** (Kanal svetog Ante), a narrow, cliff-lined waterway which leads from the bay of Šibenik out into the open sea. At the far end of the channel lies the sixteenth-century **St Nicholas's Fortress** (Tvrđava svetog Nikole), a monumental triangular gun battery placed here by Venetian engineers to keep enemy shipping away from Šibenik's port.

ARRIVAL AND DEPARTURE — ZLARIN AND PRVIĆ

By ferry The islands are served by the four daily Šibenik–Vodice passenger ferries (though only 2 on Sun), which call in at Zlarin (30min) before proceeding to Prvić Luka (another 15min) on the southeastern side of Prvić, and Šepurine on the island's northwestern shore. From Šibenik, you could feasibly fit all three villages into a single day's sightseeing, although most visitors favour a more relaxing approach.

Zlarin

Thirty minutes out by boat from Šibenik, the village of **ZLARIN** is an attractive huddle of houses at the apex of a broad bay. Coral fishing and processing used to be the island's main employer, until overharvesting led to a shutdown of all but one of the coral workshops in the 1950s. Nowadays the island has a winter population of around 25 souls, although the figure increases hundredfold in July and August. Largely lacking in modern buildings, the village is an almost perfect example of what a typical Dalmatian settlement looked like in the early twentieth century. There's a brace of coral souvenir shops in the alleyways behind the harbour, and a seasonally open **coral museum** that allows a glimpse of how the coral is polished and processed. Zlarin's rarely open **parish church** is famous for housing the body of fourth-century Roman martyr St Fortunatus, a relic obtained for the island by a resourceful local priest in 1781. Every fifty years the remains are paraded through the village on April 23 – the next celebration is due in 2050, so there's no need to pack your bags just yet.

Paths on the western side of the bay will take you to an abundance of rocky **bathing areas** backed by pines.

INFORMATION — ZLARIN

Tourist office On the harbour (July & Aug daily 10am–1pm & 6–8.30pm; ⓣ022 553 557, ⓔtzzlarin@net.hr), which can organize private rooms (180Kn).

ACCOMMODATION AND EATING

Aldura Sunčana obala bb ⓣ022 553 628. Right opposite the ferry jetty, *Aldura* serves up risottos, salads and seafood in an elegantly restored, wooden-beamed old house, with a couple of nineteenth-century oil presses in the dining room. May–Oct daily noon–11pm.

Konoba Vuneni Zlarin bb. In a narrow street opposite the coral museum, *Vuneni* prepares excellent mussels and grilled fish, although the house speciality is veal, lamb or octopus baked with potatoes under a *peka* (order 24hr in advance). The indoor dining room has an open kitchen and a bicycle hanging from the ceiling, the outdoor terrace is decorated with tin cans, driftwood and other seaborne junk. June–Sept daily 6–11pm.

Koralj Obala boraca 15 ⓣ022 553 621, ⓦ4lionszlarin.com. Zlarin's lone hotel is set right on the seafront a short walk from the ferry landing, with simple en-suite rooms and a spacious garden in the back. The ground-floor *Four Lions* café-restaurant offers a broad-based menu of Adriatic seafood with benches set out under a huge harbourside awning. May–Sept. **600Kn**

Prvić Luka and around

A fifteen-minute ferry journey away from Zlarin, the main settlement of Prvić, **PRVIĆ LUKA**, is another unassuming, bay-hugging village with a charmingly soporific atmosphere. The **parish church**, just up from the harbour, boasts an extrovert collection of Baroque altarpieces as well as the tomb of Šibenik-born humanist and all-round brainbox Faust Vrančić (see box below). Nearby, the Faust Vrančić **memorial centre** (currently under construction) will display models of the contraptions that he dreamt up in his book of inventions, *Machinae Novae.*

Šepurine

A single road leads northwest out of Prvić Luka, passing olive groves and offering some great vistas before arriving after fifteen minutes in **ŠEPURINE** (which is also the next stop for the Šibenik–Vodice ferry), an attractive and beautifully preserved fishing village spread beneath a mushroom-topped church tower. Šepurine has the best **beach** in the area, a wonderful S-bend of shingle stretching away south of the ferry dock.

INFORMATION — PRVIĆ LUKA AND AROUND

TOURIST OFFICES

Prvić Luka Prvić Luka bb, just beyond the church on the main road to Šepurine (May–Sept Mon–Sat 11am–1pm & 6–9pm, Sun 9am–noon; ⊕ 022 448 083).

Šepurine The sporadically open tourist office (May–Sept Mon–Sat 9am–11am), 200m south of the landing stage and housed in the local primary school, will put you in touch with local landladies offering rooms (180Kn).

ACCOMMODATION AND EATING

Hotel Maestral Prvić Luka ⊕ 022 448 300, ⊕ hotelmaestral.com. One of the most stylish small hotels on this stretch of coast, the *Hotel Maestral* is housed in a beautifully restored school building smack in the centre of the village. There are twelve tastefully furnished a/c, en-suite rooms with original details, including cool stone interiors and wooden shutters. It also has the excellent *Val* restaurant on the ground floor (with an impressive wine list), a lovely breakfast terrace and a gym. April to mid-Nov. **900Kn**

FAUST VRANČIĆ (1551–1617)

Renaissance Šibenik produced many learned minds, most famously **Faust Vrančić** (Faustus Verantius), the author of **Machinae novae** (1615) – a book of machines and contraptions whose inventiveness rivalled the mechanical fantasies of Leonardo da Vinci. The album of 49 copper engravings included suspension bridges, wind-powered mills with rotating roofs and, most famously, **Homo volans** – a picture of a man jumping from a tower with a primitive parachute. Equipped with a square of sail-canvas, Vrančić opined in the accompanying text, "a man can easily descend securely and without any kind of danger from a tower or any other high place". According to seventeenth-century British scientist Bishop John Wilkins, Vrančić succesfully tested his parachute by jumping out of a window in Venice, although Wilkins' account was written thirty years after the event and remains tantalizingly unconfirmed by other sources.

Vrančić compiled *Machinae Novae* towards the end of a busy intellectual life. As the nephew of imperial diplomat and Archbishop of Hungary, Antun Vrančić, the young Faust served as secretary to the court of Emperor Rudolf II in Prague – a renowned meeting place for humanists from all over Europe. He subsequently retired to become a monk in Rome, where he probably became acquainted with Leonardo's drawings, and was moved to compile his *Machinae*. Vrančić's other major work was his *Dictionarium quinque nobilissimarum Europae linguarum* ("Dictionary of the Five Most Noble Languages of Europe", 1595), a lexicon including Latin, Italian, German, Hungarian and "Dalmatian" (Croatian). It was the first real dictionary in either Croatian or Hungarian, and had a profound influence on the subsequent development of both languages.

Krka National Park

Inland of Šibenik lies one of the most spellbinding landscapes in Croatia, with a canyon-bound sequence of gorges, lakes and rapids marking the progress of the River Krka towards the sea. Falling under the protection of the **Krka National Park**, the stretch of the Krka valley between the towns of Knin (see p.278) and **Skradin**, 12km out from Šibenik, is visited by almost three quarters of a million trippers per year. The huge majority of these visitors gravitate towards **Skradinski buk**, a sequence of waterfalls and cataracts just above Skradin. The upper reaches of the river are much less swamped by crowds, although there's a good deal worth seeing here, including two historic **monasteries** and another stretch of falls at **Roški slap** – all of which are accessible by national park-operated excursion boats. Travelling by car, you can combine visits to Skradinski buk and Roški slap with a stop-off at the former Roman legionary camp at **Burnum** just to the west.

ARRIVAL AND DEPARTURE — KRKA NATIONAL PARK

There are several main entrance points to the national park: for Skradinski buk, the town of **Skradin** itself, 4km north of Skradinski buk, from where national park boats ferry visitors to the falls; **Lozovac**, on the hill just above Skradinski buk, from where a path (15min) or bus shuttle service (April–Oct only) leads down to the river. Upstream, there is a road-accessible entrance at **Roški slap**; and another near the northern end of the park at **Burnum** (on the Kistanje–Knin road).

By bus There are several buses daily from Šibenik to Skradin (only two on weekends), passing through Lozovac on the way, making it possible to visit as a day-trip from the city. An early start is advised if you want to explore more than just the area around Skradinski buk – boat timings mean that a full day is required if you want to venture into the upriver sections of the park.

By car If travelling by car, note that there is ample parking at Skradin and Lozovac, but limited space at Roški slap or Burnum.

Tickets The entrance fee (March–June, Sept & Oct 80Kn; July & Aug 95Kn; Nov–Feb 30Kn) is payable at pavilions sited at each of the entrance points. The fee includes travel on the shuttle boats and buses linking Skradin and Lozovac with Skradinski buk, but lengthier boat excursions to Roški slap and the upper stretches of the river cost extra.

Skradin

The classic approach to the park is via **SKRADIN**, a beautifully situated huddle of houses squeezed into one of the river's large lagoon-like inlets. It's a good place to stay if you're visiting the park, and is also the site of the park's **visitors' centre** (see below). Although limited to a single main street overlooked by the crumbling remains of a castle keep, Skradin is an evocative place for a stroll. The town's marina is busy with expensive yachts for much of the summer, and Skradin's **restaurants** – known for a hybrid cuisine that mixes the best of the Adriatic with inland fare – are among the best in Dalmatia and are not outrageously expensive by any means.

INFORMATION — SKRADIN

Tourist office Obala bana Šubića 1 (mid-May to mid-Sept daily 8am–8pm; rest of the year Mon–Fri 9am–4pm; ☎ 022 771 329, Ⓦ skradin.hr).

National Park Visitors' Centre Šibenska bb (daily: June to mid-Sept 8am–8pm; mid-Sept to May 8am–6pm; ☎ 022 771 688, Ⓦ www.npkrka.hr). Housed in a modern pavilion, the visitor centre sells tickets, doles out information and mounts displays relating to nature conservation.

ACCOMMODATION

Skradinski buk Burinovac bb ☎ 022 771 770, Ⓦ skradinskibuk.hr. The *Skradinski buk* hotel, bang in the centre of the village, has swanky en-suite rooms equipped with cool Scandinavian-style furnishings, TV and a/c. **650Kn**

Villa Marija B&B Dr Franje Tuđmana 2 ☎ 022 771 110, Ⓦ pini.hr. Right on Skradin's central street, this B&B above the *Pini* restaurant offers neat rooms with small TVs. **350Kn**

EATING

★ **Bonaca** Rokovača 5 ⓣ 022 771 444. Fresh-caught fish and shellfish from the Adriatic, eel from the Krka river, lamb from the inland pastures – all served up on an outdoor terrace slightly uphill from the marina. April–Oct noon–midnight.

★ **Cantinetta** Skradinskih svilara 7 ⓣ 091 150 6434, ⓦ cantinetta-skradin.com. Quality restaurant in a walled courtyard whose menu of traditional local treats includes fish soups, local mullet (*cipalj*), lamb dishes and game. Feb–Dec daily noon–midnight.

★ **Zlatne školjke** Grgura Ninskog 9 ⓣ 022 771 022, ⓦ zlatne-skoljke.com. Seafood pastas, shellfish, fresh fish and local treats such as *skradinski rižot* (slow-cooked meat risotto) and *skradinska torta* (ground almonds, walnuts and rose-petal brandy), served in a snug dining room hung with nautical pictures. Daily Noon–11pm.

Skradinski buk

Krka National Park boats leave hourly from Skradin's harbourfront (20min); if you miss the boat you can go on foot along the road, which follows the river's right bank (50min)

Skradinski buk is one of nature's most unforgettable water features – a 500m sequence of seventeen mini-cascades spilling over barriers of travertine (limestone sediment), behind which lie pools surrounded by reeds and semi-submerged forest. One of the more dramatic sequences is just up from the boat landing, with several tiers of waterfall tumbling into a broad, shallow pool – it's the only part of the park where **swimming** is permitted, and is full of holiday-makers on warm summer days. From here the path crosses over to the eastern side of Skradinski buk, climbing past a nineteenth-century hydro-electric power station ("Jaruga 1"; opened in 1895) that was almost the first of its kind in the world – the Forbes dam on the Niagara falls beat it by a matter of months. The route ascends towards a collection of stone watermills positioned directly above the rushing Krka. There's also a network of wooden walkways that break off from the main path, leading you above gurgling waters and through thick riverine vegetation. It's a beautiful location, and you could spend an entire day here, lolling around on the rocks beside the tumbling water.

Visovac

Skradinski Buk–Visovac–Roški slap excursion boats depart from a jetty at the northern end of the Skradinski buk falls (around 2hr there and back; April–Oct only; 130Kn)

The most popular northbound trip from Skradinski buk takes you to the islet of **Visovac** just upstream, where you can visit a Franciscan monastery nestling among a thick cluster of cypresses. The monastery has a small collection of seventeenth-century paintings and, in its valuable library, some incunabula and a beautifully illustrated fifteenth-century *Aesop's Fables*, one of only three in the world.

Roški slap

Accessible by road, and also the final destination for those on the Skradinski buk–Visovac–Roški slap excursion boat, the **Roški slap** falls are only slightly less dramatic than those at Skradinski buk. You can explore another set of wooden walkways beside the frothing waters, and visit a cluster of traditional watermills (open April–Oct only) where weaving, carpet-washing and other beside-the-riverbank activities are demonstrated by staff in local costume.

Krka monastery

Boats leave from the northern end of Roški slap (2hr 30min return; 100Kn; March–Oct only)

Boats run from Roški slap through a rugged canyon-scape to the **Krka monastery**, a Serbian Orthodox foundation nestling in a lovely rustic setting on the western bank of the river, with a church rich in incense and icons. On the way to the monastery you'll

5

catch sight of the medieval Croatian fortresses of Trošenj and Nećven, clinging to crags high above the river.

Burnum

Rising from the shrub-covered maquis on the western side of the Krka canyon are the ruins of **Burnum**, a first-century legionary base that subsequently grew to become a medium-sized market town. There's not a great deal of Burnum still standing, although what is left is starkly evocative, with the graceful arches of some former palatial structure rising above one side of the Kistanje-Knin road. On the other side of the road there's a car park and a path to an amphitheatre – it's fascinating to think how this scrub-covered wasteland once played host to gladiator fights and wild beast hunts.

Burnum is the starting point for a footpath that descends into a steep-sided canyon of the upper Krka, emerging at the **Manojlovac rapids** – a smaller but much less visited version of the cataracts at Skradinski buk and Roški slap.

Knin

Set dramatically amid the stark, arid scenery typical of inland Dalmatia, the fortress town of **KNIN** occupies an indelible place in the Croatian national psyche, both as an important centre of the medieval kingdom and as a bone of bitter contention in the Homeland War of 1991–95. It was during the latter conflict that Knin became notorious as the capital of the so-called **Republic of the Serbian Krajina** (RSK).

Despite being surrounded by a patchwork of both Serbian and Croatian villages, Knin itself had a Serbian majority in 1990 and became the epicentre of the Serbian armed rebellion. Many of the key players in the Serb–Croat conflict started out in Knin, only to end up in the International War Crimes Tribunal in The Hague a decade or two later: Milan Babić, the RSK's first leader; Milan Martić, the Knin police chief who built up the Krajina's armed forces; and Colonel Ratko Mladić, commander of the Knin military garrison, who practised ethnic cleansing here, forcibly ejecting Croat families from nearby villages, before becoming head of the Bosnian Serb army in 1992. In the end, Serbian forces melted away when the Croatian army launched the Oluja (Storm) offensive in August 1995, and Knin's recapture on the morning of August 5, 1995 brought the war in Croatia to a rapid conclusion. Fearing Croatian reprisals, most Serb civilians fled in the wake of their defeated army, and only a handful have since returned. Otherwise Knin has largely reverted to what it was in the pre-1990 period: a provincial railway-junction town that accommodates a trickle of day-trippers drawn to its spectacular hilltop castle.

The fortress

Daily dawn–dusk • Free

Knin **fortress** (Kninska tvrđava) is pretty much everything you would expect from a medieval castle, with grey walls and turrets striding proudly along a ridge overlooking the Krka river. There's been a castle here since at least the tenth century, and it was the seat of the medieval Croatian state's last effective king, Zvonimir, towards the end of the eleventh century. The castle later fell to the Turks in 1522, and was retaken by the Venetians in 1688. The shell of the fortress has been impressively restored, and it is great fun to scramble around its central keep, which is defended by several layers of walls with outlying towers squatting on craggy outcrops. The battlements offer an extensive panorama of the surrounding countryside, with a view of Knin below in its bowl of brownish hills and the grey ridge of the Dinaric mountains to the northeast on the border with Bosnia-Hercegovina. Near the summit of the fortress hill is a flagpole bearing a huge Croatian flag. President Tuđman's 1995 visit to the fortress, when he arrived to kiss the flag the day after Knin's recapture, provided one of those iconic TV moments that most Croatian adults will forever retain in some corner of their brain.

ARRIVAL AND INFORMATION — KNIN

By train and bus Knin's train and bus stations are next to one another on the main street, Tuđmanva, a 20min walk from the fortress.

Train destinations Šibenik (4 daily; 2hr); Split (4 daily; 1hr 30min–2hr 30min); Zagreb (4 daily; 4hr 30min–7hr)

Bus destination Šibenik (8 daily; 1hr 20min).

Tourist office Dr Franje Tuđmana 24 ⊕022 664 822, ⊛tz-knin.hr).

EATING

Tvrđava Tvrđava bb ⊕022 663 155. The fortress's erstwhile gatehouse provides a suitably evocative home to a restaurant that concentrates mainly on the meaty fare of inland Croatia, with grilled pork and roast lamb predominating. Outdoor seating on a grass-covered bastion offers expansive views of the Dinaric mountains. Daily 9am–midnight.

Primošten

Heaped up on an island that's joined to the mainland by a short causeway, **PRIMOŠTEN**, 20km south of Šibenik, is enchanting when seen from a distance, although the place comes over as blandly packagey once you get up close. Its main attribute is the ultra-clear water that laps the pebble and rock **beaches** of the wooded promontory north of town, where there are also a number of hotels. The landscape around Primošten is famous for having preserved a patchwork of dry-stone walls, vineyard plots and olive groves that has changed little for centuries. Much of the Šibenik region's best **Babić wine** is produced around here, and you should definitely make the effort to down a glass or few of the stuff if you are sticking around here for an evening or longer.

ARRIVAL AND INFORMATION — PRIMOŠTEN

By bus Primošten's small bus station is uphill on the landward side of the causeway.

Tourist office Trg biskupa Arnelića 2, just inside the Old Town (June, Sept & Oct daily 8am–9pm; July & Aug daily 8am–10pm; Nov–May Mon–Fri 8am–2pm; ⊕022 571 111, ⊛summernet.hr/primosten).

ACCOMMODATION

Private **rooms** (200Kn) and **apartments** (two-person apartments 380Kn, four-person apartments 520–710Kn) are available from **Nik** agency at Raduča 2 (daily 8am–10pm; ⊕022 571 200, ⊛nik.hr) and **Dalmatinka Turist Buro** on Zagrebačka 8 (⊕022 570 323, ⊛dalmatinka.hr).

Camping Adriatiq Huljerat bb ⊕022 571 223, ⊛autocamp-adriatiq.com. About 3km north of town on the main coastal road, this occupies a terraced site overlooking the shore, has good pine-tree cover and an attractive rocky beach. Mid-April to mid-Oct. **60Kn** per person, from **55Kn** per pitch

EATING AND DRINKING

Mediteran Put briga 13 ⊕098 445 945, ⊛mediteran-primosten.hr. In an Old Town alleyway just uphill from the tourist office, *Mediteran* offers an extensive range of grilled fish and seafood, with a constant flow of house Babić keeping the evening well oiled. Mid-April to mid-Oct 1pm–midnight.

Popaj Franje Tuđmana 24 ⊕022 570 684. Garden café attached to a house on the mainland side of Primošten, a must for coffee and cakes during the daytime and a laid-back drinking choice come the evening. The next-door *Popaj* fast-food kiosk sells *ćevapi* and sandwiches. Daily 9am–midnight.

NIGHTLIFE

Aurora Kamenar ⊕098 523 343, ⊛auroraclub.hr. Two kilometres uphill from the town centre, this is one of the most popular clubs in central Dalmatia, with a summer-long repertoire of techno and house DJs, and gigs by Croatian and ex-Yu pop stars. It's a big place with several floors, a garden terrace and a pizzeria. Check the website for details. Daily 10pm–4am.

MUSIC SHOP

Split and the south Dalmatian coast

PAVEMENT CAFÉ, SPLIT

6

Split and the south Dalmatian coast

Southern Dalmatia possesses one of Europe's most dramatic shorelines, as the stark, grey wall of the coastal mountains sweeps down towards a lush seaboard ribbon dotted with palm trees and olive plantations. It is one of the most urbanized parts of the Adriatic coast, with suburban Split creeping earnestly along the shore in both directions, and the resorts of the Makarska Riviera strung together towards the south. However it is also home to antiquated villages and harsh natural wildernesses, which can often be found just a few minutes' walk uphill from the coastal strip.

The hub around which everything on this stretch of coast revolves is **Split**, a teeming, chaotic but ultimately addictive city that also serves as the Adriatic's main ferry port. Just outside the city, the ruins of Roman **Salona**, the Renaissance town of **Trogir** and the medieval Croatian stronghold of **Klis** are the main draws. The coast south of Split is probably mainland Dalmatia's most enchanting stretch, with the mountains glowering over a string of long pebble beaches, although along the **Makarska Riviera** crowded resorts are beginning to put the squeeze on the fishing villages. The dramatic **Cetina gorge** and the weird lakes of **Imotski** provide ample excuses for excursions inland.

Split has good **bus** links with the towns along the coast, and is also the main **ferry** port for the southern Dalmatian islands (see p.326).

Split

With its seafront cafés and ancient alleyways, shouting stallholders and travellers on the move, bustling, exuberant **SPLIT** is one of the Mediterranean's most compelling cities. It has a unique historical heritage too, having grown out of the **palace** built here by the Roman Emperor Diocletian in 295AD. The palace remains the city's central ingredient, having been gradually transformed into a warren of houses, tenements, churches and chapels by the various peoples who came to live here after Diocletian's successors had departed. Lying beyond the Roman/medieval tangle of central Split lie suburban streets full of palms and exotic plants, followed by stately rows of socialist-era housing blocks that look like something out of a modernist architectural stylebook.

As Croatia's second city, Split is a hotbed of regional pride, and disparagement of Zagreb-dwellers is a frequent, if usually harmless, component of local banter. The city is famous for the vivacious outdoor life that takes over the streets in all but the coldest and wettest months: as long as the sun is shining, the swish cafés of the waterfront Riva are never short of custom.

KLIS FORTRESS

Highlights

❶ **Diocletian's Palace, Split** With its unique tangle of Roman and medieval remains, Diocletian's former palace forms the vibrant heart of today's Split. **See p.286**

❷ **Bačvice beach** This has long been Split's main focus of summer leisure, with real sand underfoot and a shoreline promenade lined with cafés. **See p.298**

❸ **Salona** Roam the expansive site of this ruined Roman city, set among olive groves and only a short bus ride from Split. **See p.306**

❹ **Klis Fortress** One of the most dramatic medieval castles in the country, perched on a rock high above the city of Split. **See p.307**

❺ **Trogir** A warren of stone-paved streets presided over by a stunning Romanesque cathedral. **See p.308**

❻ **Biokovo** Perfect for demanding hikes on the heights, or easier strolls in through the foothill villages, this mountain range inland from Makarska is one of the natural wonders of the Adriatic. **See box, p.320**

❼ **Frog and eel stew** Restaurants near Metković specialize in this spicy dish indigenous to the wetlands of the Neretva delta. **See p.324**

HIGHLIGHTS ARE MARKED ON THE MAP ON P.284

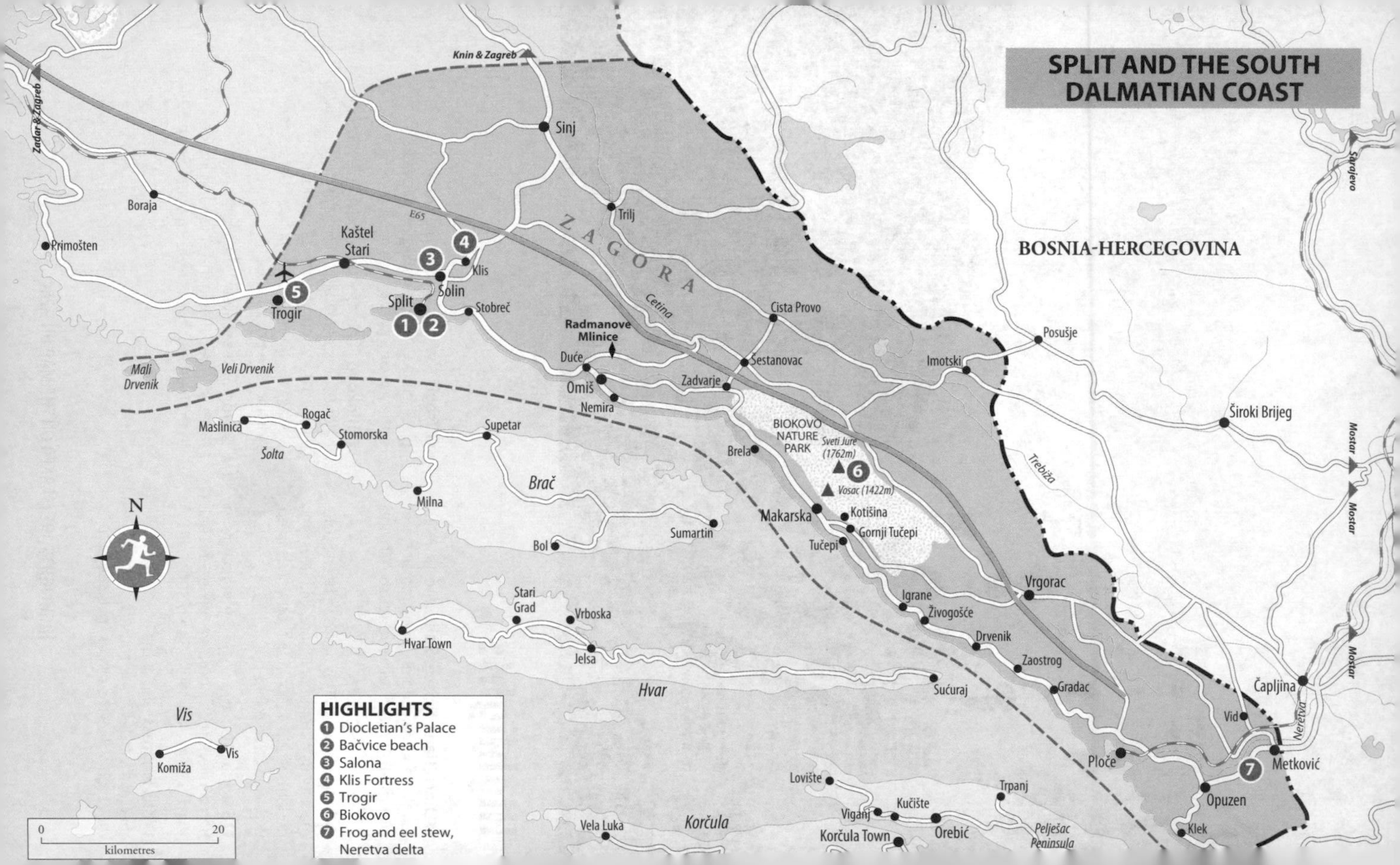

SPLIT AND THE SOUTH DALMATIAN COAST
BOSNIA-HERCEGOVINA
Zadar & Zagreb
Knin & Zagreb
Sarajevo
Mostar
Mostar
Mostar
Sinj
Boraja
Primošten
Trilj
ZAGORA
E65
Kaštel Stari
Klis
Solin
Split
Stobreč
Trogir
Cetina
Cista Provo
Posušje
Radmanove Mlinice
Duće
Omiš
Nemira
Šestanovac
Zadvarje
Imotski
Široki Brijeg
Mali Drvenik
Veli Drvenik
Maslinica
Rogač
Stomorska
Šolta
Supetar
Milna
Brač
Bol
Sumartin
Brela
BIOKOVO NATURE PARK
Sveti Jure (1762m)
Vosac (1422m)
Makarska
Kotišina
Gornji Tučepi
Tučepi
Trebiža
Vrgorac
Igrane
Živogošće
Drvenik
Zaostrog
Gradac
Stari Grad
Vrboska
Hvar Town
Jelsa
Hvar
Sućuraj
Čapljina
Neretva
Vid
Ploče
Metković
Opuzen
Klek
Lovište
Trpanj
Kučište
Viganj
Orebić
Korčula Town
Vela Luka
Korčula
Pelješac Peninsula
Vis
Komiža
Vis
N
0
20
kilometres
HIGHLIGHTS
1 Diocletian's Palace
2 Bačvice beach
3 Salona
4 Klis Fortress
5 Trogir
6 Biokovo
7 Frog and eel stew, Neretva delta

FOOD AND DRINK IN SOUTHERN DALMATIA

The traditional Adriatic repertoire of grilled fish, fried squid and seafood stews is central to the cuisine of southern Dalmatia. In addition, Dalmatian **pašticada** (slabs of beef stewed in prunes) is particularly good in Split and Makarska, where it features on the lunchtime menus of almost every *konoba*. The towns inland from the coast and along the Neretva delta are famous for their **frogs' legs** – which are either fried in breadcrumbs, grilled with garlic, or wrapped in slivers of *pršut*. The Neretva is also famous for its tangy, succulent **eels**, especially when used as the key ingredient of *brodet* – a spicy red stew that's often accompanied by a glossy yellow mound of polenta.

Brief history

According to conventional wisdom, Split didn't exist at all until the Emperor Diocletian (see box, p.289) decided to build his retirement home here, although recent archeological finds suggest that a Roman settlement of sorts was founded here before Diocletian's builders arrived. **Diocletian's Palace** was begun in 295 AD and finished ten years later, when the emperor came back to his native Illyria to escape the cares of empire, cure his rheumatism and grow cabbages. Even in retirement Diocletian maintained an elaborate court here in a building that housed both luxurious palatial apartments in the south of the complex and a military garrison in the north. The palace as a whole measured some 200m by 240m, with walls 2m thick and almost 25m high, while at each corner there was a fortified keep, and four towers along each of the land walls.

The palace was home to a succession of regional despots after Diocletian's death, although by the sixth century it had fallen into disuse. In 614, it was suddenly repopulated by refugees fleeing nearby Salona, which had just been sacked by the Avars and Slavs. The newcomers salvaged living quarters out of Diocletian's neglected buildings, improvising a home in what must have been one of the most grandiose squats of all time. They built fortifications, walled in arches, boarded up windows and repelled attacks from the mainland, accepting Byzantine sovereignty in return for being allowed to preserve a measure of autonomy. The resulting city developed cultural and trading links with the embryonic Croatian state inland, and was absorbed by the Hungaro-Croatian kingdom in the eleventh century.

Venetians, Ottomans and Austrians

By the fourteenth century, Split had grown beyond the confines of the palace, with today's Narodni trg becoming the new centre of a walled city that stretched as far west as the street now known as Marmontova. **Venetian rule**, established in 1420, occasioned an upsurge in the city's economic fortunes, as the city's port was developed as an entrepôt for Ottoman goods. Turkish power was to be an ever-constant threat, however: **Ottoman** armies attacked Split on numerous occasions, coming nearest to capturing it in 1657, when they occupied Marjan hill before being driven off by reinforcements hastily shipped in from Venice, Trogir and Hvar.

During the nineteenth century, **Austrian rule** stimulated trade and helped speed the development of Split's port.

Twentieth-century Split

Split's biggest period of growth occurred after World War II, when **industrial growth** attracted growing numbers of economic migrants from all over the country. Many of these newcomers came from the Zagora, the rural uplands just inland, and ended up working in the enormous **shipyards** – colloquially known as the Škver – on Split's northwestern edge, providing the city with a new working-class layer. It was

For a history of Dalmatia see the box on pp.246–247.

MILJENKO SMOJE (1923–95)

Split is famous for its self-deprecating humour, best exemplified by the writings of **Miljenko Smoje**, a native of the inner-city district of Veli Varoš. Smoje's books, written in Dalmatian dialect, document the lives of an imaginary group of local archetypes and brought the wit of the Splićani to a nationwide audience. An adaptation of his works, *Naše malo misto* ("Our Little Town"), and its follow up, *Velo Misto* ("Big Town"), were the most popular comedy programmes in Croatian – and probably Yugoslav – television history.

6

always said that productivity at the Škver was directly related to the on-the-pitch fortunes of **Hajduk Split** (see box, p.305), the football team which more than anything else in Split served to bind traditional inhabitants of the city with recent arrivals. Beginning with the big televised music festivals of the 1960s, Split also became the nation's unofficial **pop music** capital, promoted as a kind of Croatian San Remo. Since then generations of balladeering medallion men have emerged from the city to regale the nation with their songs of mandolin-playing fishermen and dark-eyed girls in the moonlight.

Into the present

Split entered the twenty-first century as a transit city in which people spent a few hours before boarding their ferries. However the last decade has seen an enormous boost in **tourism**, with new hostels and new hotels (with ever higher prices) catering for travellers who want to experience the city's unique urban buzz. As Split becomes wealthier, however, it is also becoming socially more **conservative** and provincial – the kind of place where moral-majority citizens campaign to have Gay Pride marches banned from the streets. The current expansion of **Split University** may help to alleviate this slide towards philistinism, with more and more young talents being encouraged to stay in the city rather than drift off to Zagreb.

The palace

Adapted long ago to serve as Split's town centre, **Diocletian's Palace** (see map, p.288) is certainly not an archeological "site". Although set-piece buildings such as Diocletian's mausoleum (now the cathedral) and the Temple of Jupiter (now a baptistry) still remain, other aspects of the palace have been tinkered with so much by successive generations that it is no longer recognizable as an ancient Roman structure. Little remains of the imperial apartments, although the medieval tenements, shops and offices that have taken their place were built in large part using stones and columns salvaged from Diocletian's original buildings. Despite its architectural pedigree, the palace area hasn't always been the most desirable part of the city in which to live. During the interwar period it was dubbed the *get* ("ghetto") and – abandoned to the

SPLIT ORIENTATION

Nearly everything worth seeing in Split is concentrated in the compact **Old Town** behind the waterfront Riva, made up in part of the various remains and conversions of **Diocletian's Palace** itself, and the medieval additions to the west of it. You can walk across this area in about ten minutes, although it would take a lifetime to explore all its nooks and crannies. On either side the Old Town fades into low-rise suburbs of utilitarian stone houses grouped tightly around narrow alleys – **Veli Varoš**, to the west, and **Manuš**, to the east, are the most unspoiled – and, although there are no specific sights, worth a brief wander. West of the city centre, the wooded **Marjan peninsula** commands fine views over the coast and islands from its heights. The best of the **beaches** are on the north side of Marjan, or east of the ferry dock at **Bačvice**.

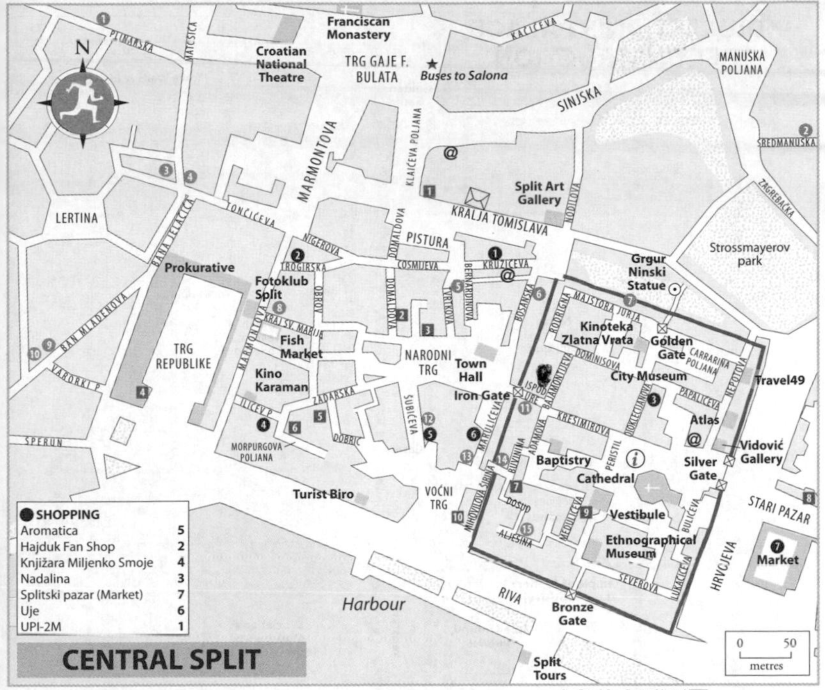

Bus, Train & Ferry Terminal (300m)

HOTELS		HOSTELS		SNACKS AND FAST FOOD				CAFÉS AND BARS	
Bellevue	4	Adriatic Hostel	8	Kantun Paulina	3	Konoba Dioklecijan	15	Bifora	5
Kaštel	10	Goli & Bosi	6	Keko	6	Konoba kod Jože	2	Bobis	11
Marmont	5	Silver Central	1	**RESTAURANTS**		Konoba Varoš	10	Figa	14
Palace Suites	3	Split Hostel/ Booze N Snooze	2	Galija	4	Le Monde/ Kavana Bistro Anika	1	Galerija Plavca	13
Slavija	7			Hvaranin	9	Noštromo	8	Po Bota	12
Vestibul	9							Teak	7

urban poor, down-at-heel White Russian émigrés and red-light bars – became synonymous with loose morals and shady dealings. Nowadays the palace area is once more the centre of urban life, hosting a daily melee of tourists and shoppers.

The Riva

Best place to start exploring the seaward side of the palace is Split's broad and lively **Riva** (officially the Obala hrvatskog naradnog preporoda). Running along the palace's southern facade, into which shops, cafés and a warren of tiny flats have been built, the Riva is where a large part of the city's population congregates day and night to meet friends, catch up on gossip or idle away an hour or two in a café. In 2007 the Riva was subjected to an expensive facelift by architecture bureau 3LHD, with pristine Brač-marble flagstones laid beneath the palm trees, and neat new café awnings held up by what look like huge hockey-sticks. It's a new look that will take the notoriously conservative Splićani decades to get used to.

The Bronze Gate

The main approach to the palace from the Riva is through the **Bronze Gate** (Mjedena vrata), a functional and anonymous gateway that originally gave access to the sea, which once came right up to the palace. Inside is a vaulted space which once formed the basement of Diocletian's central hall, the middle part of his residential complex, now occupied by arts and crafts stalls.

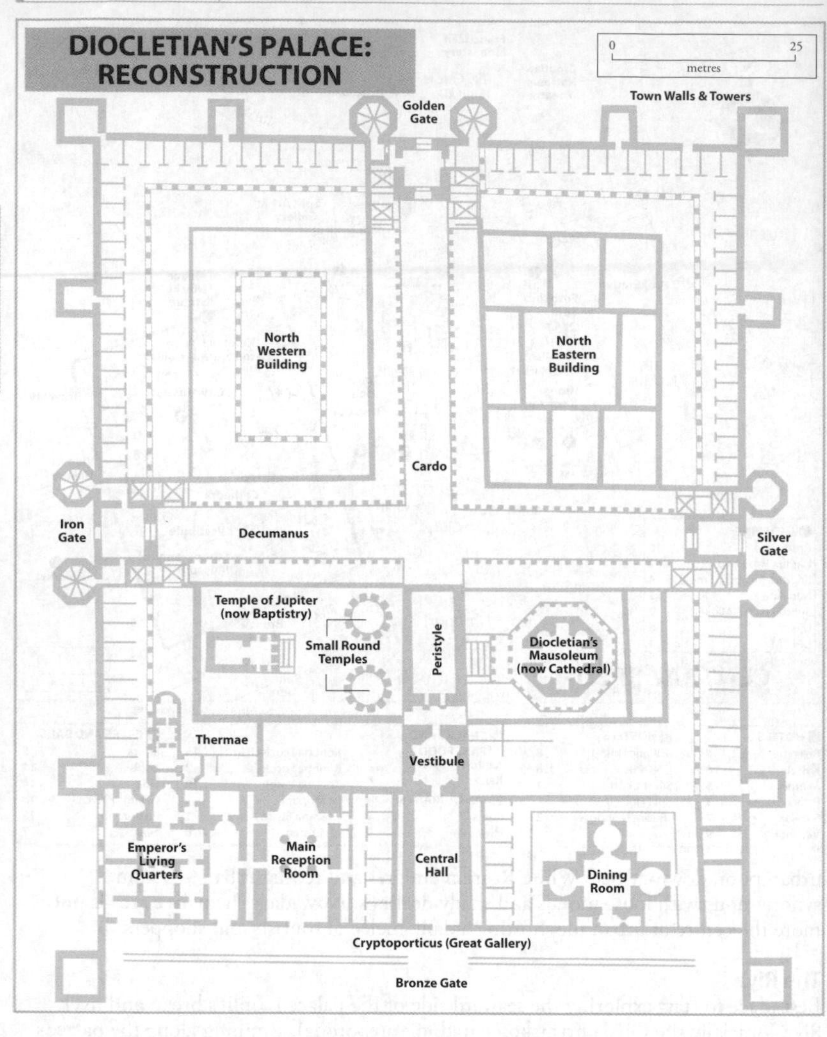

The palace basement

Daily: summer 8am–8pm; winter 8am–noon & 4–7pm • 10Kn

Accessible from the Bronze Gate entrance is the so-called **basement** (*podrum)*, built in Diocletian's time to support the apartments above – until 1956 they remained unexplored and full of centuries of debris. Now largely empty, the basement is a marvellously evocative subterranean space which provides a good idea of what the palace must have once looked like; the basement's ground plan is an exact mirror of the imperial living quarters that formerly stood above. The long corridor that stretches east and west of the Bronze Gate corresponds to the **cryptoporticus**, or great gallery, along which the emperor would have promenaded. The large hall off the western end of the corridor stood beneath Diocletian's main reception room, while the cruciform group of chambers off its eastern end stood beneath the triclinium, or dining room. The basement is sometimes used as the highly atmospheric venue for contemporary art exhibitions.

DIOCLETIAN (245–312)

Born the son of slaves, **Diocletian** was a native of Dalmatia – and possibly grew up in Salona, next door to Split. Despite his humble origins he proved himself quickly in the Roman military, becoming emperor in 284 at the age of 39. For 21 years he attempted to provide stability and direction to an empire under pressure – goals he achieved with some measure of success. Believing that the job of running the empire was too big for one man, however, Diocletian divided the role into four, the **Tetrarchy**, carefully parcelling out responsibility among his partners – a decision which some historians believe led directly to disintegration and civil war. Diocletian was also renowned for his persecution of Christians: those martyred during his reign included the patron saints of Split, Domnius and Anastasius, along with many other leading religious figures – Sebastian, George, Theodore and Vitus among them.

The motives for Diocletian's early **retirement** have been the subject of much speculation. It was obviously planned well in advance by a man who feared he was no longer up to the rigours of government. As a highly innovative emperor, Diocletian obviously saw the very concept of retirement – a total novelty among Roman rulers – as a logical adjunct to his other reforms. However, the power-sharing system he left behind soon disintegrated once he was no longer at the helm, leading ultimately to the rise of a new strongman, **Constantine the Great** (ruled 309–38).

6

The Peristyle

Symbolic heart of Diocletian's Palace is the **Peristyle** (Peristil), once the central courtyard of the palace complex and the crossing point of its main streets. These days it's a lively square and meeting point, crowded with café tables and surrounded by the stately arches that once framed the courtyard. On the east side of the Peristyle stands a black granite Egyptian **sphinx**, dating from around 1500 BC, one of the two that originally flanked the entrance to Diocletian's mausoleum.

The Peristyle has been the site of two major cultural scandals in modern times, the first in 1968, when three students used the cover of darkness to paint the square's paving stones red – the colour of both revolutionary socialist idealism and the ossified political elites in socialist states such as Yugoslavia. The action, which became known as **Red Peristyle**, has gone down in history as one of the key events in Croatian conceptual art, although the authorities were quick to condemn it as vandalism at the time. The thirtieth anniversary of Red Peristyle was marked on the night of January 10, 1998, when Igor Grubić painted a black circle in the centre of the Peristyle (black being the colour of the extreme right and, by implication, the Croatia of the 1990s) – a gesture which engendered much the same official response.

The cathedral

Peristil • Mon–Sat 7am–noon & 5–7pm • Cathedral 10Kn; Campanile 5Kn; Treasury 10kn; Crypt 5kn

Towering above Split's Palace precinct is the belfry of the **Cathedral of St Domnius** (Katedrala svetog Dujma), a medieval conversion of a building that initially served as Diocletian's mausoleum: the octagonal building surrounded by an arcade of Corinthian columns, it housed Diocletian's body for at least 170 years until it mysteriously disappeared – no one knows where.

The cathedral porch is entered through an arch guarded by two Romanesque lions with a motley collection of human figures riding on their backs, including Greek-born Maria Lascaris, wife of Hungarian King Bela IV, who briefly took refuge from the Tatars in the nearby stronghold of Klis. The walnut-and-oak main **doors** – carved in 1214 by local artist Andrija Buvina with an inspired comic-strip-style sequence showing 28 scenes from the life of Christ – are scuffed and scraped at the bottom, but in fine condition further up. On the right looms the six-storey **campanile**, begun in the thirteenth century but not finished until 1908 – the climb up is worth the effort for the panoramic view over the city and beyond.

6

ROBERT ADAM AND DIOCLETIAN'S PALACE

Our knowledge of Diocletian's Palace owes much to the eighteenth-century Scottish architect **Robert Adam**, who set out to provide a visual record of what remained of the palace, believing that contemporary European builders had much to learn from Roman construction techniques. Adam arrived in Split in 1757 with a team of draughtsmen; they spent five weeks in the city despite the hostility of the Venetian governor, who almost had them arrested as spies. This didn't prevent Adam from enjoying the trip: "the people are vastly polite, everything vastly cheap; a most wholesome air and glorious situation" was how he summed the town up. The resulting book of engravings of the palace caused a sensation, offering inspiration to Neoclassical architects all over Britain and Europe. Adam's work was certainly seminal in the development of the Georgian style in England, and large chunks of London, Bath and Bristol may be claimed to owe something of their space, symmetry and grace to Diocletian's buildings in Split.

Inside, the **dome** is ringed by two levels of Corinthian columns dating from the first century BC, while running around the base is a frieze depicting racing chariots, hunting scenes and, in one corner, portraits of Diocletian and his wife Priscia. Immediately to the left of the entrance, the **pulpit** is a beautifully proportioned example of Romanesque art, sitting on capitals tangled with foliage, snakes and strange beasts.

The altars

Moving clockwise round the nave, the first of the major altars is the **Altar of St Domnius**, honouring the first bishop of Salona's underground Christian community, who was beheaded in 304. Built by Giovanni Morlaiter in 1767, it features a pair of angels holding a reliquary on which a group of celestial cherubs cavort – a symbol of man's journey to the afterlife.

Farther around lies the church's finest feature, the **Altar of St Anastasius** (Staš), which preserves the bones of a martyr who, on Diocletian's orders, was thrown in a river with a stone tied to him. The saint's sarcophagus bears Juraj Dalmatinac's *Flagellation of Christ*, a relief of 1448 showing Jesus pawed and brutalized by some peculiarly oafish persecutors. The Baroque **high altar**, occupying the arch which leads through to the choir, features a pair of delicate, gilded angels supporting what looks like a cherub-encrusted carriage clock.

Moving onwards, Bonino of Milan's fifteenth-century **Altar of St Domnius** is where the saint's bones were once kept. Sheltered beneath a flowery Gothic ciborium, this uses an ancient Roman sarcophagus bearing a relief of a man with hunting dogs as a base, on which rests a larger sarcophagus etched with a reclining figure of the bishop.

Choirstalls and treasury

Behind the cathedral's high altar stands a row of delicately carved wooden **choirstalls**, dated to about 1200. To the right, a flight of steps leads up to the **treasury** (*riznica*), which holds handwritten missals, thirteenth-century Madonnas and reliquary busts of the city's three great martyrs – Domnius, Anastasius and Arnerius (Arnir), a bishop of Split who was stoned to death in 1180.

Crypt

Heading outside and round the back of the cathedral brings you to the early medieval **crypt** (*kripta*), where a tomb-like passageway emerges into a circular space surrounded by pointy-arched niches. There are few exhibits down here, but the architectural simplicity of the place exerts a wonderful chill-out effect.

The baptistry

Kraj sv. Ivana • Mon–Sat 7am–noon & 5–7pm • 10Kn

Opposite the cathedral, a narrow alley runs down to the attractive **baptistry** (*krstionica*), a temple built in Diocletian's time and variously attributed to the cults of

Janus or Jupiter. It has an elaborate coffered ceiling and well-preserved figures of Hercules and Apollo on the eastern portal, while later Christian additions include a skinny statue of John the Baptist by Ivan Meštrović (a late work of 1954) and, more famously, an eleventh-century baptismal font with a relief showing a Croatian ruler receiving homage from a man prostrate at his feet – most probably a priest being ritually inducted into the service of both God and king. Above the two figures runs a swirling pleated pattern known as *plutej*, a design typical of the Croatian Romanesque which has subsequently been adopted as a national symbol.

The vestibule and around

At the southern end of the Peristyle, steps lead up to a cone-shaped, roofless chamber which once served as the palace **vestibule**, in which visitors would wait before being summoned into the presence of the ex-emperor.

The vestibule marks the entrance to the area once occupied by Diocletian's private apartments, nowadays made up small interlocking squares where medieval tenement buildings brush up against the sea-facing walls of the palace. The area used to be the favoured meeting-place of Split's prostitutes and drug addicts, and is still fondly referred to by locals as the *kenjara* ("shit hole"). At the south end of this area, along Severova, windows in the palace wall provide an excellent vantage point from which to spy on goings-on down on the Riva while, to the west, Alješina threads its way through one of the most abandoned and mysterious parts of the palace, eventually bringing you out at Mihovilova širina (see p.292).

Ethnographic Museum

Severova 1 • June–Sept Mon–Fri 9am–7pm, Sat 9am–1pm; Oct–May Mon–Fri 9am–4pm, Sat 9am–1pm • 10Kn • ⓣ 021 344 164, ⓦ etnografski-muzej-split.hr

On the far side of the vestibule, the medieval Božičević Palace is home to Split's **Ethnographic Museum**, where a suite of superbly renovated medieval rooms provides the perfect backdrop to a display of Dalmatian folk costumes. The museum extends into the beautifully restored St Andrew's Church (Crkva svetog Andrije), a former imperial bedroom adapted for Christian purposes in the ninth century.

The Vidović Gallery

Poljana kraljice Jelene • June–Sept Tues–Fri 9am–9pm, Sat & Sun 9am–4pm; Oct–May Tues–Fri 9am–4pm, Sat & Sun 10am–1pm • 10Kn • ⓣ 021 360 155, ⓦ galerija-vidovic.com

Just inside the Silver Gate (Sebrna vrata), the palace's main eastern entrance, the **Vidović Gallery** (Galerija Vidović) is a beautifully restored Romanesque house holding the works of local painter Emanuel Vidović (1872–1953), whose paintings of Venice, Trogir and Split convey a compelling sense of atmosphere. Vidović developed a famously murky style, as if trying to catch the look of a landscape in twilight, or during a rainstorm – imagine J.M.W. Turner painting at nightfall and you'll get the idea. Vidović was also a keen collector, and his re-created studio is full of fascinating *objets d'art*, notably the delightful wooden statues of Dalmatian villagers by self-taught sculptor Petar Smajić (1910–85).

The City Museum

Papalićeva 1 • May–Oct Tues–Fri 9am–9pm, Mon, Sat & Sun 9am–4pm; Nov–April Tues–Sun 9am–4pm, Sat & Sun 10am–1pm • 10Kn • ⓣ 021 360 171, ⓦ mgst.net

Set amidst rows of tottering medieval houses, the **City Museum** (Gradski muzej) is housed in the Juraj Dalmatinac-designed **Papalić Palace**, a typical example of the sturdy Gothic mansions built by Split's fifteenth-century aristocracy. An unobtrusive gateway leads through to a secluded, ivy-covered courtyard centred on a well adorned with the star-and-feathers symbol of the Papalić family, with a delicate loggia at ground level and an outdoor stone stairway leading to the first-floor apartments. Inside are well-laid-out displays of medieval weaponry and sculptural fragments, including a serene Pietà by Nikola Firentinac. A first-floor reception room with a restored wooden-beam ceiling contains pictures and manuscripts relating to Marko Marulić (1450–1524), author of the biblically inspired epic *Judita*, one of the first poems to be written in the Croatian language.

The Golden Gate

Grandest of the palace gates is the **Golden Gate** (Zlatna vrata), the northern entrance to the palace and the beginning of what was the main road to Salona. The arched niches (now empty) originally contained statues, and the four plinths on top of the gate once supported likenesses of Diocletian and his fellow tetrarchs.

Just outside the gate there's another Meštrović work, the gigantic statue of the tenth-century Bishop **Grgur Ninski**. It was completed in 1929 to mark the 1000th anniversary of the Synod of Split, at which Grgur, Bishop of Nin, fought for the right to use Croatian in the liturgy instead of Latin. Catching the bishop in stiff mid-gesture, it's more successful as a patriotic statement than as a piece of sculpture. This bronze mammoth used to stand in the Peristyle before it was moved during World War II, when the Italian occupiers attempted to cleanse the town centre of anything resembling a Croatian national symbol.

Narodni trg and around

Standing at the heart of medieval Split is **Narodni trg** (People's Square, although it's colloquially known as "Pjaca" or piazza), the public space that stretches just outside the **Iron Gate** (Željezna vrata), the palace's western entrance. Narodni trg replaced the Peristyle as the city's main square in the fourteenth century, and is overlooked to the east by a Romanesque clock tower with the remains of a medieval sundial. The north side of the square is dominated by the fifteenth-century **Town Hall** (Gradska vijećnica), with a ground-floor loggia of three large pointed arches supported by stumpy pillars – it frequently plays host to major art or history exhibitions in the summer.

West of the square lie the bustling narrow streets and passages of the medieval town. To the south, Marulićeva leads down towards **Mihovilova širina**, a small square whose café-bars get packed on warm summer evenings, and the adjoining Trg braće Radića, more popularly known as **Voćni trg** (Fruit Square) because of the market that used to be held here. There's a large statue of Marko Marulić, supplied by the industrious Meštrović, in the middle, and an octagonal tower that once formed part of the fifteenth-century Venetian castle, or *kaštel* – most of which has now either disappeared or been incorporated into residential buildings.

Split Art Gallery

Kralja Tomislava 15 • May–Sept Mon 11am–4pm, Tues–Fri 11am–7pm, Sat 11am–3pm; Oct–April Mon 9am–2pm, Tues–Fri 9am–5pm, Sat 9am–1pm • 20Kn • ⓣ 021 350 112, ⓦ galum.hr

Opened in May 2009 in the expansive halls of a former hospital, the **Split Art Gallery** (Galerija Umjetnina) kicks off with a collection of medieval altarpieces from all over Dalmatia. After a frankly boring Baroque section, the display comes startlingly back to life with the reclining lady that forms the subject matter of Vlaho Bukovac's *Divan* (painted in 1905), followed by a handful of Emanuel Vidović's strange, unsettling seascapes in semi-darkness. Moving on, two Dalmatian painters who loved to splash their colours around were Ignjat Job (1895–1936), represented here by views of Brač, and Ivo Dulčić (1916–75), whose Adriatic island-scapes have a jazzy modernity. Arguably the most gripping section of the gallery is the contemporary collection on the ground floor, where Boris Bućan's theatre posters, Dalibor Martinis's video works and Lovro Artuković's painterly portraits show the breadth of the Croatian art scene. The gallery's café is a cool place to relax over coffee.

Marmontova

At the western exit from the Old Town, **Marmontova** is a pedestrianized thoroughfare that marks the boundary of medieval Split. Marking the southern end of Marmontova is **Trg republike**, an elongated square set back from the water and surrounded on three sides by the grandiose neo-Renaissance city-council buildings known as the **Prokurative** – it's put to good use as a venue for outdoor concerts in summer.

Halfway up Marmontova, on the eastern side of the street, is an animated and pungent **fish market**, the scene of shopping frenzy most mornings, especially Fridays.

Fotoklub Split

Marmontova 5 • Mon–Fri 10.30am–12.30pm & 6.30–9.30pm, Sat 10.30am–12.30pm • Free • ⓣ 021 347 597, ⓦ fotoklubsplit.hr

Fotoklub Split offers an inviting range of themed photography exhibitions. Not only does it showcase the amateur and professional work of the Fotoklub's members, but features occasional international shows too.

Franciscan Monastery

Trg Gaje Bulata

Presiding over Trg Gaje Bulata at the northern end of Marmontova, the church of the **Franciscan Monastery** (Franjevački samostan) is worth a peek for the large fresco behind the high altar, a flamboyantly expressionistic work by Dubrovnik artist Ivo Dulčić. A central figure of Jesus hovers above the Adriatic coastline, offering salvation to the matchstick forms below, most of which are dressed in colourful Dalmatian costumes. On his left are Cyril and Methodius, inventors of Glagolitic, the script used by the medieval Croatian church, while floating in the sky are a bull, lion and eagle – symbolizing saints Luke, Mark and John the Evangelist respectively.

Archeological Museum

Zrinsko-Frankopanska 25 • June–Sept Mon–Sat 9am–2pm & 4–8pm; Oct–May Mon–Fri 9am–2pm & 4–8pm, Sat 9am–2pm • 20Kn • ⓣ 021 329 340, ⓦ armus.hr

Much of southern Dalmatia's considerable ancient heritage is on display at the **Archeological Museum** (Arheološki muzej), a sizeable collection of Illyrian, Greek, medieval and – particularly – Roman artefacts, mostly plucked from the rich excavation sites at nearby Salona. Exhibits include delicate votive figurines, amulets and – in a section entitled "domestic life" – an oil lamp embellished with a tiny peepshow of lewd love-making. Outside, the arcaded courtyard is crammed with a wonderful array of Greek, Roman and early Christian stelae, sarcophagi and decorative sculpture. Of particular note are the third-century **Salonan sarcophagi** to the left of the entrance: one depicts the Hippolytus and Phaedra legend and is in superb condition – the marble still glistens – while the other is of a Calydonian boar hunt, which in Robert Adam's pictures stood outside Split's baptistry. To the right of the entrance is a fourth-century sarcophagus known as the "Good Shepherd", which appears to mix up the Christian motif of the shepherd with pagan symbols of Eros and Hades on its end panels.

The Marjan peninsula

Bus #12 from Trg republike (every 30min) runs along the south side of the peninsula to Bene bay

Crisscrossed by footpaths and minor roads, the wooded heights of the **Marjan peninsula** offer the easiest escape from the bustle of central Split. From the Old Town it's an easy ten-minute walk up Senjska, which ascends westwards through the district of Veli Varoš, arriving after about ten minutes at the *Vidilica* café on Marjan's eastern shoulder (see p.304). There's a small Jewish graveyard round the back of the café, and to its right a stepped path climbs towards **Vrh Marjana**, where there's a wider view of the coast and islands.

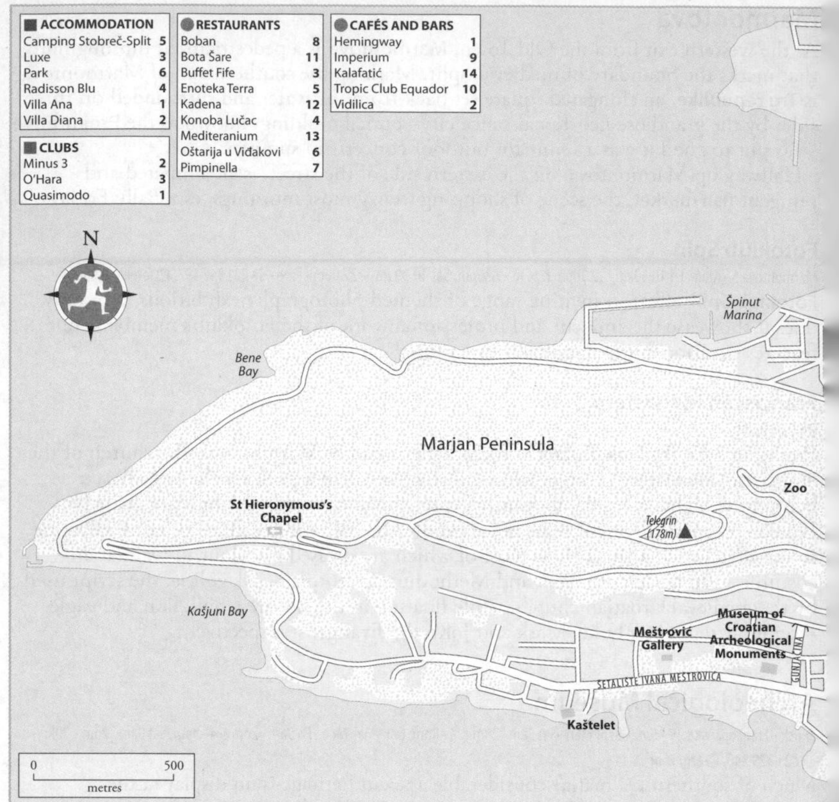

About 1km further west, there's an even better panorama from the peninsula's highest point, 178-metre-high **Telegrin**. Keeping to the left of the *Vidilica* brings you to a path which heads round the south side of the hill, arriving after about five minutes at the thirteenth-century **St Nicholas's Chapel** (Sveti Nikola), a simple structure with a sloping belfry tacked on to one side like a buttress. From here, the path continues for 2km, with wooded hillside to the right and the seaside suburbs of Marjan's south coast on the left, before arriving at **St Hieronymous's Chapel** (Sveti Jere), a simple shed-like structure pressed hard against a cliff – medieval hermits used to live in the caves that are still visible in the rock above. From here you can descend towards the road which leads round the base of the peninsula, or cross its rocky spine to reach Marjan's fragrant, pine-covered northern side. Paths emerge at sea level near **Bene bay**, where you'll find a combination of rocky and concreted bathing areas and a couple of cafés.

Marjan's main cultural attractions are on its southern side, in the suburbs of Zvončac and Meje.

The Museum of Croatian Archeological Monuments

Stjepana Gunjače bb • Mon–Fri 9am–4pm, Sat 9am–2pm • 20Kn • ☎ 021 323 901, Ⓦ mhas-split.hr • The museum is a 20min walk from the centre or a short ride on bus #12 from Trg republike

Housed in an oversized concrete edifice with huge open-plan halls and piped-in organ muzak, the **Museum of Croatian Archeological Monuments** (Muzej hrvatskih arheoloških spomenika) makes a concerted attempt to remind people of Split's

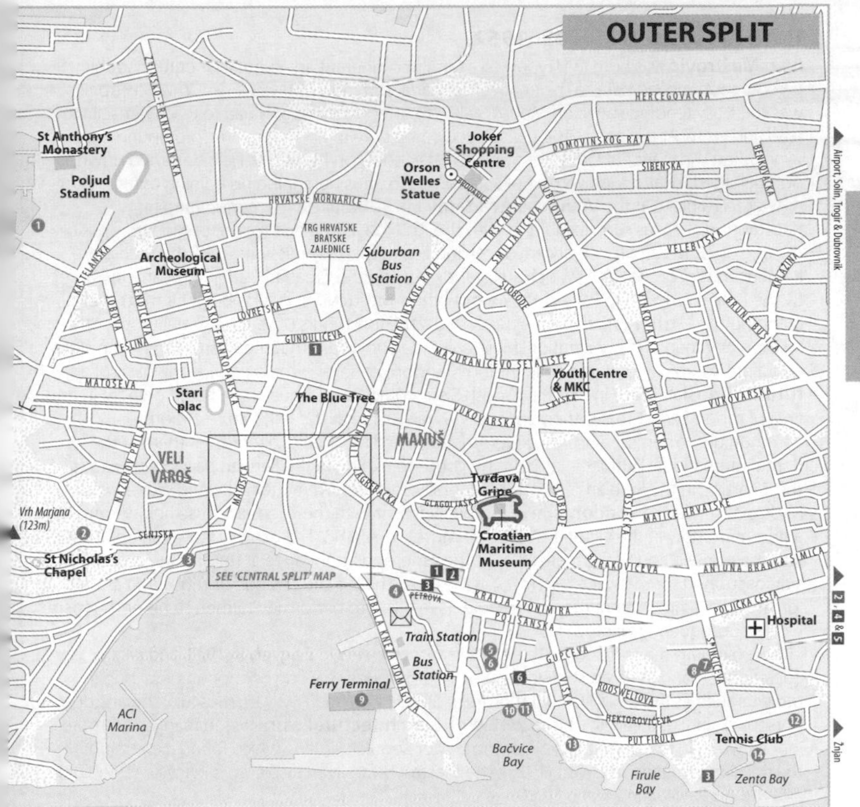

medieval Croatian heritage, a phase of local history that's often forgotten in the enthusiasm for all things connected with Diocletian. Displays include a motley collection of jewellery, weapons and fragmentary reconstructions of chancel screens and ciboria (the canopies built over a church's main altar) from ninth- and tenth-century Croatian churches.

The Meštrović Gallery

Šetalište Ivana Meštrovića 39 • May–Sept: Tues–Sun 9am–7pm; Oct–April: Tues–Sat 9am–4pm, Sun 10am–3pm • 30Kn, includes admission to the Kaštelet • ⓣ 021 340 800, ⓦ mestrovic.hr • The gallery is a 30min walk from the centre or bus #12 from Trg republike

Presiding regally over Šetalište Ivana Meštrovića, the **Ivan Meštrović Gallery** (Galerija Ivana Meštrovića) is housed in the ostentatiously palatial building that the country's most famous modern sculptor (see box, p.296) planned as his home and studio. Fronted by a veranda supported by Ionic columns, the house was completed in 1939 – Meštrović lived in it for just two years before fleeing to Zagreb to escape the Italian occupation in 1941.

Even if you're not mad about Meštrović, this is still an impressive collection. Some of the religious pieces have considerable emotional depth (look out for a particularly tortured *Job* from 1946), although his other work can sometimes appear facile – such as the frankly daft *Joyful Youth* or the ungainly *Adam and Eve*. Portraits of members of his immediate family in the ground-floor drawing room are refreshingly direct, especially the honest and sensitive *My Mother* from 1909.

6

IVAN MEŠTROVIĆ (1883–1962)

Ivan Meštrović was born in Slavonia to a family of itinerant agricultural labourers, but his parents soon moved back to their native Dalmatia, settling in Otavice near Drniš. Meštrović was too busy tending sheep on Mount Svilaja to attend school, and had to teach himself to read and write. At the age of 16 he displayed some drawings in a local inn, prompting locals – including the mayor of Drniš – to apply to art schools on his behalf. He was turned down, but managed to land a job with a Split stonemason, thus beginning his training as a sculptor.

Awarded a place at the **Viennese Acadamy** in 1901 (quite a feat considering his background), he was soon exhibiting with the Art Nouveau-influenced Secession group. At the age of 22, Meštrović was already receiving big public commissions – like the Secession-influenced *Well of Life* (1905) which still stands outside the Croatian National Theatre in Zagreb. By the time he moved to Paris in 1907 a distinctive Meštrović style was beginning to emerge, blending the earthy Romanticism of Rodin with the folk motifs of southeastern Europe.

Like many men of his generation, Meštrović was convinced that the Austro-Hungarian state could not survive, and that the expanding Kingdom of Serbia would provide the basis of a **future Yugoslav state** in which all South Slavs could live as equals – he had grown up in an area of mixed Serb–Croat settlement and was familiar with the folk culture of both communities. When the Austrian government invited Meštrović to represent them at the Rome International Exhibition of 1911, he chose to exhibit in the Serbian pavilion instead (of the 23 artists in the Serbian pavilion, incidentally, fourteen were Croat). During World War I Meštrović moved to **London**, where his involvement with the Yugoslav cause helped land him a one-man show at the Victoria and Albert Museum in 1915. The exhibition was an enormous success – Britain and Serbia were allies at the time, and attendance at the show was seen as a sign of support for the war effort. In 1918 Meštrović hailed the creation of Yugoslavia as the "greatest accomplishment that our people have hitherto performed", although his enthusiasm would subsequently wane.

Meštrović was made Rector of the Academy of Fine Arts in **Zagreb** in 1923, and was in constant demand as an artist over the next two decades, working on monumental public projects such as the *Grgur Ninski* sculpture in Split (1928) and two vast, muscular Indians on horseback for Grant Park in Chicago (1928). His **architectural work** was in many ways more innovative than his sculpture, developing a cool, sepulchral style which found expression in the Račić mausoleum in Cavtat (1923), the Meštrović family mausoleum in Otavice (1927–31) and the Art Pavilion in Zagreb (1939).

In 1941, Meštrović was **imprisoned** by the Ustaše because of his history of pro-Yugoslav activity, but was subsequently allowed to emigrate. Meštrović eventually made his way to the US, where he became Professor of Sculpture at the University of Notre Dame, Indiana. Much of his **later work** was religious, although he'd been tackling sacred subjects on and off ever since 1916, when the cycle of reliefs displayed in Split's Kaštelet was begun.

The Kaštelet

Šetalište Ivana Meštrovića 39 • May–Sept Tues–Sat 9am–7pm, Sun 10am–7pm; Oct–April Tues–Sat 9am–4pm, Sun 10am–3pm • Admission with Meštrović Gallery ticket (30Kn) • ⓣ 021 340 800, ⓦ mestrovic.hr

Ivan Meštrović's best work can be seen in the so-called **Kaštelet**, just up the road from the Meštrović Gallery. Built in the sixteenth century as the fortified residence of the Capogrosso family, but long used for other purposes (it was at various times a tannery and a hospital), the Kaštelet was virtually a ruin when Meštrović bought it in 1939 to house his **Life of Christ** cycle, a series of reliefs in wood that he'd been working on since 1916. Presided over by a mannered but moving *Crucifixion*, the cycle spreads like a comic strip across all four walls of the church, borrowing stylistically from Assyrian bas-reliefs, Egyptian tomb paintings and Archaic Greek art. The result is an immensely powerful piece of religious sculpture, with rows of rigidly posed, hypnotically stylized figures in which the sum of Meštrović's eclecticism is for once greater than its parts. It's said that Meštrović began the cycle in response to the horrors of World War I, which may go some way to explaining its spiritual punch.

FROM TOP SPLIT HARBOUR; SARCOPHAGUS DETAIL, ARCHEOLOGICAL MUSEUM (P.293)

Bačvice beach

The main visitor-magnet east of the city centre is **Bačvice beach**, a few minutes' walk east of the ferry terminal. This simple crescent of sand and shingle can't compare with the beaches farther south, but it remains a popular – and crowded – destination for Splićani of all ages. Bačvice is also the spiritual home of **picigin**, a game only played in and around Split, which works rather like a netless version of volleyball in the sea, involving a lot of acrobatic leaping around as players try to prevent a small ball from hitting the water. Immediately behind the beach is a chic modern three-tier pavilion, resembling a cross between an Art Deco seaside building and a high-tech metal tent. With several cafés and a couple of swanky **eating places** inside (see p.302), it's a popular venue for after-dark drinking and feasting throughout the year. A coastal path leads east from Bačvice past a couple of smaller bays, passing the tennis club where 2001 Wimbledon champion **Goran Ivanišević** honed his skills. There are plenty more cafés along the way, and the whole stretch is a popular strolling area all year round.

The Croatian Maritime Museum

Glagoljaška 18 • Mid-June to mid-Sept Mon–Sat 9am–7pm, Sun 9am–2pm; mid-Sept to mid-June Mon–Wed & Fri 9am–2.30pm, Thurs 9am–7pm, Sat 9am–1pm • 10Kn • T 021 347 346, W hpms.hr

Uphill from the Old Town to the northeast is **Tvrđava Gripe** (Gripe Fortress), an imposing seventeenth-century bastion built by the Venetians to keep Ottoman armies at bay. One of the former barrack buildings inside holds the **Croatian Maritime Museum** (Hrvatski pomorski muzej), an entertaining collection of nautical knick-knacks ranged over several halls. The display opens with a huge Roman storage vessel unearthed by marine archeologists – it was probably used to store a catch of fish, although it looks big enough to accommodate an average-sized family of humans. Elsewhere there's a fantastic array of model ships through the ages, and an attractive collection of sleek nineteenth-century torpedoes, built for the Austro-Hungarian navy in Rijeka by pioneering Croatian engineer Ivan Blaž Lupis and his English colleague Robert Whitehead. Look out for a model of former Yugoslav Navy destroyer *Split*, which, somewhat ironically, briefly shelled the city it was named after in autumn 1991.

The Youth Centre

Savska • MKC Tues–Sat 10am–1pm & 5–9pm; Sun 10am–1pm • W mkcsplit.hr

Lurking behind the Croatian TV and Radio building on the corner of Slobode and Mažuranićevo šetalište is a notorious concrete ugly duckling known as the **Youth Centre** (Dom Mladih). Begun in the 1970s to serve as an umbrella organization for all kinds of cultural initiatives, the building has never been properly finished. However it does house the best of Split's contemporary art galleries, the **MKC** (Multimedijalni kulturni centar), and occasionally hosts the odd theatre or film event. Alternative club *Kocka*

ORSON WELLES IN SPLIT

Head for the Joker shopping centre on put Brodarice (ten minutes' walk northeast of the Old Town along Dovominskog rata) and you'll come face to face with a bolero-hatted bronze sculpture of Hollywood director **Orson Welles**, unveiled in 2007. The statue was designed by Welles's long-time companion, Croatian-born actress and sculptor **Oja Kodar**, who he met while shooting gloomy central European exteriors for his adaptation of Kafka's *The Trial* in Zagreb in 1961. Croatia became a second home to Welles, who acted in local-made films (including the partisan war epic *Battle on the Neretva* in 1969), had a holiday villa at Primošten (see p.279) and – according to local lore – was an eager follower of Hajduk Split (see box, p.305).

occupies the building's basement, although it has led an on-off existence over the last few years and may not be open by the time you read this.

The Blue Tree

Vukovarska

Looming surreally over the junction of Vukovarska and Riječka is the **Blue Tree** (Plavo Stablo), a 7.5m bouquet of prickly steel designed by sculptor Vasko Lipovac (1931–2006). Famous for his playful Pop Art canvases and sculptures, Lipovac originally created the tree for temporary display in the Swiss town of Bad Ragatz in 2003. Unveiled in July 2011 to mark what would have been Lipovac's eightieth birthday, it has quickly become something of a cult landmark in a city not usually noted for its public art.

ARRIVAL AND DEPARTURE — SPLIT

By plane Split's airport (T 021 203 555, W split-airport.hr) is around 20km northwest of town between Kaštela and Trogir. Croatia Airlines buses (30Kn) connect with all of that airline's incoming flights, dropping passengers at Split bus station. Alternatively, the #37 Trogir–Split bus (every 20–30min; 16Kn) passes along the main road some 200m in front of the airport, terminating at the suburban bus station on Domovinskog rata, a 20min walk north of the centre. A taxi to Split from the airport will cost 160–200Kn.

Destinations Zagreb (April–Sept 4 daily, Oct–March 3 daily; 45min).

By train The train station is next to the bus station on Obala kneza Domagoja, a 5min walk from the Old Town.

Destination Zagreb (3 daily [one of which is overnight]; 6hr 20min–8hr 50min).

By bus The bus station is on Obala kneza Domagoja, opposite the ferry terminal.

Destinations Dubrovnik (hourly; 4hr 40min); Imotski (10 daily; 2hr 15min); Klis (every 30min; 35min); Makarska (hourly; 1hr 10min); Omiš (every 30min; 40min); Plitvice (4 daily; 6hr 30min); Ploče (hourly; 2hr 30min); Rijeka (8 daily; 8–9hr); Šibenik (hourly; 2hr); Sinj (hourly; 1hr); Zadar (hourly; 4hr); Zagreb (10 daily; 5–9hr).

International destinations Belgrade (1 daily; 15hr); Ljubljana (1 daily; 12hr); Međugorje (3 daily; 5hr); Mostar (8 daily; 5hr); Sarajevo (5 daily; 7hr).

By ferry, catamaran and hydrofoil The main passenger terminal is at Gat sveti Duje. The berths for ferries and catamarans are quite spread out, however, so always arrive early to locate the correct boat. Tickets and reservations for most ferry and catamaran services can be made through Jadrolinija, which runs a couple of ticket kiosks along Obala kneza Domagoja and a larger sales counter in the main passenger terminal at Gat sveti Duje (T 021 338 333, W jadrolinija.hr). SNAV Croatia Jet tickets are available from the SNAV ticket counter inside the passenger terminal (T 021 322 252, W snav.it). In addition, Split Tours sells tickets for the Blue Line ferries to Ancona and the LNP catamarans to Milna on Brač and Rogač on Šolta (offices in the passenger terminal or at Obala Lazareta 3, just off the Riva; T 021 352 533, W splittours.hr).

Ferry destinations Dubrovnik (June–Sept 2 weekly; 11hr); Lastovo (2 daily; 4hr 30min); Rijeka (June–Sept 2 weekly; 11hr); Rogač/Šolta (4–6 daily; 1hr); Stari Grad (3–5 daily; 2hr); Supetar (7–13 daily; 1hr); Vela Luka (2 daily; 2hr 40min–3hr 45min); Vis (2–3 daily; 2hr 30min).

International ferry destinations Ancona (3–4 daily; 10hr).

International high-speed ferry destinations Ancona (SNAV Croatia Jet; mid-June to mid-Sept 1 daily; 4hr 30min).

Catamaran destinations Bol (1 daily; 45min); Hvar Town (1–2 daily; 1–2hr); Jelsa (1 daily; 1hr); Korčula Town (1 daily; 2hr 30min); Lastovo (1 daily; 2hr 45min); Milna /Brač (1–2 daily; 1hr); Rogač/Šolta (4 daily; 40min); Vela Luka (1 daily; 2hr); Vis (1 daily; 1hr 40min).

By car Car rental is available from Sub Rosa (W subrosa.hr), Gat sveti Duje bb (T 021 399 000), and at the airport (T 021 895 320); and Hertz, Trumbićeva obala 2 (T 021 360 455, W hertz.hr).

INFORMATION

Tourist office Chapel of St Rock, Peristil (June–Sept Mon–Fri 8am–8pm, Sat 8am–7pm, Sun 9am–1pm; Oct–May Mon–Fri 9am–5pm; T 021 345 606, W visitsplit.com). The staff here can provide a free map and a list of museums and their opening times, as well as giving out general advice.

TOURS AND ACTIVITIES

Atlas Nepotova 4, east of the Golden Gate T 021 346 333, W atlas-croatia.com. Organizes yacht charter, rafting on the River Cetina and trips to Međugorje.

Split Tours Obala Lazareta 3, at the eastern end of the Riva T 021 352 533, W splittours.hr. Offers canyoning trips on the Cetina alongside other local excursions.

6

GETTING AROUND

It's generally easiest to **walk** around the city, though for journeys out to the Marjan peninsula and some of Split's museums you may need to take one of the city's **buses**.

By bus Buses are frequent and operate between 5am and midnight; tickets can be bought from the driver or conductor (11Kn) or from newspaper and tobacco kiosks (18Kn, valid for two journeys) and should be punched when you board. Tickets for Salona, Kaštela and Trogir are priced according to a zonal system – Salona is in zone 2 (13Kn one-way from the conductor or 22Kn return from a kiosk); the airport is in zone 3 (17Kn/27Kn); Trogir is in zone 4 (21Kn/32Kn). The principal nodal points for the municipal bus network are: Trg republike, at the western end of the Riva (for the Marjan peninsula and Solin/Salona); Zagrebačka, opposite the market on the eastern side of the Old Town; and the suburban bus station on Domovinskog rata (for Kaštela and Trogir).

By taxi There are taxi ranks outside the train and bus stations, and at both the eastern and western ends of the Riva. Otherwise ring T 970.

By bike/scooter Bikes (100Kn/day) and scooters (200–300Kn/day) can be rented from Travel49, Nepotova 6 (T 098 858 141, W travel49.com).

ACCOMMODATION

There are plenty of private **rooms** (doubles from 250Kn) in Split, and it's easy to find one even in high season providing you arrive early in the day – contact the **Turist Biro** on the waterfront at Riva 12 (Mon–Fri 8am–8pm, Sat 8am–7pm, Sun 9am–1pm; T 021 347 100, W turistbiro-split.hr), or **Travel49** (see above). There are very few rooms available in the Old Town, though the nearby residential districts of Manuš and Veli Varoš can be equally atmospheric. The unregistered rooms offered by touts at the bus station may work out cheaper, but bear in mind that there's no quality control, and your black-market hosts are highly unlikely to be paying their taxes. There's a moderately good choice of **hotels** and **hostels** in Split, but prices are high and beds are scarce from June to September, when you should definitely book ahead.

HOTELS

CENTRAL SPLIT

Bellevue Bana Jelačića 2 T 021 345 644, W hotel-bellevue-split.hr; map p.287. A once-elegant nineteenth-century pile superbly situated at the western end of the Riva. Rooms come with TV and WC/shower, but are dowdily furnished – those overlooking the flagstoned expanse of Trg republike have a good deal of charm; others can be gloomy and depressing. **850Kn**

Kaštel Mihovilova širina 5 T 021 343 912 and T 091 120 0348, W kastelsplit.com; map p.287. Historic stone building in a bustling location inside the palace walls, offering a mixture of doubles, triples and apartments. Rooms come with laminated floors, bright colours and smallish WC/shower. **760Kn**

Marmont Zadarska 13 T 021 308 060, W marmonthotel.com; map p.287. This ancient stone house harbours 22 smart, modern rooms, each decked out in soft colours. Fancy bathrooms, large-screen TVs and wi-fi make it a comfortable downtown choice. **2100Kn**

Palace Suites Narodni trg 13 T 021 332 507 and T 091 444 4065, W palacesuites-split.com; map p.287. Renovated medieval building right on the main square, offering a handful of spacious rooms with hardwood floors, stylish modern furnishings, some lovely exposed stone- and brickwork and swish contemporary bathrooms. Breakfast is served in a restaurant across the square. Wi-fi throughout. **1125Kn**

Slavija Buvinina 2 T 021 323 840, W hotelslavija.com; map p.287. Fully renovated Old Town hotel featuring smallish, comfortable doubles (plus some triples and quads) with modern furnishings, en-suite shower, a/c and TV. Rooms on the fourth floor have fantastic roof-level views from their terraces. Some rooms are subject to noise from nearby cafés, but providing you stay out until closing time this is unlikely to be a problem. **1080Kn**

Vestibul Iza vestibula 4 T 021 329 329, W vestibulpalace.com; map p.287. Swanky designer hotel occupying a Renaissance town house in an atmospheric Old Town location. Rooms are modest in size, but feature exposed brickwork, matt-black textiles, moody lighting and modern bathrooms. You can take breakfast in a plant-filled atrium, or outside in a courtyard where the central hall of Diocletian's palace once stood. **1820Kn**

OUT FROM THE CENTRE

★ **Luxe** Kralja Zvonimira 6 T 021 314 444, W hotelluxesplit.com; map pp.294–295. Newly opened design hotel a stone's throw from bus station, ferry port and Old Town – its combination of pristine white walls and surfaces and boldly striped carpets and textiles (think purple) will suit anyone who wants groovy contemporary design in large spoonfuls. Rooms come in different sizes but all are comfortable, with 1960s retro chairs and light fittings and "open" bathrooms visible through a glass partition. Rooms on upper storeys come with excellent views of Split's animated ferry docks. **1760Kn**

Park Hatzeov perivoj 3 T 021 406 400, W hotelpark-split.hr; map pp.294–295. Recently renovated hotel 500m southeast of the centre, directly above Bačvice beach. Smart rooms and chic reception areas give the place a somewhat more exclusive air than the rest. Formerly known as the *Imperial*, it was Split's top hotel in the 1920s and 30s, and the place where Italian forces formally surrendered Split to the Partisans in 1943. The refined hotel restaurant serves quality international food. 1125Kn

Radisson Blu Put Trstenika 19 ⓣ021 303 030, ⓦradissonblu.com/resort-split; map pp.294–295. Located 3.5km east of the centre but enjoying an excellent seaside location, this is a good four-star with an on-site restaurant, spa centre and indoor pool. It is also a good base for shoreline walks. 950Kn

Villa Ana Vrh Lučac 16 ⓣ021 482 715, ⓦvillaana-split.hr; map pp.294–295. Refurbished stone house in the atmospheric Radunica district, just east of the Old Town and ideally situated for the port and stations. Rooms are bright, spacious, pine-floored affairs with en-suite shower, TV and minibar – but there are only five of them, so ring in advance. 700Kn

Villa Diana Kuzmanića 3 ⓣ021 482 460, ⓦvilladiana.hr; map pp.294–295. Virtually next door to the *Villa Ana* and occupying a similarly tastefully restored old house, the *Villa Diana* offers small but neat doubles with parquet floors, exposed stonework, warm colours and flat-screen TVs. Only four doubles and one three-person apartment, so book ahead. 970Kn

HOSTELS

Adriatic Hostel Stari Pazar 2 ⓣ021 332 589, ⓦadriatichostel.com; map p.287. Classy hostel run by Canadian-Croatians, featuring high-ceilinged dorms with parquet floors, flat-screen TVs and fancy chandeliers. Situated just outside the palace walls, some rooms overlook the market and there is access to a roof terrace with views of the city and nearby mountains. Common room-cum-kitchen, internet terminals and a laundry service (40Kn). Dorms 195Kn

★ **Goli & Bosi** Morpurgova Poljana ⓣ021 510 999, ⓦgolibosi.com; map p.287. If living inside a giant lemon-meringue pie is your idea of holiday heaven then *Goli & Bosi* will be a dream come true. This former department store, beautifully converted into a three-storey designer hostel, consists entirely of mellow-yellow corridors and minimalist white rooms. This doesn't mean that it feels odd: dorms are smart and airy (and each bed is in a little cubicle to afford a minimum of privacy); en-suite doubles (breakfast included) are up to hotel standard; and there's a bar-restaurant right next to reception. Wi-fi throughout. Dorms from 240Kn; doubles 800Kn

Silver Central Kralja Tomislava 1 ⓣ021 490 805, ⓦsilvercentralhostel.com; map p.287. Four bright, high-ceilinged dorms sleeping six to eight, each with a/c and locker space. There are toast-making and tea-brewing facilities in the reception area-cum-common room, and the washing machine is available for a few extra kuna. The same crew run the equally spick-and-span *Silver Gate*, just outside the Old Town at Hrvojeva 6. Dorms 195Kn

Split Hostel/Booze N Snooze Narodni trg 8 ⓣ021 342 787, ⓦsplithostel.com; map p.287. Located in an alleyway just off the Old Town's bustling main square, the hostel offers a trio of six-person dorms – and a cosy five-bed space in the attic that comes with bird's-eye views of the neighbourhood washing lines. There's also a newly opened annexe, *Fiesta Siesta*, on nearby Kružićeva, with six-bed dorms and *Charlie's Bar* in the basement. Free wi-fi throughout. 199Kn

CAMPSITE

Camping Stobreč-Split Stobreč ⓣ021 325 426, ⓦcampingsplit.com; map pp.294–295. Some 6km southeast of the centre and well-signed off the main coastal road, this site occupies the wooded fringes of a shallow bay. Local bus #25 stops outside, and the #60 Split–Omiš service also passes nearby. 60Kn per person; car-plus-tent pitches from 115Kn

EATING

Good sit-down **restaurants** are in relatively short supply in the Old Town itself, although there are plenty of good options located a short walk away. Most establishments have a separate menu of *marende* (cheap brunches), which is often chalked up on a board outside. For self-catering and snacks, the daily **market** at the eastern edge of the Old Town is an excellent place to shop for fruit, veg and local hams and cheeses.

SNACKS AND FAST FOOD

Kantun Paulina Matošića 1 ⓣ021 395 973; map p.287. Steer clear of the international burger franchises and join the queue at *Paulina*'s for a portion of *ćevapi* (mincemeat cylinders) served with raw onion and a *somun* (flat-bread bun). No seats, but you can perch on a bench outside. Mon–Sat 8am–11pm, Sun 5–11pm.

Keko Bosanska 10 ⓣ021 343 445; map p.287. One of the few bakeries in the centre that still serves traditional Dalmatian *soparnik*, a thin pastry pie stuffed with garlic and *blitva* (Swiss chard). They do the full range of regular sandwiches, loaves and pastries too. Mon–Fri 7am–10pm, Sat 7am–3pm.

RESTAURANTS

CENTRAL SPLIT

Galija Tončićeva 12 ⓣ021 347 932; map p.287. Long regarded as one of the city's best pizzerias – a small, unpretentious and cheap place with breezy service and wooden-bench seating on the western fringes of the Old

Town. The recent addition of an outdoor terrace has given it added summertime appeal. Mon–Sat 8am–11pm, Sun noon–11pm.

Hvaranin Ban Mladenova 9 ⓣ 091 767 5891; map p.287. Family-run restaurant that has become something of a cult among Split's art and literary sets, serving up grilled fish, seafood risottos, *gregada* (fish stew from Hvar) and Dalmatian *pašticada*, and a choice of herbal *rakijas* with which to start and finish the evening. Daily 11am–midnight.

Konoba Dioklecijan Dosud 9 ⓣ 021 346 683; map p.287. Also known as *Tri volte* ("The Three Arches"), this unpretentious wine-bar-cum-eatery is a cult location among Split bohemians, partly owing to its atmospherically gloomy interior and outdoor terrace built into the walls of Diocletian's Palace. Turns into a laid-back restaurant in summer, when there's a limited but well-chosen menu of cheap local seafood standards. The *pršut* is among the best in town and makes for an excellent nibble-snack. Daily 10am–midnight.

Konoba kod Jože Sredmanuška 4 ⓣ 021 347 397; map p.287. In a back alley a 10min walk northeast of the Old Town (head north along Zagrebačka and turn right into Sredmanuška after you've passed Strossmayerov Park), this is one of Split's best seafood restaurants – with a homely, intimate atmosphere and fishing nets hung from the walls – and not too expensive. Choose between quick and cheap meals like *crni rižot* (squid risotto) or opt for the best fresh fish and lobster. Mon–Fri 9am–midnight, Sat & Sun noon–midnight.

Konoba Varoš Ban Mladenova 7 ⓣ 021 396 138, ⓦ konobavaros.com; map p.287. Handily situated just west of Trg republike – it's up an alley behind the *Hotel Bellevue* – this is a good place for reasonably priced *marende* (brunch) as well as expensive slap-up evening meals featuring excellent fresh fish. Much patronized by locals, it soon fills up. Daily 11am–midnight.

Le Monde/Kavana Bistro Anika Plinarska 6 ⓣ 021 322 265; map p.287. A café and restaurant tucked into an old stone house among the alleys of the Varoš district. The menu has a good range of meat and seafood dishes, including fillets of fish with imaginative sauces, though the real advantage is the cosy living-room ambience of a dining room crowded with photos and mementoes, and the charming and secluded courtyard down below. Mains in the 100–140Kn range. Mon–Sat 10am–midnight, Sun 10am–3pm; closed Jan.

★ **Noštromo** Kraj sv. Marije 10 ⓣ 091 405 6666, ⓦ restoran-nostromo.hr; map p.287. Right next to the fish market, this is an engaging cross between informal café-bar and smart restaurant – downstairs locals smoke, argue and watch TV, while upstairs diners tuck in their napkins and gorge on some of the best seafood in town. It's always a good bet for grilled fish, scampi, tuna steaks and *gregada* (seafood stew). Risottos 100Kn, mains from about 150Kn. No cards. Daily 6am–midnight.

OUT FROM THE CENTRE

Boban Hektorovićeva 49 ⓣ 021 543 300, ⓦ restaurant-boban.com; map pp.294–295. Smart but never-too-formal restaurant in a residential street some 2km east of the Old Town, with a long tradition of serving top-notch seafood. Superb fish dishes, elegantly presented, and an extensive wine list. Daily 10am–midnight; closed Jan.

Bota Šare Bačvice bb ⓣ 021 488 648, ⓦ bota-sare.hr; map pp.294–295. *Bota Šare*'s parent restaurant is set beside the oyster farms of Mali Ston (see p.382), and the Split branch rolls out the same menu with fresh fish and shellfish the order of the day. Tucked into an upper corner of the Bačvice beach pavilion, it's not in the most convincing of locations in terms of ambience, but the food is a major plus. Daily 11am–midnight.

Buffet Fife Trumbićeva obala 11 ⓣ 021 345 223; map pp.294–295. Is it cool to eat in a place that has a TripAdvisor sticker in the window? In the case of *Fife* it still is. This legendary feeding station just west of the Old Town is renowned for its inexpensive home cooking – usually served up in enormous portions – with cheap standards such as *ribice* (small fish, deep-fried) and *fažol*, augmented by daily seafood specials. The house wine is unsophisticated but potent. Popular with tourists, popular with locals. Daily 6am–midnight.

Enoteka Terra Prilaz braće Kaliterna 6 ⓣ 021 314 800, ⓦ vinoteka.hr; map pp.294–295. Upmarket wine cellar in stone-clad surrounds, offering an intoxicating array of top-quality Croatian wines (available by the glass as well as by the bottle), and a small but delicious choice of seafood – the marinated fish carpaccio makes for a deluxe dainty nibble-snack, and there are plenty of grilled or baked fish main courses, too. Daily noon–midnight.

Kadena Ivana pl. Zajca 4 ⓣ 021 389 400, ⓦ restorankadena.com; map pp.294–295. Quality Adriatic fare, attentive service and a sweeping seafront terrace in a residential area just above the Zenta marina. If you're strolling along the seafront path from Bačvice beach, this makes for a fitting target. Daily 10am–midnight.

Konoba Lučac Petrova 2 ⓣ 021 490 266; map pp.294–295. No-nonsense local nosh served in large, cheap portions, with a dining room boasting 1970s-era wood-panelling and wooden benches, and a small terrace overlooking the port area. Dishes vary from day to day and are chalked up on a board outside – expect to see staples such as squid risotto, calf knuckle and *pašticada* with home-made gnocchi (mains 40–50Kn). Mon–Sat 7am–10pm, Sun 8am–3pm.

Mediteranium Put Firula 6 ⓣ 021 782 379, ⓦ mediteraniumsplit.com. Formerly known as *Šumica*, this restaurant and lounge bar overlooking the shoreline path arguably offers the best option in Split when it comes to fine food in a fine location. Smart but not too showy, the restaurant is a small seven-table affair at the far end of the lounge bar, with a semi-open kitchen glimpsed through a long rectangular window. Everything is good quality here, from the basket of fresh rustic bread you get at the beginning to the sweet course at the end. Mains (100–150Kn) include a good selection of local pastas, fish and grilled meats. Daily noon–midnight.

Oštarija u Viđakovi Prilaz braće Kaliterne bb ⓣ021 489 106; map pp.294–295. Traditional Dalmatian fare cooked to a high standard, with tasty home dishes like *fažol* or *riba na lešo* (stewed fish) weighing in at around 60Kn, and more expensive grilled seafood filling out the top end of the menu. Choose between a cosy ground-floor room filled with photos of Split past and present, or the bigger basement dining room decorated with domestic knick-knacks and pictures of baggy-trousered Hajduk teams of the 1930s. Daily 11am–midnight.

Pimpinella Spinčićeva 2a ⓣ021 389 606; map pp.294–295. Set in a residential street above Zenta bay, this unassuming conservatory-like space with a few tables strewn outside is a great place for grilled meats and simple seafood. There is also a chalked-up menu of typical Dalmatian lunches, with favourites such as calf knuckle, stuffed peppers, and meatballs and mashed potato weighing in at around 50Kn each. Daily 9am–midnight.

6

DRINKING AND NIGHTLIFE

There are plenty of **pavement cafés** in the Old Town for daytime and evening drinking. The Riva is the classic venue for hanging out and people-watching; there's not much to choose between the numerous cafés along it, although those at its western end are slightly more posey and expensive than those to the east. From the Riva, evening crowds flow into the Old Town, where crumbling palaces and squares provide the perfect ambience for late-night supping. Most café-bars in the centre stay open until 2am in summer, 11pm or midnight in winter; longer hours are observed by the establishments in the pavilion at Bačvice beach (see p.298), and in the next two bays along the coastal path to the east.

CAFÉS AND BARS

CENTRAL SPLIT

Bifora Bernardinova 5 ⓣ095 822 5012; map p.287. Decorated with images of fairies and dwarves that look childish, psychedelic or pervy depending on what you've been drinking, *Bifora* has outdoor seating on a secreted-away small piazza and a genre-bashing music policy that takes in anything from punk to techno. Daily 7am–midnight.

Bobis Marulićeva 6, cnr Ispod ure ⓣ021 344 184, ⓦbobis-svagusa.hr; map p.287. Classic venue for coffee and a nibble, offering a wide variety of cakes, pastries and *crostata* (a cheesecake with crusty topping). They also sell packets of *bobići* ("beans"), sugary balls with a biscuity texture that used to be eaten on the Day of the Dead (Nov 2), but are nowadays safe to consume whatever the occasion. Other branches throughout the city. Mon–Sat 7am–10pm, Sun noon–5pm.

★ **Figa** Buvinina 1 ⓣ021 274 491; map p.287. The purists may be choking on their macchiato, but this Split legend (formerly known as *Puls*) has been relaunched as a designer bar with a flashy-looking menu of sandwiches and light bites. It is obviously aimed at tourists, but its location on the Old Split bar circuit (with outdoor seating on the steps of Dosud) looks set to guarantee its enduring popularity with the locals. Daily 8am–1am.

Galerija Plavca Marulićeva 3; map p.287. This bright L-shaped space is not the most atmospheric in town, but it's popular with an arty-but-not-too-earnest local clientele and has a supremely soothing courtyard with outdoor seating. Sun–Thurs 7am–11pm, Fri & Sat 7am–1am.

★ **Po Bota** Šubićeva 2 ⓣ095 877 8899, ⓦpo-bota.com; map p.287. Half-hidden in an alley just off Voćni trg, this tiny café-cum-art gallery has an optimum capacity of about seven/ten people – anything more than that and you can't get in. Most people end up standing or perching outside, where there's a table or two just beside the door. Owned by the family of celebrated singer-songwriter Toma Bebić (1935–90), whose picture can be seen above the door. The name means "half past midnight"' – ie, the time you should be making tracks. Daily 7am–midnight.

Teak Majstora Jurja ⓣ021 362 596; map p.287. Split-level café featuring lots of wooden beams and cast iron, a chunky piece of Diocletian's Palace forming one wall, and outdoor seating crammed into one of the Old Town's more café-filled alleyways. Daily 9am–midnight.

OUT FROM THE CENTRE

Hemingway Osmih Mediteranskih igara 5 ⓣ099 211 9993, ⓦhemingway.hr; map pp294–295. Top DJs, cocktails and a swimming pool. North of the centre near the Poljud Stadium (see box, p.305), this is the best place to catch Split's beautiful young things at play. Daily 8am–midnight, later on summer weekends.

Imperium Gat sv. Duje bb ⓣ021 388 555, ⓦimperium.hr; map pp.294–295. Megalomaniac project on the first floor of the ferry terminal incorporating a café, restaurant and club, offering designer furnishings, retro 1970s stylings and superb views of the city. As a place to wait for your ferry, it's as exotic as they come. Live gigs and DJs on summer evenings. Daily 7am–1am, later at weekends.

6

Kalafatić Cvjetna 1, Zenta ⓣ 021 571 309; map pp.294–295. A good place to aim for if you're walking along the coast from Bačvice beach. Great for coffee and cakes during the daytime, and a relaxing place for waterside supping at night. Sun–Thurs 7am–midnight, Fri & Sat 7am–1am.

Tropic Club Equador Bačvice ⓣ 098 569 135, ⓦ tropic.hr; map pp.294–295. Snazzy Latin-themed bar in the pavilion above Bačvice beach, with deep, comfy chairs and a range of cocktails, nibbles and salads. Daily 7am to early morning.

Vidilica Nazarov prilaz 1 ⓣ 021 394 925; map pp.294–295. The terrace out front from this café en route between the Old Town and Marjan (see p.293) offers fantastic views of Split and the offshore islands – in summer, arrive here at about 6pm to see the whole landscape bathed in evening sunshine. Daily 8am–10pm.

CLUBS

Minus 3 Ruđera Boškovića 18 ⓦ minus3.hr; map pp.294–295. Underground in more than just the musical sense, *Minus 3* is a classy alternative club located in a nuclear shelter deep below the suburb of Split 3, 3km east of the Old Town and entered via an unmarked white door in the middle of a car park. The minimalist interior has ceiling reliefs by local designer Damir Gamulin Gamba, and a stage that hosts indie bands, DJs and occasionally literary events. Run by the same team as the *Goli & Bosi* hostel (see p.301) – you can pick up what's on information from there. Sat & Sun; opening hours depend on event.

O'Hara Uvala Zenta 3 ⓣ 091 794 1349, ⓦ ohara.hr; map pp.294–295. Popular bar and disco club on the seafront path east of Bačvice beach, with frequent live pop-rock bands or DJ-driven events. A good option for late drinking when the bars in the city centre close. Named after cult New York poet Frank O'Hara. Summer daily 8am–5am; winter opening hours depend on event.

Quasimodo Gundulićeva 26 ⓣ 095 856 5125, ⓦ facebook.com/quasimodoklub; map pp.294–295. Main venue for medium-sized rock bands and a cool place to hang out on non-gig nights, although it's initially a bit difficult to find – it's in what looks from outside like an office block, then up a flight of steps. Daily 9pm–2am.

ENTERTAINMENT

Split has a good theatre and a handful of worthwhile festivals (see box below), but is otherwise far from being the cultural powerhouse that its size might suggest. It's only in the sphere of popular song that the city continues to punch its weight, with old-school easy-listening chansonnier Oliver Dragojević (born 1947), and younger-generation, highly literate rappers like TBF and Dječaci (check them all out on YouTube) acting as cultural ambassadors for a city that in all other artistic spheres promises a lot more than it ever delivers.

THEATRE

Croatian National Theatre (HNK) Trg Gaje Bulata 1 ⓣ 021 306 908, ⓦ hnk-split.hr. Top-class drama, classical music, opera and ballet are staged at the prestigious National Theatre (Hrvatsko narodno kazalište). Box office Mon–Fri 9am–2pm & 3–7.30pm, Sat 9am–noon & 6–7.30pm.

CINEMA

Kino Karaman Ilićev prolaz ⓣ 021 343 813, ⓦ ekran.hr. One of the few remaining single-screen city-centre cinemas in Dalmatia, showing mainstream movies and also used as a venue for film festivals (see box below).

Kinoteka Zlatna Vrata Dioklecijanova 7 ⓣ 021 361 524, ⓦ pouciliste-split.hr. A boutique cinema in a medieval palace which has a regular programme of art-house and cult films.

SPLIT FESTIVALS

Feast of St Domnius (Sveti Dujam or, more colloquially, Sveti Duje) May 7. The city's protector is celebrated with processions, masses and general festivity. Domnius is also the patron saint of woodwork, and you'll see craftsmen selling chairs, tables, barrels and carvings in Split market on the days surrounding the feast.

Mediterranean Film Festival (Festival mediteranskih filmova) Early June ⓦ fmfs.hr. Features and documentaries with a strong regional focus, with showings at open-air cinema Bačvice and Kinoteka Zlatna Vrata, and DJ-led after-parties.

Split Summer Festival (Splitsko ljeto) Mid-July to mid-August ⓦ splitsko-ljeto.hr. In the summer Split hosts a spate of cultural events – including top-quality theatre, a lot of classical music and at least one opera – many performances of which take place on outdoor stages in the Peristyle and other Old Town squares. Seats for the operas cost between 100Kn and 250Kn, significantly less for other events; tickets are available from the HNK box office (see above).

Split Film Festival September ⓦ splitfilmfestival.hr. Independent, radical and subversive features, shorts and documentaries. The main venues are Kino Karaman and Kino Zlatna Vrata.

SHOPPING

There are a number of classy boutiques, bookshops and souvenir shops squeezed into the narrow alleys and tiny squares of the Old Town. Otherwise high-street Split has retreated to the out-of-the-centre **shopping malls**, such as Joker, put Brodarice 6.

BOOKSHOPS

Knjižara Miljenko Smoje Ilićev prolaz 1 ⓣ 021 332 380; map p.287. A wide selection of English-language paperbacks, international art and design books, and guidebooks. Mon–Fri 8am–8pm, Sat 8am–3pm.

UPI-2M Kružićeva 5 ⓣ 021 344 024, ⓦ upi2mbooks.hr; map p.287. Art and architecture bookshop with a fascinating collection of both local and global interest, English-language guidebooks and some kooky stationery. Mon–Fri noon–8pm, Sat 10am–2pm.

FOOD AND DELI PRODUCTS

Aromatica Šubićeva 2 ⓣ 021 344 061, ⓦ romatica.hr; map p.287. Herbal soaps, essential oils, herbal teas and massage creams. Mon–Sat 10am–7.30pm.

Nadalina Dioklecijanova 6 ⓣ 091 210 8889, ⓦ nadalina-cokolade.com.hr; map p.287. Local firm Nadalina make rich dark chocolate bars with Dalmatian flavourings such as lavender, carob and Plavac wine. Mon–Fri 8am–8pm, Sat 9am–2pm.

Splitski pazar (Market) Zagrebačka; map p.287. In amongst the fruit and veg you'll find Dalmatian dried figs, mandarins from the Neretva valley and local cheeses and hams. Stalls selling clothes, bags and other bits and bobs stretch beyond the market proper along neighbouring northbound alleys. Daily from early till late.

HAJDUK SPLIT

Few football teams are as closely associated with their home city as **Hajduk Split**. Formed in Prague's U beer hall in February 1911 by Croatian students inspired by Czech teams Sparta and Slavia, the club is named after the Robin Hood-like brigands who opposed both Ottoman and Venetian authority from the Middle Ages onwards. Hajduk was an explicitly Croatian team at a time when Split was still part of the Austro-Hungarian Empire and, later, towards the end of World War II, the entire squad was shipped to Italy by the Partisans in order to play demonstration matches as an explicitly anti-fascist team. They were also the first team in Yugoslavia to play with a *petokraka* (communist five-pointed star) on their jerseys, and the first team to remove it when it became clear that Yugoslavia's days were numbered.

A large part of the Hajduk mystique comes from their success on the pitch: they were Yugoslav champions twice in the 1920s, three times in the 1950s, four times in the 1970s and went on to become champions of Croatia five times between 1992 and 2005. They're also famous for their loyal fans, known as the **torcida** (after the Brazilian fans that Hajduk supporters had seen footage of during the 1950 World Cup). Split's version of the *torcida* launched itself in October 1950, providing the team with maximum, Rio-style support for the title-decider against Red Star Belgrade – the first time that torches, banners and massed chanting had been seen on the terraces in this part of Europe. Hajduk won the match, but the communist authorities were shocked by the levels of popular frenzy displayed. Horrified by the idea that football supporters could organize themselves without the leadership of the Party, the government came down hard on the *torcida*. Today, Hajduk and their fans remain an unavoidable part of the urban landscape, and victories over traditional enemies like Dinamo Zagreb are still celebrated with citywide rejoicing. Some would argue that the team has become all-important to the local population as other symbols of Dalmatian identity are gradually eroded and the act of supporting Hajduk becomes one of the few communal experiences left. And although over the last two decades they've fallen from being a major European force to ineffectual east European minnows, if the number of freshly painted Hajduk murals is anything to go by, they still retain the status of number-one local religion.

The team plays in the **Poljud Stadium** (8. Mediteranskih igara 2; ⓣ 021 323 650, ⓦ hajduk.hr), a strikingly organic structure originally built for the 1979 Mediterranean Games. The season lasts from September to April and matches take place on Saturday or Sunday; **tickets** (20–50Kn) are sold from kiosks at the southern end of the ground. Most of the *torcida* congregate in the northern stand (*tribina sjever*), while the poshest seats are in the west stand (*tribina zapad*). Beer and popcorn are available inside, and there are numerous snack bars offering drinks and grills immediately outside.

Uje Marulićeva 1 ⓣ 021 490 990, ⓦ uje.hr; map p.287. *Uje* is local dialect for olive oil and this shop sells innumerable local varieties of the stuff – alongside herbal soaps, domestic sweets and other natural products. Mon–Fri 8am–8.30pm, Sat 8am–2pm.

RELIGIOUS ITEMS

Hajduk Fan Shop Trogirska 10 ⓣ 021 343 096, ⓦ cro-fan-shop.com; map p.287. Get your replica shirts here. There's also a good choice of scarves, kit bags and other mementoes. Mon–Fri 8am–8pm, Sat 8am–6pm.

DIRECTORY

6

Consulates UK, Riva 10, 3rd floor ⓣ 021 346 007.

Hospital Firule, Spinčićieva 1 ⓣ 021 556 111.

Internet access Cyber Club 100D, Sinjska 2/4 (Mon–Sat 9.30am–10pm, Sun 5–10pm); Internet Caffe Net Com, Grgura Ninskog 9 (daily 10am–10pm).

Launderette Modrulj, Šperun (daily: April-Oct 8am–8pm; Nov–March 9am–5pm).

Left luggage At the bus station (daily 7am–9pm) and the train station (daily 6.30am–10pm).

Pharmacy Dobri, Gundulićeva 52, just south of the suburban bus station, is open 24hr.

Police Trg hrvatske bratske zajednice 9 (ⓣ 021 307 111), west of the suburban bus station.

Post office Northwest of Diocletian's Palace at Kralja Tomislava 7 and southeast of the palace at Obala kneza Domagoja 3 (both Mon–Fri 7.30am–7pm, Sat 7.30am–2.30pm).

Telephones At the post office.

Around Split

Just a few kilometres outside Split, the Roman city of **Salona** and the medieval fortress of **Klis** are both worthwhile half-day excursions. Each is easily reached on local buses.

Salona

Five kilometres inland from Split, at the foot of the mountains that divide the coastal plain from the Zagora, is the sprawling dormitory suburb of **Solin**, a characterless modern town which has grown up beside the ruins of **Salona**, erstwhile capital of Roman Dalmatia and probable birthplace of Diocletian. The town once boasted a population of around sixty thousand and was an important centre of Christianity long before Constantine legalized the religion throughout the empire – prominent leaders of the faith (future saints Domnius and Anastasius among them) were famously put to death here by Diocletian in 304. It was later the seat of a powerful Byzantine bishopric until 614, when the town was comprehensively sacked by a combined force of Slavs and Avars, and the local population moved off to settle in what would subsequently become Split.

The ruins of Salona

June–Sept Mon–Fri 9am–7pm, Sat 10am–7pm, Sun 4–7pm; Oct–May Mon–Fri 9am–3pm, Sat 9am–4pm • 20Kn • Bus #1 (Mon–Sat every 25–35min, Sun hourly) from central Split – pick it up from the square in front of the Croatian National Theatre – passes the main entrance to the ruins

Located on the northwestern fringe of Solin, the **ruins of Salona** stretch across a hillside just above the main road to Trogir. Salona was extensively excavated at the end of the nineteenth century, and although most movable remains were packed off to museums years ago there's still a great deal to see. Despite the hazy industrial suburbs across the bay, the location is an evocative one, with ancient ruins scattered among meadows, olive groves and vineyards.

The part of the site closest to the entrance is **Manastirine**, an early necropolis for Christian martyrs piled high with sarcophagi around the impressive ruins of a fifth-century basilica. Within its walls are the graves of Domnius and his nephew Primus, Salona's first bishop. Nearby is the **Tusculum** or former summer villa of pioneering archeologist Don Frane Bulić, who spent the first half of the twentieth century digging here. Bulić had his drawing room decorated in the style of a Roman villa, and photographed himself lounging around in togas.

Below Manastirine, the path leads along a stretch of old city wall as it zigzags above the fields, providing a superb view of a spectacular stretch of ruined basilicas – most complete of which is Salona's fifth-century **cathedral**. Downhill to the south, the arched form of the first-century **Porta Caesarea** is easily identified, marking the boundary between the oldest quarters of Salona (to the west) and the so-called Urbs Nova (New Town) to the east. What was once Salona's main east–west street heads through the gate, soon disappearing into the private gardens and orchards of modern-day Solin. Sticking instead to the wall-top westward path takes you past another early Christian basilica before arriving at the second century **amphitheatre**. A reasonably well-preserved structure, it originally seated around eighteen thousand spectators and is probably the most extensive relic on the site. From here you can descend to the busy Split–Zadar highway and catch a bus back to town (there's a stop served by the #37 Split–Trogir service 100m to the right and through the pedestrian underpass), or return the way you came.

Klis

The town of **KLIS** grew up around a strategic mountain pass linking the coast with the hinterland of the Zagora. The steep rock pinnacle around which the modern town huddles was first fortified by the Romans before being taken over by the expanding medieval kingdom of the Croats; kings Mislav (835–45) and Trpimir (845–64) both based their courts here. Klis remained in Hungaro-Croatian hands until the sixteenth century, when the Turks, already in command of Bosnia, began pushing towards the coast. Commanded by Captain **Petar Kružić**, Klis withstood sieges in 1526 and 1536, but finally succumbed to Ottoman attack in 1537, when attempts to relieve the citadel ended in failure. Kružić himself – who had left the fortress to make contact with the hapless reinforcements – was captured and executed; the sight of his head on a stick was too much for Klis's remaining defenders, who gave up the fortress in return for safe passage north, where they resumed the struggle from the security of Senj (see box, p.222).

The present-day town straggles up the hillside beneath the fortress and is divided into three parts: **Klis-Varoš**, on the main road below the fortress; **Klis-Grlo**, at the top of the hill where the Drniš and Sinj roads part company; and **Klis-Megdan**, off to one side, where you'll find the main gate to the site.

The fortress

Tues–Sun: June–Sept 9am–7pm; Oct–May 10am–4pm • 20Kn

The **fortress** (*tvrđava*) is a remarkably complete structure, with three long, rectangular defensive lines surrounding a central strongpoint, the Položaj maggiore (Grand Position, a mixed Croatian–Italian term dating from the time when Leonardo Foscolo captured the fortress for the Venetians in 1648), at its eastern end. There's no real museum display and very little labelling, but the fortress interior is immediately impressive, with cobbled walkways zigzagging their way up through a succession of towered gateways. You can peek inside several dusty storehouses, barrack blocks and – near the fortress's highest point – an ancient stone chapel that briefly served as a mosque during the Ottoman occupation. The views from the walls are truly breathtaking, with the marching tower blocks and busy arterial roads of suburban Split sprawling across the plain below, and the islands of Šolta and Brač in the distance.

ARRIVAL AND INFORMATION — KLIS

By car Driving to Klis, take the old road which heads inland from Solin (rather than the new dual carriageway which skirts Klis to the east), go through the tunnel that separates Klis-Varoš from Klis-Grlo, and turn left when you see the sign for the *tvrđava*.

By bus Bus #34 goes from Split to Klis-Megdan, but it's relatively infrequent, so it may be better to catch a Split–Sinj bus (most, but not all, go through Klis), get off opposite the *Castel* café in Klis-Varoš, and walk up the steps just uphill from the café, subsequently bearing left to follow the road that winds its way up and round the hill (15min).

Tourist office The enthusiastic tourist office (021 240 578, www.tzo-klis.htnet.hr; open sporadically in summer) is behind the *Belfast* café, on the square just below the fortress entrance.

EATING

Perlica Klis-Grlo 3 021 240 004. For succulent spit-roast lamb (*janjetina na ražnju*) head for this restaurant by the road junction in Klis-Grlo, which may well have a carcass or two slowly revolving over an open fire by the roadside. Portions are priced by the kilogram and are invariably served with spring onion (*kapulica*). Daily 9am–11pm.

Trogir and around

Twenty kilometres west of Split, **TROGIR** is one of the most seductive towns on the Dalmatian coast, its old-town cluster of palaces, belfries and cobbled alleys fanning out from an antique central square. Founded by Greeks from Vis in the third century BC, Trogir can compare with any of the towns on the coast in terms of historic sights, and its **cathedral** is one of the finest in the Adriatic. It's also a good holiday base: it is nearer to Split airport than Split itself, and has ferry connections to the relatively quiet Drvenik islands.

Trogir's Old Town occupies an oval-shaped island squeezed between the mainland and the larger island of Čiovo. It is entered via the seventeenth-century **Land Gate** (Kopnena vrata), a simple arch topped with a statue of the town's protector, St John of Trogir (Sveti Ivan Trogirski), a miracle-working twelfth-century bishop.

St Lawrence's Cathedral

Trg Ivana Pavla II • Mon–Sat 8am–8pm, Sun 11.30am–7pm • 20Kn

Dominating Trogir's main square is **St Lawrence's Cathedral** (Katedrala svetog Lovre), a squat Romanesque structure begun in 1213 and only finished some three centuries

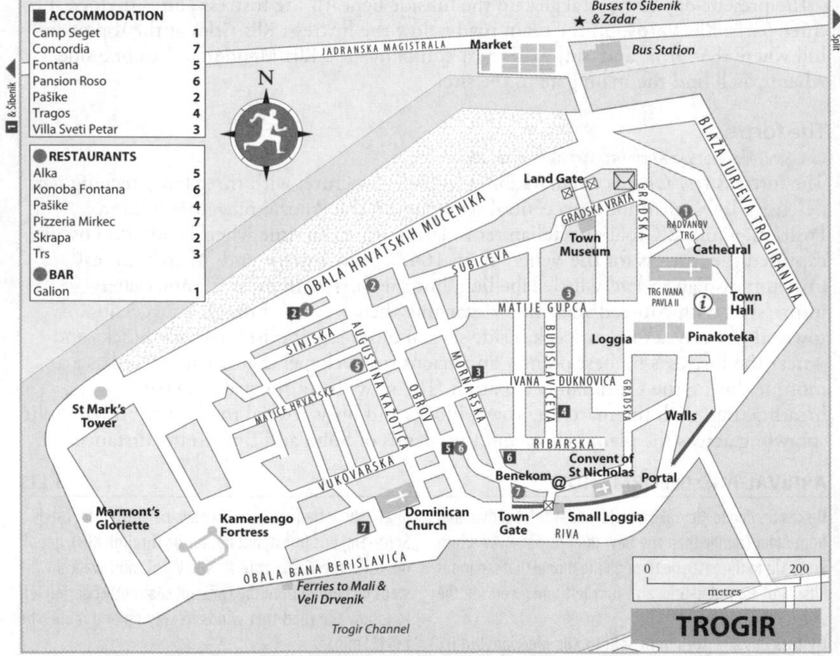

later. The soaring Venetian Gothic **tower**, climbable via dizzying flights of steps, provides an unparalleled view over town.

The west portal

The cathedral's most distinctive feature is its **west portal**, an astonishing piece of work carved in 1240 by the Slav master-mason **Radovan**. Radovan described himself "most excellent in his art" in an immodest inscription above the door – a justifiable claim given the doorway's intricate mix of traditional iconography, daily life and popular myth, with figures of apostles, woodcutters and centaurs jostling for attention. Roughly speaking, there is a gradual movement upwards from Old Testament figures at the bottom to New Testament scenes on the arches and lunette. Adam and Eve frame the door and stand with anxious modesty on a pair of lions. On either side, a series of receding pillars sit upon the bent backs of the undesirables of the time – Jews and Turks – while above is a weird menagerie of writhing creatures, laced together with tendrilled carvings symbolizing the seasons. The sequence begins on the left with March (the year started with the Annunciation as far as the Church was concerned), symbolized by a man pruning vines, and a wild-haired youth blowing a horn (a reference to the March winds). Near the top of the right-hand pillar, a man killing a pig represents the autumn, while another character in clogs cooks what look like sausages. The lunette above comprises scenes of both the Nativity and the Bathing of Christ, fringed by curtains, in imitation of the two-level stages on which medieval miracle plays were presented. Above the lunette, the uppermost arch is decorated with scenes from the life of Christ.

The baptistry

Left of the portal lies the fifteenth-century **baptistry**, a fine piece of Renaissance stonework executed by **Andrija Aleši** of Dürres, thought to have been an Albanian noble who fled the Turks and had to learn a trade in order to earn a living. He was apprenticed to Juraj Dalmatinac (see box, p.269) at Šibenik, and was in many ways his stylistic successor. The portal, topped by a relief of the Baptism of Christ, gives way to a coffer-ceilinged interior, where a frieze of cherubs carrying a garland leads round the walls, overlooked by a relief in smooth milky stone of St Hieronymous in the cave.

The interior

The **interior** of the cathedral is atmospherically gloomy, its pillars hung with paintings illustrating scenes from the life of St John of Trogir. At the head of the nave stand a Romanesque octagonal pulpit, its capitals decorated with griffins and writhing snakes, and a Baroque high altar canopied by an ornate thirteenth-century ciborium. The beautiful set of mid-fifteenth-century choirstalls was carved in Venetian Gothic style by local artist Ivan Budislavić.

St John of Trogir's Chapel

The north aisle of the cathedral opens up to reveal **St John of Trogir's Chapel** (Kapela svetog Ivana Trogirskog), another spectacular example of Renaissance work, mostly carried out by Juraj Dalmatinac's other pupil Nikola Firentinac, together with the Trogir sculptor Ivan Duknović. God the Creator is pictured at the centre of a barrel-vaulted ceiling, from which a hundred angels gaze down. The space below is ringed by life-size statues of saints, each of which occupies a niche framed by cavorting cherubs. Firentinac's statues of St John of Trogir and St Paul, both portrayed as bearded sages pouring over their prayer books, are masterpieces of sensitive portraiture. Duknović's equally impressive statue of St John the Evangelist, here depicted as a curly-haired clean-shaven youth, is thought to bear a deliberate resemblance to a favourite son of Trogir aristocrat Koriolan Ćipiko, who may well have provided funding for the chapel. At floor level there are more cherubs, this time peeping cheekily from behind half-open doors – which here symbolize the passage from life to death.

Treasury

June–Sept Mon–Sat 9am–8pm, Sun 4–7pm • 10Kn

Further along the north aisle from St John's Chapel lies the **Treasury** (Riznica), a mundane collection of ecclesiastical bric-a-brac. The best exhibits are the fine inlaid storage cabinets carved by Grgur Vidov in 1458; a fourteenth-century Gothic jug, scaled and moulded into snake-like form; and a silver-plated reliquary of St John of Trogir which is paraded around town on his feast day.

The Town Loggia

Trg Ivana Pavla II

Standing on the same square as Trogir Cathedral is the fifteenth-century **Town Loggia** (Gradska loža), with its handsome clock tower and classical columns. The large relief on the east wall of the loggia, showing Justice flanked by St John of Trogir and St Lawrence (the last holding the grill on which he was roasted alive), is another work by Firentinac – identifiable by the presence of his personal "signature", the flower-covered pillars on either side. The relief was damaged in 1932, when a Venetian lion occupying the (now blank) space beneath the figure of Justice was dynamited – an act carried out by locals keen to erase Italian symbols from a town which was still coveted by Italian nationalists. The loggia's south wall has been disfigured by a surprisingly lifeless Ivan Meštrović relief of Petar Berislavić, sixteenth-century Bishop of Zagreb and Ban of Croatia, who fought a losing battle against the advance of Ottoman power.

The Pinakoteka

Trg Ivana Pavla II • June–Sept Mon–Fri 8am–8pm, Sun 11.30am–7pm • 20Kn

Next to the loggia, the former bishop's palace provides a fine setting for the **Pinakoteka**, a display of sacred art culled from Trogir's churches. Among a number of painted crucifixes and altarpieces is Blaž Jurjev's fifteenth-century polyptych showing a Madonna and Child flanked by six saints, in which the Virgin proffers a pear-shaped breast to the infant. There are also full-length, life-size portraits of John the Baptist and St Jerome, painted to decorate the cathedral organ shutters by Gentile Bellini in 1489.

Town Museum

Gradska Vrata 4 • June & Sept daily 9am–noon & 5–8pm; July & Aug daily 9am–1.30pm & 4–10pm; Oct–May Mon–Fri 9am–2pm • 20Kn • ⓣ 021 881 406

The outwardly unassuming Garagnin Palace now houses the **Town Museum** (Gradski muzej), a largely disappointing collection of pictures and documents which boasts one stand-out exhibit, a serene fifteenth-century relief of the Virgin and Child rendered in milky-white marble by local sculptor Ivan Duknović. The museum's lapidarium, accessed by a separate entrance round the corner, boasts Roman tombstones, sundry chunks of early Christian masonry and Renaissance family crests which once hung above the portals of patrician houses.

The Convent of St Nicholas

Gradska 2 • June to mid-Sept 10am–noon & 4–6pm; rest of the year on request at the tourist office • 20Kn

South of Trg Ivana Pavla II, on the ever-narrowing Gradska, is the **Convent of St Nicholas** (Samostan svetog Nikole), whose treasury is famous for an outstanding third-century Greek relief of Kairos, discovered in 1928. Sculpted out of orange marble, it's a dynamic fragment representing the Greek god of opportunity – once passed he's impossible to seize hold of, and the back of his head is shaved just to make

FROM TOP MAKARSKA (P.319); TOWN LOGGIA, TROGIR

it even more difficult. The rest of the collection focuses on Byzantine-influenced sacred paintings from the sixteenth century, and the painted chests in which girls new to the convent brought their "dowries" (gifts to the convent in the form of rich textiles and ornaments) in anticipation of their wedding to Christ.

Along the Riva

6

Gradska emerges through the **Town Gate** (Gradska vrata) onto the **Riva** (officially known as Obala bana Berislavića, although hardly anyone uses the full title), a seafront promenade facing the island of Čiovo. Hard up against the gate stands the so-called **Small Loggia** (Mala loža), nowadays occupied by souvenir sellers. On either side of the gate are a few stretches of what remain of the medieval **town walls**, large chunks of which were demolished by the Napoleonic French, who hoped the fresh sea breezes would help blow away the town's endemic malaria.

Dominican Church

Riva

West along the Riva from the Town Gate, past a gaggle of cafés, is the campanile of the **Dominican Church** (Crkva svetog Dominika), a light, high building with a charming relief in the lunette above the main door; it shows a Madonna and Child flanked by Mary Magdalene, clad in nothing but her own tresses, and Augustin Kažotić (1260–1323), Bishop of Trogir. A small praying figure next to Kažotić represents his sister Bitkula, who commissioned the work. The main feature inside is the tomb of Šimun and Ivan Sobota, which bears a Firentinac relief of the Pietà surrounded by mourners. The coffin below is decorated with more of Firentinac's trademark flowery pillars.

Kamerlengo Fortress and St Mark's Tower

Riva • May–Oct daily 8am–10pm • 10Kn

The fifteenth-century **Kamerlengo Fortress** was named after the Venetian official – the *kamerling* – who ran the town's finances. An irregular quadrilateral dominated by a stout octagonal tower, it's a wonderfully atmospheric venue for a quick stroll on the battlements and hosts concerts and theatre and dance performances in summer months.

Beyond lies the town's football pitch, on the opposite side of which looms the tapering cylinder of **St Mark's Tower** (Kula svetog Marka), a sandcastle-style bastion built at the same time as the Kamerlengo.

Marmont's Gloriette

Riva

At the far western end of the island is **Marmont's Gloriette**, a graffiti-covered, six-pillared gazebo which looks out onto Čiovo's rusting shipyard. It was built for Marshal Marmont, the French governor of Napoleon's Illyrian Provinces; just and progressive, Marmont was probably the best colonial ruler Dalmatia ever had, and the Gloriette serves as some sort of modest tribute.

ARRIVAL AND INFORMATION — TROGIR AND AROUND

By bus Both inter-city buses and the local #37 service from Split arrive at the bus station (left luggage daily 6am–9pm) on the main coastal road, just by the bridge that leads into the Old Town.

Destinations Šibenik (hourly; 1hr); Split (every 20min; 30–50min); Zadar (hourly; 3hr).

By ferry Ferries to the nearby islands of Mali and Veli Drvenik (see p.314) depart daily from the western end of Trogir's Riva (Obala bana Berislavića); tickets can be purchased on board.

Destinations Mali Drvenik (2 daily; 50min); Veli Drvenik (2 daily; 1hr 10min).

Tourist office Ivana Pavla II (daily: June–Sept 8am–9pm; rest of the year 8am–2pm; ☎ 021 885 628, ⓦ tztrogir.hr). The tourist office has basic town maps and brochures.

Internet Benekom, Ribarska 2 (Mon–Sat 9am–10pm, Sun 2–10pm).

ACCOMMODATION

There's a generous handful of small **hotels** in or around Trogir's Old Town, although prices are slightly higher here than in the rest of central Dalmatia. **Portal**, Obala bana Berislavića 3 (021 885 016, portal-trogir.com), has a range of **rooms** (doubles from 250Kn) and **apartments** (two-person studios from 380Kn, four-person apartments from 540Kn) in Trogir, Čiovo and the offshore island of Veli Drvenik – although if your heart is set on something in the Old Town, reserve well in advance.

HOTELS AND GUESTHOUSES

Concordia Obala bana Berislavića 22 021 885 400, concordia-hotel.net. Attractive fourteen-room hotel in an old stone house on the Riva. The en-suite rooms have TV and a/c but are a bit cramped. Some of the more expensive ones come with sea views. **720Kn**

Fontana Obrov 1 021 885 744, fontana-trogir.com. Smart en-suite rooms in another old stone house, tucked away in a side alley just off the Riva. A couple of the more expensive rooms have jacuzzis, and there's also a two- to three-person apartment with living room and kitchenette. Guests get a ten percent discount in the (excellent) hotel restaurant (see below). **690Kn**

Pansion Roso Ribarska 21 021 882 602. Rooms with en-suite WC and shower, TV and electric fan in a handy Old Town location. Can get stuffy in summer, but you can always chill out on the top-floor roof terrace. No breakfast, but you can use the kitchen and fridge. **360Kn**

Pašike Sinjska bb 021 885 185, hotelpasike.com. Inviting, family-run hotel occupying a beautifully restored historic building with original stone interiors. Rooms feature classy repro furniture, TV, a/c and minibar, with an elaborate breakfast buffet served on a sunny rooftop terrace; you also get free parking and round-trip airport pick-up. Rooms can be noisy in summer. **850Kn**

Tragos Budislavićeva 3 021 884 729, tragos.hr. Tastefully refurbished stone house offering twelve rooms, each with pine beds and cheerful blue-and-orange colour schemes, satellite TV and modern WC and bathroom (half come with shower cabinets, the others have tubs). **970Kn**

Villa Sveti Petar Ivana Dukovića 14 021 884 359, villa-svpetar.com. Another thoughtfully restored town house in the old centre, offering small but very neat en suites with a/c, hard-wood floors, patches of exposed stonework and traditional green window shutters. Breakfast is available for a few extra kuna. **1010Kn**

CAMPSITE

Camp Seget Hrvatskih žrtava 121 021 880 394, kamp-seget.hr. Part-shaded, part grassy site 4km north of town in the suburb of Seget (Split–Trogir–Šibenik buses pass by), with pitches set out on a sequence of terraces overlooking a small beach. Open March–Oct. From **36Kn** per person, **40Kn** per tent pitch

6

EATING AND DRINKING

Eating out in Trogir is a joy, with dozens of restaurants tucked away in the courtyards of the centre. There's also a hugely enjoyable **market** opposite the bus station, where you'll find fruit, veg, cheeses, hams, and home-made wines and spirits offered by local farmers, haphazardly bottled into all kinds of containers. As far as **drinking** is concerned, all the Old Town's squares are stuffed with café tables in summer, and it's simply a question of picking a space that suits.

RESTAURANTS

Alka Augustina Kažotića 15 021 881 856, restaurant-alka.hr. Don't be fooled by the touristy signs pointing the way, this is one of the longest-established and best restaurants in Trogir, serving up superb grilled fish and shellfish, and a mean *pašticada*. Pleasant courtyard seating down an alley opposite the restaurant entrance. April–Oct daily 9am–midnight.

Konoba Fontana Obrov 1 021 884 811, fontana-trogir.com. With an outdoor terrace right on the Riva, this is one of the classiest places in town, offering the widest range of meat and fish dishes, all excellently prepared and presented. Daily noon–midnight.

Pašike Obala hrvatskih mučenika 021 885 185, hotelpasike.com. On the main thoroughfare in front of the *Pašike* hotel, this place has a 26-year-old tradition of dishing up well-prepared traditional specialities like squid risotto and anchovies, *Kaštelanski makaruni* (home-made pasta in meat sauce) and grilled fish and shellfish. Live folk music and waiting staff clad in traditional dress are part of the experience. Daily 8am–midnight.

Pizzeria Mirkec Budislavićeva 15 021 883 042, pizzeria-mirkec.hr. Popular joint right on the seafront offering good pizza and pasta, as well as other Dalmatian mainstays. Daily 11am–11pm.

Škrapa Augustina Kažotića 021 885 313. Cheap and cheerful feeding station serving up seafood risottos, *lignje na žaru* (grilled squid) and other standards, with wooden bench seating on the street outside. Fills up early. Daily noon–11pm.

Trs Matije Gupca 14 021 796 956, konoba-trs.com. Workaday *Trs* might not be your first choice in summer, but it's a life-saver out of season, when it's the only place in town that keeps regular hours. The menu is respectable Dalmatian fare, with grilled fillets of fish and steak-with-chips dishes predominating. Daily 11am–11pm.

BAR

Galion Radovanov trg 8 ⊕091 944 3630. Old-style café-bar with an S-bend of a bar and 1970s-style let's-do-everything-in-brown interior design. Cute outdoor terrace on a tiny piazza. Daily 7am–midnight.

Mali Drvenik and Veli Drvenik

There's little in the way of decent beaches around Trogir, and it's well worth considering a ferry trip to **Mali Drvenik** or **Veli Drvenik** if a lazy day by the sea is what you're after. Lying some 12km west of town, these small, sparsely populated islands are increasingly popular with yachtspeople, but are little visited by other travellers, making them perfect for a quiet getaway. Boats sail from Trogir twice a day – although occasionally the return times may make it impossible to visit the islands on a day-trip, more often than not you will be able to spend a day on one of the islands and be back in town by nightfall. There are precious few roads on the islands (wheelbarrows and mini-tractors provide the only forms of transport), but they're crisscrossed by farm tracks, making them perfect for relaxed rambling. You'll find accommodation, food and drink on Veli Drvenik should you wish **to stay**.

Veli Drvenik

Veli Drvenik is the livelier of the two islands, with its eponymous main village sprawling attractively on either side of a deep bay. The village itself is popular with second-home owners from the mainland, while its harbour frequently fills with touring yachts – all of which helps to keep the village shop and a couple of cafés in business. The water in the bay is clean enough to swim in, and there are several attractive coves elsewhere on the island – **Krknjaši bay**, a ninety-minute walk to the east, has a partly pebbly beach and views southeast towards the island of Šolta. *Konoba Krknjaši*, immediately behind the beach, serves up freshly caught fish in a garden filled with rosemary, lavender and other fragrant shrubs. The interior of the island, covered in prickly bushes, abandoned olive plantations and fig trees, is a great place for walks – there's little real tree cover, however, so it's best to bring a hat.

Mali Drvenik

Lying a few kilometres off Veli Drvenik's western shore, maquis-covered **Mali Drvenik** has a much wilder, untouristed air. The main port is a grubby little place with few amenities, and is little more than a staging post on the way to **Vela Rina**, a broad bay twenty minutes' walk away on the other side of the island. There's not much here apart from bare rocks and a view of the open sea, but it's an undeniably beautiful spot – you could easily while away several hours here if you come well prepared (there's precious little shade and certainly no cafés).

ARRIVAL AND DEPARTURE — MALI DRVENIK AND VELI DRVENIK

By boat Boats sail from Trogir twice a day to Veli Drvenik (50min) and Mali Drvenik (1hr 20min).

ACCOMMODATION AND EATING

VELI DRVENIK

There's no tourist office on the island, but private **rooms** (from 250Kn double) can be arranged in advance through the Portal agency in Trogir (see p.313) – the Trogir tourist office (see p.312) will also have a list of Drvenik addresses, but might not ring up hosts on your behalf. A couple of harbourside **restaurants** serve up fresh fish, although they tend to open only when yachts appear in the bay.

Atelje Tramontana Veli Drvenik bb ⊕021 893 031, ⓦateljetramontana.com. The coolest place to hang out on the island is an art gallery just below the *Mia* pension. Run by a Finnish–Croatian couple, it also serves grilled fish and local wines in a secluded garden courtyard. Daily 6–11pm.

★ **Mia** Veli Drvenik bb ⊕021 893 038 and ⊕091 163 3325, ⓦmia-drvenik.com. An excellent family-run pension, overlooking Veli Drvenik's harbour and offering a range of cosy rooms and two- to four-person apartments, all with TV, a/c and fridge. The owner is an expert on local herbs, and makes invigorating *rakija*, marmalade and massage oils from the grasses he's collected round the island. He will also drive you round the island on his tractor buggy for a small extra fee. Half board 70Kn extra per person **400Kn**

The southern Dalmatian coast

The coast **south of Split** is perhaps the most dramatic in the country, with some of the Adriatic's finest pebble beaches sheltering beneath the papier-mâché heights of the karst mountains, all easily accessible on the frequent coastal bus service.

Some 25km south of Split, the historical town of **Omiš** makes the ideal base from which to visit the rugged **Cetina gorge** and the strange and wonderful lakes at **Imotski** just inland. North of the gorge lies the Marian pilgrimage centre of **Sinj**, while south from Omiš stretch the celebrated beaches of the **Makarska Riviera** – which runs from Brela to Gradac – dramatically perched at the base of the **Biokovo mountains**. Beyond Makarska, the **Neretva delta** comprises a fascinating landscape of canals and mandarin groves, and contains at least one major archeological site in the shape of Roman **Narona**.

ARRIVAL AND DEPARTURE **THE SOUTHERN DALMATIAN COAST**

By bus Plentiful buses zoom up and down the coastal road from Split to Dubrovnik, though Makarska and Ploče are the only places along this stretch of coast that have proper bus stations with timetable information. Elsewhere, you'll just have to wait by the roadside until something turns up (during the day, it's unlikely you'll have to wait more than an hour). Note that travelling between Makarska and Dubrovnik entails passing through a small chunk of Bosnia-Hercegovina – visas aren't required for this, but be prepared for passport checks.

By ferry Makarska and Ploče are also useful ferry hubs: the former has links with Sumartin on Brač, the latter has regular services to Trpanj on the Pelješac peninsula.

Omiš

The first town of any size south of Split is **OMIŠ**, at the end of the Cetina gorge, a defile furrowed out of the bone-grey karst by the River Cetina (see p.316). For centuries, Omiš was an impregnable pirate stronghold – repeated efforts to winkle them out, including one expedition in 1221 led by the pope himself, all failed. The main coastal road runs right past the **Old Town**, a huddle of cramped alleys spread either side of the pedestrianized Knezova Kačića. Remnants of the old city walls survive, and two semi-ruined Venetian fortresses cling to the bare rocks above.

South of Omiš's Old Town lies a long stretch of **beach**, largely composed of a hard and uninviting mix of sand and gravel – you're better off heading for the long shingle beaches of **Duće**, about 2km north up the coast, or for the nice shingle beach at the village of **Nemira**, 3km southeast.

Mirabela

June–Sept daily 8am–noon & 4.30–8.30pm • 10Kn

The lower of Omiš's two fortresses is the **Mirabela**, reached by a zigzagging path that begins behind Omiš parish church. A steep scramble up staircases affords access to the roof of its tower, which offers a good view of the offshore island of Brač.

Fortica

Perched precariously on a pinnacle of rock high above Omiš is the largely ruined stronghold known locally as the **Fortica**. It can be reached from the southeastern end of town, just behind the harbour, via a steeply ascending road, then a goat track, in about ninety minutes. You'll be rewarded with a stunning panorama of the offshore islands.

6

OMIŠ KLAPA FESTIVAL

Omiš is famous for its festival of local **klape** – the traditional male- and female-voice choirs of Dalmatia – which takes place over weekends throughout July, usually culminating with open-air performances in the Old Town over the last weekend of the month. *Klape* are an important feature of Dalmatian life, and almost every town or village has at least one of them. Songs deal with typical Dalmatian preoccupations such as love, the sea and fishing, and are usually sung in local dialect. The festival is well worth a trip from Split; the Omiš tourist office will have details.

ARRIVAL AND INFORMATION — OMIŠ

By bus Omiš is served by inter-city buses on the Split–Makarska route as well as local bus #60 from Split (every 20–30min), which runs from the Lazareti bus stop at the eastern end of Split's Riva.

Tourist office Trg kneza Miroslava (T 021 861 350, W tz-omis.hr; mid-June to mid-Sept Mon–Fri 8am–8pm, Sat 8am–noon; mid-Sept to mid-June Mon–Fri 8am–3pm). The tourist office has details of local excursions up the Cetina gorge.

ACCOMMODATION

Slap, Poljički trg (T 021 757 336, W hrslap.hr), can arrange private **rooms** (180Kn) and apartments.

Camp Galeb Vukovarska T 021 864 430, W kamp.galeb.hr. Large, partly shaded site just north of town and handy for the beaches of Duće. Strangely, the site is owned by Omiš-based underwear manufacturer Galeb and there's an annual lingerie catwalk show on the beach. Tent pitches from 112Kn, plus 56Kn per person

Villa Dvor Mosorska 13 T 021 863 444, W hotel-villadvor.hr. Perched dramatically on a rocky outcrop on the opposite side of the river to the town centre, the *Villa Dvor* hotel is an intimate, medium-sized place with bright en-suite rooms, each equipped with a/c, flat-screen TV and internet connection; many have sweeping views of either the coast or the canyon inland. The hotel's elevated position meant that it could only be reached by a steep flight of steps until 2012, when a lift shaft and tunnel were bored through the rock. 810Kn

EATING AND DRINKING

There are plenty of **places to eat** on Knezova Kačića, while the **cafés** of Trg Stjepana Radića, at the eastern end of Knezova Kačića, are lovely places to sit outside in the summer.

Pod odrnom Ivana Katušića 3 T 021 861 918, W pod-odrnom.hr. This is a reliable pizzeria and restaurant, good for shellfish, scampi and grilled cuts of meat. Feb–Nov daily 11am–midnight.

U našeg Marina Knezova Kačića 4 T 021 861 328. Not so much a full restaurant as a wine bar with nibbles, this atmospheric *konoba* serves up potent local tipples accompanied by *pršut*, local cheeses or anchovies. Daily 9am–2pm & 6–10pm.

The Cetina gorge

The River Cetina rises just east of Knin (see p.278) and flows down to meet the sea at Omiš, carving its way through the karst of the Zagora to produce some spectacular **rock formations** on the way. The most eye-catching portions are those just outside Omiš, and another set 23km upstream near Zadvarje.

Out of Omiš, the first few kilometres of the **Cetina gorge** are truly dramatic, with the mountains pressing in on a narrow winding valley. Six kilometres up, the valley floor widens, making room for some swampy stretches of half-sunken deciduous forest; there's a string of popular restaurants along this stretch of the gorge. Most boat excursions and tourist trains from Omiš terminate at the *Radmanove Mlinice* restaurant (see opposite), where there's also a children's playpark and a beach.

Soon after the *Radmanove Mlinice* the road turns inland, twisting its way up onto a plateau surrounded by dry hills streaked with scrub. The village of **ZADVARJE**, at the top of a steep sequence of hairpins, offers views of the most impressive stretch of the

6

RAFTING DOWN THE CETINA

Rafting down the River Cetina is fast becoming the premier activity-holiday attraction in southern Dalmatia, with a growing number of local travel agents offering the trip. Excursions usually start at Penšići, 16km upstream from Omiš, and end up at *Radmanove Mlinice* 10km farther down. The river only gets wild after strong rains, so most trips involve a gentle descent rather than a white-knuckle, whitewater ride – giving you plenty of time to admire the dense riverine vegetation and rugged cliffs on either side. Expect to pay 230–260Kn per person. Numerous local agents in Split, Trogir or Makarska will organize the trip; in **Omiš**, excursions can be arranged through:

Active Holidays 021 861 829, activeholidays-croatia.com.
Dalmatian Adventurs Fošal 19 021 863 161, raft.hr.
Pinta 021 734 016, rafting-pinta.com.
Slap Poljički trg 021 757 336, hrslap.hr.

gorge. Follow a sign marked *Vodopad* (waterfall) in the centre of the village to a scruffy car park on the edge of a cliff, from where there's a view northeast towards a canyon suspended halfway up a rock face, with the river plunging down via two waterfalls to a gorge deep below. The cliffs lining the canyon sprout several more minor waterfalls whenever the local hills fill up with rain.

From Zadvarje, you can either head south to rejoin the main coastal road (Magistrala), or carry on northwards through **Šestanovac** to a major T-junction 7km beyond at **Cista Provo**, where you're faced with a choice of routes – eastwards to the lakes of Imotski (see p.318), or westwards to the village of **Trilj**, where you can stay.

ARRIVAL AND DEPARTURE — CETINA GORGE

There's no public transport along the valley so you'll need a **car** to see all the interesting bits. You can also **raft** down the upper stretches of the gorge (see box above).

By boat Over the summer, boat trips are advertised on Omiš's quayside (40Kn per person; they depart when full), but they only go about 6km upstream before stopping at the *Radmanove Mlinice* restaurant.

By tourist train A tractor-pulled "tourist train" makes the journey from Omiš to the *Radmanove Mlinice* a couple of times a day in season – the timetable will be pinned up at numerous points around town.

ACCOMMODATION AND EATING

Kaštil Slanica 4km out of Omiš 021 861 783, radmanove-mlinice.hr. This restaurant specializes in freshwater fish as well as *žablji kraci* (frogs' legs) and the tasty *brudet od jegulje* (spicy eel soup). Daily 10am–11pm.

Radmanove Mlinice 5.5km out of Omiš 021 862 073, radmanove-mlinice.hr. A seventeenth-century water-milling complex now home to a restaurant known for its frogs' legs, trout and lamb-baked *ispod peke*. It's a big place, but it soon fills up – excursions from Omiš often end up here. April–Oct daily 9am–11pm.

Sveti Mihovil Bana Jelačića 8, Trilj 021 831 790, svmihovil.com. Smart rooms with private bathroom and TV in a riverside location. The hotel is also an excellent base for adventure tourism, arranging rafting and kayaking on the Cetina, horseriding in the hills and mountain-bike rental (100Kn/day). The same family runs the nearby *Čaporice* restaurant (021 831 770; daily 7am–midnight), with Zagora specialities such as *arambašići* (stuffed cabbage leaves) and the ubiquitous *žablji kraci*. 485Kn

Sinj

The main urban centre of the arid south Dalmatian interior is **SINJ**, a provincial market centre laid out in a bowl between hills. It's famous locally for the **Our Lady of Sinj** (Sinjska gospa), a miraculous image of the Virgin dating from around 1500 which hangs in the local parish church (on the last altar on the left-hand side as you enter). It's claimed that prayers to the Sinjska gospa saved the town on Ascension Day 1715, when the locals drove away a superior force of Ottoman Turks – the

JOUSTING IN SINJ

Sinj is famous for its annual **Sinjska alka** (usually the first weekend of August), a medieval joust that celebrates the townsfolk's victory over the Ottomans (see p.317) – contestants, clad in eighteenth-century costume, gallop down a steeply sloping street at the southern end of town and attempt to thread their lances through a ring dangled from a rope. First recorded in 1715, the Alka is one of the few remaining examples of the contests that once took place in all the Adriatic towns, and its survival in Sinj is seen as a powerful symbol of regional identity. Membership of the Alkarsko Društvo, the association of riders allowed to take part in the Alka, is still seen as a badge of knightly prowess in a part of the country where traditional patriarchal values still rule. It remains an authentic expression of living folklore, involving all the surrounding villages and taking up a whole riotous day of colour and procession. Tickets for the main spectator stand are hard to get hold of (costing from 80Kn to 150Kn, they usually go on sale in travel agents in Split and Makarska a few weeks before the contest), but the atmosphere is worth savouring whether you get a grandstand view or not.

image still draws pilgrims from all over Dalmatia, and is paraded through the town every year on August 15.

ARRIVAL AND INFORMATION — SINJ

Bus The hourly bus from Split takes 1hr and arrives at Sinj bus station, a 5min walk downhill from the town centre.

Tourist office Put Petrovca 12 (T 021 826 352, W tzsinj.hr; Mon–Fri 9am–3pm).

Imotski and around

Set amid stony hills on the Hercegovinian border, **IMOTSKI** is famous for its Red and Blue Lakes, gawp-inducingly deep pools located on the outskirts of town. Once you've seen the lakes there's no compelling reason to stay, although the attractive string of **cafés** along Šetalište Stjepana Radića will ensure that you're well watered before you leave.

Blue Lake

A short walk west of central Imotski, the **Blue Lake** (Modro jezero) occupies a monstrous hole in the karst, formed by the collapse of underground caverns. The depression is 290m deep, and fissures near the bottom keep the lake fed with water whenever the local rock is saturated with rainfall. During dry summers the water level drops dramatically, revealing a deep basin with sheer cliffs on one side and steep scree-covered slopes on most others. A path switchbacks its way down into this veritable moon-crater of a place, offering several vantage points en route before arriving at the water's edge. The going is rough and gravelly, so don sensible footware (and try to ignore the locals nonchalantly traipsing down in their flip-flops).

Red Lake

Fifteen minutes' walk along the main road west out of Imotski, the **Red Lake** (Crveno jezero) owes its name to the russet hues of the surrounding cliffs, and is if anything an even more astonishing sight than its Blue counterpart. The lake stands at the bottom of a pit some 300m wide and 500m deep – water usually fills up to 250–300m. You can't get down to the water's edge, but you get a marvellous view of this awesome hole in the ground from the roadside viewing point, which is right on the rim of the depression.

The Makarska Riviera

Lying at the foot of the Biokovo mountains south of Omiš, the **Makarska Riviera** is Dalmatia's most package-tourist-saturated stretch of coast. However it has much to offer independent travellers too, most notably its long pebble beaches and rugged unspoilt hinterland. The town of **Makarska**, roughly in the middle of the region, has the most to offer year round, is a good base from which to tackle the ascent of the **Biokovo range**, and offers boisterous nightlife in the summer peak season. Many of the other coastal settlements are bland and packagey in comparison, although archaic hill villages above Makarska and **Tučepi**, and a quirky monastery at **Zaostrog**, provide the area with plenty of character.

6

Makarska

A lively seaside town ranged round a broad bay, **MAKARSKA** is dramatically framed by the Biokovo massif behind and two stumpy pine-covered peninsulas on either side. A leading package-holiday centre since the 1960s, the town offers some of the liveliest nightlife on the coast, and is exceedingly popular with the youth of Croatia and Bosnia-Hercegovina as a result. Though the seafront can be frenetic with activity in July and August, the place can be soothingly quiet in May, June and September, when it makes the perfect base for exploring the arid, rocky landscapes of Mount Biokovo (see box, p.320).

Central Makarska is a pleasant mixture of old and new, with a huddle of stone houses hiding behind a seafront lined with Habsburg-era buildings and modern blocks.

Kačićev trg

Just behind the waterfront, the main **Kačićev trg** is home to the Baroque **St Mark's Church** (Crkva svetog Marka). Outside is Ivan Rendić's statue of **Andrija Kačić-Miošić** (1704–60), the Franciscan friar whose *Razgovor ugodni naroda slovinskoga* ("A Pleasant Conversation of the Slav People") was the most widely read book in the Croatian language until the twentieth century, after which its archaic style fell out of fashion. Kačić's work, a history of the Croats written in verse, and containing material taken from folk poems recounting Slav heroism in the face of the Ottoman Turks, was a landmark in the creation of a modern Croatian consciousness.

The Franciscan monastery

Franjevački put 1

The **Franciscan monastery** (Franjevački samostan), just east of the centre, is worth visiting for the enormous contemporary mosaic in the apse of its church. Completed

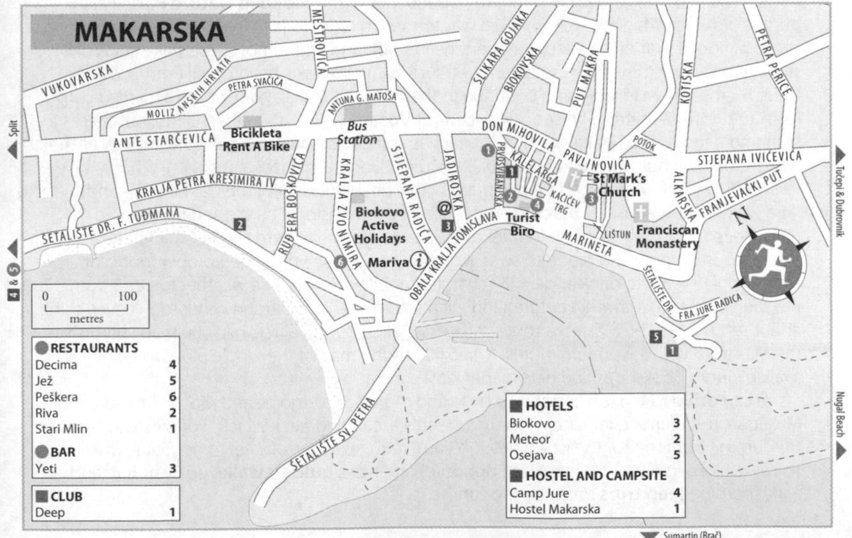

by Josip Bifel in 1999, it's rich in greens and turquoises, with Christ the Pantokrator presiding over an array of colourful sea creatures.

The Seashell Museum

Franjevački put 1 • Mon–Sat 11am–noon & 5–7pm, Sun 11am–noon • 10Kn • ☎ 021 611 256

The **Seashell Museum** (Malakološki muzej), in the monastery courtyard, is more engrossing than you might expect, its colourful exhibits shown to maximum advantage in a stylish and well-planned display.

6

Beaches

The main **beach** is west of town, where a seafront path backed by the main package hotels stretches for some 2km. Far more attractive is naturist-friendly **Nugal**, an enticing stretch of pebble squeezed between red-streaked cliffs 3km southeast of town – to get there, head to the eastern end of Makarska's Riva and pick up the marked trails leading up into the woods.

Villages around Makarska

Behind Makarska lies a verdant zone of olive groves and orchards peppered with ancient stone-built **villages**, all set on a steep slope that rises to meet the sheer rock wall of the Biokovo ridge. Providing your calf muscles are up to the gradients, the area is easily accessed by following Put Makra north from Makarska's main square and simply heading straight on; once you get above the town there's any number of gravel-track itineraries you can follow.

Biokovo Botanical Garden

Assuming you're not scaling Biokovo itself (see box below), the most obvious destination to aim for among the surrounding villages is the so-called **Biokovo Botanical Garden** (Biokovski botanički vrt), a well-signed seventy-minute walk northeast of town

BIOKOVO

The long grey streak of the **Biokovo ridge** hovers over the Makarska Riviera for some 50km, and its highest point – 1762m **Sveti Jure**, just above Makarska – is the highest point in Croatia. Much of the range falls within the boundaries of the **Biokovo Nature Park** (Park prirode Biokovo; ⓦ biokovo.com), which was formed in order to preserve the area's unique combination of lush pine forests, Mediterranean scrub and arid, almost desert-like fields of stone. It takes five to six hours to climb Sveti Jure from Makarska: head uphill from St Mark's Church, cross the Magistrala and continue to the village of Makar, from where a marked path leads to the 1422-metre-high subsidiary peak of **Vošac** (3–4hr). It's a steep climb, but there's a stunning panorama of Makarska and its beaches at the top. You can break your journey at the *Vošac* mountain hut (weekends only; ☎ 021 615 422), or press on for a further two hours' hike to Sveti Jure itself, where you'll be rewarded with a beautiful view of the Dalmatian islands.

Be warned, however, that Biokovo is not suitable for occasional hikers, and ill-prepared tourists are more likely to come to grief on its slopes than anywhere else in Croatia. The ascent is strenuous, slippery and prone to swift weather changes, so you'll need proper footwear, waterproofs, plenty to drink and a fully charged mobile phone. Get a weather forecast from the tourist office in Makarska beforehand – if there's a chance of strong winds, don't even think about setting out. The Makarska tourist office can also provide a free 1:20 000 map charting the Makarska-Vošac-Sveti Jure routes. A 1:25,000 hiking map of the whole Biokovo range is available from bookshops and newspaper kiosks.

You can **drive** to the top in summer by taking the road to Vrgorac and Mostar just south of Makarska, then turning left after 7km up a steeply ascending track which works its way up to the summit from the southeast – although you'll require nerves of steel to negotiate the hairpins. Biokovo Active Holidays (see opposite) organizes **guided walks** up Sveti Jure and early morning **jeep trips** to watch the sunrise.

just above the attractively weathered hamlet of Kotišina. Established in the interwar years by local priest Jure Radić, the garden occupies a part-scree-covered slope directly below the grey cliffs of Biokovo. Seeded with plants indigenous to the rocky, arid regions of central Dalmatia, the garden has lost much of its orderly layout since Radić's time, and nowadays doesn't look any different from the surrounding maquis. It's a beautiful spot nevertheless, and the walk here is accompanied by great views back across Makarska with the islands of Brač and Hvar in the background.

From here you can follow lateral paths eastwards towards Gornji Tučepi (see p.322).

6

ARRIVAL AND INFORMATION — MAKARSKA

By bus The town bus station is on the main road through town, a 5min walk from the seafront.
Destinations Tučepi (hourly; 15min); Zaostrog (hourly; 40min).
By ferry The car ferry from Sumartin on Brač docks right on central Makarska's seafront (June–Aug 5 daily, Sept–May 3 daily; 50min).
Bikes and scooters can be rented from numerous outlets in town, including Bicikleta Rent A Bike, west of the bus station at A. Starčevića 24.

INFORMATION AND ACTIVITIES

Tourist office Obala kralja Tomislava bb (June–Sept daily 7am–9pm; Oct–May Mon–Fri 9am–2pm; ⓣ 021 612 002, ⓦ makarska-info.hr). The tourist office, on the seafront, can provide a free town map, advice on hiking Mount Biokovo and a leaflet detailing local mountain-bike trails.
Internet You can surf the net at Internet club m@ster, just off the Riva at Jadranska 1 (daily 9.30am–midnight).
Activities Biokovo Active Holidays, Kralja Petra Krešimira IV 7b (ⓣ 021 679 655, ⓦ biokovo.net), offers trips up to Sveti Jure (see box opposite).

ACCOMMODATION

The town's **hotels** are mostly package-oriented establishments and are full to the rafters in July and August, so don't bank on getting a room if you're just turning up on spec. **Rooms** (doubles from 250Kn) and **apartments** (two-person apartments from 275Kn, four-person apartments from 500Kn) are on offer from innumerable agencies around town; most are open mornings and evenings with a long siesta break in the afternoon. Two of the longest-established are Mariva, Obala kralja Tomislava 15a (ⓣ 021 616 010, ⓦ marivaturist.hr); and Turist Biro, Obala kralja Tomislava 2 (ⓣ 021 611 688, ⓦ turistbiro-makarska.com).

HOTELS

Biokovo Obala kralja Tomislava bb ⓣ 021 615 244, ⓦ hotelbiokovo.com. Hogging a waterside position right on the Riva, this is the handiest hotel for the town centre, although its popularity with tour groups ensures that it fills up fast. The rooms are tastefully decorated and en suite, with shower. Half board is 75Kn extra per person. **870Kn**

Meteor Kralja Petra Krešimira IV bb ⓣ 021 602 600, ⓦ hoteli-makarska.hr. Something of an architectural statement when first built in the 1970s, this pale beachside ziggurat 1km west of the centre offers modernized four-star rooms with en-suite bathtubs, minibar and a/c. There's also an outdoor pool and a sauna on site. Prices vary greatly according to room position and size of balcony. From **900Kn**

Osejava Šetalište dr fra Jure Radića ⓣ 021 604 300, ⓦ osejava.com. Bright rooms with modern bathrooms in a well-equipped four-star, an almost total rebuild of a historic Makarska hotel – Jan Masaryk and Alberto Moravia are among the former guests. Small swimming pool out front. From **1260Kn**

HOSTEL AND CAMPSITE

Camp Jure Ivana Gorana Kovačića ⓣ 021 784 5951, ⓦ kamp-jure.com. Pleasant, shaded campsite at the western end of town, a 25min walk from the centre. Makarska's famous pebble beach is just downhill. **45Kn** per person, **130Kn** per pitch.

Hostel Makarska Prvosvibanjska 15 ⓣ 091 256 7212, ⓦ hostelmakarska.com. Bang in the middle of town, this is a welcoming family set-up with private rooms and apartments (some with kitchenette) in the main house and a ten-bed dorm in the garden. There's an outdoor kitchen for summer barbecues, and the usual extras – wi-fi is free, and washing and bike hire can be arranged for a few extra kuna. Dorms from **90Kn**, doubles from **250Kn**

EATING, DRINKING AND NIGHTLIFE

The town centre has scores of **restaurants** along the Riva, although in many of these establishments price and quality tend to vary from one season to the next; standards are reasonably reliable in those we've listed below. Simply cruise the Riva to find a place to **drink**: the nightly *korzo* flows past the string of lively café-bars crowded into the Lištun, the narrow pedestrian street that connects Kačićev trg with the far end of the Riva. Most of the bars are indistinguishable from each other save for the music they're blaring out – and it can get so crowded here at weekends that the main priority is simply to grab a table wherever you can.

6

RESTAURANTS

Decima Trg Tina Ujevića ⓣ021 611 374, ⓦkonoba-decima.com. Unpretentious *konoba* just behind the Riva, which seems to keep both tourists and locals satisfied with a filling and not-too-pricey range of Dalmatian standards such as *pašticada*, *crni rižot* and fish – grilled mackerel will set you back 35Kn. Daily 10am–midnight.

★ **Jež** Kralja Petra Krešimira IV 90 ⓣ021 611 741. Tucked away on a residential street behind the large and prominent block-shaped *Dalmacija* hotel, *Jež* has worn the best-restaurant-in-town tag for quite some time. It remains unpretentious, enjoyable and affordable, with fine steaks and seafood a speciality. For a good, mid-priced meal go for the grilled fillet of fish with *blitva* (120Kn). Daily 10am–midnight; closed Nov.

Peškera Kralja Zvonimira 7 (entered from Šetalište dr. Franje Tuđmana) ⓣ021 613 028, ⓦsusvid.com. A good choice of quality seafood, and with inexpensive lunch menus chalked up on a board. Nicely situated midway between the town centre and the package hotels. Daily 7am–1am.

Riva Obala kralja Tomislava 6 ⓣ021 616 829. Classy restaurant with a plush interior decorated with nautical bric-a-brac and a large outdoor terrace shaded by ancient, twisting trees. Fresh fish and seafood are very good indeed: the meat dishes, by comparison, are rather ordinary. The wine list rounds up most top Croatian labels, and a few French ones too. Daily 10am–midnight.

★ **Stari Mlin** Prvosvibanjska 43 ⓣ021 611 509. A warm and atmospheric stone building decorated with the owner's own artwork, the *Old Mill* has a lovely shaded porch where steaks and fish are cooked up on an open grill. It's family run but imaginative with it; Thai dishes occasionally appear on the list of daily specials, and exotic spices are in much more regular use here than elsewhere in Dalmatia. Daily 10am–2pm & 4–11pm.

BAR

★ **Yeti** Kačićev trg ⓣ095 538 4318. With bare floorboards, a jumble of furnishings and pop-culture references crowding the walls, this is the best place to drink in Makarska by a long distance. The coffee is reliably strong and there's a cute terrace overlooking the main square. Mon–Sat 7am–midnight, Sun noon–11pm.

CLUB

Deep Šetalište dr. fra Jure Radića 21 ⓦdeep.hr. Located on the Osejava peninsula just beyond the Riva's eastern end, this cave-bound nightclub attracts the best in the way of top DJs and hedonistically-inclined punters, although the party season is pretty short: it's at its peak from mid-July to mid-August. May–Sept 10pm–4am.

Tučepi and Gornji Tučepi

While Makarsksa preserves something of its historic character, its near neighbour to the southeast, **TUČEPI**, is almost wholly modern, with off-white concrete hotels and holiday villas lining a neatly manicured seafront. However it has a great beach, and there's a great deal of character in the villages just uphill from the shore, most notably **GORNJI TUČEPI** (Upper Tučepi), a knot of stone houses that can be reached by car via the main Makarska–Vrgorac road or on foot by heading uphill from Tučepi itself (45min). There's a lot to enjoy up here, with a network of minor roads and farm tracks leading past vineyards and olive groves towards a succession of half-abandoned hamlets, all cowering under the shadow of the Biokovo massif.

ARRIVAL AND INFORMATION — TUČEPI AND GORNJI TUČEPI

By bus Buses from Makarska run hourly (10min).

On foot You can walk to Tučepi from Makarska in under an hour by following paths that cross the wooded Osejava peninsula.

FESTIVALS IN MAKARSKA

Running throughout July and August, the **Makarska Cultural Summer** (Makarsko kulturno ljeto) features concerts and theatre performances in town squares, chamber music in the town church and carnival-style events on the Riva – pick up a schedule from the tourist office. The **Fishermen's Night** (Ribarska večer), held every Friday in July & August, is a great opportunity to cruise the seafood snack stalls and catch a bit of open-air music.

Tourist office Donji ratac (June–Sept daily 8am–9pm, Oct–May Mon–Fri 8am–3pm; ☎ 021 623 100 ⓦ tucepi.com). They can provide a rudimentary map of the town and the hillside settlements.

ACCOMMODATION AND EATING

Ratours, Donji ratac 24 (☎ 021 623 200, ⓦ ratours.com) is an agency offering **private rooms** (doubles from 150Kn) and **apartments** (two-person studios from 300Kn, four-person apartments from 450Kn).

Jeny Gornji Tučepi 49 ☎ 021 623 704, ⓦ restaurant-jeny.hr. *Jeny* enjoys a Croatia-wide reputation for serving up a mixture of traditional dishes and modern European concoctions, with the menu changing seasonally according to what's fresh. Daily: April–Oct 11am–midnight; Nov–March 6pm–midnight.

Veza Gornji Tučepi/Srida Sela ☎ 021 623 224. Further proof that the food is better in Gornji Tučepi than down on the coast, with a solid repertoire of steaks, fish fillets and pasta dishes in a homely stone house with natural colours and timber beams. Try the *pašticada* (65Kn), one of the best on the Makarska coast. Daily 9am–midnight.

6

Zaostrog

After a cluster of unremarkable resorts around Igrane and Živogošće, the next point of interest beyond Tučepi is quiet and charming **ZAOSTROG**, 30km to the southeast. There's a long family-friendly pebble **beach**, and the path leading north out of town leads to some attractive rocky coves. Twenty or thirty minutes' walk north of Zaostrog is **Drvenik**, a pretty seaside village with beaches ranged around two crescent-shaped bays.

Franciscan monastery

May–Sept daily 4.30–7.30pm • 10Kn

Zaostrog is built around a sixteenth-century **Franciscan monastery** (Franjevački samostan), which has a simple, plant-filled cloister and a small **museum**, displaying church silver, religious manuscripts and a collection of traditional agricultural implements.

ACCOMMODATION — ZAOSTROG

CampViter A. K. Miošića 1 ☎ 021 629 190, ⓦ camp-viter.com. Occupying a partly shaded site among olive groves in the centre of the village, *Viter* offers easy access to the beach, and a well-equipped shop and restaurant. Open May–Oct. Tent pitches from 32Kn, plus 40Kn per person.

TRAVELLING ON TO BOSNIA-HERCEGOVINA

Bosnia-Hercegovina, or **BiH** (pronounced "bey-ha"), as it is colloquially known, is in theory a unified state comprising two "entities" – the so-called **Serbian Republic** (Republika srpska; RS), which roughly covers the east and northwest of BiH, and the **Muslim-Croat Federation**, which covers the rest. Within the Muslim–Croat entity, Croatian-dominated western Hercegovina is virtually a state within a state, paying little heed to the government in Sarajevo. Despite the political differences between them, travel between the entities is unrestricted. Most of what you are likely to want to see – dramatic, still-beautiful Sarajevo, Ottoman-influenced Mostar and the Catholic pilgrimage centre of Međugorje – are all in the Muslim-Croat Federation.

Citizens of the EU, USA, Canada, Australia and New Zealand do not need a **visa** to enter Bosnia-Hercegovina; nationals of other countries should check current regulations with the Bosnian consulate in their home country before setting out.

Public transport from Croatia to the Muslim-Croat Federation is relatively straightforward. The Ploče–Mostar–Sarajevo **rail** line was reopened in 1999, and there are numerous **buses**, with at least one departure a day from Zagreb, Split and Dubrovnik to destinations like Sarajevo, Mostar and Međugorje. The official **currency** of Bosnia-Hercegovina is the convertible mark (konvertabilna marka; KM), although you'll find that euro notes are accepted in most parts of Bosnia, and Croatian kuna often come in handy in western Hercegovina.

Large tracts of Bosnia-Hercegovina are still heavily **mined**. Stick to roads and pavements, and never go wandering off across waste ground or into the countryside.

6

The Neretva delta

Beyond the Makarska Riviera, the main road southeast to Dubrovnik ploughs across the broad, green delta of the **River Neretva**, which includes some of the most fertile land in the country. Standing in lush green contrast to the arid landscape of limestone and scrub that characterizes much of the Croatian coast, the delta comprises a dense patchwork of melon plantations, tangerine orchards and reedy marsh. Local farmers get to their fields by boat, navigating a shimmering grid of irrigation channels: it's not uncommon to see a row of waterside houses with a motor launch bobbing outside each one. **Frogs and eels** abound in the delta's waterways, and play an important role in the local cuisine.

Ploče

Standing near the mouth of the Neretva is the industrial port of **PLOČE**, an important transport hub, offering rail services to the Bosnian capital Sarajevo and daily ferries to Trpanj on the Pelješac peninsula, where you can pick up buses to Orebić (see p.380). There's no other reason to keep you here, however, and it's best to press on towards Dubrovnik or make a short detour inland to Metković (see below)

ARRIVAL AND DEPARTURE — PLOČE

By bus Buses run to and from Dubrovnik (hourly; 2hr 15min); Split (hourly; 2hr 30min).

By ferry Regular ferries run to Trpanj (summer 7 daily, winter 3 daily; 1hr).

Metković and around

METKOVIĆ is a scruffy little town but it makes an ideal jumping-off point for **Narona**, a fascinating archeological site in the village of **Vid**, a village set among the reeds and irrigation canals 5km northwest of Metković.

Narona Archeological Museum

May–Oct Tues–Sat 9am–8pm, Sun 9am–1pm; Nov–April Tues–Sat 9am–5pm, Sun 9am–1pm • 20Kn • ⓣ 020 691 596, ⓦ a-m-narona.hr • The museum is a 1hr walk from Metković bus station to Vid, with very little shade

Once a thriving Roman market town, the ancient settlement of Narona is now partially preserved beneath the **Narona Archeological Museum**, an impressively stark concrete structure standing in the middle of Vid. The museum is built on top of Narona's original forum – the excavations are visible beneath the museum's glass floors. Occupying centre stage is the Temple of Augustus, guarded by a row of fourteen statues which – despite being headless – are believed to represent members of the imperial family and are among the most impressive examples of stone carving found in southeastern Europe. One armour-clad figure is thought to represent Augustus himself, while the female next to him is probably his consort Livia. Livia's presumed head was unearthed by locals in the 1870s and sold to British archeologist Arthur Evans, who carted it back to the Ashmolean Museum in Oxford. The museum's roof terrace provides excellent views of the reedy landscape of the Neretva delta.

ARRIVAL AND DEPARTURE — METKOVIĆ AND AROUND

By bus Metković bus station is served by regular buses from Split and Dubrovnik.

ACCOMMODATION AND EATING

Đuđa i Mate Vid ⓣ 020 687 500, ⓦ djudjaimate.hr. Right opposite the museum, this restaurant dishes up frog risotto and other local treats, with an outdoor terrace overlooking a canal (daily 11am–10pm). It also offers cosy B&B accommodation. **360Kn**

Villa Neretva Splitska 14, Krvavac II, Metković ⓣ 020 672 200, ⓦ hotel-villa-neretva.com. On the main route between Metković and Opuzen, this roadside hotel has a smart restaurant (daily 9am–11pm) serving up a famously tasty *brudet* with eel and frog. Fried frogs' legs, frogs' legs with *pršut* and other regional delicacies fill out the menu. **400Kn**

Vrilo Prud ⓣ 020 687 139. Some 2km northwest of Vid in the village of Prud, this unpretentious but welcoming *konoba* is famous for its frog and eel *brudet*. Daily noon–10pm.

The Neum Corridor

South of the Neretva delta the coastal highway passes the nine-kilometre stretch of coast that is actually part of **Bosnia-Hercegovina** (keep passports handy). This corridor was awarded to the Republic after 1945 in order to give it access to the sea, although it has no strategic or economic value at present – Bosnia-Hercegovina's trade, such as it is, still goes through Ploče. The corridor's only real settlement is the ghastly holiday village of **Neum**. Food and cigarettes here are slightly cheaper than on the Croatian side of the border, and most Croatian inter-city buses make a pit-stop here so that passengers can do a spot of shopping. Whether the corridor continues to be of significance largely depends on the pending decision on how to extend the Dubrovnik-bound motorway: by land through Neum, or – more expensively – by bridge to the Pelješac peninsula (thereby missing out Bosnian-Hercegovinian territory entirely).

The southern Dalmatian islands

ZLATNI RAT BEACH, BRAČ

The southern Dalmatian islands

If the Croatian Adriatic has an increasing reputation for mixing Mediterranean tradition with modern chic, then it's arguably on the southern Dalmatian islands that most people expect to find it. A few resort settlements apart, local tourism has avoided megalomaniac corporate development, and a contemporary boutique approach to hotels, restaurants and yachting marinas goes hand in hand with a much older holiday culture of private accommodation and local food and wine. The sense of insular uniqueness is enhanced by the fact that the vast majority of travellers have to cross at least part of the Adriatic Sea in order to get here – first impressions of arriving in ancient ports fringed by palms and overlooked by arid hills are not likely to be forgotten in a hurry.

Easiest to reach from the mainland is the island of **Brač**, boasting some good beaches at **Supetar** and a truly wonderful one at **Bol**, while lying off the northern coast of Brač is relatively unsung **Šolta**, with its quiet country lanes and yacht-sprinkled inlets. Further south is the long thin ridge of **Hvar**, whose capital, **Hvar Town**, rivals Dubrovnik in terms of stone-built architectural beauty. It's also a fashionable hang-out for urbane travellers: chic bars rub shoulders with Gothic palaces and chapels, and water taxis convey bathers to idyllic offshore islets. Hvar Town's hedonistic buzz contrasts with the rest of the island, where small-town destinations like **Stari Grad** and **Jelsa** offer a much more laid-back take on the Dalmatian island experience. Much the same can be said of the island of **Korčula**, south of Hvar, whose fascinating medieval capital, **Korčula Town**, offers a mixture of urban tourism and lazy beachcombing. Farther out, but still only a few hours by boat from Split, the island of **Vis** was only opened up to foreign tourists in 1989, after previously serving as a naval base. Wilder and less visited than Brač or Hvar, it's an obligatory destination for travellers who want a piece of the Adriatic to themselves. Far-flung **Lastovo** is another favourite destination for the independent-minded, with a supremely relaxing main village ringed by unspoiled bays. You can rejoin the mainland from Korčula by a short ferry-ride to the **Pelješac peninsula** – virtually an island itself – which is joined to the coast by a slim neck of land at **Ston**, whose magnificent town walls were built to defend the northernmost frontiers of the Dubrovnik Republic.

ARRIVAL AND DEPARTURE — THE SOUTHERN DALMATIAN ISLANDS

By boat Split is the fulcrum of the transport network, with car ferries and passenger-only catamarans serving each island at least once a day, all year round (with increased services in summer). Travelling from one island to the next is feasible up to a point, with a handful of connections between Hvar, Korčula and Lastovo; otherwise island-hopping necessitates back-tracking to Split.

ST STEPHEN'S CATHEDRAL, HVAR TOWN

Highlights

❶ **Maslinica** This cute fishing harbour on the western coast of Šolta could be the Adriatic's best-kept secret. **See p.332**

❷ **Brač's northeastern coast** succession of picturesque bays lapped by clear seas, and hardly a package hotel in sight. **See p.336**

❸ **Hvar Town** Beautifully proportioned Renaissance town that also happens to be the swankiest resort on the Croatian coast. **See p.342**

❹ **Stari Grad** If Hvar Town is the celebrity magnet, Stari Grad represents the other side of the Adriatic coin – laid back, unhurried and full of charm. **See p.349**

❺ **Vis** Enjoy the unspoiled nature and clear seas of the independent traveller's favourite island. **See p.357**

❻ **Vela Luka** Korčula's surprise package, never too crowded and with fantastic beaches nearby on the island of Proizd. **See p.374**

❼ **Mali Ston** A must-visit for the epicurean traveller, with a brace of fine restaurants serving up locally harvested oysters. **See p.382**

HIGHLIGHTS ARE MARKED ON THE MAP ON P.330

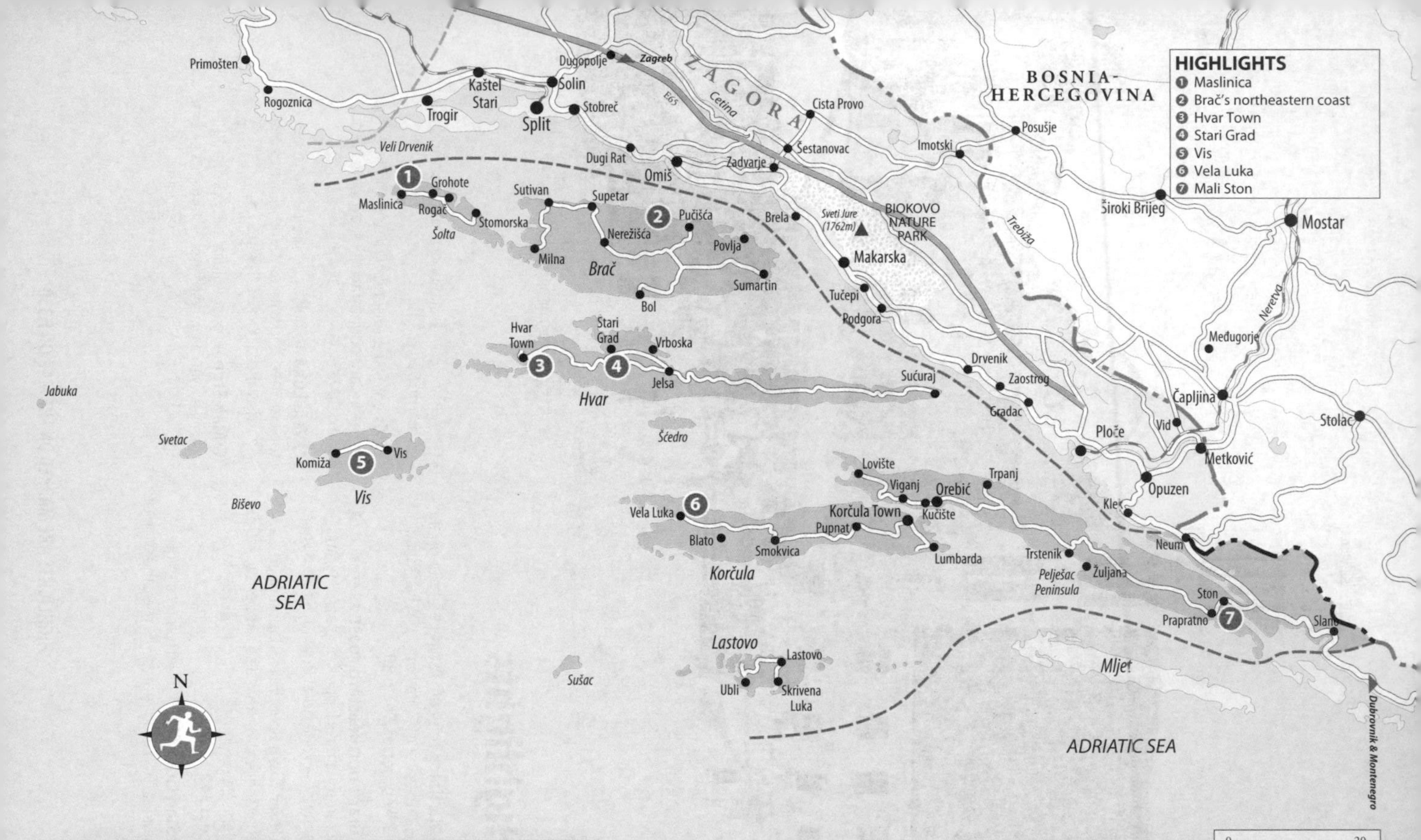

THE SOUTHERN DALMATIAN ISLANDS

For a history of Dalmatia, see the box on pp.246–247.

Šolta

Despite its proximity to Split, **ŠOLTA** is one of southern Dalmatia's more sleepy and understated islands, with a landscape of Mediterranean maquis and olive groves interspersed with a collection of stone-house villages and attractive harbours. Small, compact and not dramatically mountainous, it's ideal for walking and cycling, especially once you get away from the island's single main east–west road. Apart from a bland (and not particularly recommended) apartment complex at Nečujam, accommodation is limited to private rooms and the odd hotel. Main attractions are the picture-perfect harbour villages of **Maslinica** and **Stomorska** and the half-forgotten, kasbah-like villages of the interior.

Note that facilities on Šolta are limited: there is an ATM and a petrol station in the port of **Rogač**; and a post office and supermarket in the central village of **Grohote**.

Rogač

Ferries and catamarans from Split arrive at **ROGAČ**, a settlement that is not much more than a huddle of houses overlooking a harbour. In the crook of the bay (well to the east of the ferry dock) is a fine stretch of pebble **beach** perfect for families.

ARRIVAL AND INFORMATION — ROGAČ

By ferry From Split, ferries are operated by Jadrolinija (June–Sept 5 daily; 1hr), and catamarans by G&V Lines (tickets from Split are sold by Split Tours; see p.299). Ticket kiosks for both services are located beside Rogač harbour.

By bus Buses (5 daily) to Grohote (10min), Maslinica (20min) and Stomorica (30min) meet incoming ferries at Rogač.

Tourist office In a kiosk opposite the ferry landing (Mon, Wed & Fri–Sun 7.30am–9.30pm; Tues & Thurs 9am–4pm; ⊕021 654 491, ⓦvisitsolta.com).

EATING

Pasarela Obala svete Tereze 29 ⊕021 654 505, ⓦrestoran-pasarela.hr. Above the beach, with a shaded terrace adjoining the restaurant itself, and down below a cluster of straw-covered mini-terraces overlooking the water. Good pizzas, and sandwiches made from home-baked bread. Daily 8am–11pm.

Grohote

Three kilometres uphill and inland from Rogač, the island's main settlement of **GROHOTE** centres on a tightly bound knot of green-shuttered old stone houses, overlooking fig-shaded alleys which have largely retained their archaic stone-slab paving.

ŠOLTA ISLAND PRODUCE

Šolta is an excellent place to pick up traditional Dalmatian delicatessen items, with local producers having banded together to form **Šoltanski trudi** (ⓦsoltanskitrudi.hr), a cooperative that sells their wares at a stall in Grohote market (at the T-junction at the centre of the village; daily 8am–noon) and a shop on Maslinica harbourfront (daily 8am–noon & 6–10pm). **Honey** produced by the Tvrdić family and Anka Burić's **fruit preserves** are well worth picking up, and the outlets also sell Dobričić **wine** – an indigenous dry red that has been revived by the Kaštelanac family winery – and Olynthia **olive oil**. You can also buy the olive oil direct from the pressing plant in Gornje Selo (⊕021 658 385, ⓦolynthia.hr).

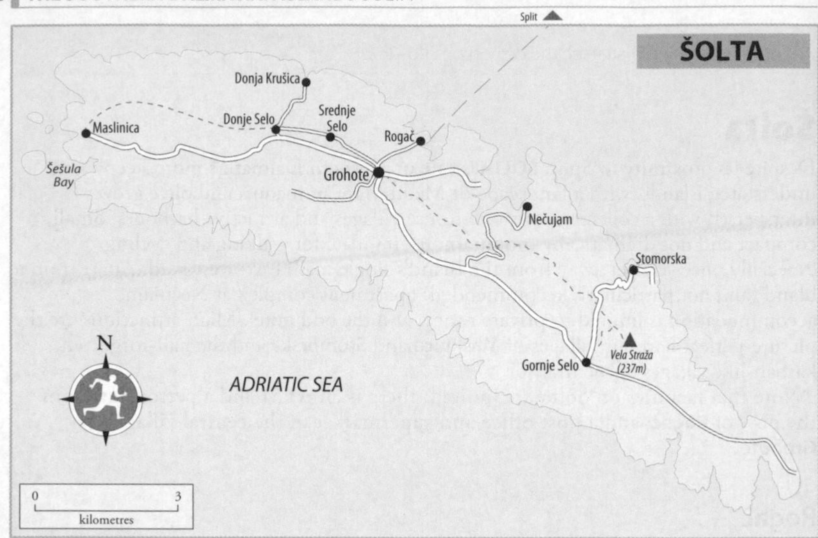

7

INFORMATION — GROHOTE

Tourist office At the back of the market on Grohote's main T-junction (Mon–Thurs, Sat & Sun 8am–12.30pm & 7–9pm, Fri 8am–11pm; visitsolta.com).

EATING

Momčin dvor Šoltanskih žrtava 18 021 654 223. A stone-walled yard shaded by vines and a lemon tree is the intimate setting for this traditional *konoba* serving grilled meats and seafood; the speciality is local lamb (either baked under a *peka* or roast on a spit), although ideally it should be ordered in advance. Daily 4pm–midnight.

Maslinica and around

Spreading along both sides of a long thin inlet, **MASLINICA** is a blissful blend of unspoiled fishing village and chic hideaway. There's a small but swanky yachting marina on the south side of the harbour, a Renaissance castle-cum-boutique hotel (*Martinis Marchi*; see opposite), and not much else save for a palm-shaded huddle of stone houses and a spread of garden-shrouded holiday villas. Walk up the north side of the

EXPLORING ŠOLTA'S INTERIOR: GROHOTE TO MASLINICA

Best way to explore Šolta's interior is to **walk or cycle** along the combination of old tarmacked roads and gravel tracks that head west from Grohote towards the villages of Srednje Selo and Donje Selo before finally arriving at Maslinica at the island's western tip. It takes around ninety minutes to do the whole lot on foot. There are no shops or *konobe* on the way.

Start by following the road west from Grohote church, which runs along the north side of **Šoltansko polje**, the strip of cultivable land that stretches along the middle of the island, passing dry-stone-walled olive groves before arriving at **Srednje Selo**, a village of chunky stone houses roofed with thick stone slabs. Domestic gardens are choked with bougainvillea, palms and fruit trees. Continue west to the next village, **Donje Selo**, where you will see more of the same. If you have time for a side-trip, a road leads north out of Donje Selo and over the hump of a hill before descending through olive groves to **Donja Krušica**, a small cove with an attractive beach. West of Donje Selo, a signed gravel track continues through maquis towards **Maslinica**, where you will be rewarded with fine maritime views before descending into the village.

bay to reach a pebbly promontory known as **Česka plaza** (Czech Beach), a good place for bathing and a great place to watch the sun setting over nearby islets. On the south side of Maslinica's harbour, a path leads beyond the yachting marina and round the headland towards Šešula Bay (Uvala Šešula), a beautiful S-shaped inlet popular both as a yachting anchorage and a rocky-beach bathing spot.

INFORMATION — MASLINICA AND AROUND

Tourist office Obala brace Marchi bb (Mon–Wed 8am–3pm; Thurs 3–6pm, Fri–Sun 2–9pm; ☎ 021 659 220).

ACCOMMODATION

Anka i Zlatko Burić Maslinica bb ☎ 021 659 202, ⓦ saskinja.de. Homely, well-maintained apartments with neat modern furnishings, right above Česka plaža beach. The owners sell their own olive oil and fruit preserves. Fluent German spoken, and other languages understood at a pinch. **450Kn**

Martinis Marchi Maslinica bb ☎ 021 572 768, ⓦ martinis-marchi.com. A former aristocratic seat with rooms and apartments grouped around a swimming pool-filled courtyard, this is a soothing, attention-to-detail location that includes extensive gardens, a large library-cum-sitting room and hallways filled with artworks. Furnishings feature a mixture of restored antiques and swish modernity, and the buffet breakfast is exquisite. **1275Kn**

Maslinica Net ☎ 021 659 011, ⓦ maslinica.net. Agency booking rooms and apartments: two-person studios **375Kn**, four-person apartments from **475Kn**

7

EATING AND DRINKING

Beach Bar Punta Česka plaza ☎ 095 904 5722. An uncomplicated beachside kiosk serving rather good cocktails (including potent own-recipe combinations like *Šolta na dlan*, which includes a representative mix of local *rakijas*). Daily 9am–2am.

Saskinja Obala brace Marchi 15 ☎ 021 659 205. This traditional restaurant is a good bet for fresh fish and lobster, with a covered terrace right beside Maslinica's small-boat harbour. Daily 9am–10pm.

Šišmiš Šešula bb ☎ 095 904 5546, ⓦ restaurant-sismis-sesula.com. Located above the north side of Šešula bay, a good 20min walk round the headland from Maslinica harbour, the "Bat" is a grill-restaurant and cocktail bar with a walled garden-terrace overlooking the yacht anchorage. Daily 11am–1am.

Stomorska

Lodged in the southeast of the island, **STOMORSKA** looks at first sight very similar to Maslinica, with its shuttered brown houses snaking along either side of a crooked-finger inlet. On closer inspection it has less of the bustle, fewer of the fancy yachts and bags of beautiful-village-with-nothing-to-do charm. Paths lead southeast along the rocky shore, passing several attractive spots for bathing.

INFORMATION — STOMORSKA

Tourist office Stomorska bb (Mon & Tues 7am–2pm, Wed 8–11am, Thurs–Sun 2–9pm; ☎ 021 658 192).

ACCOMMODATION

Auto-camp Mido Put krušice 3 ☎ 021 658 011, ⓦ camp-mido.webs.com. Squeezed into the funnel-shaped cleft of land to the rear of Stomorska harbour, this is a pleasant, small-scale site among olive trees. **50Kn** per person, pitches from **40Kn**

M-Travel Tourist Service Riva bb ☎ 021 718 309, ⓦ m-travelonline.com. Rooms and two-person studios (from 325Kn). The office is only open in July & Aug but they may deal with email requests outside that time. Rooms **250Kn**

EATING AND DRINKING

Afrika Stomorska bb. A 10min walk up the western side of Stomorska's bay, this humble hut scattered with lounge-bar furniture stands above a small crescent-shaped beach. It's a fun place to come at night when coloured lights play across the pebbles. Summer only daily 10am till late.

Volat Riva Pelegrin 17 ☎ 021 568 028. Café-restaurant handling anything from breakfast onwards, with a solid choice of pizzas and grilled seafood. Located right on Stomorska's seafront, it's the perfect place to observe comings and goings in the harbour. Daily 7am–11pm.

Brač

The third-largest of Croatia's islands, **BRAČ** is the nearest of the major islands to Split, and is the easiest to get to, with regular ferries running (hourly in high season) to the port of **Supetar**, an attractive former fishing village with shallow pebbly beaches. On the opposite side of the island is similarly picturesque **Bol**, boasting the spectacular beach of **Zlatni rat** and a mild-breeze climate that's perfect for windsurfing. The smaller coastal settlements of **Postira**, **Pučišća**, **Povlja** and **Milna** are less visited, more relaxed, and ideal for a spot of Mediterranean-island chilling. Away from the coast, the island's starkly beautiful interior has undoubted allure, its scrub-covered karst uplands dotted with fertile depressions containing vines, olives and orange trees, or by the great man-made piles of limestone built up over centuries by smallholders clearing a place in which to grow crops.

Brač was, until the development of the tourist trade, dependent on the export of its **stone** – a milky-white mix of marble and limestone – which was used in structures such as Berlin's Reichstag, the high altar of Liverpool's Catholic cathedral, the White House in Washington and, of course, Diocletian's Palace in Split.

7

ARRIVAL AND DEPARTURE — BRAČ

BY PLANE

Brač airport, near Bol (see p.339), is served by flights from Zagreb (April–Sept 1 or 2 weekly; 50min).

BY BOAT

From Split There are 7–13 ferries a day from Split to Supetar, plus daily catamarans from Split to Bol (1hr 10min) and a weekly service to Milna on the western side of the island (Tues; June–Sept only 1–2 daily; 1hr).

From Makarska Ferries run from Makarska to Sumartin on the eastern tip of Brač (June–Aug 5 daily, Sept–May 3 daily; 50min), although there are only a handful of connecting buses from here to Supetar daily.

From Hvar There is a Jelsa–Bol–Split catamaran (1 daily; Jelsa–Bol 30min; Bol–Split 1hr), and a weekly catamaran from Hvar Town to Milna (Tues; June to Sept only; 1hr). Private boats in Bol offer excursions to Hvar (they'll be chalked up on signboards in the harbour) – more expensive than catamarans but maybe more conveniently timed, and more convenient than going all the way back to Split to pick up a regular ferry.

Supetar

Despite being the largest town on the island, **SUPETAR** is a sleepy place onto which package tourism has been painlessly grafted. With a decent beach, a clutch of good restaurants and not too much noise, it's a relaxing, family-oriented resort and a good base from which to explore the rest of the island.

Much of Supetar has the appearance of an affluent suburb, with rows of neat villas nestling amid lush, well-kept gardens. Something of an **old town** survives, however, its rust-brown stone houses grouped around a horseshoe-shaped harbour. Ten minutes' walk west of town, a long pebbly **beach** curves around a shallow bay.

The town cemetery

Standing on a peninsula screened by dark cypresses just beyond the beaches, the **town cemetery** (groblje) is as much a sculpture park as a burial site, thanks in large part to **Ivan Rendić** (1849–1932), whose eclectic amalgam of Egyptian, Classical and Byzantine styles can be seen on many of the family tombs here. A native of Supetar, Rendić was repeatedly commissioned by wealthy families to design funerary monuments here, giving the cemetery a uniquely unified sculptural style.

Ironically, Rendić was passed over in favour of his contemporary **Toma Rosandić** for the cemetery's grandest monument, the **Petrinović Mausoleum**, commissioned by the Supetar-born, Chile-based shipping magnate, Francisco Petrinović. The resulting structure is a beautiful piece of sepulchral art: a neo-Byzantine dome pokes above the trees, topped by a kneeling angel, his long wings spearing skywards. The four

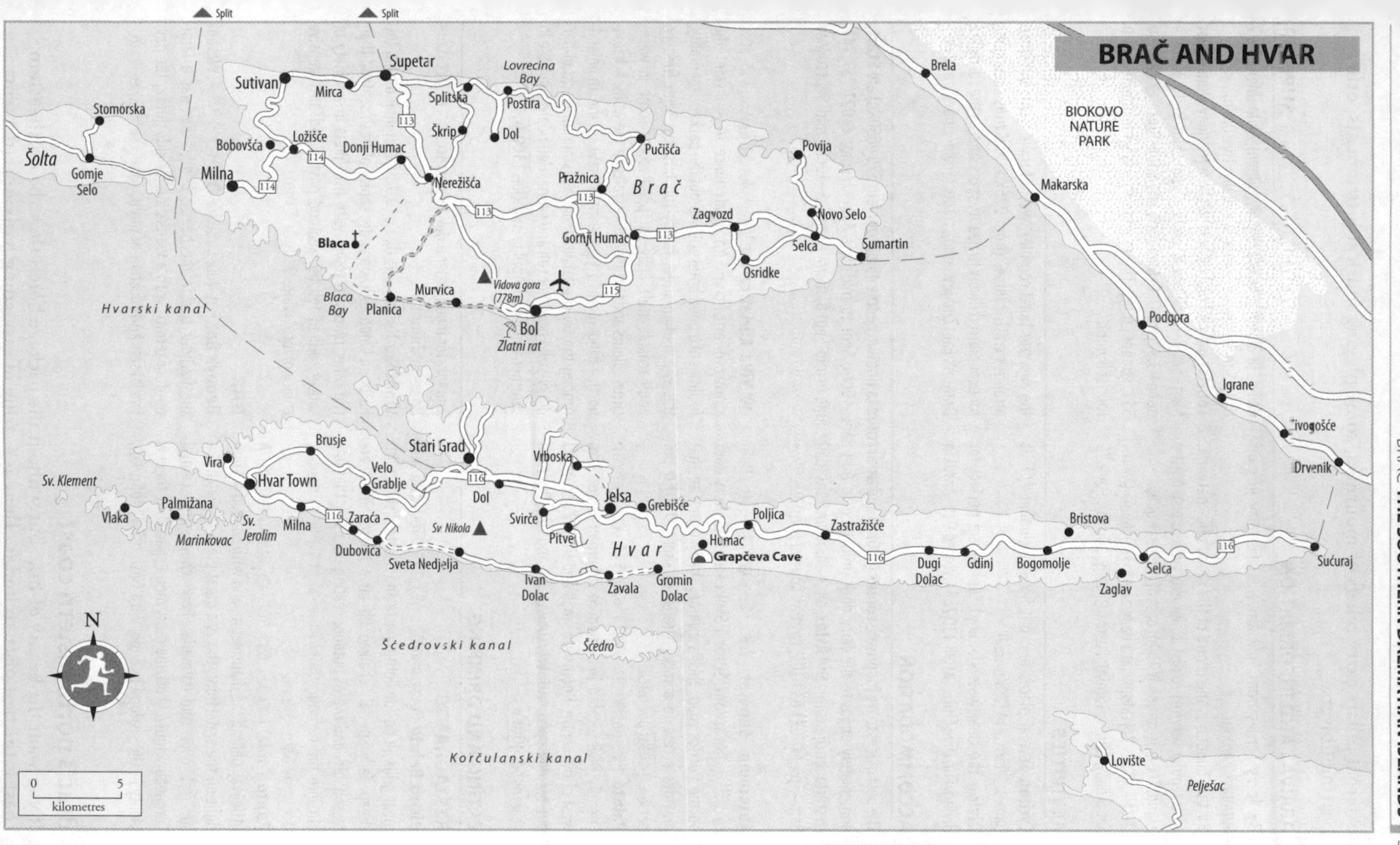
BRAČ AND HVAR
Split
Split
Supetar
Sutivan
Mirca
Lovrecina Bay
Splitska
Postira
Stomorska
Škrip
Dol
Šolta
Gornje Selo
Bobovšća
Ložišće
Donji Humac
Milna
Nerežišća
Pražnica
Pučišća
Brač
Povija
Zagvozd
Novo Selo
Gornji Humac
Selca
Sumartin
Osridke
Blaca
Vidova gora (778m)
Murvica
Blaca Bay
Planica
Bol
Zlatni rat
Hvarski kanal
BIOKOVO NATURE PARK
Brela
Makarska
Podgora
Igrane
Živogošće
Drvenik
Brusje
Stari Grad
Vrboska
Vira
Hvar Town
Velo Grablje
Dol
Jelsa
Grebišće
Sv. Klement
Palmižana
Vlaka
Sv. Jerolim
Marinkovac
Milna
Zarača
Dubovica
Sveta Nedjelja
Sv. Nikola
Svirče
Pitve
Hvar
Humac
Grapčeva Cave
Poljica
Zastražišće
Bristova
Ivan Dolac
Zavala
Gromin Dolac
Dugi Dolac
Gdinj
Bogomolje
Selca
Zaglav
Sućuraj
Šćedrovski kanal
Šćedro
Korčulanski kanal
Lovište
Pelješac
113
114
115
116
N
0
5
kilometres

7

external pillars carry reliefs of mourners, some playing musical instruments, others bearing flowers.

ARRIVAL AND INFORMATION — SUPETAR

By ferry Ferries from Split arrive at the quay just off Supetar's harbour.

By bus Supetar is the centre of the island's bus network, with regular services to just about everywhere else on the island. The bus station is 100m east of the ferry quay.

Destinations Bol (Mon–Sat 5 daily, Sun 4; 1hr); Milna (Mon–Sat 6 daily, Sun 3; 35min); Postira (5 daily; 20min); Povla (5 daily; 1hr 30min); Pučišća (5 daily; 30min); Škrip (Mon–Sat 2 daily, Sun 1; 25min); Sumartin (5 daily; 1hr 30min).

Tourist office Porat 1, next to the ferry quay (June–Sept Mon–Sat 8–11.30am & noon–10pm, Sun 8–11.30am & noon–3.30pm; Oct–May Mon–Fri 8am–3pm; ⓣ 021 630 551, ⓦ supetar.hr). The tourist office is well supplied with tourist bumph.

ACTIVITIES

7

Cycling Several places rent out bikes, including ACF at bana J. Jelačića 14 (80Kn/day).

Diving The clear waters around Supetar are perfect for diving. Fun Dive Club (ⓣ 098 130 7384; closed Oct–April) in the *Supetrus* hotel complex, west of town, rents out gear, arranges crash courses (from 225Kn) and runs excursions for experienced divers to beauty spots such as the so-called Dragon's Ear (Zmajevo uho), a spectacular undersea cave.

ACCOMMODATION

The best places to try for private **rooms** (300Kn) and **apartments** (for two people 450Kn, for four 525–650Kn) are **Start**, immediately opposite the ferry dock (mid-June to Aug 8am–10pm; Sept to mid-June 8am–2/3pm; ⓣ 021 757 741, ⓦ startagencija.com), and **Atlas**, on the harbourfront (daily: June to mid-Sept 8.30am–1pm & 6–10pm; mid-Sept to May 8am–3pm; ⓣ 021 631 105, ⓦ atlas-supetar.com).

Autocamp Supetar Vrilo bb ⓣ 021 630 088, ⓦ campsupetar.com. Some 1.5km east of the ferry dock on the Pučišća road, this is a large, shady campsite that provides access to a rocky stretch of shore. **140Kn** per person, **140Kn** per pitch

Palute Put pašike 16 ⓣ 021 631 541, ⓦ palute.hr. Friendly B&B located in a modern suburban street 1km west of the centre. Rooms are small and simply decorated but are equipped with WC/shower, TV and a/c. Open all year round. **400Kn**

★ **Villa Adriatica** Put Vele Luke 31 ⓣ 021 343 806, ⓦ villaadriatica.com. An ideal choice if you want the facilities of a good hotel but without the package mentality, this is a human-sized, family-run business with friendly, approachable staff. Fully equipped rooms come in warm citrus colours and feature quirky crafts on the walls. Ask for a north-facing room if you want a view of the mainland. Among the on-site facilities are a restaurant, cocktail bar, dinky-sized pool, hot tub and sauna. Half board available in summer. Open mid-April to mid-Oct. **1300Kn**

EATING AND DRINKING

RESTAURANTS

Bistro Palute Porat 4 ⓣ 021 631 730. Fresh fish and meat grills alongside lighter pasta and risotto dishes, with cheap daily specials chalked up on a board. Prices are reasonable, and there's outdoor seating on a pier that juts out into the harbour. Daily June–Sept 8am–midnight, Oct–May 8am–10pm.

Punta Punta 1 ⓣ 021 631 507, ⓦ villapunta.com. A little way behind the mausoleum, and with shaded seating right on the waterfront, this is a great place to watch the sun set over mid-Dalmatia. Pork chops and central European schnitzels occupy most menu space but there is plenty in the seafood line too, with fresh fish (340Kn/kg), and lobster if you order a day in advance. April–Oct daily 8am–midnight.

Vinotoka Jobova 6 ⓣ 021 630 969. Just inland from the harbour, *Vinotoka* has a wider choice of fresh seafood than the other places in town, with fish fillets in a variety of sauces, grilled lobster, seafood pastas and an extensive choice of local wine. Daily 3–11pm.

BAR

Benny's Bar Put Vele Luke bb ⓣ 091 543 7884. West of the harbour beside the beach, *Benny's Bar* has a large outdoor terrace with a waterslide for kids during the day; live DJ sets and cocktails at night. June–Sept 8am–2am.

Brač's northeastern coast

If you want the beauty of Brač but without the package hotels then the **northeastern coast** is the best place to find it. There is a string of easy-going harbour settlements along this stretch of shore, each occupying dramatically indented bays that offer a range of bathing opportunities – beaches are predominantly rocky, although there is the odd shingly cove to paddle around in.

Postira and around

Smaller than Supetar and slightly more soothing, the fishing village of **POSTIRA** is pleasantly curled around a bay, with spectacular views of mainland Dalmatia across the water. Rocky stretches of shore on either side of the bay are the perfect places to spread-eagle yourself.

Four kilometres east of town, **Lovrečina Bay** is one of those beaches that actually delivers what you read about in the brochures, with a sandy shore bordering translucent turquoise waters, and a ruined medieval church among olive groves just behind the strand. The fact that there is limited parking and no clear bus stop helps to keep it from becoming swamped.

Pučišća

Tucked into the western arm of a long Y-shaped inlet, the stone-quarrying town of **PUČIŠĆA** huddles around a grizzled pair of medieval defensive towers and a knobbly church belfry. The harbour is clean enough to swim in and there are pleasant rocky beaches at the northwestern end of Pučišća's bay – simply follow the road along the western side of the inlet for twenty minutes. Pučišća's stone industry is in big trouble (the local quarry went into receivership in 2012, provoking a wave of protests), but there is a stone-carving school in the village and characteristic white-stone souvenirs are on sale pretty much everywhere you look.

Povlja

Of all northern Brač's bay-hugging settlements, **POVLJA** is arguably the prettiest. It's a small place draped around a compact harbour, reached by a steeply descending road that comes with a marvellous view of the tiny port, the sea and the mountains of the mainland in the distance. Walk along the east side of Povlja's harbour to reach a rocky headland, where there is a beach made up of big rough pebbles and otherworldly shards of rock – you'll need sandals, and there's no natural shade, but it's a superbly scenic place for a swim.

ARRIVAL AND DEPARTURE — BRAČ'S NORTHEASTERN COAST

By bus Regular buses (5 daily) between Supetar and Sumartin (1hr 15min) call in at Postira (20min), Pučišća (45min) and Povlja (1hr 30min), although most services to the latter require a change at Gornji Humac.

ACCOMMODATION AND EATING

POSTIRA AND AROUND

Apropos Obala bb ⓣ021 717 858, ⓦapropos.hr. This agency on the harbourfront offers rooms and apartments throughout the village. Rooms **260Kn**, two-person studios from **400Kn**

Konoba Toni Dol ⓣ021 632 602, ⓦtoni-dol.info. Traditional tavern in a mountain village 3km south from Postira at the head of a fertile, narrow valley. The tree-shaded terrace is the perfect place to enjoy home-cured *pršut*, roast meats and baked fish. April–Oct daily noon–11pm.

PUČIŠĆA

Dešković Palace Put sv. Jerolima bb ⓣ021 778 240, ⓦpalaca-deskovic.com. Beautifully restored fifteenth-century palace with thirteen rooms, each kitted out in antique and repro furniture. There's a walled garden at the back, and a fine restaurant serving Dalmatian classics such as *pašticada* (90Kn), chicken with capers (80Kn) and grilled fresh fish (340Kn/kg). Restaurant open daily 6–11pm. **1170Kn**

Pansion Lučica Put Lanterne bb ⓣ021 633 262, ⓦpansion-lucica.com. A 10min walk along the western side of the inlet, with ten quiet, sea-facing doubles. The restaurant occupies a lovely first-floor terrace overlooking the water and brushed by the upper branches of a fig tree. Fresh fish (390Kn/kg) is the speciality, although the squid risotto (65Kn) is an excellent light-lunch option. Daily noon–11pm.

POVLJA

Stara Uljara Povlja bb ☎ 091 525 4765, Ⓦ neimtours.com. A please-all menu of grills, seafood and pizzas in a nautical-themed, shore-side restaurant that's perfect for lazing around and watching boats drift in and out of the harbour. Studio apartments with kitchenette are located above the restaurant. Restaurant 7am–11pm. Studios 375Kn

Škrip

Accessible by road from Supetar or by footpath and cycle track from Postira, **ŠKRIP** is the oldest continually inhabited settlement on Brač. Founded by the Illyrians, it's now a sleepy nest of stone houses with heavy stone roof-tiles that seem in permanent danger of slipping off. Its hilltop position affords views towards the terraced ridges of the Mosor massif on the mainland. The eastern end of the village is the oldest bit, with a ruined sixteenth-century **castle** and the island's museum.

The Museum of Brač

7

Daily 10am–6pm in theory, if not always in practice • 10Kn • ☎ 021 637 092

Occupying a fortified stone residence overlooked by the castle, the **Museum of Brač** (Muzej otoka Brač) displays a well-preserved Roman relief of Hercules discovered locally, and sundry nineteenth-century agricultural tools. Outside the museum lie the remains of Iron Age walls and a Roman mausoleum, which local legend says contains a wife or daughter of Diocletian.

Milna

Main settlement of Brač's western coast, **MILNA** is a delightful, picture-postcard port that curves round a deep bay. The old village climbs uphill from the shore, a pleasant enough ensemble of narrow lanes and stone houses on either side of an eighteenth-century parish church and an adjacent nineteenth-century loggia. Behind the loggia looms an ancient crumbling house that's curiously known as Anglešćina after a local myth connecting its construction with an English crusader. All in all it's a relaxing little place.

INFORMATION **MILNA**

Tourist office Riva bb, in the main square (June & Sept Mon–Sat 8am–1pm & 3–8pm, Sun 8am–noon & 4–8pm; July & Aug daily 8am–10pm; ☎ 021 636 233).

ACCOMMODATION AND EATING

Private **rooms** (300Kn) and **apartments** (two-person apartments 350Kn, four-person apartments from 460Kn) are available from **Dupin**, at the northern end of the Riva (May–Sept ☎ 021 636 082, Oct–April ☎ 021 489 024; Ⓦ dupin-tours.com).

Fjaka Riva bb ☎ 021 636 048 or ☎ 098 793 187. There's a sprinkling of cafés along the harbourfront, of which *Fjaka* is the most pleasant and is worth a stopoff by virtue of its name alone – it's Dalmatian dialect for "slobbing around in the afternoon". Daily 7am–11pm (June–Aug till 2am).

Fontana Žalo bb ☎ 021 636 285. Restaurant with a popular harbourfront terrace, serving up a satisfying repertoire of fish, shellfish, steaks and pastas. March–Nov daily 8am–11pm.

Bol

You cannot help but be overwhelmed by the beauty of **BOL**'s setting, hugging the coastal flanks of Vidova gora mountain (see p.340), or the charm of its old stone houses. Most famous the of the town's attractions is the beautiful **Zlatni rat** (Golden Cape), a 400-metre-long pebbly promontory which stretches into the sea just west of town. Both Bol and its beach fill up with visitors during high season, when accommodation is at a premium; come in early summer or September for a lower stress dose of Adriatic charm. Bol's summer crowds provide a ready-made audience for the enjoyably informal **Supertoon** animation festival, which screens short films in a variety of around-town outdoor venues in late July/early August.

Although there's a modest string of package hotels on the path to Zlatni rat, the town itself is a reassuringly low-rise affair, with a couple of rows of old stone houses set above an attractive harbour packed with small boats and pleasure craft.

Branislav Dešković Gallery

Put bolskih pomoraca bb • June–Sept Tues–Sun 10am–noon & 6–10pm; Oct–May Mon–Fri 9am–3pm, Sat 9am–noon • 20Kn • ⓣ 021 635 270

The main attraction along the seafront is the **Branislav Dešković Gallery** (Galerija Branislav Dešković) housed in a former Renaissance town house, which contains a good selection of twentieth-century Croatian art. Most big names get a look in – sculptor Ivan Meštrović, Dubrovnik expressionist Ivo Dulčić and contemporary painter Edo Murtić among them.

Dominican monastery

Anđelka Rabadana 4 • Museum daily 10am–noon & 5–8pm • 10Kn• ⓣ 021 778 000

The fifteenth-century **Dominican monastery** (Dominikanski samostan) is dramatically located high on the promontory just east of Bol's centre. Its **museum** holds crumbling amphorae, ancient Greek coins from Hvar and Vis, Cretan icons and an imposing Tintoretto *Madonna with Child* from 1563 among its small collection. An archway leads through the accommodation block to the superbly maintained monastery **gardens** overlooking the sea.

Zlatni rat

Bol's principal draw remains **Zlatni rat**, a pleasant twenty-minute walk west of the centre along an attractive tree-lined promenade. Composed of fine shingle and backed by pines, the cape juts out into the sea like an extended finger, changing shape slightly from one year to the next according to the action of seasonal winds. With a series of large hotels positioned behind the promenade, it can get crowded during summer, but the presence of extra beach space on the approach to the cape, and rockier coves beyond it, ensures that there's enough room for everyone. Naturism is tolerated on the far side of the cape, and in the coves beyond.

ARRIVAL AND INFORMATION — BOL AND AROUND

By plane Brač airport (ⓣ 021 559 711, ⓦ airport-brac.hr) is 8km inland from Bol. There is no public transport; taxis will meet incoming flights, otherwise call Taxi Bol (ⓣ 095 527 6222, ⓦ taxi-bol.com).

Destination Zagreb (April–Sept 1 or 2 weekly; 50min).

By bus Buses from Supetar (Mon–Sat 5 daily, Sun 4; 1hr) stop just west of Bol's harbour.

By boat Catamarans from Split and Jelsa dock at the western end of the Riva.

Tourist office At the eastern end of the harbour (June & Sept daily 8.30am–3pm & 5–9pm; July & Aug daily 8.30am–10pm; Oct–May Mon–Fri 8.30am–3pm; ⓣ 021 635 638, ⓦ bol.hr). The tourist office has free leaflets, and maps of the island (useful if you're walking to Blaca; see p.340).

ACTIVITIES

Windsurfing and diving There are a couple of windsurfing centres on the shore west of town, on the way to Zlatni rat, offering board rental (about 250Kn/day) and a range of courses (about 900Kn for 8hr). Reputable outfits include Big Blue, in front of the *Hotel Borak* (ⓣ 021 635 614, ⓦ www.big-blue-sport.hr; April–Nov), and Nautic Center Bol (ⓣ 021 635 367, ⓦ nautic-center-bol.com), a little farther west on the way to Zlatni rat, which organizes scuba-diving courses (taster courses from around 270Kn), and rents out gear.

Cycling Boltours (see below) and Big Blue (see above) rent out mountain bikes (from 100Kn/day) and there are plenty of smaller outfits on the path to Zlatni rat renting out cheaper bicycles (from 60Kn) and scooters (360Kn).

ACCOMMODATION

Private **rooms** (330Kn) and **apartments** (two-person studios 430Kn, four-person apartments from 750Kn) can be obtained from **Boltours**, 100m west of the bus stop at Vladimira Nazora 18 (daily: mid-April to May & Sept to mid-Oct

9am–1pm & 5–8pm; June 9am–8/9pm; July & Aug 8.30am–10.30pm; 021 635 693, boltours.com), from **More Travel Agency**, Vladimira Nazora 28 (021 642 050, more-bol.com), or from **Adria Tours**, Bračka cesta 10 (021 635 966, adria-bol.hr).

Camp Meteor Hrvatskih domobrana 1 021 635 630, campmeteor.com. One of several campsites set among olive groves about 1km uphill from the centre, well signed from the main road into town. Small, family run and perfect for small-tent travellers. **55Kn** per person, pitches from **15Kn**

Kaštil Frane Radića 1 021 635 995, kastil.hr. A historic building on the waterfront featuring 32 tastefully modernized en-suite rooms with TV and a/c. All rooms come with a sea view. **815Kn**

Villa Giardino Novi Put 2 021 635 900, dalmacija.net/bol/villagiardino. B&B just uphill from the centre offering bright, homely rooms with a/c and en-suite facilities, a lovely breakfast terrace and relaxing garden – it's booked up well in advance during July and Aug and doesn't take credit cards. Open Easter–Oct. **750Kn**

EATING, DRINKING AND NIGHTLIFE

7

Given that so many guests have half board arrangements in their hotels, it's not surprising that central Bol has a relatively meagre roster of places **to eat**. For drinking, there are several **cafés** and ice-cream parlours along the front.

RESTAURANTS

Konoba Gušt Frane Radića 14 021 635 911. Inviting place with agricultural implements and old photographs hanging on the wall. An extensive menu of traditional Dalmatian dishes features a wide range of fresh fish and a satisfying *pašticada*. Mid-April to Oct daily noon–1am.

Mlin Ante Starčevića 11 021 635 376. Midway between the harbour and the Dominican monastery, *Mlin* is a rustically decorated place with a big olive-shaded terrace overlooking the sea. Tasty eats include seafood risottos, grilled mussels, *brudet* and (if you order in advance) lamb roasted *ispod peke* style. June to mid-Oct 5pm–midnight.

Ribarska kućica Ante Starčevića bb 021 635 033, ribarska-kucica.com. Seaside pavilion right beside a rocky stretch of beach, serving seafood risottos and a broad range of fish dishes – including *gregada* (fish in a white-wine-based broth). June–Sept daily 11am–midnight.

Taverna Riva Frane Radića 5 021 635 236, tavernariva-bol.com. Fine dining on a terrace right above the Riva, with formal waitstaff, superbly prepared grilled fish and an extensive list of Croatian wines. March–Oct daily noon–3pm & 6pm–midnight.

CAFÉS AND BARS

Marinero Rudina. In the side streets up above Bol's bus stop, this animated café-bar is bypassed by many tourists and has a refreshingly local feel as a result. There's outdoor seating in a triangular park, shaded by a mulberry tree that is something of a Bol landmark. Daily 7am–midnight.

Pivnica Moby Dick Loža 11 021 635 281. A late-opening bar directly above the small-boat harbour, with a welcoming pub-like interior with a pool table, and a terrace packed with easy chairs overlooking the harbour. Also serves pizzas and grill fare. Daily 9am–2am.

Varadero Frane Radića bb. Outdoor lounge-bar set around an ancient harbour-side tree, with wicker sofas, grass parasols, pastry nibbles during the day and a suitably decadent list of cocktails. Free wi-fi. Daily 9am–2am.

Vidova gora

There's a marked walking trail (2hr each way) from the centre of Bol, heading uphill immediately beyond the *Kito* campsite; alternatively, it's accessible via an asphalt road which leaves the Supetar–Bol road just south of the village of Nerežišća

Looming over Zlatni rat to the north is the 778-metre peak of **Vidova gora**, the highest point on any Adriatic island. A small tavern at the summit sometimes serves roast lamb during summer, but most people come simply to savour the view, encompassing Zlatni rat and Bol down to the left, with the islands of Vis and Hvar visible farther out.

Blaca Hermitage

Tues–Sun 8am–5pm, though check in the tourist office at Bol or Supetar as times can vary • 20Kn

Tucked away at the head of a valley on the western flanks of the Vidova gora is the **Blaca Hermitage** (Pustinja Blaca), about 12km out of Bol. The hermitage was founded in 1588 by monks fleeing the Turks, and was occupied until the 1930s – its last resident, Niko Miličević, was an enthusiastic astronomer who left all sorts of bits and bobs, including an assortment of old clocks and a stock of lithographs by Poussin. You can also look around the ascetic living quarters and the kitchen, with its forest of blackened iron utensils surrounding an open hearth. The principal attraction, however, is the setting, with the simple buildings hugging the sides of a narrow, scrub-covered ravine. Islanders from all over Brač attend the **pilgrimage** to Blaca on the first weekend after Assumption (August 15).

ARRIVAL AND DEPARTURE — BLACA HERMITAGE

By car Take the turn-off for Vidova gora midway between Supetar and Bol, then turn right after about 2km onto the signed gravel track for Blaca (just about passable for cars, but rough on the suspension). From the end of the track, walk along the path which heads downhill past deserted hamlets before arriving at the monastery after about 40min.

By foot Following the road (which later degenerates into a track) west from Zlatni rat, passing the village of Murvica before heading inland at Blaca Bay. The route is easy to follow and takes about 3hr each way – an exhilarating but unshaded walk along a rugged hillside with the sea far below. You can cut out some of the effort by taking a boat trip (advertised in Bol harbour in high season) to Blaca Bay and continuing from there.

Hvar

From the gossip pages to the travel magazines, **HVAR** has long been the global media's favourite Croatian island, a status it shows no sign of losing. As well as being the summertime haunt of celebrities, yacht-travellers and cocktail sippers of all descriptions, it also remains robustly popular with those who want a piece of the Mediterranean that is family-oriented, unspoiled and affordable. It is certainly well endowed with natural beauty: a slim, purple-grey slice of land punctured by jagged inlets and pebbly coves, with lavender plantations, vineyards and half-abandoned stone villages clinging to its steep central ridge.

The island's capital, **Hvar Town**, is one of the Adriatic's best-preserved historic towns, and also one of its most glamorous, with paparazzi roving the Riva to see who is transiting from which yacht to which club. The other main settlements offer complete contrasts, with **Stari Grad** – the main port – **Jelsa** and **Vrboska** boasting old stone houses and an unhurried, village feel. East of Jelsa, the island narrows to a long, thin mountainous strip of land that extends all the way to isolated Sućuraj, which is linked to Drvenik on the mainland by regular ferry.

Brief history

Around 385 BC, the Greeks of Paros in Asia Minor established the colony of **Pharos** (present-day Stari Grad), developing a network of fields and enclosures on the island's central plain that can still be seen today. After a period of Roman then Byzantine

FOOD AND DRINK ON HVAR

Quality seafood restaurants are becoming the rule in Hvar Town, while traditional inns in the interior are dependable places to try baked and grilled meats. One speciality particular to Hvar is **gregada**, a stew of fish cooked in white wine – few restaurants bother to serve it in single portions, however, so you'll have to order it for two or more people to make it worthwhile.

As for **wine**, best known of the local grape varieties is the rich red Plavac mali, grown everywhere in the fertile middle of the island and along the southern coast, while the indigenous Bogdanjuša grape produces an intriguing dry white. There isn't really any bad wine on Hvar – the house wines served by local restaurants are usually from a nearby vineyard and (never less than enjoyable) are frequently very fine indeed. Bottled wines produced by the Svirče cooperative are sold in supermarkets throughout Croatia and their inexpensive Plavac Hvar red represents outstanding value. Tomić and Duboković (both based near Jelsa) are two highly regarded local wineries focusing on quality boutique production – either are well worth a splurge.

control, the island was settled by Croatian tribes some time in the eighth century. The new arrivals couldn't pronounce the name Pharos, so the place became **Hvar** instead. The settlement nowadays known as Hvar Town began life as a haven for medieval pirates. The Venetians drove them out in 1240, and encouraged the citizens of Stari Grad to relocate to Hvar Town, which henceforth became the administative capital of the island.

As in most other Dalmatian towns, the nobles of Hvar established an oligarchical government from which commoners were excluded. In 1510 this provoked a **revolt** led by **Matija Ivanić**, a representative of the mercantile middle class. After first capturing Vrboska and Jelsa, Ivanić held the central part of the island for almost four years, raiding Hvar Town (and massacring sundry aristocrats) on two separate occasions. The Venetians ultimately re-established control, hanging rebel leaders from the masts of their galleys. Ivanić himself escaped, dying in exile in Rome.

Despite all this, sixteenth-century Hvar went on to become one of the key centres of the Croatian Renaissance, with poets like **Hanibal Lucić** and **Petar Hektorović** (see box, p.350) penning works which were to have a profound influence on future generations. This golden age was interrupted in 1571, when Ottoman corsair **Uluz Ali** sacked Hvar Town and reduced it to rubble. Rebuilt from scratch, the town soon reassumed its importance as a trading post. Later, the arrival of long-haul steamships becalmed Hvar Town, which drifted into quiet obscurity until the tourists arrived in the late nineteenth century – largely due to the efforts of the Hvar Hygienic Society, founded in 1868 by locals eager to promote the island as a health retreat. The first ever guidebook to the town, published in Vienna in 1903, promoted it as "Austria's Madeira", and it has been one of Dalmatia's most stylish resorts ever since.

ARRIVAL AND DEPARTURE — HVAR

Queues for car ferries build up fast in summer, so arrive early (2hr early in Aug); ferries are loaded on a first-come-first-served basis and any remaining vehicles will have to wait for the next sailing.

From Split There are regular car ferries from Split to Stari Grad (June–Sept 6 daily; Oct–May 3 daily; 2hr), as well as passenger-only catamarans from Split to Hvar Town (June–Sept 3 daily; Oct–May 2 daily; 1hr 20min) and Jelsa (1 daily; 1hr 50min).

From Brač There is a daily catamaran from Bol to Jelsa (25min) and a weekly catamaran from Milna to Hvar Town (June–Sept; Tues only; 1hr).

From Drvenik A car ferry runs from Drvenik, south of Makarska, to Sućuraj at the eastern end of the island (June–Sept 10 daily; Oct–May 5 daily; 35min), although there's virtually no public transport between here and the rest of Hvar.

From Lastovo A daily catamaran runs from Ubli to Hvar Town (1 daily; 2hr).

From Korčula There is a daily catamaran from Korčula Town to Hvar Town (1 daily; 1hr 15min) and from Vela Luka to Hvar Town (1 daily; 1hr)

From Vis There is a weekly catamaran from Vis Town to Hvar Town (Tues only; 55min).

From Dubrovnik and Korčula The main Dubrovnik–Rijeka coastal ferry calls at Stari Grad (June–Sept: twice weekly).

From Italy Both Jadrolinija and Blue Line run ferries from Ancona to Stari Grad (June–Aug 2–5 weekly; 8–13hr; overnight).

GETTING AROUND

By bus There are regular services between Hvar Town, Stari Grad, Jelsa and Vrboska. All Stari Grad–Hvar Town services call at Stari Grad ferry port to pick up and drop off ferry passengers.

Hvar Town and around

One of the best views of **HVAR TOWN** is from the sea, with its grainy-white and brown scatter of buildings following the contours of the bay, and the green splashes of palms and pines pushing into every crack and cranny. Once you're on terra firma, central Hvar reveals itself as a medieval town full of pedestrianized alleys overlooked by ancient stone houses, providing an elegant backdrop to the main leisure activity: lounging around in cafés and watching the crowds as they shuffle round the yacht-filled harbour.

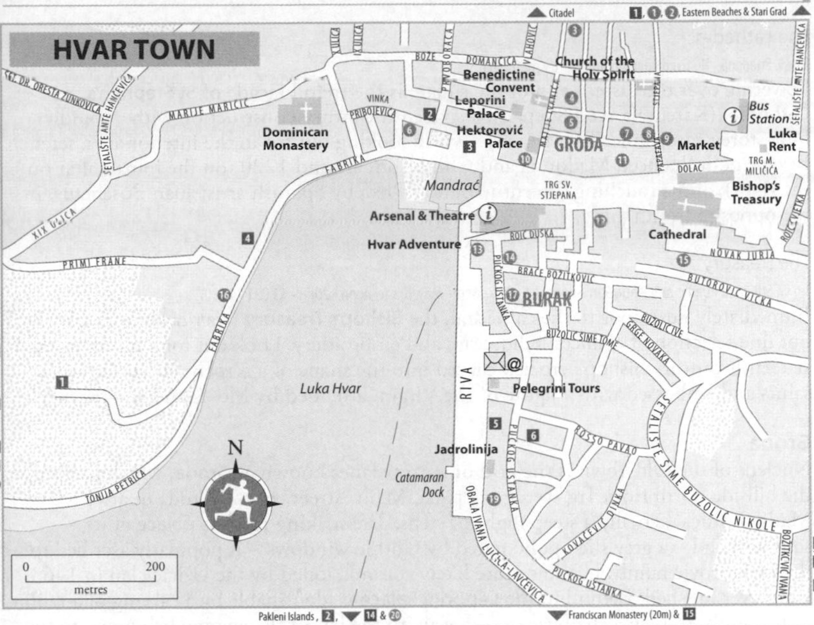

HVAR TOWN

HOTELS AND PENSIONS

Adriana	4
Amfora	7
Never Better	6
Palace	3
Palmižana Meneghello	14
Pansion Ćurin	8
Park	2
Pharia	9
Podstine	10
Riva	5
Villa Meneghello	15

HOSTELS

Green Lizard	11
Luka's Lodge	12
Orange	13

CAMPSITE

Mala Milna	1

RESTAURANTS

Giaxa	8
Kod Kapetana	16
Luna	5
Luviji	15
Macondo	4
Mala Milna	1
Palmižana Meneghello	20
Pizzeria Kogo	12
Zlatna Školjka	11
Zoraća	2

CAFÉS AND BARS

Carpe Diem	19
Hula Hula	18
Jazz	14
Ka' lavanda	9
Kiva	6
Konoba Menego	3
Loco	10
Red Baron	13
Tri pršuta	7
Nonica	17

CLUBS

Carpe Diem Beach	2
Veneranda	1

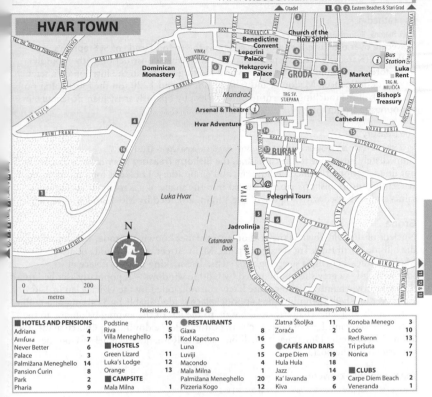

As well as being the nearest thing that Croatia has to the Côte d'Azur, Hvar Town is also very much a family destination, bringing both haute couture and howling kids to the animated *korzo* that engulfs the town at dusk.

Trg svetog Stjepana

At the centre of the town is **Trg svetog Stjepana**, a long, rectangular square which meets the sea at the so-called **Mandrać**, the balustraded inner harbour used for mooring small boats.

The theatre

Trg sv. Stjepana • Daily: summer 9am–1pm & 5–11pm; winter 11am–noon • Theatre and picture gallery 20Kn

Dominating the square's southwestern corner is the arcaded bulk of the seventeenth-century Venetian **arsenal**, with an arched ground floor into which war galleys were once hauled for repairs. The upper storey of the arsenal was adapted in 1612 to house the town **theatre** (*kazalište*), one of the oldest Baroque playhouses in Europe. It was built by the Venetian governor to assuage the distrust between nobles and commoners that had continued since the Ivanić rebellion, since the theatre was a civic amenity that all classes could enjoy together. The gaily painted interior, complete with two tiers of boxes, dates from the early 1800s, when locals revived and renovated the theatre after a period of neglect. The auditorium is entered through a small **picture gallery**, which has a modest collection of twentieth-century Croatian work. The terrace outside is the perfect place from which to observe the milling crowds on the square below.

The cathedral

Trg sv. Stjepana • No fixed opening hours – try mornings

Towering over the eastern end of the square is the trefoil facade of **St Stephen's Cathedral** (Katedrala sveti Stjepan), a sixteenth-century construction with a spindly four-storey campanile. Two artworks worth looking out for in the interior are a serene, Byzantine-influenced Madonna and Child from around 1220 (on the fourth altar on the right); and a touching fifteenth-century Pietà by Spanish artist Juan Boschetus, in the opposite (south) aisle.

The treasury

Trg sv. Stjepana • Daily: June–Aug 9am–noon & 5–7pm; Sept–May 10am–noon • 20Kn • ☎ 021 743 107

Immediately next door to the cathedral, the **Bishop's Treasury** (*riznica*) houses a small but fine selection of chalices, reliquaries and embroidery. Look out for a nicely worked sixteenth-century bishop's crozier, carved into the shape of a serpent encrusted with saints and embossed with a figure of the Virgin, attended by Moses and an archangel.

7

Groda

Nucleus of the Old Town is the grid of narrow lanes known as **Groda**, which backs up the hillside north from Trg svetog Stjepana. Main "street" of the Groda quarter is Matije Ivanića, actually a steep flight of steps. The striking roofless **palace** at its southern end – a grey shell punctuated by Gothic windows – is popularly ascribed to the Hektorović family, but was more likely commissioned by the Užičić clan in 1463, and never finished. Behind it, the **Leporini Palace** is identifiable by a carving of a rabbit – the family emblem – halfway up the wall, to the left of the awning belonging to the *Leporini* restaurant. East of here, above the cathedral, the diminutive **Church of the Holy Spirit** (Crkva svetog Duha) has a small but striking Romanesque relief of God the Creator above the portal.

The Benedictine convent

Groda bb • Mon–Sat 10am–noon & 5–7pm • 20Kn • ☎ 021 741 052

The **Benedictine convent** (Benediktinski samostan) in the centre of Groda was founded by the daughter-in-law of sixteenth-century Hvar poet Hanibal Lucić, and it still occupies parts of the Lucić family's former town house. Inside there's a small display of devotional paintings, and a unique display of lace made by the nuns – the lace is made from fibres of the agave cactus.

The Citadel

Daily: April & May 9am–4pm; June–Sept 8am–11pm • 25Kn

Above Groda a path zigzags its way up an agave-covered hillside to the **Citadel** (Fortica), built by the Venetians in the 1550s with the help of Spanish engineers – the structure is still known colloquially as Španjola by the locals. There's a marine archeology collection in one of the halls, with an attractively presented display of amphorae and other sediment-encrusted Greco-Roman drinking vessels, although the real attraction is the view from the Citadel's ramparts. Largely intact stretches of defensive wall plunge down the hillside towards the terracotta roofs of Hvar Town below, while beyond stretch the deep green humps of the Pakleni islands just offshore and the bulky grey form of Vis farther out to the southwest.

The Franciscan monastery

May–Oct daily 9am–1pm & 5–7pm • 20Kn

Occupying a headland just southeast of Hvar Town's ferry dock is the **Franciscan monastery** (Franjevački samostan), founded in 1461 by a Venetian sea captain in thanks for deliverance from shipwreck. There's a small collection of paintings in the former refectory, most famously a dramatic, near life-size seventeenth-century *Last*

Supper attributed to Matteo Ingoli of Ravenna, which covers almost the entire back wall. Smaller-scale devotional works in the neighbouring room include a tranquil *Mystical Wedding of St Catherine* painted in around 1430 by a follower of Blaž Jurjev of Trogir. Archeological exhibits include amphorae and a set of Roman cooking pots retrieved from a shipwreck near Palmižana.

The monastery church

Next door is the pleasingly simple monastic **church**, with beautifully carved choirstalls and a fanciful partition of 1583. Built to separate the commoners from the nobility, the latter is decorated with six animated scenes of the Passion. Look out for the extravagant dragon candle-holders that push out from the panel below. The floor is paved with gravestones, including that of poet and playwright Hanibal Lucić, identifiable by the fleur-de-lys and dove's wing of the family crest. In the small side chapel, there's a melodramatic *Christ on the Cross* by Leandro Bassano.

Town beaches

Working westward from Hvar harbour along the coastal path you will pass several rocky areas for sunbathing and swimming – although many are chock-full of pay-to-use sunloungers and it can be difficult to find space on which to plonk a towel. Most snobbish is Bonj/Les Bains, a small lido with exorbitant prices (sun loungers from 200Kn/day) tucked into the cove beneath the *Amphora* hotel, with a fancy cocktail bar above it. Further west, the *Hula Hula* beach bar (see p.348) rents out fancy, futon-like double beds (100Kn/day).

The Pakleni islands

Regular water taxis from Hvar's harbour (50–70Kn return)

Hvar Town's best beaches are arguably to be found on the **Pakleni islands** (Pakleni otoci – *pakleni* being a modern-day corruption of their original name, *paklinski* ["resin"], a reference to the juicy-barked trees that once covered them), a chain of eleven wooded islands just to the west of town.

Nearest to the coast, **Sveti Jerolim** is a purely naturist island which has a beach popular with same-sex couples on its far side. Immediately west, the slightly larger **Marinkovac** boasts two popular beaches, the sandy Ždrilca on the northern side and U Stipanska on the south.

Sveti Klement

West of Marinkovac, **Sveti Klement** is the largest of the Pakleni and has a correspondingly wider range of facilities. Boats disgorge their passengers at Palmižana yachting marina on the island's northern side, from where it's a short walk over the island's wooded spine to **PALMIŽANA** proper, a small hillside hamlet boasting a hotel (see p.347) and restaurants (see p.348). At the bottom of the hill lies an attractive bay with a tiny crescent of sandy beach, a smooth seabed for paddling on, and plenty of rocky bathing perches on either side. A marked path leads west from Palmižana along the island's central ridge (follow the signs to *Konoba Dioniz*), passing through maquis rich in wild rosemary before arriving at the village of **VLAKA**, a huddle of houses surrounded by groves of enormous cacti. *Dioniz* itself, on the southern side, is a great place to sample freshly caught fish, seasonal vegetables and local wine.

Beaches east of town

If you have access to a bike or a scooter, there is a handful of enticing **beaches** east of Hvar that ought to be worked in to your bathing schedule. First up is **MILNA** , 3km out of town, a bay-hugging cluster of modern houses that lies below the main Hvar–Stari Grad road. Milna's main beach is a broad swathe of pebble with rocky stretches on either side; you can rent a sunlounger if you want, but there is plenty of space for those who don't want to bother. A smaller, slightly less crowded pebble beach, **Mala Milna**, site of an excellent restaurant (see p.348) can be found five minutes' walk west through the *Mala Milna* campsite (see opposite).

A further 3km east along the Stari Grad road, a narrow lane descends to **Uvala Zaraća** (sometimes spelt Zoraća). It is in fact two bays split by a headland of smooth grey rock that looks (from a distance at least) rather like a visiting whale. Perch on the back of the whale, or sprawl on the small pebbly coves below. There's a popular restaurant (see p.348) behind the beach, but precious little parking space.

Two kilometres further on, just as the Hvar–Stari Grad route turns north towards the road tunnel, a footpath descends to **Uvala Dubovica**, one of the finest pebble beaches on the island, stretching between a pair of old manor houses. The bay is large and fairly shallow, making it good family territory, although it gets popular with yachts and motorboats in season. There's a fairly obvious parking spot, from where a path descends to the bay (a fifteen-minute walk). Otherwise, difficulty of access tends to filter out the guests – the parking strip on the main road above the bay is only big enough to accommodate about fifty vehicles.

ARRIVAL AND INFORMATION — HVAR TOWN AND AROUND

By bus The bus station is a few steps east of the main square on Trg M. Miličića.

Destinations Jelsa (Mon–Sat 8 daily, Sun 4; 55min); Stari Grad (Mon–Sat 10 daily, Sun 8; 35min); Sućuraj (Mon & Fri 1 daily; 1hr 45min); Vrboska (Mon–Sat 8 daily, Sun 4; 45min).

By catamaran Catamarans dock on the eastern side of Hvar Town's harbour, next to the Jadrolinija office (Mon–Sat 6am–1.45pm & 3–8pm; Sun 8am–1.45pm & 3.30–4.30pm).

Destinations Korčula Town (1 daily; 1hr 15min); Lastovo (1 daily; 2hr); Milna (June–Sept; Tues only; 1hr); Split (June–Sept 3 daily, Oct–May 2 daily; 1hr 20min); Vela Luka (1 daily; 1hr); Vis Town (Tues only; 55min).

Tourist office Branches in the bus station and on the corner of the main square, Trg sv. Stjepana (both offices June & Sept Mon–Sat 8am–1pm & 4–9pm, Sun 10am–noon & 6–8pm; July & Aug daily 8am–2pm & 3–10pm; Oct–May Mon–Sat 8am–1pm; T 021 741 059, W tzhvar.hr).

GETTING AROUND

Vehicle rental Luka Rent, Dolac (T 021 741 440, W lukarent.com), rents out bikes (100Kn/day), scooters (250–350Kn for 1–3 days) and boats (from 300Kn/day).

ACTIVITIES

★ **Hvar Adventure** Obala bb, in the alleyway behind the Arsenal T 021 717 813 and T 091 154 3072, W hvaradventure.com. Organizes a host of activities and special-interest day-trips, including wine tasting (420Kn), sea kayaking around the Pakleni islands (350Kn), guided hiking (300Kn), sailing (420Kn) and rock climbing (400Kn).

★ **Secret Hvar** Dolac bb T 021 717 615, W secrethvar.com. Offer 4WD trips on the rough roads of inland Hvar, exploring abandoned villages and lavender plantations. They also organize kayaking (350Kn) and hiking trips (300Kn).

ACCOMMODATION

Private **rooms** (350Kn) and **apartments** (two-person studios 450Kn, four-person apartments 600–750Kn) are available from **Pelegrini Tours**, near the ferry dock on the Riva (Mon–Sat 8am–10pm, Sun 6–8pm; T 021 742 743, W pelegrini-hvar.hr).

HOTELS AND PENSIONS

Adriana Fabrika bb T 021 750 200, W suncanihvar.com. Harbourside hotel featuring small but swish rooms with hardwood floors, a lavender-themed colour scheme and free wi-fi access. With only 55 rooms, the hotel is small enough for the staff to remember who their guests are. The spa centre offers everything from massages to mud baths, and the top-floor swimming pool is a major plus. The panoramic café-bar just below the top floor is a swanky place to unwind. **1600Kn**

Amfora Tonija Petrića bb T 021 750 300, W suncanihvar.com. Outwardly a bit monstrous, this 324-room sweep of concrete, west of town on the Veneranda headland, nonetheless has recently renovated rooms that are smart, bright and comfortable, and there are indoor and outdoor pools, a gym and casino. A popular crescent of beach lies just below the front entrance. Open May–Oct. **1600Kn**

Never Better Bučić Place ⓣ091 463 6120, ⓦnever-better.net. Seventeenth-century house just up the steps from the harbourfront, still owned by descendants of the Bučić family. Two fully equipped four-person apartments, one of which is split-level. Open June–Oct. **900Kn**

Palace Trg sv. Stjepana bb ⓣ021 741 966, ⓦsuncanihvar.com. Habsburg-era hotel on the harbourfront, part of which occupies the town loggia – breakfast is served on the loggia's roof terrace. Three-star comforts can be taken for granted throughout, although most of the rooms have showers rather than bathtubs. Rooms facing out towards the port are more expensive than those at the back. Open May–Oct. **1400Kn**

Palmižana Meneghello Palmižana ⓣ021 717 270, ⓦpalmizana.hr. Luxury villa settlement on the island of Sveti Kliment, 5km west of Hvar, connected to town by regular boat shuttle. Accommodation comes in the form of detached self-catering bungalows sleeping from two to four, each decked out with a well-chosen mixture of old and new furniture and artworks collected by the Meneghello family – all surrounded by cactus-filled gardens. From May to Sept seven-day bookings (Sat–Sat) preferred. **1200Kn**

Pansion Ćurin Majerovića bb ⓣ021 741 989 or ⓣ021 742 281. Sparsely furnished but clean en suites in a modern family house, a short walk west of town up behind the *Amfora* hotel. The owners will meet you at the port if you ring in advance. **375Kn**

Park Trg sv. Stjepana bb ⓣ021 718 337, ⓦhotelparkhvar.com. Sensitively renovated stone building just above the harbour, featuring roomy doubles and a couple of swanky two-level apartments. All but two rooms come with sea views. **1600Kn**

Pharia Majerovića bb ⓣ021 778 080, ⓦorvas-hotels.com. A range of bright rooms and two- to four-person apartments, all with modern furnishings, parquet floors and swish bathrooms, about 15min walk west of the centre. In quiet suburban streets but close enough to the seafront. Double rooms are priced depending on their view; apartments start at 1050Kn. Open May–Oct. **820Kn**

Podstine Podstine bb ⓣ021 740 400, ⓦpodstine.com. Mellow, medium-sized hotel a 20min walk west of the centre, overlooking a rocky bay which is good for swimming. The rooms are cosy, with sea views and satellite TV, and some also have a small balcony. Open April–Oct. **1450Kn**

Riva Riva bb ⓣ021 750 100, ⓦsuncanihvar.com. Prime-location hotel right beside central Hvar's yacht berths, with swanky interiors and plush rooms and the added attractions of a lounge bar and waterfront terrace. With 54 rooms it preserves a small-hotel feel. Open April–Oct. **1600Kn**

Villa Meneghello Sveti Križ ⓣ021 717 270, ⓦvillameneghello.com. A 15min walk along the coast from central Hvar, and shrouded in lush garden foliage, this hugely characterful seafront house comprises two fully equipped apartments, each of which occupies a whole floor and sleeps six to eight people. The decor incorporates the kind of modern design, handcrafted details and bohemian touches that you'd expect to see in a Mediterranean lifestyle magazine, and the walls are covered in contemporary Croatian paintings. With a small pool outside, it's an ideal location for a large-group stay. The whole house is available for rent (9300Kn). Apartments **5550Kn**

HOSTELS

★**Green Lizard** Lučica bb ⓣ021 742 560, ⓦgreenlizard.hr. Plainly decorated but clean and comfy house just uphill from the Franciscan monastery, offering a mixture of dorms, doubles and triples – mostly bright, white-walled affairs with tiled floors. Some rooms have en-suite shower/WC, others share facilities in the hallway. Breakfast isn't included, but you can use both indoor and outdoor kitchens. There is free wi-fi and a laundry service (40Kn). The terrace, with hammocks and bean bags, is an excellent place to chill out or socialize. Open April–Sept. Dorms **150Kn**, rooms **350Kn**

Luka's Lodge Lučica bb ⓣ021 742 118 and ⓣ091 734 7230, ⓦlukaslodgehvar.hostel.com. A pair of neighbouring houses just uphill from the centre, with a good proportion of doubles and triples, some with en-suite facilities and a/c. There's a common kitchen, and free internet in the lounge. Washing machine available for a few extra kuna. May to mid-Oct. Dorms **150Kn**, rooms **350Kn**

Orange Lučica 11 ⓣ021 741 432 and ⓣ091 515 7330, ⓦorange.hostel.com. Diagonally opposite *Green Lizard*, *Orange* is really a private house masquerading as a hostel but it's still a comfortable and friendly place to stay, with a collection of doubles and triples (some of which are en suite – en-suite doubles 50Kn extra), a kitchen and a wonderful plant-filled garden terrace. Free wi-fi. Doubles with shared facilities **300Kn**

CAMPSITE

Mala Milna Milna bb ⓣ021 745 013. Terraced site right by the sea, 3km east of Hvar in the village of Milna. It's mostly shaded by pines, although there's a patch of sun-exposed terracing right in the middle. With a bit of luck small-tent travellers might find a pitch right beside the shore. May–Sept. **50Kn** per person, pitches from **50Kn**

7

EATING, DRINKING AND NIGHTLIFE

There are dozens of **places to eat** in Hvar Town, and although prices are constantly spiralling upwards, several establishments offer seafood of sufficiently high standard to justify the cost. Note that many restaurants are only open from April to October. For **drinking**, the cafés and bars around the main square and along the harbour are packed from mid-morning onwards. Trade thins out for a few hours during the hottest part of the day, until the crowds return for the evening *korzo*.

RESTAURANTS

HVAR TOWN

★ **Giaxa** Petra Hektorovića ⊕ 021 741 073, ⊕ giaxa.com. Creative cuisine uniting the best of local traditions with modern European flair, served up in the bare-stone rooms of a restored palace. As much thought goes into the starters and desserts as the main courses, so this is one place where it's worth coming prepared to eat expansively and splash out a bit – most entrées are in the 150–200Kn range. Higher-end local wines fill out an extensive list of drinks. April–Nov daily noon–midnight.

7

Kod Kapetana Fabrika bb ⊕ 021 742 230, ⊕ kodkapetana.com. Homely family-run establishment boasting a big port-facing terrace. The fish, shellfish and steaks on offer are always good quality. Daily specials are chalked up outside. Daily noon–3pm & 5pm–midnight.

Luna Petra Hektorovića 1 ⊕ 021 741 400. Familiar seafood recipes, including excellent grilled fish, lobster and *gregada*, in a modern, white-walled interior with contemporary arty touches. Easter–Dec daily noon–midnight.

Luviji Jurja Novaka bb ⊕ 021 741 646. Cult family-run *konoba* behind the cathedral, serving up grilled and baked fish, an exemplary *gregada*, washed down with local wines including Pošip from their own vineyard on the island of Sveti Klement. May–Oct daily 6pm–midnight.

★ **Macondo** Groda bb ⊕ 021 742 850. This place has got style and quality yet remains informal, and for a slap-up seafood feast there are few better places: fresh white fish is always of good quality, and the *škampi buzara* is excellent. It's tucked away in a backstreet uphill from the main square (head up Matije Ivanića and take the second right). April–Oct Mon–Sat noon–2pm & 6pm–midnight, Sun 6pm–midnight.

Pizzeria Kogo Trg sv. Stjepana. The most dependable of the town's pizzerias also offers decent pasta dishes and hearty steaks too. Usually open all year round and remains popular with locals as well as tourists. June–Sept 10am–4am; Oct–May 10am–11pm.

Zlatna Školjka Petra Hektorovića 8 ⊕ 098 168 8797. An intimate covered-patio atmosphere, attentive service and great food combine in this upscale restaurant, which offers an imaginative take on local cuisine. Choose between traditional seafood dishes like *gregada* or unusual meat dishes such as rabbit in fig sauce. April–Oct Mon–Fri noon–3pm & 7–11pm, Sat & Sun 7pm–midnight.

OUT OF TOWN

Mala Milna Mala Milna bb ⊕ 021 745 027. On the beach 3km east of town, beyond the campsite of the same name, this is a simple stone structure with a large rush-shaded terrace, strings of pebbles dangling from the eaves and a small but well-tended border of succulents and cacti. Fresh seafood is fairly priced (*fruits de mer* risotto 80Kn, mussels in white wine sauce 70Kn) and augmented by daily specials chalked up on the wall. May–Sept daily 9am–midnight.

★ **Palmižana Meneghello** Palmižana bb ⊕ 021 717 270, ⊕ palmizana.hr. Restaurant of the *Villa Meneghello* hotel on Sveti Klement, serving up exquisite scampi, *gregada* and grilled fish on a terrace with dried gourds and other odd objects dangling from the ceiling. The beachside *Toto* restaurant just down the hill, is run by the same family and comes equally recommended. April–Oct daily 11am–midnight.

Zoraća Uvala Zaraća ⊕ 021 745 638. Located just above the easternmost of Zaraća's two beaches, with wooden benches set out on a pair of trellis-shaded terraces, this *konoba* serves up fresh fish and seafood risottos – it's the kind of place that may well discard the menu and tell you what they have fresh that day. House wines from local vineyards. Daily 11am–11pm.

CAFÉS AND BARS

Carpe Diem Riva bb ⊕ 021 742 369, ⊕ carpe-diem-hvar.com. Prime meeting-place for Croatia's beautiful people, with relaxing wicker chairs and cushions outside, and a brash and often crowded bar inside. Cocktail quality can be unpredictable and service veers from courteous to contemptuous, but this is still the place to see and be seen. Daily 9am–2am.

Hula Hula Majerovica bb ⊕ 021 717 261, ⊕ hulahulahvar.com. Hvar's premier après-beach bar, located on the shoreline path just beyond the *Amfora* hotel. Cold beers and cocktails are served up on a big seaside terrace scattered with stools and beds, although it's standing-room-only on summer nights. Daily May–Sept 9am–midnight.

Jazz Burak bb ⊕ 095 199 2847. Laid-back, intimate bar in the tangle of streets leading south of the main square. Jungle-themed decor, a decent list of cocktails and a playlist that features more than just top-forty sounds. Daily 9pm–2am.

Ka'lavanda Trg sv. Stjepana 1 ⊕ 021 718 721, ⊕ kalavanda.com. Squeezed into a narrow alley right beside stretches of town wall, this place features lounge-bar furnishings on the outdoor terrace, a minimalist matt-grey interior and a drinks list that runs from local *rakija* to cocktails. May–Sept daily 9am–2am.

Kiva Fabrika bb ⓦkivabarhvar.com. Raucously enjoyable black hole of a place in an alleyway just off the portside path. Can be a tight squeeze on summer weekends. Daily 9pm–2am.

Konoba Menego Groda bb ⓣ021 717 411, ⓦmenego.hr. Cosy tavern with wooden barrels for tables, on the steep street leading uphill from the main square. Wines (from Vloka, on the island of Sveti Klement) are served by the glass or by the carafe, and there's a snack menu comprising anchovies, cheese and home-made sausage. Daily 11.30am–2pm & 5.30pm–midnight.

Loco Trg sv. Stjepana. Cutest of the café-bars on the main square, with a tiny interior overlooked by the owner's paintings, an outdoor terrace for watching the world go by, and reliable, kick-start-the-day standards in the espresso and macchiato department. Daily May–Sept 8am–2am, Oct–April till midnight.

Nonica Kroz Burak 23. Small café-patisserie selling its own-baked cakes and sweets, including "Hvorski koloč", a dainty croissant-shaped biscuit. It's a great place for coffee and a nibble although space is limited, with a handful of tables inside and out. Mon–Sat 8am–2pm & 5–11pm, Sun 5–11pm.

Red Baron Riva bb. Occupying a harbourside terrace with a pine tree growing out of the middle, this is an ideal vantage point from which to look at people looking at yachts. Classy list of cocktails (including the rum, strawberry and champagne Red Baron daiquiri, 65Kn), and a wine list that takes in a lot of Hvar. May–Sept daily 8am–2am.

Tri pršuta Petra Hektorovića ⓣ098 969 6193. Elegant cubbyhole of a wine bar with a fine mix of antique furnishings and an impressive array of bottles behind the bar. If you don't know your Plavac from your Pošip then this is probably the best place to undergo a crash course. May–Sept daily 6pm–2am.

CLUBS

Carpe Diem Beach Uvala Stipanska, Marinkovac ⓦcarpe-diem-beach.com. Daytime beach bar and night-time club on the island of Marinkovac. DJ events tend to kick off at around 1am, when taxi boats moored outside the *Carpe Diem* bar (see opposite) ferry revellers to the island. The crossing costs about 40Kn and drink prices are above average, so come prepared. June–Sept daily 10am–8pm, then 1–5am.

Veneranda Veneranda bb ⓦveneranda.hr. Occupying the surviving fortifications of a Venetian fortress on the hillside on the western side of the harbour, this outdoor club comes into its own at the weekends, when international DJs are shipped in to entertain the crowds until dawn. June–Sept daily 10pm–5am.

7

Stari Grad

Twenty kilometres east across the mountains, straggling along the side of a deep bay, **STARI GRAD** is more laid-back and family-oriented than Hvar Town, although it is getting gradually more popular with the yachting fraternity and can be quite lively in high season. The narrow streets of central Stari Grad are as atmospheric as anywhere in the Adriatic: a warren of low stone houses bedecked with window boxes, and narrow alleyways suddenly opening out onto small squares.

The fertile **plain** stretching south and west of Stari Grad has recently been added to the UNESCO World Heritage list, as it is one of the few places in Europe where the ancient Greek system of field division has been preserved almost unchanged. With olive groves and vineyards divided by a grid of dry stone walls and country lanes, it is easily explored on foot or by bike.

The Tvrdalj

Priko bb • Daily: June & Sept 10am–1pm; July & Aug 10am–1pm & 5–8pm • 15Kn

Right in the centre of Stari Grad's warren of medieval stone houses is the **Tvrdalj**, the summer house and walled garden of the sixteenth-century poet and aristocrat Petar Hektorović (see box, p.350). This simple stone structure is a remarkably restful place, built around a central cloister with a turquoise pond fed with seawater and packed with mullet. Hektorović littered the place with inscriptions (carved round the pond and on the walls of the house in Latin, Italian and Croatian) to encourage contemplation: "Neither riches nor fame, beauty nor age can save you from Death" is one characteristically cheerful effusion. Beyond the cloister is Hektorović's walled garden – now largely divided up into allotments, although a portion has been tidied up and returned to its former glory.

PETAR HEKTOROVIĆ AND THE TVRDALJ

Renaissance poet and Hvar noble **Petar Hektorović** (1487–1572) is primarily remembered for his *Ribanje i ribarsko prigovaranje* ("Fishing and Fishermen's Conversations"), the first work of autobiographical realism in Croatian literature. Written in 1556, by which time he was an old man, the 1680-line poem was inspired by a three-day boat trip to Brač and Šolta in the company of two local fishermen, Paskoje and Nikola, who despite being commoners are accorded a dignity which was rare for the literature of the period. Hektorović had lived through the Ivanić rebellion of the early sixteenth century, and perhaps intended *Ribanje* as a message to his fellow aristocrats – treat the lower orders with a bit of humanity, and the bonds of society will hold.

This sense of *noblesse oblige* also underpinned Hektorović's plans for his summer house, the **Tvrdalj**, which he began in 1514 and carried on building for the rest of his life. As well as a place of repose, it was intended to be a fortified refuge for the locals in time of attack – a self-sufficient ark which would provide food from its garden and fresh fish from the mullet pond. Hektorović's typically Renaissance fondness for order and balance was reflected in the symbolic inclusion of a pigeon loft in the main tower, to emphasize the point that the Tvrdalj was a refuge for creatures of the sky as well as the sea and earth. The house was built in simple unadorned style, both because Hektorović had a taste for rusticity and because he didn't want to provoke the locals with a display of lordly luxury. Local Venetian commanders actually sanctioned the diversion of manpower resources from Hvar Town to assist Hektorović in its construction, since it freed them from the responsibility of defending the people of Stari Grad from pirates.

Hektorović died before the Tvrdalj was fully finished, though it was renovated and added to by his descendants. Ironically, the one thing which most people find so memorable about the Tvrdalj – the restful arched cloister surrounding the fishpond – wasn't part of Hektorović's original plan, added instead by the Niseteo family in 1834.

7

The Town Museum

Ulaz braće Biankini 2 • May, June & Sept Mon–Sat 10am–1pm; July & Aug daily 10am–noon & 7–9pm; Oct–April by arrangement • 20Kn • ⓣ 021 766 324, ⓦ stari-grad-museum.net

Immediately west of the Tvrdalj is a lane leading to the **Biankini Palace**, an impressively restored Renaissance pile which now holds the **Town Museum**. On the ground floor is a dramatic display of Roman amphorae, rescued by marine archeologists from a fourth-century shipwreck. Upstairs are finds from ancient Greek Pharos, including pottery fragments, clay figurines and a *louterion* – a stone basin used for washing before a ceremony or sacrifice. A picture gallery contains works by local-born artists Bartol Petrić (1899–1974) and Juraj Plančić (1899–1930), both of whom sought their fortunes in interwar Paris – where they had quite a racy time judging by the works on display here.

The Moria gallery

Vagonj 1 • Summer only; check with the tourist office for opening times • ⓦ moria.hr

The **Moria gallery** (Galerija Moria) hosts some of the best contemporary exhibitions on this part of the coast, and also boasts a well-preserved fragment of Roman mosaic in a portion of sunken floor. Precise exhibition dates are difficult to get hold of, but it's always worth popping round to see what's on.

Open Atelier Fantazam

Ivana Gundulića 6 • Open mornings and evenings • ⓣ 021 765 070, ⓦ fantazam.com

Tucked into a narrow street, **Open Atelier Fantazam** showcases Zoran Tadić's fantastical sculptures of imaginary animals (mostly made from fragments of wood, stone and bone found on the island) alongside some highly individual jewellery. Tadić's workshop is on the premises and he is usually eager to talk to visitors about what he's up to.

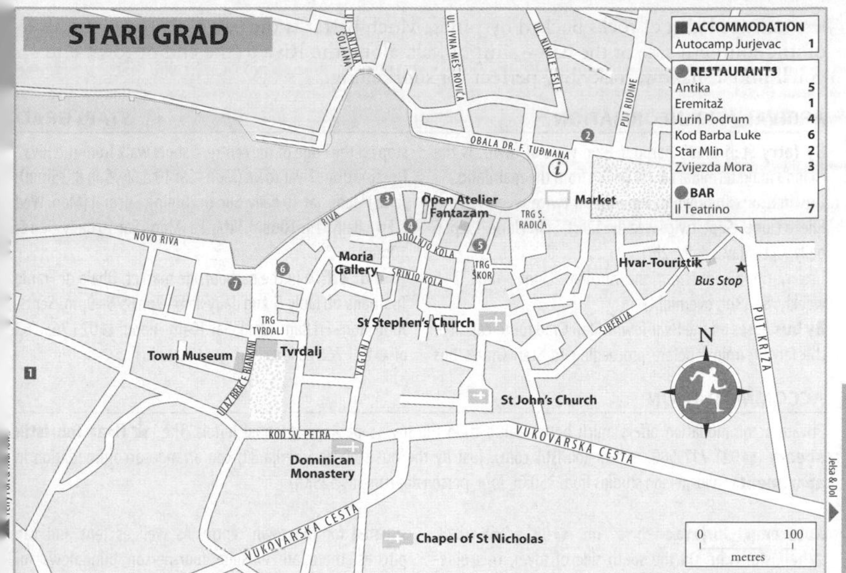

St Stephen's Church

Trg sv. Stjepana

Marking the eastern end of Stari Grad's Old Town is **St Stephen's Church** (Crkva Venetian campanile. Embedded in a wall opposite the church is a Roman-era **gravestone** relief of Winged Eros leaning nonchalantly on an upside-down torch – a classic symbol of death.

The Dominican monastery and museum

Kod sv. Petra • Museum June–Sept Mon–Fri 10am–12.30pm & 5.30–7pm • 10Kn

Marking the southern boundary of the Old Town, the **Dominican monastery** is a fifteenth-century foundation, fortified with the addition of a sturdy turret after Uluz Ali's attack of 1571. Rooms off the cloister house a **museum**, which contains an absorbing collection of Greek gravestones from Pharos, Cretan icons and a *Deposition* by Tintoretto. According to local tradition, the figures of Joseph of Arimathea and Mary Magdalene leaning over Christ's body in the picture are portraits of Petar Hektorović, his granddaughter Julija and her husband – although more sober analysts have pointed out that their faces are similar to those of many of the stock figures in the artist's paintings. There's also a small display of Hektorović's effects, including a 1532 edition of Petrarch's *Sonnets* and a copy of Polybius's *Histories*.

Chapel of St Nicholas

In the fields immediately south of the monastery, the **Chapel of St Nicholas** (Crkvica sveti Nikole) was the scene of an extraordinary demonstration of religiosity in 1554, when the hermit Lukrecija of Brač chose to be walled into a small side-room, where she lived on bread and water until her death 35 years later.

The beaches

There are rock and concrete **beaches** on the northern side of the bay in front of the package hotels, from where a path carries on beyond the *Arkada* mega-hotel to a much less sanitized area of rocks backed by pines. Much better is the bay favoured by locals on the southern side of the bay – simply walk along the Riva to the end of town and you'll find a shallow, rocky bay perfect for snorkelling.

ARRIVAL AND INFORMATION — STARI GRAD

By ferry Stari Grad's harbour, 3km west of town, is the island's main terminal for car ferries from the mainland.
Destinations Dubrovnik (June–Sept; twice weekly; 9hr); Rijeka (June–Sept; twice weekly; 12hr); Split (June–Sept 6 daily; Oct–May 3 daily; 2hr).
International destination Ancona (June–Aug 2–5 weekly; 8–13hr; overnight).
By bus Buses on the Hvar Town–Stari Grad route call in at the ferry terminal before proceeding to Stari Grad's bus stop on the edge of the centre, a short walk from the Riva.
Destinations Hvar Town (Mon–Sat 10 daily, Sun 8; 35min); Jelsa (Mon–Sat 10 daily, Sun 6; 20min); Sućuraj (Mon, Wed & Fri 1 daily; 1hr 10min); Vrboska (Mon–Sat 10 daily, Sun 6; 10min).
Tourist office In the harbourside market, Obala dr Franje Tuđmana bb (July & Aug daily 8am–2pm & 5–9pm; Sept–June Mon–Fri 8am–2pm, Sat 10am–noon; ⓣ 021 765 763 or ⓣ 021 766 231, ⓦ stari-grad-faros.hr).

7

ACCOMMODATION

Private accommodation offers much better value than the town's package-oriented hotels. The ★ **Hvar-Touristik agency** (ⓣ 021 717 580, ⓦ hvar-touristik.com), just by the bus stop at Šiberija 31, can arrange accommodation in **apartments** (two-person studios from 350Kn, four-person apartments 525Kn).

Autocamp Jurjevac Njiva bb ⓣ 021 765 843, ⓦ heliosfaros.hr. On the south side of town, this pine-shaded site in what used to be the town park is perfectly situated for the town centre. As well as tent and van pitches, there are en-suite four-person bungalows for 550Kn. June–Sept. 40Kn per person, pitches from 60Kn

EATING AND DRINKING

Eating in Stari Grad is rarely a problem, offering a clutch of restaurants that are friendlier and cheaper than the affluence-attuned establishments back in Hvar Town. The town's **drinking** scene revolves around the laid-back cafés lining the harbourfront. The wines on offer are excellent everywhere, with the nearby vineyards of Svirče, Vrbanj and Sveta Nedilja producing some of the most palatable plonk in the whole of Dalmatia.

RESTAURANTS

Antika Duolnjo kola ⓣ 021 765 479. Old Town parlour strewn with antique furniture and bric-a-brac, and serving local specialities like squid risotto, *pašticada*, baked octopus and other seafood, with a few international dishes thrown in. A touch more expensive than the others, but still affordable. There is a café section on the opposite side of the alley, and outdoor seating in a small piazza just round the corner. March–Oct daily noon–midnight.

Eremitaž Priko bb ⓣ 021 765 056. Occupying a stone structure on the shore-side path north of the Old Town, this is one of the best places in town for grilled fish and seafood. Shaded terrace out front. Mid-April to mid-Oct daily noon–3pm & 7pm–midnight.

Jurin Podrum Duolnjo kola 24 ⓣ 021 765 448. Restaurant with a stone-clad interior and outdoor tables squeezed into a narrow alley. Pastas and risotto fall in the 70Kn region, with fillets of fish for around 100Kn. April–Oct daily noon–midnight.

Kod Barba Luke Riva bb ⓣ 021 765 206. Terrace restaurant beside the harbourfront square offering superb grilled white fish, traditional stews like *brudet* and *gregada* (usually only served in two-person portions) and steak and chips for the unadventurous. Mains in the 120Kn range. Daily noon–3pm & 6pm–midnight.

Stari Mlin Obala Dr F. Tuđmana bb ⓣ 021 765 804, ⓦ stari-mlin.com. This tranquil garden restaurant located a few steps away from the tourist-trodden harbourfront is one of the best places to eat in town, serving up local treats such as stewed octopus with vegetables (70Kn), oven-baked fish (400Kn/kg) and excellent risottos. Daily noon–2pm & 6pm–midnight.

Zvijezda Mora Petra Zoranića bb ⓣ 021 766 133, ⓦ zvijezdamora.com. This is a tourist-oriented re-creation of a traditional Dalmatian *konoba* rather than the real thing, but the food is of a high order, with fine fresh fish and a mouthwatering range of own-recipe pasta dishes. Seating in an atmospheric alley just off the harbour. April–Oct daily 6pm–midnight.

BAR

Il Teatrino Riva 13 ⓣ 021 765 420. Seafront café-bar with a mix of sofas, benches and straight-backed chairs on its harbour-facing terrace, doling out good coffee in the daytime, and a broad range of shots and cocktails come the evening. DJs on weekend evenings. Daily 7am–3pm & 6pm–2am.

FROM TOP STARI GRAD; KOMIŽA HARBOUR, VIS (P.362) >

Jelsa

The former fishing village of **JELSA** sits prettily by a wooded bay 10km east of Stari Grad. There are large package hotels on either side of the bay, but the place retains a relatively laid-back feel. Tucked away behind a nineteenth-century waterfront, the old quarter is a maze of ancient alleys and lanes.

Parish church

Trg križonoše

Jelsa's fortified **parish church**, up the hill from the waterfront, managed to resist Uluz Ali's attack of 1571. Look out for the wooden Gothic statue of the Madonna (brought here from the mainland in 1539 to keep it safe from the Ottomans) on the high altar.

Chapel of St John

Between the parish church and the quayside is the charming octagonal sixteenth-century **Chapel of St John** (Crkva svetog Ivana), squeezed into a square overhung by the balconies of the surrounding Renaissance buildings.

7

Dalmacijaland

Open mornings and evenings • Ⓦ dalmacijaland.com

Tucked into the maze of streets behind the chapel, cult gallery **Dalmacijaland** has a fantastic array of paintings, graphics and subversive souvenirs for sale (including a deliciously ghoulish *I Hate Jelsa* postcard), and holds exhibitions by Croatian designers and comic-strip artists. Dalmacijaland's owner is co-creator of the (sadly, Croatian-only) comic books featuring the adventures of Jelsa's very own purple-cloaked hero Lavanderman. Note that there is a thirty percent discount for customers who enter the shop in the nude.

Beaches

Mina Bay, beyond the *Mina* campsite (see opposite), offers a mixture of rock and pebble to perch on but is quite sandy underfoot once you get in the water. Taxi boats from Jelsa harbour head for the **Glavica peninsula** near Vrboska (see p.356) and the naturist island of **Žečevo** off the tip of the cape, with limestone slabs for sunbathing and trees for shade – remember to take some food and drink.

East of Jelsa on the road to Sućuraj are a sequence of pleasant coves, most popular of which is **Grebišće**, 4km out of town. Reached by walking through the *Grebišće* campsite, the beach itself is very narrow and contains very little shade, but the bay is both very shallow and sandy underfoot, making it perfect for safe paddling and playful splashing around. Drinks and basic snacks are available at the campsite café or the *Čorni Petar* beach bar on the headland to the east.

ARRIVAL AND INFORMATION — JELSA

By catamaran Catamarans dock right in the middle of Jelsa harbour.

Destinations Bol (1 daily; 25min); Split (1 daily; 1hr 50min).

By bus Buses stop about 300m inland from the harbour.

By car There is a large car park behind the town park (8Kn/hr).

Tourist office On the western side of the harbour (June & Sept Mon–Sat 8am–2pm & 3–8pm; July & Aug Mon–Sat 8am–2pm & 3–10pm, Sun 10am–noon & 7–9pm; Oct–May Mon–Fri 8am–2pm; Ⓣ 021 761 017, Ⓦ tzjelsa.hr). The tourist office has hiking and cycling maps, as well as details of local accommodation.

ACCOMMODATION

Private **rooms** (250Kn) and **apartments** (two-person studios from 400Kn, four-person apartments from 580Kn) are available from **Atlas** (Ⓣ 021 761 038, Ⓔ atlas-jelsa@st.htnet.hr), on the harbour beside the tourist office.

Camp Grebišće Grebišće Ⓣ 021 761 191, Ⓦ grebisce.hr. Occupying a terraced site above Grebišće beach, this campsite is perfect for a bathing-based seaside holiday. There is a restaurant on site, a free wi-fi zone and olive groves – although not all of the pitches are shaded. At 4km from Jelsa, it's a bit too far to walk to/from town and there is no public transport. May–Oct. **45Kn** per person, pitches from **80Kn**

Camp Mina Račić bb 021 761 210. In front of the concrete eyesore that is *Hotel Hvar*, the *Mina* campsite occupies a pine-shaded promontory overlooking the sea and has good access to the beach on Mina bay just beyond. **40Kn** per person, pitches from **50Kn**

Pansion Murvica sv. Roka 021 761 405, murvica.net. Family-run pension, located in a residential street behind the bus station, which offers nifty studio apartments with TV and kitchenette. **570Kn**

EATING AND DRINKING

There are plenty of reasonable pizzerias and seafood places around the harbour, although it's worth heading slightly further afield for something special.

★ **Dvor Duboković** Pitve bb 098 172 1726 or 021 761 569, dvordubokovic.hr. In the hillside settlement of Pitve, 5km inland from Jelsa on the road to Zavala, *Duboković* occupies a big stone house in a village that's full of big stone houses. Most of the seating is outside in a walled and hedged garden strung with vine trellises. The food is traditional Dalmatian (seafood, grilled meats and *peka*-baked lamb or octopus; the latter need to be ordered 24hr in advance), but quality is high and reveals itself in the detail – the roast potatoes with rosemary are sufficiently divine to carry this review on their own. The Duboković house red wine is also worthy of praise. Daily 6pm–midnight.

Tarantela Pjaca. Named after a gecko lizard that lives on Hvar, this is the best place for daytime coffee on Jelsa's tiny main square, and a popular night-time haunt as well with a handsome list of cocktails, few of which break the 40Kn barrier. Daily 8am–midnight; summer till 2am.

★ **Turan** Jelsa 021 761 441. Occupying an atmospheric terraced garden in the narrow streets uphill from the octagonal chapel (follow the signs), *Turan* rolls out superb seafood and a big range of traditional Dalmatian recipes that don't always feature elsewhere – squid *brodet* and octopus fritters being just two items in a long, must-be-tried-at-least-once list. It is also known for its *peka* specialities (order 24hr in advance). And the local house wine is excellent too. April–Oct daily 5pm–midnight.

Vila Verde Jelsa vilaverde.info. A supremely attractive garden-based DJ bar with loungey seating set out under palms, *Villa Verde* has the biggest cocktail list, the widest range of drinks, but also the most irritating music, which is squarely aimed at Euro-youth. June–Sept daily 6pm–2am.

7

Vrboska

Four kilometres northwest of Jelsa, and easily reached by following the coastal path from the north side of Jelsa harbour, the sleepy little village of **VRBOSKA** is strung along both sides of a narrow inlet, which is spanned by a trio of small and picturesque bridges.

St Mary's Church

Mon–Sat 10am–noon & 7.30–9pm • 15Kn

Perched above the quayside is the strikingly angular **St Mary's Church** (Crkva svete Marije), dating from 1580. It was extensively fortified to resist attacks from seaborne raiders, resulting in a high, unadorned edifice with a crenellated tower on the southeast corner, and a hefty bastion on the northwest – a protruding structure that looks like the prow of a beached dreadnought. The interior is partly paved with grave slabs and from the sacristy you can get onto the roof for a view of the town below.

St Lawrence's Church

Mon–Sat 10am–noon & 7.30–9pm • 15Kn

Above the harbour near the much larger St Mary's Church, the Baroque **St Lawrence's Church** (Crkva svetog Lovre) has a small art collection, including a polyptych depicting St Lawrence flanked by John the Baptist and St Nicholas on the high altar, nowadays attributed to Paolo Veronese, although local tradition ascribes it to Titian. To the right, there's a *Madonna of the Rosary* by Leandro Bassano.

The beaches

Soline is a 20min walk from Vrboska; parking 4Kn/hr

There's a series of **beaches**, including a couple of naturist ones, on the Glavica peninsula 2km northeast of town. The main destination is **Soline** at the tip of the peninsula, where there is a large car park and a café-restaurant. On the right-hand side is a broad gravelly bay with a shallow paddling area; over to the left is a shoreline of rocky slabs and a more steeply shelving sea. The views on this side are terrific, with the green island of Zečevo in the foreground, the southern flanks of Brač further distant, and the stark ridge of Mount Biokovo away to the southeast.

You can find quieter spots by walking north from Vrboska over the spine of the Glavica peninsula, passing Kaštilac hill (where there's a ruined tower), towards the isolated rocky coves of the peninsula's north coast.

ARRIVAL AND INFORMATION — VRBOSKA

7

By bus Buses on the Stari Grad–Jelsa route stop in the centre of the village.

Tourist office Vrboska bb, by the main bridge (July & Aug Mon–Sat 8am–3pm & 4–10pm, Sun 8am–noon; Sept–June Mon–Fri 8am–2pm; T021 744 137, W vrboska.info).

ACCOMMODATION AND EATING

Camping Nudist Vrboska bb T021 774 034, W nudistcamp-vrboska.hr. Right next to the Soline beaches at the tip of the Glavica peninsula, this campsite occupies a partly shaded, rocky stretch of coast with its own beach. If you don't fancy camping in the buff, head for the *Mina* or *Grebišće* sites in nearby Jelsa (see pp.354–355). May–Sept. **75Kn** per person, pitches from **50kn**

Gardelin Vrboska bb T021 774 071, W gmp-art-studio.com/gardelin. With a terrace overlooking the yacht berths just east of the village on the path to Jelsa, this is the place to go for *gregada*, *brudet* and other fishy specialities. April–Oct daily 8am–midnight.

Spes tours Vrboska bb T021 774 234. This agency on the harbourfront will sort you out with apartments. Two-person studios from **350Kn**, four-person apartments from **530Kn**

Humac

Seven kilometres east of Jelsa, after several twists and turns of the serpentine route to Sućuraj, a signed road heads uphill to the semi-abandoned hamlet of **HUMAC**, a superbly preserved example of what Dalmatian rural architecture used to look like before humdrum holiday villas became the norm. Stone houses come with arched doorways and outdoor stairways, with roofs made from thick slabs of stone – a lot of the buildings are currently being renovated, a sign of oncoming rural gentrification. Paths lead from the village up onto the island's central ridge, offering fine views of the coast.

Grapčeva Cave

May–Sept Mon, Wed & Sat at 9am • Guided tours only (20Kn); meet outside *Konoba Humac* (see below) • T099 577 1770

Paths lead from the village to **Grapčeva Cave** (Grapčeva špilja), 1km away, which is famous for being one of the earliest-known sites of settled human culture on the Adriatic islands, yielding flint tools and pottery fragments around 5500 years old. It's an atmospheric place to visit if you are here at the right time, with an entrance passage leading to a large chamber decked with stalagmites and stalagtites.

EATING — HUMAC

Konoba Humac Humac T021 768 108. If location is everything then this is one of the best places on the island, with tables made out of salvaged wood spread across a terraced garden, and food prepared in an old stone barn. The food is usually great too, though you do have to be at your most carnivorous to enjoy it: grilled veal, lamb and steak are the cornerstone of the menu, and *peka*-baked veal, lamb or octopus are a speciality, but need to be ordered 24hr in advance. Reservations advised. June–Sept Mon–Sat 10am–11pm.

Vis

A compact hump rearing dramatically out of the sea, **VIS** is situated farther offshore than any of Croatia's other inhabited Adriatic islands. Closed to foreigners for military reasons until 1989, it has never been overrun by tourists, and with only two or three package-oriented hotels on the whole island, this is definitely one place in Croatia where the independent traveller rules the roost. Croatian lotus-seekers have fallen in love with the place over the last two decades, drawn by its breathtaking bays, fantastic food and wine and two great-looking small towns – **Vis Town** and **Komiža**. The latter is the obvious base for trips to the islet of **Biševo**, site of one of Croatia's most famous natural wonders, the **Blue Cave**.

Brief history

The **Greeks** settled on Vis in the fourth century BC, treating the island as a stepping stone between the eastern and western shores of the Adriatic, and founding **Issa** on the site of present-day Vis Town. Hvar took over as the major mid-Adriatic port in the late Middle Ages, and Vis became a rural retreat for Hvar nobles. When the fall of Venice in 1797 opened up the Adriatic to the competing navies of Europe's great powers, Vis fell to the British, who fortified the harbour and fought off Napoleon's navy in 1811. The **Austrians** took over in 1815, famously brushing aside Italian maritime ambitions in another big sea battle here in 1866. During World War II, Vis briefly served as the nerve centre of **Tito**'s Partisan movement (see box, p.364). After the war, the island was heavily garrisoned, a situation which, along with the decline of traditional industries like fishing and fish canning, encouraged successive waves of **emigration**. The island had ten thousand inhabitants before World War II; it now has fewer than three thousand. According to local estimates, there are ten times more Komiža families living in San Pedro, California, than in the town itself.

7

ARRIVAL AND DEPARTURE — VIS

By boat Ferries (2–3 daily; 2hr 30min) and catamarans (1 daily; 1hr 40min) run year-round between Split and Vis Town (once a week the catamarans call in at Hvar on the way).

Vis Town

VIS TOWN's sedate arc of grey-brown houses stretches around a deeply indented bay, above which looms a steep escarpment covered with the remains of abandoned agricultural terraces. Despite a scattering of new houses on the hillside, it's a good example of

FOOD AND DRINK ON VIS

The waters off the island of Vis represent one of the richest fisheries in the Adriatic, and it's no wonder that the local restaurants offer some of the freshest **seafood** in Dalmatia. Both Komiža and Vis Town contain highly rated restaurants renowned for their lobster and fish; *Pojoda* in particular (see p.361) is famous for nurturing traditional island recipes that rarely crop up anywhere else.

Harvesting the anchovy shoals around Palagruža island used to be Vis's main industry, and it's no surprise the island's principal culinary trademark is the **pogača od srdele** (anchovy pasty) – also called *viška pogača* or *komiška pogača* depending on which town you're staying in. Traditionally, the *komiška pogača* includes a richer combination of ingredients (including tomatoes), and it's this version that is sold by most local bakeries and cafés. The island's other claim to gastronomic fame is the delicious **Viški hib**, a deliciously sweet slab of compressed figs and herbs, which is served in tiny thin slices and goes down a treat with the local *rakija*.

Vis is also famous for a brace of fine local **wines** – the white Vugava, which thrives in the stony soil in the southeast of the island, and the red Viški plavac, which prefers the sandy terrain farther west.

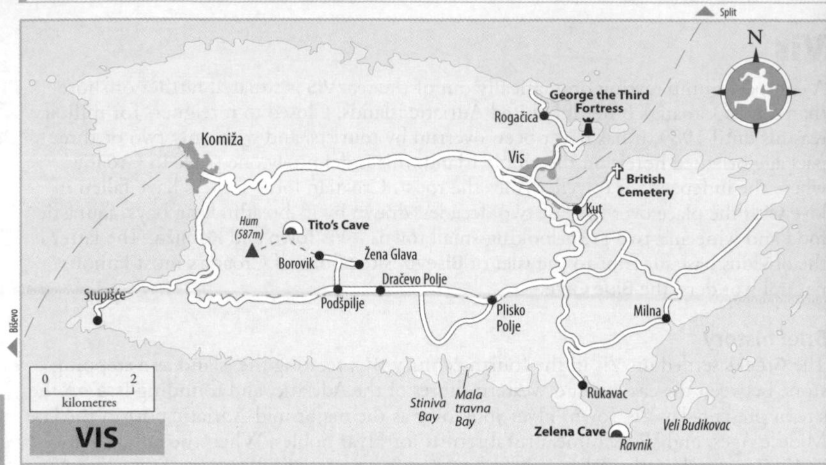

traditional Dalmatia at its best preserved. Its bay-hugging shape also makes it a highly individual place to stay – the "centre" of town is just one long, lovely seafront walk.

Town Museum

Gospina batarija • May–Oct Mon–Fri 10am–1pm & 5–9pm, Sat 10am–1pm • 20Kn • ☎ 021 771 3729

Occupying a barrack block at the rear of an Austrian-built defensive bastion, the **Town Museum** (Gradski muzej) is a small but well-organized collection of Greco-Roman finds combined with nineteenth-century wine presses and domestic furniture. The star exhibit is the bronze head of a Greek goddess, possibly Aphrodite, from the fourth century BC, which is claimed to be by a student of Praxiteles, although only a replica is on display – the original is locked up in the town vaults.

Kut

Tucked into the southeastern end of Vis's bay is the suburb of **Kut** (literally "quiet corner" or "hideaway"), a largely sixteenth-century tangle of narrow cobbled streets overlooked by the summer houses built by the nobility of Hvar – the stone balconies and staircases give the place an undeniably aristocratic air.

St Cyprian's Church

Kut • Mass Mon, Wed & Fri 7pm, Sun 8am

Kut's **St Cyprian's Church** (Crkva svetog Ciprijana) squats beneath a campanile adorned with unusual sun and rose motifs. There's a fine wooden ceiling inside, although it's difficult to gain access outside Mass times.

The British Cemetery

A fifteen-minute walk west along the seafront from Kut brings you to a small wooded peninsula, and a tiny walled garden containing a **British Cemetery** – inside lie a couple of unobtrusive monuments honouring the war dead of both 1811–15 and 1943–44. The shallow bay and pebble **beach** on the far side of the cemetery is one of the nicest places to bathe on the island.

The Ancient Greek Cemetery

Daily 4–8pm

There's not much of the ancient Greek settlement of Issa to be seen, save for the **ancient Greek cemetery** (Helenističko groblje) behind the municipal tennis courts

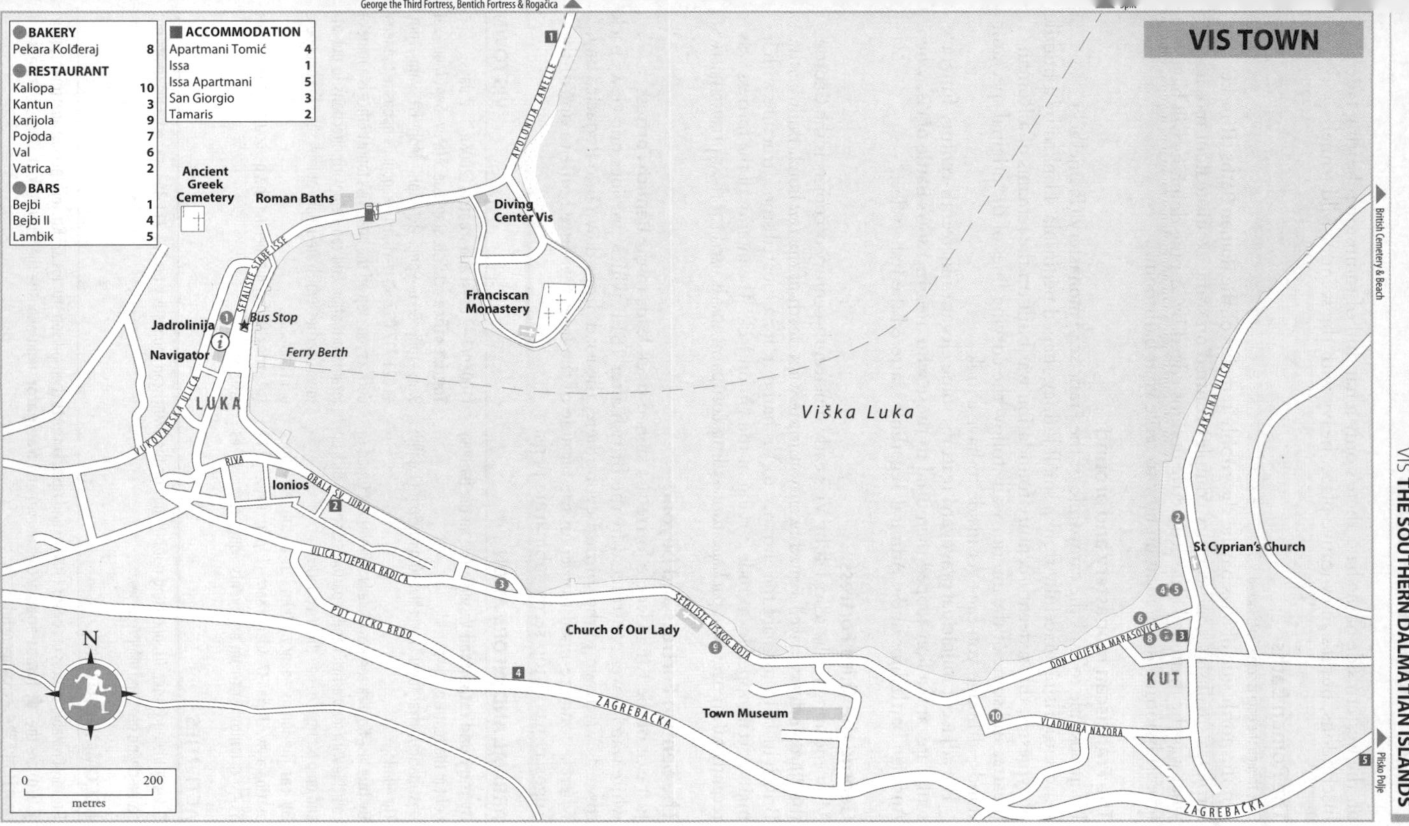
VIS TOWN
George the Third Fortress, Bentich Fortress & Rogačica
British Cemetery & Beach
Plisko Polje
Komiža
BAKERY
Pekara Kolđeraj 8
RESTAURANT
Kaliopa 10
Kantun 3
Karijola 9
Pojoda 7
Val 6
Vatrica 2
BARS
Bejbi 1
Bejbi II 4
Lambik 5
ACCOMMODATION
Apartmani Tomić 4
Issa 1
Issa Apartmani 5
San Giorgio 3
Tamaris 2
Ancient Greek Cemetery
Roman Baths
Diving Center Vis
APOLONIJA ZANELLE
ŠETALIŠTE STARE ISSE
Franciscan Monastery
Jadrolinija
Bus Stop
Navigator
Ferry Berth
LUKA
VUKOVARSKA ULICA
Viška Luka
RIVA
Ionios
OBALA SV. JURJA
ULICA STJEPANA RADIĆA
PUT LUČKO BRDO
Church of Our Lady
ŠETALIŠTE VIŠKOG BOJA
ZAGREBAČKA
Town Museum
DON CVJETKA MARASOVIĆA
KUT
VLADIMIRA NAZORA
JAKŠINA ULICA
St Cyprian's Church
N
0
200
metres

7

on the western side of the bay. There's only a handful of tombstones bearing faded inscriptions, but it's an evocative place, heavy with the scent of wild fennel.

The Roman Baths

Free, though the gate is sometimes locked

On the north side of Vis's bay lie the rubbly remains of the **Roman Baths** (Rimske terme), a smallish second-century complex centred on some exquisite floor mosaics in what was the main hall. The geometric designs edged by leaping dolphins will have you feverishly jotting down ideas on how to retile your bathroom.

The Franciscan monastery and around

It's impossible to miss the campanile of the **Franciscan monastery** (Franjevački samostan), rising gracefully from a small kidney-shaped peninsula. Flanked by a huddle of cypresses, this sixteenth-century foundation was built on the remains of a Roman theatre, and some of the interior walls follow the curving lines of the original spectator stands, although you can't get inside to have a look

The adjacent **municipal graveyard** features some elegant nineteenth-century funerary sculpture, and a lion-topped memorial to those who died in 1866's **Battle of Vis**, when Austrian battleships under Admiral Tegethoff scattered the Italian fleet.

George the Third Fortress

Most enduring of the relics left by Vis's early nineteenth-century occupiers is the **George the Third Fortress**, a well-signed twenty-minute walk north of the *Issa* hotel. Built by the British in 1813 to guard the entrance to Vis harbour, it's a moated stone structure with a main portal topped by a crude carving of the Union Jack. The interior of the fortress was recently taken over by a package-tour sailing company and is used for their private parties.

The Bentich Fortress and beyond

Just east of the King George fortress, a signed track leads to the **Bentich Fortress**, a white watchtower constructed by the British after 1811, which provides fine views back towards Vis Town to the south. Beyond here, the road drops down into **Rogačica bay**, where a concrete-lined tunnel on the far side of the inlet was once home to one of the Yugoslav navy's top-secret submarine pens.

ARRIVAL AND INFORMATION — VIS TOWN

By ferry and catamaran Vessels arrive on the harbour right in the centre of town.

Destinations Hvar Town (1 weekly; 40min); Split (1 daily; 1hr 40min).

By bus Vis–Komiža services (5 daily; 20min) are timed to coincide with ferry arrivals and departures. Services pick up and drop off right beside the ferry dock.

By car The Ionios agency, 200m left of the ferry dock at Obala sv. Jurja 37 (daily 8am–10pm; ☎ 021 711 532, ✉ ionios@st.t-com.hr), rents out cars, bikes (100Kn/1–2 days) and scooters (200Kn/1–2 days).

Tourist office Šetalište stare Isse 5 (May–Sept Mon–Sat 9am–1pm & 6–9pm; Oct–April Mon–Fri 9am–1pm; ☎ 021 717 017, 🌐 tz-vis.hr). Diagonally opposite the ferry dock as you step off the boat, Vis's tourist office is a mine of local information and can help with directions to out-of-town beaches, which are usually quieter than the ones here or in Komiža.

Internet Biliba, just behind the harbourfront on Žrtava fašizma.

ACTIVITIES

Diving Diving Center Vis, operating out of a hut by the Franciscan monastery (☎ 021 711 367, 🌐 anma.hr), rents out scuba-diving gear and offers courses.

ACCOMMODATION

The most reliable sources of **rooms** (300Kn) and **apartments** (two-person studios 375Kn, four-person apartments from 450Kn) are the ★ **Ionios agency** (see above) and **Navigator**, right opposite the ferry dock at Šetalište stare Isse 1 (☎ 021 717 786, 🌐 navigator.hr).

Apartmani Tomić Zagrebačka 3 ☎021 711 871. Studios and family-sized apartments in a modern family house slightly uphill from the seafront, most with views overlooking the town. It is very near the centre if you use the rough track that leads downhill; quite a long way around if you come by road. Two-person studio **350Kn**

Issa Apolonija Zanelle 5 ☎021 711 124, Ⓦhotelsvis.com. Modest, white-concrete 100-room hotel about 1km north of the ferry dock, offering adequate en suites within a pebble's throw of the main beach. May–Sept only. **750Kn**

Issa Apartmani Zagrebačka 156 ☎021 711 923, Ⓦissa-apartmani.com.hr. This may be the last house in Vis out on the Plisko Polje road, but the views are superb and the waterfront of Kut is only a 5min walk downhill. Five kitchenette-equipped apartments of various sizes – the cute Orange (two-person studio) and Purple (two- to four-person apartment) ones share a lovely front garden. The owners like to keep cats (so if you don't like them, don't come). **450Kn**

San Giorgio Petra Hektorovića 2 ☎021 711 362. Set amid the picturesque alleyways of the eastern suburb of Kut, this upmarket ten-room B&B offers smart, modern rooms in muted colours with hardwood floors and flat-screen TVs. Wi-fi coverage throughout. **940Kn**

Tamaris Obala sv. Jurja ☎021 711 350, Ⓦhotelsvis.com. Stately, Habsburg-era building right next to the harbourfront yacht berths, with cosy en suites with TV, a/c and squeaky parquet floors. Nifty three-person attic apartments **950Kn**, regular doubles **750Kn**

7

EATING AND DRINKING

Vis's harbour is a popular overnight stop-off for yachters, which helps to explain why the standard of **restaurants** in town is so high.

BAKERY

Pekara Kolđeraj Don Cvijetka Marasovića 10. All you need in the fresh bread and pastries line, including Vis's famous *pogača od srdele* (see box, p.357). Daily 8am–noon & 4–10pm.

RESTAURANTS

Kaliopa Vladimira Nazora 32 ☎021 711 755. If you've always fancied dining in the middle of a horticultural attraction you won't do any better than *Kaliopa*, with chairs and tables buried amid the palms and shrubs of a walled garden. The seafood here is as excellent as you would expect, but be prepared to splash out. May–Sept daily 8am–1pm & 5pm–2am.

★ **Kantun** Biskupa Mihe Pušića 17 ☎021 711 306. Fresh fish grilled over an open hearth in an interior that mixes centuries-old stone walls with abstract artworks. There's also an outdoor terrace facing the yacht-lined quay. Meat-eaters can content themselves with an excellent Dalmatian *pašticada*, and local wines and excellent herbal *rakijas* round out the picture. May–Sept daily 6pm–midnight.

Karijola Šetalište viškog boja 4. Perched on a terrace midway between the town centre and Kut, this is the best place for a quality thin-crust pizza. Settle your stomach with *Karijola*'s range of irresistible *rakijas* – the *rakija od mirte* (flavoured with mistletoe) has proven aphrodisiac qualities. May–Sept daily 1pm–1am.

★ **Pojoda** Don Cvijetka Marasovića 8 ☎021 711 575. Excellent fresh seafood, including the best fish and lobster, served on a terrace shaded by orange and lemon trees. Look out, too, for old-fashioned peasant dishes such as *orbiko* (barley, peas and shrimps) and *bronzinić* (a *brodet*-like broth of barley, lentils and squid) – both are listed as starters but are filling enough to serve as mains. Whatever you order, a bottle of local Vugava serves as the ideal accompaniment. Daily: May–Sept noon–3pm & 6pm–midnight; Oct–April 4–11pm.

Val Don Cvijetka Marasovića 1 ☎091 508 2015, Ⓦval.info-vis.net. Quality seafood on a palm-shaded terrace just back from the quay. Alongside the customary grilled fish and shellfish, house specialities include *pasta fažol na brodet* (pasta with a thick soup full of beans, shellfish and other goodies) and *caponata* (a kind of aubergine-based ratatouille). April–Nov daily noon–3pm & 5–11pm.

Vatrica Obala kralja Krešimira 15, Kut ☎021 711 574. Vine-covered terrace next to Kut's small harbour, dishing up a simple but superbly prepared seafood repertoire – and a satisfying steak and chips for the more timorous. May–Sept daily 9am–midnight; Oct–April weekends only 5–11pm.

BARS

Bejbi/Bejbi II Šetalište stare Isse; Podloža 4. Pronounced "baby", this is a laid-back coffee-drinking haunt during the daytime which bursts into life at night, with a funkily decorated café indoors and bamboo-shaded bar in the yard. There is a new branch, *Bejbi II*, in Kut at Podloža 4. Daily 6am–midnight; Bejbi until 2am in summer.

Lambik Podloža 2. A respectable list of cocktails, light meals and pizzas, to be enjoyed while sprawled across the loungey furnishings strewn across the adjoining square, or from the distressed armchairs in the beautiful arcaded courtyard at the back. June–Sept daily 7am–2am.

Komiža

Descending along the switchback road that drops down to the fishing port of **KOMIŽA** is one of the most exhilarating arrivals in the Adriatic. Wedged into a compact curving bay beneath Mount Hum, the town is achingly picturesque, with a harbourfront lined with palm trees and fringed by sixteenth- and seventeenth-century Venetian-style houses. It has a couple of good beaches and is the obvious base from which to embark on excursions to the Blue Cave on Biševo (see opposite).

The Kaštel

Riva sv. Mikule • Fishing Museum June–Sept Mon–Sat 11am–noon & 7–10pm, Sun 7–10pm • 10Kn

Dominating the southern end of the harbour is the **Kaštel**, a stubby sixteenth-century fortress with a slender clock tower protruding from one of its corners. It currently holds a **Fishing Museum** (Ribarski muzej), whose worthy displays of nets and knots are enlivened by the presence of a reconstructed *falkuša*, one of the traditional fishing boats with triangular sails that were common hereabouts until the early twentieth century – and have recently been revived by contemporary enthusiasts. What made the *falkuša* unique was its two-piece hull: the upper storey, complete with mast and sails, ensured swift arrival at the sardine fishing grounds around far-flung islands like Palagruža, but could be removed, transforming the *falkuša* into a rowing boat – ideal for fishing in coastal waters.

7

The Kaštel has been earmarked as home of the **Komiža Eko-Museum**, a collection devoted to traditional activities and sustainable industries based largely on objects and pictures donated by the inhabitants themselves. Floors of the museum will open up gradually from year to year.

Gospa Gusarica

Among the town's churches, the most notable is the sixteenth-century **Gospa Gusarica**, whose name loosely translates as "Our Lady of the Pirates" – it's said that a painting of the Virgin was stolen from the church by pirates, but floated back into port when they were shipwrecked. The church is set amid trees on a little beach at the northern end of town near the *Biševo* hotel, and has an eight-sided well adorned with reliefs of St Nicholas, protector of fishermen and patron of Komiža.

The Benedictine monastery

About a kilometre southeast of the town on a vineyard-cloaked hillock is the seventeenth-century **Benedictine monastery** (known as *mušter*, the local dialect word for monastery), which was fortified in the 1760s to provide the townsfolk with a refuge in case of attack by pirates. Surrounded by jutting defensive bastions, it's a good vantage point from which to survey the bay of Komiža below. Most of the island's population congregate beneath the monastery every year on St Nicholas's Day (Sveti Nikola; Dec 6), honouring the patron saint of seafarers by hauling an old fishing boat here and setting it alight.

Beaches

There's a busy family-oriented **beach** in front of the *Biševo* hotel, and a string of more picturesque bays to the south of town: head past the Kaštel, follow the coastal road for 1km, then take the gravel road behind the disused Neptun fish canning factory, and you'll find yourself on a coastal path that leads past a sequence of attractive coves. First of the coves is **Kamenica Bay**, a fine crescent of pebbles with a 24-hour beach bar, while there are a couple of naturist coves further on.

ARRIVAL AND INFORMATION — KOMIŽA

By bus Buses from Vis Town (5 daily; 20min) terminate about 100m behind the harbour.

Tourist office At the southwestern end of the Riva (summer Mon–Fri 8am–1pm & 6.30–8pm, Sat & Sun 6.30–8pm; winter Mon–Fri 8am–1pm; ⓣ 021 713 455, ⓦ tz-komiza.hr).

ACTIVITIES

Alternatura Hrvatskih mučenika 2 (daily 8.30am–1.30pm & 5–10pm; 021 717 239, alternatura.hr). These sustainable tourism pioneers are the people to ask about scuba diving, free climbing, sailing in a *falkuša*, hang-gliding from Mount Hum and guided tours of the island's former military facilities.

ACCOMMODATION,

Rooms (300Kn) and **apartments** (studios 450Kn, four-person apartments 500–600Kn) are available from a number of agencies in the centre, most reliably ★ **Alternatura**, Hrvatskih mučenika 2 (see above), and **Srebrna**, Ribarska 4 (daily 8am–1pm & 6–10pm; 021 713 668, srebrnatours.hr).

EATING, DRINKING AND NIGHTLIFE

Aquarius Kamenica beach aquariuskomiza.com. Popular daytime café and night-time beach club, serving grilled food and cocktails, and featuring projections beamed onto the sea, nightly DJs and dancing till dawn. Early June to early Sept 24hr.

★ **Jastožera** Gundulićeva bb 021 713 859, jastozera.com. An attractive timber structure built above a stone-walled lobster pen, *Jastožera* is famous for its fresh lobster (done any which way you choose; 750Kn/kg), and some equally mouthwatering alternatives – fish in wine sauce (180Kn), scampi *buzara* (380Kn/kg) or an outstanding fish-and-scampi *brodet* (150Kn). Cool jazzy music and gently lapping waters are the probable accompaniment. Daily 11am–11pm (July & Aug till 1am).

Kolđeraj Trg kralja Tomislava 1. The local bakery doles out a freshly baked *Komiška pogača* (15Kn) as well as other sweet or savoury pastries. Daily 6.30am–2am.

★ **Konoba Bako** Gundulićeva bb 021 713 742, konobabako.hr. A vine-shaded terrace right beside a small pebble beach provides the setting for some wonderful dishes taken straight from the traditional Vis repertoire, including amberjack with capers, and diced octopus in red wine sauce. Daily: June–Aug 4pm–2am; Sept–May 5pm–midnight; closed Jan.

Riblji Komiža Riva sv. Mikule 17 021 713 302. Long-standing harbourfront restaurant with a solid reputation. All the splash-out options are here (best white fish, lobster), as well as reasonably priced pasta and risotto dishes. Daily 8am–midnight.

Speed Škor 12. This is the café where most locals take their first coffee of the morning and relax over their first drink of the evening. Given that almost everyone entering or leaving Komiža has to pass in front of *Speed*'s terrace, it's the ideal place from which to observe and keep tabs. There are two other bars on the same square, turning the Škor into a sea of tables in summer. Daily 7am–11pm.

7

Biševo and the Blue Cave

Cave 30Kn

Each morning small boats leave Komiža harbour for the short crossing to **Biševo**, a tiny islet just to the southwest of Vis. There's a seasonally inhabited hamlet just up from Biševo's small harbour, and a couple of attractive coves, but the main attraction here is the **Blue Cave** (Modra špilja) on the island's east coast, a modestly sized but entrancing grotto which can only be reached by sea. It's been a tourist attraction since the 1880s, when Austrian aristocrat, painter and naturalist Eugen von Ransonnet-Villez suggested dynamiting the cave's entrance to widen it for boat access, and the Lloyd steamer company began advertising it as the "Austrian Capri". It probably deserves the hype: when the sun is at its height, water-filtered light shines in through a submerged side-entrance to the cave to bathe everything in the cavern in an eerie shimmering blueness. Owing to the narrowness of the entrance, the cave can't be entered when the sea is choppy, which can happen on all but the calmest of summer days; ask the tourist office in either Komiža or Vis Town about conditions.

You can take a dip in the cave if you want – although be warned that the volume of tourist traffic often means that you won't be able to spend as long there as you might wish.

ARRIVAL AND DEPARTURE — BIŠEVO AND THE BLUE CAVE

Tours Excursions are offered by numerous agencies including Alternatura and Srebrna in Komiža; and Ionios and Navigator in Vis. Tours cost anything from 150 to 250Kn (including the cave entrance fee), depending on whether a beach interlude and a lunch stop are included in the trip.

7

VIS IN WORLD WAR II

The collapse of Italy in the autumn of 1943 led to a power vacuum in the Adriatic, with both the Germans and Tito's Partisans racing each other to take control of the region's major ports and islands. Eager to support the Partisan effort, the British occupied Vis in early 1944, and in June of that year the island was chosen as the temporary headquarters of the Partisan high command, headed by Tito himself. Having narrowly escaped a German attack on Drvar in western Bosnia, Tito was taken to Vis on board the HMS *Blackmore* on June 7, entertaining the officers' mess, it is said, with a near-perfect recital of *The Owl and the Pussycat*.

Tito took up residence in a cave on the southern flanks of Mount Hum, while his staff meetings took place in another cave next door. British officers entertained all kinds of wild ideas about who this shadowy guerilla leader really was. Novelist **Evelyn Waugh** (then a British liaison officer) was obsessed with the idea that Tito was a lesbian in disguise, and continued to spread this rumour for reasons of personal amusement even after meeting the Partisan supremo in person – it's said that Tito upbraided Waugh about this during a trip to the beach, the Marshal's skimpy trunks leaving no room for further doubt about his gender.

Vis soon became a vast **armed camp**, hosting 10,000 Partisans and 700 British and American commandos. The island was an excellent base from which to harry German positions on nearby islands, although commando raids on rugged Brač (where the Scottish Highlanders indulged in a *Guns of Navarone*-style attempt to capture Vidova Gora) led to heavy casualties. The daily existence of those stationed on Vis was made bearable by the endless opportunities for swimming, sunbathing and drinking the local wine, though for the local population things were not quite so jolly: all men between the ages of 15 and 50 were called up by the Partisans, while women, children and the elderly were evacuated to the British-controlled El Shatt camp in the Egyptian desert, where many died in the stifling heat.

Vis saw the first meeting between Tito and the head of the royalist Yugoslav government in exile, Ivan Šubašić, who arrived there on June 16, 1944. After agreeing on paper that Tito would protect democracy after the war, the signatories went on a trip to the Blue Cave on Biševo, where they indulged in skinny dipping, followed by a lunch of lobster and wine. Fitzroy Maclean, Winston Churchill's envoy at Partisan HQ, noted that the sea was choppy on the way back and that "several of the party were sick".

Ultimately Tito feared that he would lose his political independence if he accepted British protection on Vis for too much longer, and decided to relocate. On September 18 he abandoned the island in the dead of night, flying to join the Soviet Red Army in a Russian plane. Vis's brief period in the political limelight was over.

By taxi-boat It's possible to take a taxi-boat from Komiža harbour to the island (100Kn both ways), from where you can walk to a spot near the cave entrance – you'll then be transferred to a small boat and ferried into the cave.

Mount Hum

Rearing up above Komiža to the southeast is **Mount Hum**, which at 587m is Vis's highest point. The summit is best accessed by following the old Komiža–Vis Town route (not the new one traversed by buses), which works its way round the southern side of the island. About 6km out of Komiža, a signed road turns up towards the summit via Žena Glava and Borovik, from where a deteriorating asphalt road heads uphill to the summit. You can also walk from Komiža (2–3hr), picking up the red-marked path that begins near the access road to the Benedictine monastery (see p.362).

Nearing Hum's summit by road, you'll pass an overgrown concrete stairway leading to **Tito's Cave** (Titova špilja), a group of caverns from which the Marshal directed the war effort during 1944. There's currently nothing inside – save for a powerful whiff of history. Once at the top, the panorama of the Adriatic reveals just why Vis was so strategically important: you can pick out the pale grey stripe of the Italian coastline far away to the west, and the mountains of the Croatian mainland to the east. Also visible are the uninhabited islands of the mid-Adriatic: the hump of Svetac immediately to the west, the unearthly volcanic pyramid of Jabuka beyond it and, to the southeast, Croatia's farthest-flung Adriatic possession, Palagruža.

Plisko Polje

At the village of **PLISKO POLJE**, on the road that runs along the south of the island, the British constructed a speedily improvised airstrip in 1944 by linking together innumerable metal plates. It was long ago pulled up and replaced by vineyards, the fruits of which can be sampled at *Konoba Roki's*.

EATING — PLISKO POLJE

★ **Konoba Roki's** Plisko Polje ⓣ 021 711 226, ⓦ rokis.hr. The shady courtyard here is a great place to sit and try out the local *rakija* (flavoured with *rogač*, carob) and red and white wines, accompanied by *pršut*, home-made cheese and fishy main courses. *Roki's* speciality is octopus or lamb baked *ispod peke* (beneath a lid covered with hot embers), although for these dishes advance reservations are advised. May–Sept daily noon–11pm.

7

Korčula

Cloaked in vineyards, olives and Aleppo pines, **KORČULA** is one of the greenest of the Adriatic islands. It is also one of the most popular, thanks largely to the charms of its main settlement, **Korčula Town**, whose surviving fortifications jut decorously out to sea like the bastions of an overgrown sandcastle. The island has a varied collection of inviting **beaches** too, with sandy affairs at **Lumbarda**, 7km away from Korčula Town, secluded pebbly coves on the south coast, and dramatic slabs of rock on the islet of **Proizd**, just off the port town of **Vela Luka**.

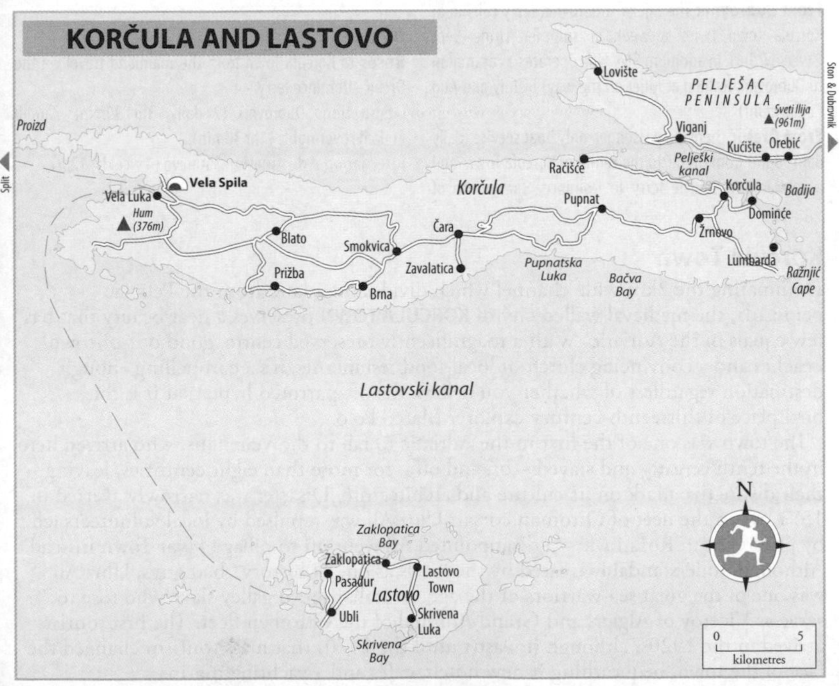

FOOD AND DRINK ON KORČULA

As well as seafood, Korčula excels in **lamb and goat**. These meats are usually baked under a *peka* (ember-covered lid) or served, goulash-style, with **Žrnovski makaruni**, a succulent, hand-rolled, cigar-shaped local pasta. *Makaruni* are very versatile, and are increasingly served up with all kinds of sauces. Undisputed hotspot for sweet-tooth travellers is a tiny shop in Korčula Town named *Cukarin* (see p.371), a cult destination famous for its handmade **sweets** – notably the croissant-shaped, citrus-flavoured *cukarin*.

When it comes to **wine**, Korčula is famed for its indigenous dry whites: Grk only grows in Lumbarda and is produced in small quantities by a handful of local producers. Pošip, cultivated around the central Korčulan villages of Smokvica and Čara, is much more widespread, and crops up in restaurants and wine shops throughout the country.

If the east of the island has wine, western Korčula has **olive oil** – and lots of it. Most local production is a blend of local strains Lastovka and Drobnica, known for their high antioxidant content and sharp peppery taste. Marko Polo, bottled by the farmers' cooperative in Blato, is one of the best mid-priced oils in the country, while Torkul oil, produced by the family-run Fanito distillery in Vela Luka, is famous for its smooth but bitter character and is much sought after throughout Croatia.

ARRIVAL AND DEPARTURE — KORČULA

BY FERRY

From Split Ferries (2 daily; 2hr 40min–3hr 45min) arrive at Vela Luka, at the western end of Korčula island, from where there's a connecting bus service to Korčula Town. The coastal ferry from Split serves Korčula Town twice weekly in summer (June–Sept; 7hr). There is also one daily catamaran (run by Krilo Jet) direct from Split to Korčula Town (1 daily; 2hr 25min).

From Dubrovnik The Rijeka–Dubrovnik ferry calls in at Korčula Town twice a week in summer (June–Sept 2 weekly; 5hr). In addition, G&V Line operates a catamaran to Dubrovnik (calling at Mljet on the way) in July and Aug (1 daily; 3hr).

From Orebić There is a passenger-only boat service (daily 6am–8pm) from Orebić to the centre of Korčula Town, and a car-carrying shuttle ferry to Dominće, 3km south of Korčula Town (a 30min walk from the centre or a short trip by local bus).

From Hvar The Krilo Jet catamaran runs from Hvar Town to Korčula Town (1 daily; 1hr 25min). There is also a daily Jadrolinija catamaran from Hvar Town To Vela Luka (1 daily; 1hr)

From Lastovo There is a ferry (2–3 daily; 2hr) and a catamaran (1 daily; 1hr) from Ubli to Vela Luka.

BY BUS

Buses to Korčula Town from the mainland travel via the Orebić–Dominće ferry.

Destinations Dubrovnik (2 daily; 3hr 30min); Zagreb (1 daily; overnight; 11hr 30min).

International destination Sarajevo (4 weekly; 12hr).

Korčula Town

Dominating the 2km-wide channel which divides the island from the Pelješac peninsula, the medieval walled city of **KORČULA TOWN** preserves a neat beauty that has few equals in the Adriatic. With a magnificently preserved centre, good out-of-town-beaches and a convincing clutch of local-food restaurants, it's a compelling enough destination regardless of whether you believe the oft-parroted hype that it is the birthplace of thirteenth-century explorer Marco Polo.

The town was one of the first in the Adriatic to fall to the Venetians, who arrived here in the tenth century and stayed – on and off – for more than eight centuries, leaving their distinctive mark on its culture and architecture. Disaster was narrowly averted in 1571, when the fleet of Ottoman corsair Uluz Ali was repulsed by local volunteers led by priest Antun Rožanović – a disappointed Ali went off to pillage Hvar Town instead. Although understandably treated by the locals as one of history's bad guys, Uluz Ali was one of the great sea-warriors of the age, an Italian-born galley slave who rose to serve as Viceroy of Algiers and Grand Admiral of the Ottoman fleet. The first tourists arrived in the 1920s, although it wasn't until the 1970s that mass tourism changed the face of the town, bequeathing it new hotels, cafés and a yachting marina.

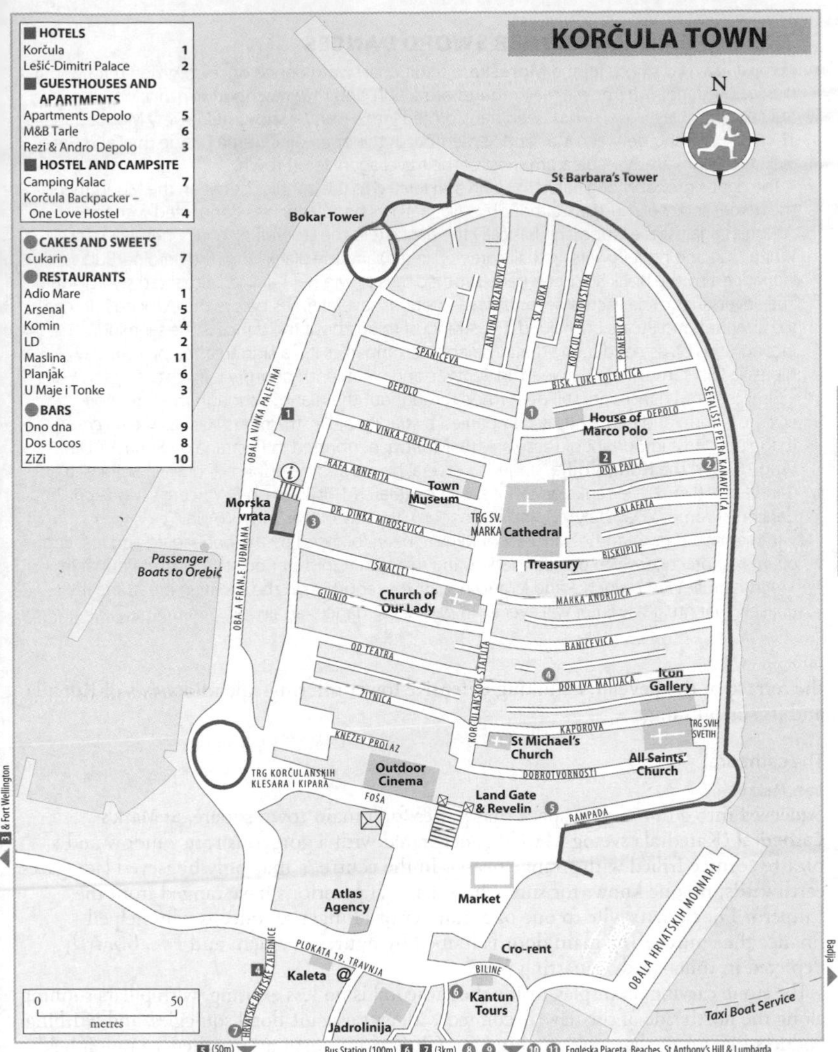

The Old Town

A well-ordered grid of grey stone houses, Korčula's **Old Town** is ribbed with a series of narrow streets that branch off the main thoroughfare like the veins of a leaf – a plan designed to reduce the effects of wind and sun.

Land Gate

Revelin tower daily 9am–9pm • 15Kn

Korčula's Old Town is entered through the fourteenth-century **Land Gate** (Kopnena vrata), dramatically located at the top of an elegant nineteenth-century staircase. The northern side of the gate takes the form of a triumphal arch built in 1650 to honour the military governor of Dalmatia, Leonardo Foscolo, who led Venetian forces against the Turks during the Candia War of 1645–69. Steps to the side of the gate lead up to

THE MOREŠKA AND OTHER SWORD DANCES

Korčula Town is famous for the **Moreška**, a traditional sword dance once common throughout the Mediterranean. It's now a major tourist attraction, and its annual performance on St Theodore's Day (July 29) has been transformed into a regular show, held every Monday and Thursday evening between May and September at the open-air cinema beside the Land Gate. Tickets (100Kn) are available from most of the travel agencies in town.

The dance probably originated in Spain and related to the conflict between the Moors (hence the name) and the Christians, although in Dalmatia its popularity was connected with the struggles against the Ottomans. Basically the dance tells the story of a conflict between the White King and his followers (actually dressed in red) and the Black King. The heroine, Bula, is kidnapped by the Black King, and her betrothed tries to win her back in a ritualized sword fight. The adversaries circle each other and clash weapons several times before the evil king is forced to surrender, and Bula is unchained. The strangest thing about the dance is the seemingly incongruous brass-band music that invariably accompanies it – a sign that the present-day Moreška falls somewhere between ancient rite and nineteenth-century reinvention.

Similar sword dances are still performed throughout the island, although they are more archaic in form and frequently accompanied by traditional instruments such as the *mijeh* (bagpipe). Most important of these are the **Moštra**, performed in Postrana on St Rock's Day (Aug 16), and the **Kumpanjija**, staged in several places at different times of year: Smokvica on Candlemas (Feb 2); Vela Luka on St Joseph's Day (March 19); Blato on St Vincent's Day (April 28); Čara on St James's Day (July 25); and Pupnat on Our Lady of the Snows (Aug 6).

In the past many of these dances would have been followed by the beheading and roasting of an ox, a practice which was banned during the communist period. Its revival in Pupnat in 1999 was followed by lurid – and largely negative – reporting in the Croatian press, and it's unlikely that ritual slaughter will ever form part of the dances again.

7

the terrace of the **Revelin**, a hulking defensive tower offering splendid views of Korčula and its surroundings.

The cathedral

Trg sv. Marka bb

Squeezed into a diminutive space that passes for a main town square, **St Mark's Cathedral** (Katedrala svetog Marka) is decorated with a gorgeous rose window and a bizarre cornice frilled with strange beasts. In the centre, a matronly bug-eyed lady gazes earthwards; no one knows for sure who she is – suggestions have ranged from the Emperor Diocletian's wife to one of a number of Hungarian queens who helped finance the church. The main door is framed by figures of Adam and Eve, bizarrely depicted in toilet-ready squatting pose.

The stone carving on display inside the cathedral is no less exciting, with pillars running along the north side of the nave decorated with extravagant floral squiggles, and writhing goddess-like forms that look anything but Christian in inspiration. There's a pulpit held aloft by griffin-topped pillars, and an elegant ciborium carved by local stonemason Marko Andrijić in the 1490s, its Corinthian columns crowned with statuettes of Archangel Michael and the Virgin. Beneath its pagoda-like canopy hangs a recently restored Tintoretto altarpiece positively bursting with colour – it depicts St Mark flanked by sts Hieronymus and Bartholomew. There's a wealth of interesting clutter in the south aisle, including some of the pikes used against Uluz Ali, and a Tintoretto *Annunciation*, with the Archangel appearing to the Virgin in a shower of sparks.

Bishop's Treasury

Trg sv. Marka bb • July & Aug daily 10am–noon & 5–7pm; rest of year ask at the tourist office • 10Kn

Next door to Korčula's cathedral, the **Bishop's Treasury** (*riznica*) is one of the most charming small art collections in the country, taking in a striking *Portrait of a Man* by Carpaccio, an imposing *Noble with Dog* by Bassano, a tiny *Madonna* by Dalmatian

Renaissance artist Blaž Jurjev of Trogir, plus some Tiepolo studies of hands. Oddities include an ivory statuette of Mary, Queen of Scots, whose skirts open to reveal kneeling figures in doublet and hose – what it's doing in Korčula remains a mystery.

The Town Museum

Trg sv. Marka 20 • Daily: April–June 10am–2pm; July–Sept 9am–9pm; Oct–March 10am–1pm • 10Kn • ⓣ 020 711 420, ⓦ gm-korcula.com

Opposite the cathedral, a Venetian palace houses the **Town Museum** (Gradski muzej), whose modest display includes a copy of a fourth-century-BC inscription from Lumbarda – the earliest evidence of ancient Greek settlement on Korčula – and, upstairs, a re-creation of a typical Korčula peasant kitchen, with an open hearth surrounded by cooking pots and bed warmers. Well-to-do town life of the nineteenth century is illustrated by a silk wedding dress hanging alluringly from the wall.

The Marco Polo House

Depolo • Daily: April–June, Sept & Oct 9am–3pm; July & Aug 9am–9pm • 20Kn • ⓦ kulturakorcula.hr/kuca-marka-pola

Rising from an alley near the cathedral is Korčula's most controversial attraction, the **Marco Polo House** (Kuća Marka Pola), which claims to be the birthplace of the famed globetrotter. Marco Polo was indeed captured by the Genoese in a sea battle off Korčula in 1298, and it is perfectly believable that he was a native of the town – De Polo is a common Korčulan surname. However, he is unlikely to have had any connection with this seventeenth-century house, which displays little of value inside but offers wonderful views of Korčula's rooftops from its upper storeys. Plans are afoot to install a more measured and informative Polo-related display in the house some time in the future.

7

The Icon Gallery

Trg svih svetih • July & Aug daily 10am–noon & 5–7pm, rest of year ask at the tourist office • 20Kn

Occupying the rooms of Korčula's All Saints' Brotherhood, the **Icon Gallery** (Galerija ikona) contains a permanent display of icons, many of which were looted from Cretan churches by the Venetians at the end of the Candia War, when Venice had to hand Crete over to the Ottomans. Among the Pantokrators and Virgins emblazoned in gold leaf is a haunting fifteenth-century triptych of the Passion.

All Saints' Church

Trg svih svetih

Korčula's **All Saints' Church** (Crkva svih svetih) contains one of the most impressive Baroque altarpieces in Dalmatia – an eighteenth-century Pietà carved from walnut wood by Austrian master George Raphael Donner. On the far side of the altar is another of Blaž Jurjev's fifteenth-century masterpieces, a polyptych centred on a chilling *Deposition*, below which the tiny figures of the All Saints' Brotherhood – identifiable from their trademark white robes – kneel in prayer.

Engleska pjaceta

From behind Korčula's bus station, Šetalište Frane Kršinića heads east towards the package-hotel end of town, passing after some 500m a curious folly in the form of a pair of obelisks and a semicircular stone bench. Known as the **Engleska pjaceta** (English piazzetta), it dates from a short-lived period of British occupation in 1813 when it was built to mark what was then the southeastern boundary of the town. The *pjaceta* becomes the outdoor terrace of a nearby café in summer.

St Anthony's Hill

A popular destination for strollers is **St Anthony's Hill** (Sveti Antun), which lies 2km southeast of town – to get there, continue beyond the Engleska pjaceta to the crossroads, go straight over onto the Lumbarda road, then bear left up a residential street at the next junction. A graceful avenue of poplars lines the approach to the hill, an easily scaled affair on top of which you'll find a small chapel and a modest circle of park. Much of Korčula's rippling eastern coast is visible from the summit, with the grey-green mountains of the Pelješac peninsula glowering from across the water.

Fort Wellington

There's easy walking on the wooded heights west of town, best reached by heading west along Put svetog Nikole and bearing left up the stepped alleyways that lead through the hillside suburbs. After ten to fifteen minutes you'll emerge onto a plateau where a legacy of British occupation, a simple grey tower known as **Fort Wellington**, rises above the maquis like an abandoned giant chesspiece. Manned by fire-watchers in summer, the tower is occasionally open to the public – when you can clamber up onto the parapet for more splendid views.

7

The beaches

The nearest **beaches** to the Old Town are southeast of the centre on the headland around the *Hotel Marko Polo*, though they're crowded, rocky and uncomfortable. A little further on, the shingle beach in front of the *Bon Repos* hotel and *Kalac* campsite is marginally preferable, although it can't compare with the sandy beach a short bus ride away in Lumbarda (see p.372).

Badija

Water taxi (20min; 45Kn) from the harbour on the eastern side of town

Largest and nearest of the islets off Korčula is **Badija**, where boats stop beside an impressive Franciscan monastery – used as a hotel for many years, it was recently returned to the order and is currently being restored. From here, numerous tracks lead to secluded beaches and a couple of elementary snack bars. Some boats continue onwards to the naturist part of the island round the corner.

ARRIVAL AND DEPARTURE — KORČULA TOWN

By bus Korčula's bus station is 200m southeast of the Old Town.

Destinations Dubrovnik (2 daily; 3hr 30min); Lumbarda (Mon–Sat hourly, Sun 5; 20min); Pupnat (Mon–Fri 6 daily, Sat 5 daily, Sun 4; 30min); Ston (1 daily; 2hr); Vela Luka (Mon–Fri 6 daily, Sat 5 daily, Sun 4; 1hr 20min); Zagreb (1 daily; overnight; 11hr 30min).

International destination Sarajevo (4 weekly; 12hr).

By ferry and catamaran Ferries and catamarans from Split and Dubrovnik dock on the harbour immediately east of the Old Town. Ferries from Orebić (see p.380) arrive at Dominće 3km east of the Old Town and are met by connecting bus. Passenger-only boats from Orebić arrive on the western side of the Old Town. Tickets for the Dubrovnik and Split car ferries are purchased at the Jadrolinija office on Plokata 19. Travnja (Mon–Fri 7.30am–8pm, Sat 7.30am–2pm, Sun 8am–1pm); tickets for other services are bought from kiosks at the relevant points of departure.

Ferry destinations Dubrovnik (June–Sept 2 weekly; 5hr); Split (June–Sept 2 weekly; 7hr).

Catamaran destinations Dubrovnik (G&V Line; July & Aug; 1 daily; 3hr); Hvar Town (Krilo Jet; 1 daily; 1hr 25min); Split (Krilo Jet; 1 daily; 2hr 25min).

INFORMATION

Tourist office Obala Franje Tuđmana 4, next to the *Hotel Korčula* (June–Sept Mon–Sat 8am–8pm, Sun 8am–3pm; Oct–May Mon–Sat 8am–noon & 5–8pm, Sun 8am–noon; T 020 715 701, W visitkorcula.net). The tourist office can tell you almost everything there is to know about the island.

Internet You can check your emails at Sirius in the bus station building, or at Media Optima, Trg svete Justine bb, just off Plokata 19. Travnja.

GETTING AROUND

Vehicle rental Cro-rent, just off Plokata 19. Travnja at Biline 5 (T 020 711 908, W cro-rent.com), rents out scooters from 150Kn/day, as well as cars and boats.

Bikes can be rented from the Kaleta and Kantun agencies (see opposite; 35Kn/2hr, 85Kn/12hr).

ACCOMMODATION

There are numerous agencies dealing in private **rooms** (300Kn) and **apartments** (two-person studios 450Kn, four-person apartments from 620Kn), most of which are grouped around the main Plokata 19. Travnja. Among the most helpful are **Kaleta**, Plokata bb (020 711 282, kaleta.hr); and **Kantun Tours**, also Plokata bb (020 715 622, ikorcula.net). Many private hosts post details of their accommodation online at korcula.net.

HOTELS

Korčula Obala Vinka Paletina bb 020 711 078, korcula-hotels.com. The *grande dame* of the town's hotels, occupying the Austrian-built former town hall and boasting an elegant waterfront terrace. Renovations in the 1980s destroyed the *belle-époque* atmosphere without putting any meaningful modern luxury in its place, but it's still a comfortable hotel in a matchless location. Former guests include overrated travel bore Rebecca West and World War I stormtrooper-novelist Ernst Jünger. **850Kn**

★ **Lešić Dimitri Palace** Don Pavla Poše 1–6 020 715 560, lesic-dimitri.com. Comprising a row of beautifully restored stone houses in the heart of town, this is certainly one of the most characterful accommodation choices in Dalmatia. On offer are six "residences" (a self-contained apartment in other words, ranging from one bedroom to four [7500Kn]) offering plush comforts in a variety of interior-design styles with fully equipped bathrooms and kitchenettes that leave nothing to chance. You'll be well looked after by attention-to-detail staff. One-bedroom apartment from **2250Kn**

GUESTHOUSES AND APARTMENTS

Apartments Depolo Hrvatske bratske zajednice 62 020 721 172 or 098 357 582, apartment-korcula.com. Modern apartments on the top two floors of a historic stone house midway between the bus station and the Old Town. They can be rented out as four- to six-person apartments or as smaller two-person units. English or Italian spoken depending on which member of the family you get hold of. Two-person apartments **600Kn**

M & B Tarle Šetalište Frana Kršinića bb 020 711 712. Roomy family house 1km east of the Old Town, offering a mixture of simply furnished en-suite doubles and family-sized apartments with kitchen (600Kn). The top-floor rooms with attic ceilings are the most popular. Big back garden. Breakfast is available on request. Open March–Dec. Rooms **300Kn**

Rezi & Andro Depolo Svetog Nikole bb 020 711 621, tereza.depolo@du.t-com.hr. Friendly family house just west of the Old Town with four rooms, each with hardwood floors, TV, en-suite shower/WC, electric kettle and – in three of the rooms – great views of the Old Town. Breakfast is available on request, and there's a nice big outdoor terrace to eat it on. Open all year; three-day minimum stay preferred in summer. **300Kn**

HOSTEL AND CAMPSITE

Camping Kalac Dubrovačka cesta 19 020 726 693, korculahotels.com. Shoreside site 3km out of town, next to the *Bon Repos* hotel and near the Dominće ferry terminal. Pitches are situated in tiny clearings between trees, guaranteeing a degree of privacy – though the site can be noisy in season. **50Kn** per person, pitches from **50Kn**

Korčula Backpacker – One Love Hostel Hrvatske bratske zajednice 6 020 716 755 or 098 997 6353, thekorculabackpacker.blogspot.co.uk. Enjoyable if occasionally cramped private hostel with friendly hosts. Its 65 beds are arranged in four- and six-bed dorms crammed into a three-storey nineteenth-century house, with a WC and shower on each floor. The cellar bar, with vaguely Middle Eastern couches and cushions, is a great place to unwind and make contacts after a day spent exploring the island. Dorms **120Kn**

EATING AND DRINKING

There are more pizzerias than you can shake a stick at in the Old Town, and a number of decent **restaurants** serving excellent local seafood. If you're planning a **picnic**, you could head for the fruit and vegetable market just below the Land Gate. As for drinking, there's a handful of cocktail **bars** on the promenade around the Old Town, although the bar-choked area around the bus station is more animated.

CAKES AND SWEETS

★ **Cukarin** Hrvatske bratske zajednice bb 020 711 055, cukarin.hr. This small shop in the narrow alley running south from Plokata 19. Travnja is famous throughout Croatia for its selection of home-baked biscuits and other crispy confections. Prime among these is the *cukarin*, a lemony-orange-flavoured biscuit that looks rather like a croissant with an extra pair of horns (and is best eaten when dipped in sweet *prošek* wine). Try also the *klašun*, a pastry ball stuffed with walnut filling; and the *Marko Polo bombica*, an asteroid-sized sphere of chocolate, cream and walnuts. Mon–Fri 8am–noon & 4–8pm; Sat 8am–noon.

RESTAURANTS

Adio Mare Svetog Roka 2 020 711 253. Located just by the alleyway leading down to Marco Polo's House, this is a long-standing tourist favourite, offering top-quality food in a

7

high-ceilinged room of medieval vintage. It's an atmospheric place to eat in spring and autumn, but should be avoided in high summer when staff and kitchen are rushed off their feet. Mon–Sat noon–11pm, Sun 6–11pm.

Arsenal Rampada 1 ☎ 020 711 720. Located beside the Land Gate, this is one of the few town-centre restaurants that can be relied upon to have traditional dishes such as those featuring lentils, chickpeas and *Žrnovski makaruni*. Locals flock here in the off season for the economically priced daily specials. Daily 10am–10pm.

Komin Don Iva Matijace ☎ 020 716 508. *Konoba Komin* has a handful of outdoor tables crammed into a narrow stepped street, plus room for a few diners in the teeny interior, and serves up consistently good fresh fish grilled over an open hearth. Specialities such as lamb or octopus baked under an ember-covered lid are also well worth trying, although they should ideally be ordered 24hr in advance. Daily except Tues noon–3pm & 6pm–midnight.

7

★ **LD** Pavla Poše 1-6 ☎ 020 715 560. The restaurant of the *Lesić Dimitri Palace* (see p.371) features contemporary cuisine with local ingredients. Mains such as bream and seabass fillets are served with imaginative combinations of textures and flavours, with Korčulan herbs and vegetables making up the supporting cast. Local wines (especially the whites: Grk from Lumbarda, Pošip from Čara) head a cosmopolitan list. The room itself is a reflection of the restaurant's mission, mixing traditional-stone-house with modern design – white surfaces, geometric patterns on the wall and low-key lighting. April–Oct daily 8am–midnight.

Maslina Lumburajska cesta bb ☎ 020 711 720. Two kilometres from the centre on the Lumbarda road, in an unpromising area characterized by car repair yards, this family-run place (owned by the same folks as *Arsenal*; see above) is nevertheless well worth the trip for its top-notch grilled fish and shellfish, as well as old-fashioned island favourites such as lamb goulash with pasta and various forms of game. Daily 11am–11pm.

Planjak Plokata 19. Travnja ☎ 020 711 015. Moderately priced, unpretentious place offering the full range of local grilled-meat fare and plenty of outdoor seating. One of those places that has been going for years, and is strongly favoured by locals outside the tourist season. Daily 8am–10pm.

★ **U Maje i Tonke** Trg Korčulanskih klesara i kipara 2 ☎ 091 799 5549. Traditional staples are given the modern bistro treatment here, with a superb range of tapas-style nibbles embracing aubergine, goats' cheese and even coast-growing samphire. Desserts employ local flavours from carob to basil. A bit too busy in season – be prepared to take your time. May–Sept daily noon–3pm & 6pm–midnight.

BARS

Dno dna Hrvatske bratske zajednice 102. Characterful café-bar near the bus station whose surreal interior looks like a cross between a submarine and a mermaid's undersea boudoir. Nice outdoor terrace running along a stretch of park. Daily 7am–11pm.

Dos Locos Šetalište Frana Kršinića. Just behind the bus station, this is the one Korčula bar that regularly gets packed out with summer-evening hedonistic drinkers. Lots of outdoor seating, frequent live music and a reasonable range of cocktails. Daily 5pm–2am.

ZiZi Šetalište Frana Kršinića. Rawest of the bars on the behind-the-bus-station strip, with TV screens permanently tuned to sport and betting-shop odds, an electric darts board and a collection of sports trophies on top of the fridge. Mon–Sat 8am–midnight, Sun 4pm–midnight.

Lumbarda

Some of the best beaches on Korčula island are at **LUMBARDA**, 8km south of Korčula Town and accessible by regular buses. Lumbarda itself is a large village that straggles along a peninsula and stretches uphill in a scattering of modern whitewashed holiday villas. From where the buses drop off, the track on the right leads through vineyards to **Prižna bay**, a glorious two-hundred-metre stretch of sand backed by a couple of cafés. The bay is relatively shallow, ensuring its popularity with children of paddling age – be warned that it soon fills up in July and August. Back at the chapel, the track on the left goes to **Bilin Žal**, a far rockier stretch of shore with brief sandy stretches and dramatic views of the coastal mountains. Heading straight on from the chapel brings you to the tip of Lumbarda's peninsula and **Ražnjić Cape**, a circular promontory of fissured rock with a small lighthouse at the end. It's a perfect location for shade-free sun roasting, and comes with an impressive panorama of the Pelješac peninsula's rocky escarpment.

ARRIVAL AND INFORMATION — LUMBARDA

By bus Buses from Korčula Town (Mon–Sat hourly; 5 on Sun) terminate at a small chapel at the southern end of town.

Tourist office In the centre near the bus stop (June & Sept daily 8am–noon & 4–8pm; July & Aug daily 8am–10pm;

Oct–May Mon–Fri 8am–2pm; 020 712 005, lumbarda.hr). The tourist office will be able to help you locate private rooms in town (200Kn), though may not be able to book them on your behalf.

ACCOMMODATION AND EATING

Bire Winery Lumbarda 020 712 208 or 098 344 712, bire.hr. Frano Bire is one of Korčula's prime winemakers, best known for cultivating the dry white Grk that is indigenous to Lumbarda and nowhere else. House wine, *rakijas* and liqueurs are served up at this farmstead signed uphill from the main road through Lumbarda, either in the stone-clad interior or on the garden terrace. Ham-and-cheese nibbles, home-grown vegetables and more substantial meals are on offer too. June–Sept daily noon–10pm.

Konoba Biin Žal Bilin Žal. The half-ruined boathouse on Bilin Žal beach is home to this atmospheric *konoba*, which serves grilled meats and seafood washed down with local wines. June–Sept daily 9am–11pm.

Marinka Lumbarda bb 020 712 007 or 098 344 712, bire.hr. Owned by the wine-producing Bire family this stone house near the Korčula–Lumbarda road has a handful of simple but neat doubles, plus a really nice garden. There are three studios (each sleeping 2–3) in a nearby building. **300Kn**

7

Inland Korčula

Away from the island's well-defended main town, most of Korčula's traditional settlements were built **inland** to avoid the unwanted attentions of pirates. Vines and olives were planted on inland plateaus and south-facing slopes, and each village maintained a seasonally inhabited fishing port at the end of a steep winding road. These ports nowadays offer quiet, avoid-the-crowds beaches (they are not served by public transport and parking spaces are at a premium), while the inland villages – still centres of wine and oil production – boast some truly outstanding *konobe*.

Žrnovo

An agglomeration of hamlets rather than a compact village, **ŽRNOVO** is scattered across stony hills inland and uphill from Korčula Town. Its southeasterly settlement, **Postrana**, is a particularly fascinating hive of stone-paved, stepped alleyways squeezed between grey houses and barns, the lack of any distractions (tourist sights, cafés, restaurants) making a stroll here all the more appealing.

Pupnat and nearby beaches

Pupnat is typical of the villages strung out along Korčula's central ridge, with stone houses ranged across a south-facing hillside, overlooking a plain filled with vegetable plots, orchards and vineyards. The village is worth a quick wander and a pause in the highly regarded local, *Konoba Mate* (see p.374), especially if you are coming back from one of the spectacular nearby beaches.

Five kilometres due south of Pupnat, a narrow road descends through thick woodland to **Bačva bay**, a long pebble beach in a U-shaped inlet. Behind the beach there are a couple of informal summer-only *konobe*, their terraces shrouded by rosemary bushes and clumps of cacti.

A similar distance southwest of Pupnat, and reached by partly asphalted road, **Pupnatska Luka** offers a beautiful crescent of pebble flanked by rocks. There's a rudimentary beach bar and *konoba* here in the summer season.

ARRIVAL AND DEPARTURE — INLAND KORČULA

By bus Buses on the Korčula Town–Vela Luka route (Mon–Fri 6 daily, Sat 5 daily, Sun 4) pass through the main inland settlements, including Žrnovo and Pupnat.

EATING

Konoba Maha Vrsilj, Žrnovo 098 494 389. Accessed by a signed turn off the main Korčula–Vela Luka road just west of Žrnovo, this farmstead set amid thick maquis serves grilled fish and *peka*-roast meats (local lamb and goat are a speciality, although you should book in advance for either). They also make their own *žrnovski makaruni* – home-made pasta twizzles customarily served with goulash. The interior is full of farmhouse nick-nacks, and there is outdoor seating in a garden bordered by stone walls and clumps of rosemary and lavender. Daily 1–11pm.

★ **Konoba Mate** Pupnat bb ☎020 717 109. Something of a temple to the art of making *makaruni*, *Mate* serves the succulent twists of pasta with a range of highly original sauces based on local ingredients – herbs and goat's cheese among them. Lamb cutlets with runner beans is a popular meat main course; rosemary sorbet is just one of several tantalisingly moreish desserts. Style-wise it is every bit the atmospheric village inn, comprising a cosy winter dining room with four tables and a log fire, and a larger summer dining area which merges with an outdoor terrace. Daily 11am–2pm & 5–11pm.

Vela Luka and around

7

At the western end of the island, the ferry port of **VELA LUKA** is totally different in character from Korčula Town, with a string of sturdy nineteenth- and twentieth-century houses stretching along an expansive, three-fingered bay. Founded much later than Korčula's other settlements (according to local lore, the men of Blato sent their illegitimate children here to ease problems of family inheritance), The town started out as a shipbuilding centre and local yards still manufacture small recreational boats. With good beaches easily accessible offshore on the island of **Proizd** but no big package hotels, today's Vela Luka radiates easy-going, unswamped affability.

The Town Museum

Ulica 26/2 • Mon–Fri 9am–1pm & 8–11pm, Sat 10am–1pm • 10Kn

There's little in the way of an Old Town to stroll around, although the Bronze Age pots and jewellery displayed in the **Town Museum** (Gradski muzej), just behind the seafront, bear sufficient witness to the town's ancient origins. Exhibitions of contemporary Croatian art are frequently put on in the summer.

Vela Spila cave

Daily 5–8pm • 10Kn • The cave is a 20min walk from town – take the alleyway behind the *Pod Bore* restaurant on the Riva and follow the path (signed with green-and-white waymarks) uphill

Most of the artefacts displayed in Vela Luka's museum were unearthed near **Vela Spila cave**, a major archeological site 2km from town, which was inhabited continuously from around 18,000 BC until the Roman era. Parts of Vela Spila's limestone roof collapsed several millennia ago, creating an eerie, tunnel-like space with light streaming in from the huge openings above. Decorated clay fragments unearthed in Vela Spila by archeologists are thought to be among the earliest known ceramic objects in the world – the finds created quite a sensation among scientific circles when first published in 2012.

Olive Oil Museum

Ulica 6 br. 13, Gudulija • June–Sept: usually mornings and evenings; check at the tourist office or ring ☎020 813 111 • 20Kn

The western end of Korčula is an important olive-growing region, and the resulting oil is highly prized for its distinctive peppery taste. If you're interested in seeing how the

THE VELA LUKA KUMPANIJA

Vela Luka's answer to the Moreška (see p.368) is the **Kumpanjija**, an archaic and rather slow sword dance performed to shrill bagpipe-and-drums accompaniment every Tuesday evening (mid-July to late August) in front of St Joseph's Church. The show begins and ends with *klapa* singing from the local folklore group, making this a good all-round introduction to island culture.

CLOCKWISE FROM TOP LEFT SNORKELLING AT VELA LUKA; TOWN WALLS, STON (P.382); FRANCISCAN MONASTERY, OREBIĆ (P.380) >

stuff is produced, the **Olive Oil Museum** (Muzej maslinovog ulja) run by the Zlokić family in Gudulija, 3km out of Vela Luka on the main road east, has an intriguing display of presses and – predictably – offers plenty of the stuff for sale.

Hum

A paved road (accessible via a turn-off about 2km out of town on the Korčula road) coils its way to the summit; there is also a (steep) marked path for hikers

Many of Vela Luka's most productive olive groves are draped around **Hum**, the dome-shaped hill that looms above Vela Luka from the southwest. At the top is a small nineteenth-century fort built by the Austrians, an abundance of wild herbs and flowers, and great views of Vela Luka. Dedicated island-spotters will be able to make out the forms of Hvar and Lastovo in the distance.

Proizd

Taxi-boats run from the harbour (40min; 40Kn return)

One of the most fantastic places to sunbathe in the whole of Dalmatia, the sloping-rock beaches of **Proizd** island will appeal to anyone who likes the idea of spreading their towel over a dramatic geological feature. Accessed from well-signed paths that spread out from Proizd's boat jetty are a clutch of celebrated beaches: **Veli Bili Bok** consists of a series of stone plates shelving gently into a pebbly bay; **Srednji Bili Bok** is even more dramatic, consisting of a smooth, steeply sloping slab of rock above turquoise waters; while the similar **Donji Bili Bok** is reserved for naturists. Nearest to the boat jetty, **Batalo** is Proizd's one shallow pebbly bay, and is popular with paddling families as a result. The island is at its most beautiful in the evening, when the rocks change colour from grey to gold to red as the sun slowly descends.

All of Proizd's beaches can be rough underfoot, so remember to take sandals and something soft to sprawl on.

ARRIVAL AND INFORMATION — VELA LUKA AND AROUND

By boat Vela Luka's ferry and catamaran dock is at the western end of the Riva, a 10min walk from the centre. There are plans to build a new ferry dock about 1km further out of town.

Ferry destinations Split (2 daily; 2hr 40min–3hr 45min); Lastovo (3 daily; 2hr).

Catamaran destinations Hvar Town (1 daily; 1hr); Lastovo (1 daily; 1hr); Split (1 daily; 2hr).

By bus Buses to Korčula Town depart from the ferry dock (Mon–Fri 6 daily, Sat 5, Sun 4; 1hr 20min).

Tourist office Obala 3 bb (June Mon–Fri 8am–2pm, Sat 8am–noon; July & Aug Mon–Sat 8am–9pm, Sun 9am–noon; Sept Mon–Sat 8am–2pm & 5–8pm; Oct–May Mon–Fri 8am–3pm; 020 813 619, tzvelaluka.hr).

Vehicle rental Mediterano (see below) rent out bikes (70Kn/1–2 days), scooters (220Kn/1–2 days) and a range of cars.

ACCOMMODATION

Korkyra Obala 3 br. 21 020 601 000, hotel-korkyra.com. From the beige pouffes of the reception area to the globe-shaped light fittings in the top-floor fitness centre, *Korkyra* gets the balance between contemporary design and old-fashioned comforts about right. The rooms feature hardwood floors and pastel-coloured fabrics, while the ground-floor restaurant (daily 7am–11pm) offers well-presented fresh seafood, steaks and a fish platter for two (200Kn). The Riva-facing terrace is a great place to soak up the sunset, and there's a small kidney-shaped pool at the back. **1200Kn**

★ **Mediterano Tourist Agency** Obala 3 020 813 832 or 091 534 9889, mediterano.hr. *Mediterano* has the biggest choice of rooms and apartments (studios 300Kn, four-person apartments 450Kn) both in Vela Luka itself and in isolated bays around the western end of the island. They also have their own apartment building just behind the Riva with neat en-suite doubles and four-person apartments with kitchenette. Rooms **225Kn**

EATING AND DRINKING

There's a string of **café-bars** along the seafront, and with locals frequently outnumbering tourists – Vela Luka has a raw vivacity that's often lacking in the considerably more twee Korčula Town.

RESTAURANTS

Konoba Lučica Ulica 5 14 ⓣ020 813 673. *Lučica*, slightly uphill from the seafront, is the best place for local seafood, serving up fresh fish and mussels in a patio with an open grill. May–Sept daily 11am–11pm.

Pizza Alfa Obala 2 bb ⓣ020 813 710. There are several pizzerias in Vela Luka and local opinion differs as to which is the best – *Alfa* is certainly reliable, serving good thin-crust pies (45–50Kn) in a compact interior divided into cosy booths. Daily 11am–11pm.

Pod Bore Obala 3/1 ⓣ020 812 123, ⓦpodbore.com. On the waterfront, *Pod Bore* has decent food and a large sea-facing terrace. It's a popular lunching spot with locals out of season, but can turn into a frantic tourist-deluged feeding-station in high summer. Steaks in the 110Kn range, and a range of grilled fish. Daily 1–3pm & 5–10pm.

BAR

Mirakul Obala 4 ⓣ095 910 2859. An archetypal rocker's bar, with album-cover art on the walls, a suitable choice of background music and live gigs in summer. There are pool tables and an electronic darts board upstairs. Summer open 24hr; winter daily 7am–midnight.

Lastovo

7

At the centre of an archipelago of some 45 uninhabited islets, tiny **LASTOVO** lies over four hours away from Split by ferry (and over three hours by catamaran), and as a result feels much more isolated than any of the other Adriatic islands. Its strong sense of regional identity is most obviously expressed in the annual **Poklad** (see box, p.378) a uniquely archaic Lenten carnival. Like Vis, Lastovo was closed to foreigners from 1976 until 1989 owing to its importance as a military outpost, and organized tourism has never caught on, but what it lacks in hotels and amenities it more than makes up for in its natural, wooded beauty. Ferries arrive at **Ubli**, a small and uneventful harbour a few kilometres short of Lastovo's one major settlement, **Lastovo Town**, where most of the remaining eight hundred islanders live.

VUKODLACI AND OTHER VAMPIRIC HOUSEGUESTS

Express an interest in **vampires** in today's Croatia and you'll probably be told that you've come to the wrong country – and yet belief in the supernatural creatures was widespread hereabouts until a couple of centuries ago. Europe's first documented case of vampirism took place in an Istrian village in the 1670s, when the nocturnal roamings of Jure Grando were recorded by Slovenian chronicler J.J. Valvasor. One of the last known outbreaks of vampire mania in Croatia took place on **Lastovo** in 1737, when officials from Dubrovnik had to dissuade the local populace from carrying out mass exhumations of those suspected of walking with the undead.

According to Croatian folk belief, the most common form of vampire was a **vukodlak** (often translated as "werewolf", although it clearly means something quite different), which basically consisted of the skin of a human corpse puffed up with the breath of the devil and further bloated with the blood of its victims. The *vukodlak* was an all-purpose bogeyman whose existence could explain away all manner of crises and conflicts: anything from listlessness among the local livestock to marital problems were blamed on the bloodsuckers (it was said that *vukodlaci* visited the beds of bored wives and pleasured them in the night). A **mora** was a female equivalent of a *vukodlak*, nightly sapping the strength of the menfolk; while **macići** were mischievious young *vukodlaci* who created envy and discord by bringing good luck to some villagers, misfortune to others – if a farmer got rich, neighbours would say that he had a *macić* in the house.

People were said to turn into *vukodlaci* after their death if a dog, cat or mouse passed under their coffin while it was being borne to the grave. The only cure was to dig up the body and cut its hamstrings to prevent it from wandering about at night. Visiting the Dalmatian hinterland as recently as the 1770s, the intrepid Venetian traveller Alberto Fortis discovered that some of the locals asked their families to carry out this operation as soon as they died, just to be on the safe side.

Ubli and around

Ferries and catamarans dock at **Ubli**, an unassuming collection of houses (plus the odd shop and café) on Lastovo's western shore. Buses run from Ubli's harbourfront to Lastovo Town, ensuring that few people stick around here for long. Three kilometres north of Ubli at the hamlet of Pasadur lies a minor resort in the shape of the *Solitudo* hotel (see below), which stands beside the narrow straight dividing Lastovo from the islet of Prezba. There's a pebble beach in front of the hotel, and plenty of rocky bathing spots along the shores of the Malo Lago inlet immediately north.

ARRIVAL AND DEPARTURE — UBLI AND AROUND

7

By boat There is a direct catamaran service from Split to Ubli, calling at Hvar Town and Vela Luka (Korčula) on the way. The car ferry service from Split to Ubli sometimes involves a change of ship at Vela Luka. Buses from Ubli to Lastovo Town (15min) connect with catamaran and ferry services.

Ferry destinations Split (sometimes via Vela Luka; 2 daily; 4hr 30min–5hr 30min); Vela Luka (3 daily; 2hr).

Catamaran destinations Hvar Town (1 daily; 2hr); Split (1 daily; 3hr 20min); Vela Luka (1 daily; 1hr).

Services The *Gušter/Lounge Lizard* café on Ubli harbour rents out mountain bikes and scooters, and may have a couple of internet terminals. There's a petrol station and a couple of shops on Ubli ferry dock.

ACCOMMODATION

Solitudo Pasadur bb ⓣ 020 802 100, ⓦ hotel-solitudo.com. Three kilometres north of Ubli, this bay-hugging hotel offers comfy en-suite rooms, gym, sauna and a restaurant. **600Kn**

Lastovo Town and around

Unusually for the capital of a Croatian island, **LASTOVO TOWN** faces away from the sea, spreading itself over the steep banks of a natural amphitheatre with a fertile agricultural plain below. There's a road at the top, a road at the bottom, and a maze of narrow alleys and stone stairways between. The town's buildings date mainly from the fifteenth and sixteenth centuries, and are notable for their curious chimneys shaped like miniature minarets.

Church of sts Cosmas and Damian

The fifteenth-century parish **Church of sts Cosmas and Damian** (Crkva svetog Kuzme i Damjana) in the centre of town is worth a look for its interior, richly adorned with

THE POKLAD

Lastovo's **carnival** is one of the strangest in Croatia, featuring the ritual humiliation of a straw puppet, the **Poklad**. Things come to a head on Shrove Tuesday, when the Poklad is led through town on a donkey by the men of Lastovo, who dress for the occasion in a uniform of red shirts, black waistcoats and bowler hats. Following this, the Poklad is attached to a long rope and hoisted from one end of town to the other three times while fireworks are let off beneath it. Each transit is met by chanting and the drawing of swords. Finally, the Poklad is put back on the donkey and taken to the square in front of the parish church, to the accompaniment of music and dancing. At the end of the evening, the villagers dance the **Lastovsko kolo**, a sword dance similar to the Moreška in Korčula (see box, p.368), and the Poklad is impaled on a long stake and burned. Drinking and dancing continues in the village hall until dawn.

Local tradition has it that the Poklad symbolizes a young messenger who was sent by Catalan pirates to demand the town's surrender, although it's more likely that the ritual actually derives from ancient fertility rites. Whatever its roots, the islanders take the occasion very seriously, and it's certainly not enacted for the benefit of outsiders. *Lastovčani* from all over the world return to their home village to attend the Poklad, when accommodation is at a premium. If you do want to attend, contact the tourist office well in advance.

sixteenth- and seventeenth-century paintings and icons, with a dainty fifteenth-century loggia opposite the entrance. Across from the church, fading propaganda slogans dating from World War II can still be made out on the facade of the village school: *Živili savjeznici SSSR, Engleska i Amerika!* ("Long live the alliance of the USSR, England and America!") is the inspiring message.

The Fort

Above the town lie the remains of the old French **fort**, built in 1810 above some much older fortifications and now used as a weather station. It's a stiff walk up, but worth it for the views from the top, with Lastovo on one side and the sea on the other.

Around Lastovo Town

Heading downhill from Lastovo Town's main square, a road hairpins its way to two tiny harbours: **Lučica**, a tiny hamlet with a mix of derelict houses and renovated holiday homes, and, a little farther over to the west, the quieter **Sveti Mihovil**.

Otherwise, you can head for **Zaklopatica**, a hamlet 3km away on the northern coast of the island, which has a yachting harbour and a couple of *konobe*, or to **Skrivena Luka**, 7km south, a deep bay backed by sandy hills, where there are several rocky places to swim.

7

INFORMATION — LASTOVO TOWN AND AROUND

Tourist office Lastovo bb (mid-June to late Aug daily 8am–2pm & 5–8pm, and later when the bus from the last ferry arrives; rest of year Mon–Fri 8am–2pm; ☎ 020 801 018, ⓦ lastovo.hr)

ACCOMMODATION AND EATING

The tourist office can advise on **private accommodation** (two-person studios 300Kn, four-person apartments 450Kn); otherwise look at those listed on ⓦ lastovo.org and ⓦ lastovo.biz.

Konoba Bačvara Pošuvalo bb ☎ 020 801 131. Hiding in the back alleys at the bottom end of the village, this *konoba* has the edge when it comes to seafood, with freshly caught fish served in a snug indoor room or on a terrace hung with fishing nets. Daily 5pm–midnight.

Triton Zaklopatica 15 ☎ 020 801 161, ⓦ triton.hr. Right beside the yacht berths in Zaklopatica bay, offering whatever's fresh from the fishermen's nets. Expect fish grilled or baked, octopus fritters, scampi-garnished risottos and lobster. Daily 3pm–midnight.

The Pelješac peninsula

Just across the Pelješac channel (Pelješki kanal) from Korčula is the **Pelješac peninsula**, a mountainous finger of land which stretches for some 90km from Lovište in the west to the mainland in the east. It's an exceptionally beautiful place, with tiny villages and sheltered coves rimmed by beaches, and although it's an increasingly popular holiday area, development remains low-key. The downside is that public transport is meagre

FOOD AND DRINK IN THE PELJEŠAC PENINSULA

The Pelješac peninsula is famous above all for its **shellfish**; the village of Mali Ston (see p.382) is particularly well known for the *kamenice* (European flat oysters) and *dagnji* (mussels) farmed in its adjacent bay. Mali Ston's **oysters** are best eaten in the clutch of excellent restaurants on the harbour; there's something special about gulping down these molluscs only yards from where they are harvested.

The Pelješac is also one of Croatia's most prolific **wine**-producing regions, celebrated for the earthy dry reds derived from the indigenous Plavac mali grape. The villages of Postup (4km east of Orebić) and Dingač (16km east) stand at the centre of the best-known vineyards, and wines bearing the Dingač label are highly rated by connoisseurs.

except along the main Korčula–Orebić–Ston–Dubrovnik route, and most of the smaller places are impossible to get to without a car.

ARRIVAL AND DEPARTURE — THE PELJEŠAC PENINSULA

From Dubrovnik There are 2–3 buses a day to Orebić (2hr 40min), calling at Mali Ston and Ston on the way.

From Korčula A car ferry runs from Dominće, 3km east of Korčula Town to Orebić, and a passenger-only ferry from the centre of Korčula Town to Orebić (see below).

From Ploče There is a car ferry (June–Sept 7 daily, Oct–May 2–3 daily; 50min) from Ploče on the mainland to Trpanj on the north coast of the Pelješac peninsula.

Orebić and around

A short ferry-hop from Korčula, the small town of **OREBIĆ** was a trading outlet of the Dubrovnik Republic for almost five hundred years. It enjoyed a period of extraordinary prosperity in the nineteenth century, when the town was home to large shipyards and an independent merchant fleet. Today, Orebić has a moderately sized package tourism industry, largely on account of its long shingle **beaches**.

7

The prettiest part of town is along **Obala Pomoraca**, just east of the ferry jetties, where generations of sea captains built a series of comfortable villas behind a subtropical screen of palms and cacti.

The Franciscan monastery

Celestinov put 6 • Museum Mon–Sat 9am–noon & 5–7pm, Sun 5–7pm • 10Kn

Squatting on a rocky spur northwest of town a twenty-minute walk from the ferry quay, the **Franciscan monastery** (Franjevački samostan) was built in the 1480s to house a miraculous icon known as Our Lady of the Angels, brought here by monks from Montenegro. Believed to protect mariners from shipwreck, the icon still occupies pride of place in the church, surrounded by an oversized frame in which gilded angels cavort in a sky full of bluish cotton-wool clouds. The monastery **museum** displays votive paintings commissioned by crews who were saved from storms after offering prayers to the Virgin, and models of ships once owned by Orebić magnates such as the Mimbeli brothers, whose onion-domed mausoleum can be seen in the graveyard outside. There's also a wonderful view of the Pelješac channel from the monastery's terrace.

Sveti Ilija

Main target for hikers on the Pelješac peninsula is the 961-metre summit of **Sveti Ilija**, the bare mountain that looms over Orebić to the northwest. A marked path to the summit (4hr walk each way) strikes uphill just east of the Franciscan monastery (look out for the red-and-white paint marks on the rocks). Bear in mind that this is a major expedition, and shouldn't be undertaken without solid footwear, head covering, waterproofs, plenty of liquid – and if possible an accurate weather forecast from Orebić's tourist office.

Trstenica beach

The best of Orebić's pebble beaches is twenty minutes' walk east from the ferry terminal at **Trstenica**, where you'll find a crescent of shingle just about fine enough to make sandcastles out of, and there are views of the ragged coast of the distant island of Mljet.

ARRIVAL AND INFORMATION — OREBIĆ AND AROUND

By bus Buses pull up beside the ferry quay.

Destinations Dubrovnik (2 daily; 2hr 40min); Kučište (Mon–Sat 3 daily, Sun 1; 10min); Ston (3 daily; 1hr 10min); Trpanj (Mon–Sat 4 daily, Sun 2; 45min); Viganj (Mon–Sat 3 daily, Sun 1; 15min); Zagreb (1 daily; 12hr).

By ferry Ferries arrive in the harbour right in the centre of Orebić. There is a passenger-only ferry from Korčula Town (summer 8 daily; 15min), and a car ferry from Dominće,

3km east of Korčula Town (summer 16 daily, winter 7 daily; 15min).

Tourist office Trg Mimbeli, a 5min walk east from the ferry quay (July & Aug daily 8am–9pm; Sept–June Mon–Fri 9am–1pm; ⓣ020 713 718, ⓦvisitorebic-croatia.hr). In summer there are additional information kiosks right by the quay and on the main road into town.

ACCOMMODATION AND EATING

Orebić Tours ul. bana Jelačića 84 ⓣ020 713 367, ⓦorebic-tours.hr. Big choice of apartments in Orebić, Kučište, Viganj and several other Pelješac villages. Two-person studios **300Kn**, four-person apartments from **420Kn**

Taverna Mlinica Obala Pomoraca bb ⓣ020 713 886. Located midway between the tourist office and Trstenica beach is this old stone house with a traditional olive press in the middle of the main dining room. It serves traditional specialities like lamb and octopus baked *ispod sača* (under an ember-covered lid). Expect to pay 200Kn for a slap-up meal. Daily 6pm–midnight.

Kučište and Viganj

West of Orebić, the road follows the coast past the relatively unspoiled villages of Kučište and Viganj, both of which have shingle beaches, a string of shoreside campsites and – in the case of Viganj at least – a burgeoning windsurfing scene. There's little in the way of package holiday development along this stretch of coast but plenty of private rooms, which can be booked through Orebić Tours (see above), making it a laid-back, low-key alternative to the bustle of Orebić and Korčula.

Five kilometres out of Orebić, sleepy **KUČIŠTE** presents a wiggly line of rust-coloured stone houses facing the water. There's a soothing lack of things to do, save for sunbathe on the small-boat jetties strung out along the shoreline, stroll in the scrub-covered foothills of Sveti Ilija above the village (see opposite), or admire the view of Korčula's woolly tree cover from a brace of waterfront cafés.

It's only a fifteen-minute walk from Kučište to the next village along, **VIGANJ**, which lies on the far side of a pebbly spur of beach from which windsurfers launch themselves into the Pelješac channel.

ARRIVAL AND DEPARTURE — KUČIŠTE AND VIGANJ

By bus There are three buses a day from Orebić (1 on Sun) to Kučište (10min) and Viganj (15min).

By boat A privately operated boat service (1–2 daily) runs from Korčula Town to Kučište and Viganj.

INFORMATION AND ACTIVITIES

Tourist office In the post office, Viganj (mid-June to mid-Sept noon & 5–8pm; ⓣ020 719 059). Offers four-person apartments from 420Kn.

Windsurfing *Liberan* In Viganj boasts a windsurfing school where it's possible to rent boards (100Kn/hr or 350Kn/day) and sign up for courses (four-day beginners' courses start at around 699Kn).

ACCOMMODATION

Antony Boy Viganj ⓣ020 719 077, ⓦantony-boy.com. Medium-sized orchard-like campsite a stone's throw from the beach. The site has its own windsurfing school. **44Kn** per person, pitches from **36Kn**

Liberan Viganj ⓣ091 6171 666, ⓦliberan-camping.com. A large and well-organized site right behind the beach, with its own windsurfing and kitesurfing centre. **35Kn** per person, pitches from **28Kn**

Pansion Mirina Viganj 115 ⓣ020 719 033, ⓦmirina-viganj.com. At the western end of Viganj village, the *Pansion Mirina* has cute rooms and a handful of apartments, many with sea-facing balconies. Rooms **270Kn**, studios from **375Kn**

EATING AND DRINKIING

Bistro Montun Viganj 81. Fish and meat grilled on an open hearth – or baked *peka*-style if you order a day in advance. Great views of Korčula from the terrace, which is right by the pebbly shore. May–Oct daily 8am–midnight.

Čiringito Viganj bb. Beach bar at the tip of Viganj's pebbly peninsula, serving cocktails and tapas-style Mediterranean nibbles. June–Sept daily 8am–midnight.

7

K2 Viganj bb. A much-favoured windsurfer hangout, this is basically a beachside hut with a something-old, something-new mixture of stools and armchairs strewn round about. Expect free wi-fi, table football, snooker and occasional live bands. June–Sept daily 8am–2am.

Ston and Mali Ston

Some 60km east of Orebić, the twin settlements of **Ston and Mali Ston** straddle the isthmus joining Pelješac to the mainland. An important salt-producing town on the southwestern side of the isthmus, Ston was swallowed up by Dubrovnik in 1333, becoming the most important fortress along the republic's northern frontier. The republic built huge defensive walls stretching across the isthmus to the nearby harbour of Mali Ston, which became the northern bastion of a unified fortification system. Nowadays the twin town is primarily known for Mali Ston's oyster beds – the aphrodisiac effect of the local molluscs makes the place an ideal venue for romantic weekend breaks.

7

Ston

Straddling the main road from Orebić to Dubrovnik, **STON**'s mix of Renaissance- and Gothic-style houses is laid out in a tight gridiron of narrow alleys stuffed with potted plants.

Town walls

Daily 9am–6pm • 30Kn

Rearing up immediately above the town, the fourteenth-century **walls** stretch for some 3km across the rugged hillside to the west. Restoration is still ongoing, although you can walk the V-shaped circuit above the town itself, visiting various defensive towers along the way, and explore a 1km stretch of the wall heading east towards Mali Ston. From the parapets you can enjoy superb views of Ston's glittering chequerboard of saltpans.

Mali Ston

Thirty minutes' walk northeast of Ston, **MALI STON** is nowadays a tranquil village of old stone houses looking out over the **oyster beds** of Mali Ston bay. The beds are marked out by wooden poles hung with ropes on which the oysters grow prior to harvesting in May and June. Following the narrow lanes up from Mali Ston's harbour, you'll soon reach a crescent-shaped **fortress** marking the northeasternmost extent of Ston's sophisticated network of defences. Nowadays it's an uninhabited shell, though steps do lead up to a parapet from where there are good views.

ARRIVAL AND INFORMATION — STON AND MALI STON

By bus Buses pull up on Ston's main street.

Destinations Dubrovnik (3 daily; 1hr 30min); Korčula Town (1 daily; 2hr); Orebić (3 daily; 1hr 10min).

Tourist office Pelješki put 1, Ston (Mon–Fri 7am–1pm & 5–7pm, Sat 7am–1pm; 020 754 452, ston.hr). The tourist office, beside the bus stop, will give you a list of local rooms (200Kn) but might not ring them up on your behalf.

ACCOMMODATION

Auto Kamp Prapratno Papratno 020 754 000, duprimorje.hr. Shoreside site 4km southwest of Ston, down a steep side road just off the main route to Orebić. It has its own beach, a couple of grill-restaurants and impressive views of the mountains of Mljet across the water. 50Kn per person, pitches from 40Kn

Ostrea Mali Ston 020 754 555, www.ostrea.hr. Intimate thirteen-room hotel with a mixture of contemporary and traditional furnishings; most rooms come with wood floors, chintzy fabrics, a/c and TV. The same family run the *Kapetanova kuća* restaurant (see opposite), and half board deals are well-worth enquiring about. 750Kn

Villa Koruna Mali Ston 020 754 999, vila-koruna.hr. This six-room, family-run pension on the harbour has small but stylish rooms boasting a/c, TV and views towards Ston's famous oyster beds. 660Kn

EATING

Bakus Angeli Radovani Branko 5, Ston ⓣ 020 754 270. *Bakus Angeli* has an inexpensive menu of grilled meats, fresh fish and seafood risottos, washed down with local Pelješac wines and served up in one of Ston's characterful narrow alleys. Daily 11am–midnight.

Bota Šare Mali Ston ⓣ 020 754 482, ⓦ bota-sare.hr. Bota means something like "barrel-vaulted roof", a reference to the medieval harbourside palace it occupies. Superb local seafood includes Ston oysters (raw, grilled or deep fried), grilled fish and scampi. Daily 11am–midnight.

★ **Kapetanova kuća** Mali Ston ⓣ 020 754 264, ⓦ www.ostrea.hr. One of the longest established of the restaurants serving locally harvested oysters, *Kapetanova kuća* delivers high standards across the board, with good grilled fish and lobster dishes available as well as the local mollusc. Daily 9am–midnight.

Dubrovnik and around

VIEW FROM THE CITY WALLS

Dubrovnik and around

A walled, sea-battered city lying at the foot of a grizzled mountain, Dubrovnik is Croatia's most popular tourist destination, and it's not difficult to see why. An essentially medieval town reshaped by Baroque planners after a disastrous earthquake of 1667, Dubrovnik's historic core seems to have been suspended in time ever since. Set-piece churches and public buildings blend seamlessly with the green-shuttered stone houses, forming a perfect ensemble relatively untouched by the twenty-first century. Outside the city walls, suburban Dubrovnik exudes Mediterranean elegance: gardens are an explosion of colourful bougainvillea and oleanders; trees are weighted down with figs, lemons, oranges and peaches.

For the Croats themselves **DUBROVNIK** serves as a powerful metaphor for freedom, having spent much of its history as a self-governing city-state independent of foreign powers. The city played a more than symbolic role in the war of 1991–95, when it successfully resisted a nine-month Serbian-Montenegrin siege. Reconstruction was undertaken with astonishing speed, and the fact that conflict took place here at all only reveals itself through subtle details: the vivid orange-red hues of brand-new roof tiles, or the contrasting shades of grey where damaged facades have been patched up with freshly quarried stone.

The success of Dubrovnik's **tourist industry** has brought a certain degree of complacency and self-satisfaction. The city's museums are the most disappointing of any major Croatian city, and – despite a few honourable exceptions – the local restauranteurs are focused on raising prices rather than culinary horizons. Certain aspects of the city's appeal remain immune to tourist numbers, however; most notably the uniquely beautiful setting and the unjaded straightforwardness of the Dubrovčani themselves.

Dubrovnik is worth a visit at any time of year, although spring and summer – when life spills out onto the streets and café tables remain packed well into the night – bring out the best in the city. Croatia's cultural luminaries visit the town during the **Dubrovnik Summer Festival** in July and August, bringing an added dash of glamour to the streets, while the main event in winter is the **Feast of St Blaise** on February 3, when the patron saint of the city is honoured by a parade and special mass, followed by much drinking and eating. Be warned though: Dubrovnik's popularity with cruise liners can lead to big crowds during the day, when the Old Town can resemble a vast theme park-cum-souvenir shop for ship-borne day-trippers. And though Dubrovnik is increasingly an all-year-round destination, note that a good half of the city's hotels are closed from November through to March, and a lot of restaurants take the whole month of January off.

The main tourist resorts south of Dubrovnik, **Župa Dubrovačka** and **Cavtat**, are within easy reach of the city by public transport. In addition, Dubrovnik's port is the natural gateway to the southernmost **islands** of the Croatian Adriatic, with the sparsely populated, semi-wild islands of **Koločep**, **Lopud** and **Šipan** providing beach-hoppers with a wealth of out-of-town bathing opportunities. Slightly farther out to sea, the

TRSTENO

Highlights

❶ **Dubrovnik's city walls** A well-trodden walkway follows the full circuit of the battlements, providing the ideal vantage point from which to enjoy the city's medieval and Baroque splendours. **See p.391**

❷ **Dominican monastery** In Dubrovnik's Old Town, the monastery's quiet cloister harbours a small but stunning collection of Renaissance art. **See p.402**

❸ **Lokrum** This densely wooded islet, a short boat ride from Dubrovnik, is the perfect place for a sunbathe or a stroll. **See p.404**

❹ **Mount Srđ** Scale the peak overlooking Dubrovnik by cable car or on foot to enjoy fantastic views of the coast. **See p.406**

❺ **Dubrovnik's Summer Festival** The annual cultural shindig brings top-class drama and music to the Old Town's courtyards and fortresses. **See p.414**

❻ **Trsteno** These Renaissance gardens, perched on a hillside overlooking the sea, provide an ideal excuse for an out-of-town excursion. **See p.415**

❼ **The Elaphite Islands** Koločep, Lopud and Šipan are among the most beautiful and unspoilt islands in the Adriatic. **See p.421**

❽ **Mljet** Lush, forested island with an easily strollable network of paths enircling its two saltwater lakes. **See p.425**

HIGHLIGHTS ARE MARKED ON THE MAP ON P.388

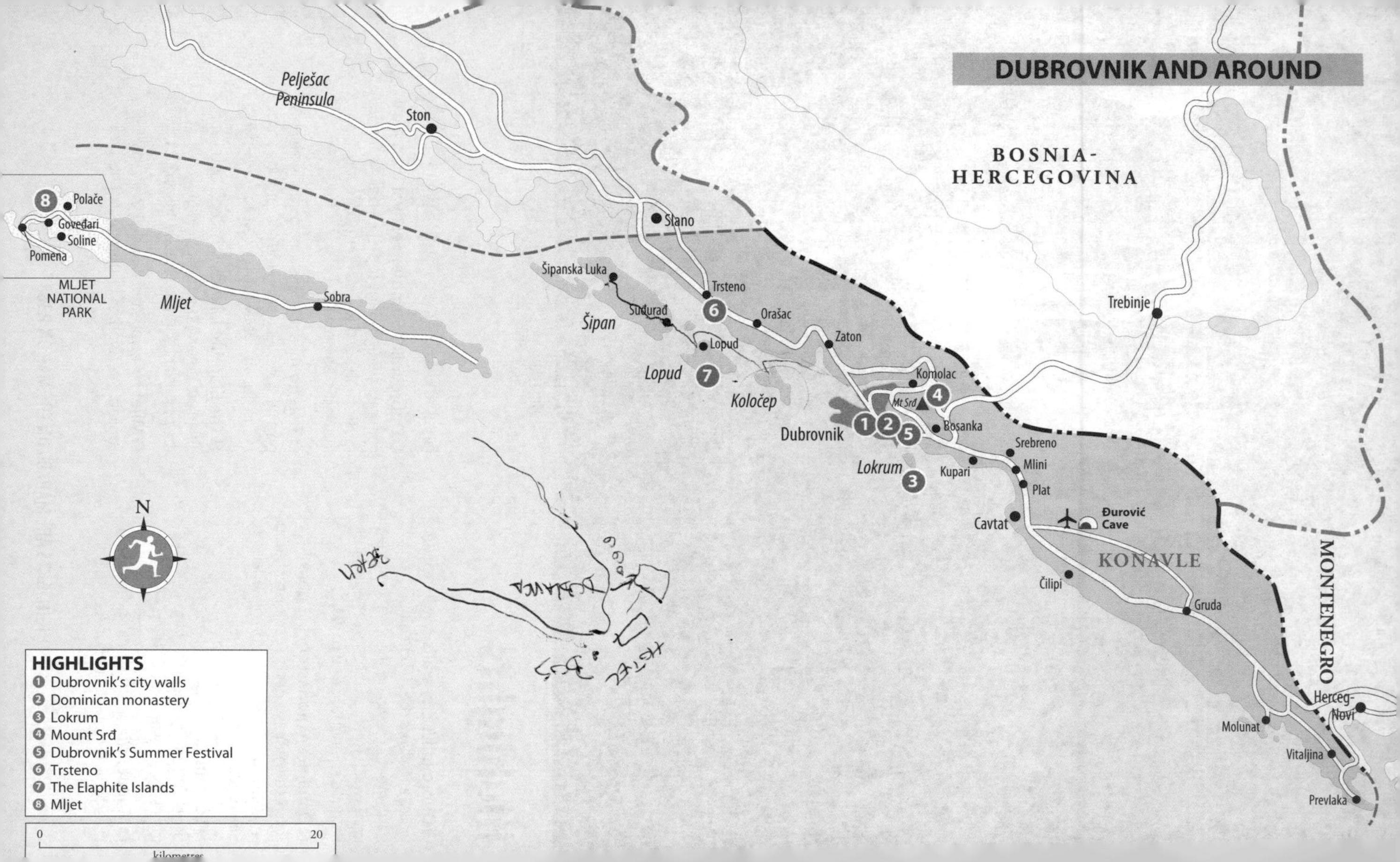
DUBROVNIK AND AROUND
BOSNIA-HERCEGOVINA
MONTENEGRO
Pelješac Peninsula
Ston
Slano
Trebinje
MLJET NATIONAL PARK
Polače
Govedari
Soline
Pomena
Mljet
Sobra
Šipanska Luka
Šipan
Suđurađ
Lopud
Koločep
Trsteno
Orašac
Zaton
Komolac
Mt Srđ
Bosanka
Dubrovnik
Lokrum
Kupari
Srebreno
Mlini
Plat
Cavtat
Đurović Cave
KONAVLE
Čilipi
Gruda
Molunat
Vitaljina
Prevlaka
Herceg-Novi
N
HIGHLIGHTS
1 Dubrovnik's city walls
2 Dominican monastery
3 Lokrum
4 Mount Srđ
5 Dubrovnik's Summer Festival
6 Trsteno
7 The Elaphite Islands
8 Mljet
0
20
kilometres

FOOD AND DRINK IN DUBROVNIK

The choice of **fish and seafood** in Dubrovnik is as fine as anywhere in the Adriatic, with the waters around Mljet and the Elaphite Islands particularly rich in squid, lobster and shells. Oysters from nearby Ston (see p.382) also feature heavily on local restaurant menus. Among the dishes associated with Dubrovnik in particular are *Šporki makaruli* ("dirty macaroni"), tubular pasta served with a goulash sauce; and *rozata*, a vanilla-flavoured custard dessert similar to crème caramel.

The vineyards of the Konavle produce respectable red **wines** of the Merlot, Cabernet Sauvignon and Plavac varieties, as well as Kadarun, an autochthonous light and fruity rosé.

green island of **Mljet** is one of the most beautiful on the entire coast – you'll need a day or two to do it justice.

Brief history

Dubrovnik was first settled in the early seventh century by Greco-Roman refugees from the nearby city of Epidauros (now Cavtat), which was sacked by the Slavs. The refugees took up residence in the southern part of what is now the Old Town, then an island known as **Laus** – a name that later metamorphosed into **Ragusa**. The Slavs, meanwhile, settled on the mainland opposite, from which the name **Dubrovnik** (from *dubrava*, meaning "glade") comes. Before long the slim channel between the two was filled in and the two sides merged, producing a symbiosis of Latin and Slav cultures unique in the Mediterranean. Ethnically, the city was almost wholly Slav by the fifteenth century, although leading families consistently claimed Roman lineage, and the nobility actively preserved the use of both Latin and Italian in official circles, if not always in everyday speech.

Initially subject to Byzantium, the city came under **Venetian** control in 1204. The Venetians stayed until 1358, when they were squeezed out of the southern Adriatic by Louis of Hungary. Officially, Dubrovnik became a vassal of the Hungaro-Croatian kingdom, although it effectively became an independent **city-state**.

The Ragusan Republic

The emergent **Ragusan Republic** was run by an elected senate – fear of dictatorship meant that the nominal head of state, the Rector (*knez*), was virtually a figurehead. However, the republic was by no means a democracy: the city's nobility was the only section of society allowed to vote. Civic peace was ensured by allowing the rest of the citizenry full economic freedom and the chance to grow rich through commerce. Dubrovnik's network of maritime contacts made it one of the major players in Mediterranean trade, but the key to the city's wealth was its unrivalled access to the markets of the Balkan hinterland. The Ottoman Empire, having absorbed the kingdoms of both Serbia and Bosnia, granted Dubrovnik this privileged trading position in return for an annual payment. Dubrovnik established a network of trading colonies stretching from the Adriatic to the Black Sea, from where wheat, wool, animal hides – and, for a time, slaves – could be shipped back to the mother republic before being re-exported to the West at a fat profit. As commerce grew, so did the need to protect it, and the republic extended its borders to include the whole of the coast from Konavle in the south to Pelješac in the north, as well as the islands of Mljet and Lastovo.

[C]ulture and diplomacy

Mercantile wealth underpinned an upsurge in culture, producing a fifteenth- and sixteenth-century **golden age** when the best artists and architects in the Adriatic were drawn to the city. It was during this period that many of the urban landmarks of present-day Dubrovnik were completed: Juraj Dalmatinac and Michelozzo Michelozzi worked on the town walls, Paskoje Miličević drew up plans for the Sponza Palace, and Onofrio della Cava designed the Rector's Palace, as well as the two fountains that still bear his name.

Suzerainty over Dubrovnik had passed from the Hungaro-Croatian kingdom to the Ottoman Empire by the early sixteenth century, but shrewd diplomacy and the regular **payment of tributes** ensured that the city-state retained its virtual independence. In the sixteenth and seventeenth centuries Dubrovnik enjoyed the protection of both Spain (Dubrovnik ships sailed with the Armada in 1588) and the papacy, but usually avoided being dragged into explicitly anti-Turkish alliances. In fact, wars between the Ottomans and the West usually led to increased revenues for Dubrovnik, which exploited its position as the only neutral port in the Adriatic.

Decline and fall

Decline set in with the **earthquake of 1667**, which killed around five thousand people and destroyed many of the city's buildings. Bandits from the interior looted the ruins, and Kara Mustafa, Pasha of Bosnia, demanded huge tributes in return for keeping the robber bands under control. Kara Mustafa's death during the Siege of Vienna in 1683 allowed the city the chance to rebuild, producing the elegantly planned rows of Baroque town houses that characterize the centre of the city to this day. However, the Austro-Turkish conflict of 1683–1718 seriously affected

THE SIEGE OF DUBROVNIK 1991–92

Few thought that Dubrovnik would be directly affected by the **break-up of Yugoslavia**: no significant Serbian minority lived in the city, and its strategic importance was questionable. However, in October 1991 units of the JNA (Yugoslav People's Army), supported by volunteers from Montenegro and Serb-dominated eastern Hercegovina, quickly overran the tourist resorts south of Dubrovnik and occupied the high ground commanding approaches to the city. The **bombardment of Dubrovnik** began in early November and lasted until May 1992. Despite considerable damage to the town's historic core, Dubrovnik's medieval fortifications proved remarkably sturdy, with the fortresses of Revelin and St John (more familiar to tourists as the site of the aquarium) pressed into service as shelters for the civilian population.

The logic behind the attack on Dubrovnik was confused. Belgrade strategists unwisely considered it an easy conquest, the fall of which would damage Croatian morale and break the back of Croatian resistance elsewhere on the Adriatic. The attack on Dubrovnik also presented an effective way of dragging both the Montenegrins and the Serbs of eastern Hercegovina into the conflict, not least because it seemed to promise them ample opportunities for pillage. Attacking forces employed a mixture of bad history and dubious folklore to justify their actions. Dubrovnik's links with medieval Serbia, and the fact that so many leading Ragusan families had originally come from the Balkan interior, were unconvincingly offered up as evidence that the early republic had been part of the Serbian cultural orbit. In a particularly twisted piece of cultural logic, opportunist Serbian intellectuals painted modern-day Dubrovnik city as a cesspit of Western corruption that could only be purified by the macho values of the Balkan hinterland. A special edition of the Montenegrin magazine *Pobjeda* published in November 1991 and entitled *The War for Peace* argued, with startling mendacity/hypocrisy, that Dubrovnik was under the control of Croatian *ustaše* (World War II fascists) and therefore deserved to be conquered.

Contrary to Serbian–Montenegrin expectations, Dubrovnik's hastily arranged defences held out, and in the end the siege was broken in July 1992 by a Croatian offensive from the north. Once Dubrovnik's land links with the rest of Croatia had been re-established, Croatian forces continued their push southwards, liberating Cavtat and Čilipi.

Dubrovnik's inland trade, a blow from which it never really recovered. By the eighteenth century Dubrovnik's nobility was dying out, and commoners were increasingly elevated to noble rank to make up the numbers; anachronistic **feuds** between the Sorbonnesi (old patricians) and Salamanchesi (newly elevated patricians, named after the universities of Sorbonne and Salamanca, where many young Ragusans studied) weakened the traditional social fabric still further.

The city-state was formally dissolved by Napoleon in 1808. The **French occupation** of the city provoked a British naval bombardment, while Russian and Montenegrin forces laid waste to surrounding territories, destroying much of suburban Dubrovnik in the process. In 1815 the **Congress of Vienna** awarded Dubrovnik to the Austrians, who incorporated the city into the newly formed province of Dalmatia. Political and economic activity was henceforth concentrated in towns such as Zadar and Split, leaving Dubrovnik on the fringes of Adriatic society.

The modern era

The symbolic importance of Dubrovnik long outlived the republic itself. For nineteenth-century Croats the city was a **Croatian Athens**, a shining example of what could be achieved – both politically and culturally – by the Slav peoples. It was also increasingly a magnet for foreign travellers, who wrote about the city in glowing terms, save for Rebecca West, for whom it was too perfect and self-satisfied: "I do not like it," she famously wrote. "It reminds me of the worst of England."

Already a society resort in West's time, Dubrovnik enhanced its reputation for cultural chic with the inception in 1949 of the **Dubrovnik Festival**, one of Europe's most prestigious, while the construction of big hotel complexes in Lapad and Babin kuk to the north, and Župa to the south, helped make Dubrovnik one of the most popular tourist destinations in Yugoslavia in the 1970s and 1980s. After repairing the damage done during the **1991–92 siege** (see box opposite) with remarkable speed, Dubrovnik quickly recovered its position as Croatia's premier vacation spot.

Pile Gate

Marking the western entrance to Dubrovnik's Old Town, **Pile Gate** (pronounced pee-leh) is many people's first taste of the city. It's just outside the gate that buses from the airport, ferry and bus terminals drop off their passengers, and day-trip tour groups are met by their guides. The gate itself is a simple archway set into an imposing, pillbox-like bastion. It is accessible by a **stone bridge** dating from 1471 which crosses the former moat, now a park full of orange trees. Occupying a niche above the gateway is a statuette of a bearded **St Blaise**, traditional protector of the city. A flight of steps descends to a second, inner gate, starting point of the Stradun, Dubrovnik's main street.

The city walls

Daily: summer 8am–7.30pm; winter 10am–3pm • 50Kn

Best way to get your bearings of Dubrovnik's Old Town is by making a tour of the still largely intact **city walls** (Gradske zidine), 25m high and stretching for some 2km, completely surrounding the city's historic heart. The full circuit takes about an hour, longer in high summer when crowds may slow down your progress. The path along the walls is narrow in places and you're not allowed up there if you're wearing a backpack.

The walls are encrusted with towers and bastions, and it's impossible not to be struck by their remarkable size and state of preservation. Although some parts date back to the

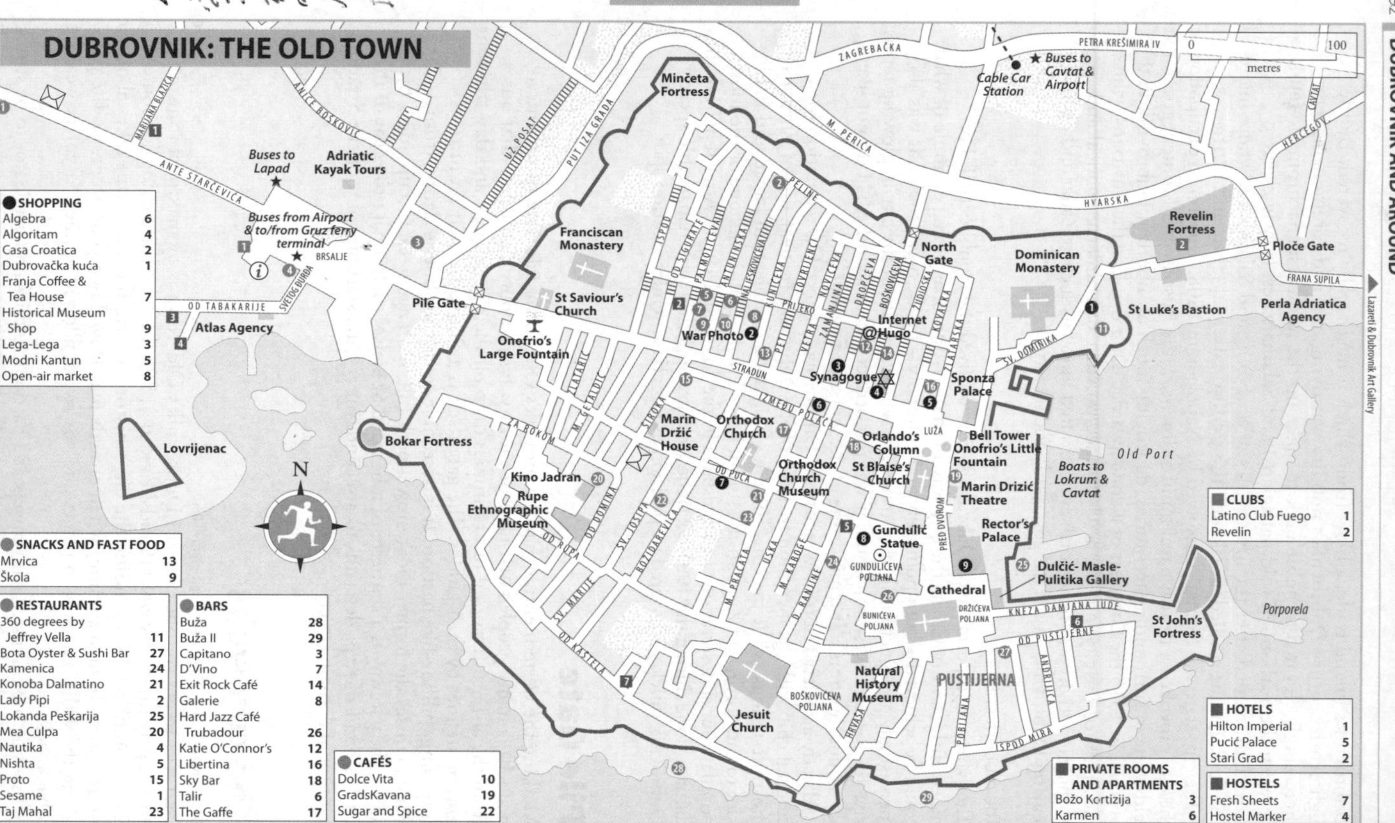
Lazareti & Dubrovnik Art Gallery
DUBROVNIK: THE OLD TOWN
8
0
100
metres
ZAGREBAČKA
PETRA KREŠIMIRA IV
Cable Car Station
Buses to Cavtat & Airport
Minčeta Fortress
M. PERIĆA
HVARSKA
HERCEGOV
CAVTAT
Revelin Fortress
Ploče Gate
FRANA SUPILA
Perla Adriatica Agency
St Luke's Bastion
Dominican Monastery
North Gate
SV. DOMINIKA
Old Port
Boats to Lokrum & Cavtat
Porporela
St John's Fortress
Dulčić- Masle- Pulitika Gallery
KNEZA DAMJANA JUDE
OD PUSTIJERNE
ANDRIJICA
PUSTIJERNA
POBIJANA
ISPOD MIRA
Natural History Museum
HRVASA
BOŠKOVIĆEVA POLJANA
Jesuit Church
BUNIĆEVA POLJANA
DRŽIĆEVA POLJANA
Cathedral
Rector's Palace
PRED DVOROM
Marin Držić Theatre
Bell Tower
Onofrio's Little Fountain
LUŽA
Sponza Palace
ZLATARSKA
KOVAČKA
ŽUDIOSKA
BOŠKOVIĆEVA
DROPČEVA
Internet @Hugo
Synagogue
ZAMANJINA
NOVIĆEVA
VETRA
LOVRIJENCA
PRIJEKO
KUNIĆEVA
War Photo
PELINE
ISPOD
OD SIGURATE
PALMOTIĆEVA
ANTUNINSKA
NALJEŠKOVIĆEVA
STRADUN
IZMEĐU POLAČA
Orlando's Column
St Blaise's Church
Gundulić Statue
GUNDULIĆEVA POLJANA
Orthodox Church Museum
Orthodox Church
OD PUČA
Marin Držić House
ŠIROKA
M. PRACATA
USKA
M. KABOGE
D. RANJINE
SV. JOSIPA
BOŽIDAREVIĆA
OD DOMINA
OD RUPA
Kino Jadran
Rupe Ethnographic Museum
SV. MARIJE
OD KAŠTELA
ZA ROKOM
M. GETALDIĆ
ZLATARIĆ
Franciscan Monastery
St Saviour's Church
Pile Gate
Onofrio's Large Fountain
Bokar Fortress
PUT IZA GRADA
UZ POSAT
Lovrijenac
N
Buses to Lapad
Adriatic Kayak Tours
Buses from Airport & to/from Gruz ferry terminal
BRSALJE
SVETOG ĐURĐA
OD TABAKARIJE
Atlas Agency
ANTE STARČEVIĆA
ANICE BOSKOVIĆ
MARIJANA BLAŽIĆA
SHOPPING
Algebra 6
Algoritam 4
Casa Croatica 2
Dubrovačka kuća 1
Franja Coffee & Tea House 7
Historical Museum Shop 9
Lega-Lega 3
Modni Kantun 5
Open-air market 8
SNACKS AND FAST FOOD
Mrvica 13
Škola 9
RESTAURANTS
360 degrees by Jeffrey Vella 11
Bota Oyster & Sushi Bar 27
Kamenica 24
Konoba Dalmatino 21
Lady Pipi 2
Lokanda Peškarija 25
Mea Culpa 20
Nautika 4
Nishta 5
Proto 15
Sesame 1
Taj Mahal 23
BARS
Buža 28
Buža II 29
Capitano 3
D'Vino 7
Exit Rock Café 14
Galerie 8
Hard Jazz Café Trubadour 26
Katie O'Connor's 12
Libertina 16
Sky Bar 18
Talir 6
The Gaffe 17
CAFÉS
Dolce Vita 10
GradsKavana 19
Sugar and Spice 22
CLUBS
Latino Club Fuego 1
Revelin 2
HOTELS
Hilton Imperial 1
Pucić Palace 5
Stari Grad 2
PRIVATE ROOMS AND APARTMENTS
Božo Kortizija 3
Karmen 6
HOSTELS
Fresh Sheets 7
Hostel Marker 4

ORIENTATION

With a population of a little over 49,000, Dubrovnik isn't as large as yc
although it sprawls along the coast for several kilometres, its real hea
Town. Doing the circuit of the city walls is the one Dubrovnik attracti
and it's worth doing this early on in order to get the feel of the place.
can easily be covered in a day and a half – although once you begin t
atmosphere you'll find it difficult to pull yourself away. Running above
the bare ridge of **Mount Srđ**, the summit of which provides expansive
the coast. The best place for swimming and sunbathing is the islet of **L**
taxi-boat ride from the Old Town.

tenth century, most of the original construction was undertaken in the twelfth and thirteenth centuries. A major campaign of renovation and expansion then took place in the mid-fifteenth century when fear of Ottoman expansion was at its height. Once you're on top, the **views** over the town are of a patchwork sea of terracotta tiles, punctuated by sculpted domes and towers and laid out in an almost uniform grid plan – the Ragusan authorities introduced strict planning regulations to take account of the city's growth as early as the 1270s, and the rebuilding programme which followed the earthquake of 1667 rationalized things still further.

Circuiting the walls

Clockwise around the walls from the Pile Gate, it's a gentle two-hundred-metre climb towards the fat, concentric turrets of the **Minčeta Fortress**, which guards the Old Town's northern corner. It was begun in 1455 by the Florentine architect Michelozzo Michelozzi who was subsequently replaced by Juraj Dalmatinac (see box, p.269) as the town's chief engineer. It was Dalmatinac who designed the eye-catching crown of battlements that has made Minčeta such a landmark. From Minčeta it's a farther 500m around the walls to the **St Luke's bastion** (Sveti Luka), where you have an excellent view of the **Revelin Fortress** and the **Old Port** area; and another 200m to St John's Fortress (see p.399), a W-shaped curve of thick stone facing out to sea. It's probably as you return towards Pile Gate along the southern, sea-facing walls that you get the best views of old Dubrovnik's tiled roofs and narrow, tunnel-like streets. At the western corner of the Old Town you'll pass the **Bokar Fortress**, also by Michelozzi and Dalmatinac, a jutting bastion which once guarded sea-borne access to the moat.

Along Stradun

A constant surge of visitors throngs the **Stradun**, the main street (also known as Placa) that runs straight across the Old Town from west to east, following the line of the channel that originally separated the island of Laus from the mainland. A constant surge of tourists throngs the Stradun in summer, and the street's limestone surface has been buffed to a slippery polish by the tramp of thousands of feet. The set-piece uniformity of this thoroughfare is a result of the 1667 earthquake, after which Stradun was reconstructed with the imposing, outwardly unadorned town houses you see today, displaying a civic commitment to purity and order characteristic of a city government that always had a rather disciplinarian streak, and which has been rigorously maintained by subsequent generations. All the houses have identical door and window frames, the latter flanked by uniform green shutters, and though they're nowadays full of tourist shops, laws forbidding conspicuous shop signs mean that the names of boutiques and restaurants are instead inscribed on the lanterns that hang over each doorway.

AKING IN DUBROVNIK

yaking is a popular pastime in Dubrovnik and shoals of orange-bibbed paddlers ing into Banje beach has become one of the city's most characteristic sights. A trip sually involves a group excursion in one-person kayaks, led by an instructor, and is an exhilarating way of seeing the walled city and its surrounding islands from a maritime perspective. Previous experience is not necessary, and the pace is gentle enough to suit most people of average health.

The most common excursions are a half-day trip round Dubrovnik's walls and the nearby island of Lokrum (around 260Kn per person), or full-day tours to the slightly more distant islands of Koločep, Lopud and Šipan (around 400Kn per person).

KAYAKING OPERATORS

Adriatic Kayak Tours Zrinsko-Frankopanska 6 T 020 312 770, W adriatickayaktours.com.

Adventure Dalmatia Ivana Matijasevića 6 T 091 566 5942, W adventuredalmatia.com.

Perla Adriatica Frana Supila 2, just outside Ploče Gate T 020 422 766, W perla-adriatica.com.

Onofrio's Large Fountain

Stradun

Dominating the western end of Stradun is **Onofrio's Large Fountain** of 1444, a circle of water-spouting heads topped by a bulbous dome. It was here that medieval visitors to this hygiene-conscious city had to wash themselves before they were admitted. Built by the Italian architect Onofrio della Cava, the fountain was the culmination of an elaborate water system that delivered water from Mount Srđ to public washing facilities right across town.

St Saviour's Church

Stradun

Near the Stradun's western end is the small **St Saviour's Church** (Crkva svetog Spasa), a simple but harmonious Renaissance structure whose facade – featuring a rose window beneath a trefoil roofline – may have influenced the cathedral at Hvar. The church's bare interior is occasionally used as a concert venue and as an exhibition space for contemporary work.

The Franciscan monastery

Stradun • Museum daily: April–Oct 9am–6pm; Nov–March 9am–5pm • 30Kn

Entered via a narrow passageway from the Stradun's northern side is the fourteenth-century **Franciscan monastery** (Franjevački samostan), whose late Romanesque cloister is decorated with rows of double arches topped by a confusion of human heads and fantastic animals. The attached **museum** is also worth a look, with manuscripts tracing the development of musical notation, together with relics from the apothecary's shop at the entrance to the cloister. Established in 1317, and still in business, it calls itself the oldest pharmacy in Europe. Among the Gothic reliquaries, a smooth, silver-plated fourteenth-century receptacle for St Ursula's head looks far too small and dainty to contain a human skull.

On the Stradun itself, on the right-hand side of the entrance to the monastery cloister, a small stone embellished with a gargoyle-like face juts out of the wall just above pavement height. For some reason, it has become a test of male endurance to stand on this stone – which is extremely difficult to balance on – and to remove one's shirt while facing the wall before falling off. A few steps beyond is the entrance portal to the monastery church, above which is a moving relief of the Pietà, carved by the Petrović brothers in 1499.

War Photo Limited

Antuninska 6 • May–Oct daily 9am–9pm • 25Kn • ☎ 020 322 166, 🌐 warphotoltd.com

Founded by a photographer who reported on the war in Croatia and stayed, **War Photo Limited** belies its rather brusque and to-the-point name with a selection of exhibitions that show contemporary photojournalism at its subtle and varied best. There are usually two or three themed exhibitions each summer, frequently featuring some of the world's best photographers, and often focusing on the victims of conflict and its social consequences rather than the activity itself – powerful, moving stuff for the most part. A side room on the top floor concentrates on the conflict in former Yugoslavia.

The synagogue

Žudioska 5 • May–Oct daily 10am–8pm; Nov–April Mon–Fri 9am–noon • 20Kn

Dating from the fifteenth century, Dubrovnik's **synagogue** (sinagoga), on Žudioska (Jews' Street), is said to be the second oldest in the Balkans. The present-day interior dates from the nineteenth century, its heavy brass lamps and candelabras hanging from a bright-blue ceiling dotted with Star of David motifs. A room below contains a museum display rich in ancient Torah scrolls, many with fancy silk and velvet bindings.

Unlike other Christian powers, Dubrovnik welcomed many of the Jews expelled from Spain in 1492, although anti-Semitism was not unknown. Even before their arrival in the city, scapegoating of Jews formed part of Dubrovnik's medieval carnival, most notably in the practice known as the *džudijata*, in which an unfortunate lunatic or criminal was dressed as a Jew before being hauled through the streets in an ox cart and either ritually killed or made to act out a make-believe death – historians are divided on how far things actually went.

8

Luža

The Stradun's eastern end broadens into a square known simply as **Luža** ("Loggia"), the centre of the medieval town and, with its pavement cafés and milling tourists, still a hub of activity today. Overlooking it is the fifteenth-century municipal **bell tower** (gradski zvonik), a smooth pillar of pale stone topped by an unassuming pimple-like cupola. Visible near the top of the tower, the bell itself is flanked by two larger-than-life statues of hammer-wielding figures, modern replicas of the fifteenth-century bell-striking originals. Thought to have been designed by the prolific Michelozzi, the statues have long served as a symbol of the city and are popularly known as the *zelenci* ("greenies") on account of their well-weathered patina.

Sponza Palace

Luža

Occupying the northern side of Dubrovnik's Luža is the **Sponza Palace** (Palača Sponza), once the city's custom house and mint, which features broad Renaissance arches on the ground floor and florid Venetian Gothic windows on the first floor. It was designed by Paskoje Miličević in 1522, although much of the stone-carving was done by Josip Andrijić, who also worked on Korčula's cathedral as well as Dubrovnik's St Saviour's Church. Inside, the majestic courtyard is given over to art exhibitions and occasional concerts in summer. A Latin inscription on the courtyard's northern wall refers to the public scales that once stood here, and puts God firmly on the side of trading standards: "Cheating and tampering with the weights is forbidden, and when I weigh goods God weighs me."

Memorial Room of the Defenders of Dubrovnik

Sponza Palace • Daily: May–Oct 9am–10pm; Nov–April 10am–3pm • Free

A room on the left-hand side of the Sponza Palace's main courtyard contains the **Memorial Room of the Defenders of Dubrovnik** (Spomen soba poginulim dubrovačkim braniteljima), with photographs of those who lost their lives during the 1991–92 siege. It's a discreet, understated and moving commemoration.

Dubrovnik State Archives

Sponza Palace • Daily: May–Oct 9am–10pm; Nov–April 10am–3pm • 20Kn • T 020 321 031, W dad.hr

A good example of how Dubrovnik's museums tend to look improvised, underfunded or both, the **Dubrovnik State Archives** (Državni arhiv u Dubrovniku) displays badly photocopied facsimiles of historical documents in a couple of rooms inside the courtyard of the Sponza Palace. The mildly diverting display of old photographs and maps may be enough to perk up flagging interest.

St Blaise's Church

Luža 3

Owing to its dominant position at the eastern end of the Stradun, many visitors make the mistake of assuming that the handsome Baroque church is in fact the city's cathedral. Completed in 1714, **St Blaise's Church** (Crkva svetog Vlaha) boasts a fine facade topped by saintly statuettes that seem poised to topple down onto the square below. Twentieth-century stained glass bathes the interior with dappled light, although it's hard to make out the statuette of St Blaise on the high altar, surrounded by a supporting cast of swooning Baroque statuary. Originally an Armenian martyr, Blaise is said to have appeared in a vision to a local priest to warn of impending Venetian attack in 791. Although the whole story is a piece of anti-Venetian propaganda cooked up in around 1000 AD, it was enough to ensure the saint's adoption as patron of the city.

Orlando's Column

Luža

Right in front of St Blaise's Church stands the carved figure of an armoured knight on a small pedestal, usually referred to as **Orlando's Column**. Surprisingly for such an insignificant-looking object, erected in 1418 as a morale-boosting monument to freedom, this was the focal point of the city-state: it was here that government ordinances were promulgated and punishments carried out. Nowadays, a flag bearing the *libertas* motto flies from atop the column, and the start of the Dubrovnik Summer Festival is formally proclaimed here every July. Orlando's right arm was also the republic's standard measurement of length (the Ragusan cubit or Dubrovački lakat, equivalent to 51.2cm); at the base of the column you can still see a line of the same length cut in the stone.

THE CULT OF ORLANDO

The **medieval cult of Orlando** (or Roland) was born in the twelfth century thanks to the popularity of the epic poem, the **Song of Roland**, which told of the knight's heroic defence of a Pyrenean pass during the Arab invasion of Europe in the eighth century. The cult was a predominantly north European affair, brought to Dubrovnik at the time the city was under the protection of the Hungarian king, Sigismund of Luxemburg, who passed through the city after his defeat by the Turks at Nicopolis in 1396. The legend of Orlando was subsequently adapted to Ragusan requirements by making him the saviour of Dubrovnik in battles against the Saracens, during which he fought a duel with a pirate called Spuzente ("Smelly breath") – nobody seemed to mind that the real Saracen siege of Dubrovnik took place almost a century after Orlando's time.

Onofrio's Little Fountain

Luža

The eastern side of Luža is flanked by a loggia, to the right of which is **Onofrio's Little Fountain**, an altogether more dainty affair than the same sculptor's fountain at the other end of Stradun, decorated with frivolous cherub reliefs courtesy of Onofrio's contemporary, Pietro di Martina of Milan.

GradsKavana and the arsenal

Luža

Facing the bare southern flank of St Blaise's Church, the terrace of **GradsKavana** (a contraction of *gradska kavana* or "town café"; see p.412) is where Dubrovnik's more stolid burghers traditionally sit to exchange gossip and observe the ebb and flow of tourists below. To the rear of the café is a wine bar occupying the city's former **arsenal**, into which galleys were hauled for repairs.

The Rector's Palace

Pred Dvorom 3

Immediately south of Luža is the **Rector's Palace** (Knežev dvor), former seat of the Ragusan government. As Dubrovnik's head of state, the rector was elected for just one month, during which he could only leave the palace on state occasions; after the end of his term, he was ineligible for re-election for the next two years. The palace housed all the major offices of state, plus a dungeon and a powder store (which caused the palace to blow up twice in the fifteenth century). The current palace, put together by a loose partnership of architects (including Dalmatinac and Michelozzi), is a masterpiece of serene proportion, fringed by an ornate arcaded loggia held up by columns with delicately carved capitals. Farthest to the right as you face them is the so-called **Asclepius Column**, bearing a relief of a bearded figure – presumably the Greco-Roman god of medicine, Asclepius – sitting in a pharmacist's laboratory. Asclepius was thought to be the patron of the ancient city of Epidauros (modern-day Cavtat, 20km south of Dubrovnik), from which the original population of Dubrovnik came, making him something of a distant guardian of the Ragusan state.

The palace's Renaissance atrium is a popular venue for summer recitals (especially during festivals such as the Dubrovnik Summer Festival and Rachlin and Friends; see box, p.414). At its centre is a bust of **Miho Pracat** (1522–1607), a rich shipowner and merchant from the island of Lopud who left most of his wealth to the city-state on his death – and was consequently the only citizen the republic ever honoured with a statue. Local folk tales sought to explain how Pracat came by his vast riches. He is said to have robbed Dubrovnik cathedral's treasury to pay for his business ventures, one of which involved exporting the city's cats to North Africa, where he had chanced upon a plague of rodents.

The Cultural and Historical Museum

Rector's Palace • Daily: April–Oct 9am–6pm; Nov–March 9am–4pm • Combined ticket with Maritime Museum, Ethnographic Museum and Revelin Fortress 70Kn • Ⓣ 020 322 096, Ⓦ dumus.hr

Much of the Rector's Palace is given over to the **Cultural and Historical Museum** (Kulturno-povijesni muzej), a poorly labelled three-floor collection of furniture and paintings that manifestly fails to tell the story of Dubrovnik in any meaningful or accessible way. It works quite well as a picture gallery though, with a respectable hoard of (mostly anonymous) Baroque works amassed by the city's aristocracy, although pride of place goes to a sixteenth-century *Baptism of Christ* by local artist Mihailo Hamzić, clearly showing the impact of Renaissance styles on Ragusan painting.

The Dulčić-Masle-Pulitika Gallery

Držićeva poljana 1 • Tues–Sun 10am–8pm • 30Kn (combined ticket with Dubrovnik Art Gallery) • ⓣ 020 323 172, ⓦ ugdubrovnik.hr

Immediately south of the Rector's Palace, a Baroque town house backing onto the city walls is now home to the **Dulčić-Masle-Pulitika Gallery** (Galerija Dulčić-Masle-Pulitika), which honours a trio of local painters – Ivo Dulčić (1916–75), Antun Masle (1919–67) and Đuro Pulitika (1922–2006) – who have been dubbed the "Dubrovnik Colourists" for their unabashed enjoyment of bright hues. There's an incendiary display of their expressionistic Mediterranean landscapes on two floors.

Đuro Pulitika Atelier

Town walls; near the St John's Fortress exit • Tues–Sun 10am–1pm • Free • ⓦ ugdubrovnik.hr

Staff at the Dulčić-Masle-Pulitika Gallery will give you directions to the nearby **Đuro Pulitika Atelier**, where the painter's former studio contains several of his characteristically colourful village scenes – full of candyfloss trees, winding roads and hilltop churches.

The cathedral

Držićeva poljana • Mon–Sat 9am–5pm, Sun noon–5pm

8

The bulky grey building rising south of the Rector's Palace is Dubrovnik's **cathedral** (katedrala), a plain but stately Baroque structure begun by Andrea Bufalini of Urbino in 1672. Construction was supervised by a succession of architects imported from Italy (the first three of whom gave up owing either to illness or non-payment) before it was finally completed by local Ilija Kalčić in 1731. According to legend, the original church – destroyed in the 1667 earthquake – was funded by a votive gift from Richard the Lionheart, who may well have been shipwrecked (and saved) off Ragusa on his way back from the Third Crusade, though traces of the original church's foundations have revealed that it actually predated Richard's visit by a couple of decades.

Inside the cathedral are a couple of Italian paintings, including Titian's polyptych *The Assumption* behind the main altar, a work originally purchased by the Brotherhood of the Lazarini – a sign of how rich some of Dubrovnik's commoners' associations really were. The west side of the nave holds the icon of Our Lady of the Port, a Veneto-Byzantine Madonna once carried through the streets in time of drought on account of its rain-making powers.

The cathedral treasury

Mid-April to Oct Mon–Sat 9am–5pm, Sun noon–5pm; Nov to mid-April Mon–Sat 10am–noon & 3–5pm, Sun 3–5pm • 15Kn

To the left of the cathedral's high altar, the **treasury** (*riznica*) occupies a specially built room hidden behind heavy wooden doors secured with three locks – the three keys were held separately by the rector, the bishop and a nobleman. Now packed with gilded shelves and small paintings, the treasury originally grew from two collections, one of which was attached to the now destroyed St Stephen's Church, while the other belonged to the old pre-earthquake cathedral. Stored in the Revelin Fortress after the earthquake, both were brought to their current home in a grandiose procession in 1721. One of the prime exhibits is a twelfth-century skull reliquary of St Blaise, fashioned in the shape of a Byzantine crown, studded with portraits of saints and frosted with delicate gold and enamel filigree work. Nearby are reliquaries containing both hands and one of the legs of the same saint. Even more eye-catching is a bizarre fifteenth-century *Allegory of the Flora and Fauna of Dubrovnik*, a jug and basin festooned with snakes, fish and lizards clambering over thick clumps of seaweed.

Pustijerna

South of the cathedral is **Pustijerna**, one of the city's oldest quarters, much of which predates the seventeenth-century earthquake. It preserves a medieval feel, with crumbling, ancient houses crowding in on narrow lanes spanned here and there by arches.

Aquarium

St John's Fortress, Kneza Damjana Jude • Summer: daily 9am–8pm; winter: Tues–Sun 10am–1pm • 40Kn • T 020 323 125, W imp-du.com

Occupying the ground floor of the impressively bulky bastion known as **St John's Fortress** (Tvrđava svetog Ivana) is Dubrovnik's gloomy **aquarium** (akvarij), containing tanks filled with pretty much every creature known to roam the waters of the Adriatic. There's also an educative display of the polluting junk left in the sea by visiting humans. Most popular exhibit is the sea turtle, into whose pool visitors throw coins for good luck.

The Maritime Museum

Trvđava sv. Ivana, Kneza Damjana Jude • Daily: April–Oct 9am–6pm; Nov–March 9am–4pm • Combined ticket with Historical Museum, Ethnographic Museum and Revelin Fortress 70Kn • T 020 323 904, W dumus.hr

The **Maritime Museum** (Pomorski muzej), which takes up the upstairs floor of St John's Fortress, is a rather better guide to Dubrovnik's history than the Cultural and Historical Museum (see p.397), tracing the history of Ragusan sea power in chronological and easy-to-follow fashion. It's still a bit old-fashioned, however, relying on display panels and texts rather than revealing exhibits, although there's an excellent collection of models of Dubrovnik boats through the ages.

8

Natural History Museum

Androvićeva 1 • Mon–Fri 10am–6pm, Sat 10am–2pm • Free • T 020 324 888, W pmd.hr

Occupying a former palace on Androvićeva is the **Natural History Museum** (Prirodoslovni muzej), which includes stuffed birds and preserved sea creatures. There are some lovely photographs of Adriatic marine life, accompanied by ethereal chill-out music.

Jesuit church

Boškovićeva poljana

At the western edge of Pustijerna, a grand Baroque staircase roughly based on Rome's Spanish Steps sweeps up to the **Jesuit church** (Isusovačka crkva), Dubrovnik's largest place of worship, modelled on the Church of the Gesù in Rome. It certainly boasts Dubrovnik's most frivolous ecclesiastical interior, with pinks and blues swirling across the ceiling, and a bombastic main altar with scenes from the life of St Ignatius, founder of the Jesuit order – the central panel shows the man renouncing all worldly things, here symbolized by a bevy of comely Baroque ladies.

Gundulićeva poljana

Site of the city's animated fruit and vegetable market, **Gundulićeva poljana** is watched over by a **statue of Ivan Gundulić** (1589–1638), the poet whose cherubic face adorns one side of the 50Kn banknote. Gundulić's epic poem *Osman*, which celebrates the victories of the Poles over the Turks, revealed a typical Ragusan paradox: despite growing rich through trade with the Ottoman state, the locals always sympathized with the empire's enemies, especially if they were Slavs. Gundulić's poetry found a nationwide audience in the nineteenth century, when a burgeoning sense of cultural patriotism generated new pride in the literary traditions of the past. The unveiling of Ivan Rendić's statue in 1893 occasioned one of the biggest demonstrations of solidarity the nation had ever seen, with the cream of Croatian society converging on the city to indulge in what amounted to a week-long street party.

Od Puča and around

Running parallel to Stradun, **Od Puča** leads west from Gundulićeva poljana, with stepped alleys branching off to meet the sea walls. Lined with boutiques, bakeries and souvenir shops, it's one of the Old Town's busiest thoroughfares.

Orthodox church and museum

Museum Od Puča 8 • May–Oct daily 9am–2pm; Nov–April Mon–Fri 10am–3pm • 30Kn

The **Orthodox Church Museum** (Muzej pravoslavne crkve) contains a display of icons packed with Virgins, Christ Pantokrators and St Georges, mostly anonymous works hailing from Crete, Greece and the Bay of Kotor in Montenegro.

A couple of paces beyond is the **Orthodox Church** itself, whose simple icon screen and functional interior are not of great artistic merit, but nevertheless exude an air of peaceful harmony.

The Marin Držić House

Široka 7 • Tues–Sun: June–Sept 10am–8pm; Oct–May 10am–4pm • 20Kn • T 020 323 242, W muzej-marindrzic.eu

Sixteenth-century playwright Marin Držić (see below) is very much the father of Croatian drama, although you wouldn't necessarily know that judging from the contents of the rather disappointing **Marin Držić House** (Dom Marina Držića). Exhibits

MARIN DRŽIĆ (1508–67)

In many ways **Marin Držić** is to Croatia what William Shakespeare is to the English-speaking world: a seminal figure who transformed the knockabout theatrical entertainments of the day into something approaching modern drama, employing an unprecedented richness of vocabulary and metaphor that helped turn the dialect of sixteenth-century Dubrovnik into a literary medium equal to the other tongues of Renaissance Europe.

Born into a family of merchants, Držić was never a member of the aristocratic elite that ran the republic, though the city did award him a scholarship to study at the University of Siena, where his involvement with the theatre began – he was thrown out in 1542 after taking part in a banned theatrical performance. Držić returned to Dubrovnik, and in 1545 entered the service of Graf Rogendorf, an Austrian then working as a diplomat for the Ottoman Empire.

It's not known precisely how and when Držić got involved with the drama troupes active in Dubrovnik. As in other Renaissance cities, satirical, farcical and moralizing performances were put on to entertain the populace at carnival time, or were given at the private parties and wedding feasts of the wealthy. It was in this environment that Držić's bawdy, but subtly plotted, comedies appeared. His first play, the now-lost *Pomet*, was performed in Dubrovnik in 1548. *Dundo Maroje* (1551), a ribald farce set among the expatriate Dubrovnik community in Rome, is the most frequently performed work today. His only tragedy, a reworking of Euripides' *Hecuba*, was interpreted as an anti-aristocratic allegory by the city authorities.

Držić left Dubrovnik for Venice in 1562, where he became an outspoken critic of the Ragusan Republic – his final literary oeuvre took the form of five letters to Cosimo de Medici asking for Florentine help in overthrowing the Dubrovnik aristocracy. The letters went unanswered, and Držić died an embittered and lonely figure. Držić's works were dusted off during Croatia's nineteenth-century cultural revival, and today play a key role in Dubrovnik's annual summer festival.

FROM TOP LEFT DUBROVNIK ALLEYWAY; PROTO (P.411); OLD PORT (P.393) >

and costumed dummies allude to characters and themes from Držić's plays, although English-language labelling is too ill-conceived and confusing to offer much in the way of illumination. If you already know something about Držić you may well make head or tail of it, otherwise give it a miss.

The Rupe Ethnographic Museum

Od Rupa 3 • Daily except Tues: April–Oct 9am–6pm; Nov–March 9am–4pm • Combined ticket with Historical Museum, Maritime Museum and Revelin Fortress 70Kn • Ⓣ 020 323 056, Ⓦ dumus.hr

The dull display of regional crafts at the **Rupe Ethnographic Museum** (Etnografski muzej Rupe) isn't half as interesting as the building itself, a former municipal grain store built in 1548 and featuring fifteen huge storage pits – the *rupe* or "holes" after which the building is named – carved out of bare rock. The Dubrovnik Republic was almost wholly reliant on imported grain, and the city imposed food-carrying responsibilities on shipowners as much as twelve months in advance. On arrival, wheat was dried in the upper storeys of the building before being sent down chutes into the storage pits below.

The Dominican monastery

Sv. Dominika 4

8

Begun in 1301, the construction of Dubrovnik's **Dominican monastery** (Dominikanski samostan) was very much a communal endeavour: owing to its position hard up against the fortifications, the city authorities provided the Dominicans with extra funds, and ordered the citizenry to contribute labour. The monastery is approached by a grand stairway with a stone balustrade whose columns have been partly mortared in, an ugly modification carried out by the monks themselves in response to the loafers who stood at the bottom of the staircase in order to ogle the bare ankles of women on their way to church. At the top of the steps a doorway leads through to a fifteenth-century Gothic Renaissance cloister, filled with palms and orange trees.

Monastery Museum

Daily: May–Oct 9am–6pm; Nov–April 9am–5pm • 20Kn • Ⓣ 020 321 423

Accessed via the monastery cloister, the Dominican monastery (Muzej dominikanskog samostana) has some outstanding examples of sixteenth-century religious art from Dubrovnik, including three canvases by **Nikola Božidarević**, the leading figure of the period, who managed to combine Byzantine solemnity with the humanism of the Italian Renaissance. Immediately on the right as you enter, Božidarević's triptych with its central Madonna and Child is famous for its depiction of Dubrovnik prior to the earthquake of 1667, when both Franciscan and Dominican monasteries sported soaring Gothic spires. Nearby, Božidarević's *Annunciation* of 1513, commissioned by shipowner Marko Kolendić, contains more local detail in one of its lower panels, showing one of the donor's argosies lying off the port of Lopud. The most Italianate of Božidarević's works is the Virgin and Child altarpiece, also of 1513, ordered by the Đorđić family (the bearded donor kneels at the feet of St Martin in the lower right-hand corner) – note the concerted attempt at some serious landscape painting in the background.

Much more statically Byzantine in style is Lovro Dobričević Marinov's 1448 polyptych of Christ's baptism in the River Jordan, flanked from left to right by sts Michael, Nicholas, Blaise and Stephen – the last was put to death by stoning, hence the stylized rock shapes which the artist has rather awkwardly placed on his head and shoulders. Cabinets full of precious silver follow, including the cross of the Serbian king, Stefan Uroš II Milutin (1282–1321), inscribed with archaic Cyrillic lettering, and a reliquary which claims to contain the skull of King Stephen I of Hungary (975–1038). The Baroque paintings in the next-door room are all fairly second-rate, save for Titian's *St Blaise and St Mary Magdalene* – Blaise holds the inevitable model of Dubrovnik while sinister storm clouds gather in the background.

Monastery church

The Dominican **monastery church** (Dominikanska crkva) is very much an art gallery in its own right. Among the highlights are a dramatic Veneto-Byzantine crucifix, attributed to the fourteenth-century Paolo Veneziano, which hangs over the main altar, and a fine pastel St Dominic by the nineteenth-century Cavtat artist Vlaho Bukovac.

The Revelin Fortress

Archeological Exhibition: daily 10am–6pm • Combined ticket with History Museum, Maritime Museum and Ethnographic Museum 70Kn

The **Revelin Fortress**, which lies east of the Dominican monastery, was begun in the mid-1400s but not finished until 1539, when fears of a coming war between the Turks and the Western powers impelled the Ragusans to hastily strengthen their defences. All other building work in the city was cancelled for four months, leaving the city's builders free to concentrate on the fortress; leading families had to send their servants to work as labourers, or pay a fine. The atmospheric, barrel-vaulted armouries inside the fortress now play host to a small **Archeological Exhibition**, displaying delicately carved stoneware from Dubrovnik's medieval churches.

Ploče Gate

Immediately beyond the Revelin Fortress lies the **Ploče Gate**, the main eastern entrance to the Old Town. It's larger than the Pile Gate, with another statue of St Blaise in the niche above (the oldest in the city) and a bridge across the moat, which dates from 1449.

Ploče

On the eastern side of Ploče gate is the modern suburb of **Ploče**, until the beginning of the twentieth century the scene of a large market where cattle and other goods arrived by caravan from the Balkan interior. Fear that such caravans brought disease prompted the construction in 1590 of a series of quarantine houses, or **Lazareti**, a row of brick-built accommodation blocks and courtyards which can still be seen on the right-hand side of the road. During times of pestilence, visitors entering the Dubrovnik Republic from the Ottoman Empire were obliged to stay here for forty days before proceeding any further. Ottoman traveller Evliya Çelebi, quarantined here in 1664, likened it to a comfortable and homely inn, although he regretted not being allowed out to enjoy Dubrovnik's nightlife. Sanitary concerns were still uppermost in Ragusan minds in the mid-nineteenth century, when British consul A.A. Paton reported with satisfaction that the market here was penned in by a chest-high stone partition in order to "permit commerce and conversation without contact".

Dubrovnik Art Gallery

Frana Supila 23 • Tues–Sun 10am–6pm • 30Kn (combined ticket with Dulčić-Masle-Pulitika Gallery) • ⓣ 020 426 590, ⓦ ugdubrovnik.hr

The main sight east of the Old Town is the **Dubrovnik Art Gallery** (Umjetnička galerija), whose permanent collection contains a good cross-section of works by the

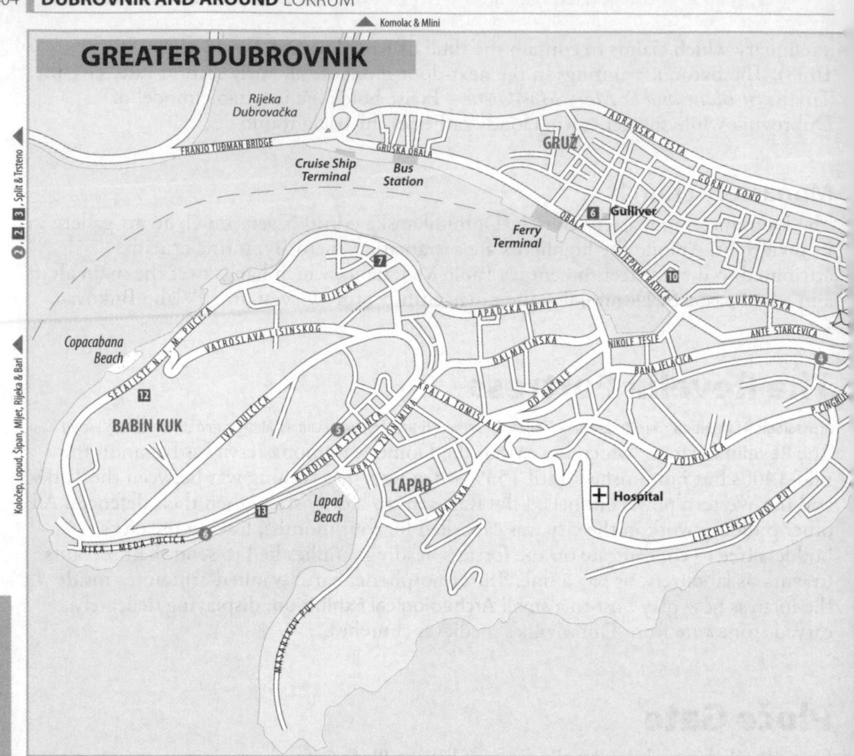

Cavtat-born painter Vlaho Bukovac (see p.417). It also hosts high-profile contemporary exhibitions – major international art shows occasionally take place here over the summer.

Lokrum

Boats leave for Lokrum from the Old Town's port and take 10min (every 30min: May–Oct 9am–6pm; 45Kn return)

Facing the suburb of Ploče is the wooded island of **Lokrum**, 1km to the southeast. Reputedly the island where Richard the Lionheart was shipwrecked, it was bought in 1859 by Maximilian von Habsburg, Archduke of Austria (and subsequently ill-fated Emperor of Mexico). He transformed a former Benedictine monastery here into his summer palace, laid out gardens and wrote bad verse about the island's beauty. Following Maximilian's execution by Mexican insurgents in 1867, the Habsburgs sold the island to a local businessman eager to turn it into a health resort, only to buy it back on behalf of Emperor Franz Josef's son Rudolf, who wintered here to soothe his bronchial difficulties.

Maximilian's largely overgrown and untended gardens stretch to the east. More interesting is the **botanical garden** of the Dubrovnik Oceanographic Institute immediately north of the monastery, filled with a spectacular array of triffid-like cacti that look as if they could swallow you whole. The best of Lokrum's rocky **beaches** are beyond the monastery on the island's southeast side, where you'll find a small salt lake named the **Dead Sea** (Mrtvo more) just inland, and a naturist beach at the island's southern tip. Shady paths overhung by pines run round the northern part of the island,

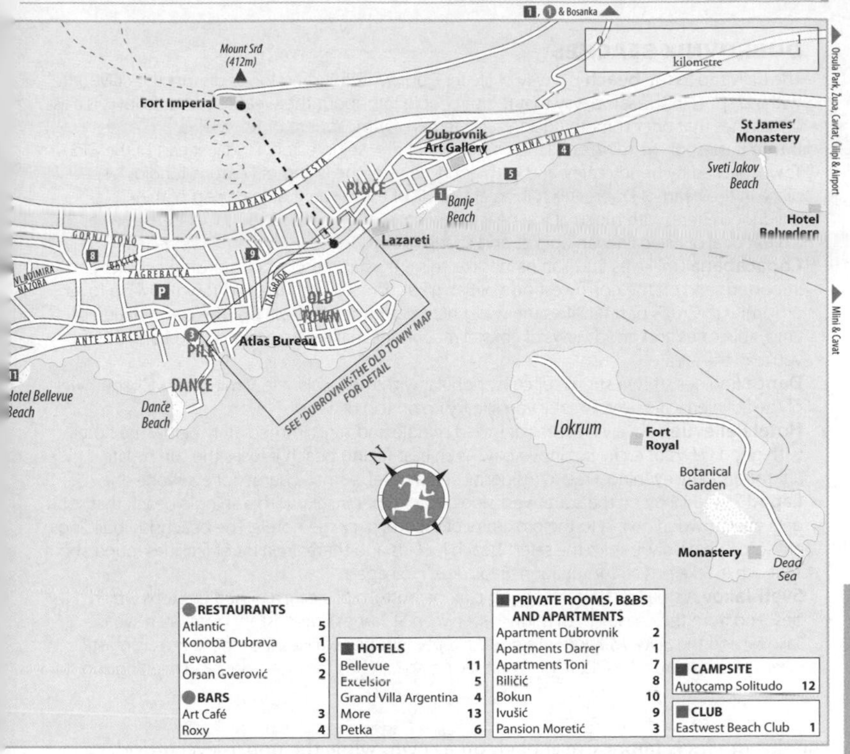

8

with tracks leading uphill towards **Fort Royal**, a gun position left by the Napoleonic French whose grey, menacing ramparts rise rather suddenly from the jungle-like greenery covering the island's central ridge.

Just up from the island's jetty, the former monastery complex contains a fascinating but largely barren network of walled gardens, one of which contains a routinely average café-restaurant.

Lovrijenac

Daily 8am–7pm • 20Kn

West of the Old Town, just outside Pile Gate, steps descend towards a small harbour overlooked by the Bokar Fortress on one side and by the monumental, wedge-shaped fortress of **Lovrijenac** on the other. Originally built in 1050, but assuming its current shape in the sixteenth century, it was the most important component of the city's south- and west-facing defences, commanding both land and sea approaches from atop a craggy cliff. In recent times Lovrijenac has become famous as the venue for performances during the Dubrovnik Summer Festival – particularly Shakespeare's *Hamlet*, when it becomes the perfect double for Elsinore castle (though it's not performed every year).

A statue of St Lawrence brandishing a model of the fort watches over the steps to the entrance, above which there's a typically proud Ragusan inscription: *Non bene pro toto libertas venditur auro* ("All the gold in the world cannot buy freedom"). There's no museum display inside the fortress but it actually works better that way, leaving you alone with the bare stones and your imagination. The triangular courtyard framed by

DUBROVNIK BEACHES

The daily trip to the **beach** is a way of life for Dubrovnik folk, and locals discuss their favourite bathing spots in the same way that British people talk about the weather. What follows is a list of beaches that offer something special in terms of atmosphere or fine views.

Banje Busiest of the town's beaches, a mixture of fine shingle and sand just east of the Old Town, backed by trendy cafés, and with good views of the island of Lokrum. It holds a special place in the heart of Dubrovnik folk, as almost all of them spent at least part of their childhoods here. With much of the beach now covered in sun-loungers for hire, Banje has lost a great deal of its egalitarian bucket-and-spade charm.

Copacabana Unlike its Brazilian namesake, this is a small crescent comprising pebbles and imported sand on the northwest side of Babin kuk (bus #6 from the Old Town). Owing to its proximity to Gruž's port facilities the water here is not the cleanest, but the combination of enjoyable cafés and good views of coastal mountains make it a good place to hang out if you're in the area.

Danče Boulder-strewn stretch of coast popular with the locals, a few minutes' walk southwest of the Lovrijenac fortress. Great if you like frying on top of a rock.

Hotel Bellevue A lovely crescent of mixed shingle and sand immediately below the hotel, with good views of rocky Boninovo bay. As an east-facing beach it loses the sun by late afternoon/early evening. Free to residents of the hotel, a small charge for everyone else.

Lapad Shallow bay on the southwest side of Lapad peninsula, with a shingle beach that soon gets overcrowded owing to the proximity of Lapad's package hotels. The beachside buildings are somewhat ugly, but it's the safest beach for kids and there are a lot of facilities round about. To reach it, take bus #6 (destination "Babin kuk") to Lapad.

8

Sveti Jakov A smallish stretch of pebble at the bottom of a cliff, reached by steps which descend from the coastal path midway between St James's Monastery (Samostan svetog Jakova) and the *Belvedere* hotel – a good twenty minutes' walk east of the centre. Fantastic views back towards the Old Town. West-facing, so catches the afternoon and evening sun.

chunky arcades is impressive enough on its own, while the upper level provides a fantastic view of the city and its walls.

Mount Srđ

Towering above Dubrovnik to the north, the 412-metre summit of **Mount Srđ** offers stunning views of the walled town below, with a panorama of the whole coast stretching as far as the Pelješac peninsula to the northwest. Quickest way to get here is by **cable car** (see below), which was destroyed by attackers in 1991 and reopened to much fanfare some twenty years later. It's a breathtaking, super-smooth ride, the only drawback being that the journey lasts a mere two minutes. At the top, the *Panorama* café-restaurant (same times as the cable car) has a viewing terrace and is only slightly more expensive than similarly touristy restaurants back in town.

The mountain seems a world away from the lush subtropical world of the coastal strip, with bare stone and scrub stretching as far as the eye can see. In spring and early summer, the scrub is covered in daisies and bright-pommelled thistles. Otherwise nothing much grows here apart from sage, which is hungrily devoured by the local sheep and goats.

The highland plateau immediately north of the summit has been earmarked as the future sight of Dubrovnik's golf course – although this anti-ecological exercise has not met with unanimous local support.

ARRIVAL AND DEPARTURE — MOUNT SRĐ

By cable car The cable car runs every day, and takes 2min (Feb, March & Nov 9am–5pm; April, May, Sept & Oct 9am–8pm; June–Aug 9am–midnight; Dec & Jan 9am–4pm; one way 50Kn, return 87Kn).

By car Srđ is accessible by car via the village of Bosanka.

By foot You can walk up Srđ on the winding footpath known as the Serpentina (90min up; 35min down). Note that the Serpentina is stony and largely unshaded – strong footwear and water are essential.

Fort Imperial

Museum daily 9am–6pm • Free

Built by Napoleon's occupying army in 1808, the summit-crowning **Fort Imperial** served as a disco in the 1980s before reverting to its original military purpose during the 1991–95 war, when it was heroically held by Dubrovnik's defenders. The fort now houses the **Museum of the Homeland War** (Muzej domovinskog rata), featuring guns, shell cartridges and a rousing collection of photos – with English-language texts providing a blow-by-blow account of Croatian resistance. The fact that the fort has otherwise been left in its raw, undecorated state only adds to the museum's powerful effect.

Walks on Srđ

There aren't any signed trails on Srđ but that shouldn't prevent you from striking out along the roads that lead east and west from the summit, crossing the kind of starkly beautiful Mediterranean scrub that Croatians call the kamejnar or "stone field". Heading **west** past the TV and radio mast then north along a gravel trail brings you to an abandoned outlying fort on a rocky outcrop (25min). Along the way you will pass memorials to the fallen from the 1991–95 war: it was Croatian resistance on Srđ that prevented the encirclement of the city and arguably saved it from enemy occupation.

Following the road **east** from the summit provides good views of both the coast and the mountains of nearby Hercegovina, descending after twenty minutes to the village of Bosanka, a mixture of traditional village and bijou rural suburb where stone houses rub shoulders with modern villas and fig, olive and fruit trees.

8

Orsula Park

To enter the park, ask at the kiosk; entrance is free if you buy a drink • ⓦ parkorsula.com • No public transport

One of the most memorable things about approaching or leaving Dubrovnik southeast via the Cavtat road is the view of the city enjoyed from a curve in the road some 3km above the town. There's a car park, a drinks kiosk and – just below – the sloping pathways and shrubs of **Orsula Park**, laid out by volunteers of the environmental and cultural association Ambient Croatia. Focus of the park is the ruined fourteenth-century chapel of St Ursula, occupying a shoulder of the hillside with commanding views towards the Old Town and Lokrum island. The rough overgrown track that passes the chapel marks the former course of the main Dubrovnik–Istanbul trade route, and it is here that long-distance wayfarers would have offered prayers on catching sight of (or leaving) the city. Above the chapel is an amphitheatre-style bank of seating pressed into use each year during the Mali Glazbeni Festival (Little Music Festival; see box, p.414), a season of concerts that runs throughout the summer.

ARRIVAL AND DEPARTURE — DUBROVNIK

By plane Dubrovnik airport (ⓦ airport-dubrovnik.hr) is situated some 22km southeast of the city, close to the village of Čilipi. Atlas buses travel into town roughly ten times a day (they're timed to coincide with Croatia Airlines flights but other passengers can use them too), dropping off at the main western entrance to the Old Town, Pile Gate, before terminating at the bus station (25min; 35Kn single). Note that buses to the airport commence at the bus station and pick up passengers at the cable-car station on Zagrebačka; they do not call at Pile Gate. A taxi from the airport will set you back between 220 and 260Kn.

Destinations Split (2 weekly; 35min); Zagreb (2–3 daily; 50min).

By bus The bus station (autobusni kolodvor; ⓣ 060 305

070, ⓦ libertasdubrovnik.com) is located 5km west of the Old Town, 1km beyond the ferry terminal – buses #1A and #1B run from there to Pile Gate, both passing the ferry terminal on the way. Flat-fare tickets for local buses can be bought either from the driver (15Kn; exact change only) or from newspaper kiosks (12Kn). For buses from Dubrovnik to Montenegro, payment must be made in euros.

Destinations Cavtat (every 30–45min; 40min); Čilipi (Mon–Sat 3 daily, Sun 2 daily; 45min); Korčula (2 daily; 4hr); Makarska (hourly; 3hr); Molunat (Mon–Sat 3 daily, Sun 2 daily; 1hr 10min); Orebić (Mon–Sat 4 daily, Sun 3 daily; 3hr); Plitvice (2 daily; 10hr); Ploče (hourly; 2hr); Pula (1 daily; 16hr); Rijeka (4 daily; 13hr); Šibenik (8 daily; 6hr 30min); Split (hourly; 5hr); Ston (Mon–Sat 6 daily, Sun 4 daily; 1hr 30min); Trsteno (hourly; 40min); Vela Luka (2 daily; 5hr); Zadar (7 daily; 9hr); Zagreb (8 daily; 12hr).

International destinations Herceg Novi (3–4 daily; 2hr); Kotor (1–2 daily; 3hr); Međugorje (1 daily; 4hr); Mostar (4 daily; 3hr 30min); Sarajevo (4 daily; 8hr).

By ferry The ferry terminal is 4km west of the Old Town in Gruž harbour. Buses #1A and #1B run to Pile Gate. Services are run by Jadrolinija (ticket office opposite the ferry quay; ⓣ 020 418 000, ⓦ jadrolinija.hr), except for the catamaran to Polače which is operated by G&V Line (ticket booth right on the ferry quay; ⓣ 020 313 400, ⓦ gv-line.hr), which continues to Korčula and Lastovo on certain days of the week in July and August.

Destinations Koločep (1–4 daily; 30min); Korčula (2–5 weekly; 3hr); Lopud (1–4 daily; 50min); Polače (1 daily; 1hr 40min); Rijeka (June–Sept 2 weekly; 22hr); Šipanska Luka (1–2 daily; 1hr 45min); Sobra (1–2 daily; 2hr 15min); Split (June–Sept 2 weekly; 10hr); Suđurađ (1–4 daily; 1hr); Stari Grad (June–Sept 2 weekly; 7hr).

By car Street-side parking is virtually impossible in central Dubrovnik; your best bet is the parking garage at Ilijina glavica (15Kn/hr or 180Kn/24hr), just west of the Old Town off Zagrebačka cesta. There is a bus service from the garage to Pile Gate, but with Pile only a 10min walk downhill (20min on the way back) you may not need to use it. Car rental is available from Budget, Obala S. Radića 24, Gruž (ⓣ 020 418 998, ⓦ budget.hr), and Gulliver, Obala S. Radića 28, Gruž (ⓣ 020 410 823, ⓦ gulliver.hr).

8

GETTING AROUND

Buses The municipal bus network is run by Libertas (their site ⓦ libertasdubrovnik.hr has full timetables) and is a quick and reliable way of getting from the Old Town to hotel-and-beach areas of the city such as Lapad and Babin kuk. The network operates until about 11.30pm in winter, 2am in summer. Flat-rate single-journey tickets cost 10Kn from a newspaper kiosk or 12Kn from the driver (exact change required).

Taxis There are ranks outside the bus and ferry terminals and at Pile Gate, or call ⓣ 0800 1441.

INFORMATION AND ACTIVITIES

Tourist office Just outside Pile Gate (daily: July & Aug 8am–10pm; May, June & Sept 9am–9pm; Oct–April 9am–5pm; ⓣ 020 321 561, ⓦ tzdubrovnik.hr).

Tours Atlas, Svetog Đurđa 1 (near the Pile Gate) handle excursions as well as air tickets (Mon–Sat 8am–8pm, Sun 9am–1pm; ⓣ 020 442 584, ⓦ atlas-croatia.com).

Diving Blue Planet, at the *Dubrovnik Palace* hotel in Lapad (ⓣ 091 899 0973, ⓦ blueplanet-diving.com), organizes PADI-approved courses (including a half-day beginners' course from 350Kn), and excursions to nearby reefs and wrecks.

Sea kayaking (see box, p.394).

ACCOMMODATION

Dubrovnik is the most expensive destination in Croatia and this is reflected in everything from the price of a hostel bed to a five-star hotel. Many of the more upmarket **hotels** occupy fantastic locations and are well worth the splurge. Otherwise, private **rooms, apartments and B&Bs** represent a better value than hotels, especially if you want to be in or near the Old Town. In addition to a handful of **hostels**, there is one **campsite** in Dubrovnik itself, and several more are located a short bus ride away in Trsteno, Kupari and Srebreno (p.416). Whatever kind of accommodation you are seeking, always reserve in advance, and be aware that long-stay guests are favoured in July and August. The high-season **prices** quoted below can fall by about twenty percent in spring and autumn, thirty percent or more in winter.

DUBROVNIK CARD

For those with serious intentions to "do" Dubrovnik, the **Dubrovnik Card** (available from the tourist office) is a sound investment. Costing 110Kn for one day, 180Kn for three days or 220Kn for one week, the card allows free rides on municipal buses, free entrance to the city walls, the Rector's Palace and Cultural and Historical Museum, the Natural History Museum, the Art Gallery, the Dulčić-Masle-Pulitika Gallery, the Marin Držić House, the Maritime Museum and the Rupe Ethnographic Museum (but not the church or monastery collections).

HOTELS

THE OLD TOWN AND AROUND

Hilton Imperial Marijana Blažića 2 ⓣ 020 320 320, ⓦ hilton.co.uk/dubrovnik; map p.392. Originally opened in 1897 and long considered the top address in town, with a guest list that includes George Bernard Shaw and H.G. Wells, the *Imperial* suffered serious shell damage in 1991 and stood empty for a decade before being laboriously restored by the Hilton chain. Plush rooms, faultless service and the glass-roofed indoor pool are the main attributes, and it's ideally situated next to Pile Gate. **2000Kn**

Pucić Palace Od Puča 1 ⓣ 020 324 111, ⓦ thepucicpalace.com; map p.392. Five-star boutique hotel in a recently renovated eighteenth-century palace, offering plush, fully equipped – but slightly cramped – doubles. Decor is on the chintzy side, but most rooms come with views of Old Town street life. **2500Kn**

Stari Grad Od Sigurate 4 ⓣ 020 322 244, ⓦ hotelstarigrad.com; map p.392. Charming Old Town hotel offering small but atmospheric rooms, all with shower and TV. The view from the roof terrace (where breakfast is served in summer) is a major plus. Only eight rooms, so reserve well in advance. **1500Kn**

OUTSIDE THE OLD TOWN

Bellevue Pera Čingrije 7 ⓣ 020 330 000, ⓦ alh.hr; map pp.404–405. Dramatically situated on a clifftop overlooking Miramare Bay, a 15min walk from Pile Gate, and with a wonderful shingle beach immediately below. Rooms feature crisp linens, luxury fittings and warm colours. **2250Kn**

Excelsior Frana Supila 12 ⓣ 020 353 353, ⓦ alh.hr; map pp.404–405. Just east of the Old Town, and recently modernized, this five-star place offers plush en-suite rooms, indoor pool and fitness centre. The terraces of the hotel's bar and restaurants have excellent views back towards the town, as do some of the room balconies. Try and avoid the viewless, north-facing rooms. **2200Kn**

Grand Villa Argentina Frana Supila 14 ⓣ 020 440 555, ⓦ alh.hr; map pp.404–405. Long-established five-star a 10min walk east of the Old Town, comprising a central building dating from the 1920s, a modern annexe and two *belle-époque* villas: the *Orsula* and the *Sheherezade*. All creature comforts, including a concrete beach and small swimming pool. **2140Kn**

More Kardinala Stepinca 33 ⓣ 020 494 200, ⓦ hotel-more.hr; map pp.404–405. Well-appointed but small enough to be cosy and intimate, *More* ("Sea") occupies an attractive cliff-hugging position just west of Lapad beach. Rooms are spacious, and breakfast is served on a lovely sea-facing terrace. Both the private beach and the outdoor pool are tiny in the extreme, but these are small quibbles. Gym and spa facilities on site. **2175Kn**

Petka Obala Stjepana Radića 38, Gruž ⓣ 020 410 500, ⓦ hotelpetka.hr; map pp.404–405. Medium-rise concrete affair opposite the ferry terminal. The en-suite rooms are plain but contain small desks and TV; those at the front offer marvellous views of the port. Wi-fi throughout. A 1km walk east of the bus station; otherwise catch bus #1A or #1B from Pile. **650Kn**

HOSTELS

★ **Fresh Sheets** Smokvina 15 ⓣ 020 322 040, mobile ⓣ 091 799 2086, ⓦ igotfresh.com; map p.392. Genuine backpacker hostel occupying a three-storey stone house in one of the most atmospheric parts of the Old Town. Containing dorms, a quad and a double, the building is decorated in relaxing colours and features a cute reception-cum-lounge-cum-kitchen area. There's a well-stocked fridge from which you can make your own breakfast as well as laundry service for an extra fee. Wi-fi throughout. **190Kn** per person, doubles **380Kn**

Hostel Marker Od Tabakarije 19 ⓣ 091 739 7545, ⓦ hostelmarkerdubrovnik.hostel.com; map p.392. A collection of private rooms and apartments sailing under the "hostel" banner, located in three neighbouring houses in the narrow streets beneath Lovrijenac fortress. Well organized and friendly, but lacks common-room areas in which to socialize. Rooms **220Kn** per person, four-person apartments **1500Kn**

8

PRIVATE ROOMS, B&BS AND APARTMENTS

Internet booking has made huge inroads into the Dubrovnik private accommodation scene. The vast majority of private rooms and apartments in Dubrovnik have registered themselves as "hotels" on websites such as ⓦ booking.com and "hostels" on sites such as ⓦ hostelworld.com – and as a consequence there are far fewer walk-in accommodation agencies in the city than you might expect. Travellers arriving at the bus station may well be besieged by landladies offering unlicensed rooms, but these are often inconveniently located and various "extra costs" may be added to any price you think you've agreed.

THE OLD TOWN AND AROUND

Božo Kortizija Od Tabakarije 27 ⓣ 020 426 085 and ⓣ 095 875 6243, ⓦ privateaccommodationkortizija.com; map p.392. Three double rooms and a three- to four-person apartment in a traditional stone house just outside the Pile Gate. The smart rooms are en suite and have a small desk with TV. Doubles from **420Kn**, apartment **750kn**

★ **Dubrovnik Apartment Source** ⓣ 00353 86 024 1834, ⓦ dubrovnikapartmentsource.com. Offers a selection of accommodation from well-maintained doubles up to deluxe family-sized apartments, conscientiously managed by an American couple. They also have a handful of apartments on Koločep, Korčula and Hvar. Studios from 800Kn

★ **Karmen** Bandureva 1 ⊕020 323 433 or ⊕098 619 282, ⊕karmendu.com; map p.392. Four cosy apartments, each with kitchenette, in a traditional stone building in the Pustijerna quarter of the Old Town. Rooms have a homely mix of furnishings and crockery and the whole place is full of books and prints – the main stairway is decked out with the kind of sepia photographs and historic maps that many a history museum would be proud of. Welcoming and unique. Two-person apartments from 600Kn

OUTSIDE THE OLD TOWN

Apartments Toni Ivana Zajca 5, Lapad ⊕091 529 4741 and ⊕098 850 578, ⊕apartmanitoni.com; map pp.404–405. Modern house on the northern side of the Lapad peninsula with a handful of cute two-person studio apartments, each with kitchenette and washing machine, and a beautiful split-level family apartment which can be rented as a whole or as individual double rooms with access to the shared kitchen-diner – which comes with fantastic views of Gruž harbour. Breakfast can be arranged, as can airport transfer. Bus #6 (destination Dubrava) from either Pile or Lapad to the INA petrol station on Lapadska obala. Doubles with breakfast 560Kn

8

Biličić Privezna 2 ⊕020 417 152 or ⊕098 802 111, ⊕dubrovnik-online.com/apartments_bilicic; map pp.404–405. Family-run guesthouse an easy walk uphill from the centre in the Gornji Kono district, offering doubles with a/c, TV and en-suite bathrooms, as well as a pleasant walled garden. It's extremely popular, and gets booked up weeks or months in advance in summer. They'll pick you up from the airport if the family schedule allows. There's no breakfast but you can use the alfresco kitchen in the porch. Doubles 450Kn, four-person apartment 900Kn

Bokun Obala Stjepana Radića 7 ⊕020 357 290 or ⊕098 969 7329, ⊕bokun-guesthouse.com; map pp.404–405. Friendly family pension located in the bustling Gruž harbour area but wonderfully secluded behind a walled garden shaded by figs, grapes and kiwi fruit. On offer are a mixture of simply furnished rooms with a/c and TV, some with en-suite facilities, others sharing a WC/shower in the hallway. There are also three two-person apartments, each with a kitchenette. There's an optional continental breakfast (35Kn), and a laundry service (60Kn per load). No credit cards. Rooms from 350Kn, apartments from 500Kn

Ivušić Bernarda Shawa 1 ⊕020 432 654 and ⊕098 162 0850, ⊕apartmani-ivusic.hr; map pp.404–405. Family house in an excellent location on the hillside just above the Old Town, with a pair of simply decorated doubles with a/c and TV, and two- to four-person apartments with kitchenette. The main selling point is the excellent view down towards the town walls and the Minčeta tower. Breakfast is available on request, and an airport pick-up can be arranged. Three-day minimum stay preferred. Doubles from 450Kn

OUTSIDE THE CITY

Apartment Dubrovnik Veliki Zaton ⊕020 744 140 and ⊕098 285 697, ⊕boutiqueaccommodationmljet.com; map pp.404–405. Two-bedroom apartment on the north side of Zaton bay, 10km out of town on the main Split road. Relatively secluded and quiet in comparison to the Dubrovnik-bound options. 600Kn

★ **Apartments Darrer** Bosanka 62a, Bosanka ⊕020 414 818, ⊕villadarrer.hr; map pp.404–405. Modern house set in the lush village of Bosanka, a 20min walk from the summit of Mount Srđ. The neat, bright apartments – either two-person studios with kitchenette, or four-person family-sized suites – come with a/c, TV and new furnishings throughout. There's a large, herb-stocked garden and a small swimming pool out front. It's a restful out-of-town location with only the odd cockerel or sheep likely to disturb your sleep in the morning. To get there, catch bus #17 from Pile or drive along the Cavtat road before taking the battered side road that leads to Mount Srđ. Two-person studios from 450Kn, four-person apartments 900Kn

Pansion Moretić Na Pržini 10, Orašac ⊕020 891 507, ⊕i-reception.net/moretic; map pp.404–405. This B&B, with English-speaking owners, is located in a rustic village 12km west of town, just off the main road to Split. It has simple en-suite doubles, some with balconies looking out onto vineyards, olive trees and orange groves. A 15min walk from the sea, and handily placed for the botanical gardens at Trsteno (see p.415), the pension is well signed from the main road, and there's a bus stop (most inter-city buses will pick up and drop off here) nearby. 400Kn

CAMPSITE

Autocamp Solitudo Babin kuk ⊕020 448 249, ⊕camping-dubrovnik@valamar.com; map pp.404–405. Roomy, well-organized but frequently crowded site on the northern side of Babin kuk peninsula, with modern facilities and a reasonable amount of tree cover. Small shop and a (currently Mexican-style) restaurant on site. Bus #6 (destination Dubrava) from Pile or the bus station. 80Kn per person; pitches from 120Kn

EATING

There's no shortage of **places to eat** in Dubrovnik, and culinary standards are reasonably high. The choice of food doesn't significantly differ from what's on offer in the rest of maritime Croatia, with grilled fish, squid and shellfish forming the backbone of local menus. Certain places are worth avoiding: **Prijeko** (maliciously dubbed "Bandit Street" by some local foodies), the street parallel to Stradun, is lined with tourist-trap establishments aggressively selling their indifferent fare with dubious offers of free wine or family discounts. Luckily, there are plenty of other places in town that base their reputation on good cooking rather than the hard sell.

SNACKS AND FAST FOOD

Mrvica Kunićeva 2; map p.392. Hole-in-the-wall fast-food bar serving up sandwiches filled with traditional Croatian home-cured meats such as *pršut*, *kulen* and *buđola* (cured pork neck). Daily 8am–2am.

Škola Antuninska 1; map p.392. Marginally fancier than *Mrvica* (see above), *Škola* offers the same kind of *pršut*-sandwich fare but with the added attractions of salads and a few tables. Daily 8am–2am.

RESTAURANTS

THE OLD TOWN AND AROUND

360 degrees by Jeffrey Vella Sv. Dominika 2 ⓣ 020 322 222; map p.392. Honeycombed with cannon ports and powder cellars, the bastion of St Luke's Fortress makes a breathtaking setting for this upscale restaurant and cocktail bar. Presided over by former head chef at Zagreb's *Regent Esplanade* hotel (see p.83) the food is Adriatic-Modern European, with a well-chosen repertoire of meat, fowl and seafood recipes to choose from. Mains are in the 250–300Kn range, while the mind-boggling choice of wines ranges from 300Kn to 100,000Kn a bottle. Daily noon–2pm & 7pm–midnight.

★ **Bota Oyster and Sushi Bar** Od Pustijerne bb ⓣ 020 324 034, ⓦ bota-sare.hr; map p.392. This Adriatic-sushi fusion venture is a worthy extension of the *Bota* empire, whose well-regarded parent restaurant is in the Dalmatian oyster capital of Ston (see p.382). Traditional Japanese-style sushi sets are handled convincingly, and the *Bota* specials – Adriatic scampi in tempura, Ston oysters in tempura – are exquisite. The location is a sweet one too, a stone's throw from the Stradun but with a secluded terrace facing the narrow alleys of the Pustijerna quarter. Daily 10am–1am.

Kamenica Gundulićeva poljana 8 ⓣ 020 323 682; map p.392. Unpretentious and cheap seafood restaurant popular with locals and tourists alike, with a cramped, functional interior and outdoor seating on one of the Old Town's finest squares. Dishes start at around 45Kn, with favourites including *girice*, *kamenice* and *mušule*. Daily 9am–midnight.

Konoba Dalmatino Miha Pracata 6 ⓣ 098 327 404; map p.392. A soothing exposed-stone interior and outdoor seating in an atmospheric tunnel-like alleyway render this a relaxing place in which to enjoy Adriatic food with a touch of Mediterranean style. Grilled fish fillets followed by chocolate mousse is one recommended way to go, backed up with a well-chosen Korčulan wine. Mains 135kn. Daily noon–11pm.

Lady Pipi Peline bb ⓣ 020 321 288; map p.392. Right beneath the city walls, and a stiff climb up the stepped street of Antuninska, this is one of the best places in the Old Town for local food simply cooked, with an outdoor grill on a vine-covered terrace pouring forth expertly singed squid, sausages and steaks. Cash only, and no reservations – expect to queue on summer evenings. April–Oct daily 9am–3pm & 6–11pm.

Lokanda Peskarija Na Ponti bb ⓣ 020 324 750, ⓦ mea-culpa.hr; map p.392. Lively place with outdoor bench-seating right beside the Old Town's port area. Frequently crowded, but somehow succeeds in retaining good standards of food and service, all at moderate prices. Trademark seafood dishes like *kozice* (shrimps) and *crni rižot* are served in big metal pots. Also a fine choice for grilled fish and big, healthy salads. Mains 80–100Kn. Daily 8am–1am.

Mea Culpa za Rokom 3 ⓣ 020 323 430, ⓦ mea-culpa .hr; map p.392. Popular pizzeria in the maze of streets south of the Stradun, which manages to combine huge pies with moderate prices. Cosy warren of tables inside, plus a long row of bench seating outside. The menu limits itself to pizzas only; no salads or desserts. Daily 8am–midnight.

Nautika Brsalje 3 ⓣ 020 442 526, ⓦ nautikarestaurant .com; map p.392. Long considered one of the best places in town for quality seafood, this is an upmarket environment with two floors of formal dining rooms, each with a small outdoor terrace. Liveried waiters, napkins folded with origami-like precision and a large list of top international wines complete the picture. Mains weigh in at around 200–300Kn, although the light bites on the lunchtime menu come significantly cheaper. Daily noon–midnight.

Nishta cnr Prijeko/Palmotićeva ⓣ 020 322 088 or ⓣ 098 186 7440, ⓦ nishtarestaurant.com; map p.392. Probably the only place on tourist-trappy Prijeko where you would want to be seen eating, *Nishta* prides itself on a well-chosen selection of Chinese-, Indian- and Middle Eastern-influenced recipes, with vegetarian dishes predominating. Long-standing favourites include Indiastic (a curry-flavoured combination of rice and vegetables) and Orsotto (barley cooked risotto-style with seaweed), and the salad bar is something of a life-saver if you're after a light lunch. Opt for tables in the street or cushioned benches inside and don't forget to pay a visit to the deliciously kitsch WC. Mains hover in the 80–100Kn range. March–Dec Mon–Sat noon–11pm.

Proto Široka 1 ⓣ 020 323 234, ⓦ esculaprestaurants .com; map p.392. Top-notch establishment bang in the heart of old Dubrovnik, with a formal indoor dining room, a rather more relaxed outdoor terrace upstairs and attention-to-detail service. As usual, fish is the main attraction, although this is one spot in Dubrovnik where the meat dishes are prepared to the same level of excellence as the seafood – you can't really go wrong whatever you order. The site has been occupied by a fish restaurant since 1886, and it's claimed that Edward VIII and Wallis Simpson ate here during one of their visits to Dubrovnik in the 1930s (see box, p.230). Expect to exceed the 350Kn mark for main course, sweet and drinks. Daily 11am–11pm.

Sesame Dante Alighieria bb 020 412 910, sesame.hr; map p.392. The likeably eccentric uncle of the Dubrovnik dining scene, *Sesame* never quite breaks through to haute-cuisine territory but offers much more variety and imagination than the tourist-dinner mainstream. Main courses (120–150Kn) feature the likes of fillets of fish in red wine sauce or with almond-based gratin, alongside lamb chops and fine steaks, and the home-made ravioli with fishy fillings (80Kn) will make a decent lunch. There's a brick-vaulted café space at the front, a dining room decked out in oriental rugs and oil paintings at the back, and outdoor seating on an upstairs terrace. Daily 8am–11pm.

Taj Mahal Nikole Gučetića 2 020 323 221, tajmahaldubrovnik.com; map p.392. Bosnian-run restaurant churning out the things that Bosnian cuisine is famous for: grilled *ćevapi* (mincemeat rissoles), *pljeskavice* (succulent mincemeat patties that make Western burgers look like wimp-food) and some of the best *burek* (filo-pastry pie filled with meat) available outside Sarajevo. Vegetarians can dine on peppers stuffed with cream cheese, or the excellent spinach *pita* (pie). Daily 10am–midnight.

OUTSIDE THE OLD TOWN

Atlantic Kardinala Stepinca 42 020 435 726, konobatlantic.com; map pp.404–405. Located just uphill from Lapad beach on an uneventful street, this is one of the city's best addresses for pasta, with home-made ravioli and a superb range of spaghetti sauces dominating the menu. The six-table interior with adjoining conservatory makes it a cosy place to eat, and you can always admire the owner's prodigious collection of sailing trophies. Mains 80–90Kn. Daily noon–11pm.

Levanat Nika i Meda Pucića 15 020 435 352, dubrovnik-online.com/levanat; map pp.404–405. Family-run restaurant on the coastal path between Lapad and Babin kuk, with a chic interior and outdoor terrace with a marvellous view of jagged offshore outcrops. The extensive seafood menu features excellent shellfish, and the kind of boiled and baked fish recipes that you might not find elsewhere – the *brancin lešo* (sea bass stewed in caper sauce) is well worth trying. A café as well as a restaurant, it's also one of the most relaxing places in this part of Dubrovnik to stop off for a drink. A full meal will set you back 250–300Kn with drinks. Daily noon–11pm.

OUTSIDE THE CITY

Konoba Dubrava Bosanka bb, Bosanka 020 416 405, konobadubrava.com; map pp.404–405. Well signposted at the eastern end of the village of Bosanka, *Dubrava* has a big covered terrace overlooking grey mountains and green meadows. Specialities include lamb baked *ispod sača* (under an ember-covered lid). Spit-roasts on Fri. Daily 10am–midnight.

★ **Orsan Gverović** Zaton Mali bb, Zaton 020 891 267, gverovic-orsan.hr; map pp.404–405. Cult seafood restaurant 8km northwest of town, right beside the coastal Magistrala at the entrance to the village of Zaton. The owner adopts a no-nonsense approach: there's little on the menu save for fresh fish and shellfish, grilled to perfection. Among the starters, the Orsan risotto, full of succulent shellfish, squid and prawn, is quite possibly the best combined seafood dish you're likely to find on the Adriatic. The terrace is right on the seashore, so you can order your food and go for a quick dip before the starter arrives. With mains at around 120–150Kn, it's slightly less expensive than the top-of-the-range seafood places back in town. Daily noon–midnight.

DRINKING AND NIGHTLIFE

Drinking in Dubrovnik is for much of the year a question of finding an outside table from which to see and be seen. The pavement cafés of **Stradun** are the best places for daytime and early evening imbibing, providing classic people-watching and postcard-writing venues. Nearby **Bunićeva poljana**, just behind the cathedral, becomes one vast outdoor bar on summer nights, with rows of tables spread out between the *Hard Jazz Café Trubadour* on one side and *Café Mirage* on the other. You could also try the streets leading uphill from Stradun, where you'll find drinkers sitting on the steps outside tiny bars with blaring music.

CAFÉS

Dolce Vita Nalješkovićeva 1 020 321 666; map p.392. *Dolce Vita's* selection of cakes has been getting a bit boring of late, but it's still one of the best places in town for eat-in or take-out ice cream. It's the kind of place that the locals take their kids for a treat. Daily 8am–midnight.

GradsKavana Pred Dvorom 1 020 321 202; map p.392. This once staid café, catering to a loyal clientele of older-generation, coffee-supping locals is now one of the most inviting places in town to pause for a caffeine break. There's also a mouthwatering selection of quality cakes and ice cream– look out for typical Dubrovnik desserts such as *torta od makarula* (pasta and chocolate cake) and *kontonjata* (hard fruit jelly). Daily 8am–midnight.

★ **Sugar and Spice** Sv. Josipa 5 091 361 9550 and 020 324 039, sugarandspicedubrovnik.com; map p.392. Many of Dubrovnik's most irresistible temptations emanate from this devilishly innovative little cake shop, whose unique range of home-baked goodies includes much that is unusual for Croatia – carrot cake, banana bread and chocolate-and-chilli torte to name but three. Tucked into a narrow Old Town alley, it offers a handful of stools inside and the odd table in the street outside. They also make refreshing lemonade and sell home-made marmalades from local seasonal fruit. Daily: March–May & Oct–Dec 9am–5pm; June–Sept 9am–10pm.

BARS

THE OLD TOWN AND AROUND

Buža Ispod Mira ⓣ 098 361 934, ⓦ cafebuza.com; map p.392. One of the most atmospheric places to drink in Dubrovnik, this is an unpretentious outdoor bar perched on the rocks just outside the Old Town's sea-facing walls. It's approached through a hole in the wall – advertised by a sign that simply reads "cold drinks". Drinks are on the expensive side but the setting is like no other. They don't bother opening if the weather is cold or windy. Daily 10am–2am.

Buža II Ispod Bosanka Mira; map p.392. Another hole in the wall offering a similar deal to the original *Buža* (see above), with a rush-shaded shack doling out drinks and tables spread across the neighbouring rocks. Entered, Narnia-style, through an unmarked doorway in the city walls. Daily 10am–2am.

Capitano Između vrta 2 ⓣ 098 366 470; map p.392. A few steps north of Pile Gate, this rather nondescript place gets raucous after around midnight, when it's a popular stopoff for young locals doing the rounds of the Old Town bars. Enjoy the crush of bodies inside or sit on the stone wall outside. Daily 9pm–4am.

D'Vino Palmotićeva 4a ⓣ 020 321 130, ⓦ dvino.net; map p.392. There are a quite a few wine bars lurking in the Old Town's alleys but *D'Vino* is one of the oldest and best, and is usually staffed by the kind of folk who can offer a few well-informed pointers on the best local tipples. The alley invariably fills with enthusiastic imbibers on warm summer evenings. Daily noon–2am.

Exit Rock Café Boškovićeva 2; map p.392. A year-round favourite with locals, although it loses out in the summer months due to its first-floor location. The tone is set with album covers and rock-star photos on the walls, and more or less permanently hard-riffing background music. Daily 6pm–2am.

Galerie Kunićeva 5; map p.392. The one bar in the Old Town that is consistently patronized by the locals, and also gets its fair share of boozing backpackers in summer. *Galerie's* two-room interior quickly gets crowded, after which the hubbub spills out onto the street. Daily 7am–2am.

Hard Jazz Café Trubadour Bunićeva poljana ⓣ 020 323 476; map p.392. Small and intimate pub-like space which explodes out onto the surrounding square as soon as the weather's warm enough for outdoor drinking. If you're a well-known face in Croatia, you have to be seen drinking here at least once in the summer. Legendary founder Marko Breśković (bassist with the big-time 1960s beat group Dubrovački Trubaduri) passed away in 2010, but his family have done their best to keep the *Trubadour* torch aflame, especially its reputation for live jazz and impromptu jamming sessions. Daily 9am–2am.

Katie O'Connor's Dropčeva 4a ⓣ 020 321 575, ⓦ katieoconnors.com; map p.392. Well patronized by locals, especially outside peak season, *Katie O'C's* inviting, semi-sunken stone room both functions admirably as a big-screen sports bar and offers a comfortingly mellow vibe when a match isn't on. Guinness, Kilkenny and Erdinger on tap, and a row of Irish whiskeys behind the bar. Daily 9am–2am.

Libertina Zlatarska 3 ⓣ 020 321 526; map p.392. Tiny watering hole in a side street next to the Sponza Palace which, despite being located in Dubrovnik's tourist-tramped centre, still has the feel of a neighbourhood bar. A cosy place, stuffed with domestic knick-knacks and garrulous local drinkers. Daily 8am–midnight.

Sky Bar Marojce Kaboge 1 ⓣ 091 220 2094; map p.392. Lurking invitingly in the narrow alleyways south of Stradun, *Sky Bar* combines sleek lounge-bar aesthetics with a good range of on-tap beers and a solid food menu taking in burgers and steaks. Occasional DJs, and major sport events on the big screen. Daily 9am–2am.

Talir Antuninska 5 ⓣ 091 896 4899; map p.392. Legendary post-performance hangout for actors and musicians during the summer festival – the walls are plastered with photographs of Croatian celebrities past and present. It's a small place, in a side street midway down Stradun, and most people end up sitting on the steps outside. Daily 8am–2am.

The Gaffe Miha Pracata 4 ⓣ 020 323 867; map p.392. The one place in Dubrovnik's Old Town that looks and feels like a cultural implant, this Irish pub is predictably popular with English-speaking tourists in season, but picks up a lot of local trade throughout the rest of the year – especially when sporting events are screened. The daily menu of cheap Croatian lunches (from 30Kn) goes down a treat in winter. Daily 9am–1am.

OUTSIDE THE OLD TOWN

Art Café Branitelja Dubrovnika 25 ⓣ 020 321 065; map pp.404–405. "Pop-Art Café" might be a more accurate moniker for this café much patronized by local student-age youth. Bold colours and swirly rainbow murals characterize the interior decor, while on the street-facing porch purple-topped tables rest on drums salvaged from washing machines. Daily 10am–2am.

Roxy Bana Jelačića 11 ⓣ 020 421 754; map pp.404–405. Nowadays a relatively quiet neighbourhood 1km west of the Old Town, Bana Jelačića was once the heart of Dubrovnik nightlife and *Roxy* was one of its main

8

landmarks. It's nowadays a soothing café-bar rather than rock'n'roll central. Album covers, photos and the odd musical instrument dangling from the wall recall the gigs that took place here in the 1980s and '90s. Daily 7am–midnight.

CLUBS

Eastwest Beach Club Frana Supila 4, Ploče T 020 412 220, W ew-dubrovnik.com; map pp.404–405. Roomy place right on Banje beach offering lounge-bar furnishings and an impressive choice of cocktails. Late-night DJs attract an uninhibited clubby crowd after the sun goes down. Daily 10am–4am.

Latino Club Fuego Brsalje 11, Pile T 020 312 870, W dubrovniknightclub.com; map p.392. Enjoyable mainstream disco aimed mostly at tourists. 11pm–6am.

Revelin Sv. Dominika bb T 091 250 2388, W clubrevelin.com; map p.392. Cavernous club in the Revelin Fortress with an expensive lighting rig, cage dancers and affordable drinks. Daily 11pm–6am.

ENTERTAINMENT

During the summer, the rich cultural diet provided by the **Summer Festival** (see box below) is augmented by informal open-air pop and jazz concerts in the Old Town. At other times, look out for regular performances mounted by the town's two main cultural institutions: the Marin Držić Theatre (see below) and the **Dubrovnik Symphony Orchestra**, which plays in the Revelin Fortress and in other venues around town (T 020 417 101, W dso.hr). Local folk ensemble Linđo (W lindjo.hr) perform in the Lazareti (see p.403) at least twice a week in summer – tourist offices and hotels will have details.

Kino Jadran za Rokom T 020 417 107, W kinematografi.org. The open-air cinema, just behind the *Mea Culpa* pizzeria, is a great place to catch a movie. June–Sept.

Marin Držić Theatre Pred Dvorom 3 T 020 426 437, W kazaliste-dubrovnik.hr. The Gradsko Kazalište Marina Držića specializes in serious drama in the Croatian language.

SHOPPING

8

Along the Stradun there's a respectable string of shops selling postcards and souvenirs, and in the alleyways nearby a smattering of high-street clothes and shoe shops. There's little in the way of specific **craft products** associated with Dubrovnik and its hinterland per se, save perhaps for the vivid geometric designs featured in embroidery from the Konavle region south of the city – tablecloths and napkins bearing Konavle motifs are on sale in the classier gift shops, although they come at a price. The gaggle of **jewellery shops** at the western end of Od Puča is the place to look for coral necklaces, filigree earrings and other traditional adornments.

BOOKS

Algebra Stradun 9; map p.392. Everything you ever wanted to read about Dubrovnik will probably be here, somewhere. Also sells postcards and souvenirs. Mon–Sat 9am–9pm.

Algoritam Stradun 8 T 020 322 044, W algoritam.hr; map p.392. Good across-the-board choice of English-language books, as well as Dubrovnik-related touristy stuff. Mon–Sat 9am–9pm, Sun 9am–1pm.

GIFTS AND SOUVENIRS

Casa Croatica Kunićeva 6; map p.392. Delicacies from

FESTIVALS

The **Dubrovnik Summer Festival** (Dubrovačke ljetne igre; July & Aug; W dubrovnik-festival.hr) stages classical concerts and theatre performances in the courtyards, squares and bastions of the Old Town. The emphasis is very much on high culture: the festival usually includes plays by Shakespeare and Marin Držić (see box, p.400), a major opera, symphonic concerts and a host of smaller chamber-music events. Seats for some of the more prestigious events often sell out well in advance, but it should be possible to pick up tickets for many performances at fairly short notice. The full programme is usually published in April; for details and ticket booking information check the website. Once the festival starts, tickets (30–200Kn) can be bought from the festival information points, usually located on Stradun or outside Pile Gate.

The festival is followed almost immediately by **Julian Rachlin and Friends** (W rachlinandfriends.com; Sept), a short season of classical concerts featuring the world-renowned violinist and a host of other big-name guests, with events taking place in atmospheric venues such as the Rector's Palace and Revelin Fortress. Lastly, the **Mali Glazbeni Festival** (W parkorsula.com; June-Sept) is a season of rock, jazz and ethno concerts in Orsula Park, on the hillside east of town.

all over Croatia including Istrian truffles, pasta from Krk, peppery biscuits from Dubrovnik and plenty in the honey, marmalade, olive oil and *rakija* line. Daily 10am–9pm.

Dubrovačka kuća Sv. Dominika bb ☎020 322 092; map p.392. Big choice of quality souvenirs, from prints and *objets d'art* to olive oil and *rakija*. Try the Lucine Gulozece, strips of candied orange peel which are absolutely delicious. Daily 10am–9pm.

Franja Coffee & TeaHouse Od Puča bb ☎020 324 816, Ⓦfranja.hr; map p.392. Offers much more than the name suggests, with local wines, herbal *rakijas*, sweets and soaps. Daily 10am–9pm.

Historical Museum Shop Rector's Palace, Pred Dvorom; map p.392. Silk ties, porcelain, glass and statuettes of Dubrovnik's protector St Blaise. Daily 9am–6pm.

Lega-Lega Dropčeva 3 ☎020 321 744, Ⓦlega-lega.com; map p.392. Kooky T-shirts sold in milk-carton packaging, highly individual stationery and drinks coasters, from the Osijek-based design outfit (*lega* is Osijek slang for "buddy"). Daily 9am–9pm.

Modni Kantun Zlatarska 3 ☎020 321 241; map p.392. Dresses by local designer Karaka, desirable bags by Croatian label baggiz, and beautiful handmade bracelets, earrings and necklaces incorporating silver and enamel by Ivana Bačura (Ⓦivanabacura.com). Daily 10am–9pm.

MARKET

Open-air market Gundulićeva poljana. As well as fruit and vegetables, there's a row of stalls selling dried figs, olive oil, herb-flavoured *rakija* and small pieces of Konavle embroidery. Daily 8am–5pm.

DIRECTORY

Hospital Roka Mišetića, Lapad, 4km west of the Old Town (☎020 431 777).

Internet access Internet Hugo, Prijeko 13 (10Kn/30min).

Laundry Sanja & Rosie's Launderette, put od Bosanke 2 (☎091 896 7509, Ⓦdubrovniklaundry.com; daily 9am–6pm) is a self-service launderette jut outside Ploče Gate.

Left luggage At the bus station (daily 4.30am–10.30pm).

Pharmacy Kod Zvonika, Stradun (Mon–Sat 7am–8pm); Ljekarna Gruž, Gruška obala (Mon–Sat 7am–8pm). Both take it in turns to be open 24hr.

Post office and telephones Main post office at Vukovarska 16 (Mon–Fri 7am–8pm, Sat 8am–3pm); Old Town branch at Široka bb (Mon–Fri 7.30am–9pm, Sat 10am–5pm).

8

Trsteno

Standing on the coastal highway 13km northwest of Dubrovnik, the straggling village of **TRSTENO** is an essential day-trip destination if you're at all interested in things horticultural. It was here in 1502 that Dubrovnik noble Ivan Gučetić built his summer villa, surrounded by formal gardens extending along a terrace overlooking the sea. Such gardens were considered de rigueur by the aristocracy of sixteenth-century Dubrovnik – sadly, those of Trsteno are the only ones which can still be enjoyed in something approaching their original form. Maintained by successive generations of the Gučetić family, the villa and its gardens were confiscated in 1948 by a communist regime eager to destroy any latent prestige still enjoyed by the Dubrovnik nobility. Soon afterwards the Yugoslav (now Croatian) Academy of Sciences took the place over and expanded it, turning it into an arboretum.

Arboretum

Trsteno • Daily: May–Oct 7am–7pm; Nov–April 8am–4pm • 35Kn • ☎020 751 019

Standing by the roadside just next to the bus stop is a majestic pair of four hundred-year-old plane trees, some 50m high and 15m in circumference. From here a path drops you down to the main entrance to the **arboretum**, where Gučetić's former villa overlooks the oldest part of the estate, a typical Renaissance garden in which patches of lavender, rosemary, oleander, bougainvillea, myrtle and cyclamen are divided up by lines of box hedge to form a complex geometrical design. A nearby orchard sports bushy grapefruit and mandarin trees, but beyond here the garden has a wonderfully lush, uncontrolled feel, as pathways begin to lose themselves in a dense woodland environment comprising trees from around the world. Amid it all, a trident-wielding statue of Neptune overlooks a pond packed with goldfish. Running northwest from the villa, beyond a small football pitch, an avenue of palm trees leads to yet more semi-wilderness areas, thick with cypresses and pines. The effects of two recent fires (the first resulting from Yugoslav artillery in 1991, the second starting accidentally in 2000), can be seen in the shape of blackened tree trunks and waste ground, dotted here and there with areas of new planting. Overlooking the shore at the northwestern end of the gardens is what looks like a ruined palace – it is in fact a purpose-built nineteenth-century folly – commanding a superb view of the surrounding coastline, with the islands of Lopud and Koločep roughly opposite. From here a staircase adorned with weird stone cactus sculptures descends towards a rocky **beach** and tiny harbour perfect for restful sunbathing.

ARRIVAL AND DEPARTURE — TRSTENO

By bus Trsteno is relatively easy to get to, with hourly Dubrovnik–Split buses dropping off and picking up in the centre of the village. The journey from Dubrovnik takes 40min.

ACCOMMODATION AND DRINKING

Auto Camp Trsteno ⓣ 020 751 060 ⓦ trsteno.hr. This idyllic tree-shaded site is just below the main road on the approach to the arboretum; the attached café is the best place in the village for a quick drink. **26Kn** per person, pitches from **20Kn**

Župa Dubrovačka

8

Ten kilometres out of Dubrovnik, the main Montenegro-bound road descends into **Župa Dubrovačka**, a string of erstwhile fishing villages which have now merged to form a six-kilometre line of apartment blocks, weekend villas, angular hotels and waterside cafés, the whole verdant strip backed by impressively stark mountains. The area was occupied by Serb and Montenegrin troops in the winter of 1991–92 and most of the hotels looted, although all but a small proportion have now been spruced up and put back in service.

Kupari beach

The beach is a 10–15min walk northwest of Srebreno (see below)

One-time holiday resort to the Yugoslav People's Army, Župa's westernmost settlement, **KUPARI**, was badly damaged in the 1991–95 war and has lain derelict ever since. It is, however, unexpectedly home to one of the Dubrovnik region's best **beaches**, a fine crescent of shingle with a few sandy bits underfoot (and a summer-only beach bar) that curls in front of the resort's evocative backdrop of shell-damaged hotels. Note that the derelict hotels are unprotected and potentially dangerous – this is not a place for kids and young teenagers to run free.

Srebreno to Plat

Your first real taste of the Župa is likely to be **SREBRENO**, the next place along from Kupari, which sits on the northwestern shoulder of Župa's broad bay. From here an enjoyable promenade runs past well-landscaped stretches of park and an inviting sequence of **beaches** – rough, pebbly affairs at first sight, although the seabed itself is luxuriantly sandy under foot.

After a kilometre or two Srebreno fades imperceptibly into **MLINI**, the most attractive of Župa's settlements, boasting a fair number of traditional stone houses, an attractive harbour and a centuries-old plane tree that looks as if it could have stepped straight out of the writings of Tolkien. Occupying the southeastern curve of the bay are Župa's remaining resorts, **SOLINE** and **PLAT** – little more than hotel settlements, they're not really worth visiting unless you're actually staying there.

ARRIVAL AND INFORMATION — **ŽUPA DUBROVAČKA**

By bus Župa is easily accessible from Dubrovnik, with Dubrovnik–Cavtat buses trundling along the main road every 30min or so.

Tourist office The tourist office is at the northwestern end of the agglomeration in Srebreno, just off the main road (Mon–Fri 8am–3pm, Sat 8am–noon; ⓣ 020 486 254, ⓦ dubrovnik-riviera.hr).

EATING

Konoba Marinero Šetalište Marka Marojice bb, Mlini ⓣ 020 487 257. Slightly uphill from the Mlini seafront in a sheltered garden, this is a good place to tuck into a leisurely meal of fresh seafood or traditionally cooked meats. May–Oct daily 11am–midnight.

Cavtat

Some 20km south of Dubrovnik, and 3km off the main coastal highway, **CAVTAT** is a dainty coastal town offering plenty in the way of traditional stone architecture and lush subtropical vegetation. It began life in the third century BC as Epidaurum, a colony founded by Greeks from the island of Vis. There's nothing left to see of the antique town: Epidaurum was evacuated in favour of Dubrovnik after a thorough ransacking by the Slavs in the seventh century, and the pretty fishing village of Cavtat subsequently grew up in its place. Discovered by Austro-Hungarian holiday-makers at the beginning of the twentieth century, Cavtat was a favourite haunt of the wealthy until a rash of high-rise hotel building in the 1980s changed the place's profile. Happily, the package hotels are set apart from the palm-dotted seafront of the original village, ranged across the neck of a sweet-smelling wooded peninsula. Much of Cavtat's former charm survives in the old part of town, which straddles the ridge behind the waterfront.

The Baltazar Bogišić Collection

Riva • Mon–Sat 9.30am–1pm • 10Kn • ⓣ 020 478 556

Occupying the former Rector's Palace at the southern end of the palm-splashed Riva, the **Baltazar Bogišić Collection** (Zbirka Baltazara Bogišića) remembers lawyer and cultural activist Bogišić (1834–1908), who spent a lifetime promoting Croatian literature and learning at a time when Italian was still considered the language of civilized discourse along the coast. Books from Bogišić's collection crowd the display cabinets, although the stand-out exhibit is Vlaho Bukovac's immense canvas of local carnival celebrations in 1901 – with the cream of Cavtat society gamely got up in fancy dress for the occasion.

The Vlaho Bukovac Gallery

Bukovčeva 5 • May–Oct Tues–Sat 9am–1pm & 4–8pm, Sun 4–8pm; Nov–April Tues–Sat 9am–1pm & 2–5pm, Sun 2–5pm • 20Kn • ⓣ 020 478 646

Lurking near the top of a narrow, stepped alleyway off Cavtat's Riva is the **Vlaho Bukovac Gallery** (Galerija Vlaha Bukovca) celebrating the Cavtat-born artist (1855–1922) who painted lucrative society portraits in Paris, London and elsewhere, and ended his career as professor at Prague's Academy of Fine Arts. The building itself once belonged to Bukovac's father, and the artist spent much of his early adulthood here. Vivid frescoes of animals, birds and exotic plants – painted by a 16-year-old Bukovac while convalescing after an accident at sea – can still be seen in the hallways and stairwell. The larger rooms contain a thorough overview of Bukovac's oeuvre, ranging from the realistic early portraits of family, friends and high-paying clients to later works influenced by Impressionism and Symbolism – notably the torrid, Dante-inspired canvases depicting Heaven, Purgatory and Hell. Scattered throughout the building are some wonderful examples of solid, rustic nineteenth-century furniture.

St Nicholas's Church

Sv. Nikole • Pinakoteka: Mon–Sat 10am–1pm • 10Kn

Work by Cavtat's Vlaho Bukovac, Croatia's most famous painter, is on display at **St Nicholas's Church** (Crkva svetog Nikole), where his paintings of the Four Evangelists look down on the main altar. A few metres up the narrow street next to the church, the **Pinakoteka** displays reliquaries, icons, a gruesome seventeenth-century painting of St Sebastian by Benedetto Gennari and a life-sized diorama of Christ's grave designed by the ubiquitous Vlaho Bukovac and displayed in church over the Easter period.

The Monastery of Our Lady of the Snow

Marking the northern end of the Riva, the rather plain-looking **Monastery of Our Lady of the Snow** (Samostan snježne Gospe) contains a couple of early Renaissance gems in its small church: the first, Vičko Lovrin's triptych of 1509 at the back of the church, shows a gold-clad Archangel Michael slaying a demon while John the Baptist and St Nicholas look on from the wings; the second, Božidar Vlatković's *Madonna and Child* (1494) on the main altar, is a small piece somewhat overpowered by its fussy Baroque frame.

Račić Mausoleum

Mon–Sat: May, June & Sept 10am–5pm; July & Aug 10am–noon & 5–7pm • 10Kn

Paths behind the monastery lead up towards the **Račić Mausoleum**, built on a prime spot high above the town in 1921 by Ivan Meštrović for a local shipowning family. It's one of Meštrović's true masterpieces, blending different historical styles in a way that works much better than in most of his sculptures. It's certainly an eclectic work: a domed structure guarded by stern, archaic Greek angels and decorated with dog-faced gargoyles, Teutonic-looking eagles and what look like neo-Assyrian winged lambs just below the cupola. Inside are impressive reliefs of the Račić family and St Rock, the patron saint, his wounds being licked by an athletic-looking whippet of a dog.

The beaches

A brace of fine shingle **beaches** lies about 1km east of the town centre in an area known as **žal** (literally, "beach"), although the proximity of the package hotels ensures that they're usually crowded. Quieter spots, if you don't mind perching on rocks, can be found at the far end of the peninsula, ten minutes' walk north from town, or on the Sustjepan peninsula immediately to the west. The latter has a naturist section, just on the other side of the *Croatia Hotel*.

ARRIVAL AND INFORMATION — CAVTAT

By bus Bus #10 runs to Cavtat roughly hourly from Dubrovnik.

By boat Privately operated boats from Dubrovnik's Old Port do the same trip for about 90Kn.

Tourist office Zidine 6 (June & Sept daily 8am–8pm; July & Aug daily 8am–9pm; Oct–May Mon–Fri 8am–3pm; ⓣ 020 479 025, ⓦ tzcavtat-konavle.hr). Cavtat's tourist office, right next to the bus stop, offers an ocean of town maps and brochures in every conceivable language.

ACCOMMODATION

Teuta, Trumbićev put 3 (ⓣ 020 479 786 ⓦ cavtat.biz; Mon–Sat 8am–8pm, Sun 9am–noon) is an agency organizing **apartments** (two-person studios from 350Kn; four-person apartments from 620Kn); as well as excursions and scooter rental.

Castelletto put od Cavtata 9a ⊕020 479 547, ⊕dubrovnikexperience.com. Thirteen-room B&B just uphill from the port. Rooms are in creamy pastel colours and come with tiled floors, reconditioned pine furnishings and attractive art prints on the walls. Some have balconies with views towards Dubrovnik; all are equipped with TV, a/c and bathroom. There's a nice garden and small outdoor pool. Airport pick up available. **730Kn**

Croatia Frankopanska 10 ⊕020 430 830, ⊕alh.hr. A vast, multi-tiered concrete five-star hogging the ridge of the Sustjepan peninsula. It's easy to get lost in its seemingly endless corridors, but it has modern a/c rooms with TV, and a private beach facing the Cavtat waterfront. The indoor swimming pool is a major feature. **1350Kn**

Villa Pattiera Trumbićev put 9 ⊕020 478 800, ⊕villa-pattiera.hr. Twelve-room hotel right on the harbourfront, housed in the former home of interwar opera singer Tino Pattiera. Rooms feature peachy and plummy colours, parquet floors and flat-screen TVs; the pricier ones have views of the palm-fringed quay, the others share a large garden terrace at the back of the house. **850Kn**

EATING AND DRINKING

There are numerous **restaurants** on or near the waterfront, offering everything from cheap pizza to more expensive local specialities. In addition, a string of **cafés** along the Riva serve salads, sandwiches and ice cream during the day, potent cocktails at night.

★ **Galija** Vulićevićeva 5 ⊕020 478 566, ⊕galija.hr. Cosy *konoba* in an alleyway behind the monastery, which in summer expands onto a large outdoor terrace with views across the bay. Succulent seafood starters include grilled squid and salmon with pasta, although the real highlights of the menu are the grilled fresh fish and the stand-out *riba u pečnici* (a whole fish roasted in a tin together with potatoes and seasonal vegetables). *Galija* can sometimes become the victim of its own success – so popular on summer evenings that neither kitchen nor wait-staff can really cope. Mains in the 120–160Kn range. April–Dec noon–midnight.

Ivan Tiha 5 ⊕020 478 485. Quiet place on the opposite side of the peninsula to the main Riva, with tables set out beside a harbour full of small boats and good views north towards Župa Dubrovačka. Familiar range of seafood and grilled meats, with mains clocking in at 100–120Kn. April–Oct 11am–midnight.

Konoba Cavtat Obala A Starčevića ⊕020 478 473. Although arguably the most ordinary of the restaurants along the seafront, *Cavtat* is certainly the most useful out of season, when it's frequently the only place open. The menu is a mainstream mix of steaks, fish and *pljeskavica*-style grill-snacks, and the risottos and pasta dishes are a reliable lunch choice. Mains 70–140Kn. Daily 10am–11pm.

Leut Trumbićev put 11 ⊕020 478 477, ⊕restaurant-leut.com. A leafy outdoor terrace a few steps back from the seafront, offering top-of-the range grilled seafood and a few oven-baked fish alternatives. Mains hover around 120Kn, while the pastas and risottos (70–80Kn) listed as starters make a good light lunch. April–Nov daily 11am–midnight.

Toranj Starčevićeva 13 ⊕020 479 577, ⊕konoba-toranj.com. A customary range of fish and shellfish, with the fish platter for two (230Kn) well worth a try. Also look out for pasta dishes with lobster or shrimp (70Kn), and try and leave room for the excellent desserts. Slightly set back from the Riva, but the charming first-floor terrace is no mean compensation. April–Nov daily 11am–11pm.

8

The Konavle

Southeast of Cavtat stretches the **Konavle**, a ribbon of fertile agricultural land squeezed between the mountains on one side and the sea on the other. It is a restfully scenic place to drive through, and offers a couple of rewarding village stopoffs to boot. Traditionally the Konavle formed the rural hinterland of the Dubrovnik Republic, keeping the city supplied with fresh victuals – as well as being the major recruiting ground for itinerant labourers and serving girls.

The Đurović Cave

Daily 10am–6pm • 50kn

Not necessarily the most spectacular of Croatia's limestone caverns, the **Đurović Cave** (Đurovića Špija) is certainly the most unusual in terms of location, stretching beneath the runway of Dubrovnik airport just east of Cavtat. Entered via a concrete passageway near the domestic departures lounge, the twisting 200-metre-long fissure contains a sequence of chambers, each concealing an array of stalagtites and rock curtains. The cave has a constant temperature of 16°C, so remember to bring a sweater.

Čilipi

The village of **ČILIPI**, 2km beyond Dubrovnik airport, is renowned for the **folklore shows** which take place on the village's flagstoned central square every summer Sunday. Organized by the local folklore society, performances are held in the late morning immediately after Mass, when locals and tourists alike perch on the church steps to observe a forty-minute medley of local songs and dances. Foremost among the latter is the *lindo*, which employs rigid, stylized gestures to mimic the rites of courtship, and is accompanied by the *lirica*, an archaic, droning fiddle. The dancers wear traditional Konavle costume – note the small pillbox hats donned by unmarried girls and the enormous white scarves worn by married women.

There are a couple of **cafés** just off the main square, and a largely tourist-oriented **Sunday market** selling folksy embroidery and textiles.

ARRIVAL AND DEPARTURE — ČILIPI

By bus Buses running from Dubrovnik to Molunat (see below) go via Čilipi.

Tours Trips to Čilipi from Dubrovnik are run by the Atlas agency (see p.408).

Gruda and Molunat

South of Čilipi the main southeast-bound road continues through a bucolic landscape of vineyards, orchards and sheep pasture, passing after 10km the downbeat village of **Gruda**. The Konavle's only coastal settlement of any real consequence is **MOLUNAT**, an unspoilt, vegetation-shrouded village at the end of a winding (and well-signed) secondary road 15km southeast of Gruda. A pleasing jumble of houses and holiday villas faces east across a shallow bay which, despite its small size, is one of the most attractive on this part of the coast, boasting a smooth, sandy seabed on one side and a more rocky section on the other – where there are plenty of offshore outcrops perfect for perching on.

ARRIVAL AND DEPARTURE — GRUDA AND MOLUNAT

By bus Buses run from Dubrovnik to Molunat (Mon–Sat 3 daily, Sun 2 daily; 1hr 15min).

ACCOMMODATION AND EATING

Koračeva kuća Gruda bb, Gruda ⓣ 020 791 557 and ⓣ 098 428 225. Just off the main road through Gruda is this family-run restaurant with bare-stone interior serving up traditional fare washed down with local wines. There is a menu but they don't always stick to it, with the choice of dishes changing according to what's seasonal. Roast lamb is a speciality of the house, but is slow-cooked and needs to be ordered in advance. Daily noon–11pm.

Monika Molunat 28, Molunat ⓣ 020 794 557, ⓦ camp-monika.hr. Campsite with pitches sheltering amid olive trees on a shingle-edged inlet, just south of Molunat's main beach. The restaurant serves up grilled seafood backed up with a list of wines from local Konavle vineyards. **50Kn** per person, pitches from **35Kn**

CROSSING INTO MONTENEGRO

Thirty-five kilometres south of Dubrovnik the road arrives at the border with **Montenegro** (Crna Gora in Croatian and Serbian). Crossing here is relatively problem-free for citizens of the EU, USA, Australia, New Zealand and Canada providing they have a valid passport – nationals of other countries should check visa requirements before leaving home.

The Elaphite Islands

An easy ferry ride away from Dubrovnik's Gruž harbour, the lush, vegetation-carpeted **Elaphite Islands** (Elafiti) present the perfect opportunity to savour the Croatian Adriatic at its unspoilt, get-away-from-it-all best. Strung out between Dubrovnik and the Pelješac peninsula to the north, the Elaphites got their name (literally the "deer islands") from first-century-AD Roman geographer Pliny the Elder, who mentioned them in his 37-volume *Historia Naturalis*. The Elaphites became part of the Dubrovnik Republic from the fourteenth century, sharing in its prosperity and then its decline – by the middle of the eighteenth century many island villages lay abandoned and depopulation had become a major problem. Today, only three of the islands are inhabited – **Koločep**, **Lopud** and **Šipan** – each of which supports a modest tourist industry. Despite the daily influx of trippers from Dubrovnik, however, tourism on the Elaphites remains reassuringly low key, the almost total absence of cars contributing to the mellow feel: private vehicles are not allowed on any of the islands except Šipan.

ARRIVAL AND DEPARTURE — THE ELAPHITE ISLANDS

By ferry All three islands are linked to Dubrovnik by a Jadrolinija ferry which runs up to Šipan and back again (up to 4 daily in summer; 1 daily in winter).

Destinations Koločep (30min), Lopud (50min), Suđurađ (1hr 15min), Šipanska luka (1hr 45min).

ACCOMMODATION

There's a handful of **hotels** on the islands, but rooms and apartments are in short supply – few if any Dubrovnik travel agencies bother to deal with accommodation on the Elaphites. Your best bet is to check the **apartment** listings on websites such as ⓦ dubrovnik-area.com and reserve things well in advance.

8

Koločep

Just thirty minutes from Dubrovnik by ferry, the islet of **Koločep** is a little over 2.6 square kilometres in area, and has a population of less than 150 concentrated in two main hamlets: **Donje Čelo**, on the north side of the island where the ferry docks, and **Gornje Čelo** to the southeast. There are no special sights, but Donje Čelo is a pleasant cluster of stone houses with an excellent curving sandy beach. Just uphill from the waterfront, a concreted path strikes inland towards Gornje Čelo, a huddle of vegetation-choked houses overlooking two small bays. From here you can follow innumerable paths into the dense, fragrant pine and deciduous forest that covers the southern part of the island.

Lopud

In Dubrovnik's heyday, **Lopud**, with a population of some four thousand (today it's less than 350), was the seat of one of the republic's vice-rectors and was the favoured weekend retreat of the city's nobles. A large part of Dubrovnik's merchant fleet was based here, and the ruined palaces of shipowners still occupy crumbling corners of the island's only village. Tourism here dates back to the 1920s, and the island's hotels were used by the Italians to intern Jews from Dubrovnik and Bosnia in 1942. They were shipped off to the notorious concentration camp on Rab the following year, though many managed to escape to join the Partisans after the collapse of Italy in 1943.

Lopud village

Located on the northern side of the island, the village of **LOPUD** is strung around a wide, curving bay boasting a long, crowded and reasonably sandy **beach**. Its most prominent monument is the fortified **monastery** which overlooks the village from a promontory just east of the quay where ferries dock. Built by the Franciscans (and funded by Lopud merchants) in 1483, it's now mostly derelict save for the erstwhile monastery (and now parish) **Church of Our Lady of the Rocks** (Crkva Gospe od Špilice), which boasts a rich collection of altar paintings. Among these is a triptych (to the right as you face the main altar) by Nikola Božidarević or his workshop depicting the Virgin and Child accompanied by a bevy of saints, the ubiquitous St Blaise among them. The main altar is separated from the main body of the church by a delicately carved stone screen, on which small mammals munch away happily on berries, and are in turn menaced by snarling dragons.

West along the seafront from the quay, steps lead up to the ruined palace and private chapel of **Miho Pracat**, the sixteenth-century merchant and shipowner whose bust stands in the Rector's Palace in Dubrovnik. A few steps beyond, the **Đorđić-Mayner Park** (Perivoj Đorđić-Mayner) is one of the nicest in the region, with trees from around the world grouped beneath soaring pines, and roses, cacti and other ornamental plantings basking beneath. Also near the seafront, the Bauhaus-influenced **Grand Hotel** is a modernist classic designed in the 1930s by Belgrade architect Nikola Dobrović. It is currently awaiting redevelopment following a long period of closure.

Around the island

Paths at the back of the village lead up onto the high ground at the centre of the island, one of which (look for signs reading "Kaštio" or "Tvrđava") climbs towards the Ragusan **fortress**, a forty-minute walk away, which looms above Lopud village to the southeast. It's a complete ruin nowadays, but the view from its crumbling ramparts is magnificent, with stark grey coastal mountains to the east, and the green, cone-shaped hills of Šipan and Pelješac to the north. The best of Lopud's beaches is **Šunj Bay** (Uvala Šunj), the only truly sandy beach in the area and highly popular in summer; it's 2km south of Lopud village and easily reached via an asphalt path.

8

INFORMATION — LOPUD

Tourist office On the seafront (May to mid-Oct daily 8am–1pm & 5–7pm; ☎020 759 086). Can provide a list of rooms and apartments on the island, though won't make bookings.

ACCOMMODATION AND EATING

HOTELS

★ La Villa Obala Iva Kuljevana 33 ☎091 322 0126, www.lavilla.com.hr. Eight-room guesthouse whose rooms come in Mediterranean colours with tiled floors, vivaciously tiled bathrooms and a/c. There's a shady breakfast terrace, an internet corner and library, and bikes and kayaks for rent. Open April–Oct. Book well in advance; three-day minimum stay preferred. **900Kn**

Villa Vilina Obala Iva Kuljevana 5 ☎020 759 333, villa-vilina.hr. Intimate and luxurious small hotel in an old stone house near the Franciscan monastery, offering a handful of tastefully furnished, plush-carpeted rooms with TV. The same company runs the *Lopudski Dvori* (same number; studios from 1500Kn), another stone building comprising seven well-appointed two-person apartments with shared garden and swimming pool. May–Oct. **1125Kn**

RESTAURANTS

Konoba Peggy Narikla bb ☎020 759 036. This *konoba* is a well-signed 5min walk uphill from the seafront and has a large terrace overlooking the town. Excellent fresh fish and squid cooked on an open hearth. April–Oct noon–midnight.

Obala Obala Iva Kuljevana 18 ☎020 759 170. A restaurant on the waterside-hugging main strip that offers good-quality seafood on a palm-shaded terrace, with baked octopus, seafood *brodet* and fish baked in salt featuring among the stand-out dishes. May–Oct daily 11am–midnight.

Šipan

The largest of the populated Elaphites, **Šipan** is a delightful island of craggy hills strung out around a long, fertile plain dotted with the occasional hamlet. There are few special sights and there's certainly no nightlife, but if you're after some peace and quiet and gentle hikes, this is one of the best places to be on the coast.

FROM TOP VELIKO JEZERO, MLJET (P.426); KOLOČEP (P.421) >

Suđurađ

The first port of call for the ferry is **SUĐURAĐ**, a bay-hugging clump of houses overlooked by an imposing pair of stone **towers**, built to guard the walled summer villa of sixteenth-century Dubrovnik shipowner Vice Stjepović Skočibuha. Parts of the villa have been lovingly restored but, somewhat frustratingly, they're only open to pre-booked groups. Running round the side of the palace, the village's main alleyway ascends towards the blockhouse-shaped **Church of the Holy Spirit** (Crkva svetog Duha), a fortified structure built to serve as a refuge for the locals in the event of pirate attack.

Walks from Suđurađ

To get a true taste of Šipan's bucolic beauty you really need to take the time to walk or cycle along some of the island's country lanes. Starting at Suđurađ's Church of the Holy Spirit, one road winds its way round the hillside hamlet of Pakljena before heading east towards an area of dense maquis broken up by agaves, olive groves and pines. After about 2km you'll chance upon the fortified **Church of Our Lady** (Crkva velike Gospe), a former monastic foundation whose crumbling outbuildings appear to be sinking into the undergrowth. The church is hardly ever open, but the sight of its crenellated sixteenth-century tower peeking above the greenery provides a convenient excuse to wander this far.

8

Heading north from Suđurađ's Church of the Holy Spirit along the island's only properly paved road, the seven-kilometre **walk to Šipanska Luka** takes you past some lovely inland scenery. Vineyards and olive groves cover the island's central plain, which is edged by the ruined summer houses of the Dubrovnik nobility, and perfumed by wild fennel, rosemary and other herbs.

Šipanska Luka

Ferries from Dubrovnik terminate at **ŠIPANSKA LUKA**, a pretty little place buried at the end of a deep inlet at the island's northern end. Grouped around an enormous plane tree that's thought to be as old as those in Trsteno, the settlement contains the odd relic of former glories: best is the neglected Stjepančić villa on the harbourfront, which boasts a balcony supported by carved lions, and seems to be crying out for restoration. Šipanska Luka's most attractive **beach** is about 500m away from the harbourfront, a tiny strip of sand pressed against a thread of rock that separates the western side of the bay from the sea. More isolated spots for bathing can be found by following the path which extends beyond the ferry jetty on the opposite side of the bay, threading its way between rocky shoreline and shady olive groves before petering out in dense undergrowth after a couple of kilometres.

INFORMATION — ŠIPANSKA LUKA

Tourist office The small tourist office at the apex of Šipan's bay (June–Sept Mon–Sat 8am–noon & 5–8pm; ☎ 020 758 084) will provide addresses of local private rooms (doubles from 240Kn) but will not book them on your behalf.

ACCOMMODATION AND EATING

Kod Marka Šipanska Luka ☎ 020 758 007. Located on the southern side of the bay, *Kod Marka* has earned cult status among the yachting fraternity with its fresh seafood, although it's eccentric with it – you might receive attentive service or simply be left waiting for hours. May–Oct 11am–midnight.

Konoba Tauris Šipanska Luka ☎ 020 758 088. Set back from the shore behind Šipan's plane tree, *Tauris* prepares deliciously succulent *lignje*, fried or grilled, as well as excellent fish. May–Oct 9am–midnight.

Sipan Šipanska Luka 160 ☎ 020 754 900, Ⓦ hotel-sipan.hr. The harbourfront hotel offers well-equipped en-suite rooms – the attic rooms on the top floor are the cosiest – and also rents out bikes. *Barka*, occupying one half of the *Šipan* hotel's restaurant, serves coffee and cakes during the daytime and cocktails after nightfall, with tables strewn across a palm-shaded lawn. Open late April to Oct. 930Kn

Mljet

The westernmost of the islands accessible by local ferry from Dubrovnik is **MLJET**, a thin strip of land some 32km long and never more than 3km wide, running roughly parallel to the Pelješac peninsula. The most visited part of the island is the green and unspoilt west, where untouched Mediterranean forest and two saltwater lakes provide the focus of the **Mljet National Park**, an area of arcadian beauty within which lie the villages of **Polače** and **Pomena**. Despite the presence of a hotel in the village of Pomena, the region remains blissfully unspoiled, full of bicycle-pedalling trippers during the daytime, and romantically quiet and stressless at night.

According to legend, Odysseus holed up here for seven years with the nymph Calypso, and Mljet also has fair claim to being the island of Melita, where St Paul ran aground on his way to Italy and was bitten by a viper before he set sail again. (Mljet's snake problem was once so bad that a colony of mongooses had to be imported from India to get rid of them, and the fat-tailed creatures are still very much in evidence in the national park.) The Romans used the island as a place of exile, and it was briefly owned by the kings of Bosnia, who sold it to Dubrovnik in 1333. The republic sent an emissary on May 1 every year to rule the island for a year, and many of Dubrovnik's admirals built summer houses here.

Polače

Main point of arrival for most day-trippers is **POLAČE**, little more than a row of houses along a small harbour – whose waters are clean enough to swim in. The harbour is bordered to the north by the impressively lofty walls of a fourth-century-AD **Roman palace**, the inner courtyard of which is now home to a couple of lemon trees.

8

Goveđari

Hugging the slopes of a rounded hill inland from Polače, the stone-built village of **Goveđari** used to be northern Mljet's main settlement, situated away from the coast as a defence against pirate raids.

Stara Skula Gallery

Daily 10am–2pm & 5–10pm • Free • Ⓦ staraskula.com

The village's former schoolhouse (originally built in 1912) has been painstakingly restored and is now home to the **Stara Skula gallery**. It hosts exhibitions by contemporary artists throughout the summer.

Pomena

Sheltering in a bay at the western tip of Mljet, **POMENA** is a seaside hamlet that came into being in the last few decades in order to service the island's small but growing tourist industry. There is a large modern hotel in the shape of the *Odisej* (see p.427), a souvenir shop or two, a small yachting marina and a row of family-run restaurants. Regular taxi-boats (check the lobby of the *Odisej* for details) run to the naturist islet of **Pomeštak**, just offshore.

Mljet National Park

100Kn; buy a ticket from one of the kiosks in Pomena, Polače or just outside Goveđari once you've settled in, and certainly before you start exploring; the kiosks also have park information and maps (50Kn)

There's no official entrance point to the **Mljet National Park** and by the time you arrive in Polače or Pomena you're already well inside it. The park's main attractions are its two forest-shrouded "lakes" (actually inlets connected to the sea by narrow channels), **Malo jezero** (Small Lake) and **Veliko jezero** (Big Lake), which together form a stretch of water some 4km long. Both are encircled by foot- and cycle paths, and the clear, blue-green waters are perfect for bathing. If Polače is your point of arrival, it's possible to walk over to the lakes by road or by a well-signed forest path (via the 253-metre Montokuc hill) in about 45 minutes. From Pomena, Malo jezero is ten minutes' walk south, by way of a stone-paved footpath that heads over a wooded ridge just up from the port. Once you hit the shore of Malo jezero, it's another ten-minute walk to **Mali most** (Little Bridge), spanning the channel feeding into Veliko jezero, edged by magnificently soothing, tree-shaded pathways.

Continuing along the bank of Veliko jezero takes you through fragrant mixed woodland before arriving at **Soline**, a cluster of houses presiding over a flat valley floor. The saltpans here used to be at the centre of a small but significant salt-extracting industry.

St Mary's Island

Boats run hourly; vouchers for the trip are included with the entrance ticket

Mali most is the departure point for the boat service down Veliko jezero to **St Mary's Island** (Otok svete Marije), where the Benedictines established a monastery in the twelfth century. Overlooked by a sturdy defensive tower, the **monastery church** features unusually chunky altarpieces carved from local stone and exuberantly coloured. The central dome is enclosed in a squat quadrangular tower, whose dog-tooth-patterned exterior can be admired from the neighbouring courtyard.

8

ARRIVAL AND DEPARTURE — MLJET

FROM DUBROVNIK

By catamaran The passenger-only *Nona Maria* catamaran (May–Sept; 020 313 400, gv-line.hr) sails daily from Dubrovnik to Polače in the morning, and leaves you with several hours to look round the park before returning to Dubrovnik in the evening. Tickets are sold on the harbourside 30min (in July and Aug 1hr) before departure so it is essential to arrive early to be sure of a seat.

By car ferry The year-round Jadrolinija car ferry sails from Dubrovnik to Sobra in the eastern part of the island (it's a good 20km short of the park; Sobra–Polače–Pomena buses await incoming ferries).

FROM THE PELJEŠAC PENINSULA

By ferry There is a summer-only car ferry from Prapratno on the Pelješac peninsula to Sobra (June–Sept 5 daily; 50min).

FROM KORČULA OR OREBIĆ

By hydrofoil Approaching from Korčula or Orebić, you can reach Mljet on the regular hydrofoil excursions (arriving at either Polače or Pomena) run by local travel agents – expect to pay 300–350Kn per person, including the park entrance fee.

INFORMATION

Tourist office A small white house on Polače harbour contains a tourist office (mid-June to mid-Sept Mon–Sat 8am–noon & 4–6pm; mid-Sept to mid-June Mon–Fri 8am–1pm; 020 744 186, mljet.hr), which can point you in the direction of locals offering rooms (doubles from 200Kn).

GETTING AROUND

Bikes are the ideal way to get around the national park: they can be rented from a number of private operators right on the seafront in Polače, or in front of the *Odisej* hotel in Pomena (45Kn/hr, 120Kn/day).

Kayaks can also be rented at Mali most (45Kn/hr, 120Kn/day).

ACCOMMODATION AND EATING

GOVEĐARI

★ **Boutique Accommodation Mljet** Goveđari 14 020 744 140 and 098 285 697, boutiqueaccommodationmljet.com. Family run, friendly and ideally situated in the middle of the national park, these apartments occupy the restored village schoolhouse that is also home to the Stara Skula Gallery (see p.425). Features include wooden floors, exposed stonework and well-chosen furnishings that mix farmhouse chic with modern comforts. Two doubles come with kitchenettes and TVs, a simply decorated third one can be used as a kids' room if you are travelling as a family. 525Kn

POMENA

Hotel Odisej Pomena ⓣ 020 362 111, ⓦ hotelodisej.hr. A prim collection of whitewashed modern blocks containing en-suite rooms with a/c and TV. There is a café and restaurant on site. **1300Kn**

Konoba Nine Pomena 6 ⓣ 020 744 037. A family-run restaurant that's been going since 1958, *Nine* is good for grilled fresh fish and absolutely great for traditional Dalmatian fish-stew recipes such as *gregada* (with white wine and herbs) or *brudet* (with red wine and spices). They do their own fishing, make their own goat's cheese and also keep fresh lobsters and slipper lobsters (bug-like monster crabs with succulent white meat) in wood-covered stone pens underneath the harbourfront. June–Sept noon–11pm.

SOLINE

Pikala Soline 3 ⓣ 020 744 023. Named after a grandad who was nicknamed Piccolo for being the small one of the family, restaurant and pension *Pikala* serves up food and drink on a covered terrace surrounded by vines and fig trees. Alongside the usual grilled fish, house specialities include baked octopus and squid goulash (although both need to be ordered a day in advance). Accommodation consists of simple en-suite doubles with functional furnishings, and swisher two- to three-person studio apartments with kitchenette and balcony. **450Kn**

8

SINJSKA ALKA FESTIVAL, SINJ

Contexts

History

History is a serious business in a country that has spent so much of its past under the sway of foreign powers. It's also exceedingly complicated, as the history of Croatia is interlinked, for lengthy periods, with the histories of Hungary, Austria and Venice, not to mention that of the former Yugoslavia.

Croatia before the Croatians

Our knowledge of the first humans to inhabit Croatia is patchy, although a form of Neanderthal – named **Krapina Man** after the town in which remains have been found (see p.103) – is known to have roamed the hills north of Zagreb some thirty millennia ago. By about the seventh millennium BC, Neolithic farmers had spread out along the coast, and were increasingly using the islands as stepping stones to cross the Adriatic. Advanced Neolithic cultures certainly existed on Hvar, where five thousand-year-old painted pottery offers evidence of the so-called Hvar Culture, and beside the River Danube in eastern Slavonia, where similarly rich ceramics have been unearthed at Vučedol, near Vukovar.

By the first millennium BC the indigenous peoples of the region now covered by Croatia, Bosnia, Albania and Serbia had begun to coalesce into a group of tribes subsequently known as the **Illyrians**. Although they were united by common styles of fortress building and burial-mound construction, it's not clear whether the Illyrians ever existed as a culturally homogenous group, and they were never politically united. They did, however, produce some powerful tribal states: the Histri in Istria and the Liburnians in the Kvarner and northern Dalmatia were minor maritime powers, building towns whose names – in modified, Slavonic form – still survive, like Aenona (Nin) and Jadera (Zadar).

Greeks, Romans and Byzantines

Greek city-states, led by Syracuse in Sicily, began dispatching settlers to the Adriatic from the fourth century BC onwards, founding colonies such as Issa (on present-day Vis) and Paros (on Hvar). There were various attempts by the Illyrians to drive the new colonists out, the most serious coming from Queen Teuta, whose territory stretched from Zadar in the north to what is now Albania in the south.

In 229 BC the Greeks asked for Roman help against Teuta, beginning a period of **Roman expansion** that continued until 9 AD, when the eastern Adriatic and its hinterland were annexed by the future emperor Tiberius. The seaboard became the Roman province of Dalmatia, while northern and eastern Croatia were divided between the provinces of Noricum (which covered much of present-day Austria) and Pannonia (which stretched into modern Hungary). The older Greek settlements continued to flourish, but were outshone as political and cultural centres by new Roman cities, often founded on sites that had previously served as power bases for the Illyrian tribes. The main Roman centres were Salona (Solin, near Split) and Jadera (Zadar), although the vast amphitheatre at Pula attests to the prosperity of Istria during this period. The Illyrians were either romanized or absorbed by later immigrants like the Slavs.

c. 2500 BC	**4th century BC**	**305 AD**	**641**
Late Stone Age tribes at Vučedol, near Vukovar, produce exquisite ceramics, notably the Vučedol Dove.	Issa (Vis) is founded by Greeks from Syracuse.	Emperor Diocletian builds his retirement palace at Split.	Byzantine Emperor Heraclius invites migrating Croats to settle on the Adriatic seaboard.

THE ORIGINS OF THE CROATS

The name "Croat" (Hrvat) is considered by many to be of Persian rather than Slav origin, suggesting that the Croats were subject to Persian-speaking tribes before moving towards southeastern Europe, or even that the Croats were themselves of Iranian origin and picked up the Slav tongue from neighbours as they migrated. The latter theory has always been popular among Croatian nationalists keen to emphasize the uniqueness of their people, although it's disputed by more mainstream scholars. Recent DNA research suggests that the majority of people living in today's Croatia represent bloodlines that go back to the period before the arrival of the Croats in the Balkans – which implies that the Croats conquered, intermarried with and gave their language to the indigenous people of the Adriatic, rather than supplanting them altogether.

The Romans lost the Adriatic to the Ostrogoths in 493, although Justinian, emperor of the eastern half of the Roman Empire, whose capital was at **Byzantium**, reconquered the area in 544. The **Avars**, a warlike central-Asian people, briefly forged a central European empire at the beginning of the seventh century, and even reached the coast, sacking Salona and Epidaurum in 614. Refugees from these cities went on to found Split and Dubrovnik.

The arrival of the Croats

Spurred on by the Avar threat, Byzantine Emperor Heraclius shored up his Adriatic defences by inviting in the **Croats**, a Slav tribe who had come to southeastern Europe from an area north of the Carpathians. The Croats probably migrated to the region at the same time as the **Serbs**, who settled in the middle of the Balkan peninsula. The fact that the groups share a common language suggests that they originated in the same area, and Serbs and Croats – along with other tribes speaking similar Slav dialects such as the Slovenes, Bulgarians and Macedonians – were subsequently to be known collectively as the **South Slavs**.

The medieval Croatian state

The Croats who settled along the Dalmatian seaboard established a tribal state ruled by a **knez** (prince or duke), who assumed leadership of any Avars, Illyrians and Romans still living there. Inland areas to the north, such as present-day Slavonia, fell under independent chieftains loosely allied to the Croats on the Adriatic. The existence of two Croatian heartlands – a southern one oriented towards the Mediterranean and a northern one looking towards Central Europe – has had a profound effect on Croatian culture ever since.

Both areas maintained a tenuous independence until squeezed by neighbouring empires: the Byzantines, who still held several Adriatic towns and islands, and the Carolingian Empire of the Franks, which was expanding into Central Europe by the late 700s. Croat leaders boosted their legitimacy by accepting **Christianity**, and although the northern Croatian state became subject to the Franks in the 790s, the southern state played one predator off against another and prospered. Ruling from

810
Ljudevit Posavski emerges as leader of the inland Croats, ruling from Sisak.

925
Adriatic and inland Croats are united in a single state by King Tomislav.

1060s
Petar Krešimir IV extends Croatia's boundaries to include much of the Adriatic coast, Slavonia and Bosnia.

1102
The Pacta Conventa places Croatia under the Hungarian crown.

their citadel at **Klis** (see p.307), Croatian princes paid homage to either Byzantines or Franks as necessary, while preserving de facto independence and simultaneously beating off two newcomers to the Adriatic: the Venetians and the Arabs.

The Croatian kingdom reaches its zenith

With the Croatian state growing stronger, Branimir (879–892) threw off Byzantine vassalage and was recognized by Pope John VIII as an independent ruler. His successor-but-one, **Tomislav** (910–928), pushed things further, defeating the Hungarians to gain control of northern Croatia and battling the Bulgarians to win northwestern Bosnia. Declaring himself king in 925 (previous Croatian leaders had kept to the title *knez*), Tomislav reorganized the Croatian Church, placing all his lands under the control of a Croatian archbishop at Split, thereby lessening papal influence without actually questioning his ultimate loyalty to the pope.

For the seventy years following Tomislav's death Croatia was financially, militarily and dynastically stable, until a succession crisis in the early eleventh century allowed both Venice and Byzantium to regain footholds on the Adriatic coast, while northern Croatia was lost to the Hungarians. **Petar Krešimir IV** (1058–75) presided over a revival of fortunes, and reunion with northern Croatia was achieved by appointing Slavonian leader **Dimitr Zvonimir** as co-ruler. Petar Krešimir died childless, and power passed to Zvonimir (1075–89), though he too died without issue, leaving the nobles to choose Stjepan II (1089–91), who also failed to produce an heir.

Disintegration and decline

After Stjepan II the kingdom began to disintegrate, leaving Zvonimir's brother-in-law, King Ladislas of Hungary, free to secure control of the north, while a group of nobles in the south regrouped under King Petar (1093–97). Independent Croatia's last monarch was defeated by a Hungarian army under Ladislas's successor, Koloman, at **Gvozd** (subsequently named Petrova gora or Peter's Mountain), the highland region south of Zagreb.

Hungarian control of Croatia was confirmed by the **Pacta Conventa** of 1102, according to the terms of which Croatia and Hungary remained separate states united by the same royal family. Croatia retained its own institutions – a **Ban** (governor) appointed by the king, and the **Sabor** (parliament) representing the nobility – but, despite these provisions, the Hungarian Crown steadily reduced the power of the Croatian aristocracy in the years that followed, speeding Croatia's demise as a united and distinct state.

Croatia under the Hungarians

Life in what became known as the **Hungaro-Croatian kingdom** was characterized by a strengthening of the feudal order, with the landed nobility growing stronger at the expense of the rural population. Town life, especially in northern Croatia, underwent rapid development as Varaždin, Vukovar, Samobor and Zagreb were earmarked as centres of trade.

The kingdom was overrun by the **Tatars** in 1242, but King Bela IV managed to keep royal authority alive by moving from one coastal stronghold to the next. The material damage was enormous, however, and much medieval Croatian architecture was lost.

1240	**1409**	**1460s**	**1521**
Stonemason master Radovan completes the west portal of Trogir's Romanesque cathedral.	Venice gains control of most of the Adriatic coast.	Under chief engineer Michelozzo Michelozzi, Dubrovnik's city walls reach their greatest extent.	Marko Marulić publishes the first ever book in the Croatian language, the epic poem *Judita*.

Hungarian control of the Adriatic seaboard was slowly eroded by the Venetians during the thirteenth century, but Hungarian King **Louis of Anjou** (1342–82) threw them out of Dalmatia in 1358. Louis died without a male heir, and the nobles of southern Croatia invited **Ladislas of Naples** to assume the crown in 1403. Ladislas's reign was a disaster: he lost control of inland Croatia to Sigismund of Hungary before notoriously selling Dalmatia to the Venetians for 100,000 ducats in 1409.

Venice was now in command of almost all of Istria and Dalmatia apart from the independent city-state of **Dubrovnik**. The Venetians were to stay for over 350 years, flooding the Adriatic seaboard with Italianate art and architecture, but taking away the traditional autonomy of the towns at the same time.

Cut off from the Adriatic, the Croatian lands to the north were being squeezed by the rulers of **Bosnia**, a mountainous inland region which had long been a buffer zone between Croatia, the Byzantine Empire and Serbia. The inhabitants of Bosnia were the ethnic kin of the Serbs and Croats, and large parts of Bosnia – especially the north and west – had long been in the Hungaro-Croatian sphere of influence. Powerful and resourceful rulers like Kulin (1180–1204), Stjepan II Kotromanić (1322–53) and Tvrtko I (1353–91) were nevertheless able to expand their territory at the expense of the south Croatian aristocracy. By the fifteenth century, however, the northward expansion of the **Ottoman Turks** had begun to threaten Bosnia, something that would have grave consequences for the Croats.

The Ottoman threat

From their heartland in Anatolia, the Ottoman Turks had gained a foothold in southeastern Europe in the early 1300s and soon expanded their territory, fatally weakening Byzantium, swallowing Bulgaria and reducing Serbia to vassal status within a century. The conquest of Bosnia by the Ottomans in the 1470s now left Croatia in an extremely vulnerable position.

In 1493, a large Hungaro-Croatian force assembled at **Krbavsko polje** (just south of Plitvice) and was smashed by the Turks, leaving the Adriatic open to Ottoman raids. In 1517, Pope Leo X called Croatia *antemurale christianitatis* ("the ramparts of Christendom") in recognition of its front-line status. To the east, the defeat of Hungary at the **Battle of Mohács** in 1526 left the Ottomans in command of much of Pannonia, with Slavonia and northwestern Croatia at their mercy.

The Hungarian King Louis II had died childless at Mohács, leaving the throne to the Austrian **Ferdinand I of Habsburg**. Inland Croatia was thus absorbed into the growing Habsburg Empire. The Habsburgs could do little to stem the Ottoman advance, however, and by the 1540s the Turks had overrun the whole of Slavonia as far as Sisak, only 50km south of Zagreb. By the end of the century Croatia had been reduced to a belt of territory running from the Kvarner Gulf in the southwest to the Međimurje in the northeast, with Zagreb at its centre. The Venetians continued to hold Istria and the Dalmatian coastal strip, and the city-state of Dubrovnik further south retained its independence by paying tribute to the Ottoman Empire.

Vlachs and Serbs

The expansion of Turkish power had also set in train a sequence of population movements, with refugees fleeing to areas that were still under the control of Christian

1527	1551	1573	1625
Inland Croatia becomes part of the Habsburg Empire.	Dubrovnik playwright Main Držić pens his best-known comedy, *Dundo Maroje*.	Matija Gubec leads a peasants' revolt in northern Croatia and is executed in Zagreb.	Dubrovnik poet Ivan Gundulić writes *Osman*, an epic tale of Central Europe's struggle against the Ottoman Turks.

powers. Areas depopulated by war and migration were often filled by itinerant stockbreeders, or **Vlachs**, many of whom were descended from the romanized inhabitants of ancient Illyria and still spoke a dialect of Latin akin to modern Romanian. A mixture of Catholic and Orthodox Christians, the Vlachs fell under the influence of the Croatian and Serbian churches, and were soon slavicized, coming to identify themselves as Croats or Serbs as time went on.

The Habsburgs used the Vlachs as frontier guards, giving them lands along Croatia's borders in return for military service. This belt became known as the **Military Frontier** (Vojna krajina), a defensive cordon ruled directly from either Graz or Vienna. It was to remain in existence until the mid-nineteenth century, by which time the Ottoman threat had long receded.

The seventeenth and eighteenth centuries

Habsburg forces – with many Croats in their ranks – scored an important victory over the Turks at the **Battle of Sisak** in 1593, ending the myth of Ottoman invincibility and stabilizing the Habsburg–Ottoman frontier. A further Ottoman attack on Vienna in 1683 was thrown back by a combined force of Austrians, Germans and Poles. In the decades that followed, Habsburg armies led by **Prince Eugene of Savoy** gradually drove the Ottomans out of Central Europe. The Venetians, who had often avoided all-out war with the Turks owing to the precariousness of their position in Dalmatia, exploited Austrian gains by winning back parts of the Dalmatian hinterland. By the time of the **Peace of Passarowitz** in 1718, the Habsburgs had won back the whole of Slavonia, while the Venetians gained control of a belt of highland territory running from Knin to Imotski. Significantly, the Turks retained Bosnia and Hercegovina – the frontiers agreed at Passarowitz are very close to those still dividing Bosnia-Hercegovina from Croatia today.

Because the Habsburg lands were made up of a multitude of states – its rulers were simultaneously Duke of Austria, Holy Roman Emperor and King of Hungary – political authority within the empire was often confused. In Croatia, the Military Frontier remained under the direct control of Vienna, while the rest of Croatia nominally belonged to the Hungarian Crown. The Croatian aristocracy was progressively Hungarianized from the late seventeenth century on (when its last great magnates, **Petar Zrinski** and **Fran Krsto Frankopan**, were executed for treason), and took little interest in Croatian culture.

The nineteenth century

In 1797 the Venetian Republic was dissolved by **Napoleon.** Napoleon subsequently gained control of the whole eastern Adriatic seaboard, forming a French protectorate named the **Illyrian Provinces** ruled by a French governor, Marshal Marmont. Marmont set about building roads, developing the education system and promoting Slav-language publishing, although the provinces were soon abandoned to the Austrians following Napoleon's defeat.

Habsburg dominance of Dalmatia was confirmed by the **Treaty of Vienna** in 1815, and the economic fortunes of the Adriatic began to revive under Austrian stewardship. The main language of the Adriatic sea trade, however, was Italian, and economic development went hand-in-hand with the Italianization of maritime Croatia,

1737	**1808**	**1815**	**1835**
One of Europe's last documented cases of vampirism is recorded on the island of Lastovo.	The Republic of Dubrovnik is abolished by Napoleonic France.	Dalmatia and Dubrovnik become part of the Habsburg Empire.	Ljudevit Gaj publishes the first edition of the *Danica* periodical, bringing Croatian language and literature to a growing audience.

ILLYRIANISM

The language reforms of Ljudevit Gaj in the early nineteenth century (see below) gave birth to a movement known as **Illyrianism** (*Ilirizam*) – a name that harked back to the ancient Roman province of Illyria and therefore avoided too close an identification with any single ethnic group. Illyrianism contributed enormously to the flowering of Croatian language and culture in the mid-nineteenth century known as the **Croatian National Revival.** Although the movement was originally intended to provide a bridge between Croats and Serbs, it remained a purely Croatian affair: the fact that the Croats used the Roman alphabet and the Serbs wrote in Cyrillic characters made it unlikely that the two languages and cultures would ever be harmonized. The infant Serbian state was in any case much more interested in expansion than in cooperation with its Slav neighbours.

Vienna initially tolerated Illyrianism as a politically useful counterweight against the boisterous nationalism of the Hungarians, but eventually took fright and came down heavily, banning any mention of the word "Illyria" in 1843. The movement lived on, however, with the formation of the Narodna stranka – the "National Party", whose members were known as the **Narodnjaci** – which from this point onwards was to be the country's main pro-Croat, anti-Hungarian force.

disappointing many who had seen the return of Austrian power as an opportunity to renew links between the Croats of Dalmatia and the Croats of the north.

The Croatian national revival

One of Napoleon's aims in the creation of the Illyrian Provinces had been to encourage the growth of South Slav consciousness, in the hope that Croats, Slovenes and Serbs could be weaned away from other great powers that might pose as their protectors, notably Austria and Russia. For the Croatian elite, the example of Serbia itself was increasingly important. Subject to the Ottoman Empire since the fifteenth century, the Serbs had risen up against the Turks in 1804 and 1815, and the emergence of an **autonomous Serbian principality** in 1830 was greeted by many Croat intellectuals as an example of what South Slavs could achieve. Apart from an undercurrent of distrust between the Catholic and Orthodox churches, the Serbs had never been regarded as historic enemies, and the development of common links between Serbs and Croats became a popular intellectual theme.

The closeness of the Croat and Serb languages sparked a renewed interest in language reform. A literary version of colloquial Serbian was developed by Vuk Karađić (1787–1864) in the 1820s, an example that was followed by the Croatian writer **Ljudevit Gaj** (1809–72), who set about developing a form of literary Croatian close enough to Serbian for the two to be mutually intelligible. He based it on the Štokavski dialect used by Croats in Slavonia, Hercegovina and Dubrovnik, rather than the *kajkavski* dialect spoken in Zagreb and the north. *Danica*, the cultural supplement of his own newspaper, *Novine Hrvatske*, changed over to the new, Štokavski-based written language in 1835.

1848 and after

With the outbreak of **revolution in Paris** in February 1848, a wave of reforming fervour spread through Europe. In Hungary, ambitious nationalist Lajos Kossuth agitated for

1848

Led by Viceroy Jelačić, Croatia presses for autonomy within the Habsburg Empire.

1866

Rijeka-based engineers Luppis and Whitehead demonstrate the world's first torpedo.

1867

The Habsburg Empire is divided into Austrian-ruled and Hungarian-ruled spheres; Croatian autonomy is quietly forgotten.

the introduction of a constitutional monarchy, while mobs on the streets of Vienna demanded democratic reforms. Croatian opinion saw the 1848 revolution as a means of winning autonomy from the Hungarians and forging a new South Slav unit within the Habsburg Empire. This conflict of national interests pitched Croatian radicals against the Hungarian radicals under Kossuth who, despite their liberal credentials, continued to regard Croatia as a junior partner in a reinvigorated Hungary.

Fast losing control of a complex situation, the Habsburg court had no choice but to tolerate the emergence of Croatian national sentiment, in the hope that it would serve to counterbalance the Hungarians. The popular Colonel **Josip Jelačić** was appointed Ban or Viceroy of Croatia, and he immediately called elections to the Croatian Sabor in order to provide himself with a popular mandate. Armed with the Sabor's support, Jelačić first broke off relations with the Hungarians, then declared war on them. Ultimately, however, he became a pawn in a wider game: after relying on his support to crush the revolutionaries in Hungary and Austria, reactionaries at the Viennese court gradually forgot about Croatian demands for autonomy and reintroduced centralized rule.

The Habsburg Empire's twilight years

In the aftermath of 1848 the Habsburg Empire, headed by arch-conservative **Franz Josef I** (1848–1916), attempted to reorganize itself as a centralized state in which all regionalist aspirations were suppressed in favour of loyalty to the dynasty. Continuing tension between Vienna and Budapest did however force a major constitutional change in 1867, when the Habsburg state was renamed the **Dual Monarchy of Austria-Hungary**. Franz Josef was to be emperor of Austria and king of Hungary simultaneously, and Vienna was to retain overall control of defence and foreign policy, but in all other respects the Austrian and Hungarian halves of the empire were to run their own affairs. This had serious consequences for the Croats: while Dalmatia was to remain in the Austrian half, the bulk of Croatia found itself in a semi-independent Hungary, thereby preventing the emergence of a unified Croatian national movement with clear goals.

Yugoslavism and Croatian nationalism

There were two strands to Croatian nationalism in the second half of the nineteenth century: one emphasized the cultural similarities between all South Slavs, while the other had a more exclusively Croat perspective. The principal representative of the former strand was **Juraj Strossmayer** (1815–1905), Bishop of Đakovo and leader of the Narodnjaci, who thought that Croats and Serbs within the Habsburg Empire could unite to form a South Slav state within a federal Austria-Hungary. Strossmayer also seriously considered the possibility of Austria-Hungary's collapse, concluding that an independent Yugoslav (which literally means "South Slav" in Croatian and Serbian) state would be the best solution. Strossmayer used the income from his episcopal estates to create the Yugoslav Academy of Science and Arts in Zagreb in 1867. Opposition to Strossmayer's nascent Yugoslavism was supplied by **Ante Starčević** (1823–96), who formed the **Croatian Party of Rights** in 1861. Starčević favoured the formation of an independent Croatian state under Habsburg auspices and was suspicious of any deal with the Serbs, believing that they would never treat the Croats as equals.

The question of Serb–Croat cooperation became more acute after 1881, when Vienna abolished the Military Frontier and reabsorbed it into Croatia – thereby increasing the

1888

Croatian-born inventor Nikola Tesla patents the AC induction motor in the USA.

1902

Reconstruction of Zagreb's Neogothic Cathedral reaches completion.

1914

World War I breaks out; Croatians fight and die for Austro-Hungarian armies on all fronts.

number of Orthodox Serbs in the country. The Hungarian administration in Zagreb played one side off against the other, fearful that the Serbs and Croats would join together in an anti-Hungarian alliance.

The early twentieth century

A wave of anti-Hungarian protests in northern Croatia in 1903 created new political opportunities. In 1905 Croatian deputies joined with the Hungarian opposition in signing the **Rijeka Resolution**, which called for democratic reforms and the unification of Dalmatia with the rest of Croatia. Almost immediately, Serb politicians from northern Croatia and Dalmatia followed with the **Zadar Resolution**, which promised support for the aims of the Rijeka Resolution providing that the equality of Serbs in Croatia could be guaranteed. The two sides came together to form the **Croat–Serb Coalition**, which scored a resounding success in the 1906 elections to the Croatian Sabor. The Ban of Croatia (appointed by Budapest) frustrated attempts to form a Serb–Croat majority, and the Sabor was suspended in 1911.

Austria-Hungary formally annexed the Ottoman territory of Bosnia-Hercegovina in 1908, assuming responsibility for its mixed population of Catholic Croats, Orthodox Serbs and Muslim Slavs. The annexation went down badly in Serbia, which viewed Bosnia-Hercegovina as a potential area for Serbian expansion. The ultimate goal of Serbian foreign policy – to forge a state which would include all Serbs wherever they lived, was a serious challenge to Austria-Hungary, which had a large Serbian population within its own borders. Serbian successes in the **Balkan Wars** of 1912–13, when Ottoman forces were driven out of Macedonia, increased Serbian prestige, especially among those Croats who saw Serbia as the potential nucleus of a future South Slav state.

World War I

Tension between Austria-Hungary and Serbia was already high when Franz Josef's nephew and heir, **Archduke Franz Ferdinand**, was assassinated in the Bosnian capital Sarajevo on June 28, 1914, by Gavrilo Princip, a young Bosnian Serb who had been supplied with weapons by Serbia's chief of military intelligence. The anti-Serbian mood in Viennese court circles had achieved critical mass, and Austria-Hungary declared war on Serbia on July 28. Germany was pulled in on the Austrian side, making a response from the anti-German alliance of Russia, France and Great Britain inevitable, and **World War I** was under way.

Initially Croats fought loyally on the Habsburg side, but the longer the war went on, the clearer it became that Austria-Hungary might not survive. Faced with the possibility of a future without the Habsburgs, few Croatian politicians considered it practical to work for the establishment of an independent Croatia – such a state would be vulnerable to predatory Hungarian, Italian and Serbian neighbours. Instead they increasingly embraced the idea of **Yugoslavia** – a South Slav state which would include Serbs, Croats and Slovenes and be strong enough to stand up to outside powers. With Italy joining the war in the hope of gaining territory in Dalmatia, the need to promote the Yugoslav ideal was paramount.

1915

Croatian sculptor Ivan Meštrović has a one-man show at London's Victoria and Albert Museum.

1918

With the collapse of the Habsburg Empire, Croatia joins the Kingdom of Serbs, Croats and Slovenes (later renamed Yugoslavia).

1921

Ljubomir Micić launches Dadaist art movement Zenit in Zagreb.

THE AUSTRO-HUNGARIAN EMPIRE AND THE SUCCESSOR STATES (1914–18)

The creation of Yugoslavia

In 1915, veteran Dalmatian politicians Frano Supilo and Ante Trumbić formed the **Yugoslav Committee** in Paris in order to lobby foreign governments and make contacts with Serbian leaders. The Serbs were initially unwilling to treat the committee as an equal partner, but negotiations culminated in the signing of the **Corfu Declaration** of July 1917, in which both sides agreed that any future South Slav state would be a constitutional monarchy in which Serbs, Croats and Slovenes would enjoy equal rights, but which would be headed by Serbia's Karađorđević dynasty. In October 1918 the political leaders of Austria-Hungary's Serbs, Croats and Slovenes formed the **National Council** in Zagreb and declared their independence from Budapest and Vienna.

Austria-Hungary collapsed on November 3, and Italian troops landed in Dalmatia ready to stake a claim to the parts they coveted. The territory ruled by the National Council was in chaos: they had no army, bands of deserting soldiers were roaming the countryside and fear of social revolution was rife. Desperate to restore order and keep the Italians out, the National Council rushed to declare union with Serbia on the basis of the Corfu Declaration, and the Serbian Prince Aleksandar Karađorđević declared the creation of the **Kingdom of Serbs, Croats and Slovenes** on December 1, 1918. The name "Yugoslavia" had been quietly dropped because Belgrade didn't think it sounded Serbian enough. The other areas incorporated into the new state were the Principality

1922

Miroslav Krleža's short-story collection, *The Croatian God Mars*, presents an agonized portrait of Croatia's World War I experience.

1927

Hajduk Split win the first of their nine Yugoslav League titles.

1929

Yugoslavia becomes a royal dictatorship.

of Montenegro (Crna gora), which had strong ties to Serbia, and Macedonia, which had been conquered by Serbia during the Balkan Wars.

The first Yugoslavia

Many Croats entered the new state on the assumption that it would have a federal constitution. Unfortunately, the leading Serb politicians of the time had other ideas. Leading Serbian politicians were keen to draw Croats and Slovenes into a state in which the Serbs played the leading role, arguing that because large numbers of Serbs were scattered throughout Croatia and Bosnia, only a unitary state could protect their interests.

The Croats were against the idea of a unitary state because they feared that they would always be outvoted by the numerically superior Serbs, and they gravitated towards the **Croatian Republican Peasant Party** (**HRSS**), a republican movement that backed the interests of farmers against the urban bourgeoisie and which was also suspicious of Serbian centralism. When elections to the new kingdom's constituent assembly took place on November 28, 1920, the HRSS won fifty of the 93 seats allocated to Croatia. HRSS leader **Stjepan Radić** claimed that the party's victory had given him a mandate to declare Croatia an independent republic, and spoke enthusiastically of replacing the Kingdom of Serbs, Croats and Slovenes with a Balkan peasant federation comprising Slovenia, Croatia, Serbia and Bulgaria (where a democratically elected pro-peasant government under Alexander Stamboliiski was already in power). Belgrade kept a lid on the situation by packing Radić off to prison and sending in the troops, but the HRSS's reputation as the main defender of Croat interests was secured.

The 1920s

Croatian deputies were unable to prevent the Constituent Assembly from passing the 1921 **Vidovdan Constitution**, which declared the new kingdom a unitary state and convinced many Croats that their new homeland was merely Greater Serbia under a different name. Radić immediately withdrew the HRSS from parliament and tried to raise support for the Croatian cause abroad, although Great Britain, France and the US were far too committed to the idea of a strong Yugoslavia to aid those hostile to the central government in Belgrade.

By the mid-1920s the complete freeze in relations between Belgrade and the Croatian political elite had persuaded Radić to change tack. He began working for Croatian autonomy rather than outright independence, and joined Serbian politician Svetozar Pribićević in forming a new opposition bloc, the **Peasant–Democratic Coalition**. The Radić–Pribićević alliance was a serious threat to the Belgrade establishment, and passions were already running high when Stjepan Radić was shot in the parliamentary chamber by the pro-Belgrade deputy Puniša Račić on June 20, 1928. Radić died two months later; his funeral in Zagreb was attended by 100,000 people. Fearful of further inter-ethnic violence, King Aleksandar suspended parliament and launched the **Sixth of January Dictatorship** at the beginning of 1929. The name of the state was changed to **Yugoslavia** later the same year, in the hope that an appeal to South Slav idealism might help paper over the country's cracks.

1934

King Aleksandar of Yugoslavia is assassinated by Macedonian and Croatian terrorists.

1937

Josip Broz Tito becomes leader of the illegal Yugoslav Communist Party.

1939

Vukovar-born Lavoslav Ružička wins the Nobel Prize in Chemistry.

The 1930s

Radić was succeeded as leader of the HRSS – now the HSS, having dropped the word "Republican" from its name due to its anti-royalist connotation – by **Vlatko Maček**, who broadened the party's appeal to make it a national movement representing all classes of Croats. Banned from political activity, the HSS sponsored various front organizations such as the Peasant Accord, which supported cultural activities in rural areas, and the Croatian Peasant Defence Force, a paramilitary organization which was tolerated by the government because its members occasionally beat up socialists.

One other organization that opposed the unitary nature of the Yugoslav state was the **Communist Party of Yugoslavia** (**KPJ**), which despite being banned in 1920 continued to exert a strong influence over the intelligentsia. The communists envisaged Croatia as part of a federal Yugoslavia, and it was this concept that was inherited by **Josip Broz Tito**, whom Moscow appointed leader of the KPJ in December 1937.

Diametrically opposed to communism was the **Ustaše** – a right-wing Croatian separatist organization, founded by **Ante Pavelić** in 1929, which was inspired by Italian fascism and dedicated to the violent overthrow of the Yugoslav state. Together with the similarly inclined Internal Macedonian Revolutionary Organization (IMRO), the Ustaše orchestrated the assassination of the Yugoslav King Aleksandar in Marseilles in October 1934.

Fearful that the Croat question would tear Yugoslavia apart, prime minister Milan Stojadinović tried to reach an accommodation with the HSS, relaxing the ban on its activities. Maček, however, turned to the Serbian opposition instead, joining up with the Serbian Radical and Peasant parties to put together the **Alliance for National Agreement**, which won 37.5 percent of the vote in the government-manipulated elections of 1935, rising to 44.9 percent in 1938. New Yugoslav prime minister **Dragiša Cvetković** was charged with the task of making a deal with the Croats amid a worsening international situation and the fear that Yugoslavia's internal weaknesses could be exploited by predatory neighbours. The result was the Cvetković–Maček Agreement, or **Sporazum**, signed on August 26, 1939, according to which an autonomous Croatian territory, the **Banovina**, was created within the borders of Yugoslavia. It included all of present-day Croatia as well as those portions of western Bosnia inhabited by large numbers of Croats. Maček became deputy prime minister in the Yugoslav government, while fellow HSS leader **Ivan Šubašić** became Ban of Croatia. Inside the Banovina the HSS became the party of government, although they were supported by the Serbian Democratic Party (SDS), which represented Serbs in Croatia.

World War II

Yugoslavia initially opted for a policy of neutrality when **World War II** broke out in September 1939, although German pressure eventually forced Cvetković to sign up to the Tripartite Pact (the alliance forged by Germany, Italy and Japan) on March 25, 1941. Pro-British officers in the Yugoslav Army launched a successful coup on March 27 and denounced the pact, but most of the leading figures in the coup were Serbs, and the new regime didn't enjoy the loyalty of Croats. When the Germans declared war on Yugoslavia on April 6, resistance quickly melted away.

1941	1943	1944
Germany invades Yugoslavia and installs Nazi puppet Ante Pavelić as head of the so-called Independent State of Croatia.	Communist-led partisans hold a congress at Jajce, promising to recast Yugoslavia as a federation of national republics.	Tito meets Churchill in Naples to discuss Yugoslavia's future.

The NDH

German troops entered Zagreb on April 10, 1941, and quickly established a puppet government, the **Independent State of Croatia (NDH)**, with Ante Pavelić styling himself the "Poglavnik" (a Croatian rendering of "Führer") in imitation of Hitler. The rest of Yugoslavia was carved up between Germany and her allies, although a rump of Serbia was allowed to survive under German occupation. Bosnia was awarded to the NDH, although large chunks of northern and middle Dalmatia, together with the islands, were given to Italy, something for which many Croats never forgave the Ustaše. Even the NDH's own territory was split into German and Italian spheres of influence, and NDH military commanders were under the supervision of their German and Italian colleagues.

As a result of the inclusion of Bosnia, the NDH now included large numbers of Serbs and Bosnian Muslims. The Muslims were regarded as allies, while the Serbs were regarded as a potentially traitorous element which had to be eliminated – it soon became clear that the Ustaše's attitude to Serbs was little different from the Nazi Party's attitude to Jews. The NDH immediately embarked on three main **anti-Serbian policies**: the deportation of Croatian and Bosnian Serbs to Serbia proper, their mass conversion to Catholicism, or their mass murder. It's estimated that one in six Croatian Serbs died between 1941 and 1945, many of them killed in concentration camps like Jasenovac (see p.120), where Jews, Gypsies and anti-fascist Croats were also murdered.

Partisan resistance

The sheer ferocity of the Ustaše campaign against the Serbs led to an immediate increase of resistance activity. The most important group early on were the **četniks**, Serbs loyal to the Yugoslav government-in-exile, who often carried out vicious revenge attacks upon Croats and Muslims, but they were soon eclipsed by Tito's communist **Partisans**, who played down ethnic differences in order to forge a popular anti-fascist movement that drew support from all races and areas of society. The collapse of Italy in September 1943 allowed the Partisans to capture weaponry and take command of large chunks of territory in Istria and Dalmatia, although they were soon chased out by the Germans. In 1944 the Partisans were recognized by the British, who withdrew all remaining support from the *četniks* and persuaded the Yugoslav government-in-exile in London to sign an agreement recognizing Tito's authority.

The Partisans entered Zagreb on May 8, 1945. Thousands of Croatian **Domobrani** (home guardsmen), the majority of whom were no great supporters of the Ustaše, had been mobilized by Pavelić in the preceding weeks and ordered to retreat to Austria in the hope that they could surrender to the Allies and preserve themselves as the nucleus of some future anti-communist force. The British unit that received them at the town of Bleiburg shipped them back across the border to the waiting Partisans. As many as fifty thousand of these Croatian prisoners were murdered in the weeks that followed: some were shot immediately and thrown into mass graves; others were marched to internment camps in the deep south of Yugoslavia – a journey subsequently dubbed the *Križni put* or Way of the Cross. Pavelić himself escaped to South America, and then to Spain, where he died in 1959.

1945	1948	1950	1952
Croatia becomes part of the communist-ruled Yugoslav federation.	Stalin kicks Yugoslavia out of the Soviet bloc.	The Dubrovnik Festival is founded, promoting the city as an elite resort.	An exhibition of abstract art by the EXAT 51 group helps to relaunch the Croatian avant-garde.

Tito's Yugoslavia

Yugoslavia's first postwar elections produced a landslide victory for the **People's Front**, an organization dominated by the communists. Although the ballot was nominally secret, anyone voting against the People's Front had to place their ballot papers in a separate box – sufficiently intimidating to ensure that few people took the risk. The resulting National Assembly voted unanimously to declare Yugoslavia a republic on November 29, 1945. A new Soviet-inspired constitution was adopted, creating a federation of six national republics – Slovenia, Croatia, Bosnia-Hercegovina, Serbia, Montenegro and Macedonia. The rigid discipline of the Communist Party was to hold the whole structure together.

In Croatia, the communists' elimination of political opponents went hand in hand with an attack on the **Catholic Church**. Some members of the church hierarchy had been enthusiastic supporters of the NDH, and it wasn't difficult to discredit the whole organization using the charge of collaboration. Alojzije Stepinac, Archbishop of Zagreb, was offered a role in the new order if he broke off links with the Vatican – and was rewarded with a sixteen-year prison sentence when he refused.

The birth of Yugoslav socialism

The Yugoslav economy was in a state of ruin in 1945, and the new government used the need for speedy reconstruction as an excuse to rush ahead with wholesale revolutionary change. Large estates were confiscated, businesses were nationalized and a five-year plan that emphasized heavy industry was instituted. Yugoslavia's efforts to ape the USSR made it look like the model pupil, but in June 1948 Soviet leader **Josef Stalin** denounced the Yugoslav party for indulging in ideological deviations, expecting the Yugoslavs to ditch Tito and appoint a more pliant leader: with Cold War tensions rising in Europe, it's likely that Stalin wanted to enforce unity among his satellites by making an example of Tito, the only Eastern European leader who had risen to power independently of the Red Army. Yugoslavia was expelled from the Cominform, the Soviet-controlled organization of European communist countries, and the Soviets appealed to Yugoslav communists to overthrow Tito.

In the event, Tito's wartime Partisan colleagues stood by their leader, and Yugoslavia's resistance to Soviet pressure won Tito new levels of popularity both at home and abroad. Party members who sided with Stalin were dubbed "Cominformists" and shipped off to endure years of harsh treatment on the infamous Goli otok, or "Bare Island" (see box, p.235).

Market socialism and self-management

Stalin's economic blockade, coupled with a string of bad harvests brought about by bungled attempts at collectivization, led Yugoslavia to the brink of economic collapse. Aid from the capitalist West was gratefully received, and a drastic rethink of the country's political objectives followed. The support of industrial workers was cultivated by introducing a system of **workers' self-management**, in which all enterprises would be controlled not by the state but by the people who worked in them – on the surface, a decisive move away from Stalinism. State-owned companies were encouraged to compete against each other, encouraging the emergence of a market economy. The Communist Party itself was renamed the **Yugoslav League of Communists** in a (largely cosmetic) attempt to suggest that it would play a less overbearing role in the country's

1961	1961	1964
Tito forms the Non-Aligned Movement with Indian PM Nehru and presidents Sukarno of Indonesia, Nasser of Egypt and Nkrumah of Ghana.	Orson Welles films Kafka's *The Trial* in Zagreb.	Yugoslav citizens are given passports and allowed to travel freely.

YUGOSLAVIA 1945–90

future. The League of Communists in each republic was allowed increasing autonomy, with the personal authority of Tito and his wartime comrades holding the whole thing together. Meanwhile, Tito joined Nehru of India and Nasser of Egypt to form the **Non-Aligned Movement** in 1961 and, although the movement itself was largely ineffective, Tito's delicate balancing act between East and West gained Yugoslavia international credibility far in excess of its size or power.

1967

Football team Dinamo Zagreb win the European Inter-Cities Fairs Cup, defeating mighty Leeds United in a two-leg final.

1970

Indira Gandhi presents Tito with the elephants Sony and Lanka, who go on to become Croatia's most famous safari-park attractions.

1971

Tito encourages the "Croatian Spring" reform movement, and then clamps down on it hard.

Throughout this period **Croatia** was in the firm grip of Tito's trusted sidekick Vladimir Bakarić, who did his best to protect Croatian interests in the Yugoslav federation without going too far. Above all, the break with the Soviet Union removed the Stalinist straitjacket, allowing Croatia to renew its spiritual and cultural links with the West. As one of the more developed republics in the federation, Croatia was well placed to profit from the economic boom of the 1960s, a decade which saw real wages almost double. The relaxation of visa requirements for visitors from capitalist countries led to a **tourism explosion** on the Adriatic – although the role of Belgrade-based travel companies in creaming off some of the profits was always resented.

The Croatian Spring

During the 1960s the quickening pace of economic liberalization created a rift between the conservative communists and their more reform-minded colleagues. Tito initially sided with the reformists, moving in 1966 to oust **Aleksandar Ranković**, Serbian head of the Yugoslav secret police. However, the expected democratization never really materialized, petering out in a morass of inter-republican disputes. In Croatia, growing national sentiment first expressed itself in the cultural sphere. In 1967, an attempt to promote the idea of a unified Serbo-Croatian language provoked a backlash from Croatian intellectuals, who issued a **declaration** on the unique nature of the Croatian language.

By the beginning of the 1970s, the leaders of the **Croatian League of Communists** (the Yugoslav League of Communists was divided into six republican parties) were increasingly keen to play the nationalist card, hoping to gain domestic support in bargaining with central institutions for more republican autonomy. When nationalists won control of the Zagreb university students' union in April 1971, the republican authorities pointedly failed to take action against them. Mixing demands for economic liberalization with calls for more republican autonomy, the ferment of ideas and debate that characterized Croatia throughout 1971 came to be dubbed the "**Croatian Spring**". Tito initially tolerated the Spring, seeing it as a useful counterweight to Serbian nationalism. By late 1972, however, he was beginning to fear for the survival of the Yugoslav federation and opted for a clampdown. The leaders of the Croatian League of Communists were forced to resign, student leaders were put on trial and the short-lived Spring was at an end.

Croatia after the Spring

The crackdown on the Croats sounded the death knell for liberalization all over Yugoslavia. The silencing of reformists in Serbia soon followed, and Yugoslav socialism entered a period of ideological stagnation from which it never really recovered. Tito's personal authority kept the lid on any further outbreaks of inter-republican animosity; in Croatia itself, nationalism was once more a taboo subject, while a disproportionate number of Serbs were appointed to top posts, storing up more resentment for the future. Outside the country, Croatian exiles assassinated the Yugoslav ambassador to Sweden in 1971 and hijacked a TWA airliner in 1976, giving Western observers the impression that Croatian nationalism was a volatile and terrorist force that was not to be encouraged. Tolerated by Western governments, the Yugoslav secret services sent hit squads abroad to silence the state's critics.

1972

Bob Guccione opens the Penthouse Adriatic Club Casino on the island of Krk.

1976

A club in Rijeka hosts the first punk concert in communist Europe.

1977

Brotherly Leader and Guide of the Revolution Muammar Gaddafi cruises the Kvarner coast on one of his many state visits to Yugoslavia.

The 1980s

Tito died on May 4, 1980, leaving the country without an effective leader. He was replaced by an eight-man presidency in which each republic took turns to supply a head of state. The federal government was relatively weak compared with those of the individual republics, making it difficult to adopt nationwide policies capable of dealing with Yugoslavia's worsening economic problems – the economic boom of the 1960s had been financed by Western loans, but the oil-crisis-ridden 1970s had seen a drying-up of credit, leaving Yugoslavia with crippling foreign debt, galloping inflation and high unemployment.

Problems began in **Kosovo**, a province of southwestern Serbia that had been given autonomous status because the majority of its inhabitants were ethnic Albanians. In 1981, Albanian demonstrations in Kosovo demanding that the province be upgraded to a full republic had been put down by the army. In 1986, the Serbian Academy of Sciences issued a **Memorandum** which stated that the Serbian minority in Kosovo was under threat from Albanian nationalists, adding (without much supporting evidence) that the Serbian community in Croatia was also under pressure from Croatian cultural hegemony. The Memorandum was eagerly seized upon by Serbian intellectuals who argued that the constitution of Yugoslavia should be re-centralized in order to give the Serbs (numerically superior to the other nations) more power.

The Serbian League of Communists, loyal to the federalist ideal, was initially against the Memorandum. Then, on April 24, 1987, **Slobodan Milošević**, a little-known apparatchik recently installed as Serbian party chairman, visited the town of Kosovo Polje to meet leaders of the Serbian minority in Kosovo. When local police started jostling Serb demonstrators, Milošević intervened with the now famous words "Niko ne sme da vas bije!" ("Nobody has the right to beat you!"). Propelled to national prominence as a defender of Serbian rights, Milošević realized that nationalism was the tool with which he could remould Yugoslav communism in his own image. Using support for the Serbs in Kosovo as the issue on which all other politicians should be judged, he expelled liberals from the Serbian League of Communists and promoted hard-line nationalists in their place.

Many of the Serbs who joined the mass meetings in support of Milošević mistakenly thought that they were taking part in some kind of democratic revolution: in fact, they were accessories to a neo-Stalinist putsch. In March 1989 a new Serbian constitution ended the autonomy of Kosovo and Vojvodina (the Serbian republic's other autonomous province), while shortly afterwards Milošević supporters succeeded in winning control of the leadership of another republic, Montenegro; he also found allies in the Macedonian and Bosnian parties. Milošević hoped that this growing bloc of support would be sufficient to outvote his remaining opponents in federal institutions, thereby making it possible to recast Yugoslavia in a new and more centralized form.

In November 1989 the Berlin Wall came down. As the rest of Eastern Europe prepared for multiparty rule, the biggest republic in Yugoslavia was reverting to hard-line communism. The Slovenes and Croats had to assert themselves before it was too late.

1980	1982	1987	1989
Death of President Tito, aged 87.	Croatian politician Milka Planinc becomes Yugoslavia's first female prime minister.	Zagreb undergoes a facelift in order to host the Univerzijada, or World Student Games.	Zadar-based pop-group Riva win the Eurovision Song Contest in Lausanne, representing Yugoslavia with the song *Rock Me*.

The break-up of Yugoslavia

By 1989, Slovenia, the most westernized and liberal of Yugoslavia's republics, was moving inexorably towards multiparty elections. Croatia was initially slow to follow this lead, and by the late 1980s the phrase **Hrvatska šutnja** (Croatian silence) had been coined to describe the unwillingness of the republic's politicians to discuss the future of Yugoslavia or to champion Croatian interests. The crunch came when the Slovenes insisted on changes to the Yugoslav constitution which would guarantee the autonomy of individual republics: the Croats had to choose between supporting Slovenia or being left to the mercy of Milošević. At the last ever congress of the Yugoslav League of Communists in January 1990, the Slovenes called for complete independence for each of the republican communist parties, a move rejected by the Serbs and their allies. The Slovene delegates walked out of the congress, followed by the Croats, who were now led by the reform-oriented **Ivica Račan**, effectively burying the Yugoslav League of Communists for good.

Democratization was moving at different speeds in different republics, however, making a smooth, pan-Yugoslav transition to noncommunist rule impossible. May 1989 saw the creation of Croatia's first noncommunist political organizations, among them the Croatian Democratic Union, or **HDZ**, led by former army general and dissident historian **Franjo Tuđman** (1922–99). The HDZ held their first congress in February 1990, calling for Croatia's right to secede from Yugoslavia and for a reduction in the number of Serbs in Croatia's police force and state bureaucracy. This anti-Yugoslav tone caught the mood of a country increasingly frustrated by the state's failure to offer any resistance to Milošević, and the HDZ easily won Croatian **elections** in April 1990. On May 13, a football match between Dinamo Zagreb and Red Star Belgrade was abandoned on account of a three-way fight between the two sets of fans and the Serb-dominated police, worsening relations between Croatia and Serbia still further. When the Sabor met on May 30, Tuđman was sworn in as president, and Croatian "statehood" (a potential step to full independence) was declared. The HDZ's **Stipe Mesić** became Croatia's first post-communist prime minister. The Sabor immediately began work on a new **constitution**, which contained one highly controversial passage: the Serbs who lived in Croatia were no longer to be classified as one of the constituent nations of the republic, but as a national minority – a wording which caused understandable anxiety among the Serbs themselves.

The rebellion of Croatia's Serbs

Ever since Milošević's rise to power, the Serbs of Croatia (numbering 580,000 according to the 1991 census, most of whom lived in the arc of territory that ran alongside Croatia's border with Bosnia-Hercegovina) had been subjected to a Belgrade media campaign designed to make them feel endangered by their Croatian neighbours. In February 1990, the Serbian Democratic Party (**SDS**) was formed in the largely Serbian town of Knin, just inland from Šibenik, and soon assumed leadership of a community fearful of what might happen to them in a Croatia increasingly independent of Belgrade. On June 2 the SDS organized a referendum on autonomy for Serbs living in Croatia. The Croatian authorities banned the referendum, but weren't able to prevent it. Not surprisingly, the vote was massively in favour of autonomy.

1990

Croatia holds its first multi-party elections in April. Split basketball team Jugoplastika win the Euroleague for the second year in a row in the same month.

1990

Leaders of Croatia's Serbian community declare autonomy in December.

1991

A clash between Yugoslav forces and Croatian police near the Plitvice Lakes in March is symptomatic of escalating tension.

Throughout the spring and summer of 1990 the Knin Serbs had been arming themselves with the connivance of the intelligence services in Serbia proper, aided by pro-Serb officers in the **Yugoslav People's Army**, the **JNA**. In July of that year the SDS declared the autonomy of the Knin region, creating the so-called **Kninska Krajina**. The Krajina declared its independence from Croatia in February 1991, seeking union with Serbia. The rebellion now spread to other areas of the republic: in March, the Serb-dominated town council of Pakrac in Slavonia stated that it no longer recognized the Croatian authorities, provoking the latter to send in the police to re-establish control of the town. The JNA moved in to keep the peace.

The drift to war

Despite the installation of democratically elected governments in Croatia and Slovenia, the state of Yugoslavia still existed at the end of 1990, and many feared that the JNA – possibly with the connivance of Milošević – would launch a military coup to prevent its break-up. However the JNA surprised everyone by failing to act, despite numerous promptings from the Serbian leader. Sensing that the break-up of Yugoslavia was now inevitable, Milošević began instead to plan for the next best thing: the creation of a **Greater Serbia** which would include all the parts of Croatia and Bosnia-Hercegovina where Serbs lived.

Belgrade subsequently stepped up aid and encouragement to the Knin Serbs, and in March 1991 Knin paramilitaries took control of the Plitvice National Park. Croatian police units were dispatched to arrest them, and the resulting shoot-out produced the first casualties of the Serb–Croat conflict, with two Serbs and one Croat killed. The JNA moved in, ostensibly to keep the two factions apart, but in reality sealing off the area from Croatian civilian control, a pattern to be repeated elsewhere as the spring and summer progressed. On April 29 the Croat village of Kijevo near Knin was surrounded by Serb irregulars and its inhabitants were either forced to leave or shot – the first step in a campaign to **ethnically cleanse** the Serb-held parts of Croatia of any remaining Croats.

On May 17 the head of Yugoslavia's presidency, the Serb Borislav Jović, came to the end of his one-year term. The next incumbent was due to be Croatia's delegate, Stipe Mesić. Other members of the presidency were split on whether to endorse his accession: four members voted for Mesić and four against, leaving Yugoslavia without a head of state.

The Slovenes had voted for full independence from Yugoslavia in a referendum in December 1990; on May 19, 1991, the Croats followed suit. Coordinating their actions, both Slovenia and Croatia declared their **independence** on June 26. Yugoslav Prime Minister Ante Marković, still believing that the federation could be saved, ordered the JNA to secure the country's borders, but Slovene territorial units quickly surrounded and neutralized JNA columns, and the "war" came to an end ten days later with the EU offering to mediate. The Slovenes and Croats agreed to place a three-month moratorium on independence, while the JNA withdrew from Slovenia and the Serbs and their allies agreed to recognize Stipe Mesić as Yugoslav president. In terms of injecting new life into Yugoslavia the agreement was meaningless – Slovenia had won de facto independence if not outright recognition, while the fate of Croatia was left to be fought over.

1991

Croatia declares its independence from Yugoslavia in June. It re-declares its independence on October 8 following an EEC-sponsored moratorium.

1991

The Croatian National Guard, the nucleus of the future national army, is formed in April.

1991

Sporadic violence turns into full-scale war in August; the Yugoslav People's Army begins its assault on Vukovar.

The war in Croatia

The withdrawal of the JNA from Slovenia meant that military strength could now be concentrated in the Serb-inhabited areas of Croatia. In late August the JNA and Serb irregulars launched a major offensive to gain control of eastern Slavonia, beginning with air bombardments of Vukovar and Vinkovci. In response, the newly formed Croatian National Guard began a blockade of all JNA barracks in Croatia. Areas under firm JNA and Serb control – a chain running from Knin in the southwest through the Plitvice area, Slunj, Glina and Petrinja to the environs of Pakrac in the west – were organized into the **Republic of the Serbian Krajina** (**RSK**), and Croats who lived in the region were expelled, creating almost half a million refugees. In October, JNA and Montenegrin forces began the siege of **Dubrovnik**, an operation designed to weaken Croatian morale and reward Montenegro for its support of the Serbs with opportunities for territorial aggrandizement and plunder.

The Serb advance in eastern Slavonia was held up by the defenders of **Vukovar**, who displayed incredible heroism against vastly superior odds. Many believe that Zagreb could have done more to aid Vukovar's defenders, but saw a prolonged siege as a useful way of gaining international sympathy for the Croatian cause. Vukovar fell on November 18, after which the Serb–JNA forces began the bombardment of the next big city to the north, **Osijek**.

The Croatian fightback

The defence of Croatia had initially been a hastily improvised affair, but as fighting continued, the Croats gradually assembled a highly motivated military force armed with weapons captured from JNA barracks. Serb advances were halted, while a counteroffensive won back portions of western Slavonia in December. Both Croatian paramilitaries and regular forces committed acts of revenge: the murder of civilians, torture of prisoners and dynamiting of Serb-owned houses was widespread throughout Croatia.

The EU made consistent attempts to bring the two warring sides to the table, however, and agreement became possible once it became clear that the Serb–JNA offensive had been stalled by tenacious Croatian defence. The **Geneva Agreement** brokered a ceasefire: the Croats agreed to end the siege of all remaining JNA barracks, and the JNA agreed to withdraw from Croatia. A UN peacekeeping force, UNPROFOR, was deployed to police the ceasefire line.

Meanwhile, Croatia was emerging from its diplomatic isolation. The Germans believed that pan-European recognition of Slovenia and Croatia would dissuade the JNA from further aggression, and despite initial opposition from the French and British, **Croatian statehood** was recognized by all the EEC countries on January 15, 1992.

The ceasefire wasn't perfect, and shells continued to fall on Osijek, Dubrovnik and other Croatian towns. Summer 1992 saw a Croatian counterattack break the siege of Dubrovnik, and in January 1993 the Croats recaptured the area around Maslenica in northern Dalmatia, taking the pressure off Zadar. When the Croats took the Medak Pocket (Medački džep) near Gospić in September, irregular troops allegedly murdered more than a hundred Serb civilians and prisoners. The international community protested at Croatia's breaches of the truce, but was too preoccupied with events in neighbouring **Bosnia** to take action.

1991	**1991**	**1992**	**1992**
Yugoslav forces begin the bombardment of Dubrovnik on October 9.	Vukovar falls on November 18 after a three-month siege.	The EU officially recognizes Croatian independence in January. The USA follows suit in April.	Violence flares in the multi-ethnic republic of Bosnia-Hercegovina, sparking a three-year war involving Serbs, Bosniaks and Croats.

The war in Bosnia

The ethnic balance in **Bosnia-Hercegovina** was more delicate than that of any other Yugoslav republic, with a three-way split between Serbs, Croats and Muslims. The Croats, who made up about twenty percent of the population, were scattered throughout central Bosnia, and made up the majority in western Hercegovina near the border with Dalmatia.

EU leaders had recognized Bosnia-Hercegovina's independence in April 1992 in the hope that it would discourage any attempts to partition it. In fact it had the opposite effect, and a Serbian community which wanted no part in an independent Bosnia moved towards armed rebellion. A familiar pattern of events ensued: Serbian irregulars aided by the JNA quickly gained control of areas where Serbs lived, together with any strategic towns that potentially stood in their way, ejecting or murdering a large portion of the non-Serb population.

Initially, Bosnian Croats and Bosnian Muslims cooperated in the struggle against the Serbs, although the highly organized Bosnian-Croat army – the Croatian Defence Council or **HVO** – remained independent of the largely Muslim army of the Bosnian government in Sarajevo. With Croats and Muslims in central Bosnia increasingly squeezed by Serbian successes, the two sides started fighting each other for territory, beginning a vicious Croat–Bosnian war which began in spring 1993 and continued sporadically for a year. The conflict was disastrous for the Croats of central Bosnia, who were forced to flee towards Hercegovina or Croatia proper. It was also disastrous for the international reputation of the Croatian state, whose support for the HVO in Bosnia led to accusations that Tuđman was as cynical as Milošević in his attempts to destroy Bosnia by carving it up into ethnically pure units. Croatian atrocities in Bosnia – the massacre of at least 104 Muslim civilians in the village of Ahmići, the internment of Muslim men in Dretelj concentration camp and the destruction of the five hundred-year-old Turkish bridge at Mostar – were propaganda disasters for the Croatian cause.

The road to Dayton

In the end the Croat–Muslim conflict was brought to an end by the US, which had adopted a harder line against the Serbs since the election of President Clinton in 1992. United States sympathies were primarily with the Bosnian Muslims and their besieged capital of Sarajevo, but it was widely recognized that Croat military power would have to play a part in any solution. The US-sponsored **Washington Agreement** of March 1994 created a federation of Croats and Muslims in Bosnia-Hercegovina, and an alliance between this Croat–Muslim Federation and the state of Croatia. The Croats of western Hercegovina continued to run their territory (so-called "**Herceg-Bosna**") as if it was an independent statelet, although this was overlooked in the interests of unity.

In Croatia proper, the Croats threw the Serbs out of western Slavonia in the operation known as **Blijesak** (Flash) on May 1–2, allowing the Croatian army to liberate Serb-held parts of Bosnia near the Croatian border. On August 4, the **Oluja** (Storm) offensive was launched with an artillery bombardment of Knin, and the Serbian Krajina collapsed within three days. Fearing reprisals, the Serbian population fled through Serb-controlled Bosnian territory into Serbia proper. Oluja was followed by successful Croat–Muslim operations in Bosnia which, combined with NATO air

1993

Bosnian Croatian forces destroy the sixteenth-century Stari Most bridge in Mostar.

1995

Croatia's successful Oluja offensive brings the war in Croatia to an end in August.

1995

The Dayton Accords formally end the war in Bosnia-Hercegovina in December.

strikes in September, persuaded both the Bosnian Serbs and their masters in Belgrade to seek a negotiated peace.

The war in Croatia had virtually ended with the Oluja campaign, although the Serbs remained in control of eastern Slavonia. According to the US-sponsored **Erdut Agreement**, eastern Slavonia would be governed by the UN for a transitional period before being returned to Croatia in January 1998. The war in Bosnia was formally brought to an end by the **Dayton Accords** of November 10, 1995, which created a unified Bosnian state comprising two so-called "entities": one Serbian and one Croat–Muslim.

Croatia after the war

The HDZ, which had come to power in 1990, was a broad movement which aimed to unify all Croats in the face of an outside menace. If it had any ideology at all, it was right of centre, preaching traditional family values, respect for the Catholic Church and national solidarity. The movement's creator, and Croatia's first president, **Franjo Tuđman**, was not a great admirer of Western democracy and did not want to be constrained by a strong parliament. From the start, the advisory bodies assembled by the president had more power than the Sabor or the prime minister, and policy was usually decided by Tuđman's inner circle of confidants.

The HDZ's authoritarian streak was seen as a necessary evil while the nation was fighting for its survival in 1991, but began to look increasingly anachronistic as the years progressed, while the government's actions at home and in Bosnia helped significantly to tarnish the reputation of the new nation. After 1995, Croatia dragged its feet in helping Serbs who had fled the country to return and seemed to be providing the Croats of Hercegovina with moral support in their attempts to frustrate full implementation of the Dayton Accords, something which led the West to believe that Tuđman was still secretly working for the partition of Bosnia-Hercegovina. Croatia was threatened with UN sanctions in 1996 and again in 1999 following her refusal to extradite suspects to the Hague war-crimes tribunal, while the country's unsatisfactory state of democracy – with free and fair elections rendered impossible by the fact that the state-owned TV network was a blatant government mouthpiece – ensured that Croatia was held at arm's length by the EU.

In the meantime, daily life for many Croats was becoming increasingly hard. The country ended the decade with twenty percent unemployment, an average wage of around US$400 a month and many companies unable to pay salaries with any regularity.

The January 2000 elections

Tuđman died on December 10, 1999 without a clear successor as head of the HDZ. The opposition parties, united by a desire to defeat the HDZ, had formed a five-party alliance led by the **SDP** (**Social Democratic Party**; basically rebranded former communists) and the **HSLS** (right-of-centre liberals). The SDP–HSLS coalition easily won the elections of January 2000, with the SDP's **Ivica Račan** taking over as prime minister. Presidential elections at the end of January produced a surprise win for

1998

Vukovar and Ilok return peacefully to Croatian control in January.

1998

Croatia's football team comes third in the World Cup; striker Davor Šuker is the tournament's top scorer.

2000

In Croatia's fourth post-communist parliamentary election, the HDZ loses its majority for the first time.

centrist candidate **Stipe Mesić**, the jocular charmer who had once served as the unenthusiastic president of a dying Yugoslavia. The results were greeted with glee by an international community desperate to see some signs of genuine democratic development in Croatia, and the country's diplomatic position began to improve almost overnight.

The post-Tuđman era

Despite an increase in foreign investment and a boom in sectors of the economy such as tourism and property, the vast majority of Croats didn't experience any appreciable rise in living standards during the Račan administration's four-year term. The biggest strain on the government came from the demands made on it by the **International War Crimes Tribunal** in The Hague – an institution with which Croatia had to cooperate in order to be accepted as a candidate for EU and NATO membership. Most Croats accepted that individuals had committed atrocities during the 1991–95 war, but expected The Hague to concentrate on rounding up prominent Serbian perpetrators rather than focusing attention on Croatian suspects.

Things got serious in July 2001 when The Hague put popular general **Ante Gotovina** on its wanted list. Gotovina – a former Foreign Legionary with a criminal record in France – was an officer-in-charge during the Oluja campaigns of 1995, when numerous atrocities are alleged to have taken place. There was never any suggestion that Gotovina had taken part in atrocities himself, however, and most Croats felt that Gotovina was being scapegoated by an international community that wanted all ex-Yugoslav nations to accept equal blame for the war regardless of what took place on the ground. Gotovina himself went into hiding, evading capture until December 2005 when he turned up in Tenerife.

The Hague controversy left Račan in charge of a coalition seriously weakened by defections to the opposition. The HDZ re-emerged to present themselves as the true guardians of patriotic values. However, HDZ leaders studiously avoided direct links with the right-wing groups who organized mass demonstrations in Gotovina's defence, preferring instead to project a moderate image. Aware that Croatian voters were more interested in managerial competence than ideological extremes, new HDZ leader **Ivo Sanader** ditched many of the hard-liners of the Tuđman era and promoted technocrats in their place.

The HDZ emerged from the **parliamentary elections** of November 2003 as the single largest party in the Sabor and Sanader took over as prime minister. Despite a few changes of emphasis however, the main themes of post-Tuđman politics – economic reform at home and candidature for both the EU and NATO – remained essentially unchanged. Despite its earlier support for war-crimes suspects, the HDZ in government showed more willingness in cooperating with the Hague Tribunal than anyone expected.

The political present

The peaceful post-Tuđman changeover from HDZ to SDP and back again seemed to confirm that Croatia was becoming an ordinary European democracy. In January 2005

2001	2002	2005
Goran Ivanišević becomes Wimbledon champion, defeating Pat Rafter in five sets.	Skier Janica Kostelić wins three golds at the Salt Lake City Winter Olympics.	The Zagreb–Split motorway opens for business.

Stipe Mesić won another five-year term in presidential elections, while Sanader's HDZ won another general election in 2007. The country's **accession to NATO** in April 2009 appeared to cement Croatia's position on the international stage.

By 2009, however, the onset of the global financial crisis forced the government to cut public spending, provoking outcry from an embittered public. A spate of mafia-related crimes focused attention on the government's failure to deal with large-scale corruption, throwing doubt on whether the country was ready for EU membership. The timetable for Croatia's accession to the Union was disrupted by a dispute over territorial waters with Slovenia, the Slovenes vowing to veto Croatia's European entry until the argument had been resolved in their favour.

Beset by problems, Prime Minister Ivo Sanader abruptly resigned in July 2009. His successor as prime minister, **Jadranka Kosor**, quickly patched up the border dispute with Slovenia, but had few fresh answers to the country's economic woes. The **presidential elections** of December 2010 were won by the centre-left candidate – mild-manned lawyer and contemporary-music composer **Ivo Josipović** – promising a pro-EU course and a renewed campaign against corruption.

Corruption and protests

The attentions of Croatia's **anti-corruption** investigators caused former PM Sanader to flee the country in December 2010. He was extradited from Austria to Croatia six months later – and promptly charged with accepting a succession of bribes while in office. The Sanader case opened up the whole question of how much progress Croatian public life had actually made in the twenty years since the fall of communism: was Croatia more corrupt than anywhere else in Central Europe? Was the state administration rotten to the core? Or was Croatia simply under more scrutiny than any other country?

A wave of **anti-government protests** organized via Facebook and other social networks in early 2011 suggested that the public were deserting traditional party leaders in favour of direct action. The protests united both the student left and the nationalist right, and had a strong anti-EU component. Resentment towards Europe and the international community reached a peak in April 2011, when the Hague Tribunal found former general Ante Gotovina guilty of war crimes and sentenced him to 24 years in prison. Croatians gathered spontaneously on Zagreb's main square to protest the verdict, but public anger petered out in the days and weeks that followed.

Accession to the EU

Croatian–EU negotiations were completed in summer 2011 and a date (July 1, 2013) was set for the country's induction into the union. In the **parliamentary elections** of December 2011, the centre-left coalition led by the SDP won a convincing victory, and the extreme right did rather badly – suggesting that the street protests of 2011 had had a negligible effect on radicalizing the electorate. The victors consolidated their success by calling a snap **referendum** on EU membership in January 2012. The turnout was poor (43.5 percent), but the "yes" vote was overwhelming.

While Croatia's tourist industry continues to generate increasing revenue, other sectors of the economy remain mired in recession. The government has little choice but to cut budgets, slash wages for state employees and hope that EU membership will bring increased investment.

2009	2010	2012	2013
Croatia joins NATO.	Serbian president Boris Tadić visits Vukovar, paying his respects to Croatian war victims.	Croatian footballer Luka Modrić signs for Real Madrid for a €37 million fee.	Croatia joins the EU.

A history of Croatia in ten albums

Croatia has always been at the heart of pop and rock culture, and music has often gone hand in hand with social and political change. This was particularly true in the 1970s and 80s, when a stagnant communist regime lost control over youth culture, opening the doors to a vibrant home-grown music scene. Locals are still proud to point out that the Zagreb New Wave (Zagrebački novi val) of the 1980s produced some of the finest post-punk music east of the English Channel. For foreigners brought up on Western pop, the breadth and vision of Croatian popular music can be quite a revelation – the list that follows is a highly subjective guide to further exploration.

Arsen Dedić *Čovjek kao ja* (A Man Like Me; 1969). Croatian pop was born out of the Adriatic tourist boom of the 1960s, when Eurovision-inspired song festivals were staged in Croatia's coastal cities. It was classically trained musician Arsen Dedić who transformed the variety-show music of the day into poetic gold, crafting songs that deserve comparison with Serge Gainsbourg, Jacques Brel and Leonard Cohen. His achingly romantic debut album was one of the first LPs to find its way into every self-respectingly stylish Croatian home, and it remains a treasure-trove of blissfully melancholic songs. Standout track: *Kuća pored mora* (House Beside the Sea).

Josipa Lisac *Dnevnik jedne ljubavi* (Diary of a Love Affair; 1973). Another product of the easy-listening song contests of the Sixties, Josipa Lisac combined a gutsy, blues-tinged voice with an extravagant on-stage persona to become the one true diva Croatian showbiz has produced. *Dnevnik* occupies a unique niche in Croatian pop: a concept album charting the course of an affair (significantly, from the female point of view) through a rich blend of jazz, soul, funk and rock. The percussion breaks in particular will have would-be DJs scrambling for their samplers. Standout track: *Kao stranac* (Like a Stranger).

Prljavo kazalište *Prljavo kazalište* (1979). According to legend, Zagreb band Prljavo kazalište (Dirty Theatre) were Rolling Stones fans who were so bad at playing their instruments that they took to the three-chord style of punk rock instead. Whatever the story, they produced Croatia's first punk album, an epochal collection of adrenalin-rush riffs that set the standard for Zagreb's emerging New Wave. With lyrics tackling previously no-go subjects such as suburban boredom and social hypocrisy, the album was also a landmark in demonstrating that you could be ironic about socialism without getting arrested. Standout track: *Sretno dijete* (Happy Child).

Azra *Ravno do dna* (Straight to the Bottom; 1982). Azra were by far the most popular outfit to emerge from the Zagreb New Wave and still inspire mass adoration – although they remain the most difficult of Croatian bands for foreigners to get a grip of. Ranging from melodic punk to plodding white reggae, their songs were really about the lyrics of frontman Johnny Stulić, whose tales of urban angst and political directionlessness caught the mood of the times. Stulić emigrated to the Netherlands in 1990, adding to his enduring mystique as the missing spokesman for a lost generation. *Ravno do dna* captures the group at their energetic best, performing live at the legendary (but now defunct) *Kulušić* club in 1981 – when Azra famously sold out the venue for nine nights in a row. Standout track: *Poljska u mome srcu* (Poland in My Heart).

Haustor *Treći svijet* (Third World; 1984). The most innovative act to emerge from the Zagreb New Wave was Haustor, a group that melded post-punk, ska and world music to become the most intelligent ex-Yugoslav pop act of all time. All four of their 1980s albums sound remarkably fresh today, although *Treći svijet* is by far the strangest. It's basically an avant-garde reggae album, packed with skeletal rhythms, jagged guitars and idiosyncratic melodic surprises. Erstwhile Haustor frontman Darko Rundek is still pushing the musical boundaries with his Paris-based project Cargo Orkestar – their 2008 album *Mhm a-ha oh yea da-da* garnered Europe-wide critical acclaim. Standout track: *Treći svijet*

Mance *Čovjek s Katange* (Man from Katanga; 1996). Croatia's music scene went into deep hibernation during the war years of the early 1990s, and it was only due to the enthusiasm of grass-roots enthusiasts that the gigging scene finally recovered. Nothing better illustrates the do-it-yourself spirit of the times than the debut album by Mance, a reclusive singer-songwriter with a surreal storytelling style. Recorded at home on primitive equipment (passing traffic and birdsong can be heard in the background), *Man from Katanga* started out as a cassette-only release on Kekere Aquarium – a label that basically consisted of a Zagreb student with a borrowed tape recorder and lofty dreams of selling at least twenty copies of the album. Although subsequently re-released on CD, it remains Croatia's greatest cult record. Standout track: *Ja noćas ništa nisam jeo* (I Didn't Have Anything To Eat Tonight).

Urban *Žena dijete* (Woman Child; 1998). With the Nineties in full swing, the first real signs that Croatian rock had returned from the dead came not from Zagreb but Rijeka – the only other city in the country that could boast a New Wave past. With a sprightly collection of well-crafted songs and a mixture of both guitar-based and electronic arrangements, Damir Urban demonstrated that Croatia could still produce rock albums of originality and scope. Standout track: *Mala Truba* (Loser).

Edo Maajka *No Sikiriki* (No Worries; 2004). The cadences of the Croatian language are ideally suited to rap music, and it's no surprise that hip-hop played a major role in Zagreb's recovery as a musically relevant city in the late Nineties. The one undisputed classic to emerge from the genre came courtesy of Edo Maajka (real name Edin Osmić), a refugee from the Bosnian town of Brčko who had stayed in Zagreb after the war. Edo Maajka's texts about war, displacement and ethnic angst came from personal experience and left no raw nerves untouched. Packed with wit, humanity and righteous anger (and musically innovative to boot), *No Sikiriki* is everything a good hip-hop album should be. Standout track: *Mater Vam Jebem* (Screw You).

Let 3 *Bombardiranje Srbije i Čačka* (The Bombardment of Serbia and Čačak; 2006). Doyens of the Rijeka alternative scene since the late 1980s, Let 3 (Flight No. 3) are Croatian pop's prime provocateurs, whether performing in drag, releasing albums containing nothing but silence or baring their buttocks on live TV. Filled with in-jokes, infantile vulgarity and bone-crunchingly good riffs, much of their musical output is a viciously sarcastic reflection on mainstream Croatian culture. *Bombardiranje* went one step further, re-creating a kitsch Yugoslavia filled with country-dancing peasants and bombastic folk-pop anthems. The result was a profoundly humane work of art, parodying – among other things – the flag-waving chauvinism of stadium-filling folk-rockers all over the Balkan peninsula. Standout track: *Riječke pičke* (Rijeka girls).

TBF *Galerija Tutnplok* (2007). If you're after a state-of-the-nation snapshot of contemporary Croatian society then look no further than TBF (short for "The Beat Fleet"), a Split-based rap collective whose songs describe the Croatia that has emerged from two decades of post-communist transformation. Combining alternative attitude with melodic pop instincts, TBF have become a national institution by expressing general concerns about power, corruption and bourgeois greed in wry, I-don't-know-whether-to-laugh-or-cry style, and the fact that their songs are delivered in Dalmatian dialect only adds to the sense of down-to-earth jocularity. They also have a habit of sampling the Dalmatian crooners who kick-started Croatian pop culture in the Sixties: never have Croatia's diverse musical histories been so successfully united in one band. Standout track: *Fantastična* (Fantastic).

Books

There's a dearth of good books about Croatia in the English language. Many of the most entertaining accounts are by nineteenth-century travellers to the Adriatic, though sadly their books are often only available from larger public libraries or specialist book dealers. The number of publications devoted to the break-up of the former Yugoslavia is considerable: we've listed the best of them, rather than trying to offer an exhaustive survey of the entire field. In the reviews that follow, titles marked ★ are especially recommended.

HISTORY AND POLITICS

Phyllis Auty *Tito*. Originally researched when the dictator was still alive, this book is over-deferential towards its subject and offers little in the way of salacious gossip. However, it's still the best available chronology of the man and his career, and works quite well as a general history of twentieth-century Yugoslavia.

Catherine Wendy Bracewell *The Uskoks of Senj: Piracy, Banditry and Holy War in the Sixteenth-century Adriatic*. Definitive and scholarly account of the Uskoks, which lays to rest some of the more romantic myths surrounding their freebooting activities. It's also an excellent introduction to sixteenth-century Adriatic life in general.

Milovan Djilas *Tito: the Story from Inside* (o/p). Montenegrin communist Djilas was Tito's right-hand man in the 1940s, before falling foul of the regime and becoming Yugoslavia's most celebrated dissident. As lighthearted as it is bitter, this is an entertaining series of digressions on the nature of power rather than a straightforward biography. The same author's *Conversations with Stalin* and *The New Class* offer further insights into the workings of the communist mind.

Robin Harris *Dubrovnik: A History*. Elegantly written journey through the past of one of the Mediterranean's most fascinating cities. As definitive an account as there is.

★ **John R. Lampe** *Yugoslavia as History*. If a general account of Yugoslavia and its peoples is what you're looking for, then this is the best place to start – the author has carefully sifted all the existing scholarship on the subject to produce an objective, accessible history.

★ **Branka Magaš** *Croatia Through History: the Making of a European State*. Thoroughly engrossing history of Croatia from the earliest times to the declaration of independence in 1991. Weighing in at almost 750 pages it's a bit too heavy to take on holiday, but makes an ideal choice if long-term reference is what you need.

Michael McConville *A Small War in the Balkans*. Chapter and verse on British commando campaigns in the former Yugoslavia during World War II, written – with an eye for telling detail rather than dewy-eyed nostalgia – by one of the old soldiers themselves.

★ **Marcus Tanner** *Croatia: a Nation Forged in War*. The best concise history of Croatia currently available. Balanced, thorough and written with verve by an *Independent* journalist who observed Yugoslavia's disintegration at first hand.

Rebecca West *Black Lamb and Grey Falcon*. Based on West's journey through Yugoslavia in the 1930s, this doorstop of a book has long been considered a classic of travel writing – so "classic" in fact that people have tended to become over-reliant on West as a source of insight. Mixing opinionated observations with character sketches and extensive forays into history, it is definitely an acquired taste, particularly the sweeping generalizations about the Balkan Slavs, about whom West has a tendency to be over-rhapsodic. The first quarter of the book covers Croatia, after which the intrepid author moves on to Bosnia, Serbia, Macedonia and Montenegro.

THE BREAK-UP OF YUGOSLAVIA

Christopher Bennett *Yugoslavia's Bloody Collapse*. Scholarly and informed account from a journalist who was resident in Zagreb when war broke out. His central thesis – that Yugoslavia's break-up was far from inevitable until the rise of Serbian national communism under Milošević – is convincingly argued.

★ **Misha Glenny** *The Fall of Yugoslavia*. A vivid and often moving front-line reportage of the conflict by the BBC's former Central Europe correspondent, this is a classic of modern reporting. The same author's *The Balkans* is a compendious account of southeastern European history from the early nineteenth century onwards, in which Croatia plays a walk-on part. It's sometimes too wide-ranging for its own good, but Glenny's attempt to explain the history of the Balkans – and the outside world's meddling in Balkan affairs – is consistently readable and thought-provoking.

★ **Laura Silber and Alan Little** *The Death of Yugoslavia* (UK)/*Yugoslavia: Death of a Nation* (US). Combining journalistic immediacy with prodigious research, this is by far the best blow-by-blow account of the war, although it sheds little light on the long-term causes of Yugoslavia's demise. The authors had access to many of the key players in the events described, resulting in a wealth of revealing quotes.

Brendan Simms *Unfinest Hour: Britain and the Destruction of Bosnia*. Masterly dissection of the cynicism, incompetence and pure intellectual cowardice that characterized British policy towards the former Yugoslavia in the 1990s. Simms convincingly argues that British dithering was crucial in prolonging the Bosnian war (and the misery of its inhabitants), although he rejects the theory – popular among Croatian nationalists – that the British secret services deliberately stoked the conflict between Bosnia's Croats and Muslims.

Mark Thompson *A Paper House*. Thompson travelled throughout Yugoslavia on the eve of its break-up to produce this insightful book, part travelogue, part analysis of a fragmenting society. The same author's *Forging War: the Media in Croatia, Serbia, Bosnia and Hercegovina* examines the role of the Yugoslav press in stoking ethnic hatred.

FICTION

Ivo Andrić *The Bridge on the Drina*. A Croat who grew up in Bosnia and wrote in the Serbian literary language, Andrić left a vast body of work which currently lies unclaimed by any of Yugoslavia's successor states – despite the fact that he won the Nobel Prize for Literature in 1960. A complex, generation-spanning narrative set in Bosnia under the Ottoman Empire, this book is typical of Andrić's oeuvre.

Daša Drndić *Trieste*. Highly regarded historical novel dealing with the Jews of northeastern Italy during the Holocaust. Drndić's method of mixing fiction and fact may not be to everyone's taste, with already-published memoirs and documentary materials propelling the narrative forward, but this remains a compelling piece of work.

Jean Echenoz *Lightning*. From Goncourt Prize-winning author Echenoz comes this eccentric tale of eccentric electrical engineer Gregor, an East European genius at large in North America. The character is firmly based on real-life inventor Nikola Tesla (see box, p.75).

Zoran Ferić *Death of the Little Match Girl*. Zagreb's answer to the Coen brothers, Ferić is a master at mixing the everyday with the grotesque. Set on the island of Rab, this compelling slice of Croatia noir explores the deviant underbelly of an outwardly idyllic Mediterranean community.

★ **Miljenko Jergović** *Sarajevo Marlboro*. A Bosnian Croat who grew up in Sarajevo and currently lives outside Zagreb, Jergović is one of Croatia's most productive novelists, essayists and magazine feature-writers. This sparkling collection of short stories recounts Balkan lives, loves and tragedies with the kind of wry, self-deprecating humour that's typical of the city in the title. Also available in English, and highly recommended, are the novels: *Ruta Tannenbaum*, dealing with the fate of a Zagreb Jewish family on the eve of World War II; *Mama Leone*, about the experiences of growing up in Yugoslavia and being exiled after its collapse; and *The Walnut House*, a century-long family saga with Dubrovnik one of the key locations.

★ **Miroslav Krleža** *The Return of Philip Latinowicz*. The best-known novel by Croatia's leading twentieth-century writer, in which a painter returns home to a provincial Slavonian town sometime in the 1920s and embarks on an affair which ends in tragedy. Intended as a dissection of Croatia's directionless upper classes in the wake of World War I, it's not as powerful as his *On the Edge of Reason*, set in the same period, which convincingly preaches the message that bourgeois society is a form of self-deluding madness, but to rebel against it drives you insane.

Jo Nesbø *The Redeemer*. A lot of Western authors have fed upon Croatia's Homeland War of 1991–95 in search of lurid thriller material, and this Scandinavian crime bestseller is one of the most obvious examples. A great holiday read, but don't expect to learn much about Croatia in the process.

★ **Robert Perišić** *Our Man in Iraq*. This comic and incisive satire on the Croatian media could have been written in any country where the demands of corporate news-gathering are slowly taking over from the old-fashioned newspaper values of the past. It's also a wry portrayal of contemporary Zagreb's shifting moral landscape, pitting local against global, alternative culture against mainstream entertainment, and old-fashioned family values against get-ahead-in-the-world hypocrisy and betrayal.

Edo Popović *Zagreb Exit South*. Few writers are as agile and entertaining as Popović when it comes to giving a creative stir to Zagreb's social goulash – especially the concrete suburbs of Novi Zagreb hinted at in this book's title. Describing the trajectories of characters who once belonged to the cool, New Wave Croatia of the 1980s – only to be left on the cusp of middle age bewildered by the fact that society never delivered any of the things they really expected – *Zagreb Exit South* is a typical example of Popović's work. It's just a shame that so little else of his oeuvre has been translated into English.

Dubravka Ugrešić *The Museum of Unconditional Surrender*. Dismayed by Croatia's descent into right-wing authoritarianism, Ugrešić spent most of the 1990s living outside Croatia, and this largely autobiographical novel is a powerful meditation on memory and exile. The same author's more recent *Ministry of Pain* is if anything an even starker read, exploring the loss of homeland experienced by a group of Yugoslav exiles in Amsterdam. Ugrešić's heavyweight collection of essays *Culture of Lies* is an essential read for anyone interested in the negative side of Croatian culture and nationalism in the 1990s.

Croatian

Croatian is a difficult language to learn, and the locals rarely expect anyone to bother, making them all the more pleasantly surprised if you make the effort to learn a few phrases. The vast majority of Croatians speak at least one foreign language: most people – especially the young – speak good English, while German and Italian are also widely spoken on the coast.

Croats, Serbs, Bosnians and Montenegrins can understand one another perfectly well, despite developing separate literary languages at different times in their history. All four languages are traditionally regarded as dialects of a single Slavonic tongue once referred to as Croato-Serbian or Serbo-Croat, although these names are hardly ever used nowadays.

The best of the **self-study courses** available are *Colloquial Croatian* by Celia Hawkesworth (Routledge), closely followed by *Complete Croatian* by David Norris and Vladislava Ribnikar (Teach Yourself).

Grammar and pronunciation

There are three **genders** in Croatian – masculine, feminine and neuter. Masculine nouns usually end with a consonant, feminine nouns with *-a*, neuter nouns with *-o* or *-e*. **Plurals** are usually formed by adding *-i*, *-ovi* or *-evi* to masculine nouns (*autobus*, bus, becomes *autobusi*, buses; *vlak*, train, becomes *vlakovi*, trains); *-e* to feminine nouns (*plaža*, beach, becomes *plaže*, beaches); and *-a* to neuter nouns (*auto*, car, becomes *auta*, cars) – although there are plenty of irregular nouns which don't follow these rules exactly. It's also worth bearing in mind that there are six noun **cases** in Croatian, ensuring that each noun (and any adjectives qualifying it) changes its ending according to what part of the sentence it occupies. Travelling around the coast, for example, you'll notice that "*u Dubrovnik*" means "to Dubrovnik", "*u Dubrovniku*" means "in Dubrovnik" and "*iz Dubrovnika*" means "from Dubrovnik". Similarly, look out for *u Pulu* (to Pula), *u Puli* (in Pula) and *iz Pule* (from Pula).

Pronunciation is not as difficult as it first appears. Every word is spoken exactly as it's written, and each letter represents an individual sound. The only letters you're likely to have problems with are the following consonants, which differ from their English equivalents.

c "ts" as in cats
č "ch" as in church
ć a softer version of č; similar to the "t" in future
đ somewhere between the "d" in endure and the "j" in jam
g always hard, as in get
j "y" as in youth
r always rolled; fulfils the function of a vowel in words like Hrvatska ("Croatia")
š "sh" as in shoe
ž "s" as in pleasure

REGIONAL DIALECTS

You'll find variations in dialect all over Croatia itself, the principal ones being named after the three different ways of saying "what?" – *kaj?*, *ča?* and *što?* In **Zagreb and the Zagorje** people speak *kajkavski*, because of their use of the word *kaj* for "what", while on the **Adriatic coast** people speak *čakavski*, and in Hercegovina and **Slavonia** *štokavski*. The literary language is based on *štokavski*, although the other dialects are heard on the streets and frequently feature on the radio and TV – Croatian soap-operas are full of Dalmatian characters jabbering away melodramatically in *čakavski*.

There are no hard-and-fast rules governing **stress** in Croatian, save to say that it rarely falls on the last syllable of a word, and quite frequently falls on the first.

USEFUL WORDS AND PHRASES

GREETINGS AND CIVILITIES

hello/good day	dobar dan
hi!/bye!	bog!
how are you? (polite)	kako ste?
how are you? (informal)	kako si?
fine, thanks	dobro, hvala
good morning	dobro jutro
good evening	dobra večer
good night	laku noć
goodbye	do viđenja
please	molim
thank you (very much)	hvala (lijepo)
excuse me	izvinite
sorry	oprostite or sorry
here you are	izvolite
let's go!	hajdemo!

BASIC TERMS AND PHRASES

yes	da
no	ne
when?	kada?
where?	gdje?
why?	zašto?
how much?	koliko?
large	veliko
small	malo
more	više
less	manje
good	dobro
bad	loše
cheap	jeftino
expensive	skupo
open	otvoreno
closed	zatvoreno
hot	toplo
cold	hladno
with/without	sa/bez
do you speak English?	govorite li engleski?
I don't understand	ne razumijem
I don't know	ne znam
what is this called in Croatian?	kako se zove ovo na hrvatskom?
Croatia	Hrvatska
Croatian person (m)	Hrvat
Croatian person (f)	Hrvatica
Croatian language	Hrvatski
where are you from (polite)?	odakle ste?
where are you from (familiar)?	odakle si?
I am from…	Ja sam iz…
Australia	Australije
Canada	Kanade
Great Britain	Velike Britanije
England	Engleske
Scotland	Škotske
Wales	Walesa
Northern Ireland	Sjeverne Irske
Ireland	Irske
New Zealand	Nove Zelandije
South Africa	Južne Afrike
the US	Amerike

DIRECTIONS AND GETTING AROUND

where to?	kamo?/kuda?
where is…?	gdje je?/gdje se nalazi…?
the nearest bank	najbliža banka
the nearest hotel	najbliži hotel
here	ovdje
there	tamo
left	lijevo
right	desno
straight on	pravo
backwards	natrag
above; upstairs	gore
below; downstairs	dolje
north	sjever
south	jug
east	istok
west	zapad
I'm lost (m)	Izgubio sam se
I'm lost (f)	Igubila sam se
is it nearby?	je li to blizu?
how far is it?	koliko je daleko?
airport	zračna luka
(bus/train) station	(autobusni/željeznički) kolodvor
platform	kolosijek
bus stop	stajalište autobusa
tram stop	tramvajsko stajalište
port	luka
ferry terminal	trajektna luka
pier	gat
mooring	vez
left-luggage office	garderoba
arrival	polazak
departure	odlazak
what time does the train/bus/ ferry leave?	u koliko sati polazi vlak/ autobus/trajekt?

when does the next bus/ ferry/train leave for...?	kada polazi sljedeći autobus/trajekt/vlak za...?
is it running late?	ima li zakašnenja?
a ticket for ...please	jednu kartu za ...molim
single	u jednom pravcu
return	povratnu kartu
can I reserve a seat?	mogu li rezervirati sjedište?
no smoking	zabranjeno pušenje
entrance	ulaz
exit	izlaz
beach	plaža
car park	parkiralište
cinema	kino
embassy	veleposlanstvo
gallery	galerija
hospital	bolnica
market	tržnica
museum	muzej
optician	optičar
petrol station/gas station	benzinska stanica
pharmacy	ljekarna
police station	policijska stanica
post office	pošta
shop	dućan
stadium	stadion
supermarket	samoposluga
swimming pool	bazen
theatre	kazalište
tourist office	turistički ured/turistički informativni centar

ACCOMMODATION

do you have ...?	imate li...?
a (single/double) room?	(jednokrevetnu/ dvokrevetnu) sobu?
an apartment	apartman
a private room	privatnu sobu
with...	sa...
a double bed	francuskim ležajem
a shower/bath	tušem/banjom
a sea view	pogledom na more
can I see the room?	mogu li pogledati sobu?
do you have anything cheaper?	imate li nešto jeftinije?
bed and breakfast	noćenje i doručak
full board/half board	pansion/polupansion
I have a reservation	imam rezervaciju
can I book a room?	mogu li rezervirati sobu?
key	ključ
where's the nearest campsite?	gdje je najbliži autokamp?
tent	šator
caravan	prikolica
sleeping bag	vreća za spavanje

SHOPPING

where can I buy...?	gdje mogu kupiti...?
bathing costume	kupaći kostim
batteries	baterije
cigarettes	cigarete
cigarette lighter	upaljač
corkscrew	vadičep
food	hranu
matches	šibice
phonecard	telekartu
postage stamps	poštanske marke
postcards	razglednice
soap	sapun
toilet paper	toaletni papir
toothpaste	pastu za zube
towel	ručnik
washing powder	prašak za pranje
how much does it cost?	koliko stoji/koliko košta?
that's expensive	to je skupo

NUMBERS

0	nula
1	jedan
2	dva
3	tri
4	četiri
5	pet
6	šest
7	sedam
8	osam
9	devet
10	deset
11	jedanaest
12	dvanaest
13	trinaest
14	četrnaest
15	petnaest
16	šesnaest
17	sedamnaest
18	osamnaest
19	devetnaest
20	dvadeset
21	dvadeset i jedan
30	trideset
40	četrdeset
50	pedeset
60	šezdeset
70	sedamdeset
80	osamdeset
90	devedeset
100	sto

200	dvjesta
300	trista
1000	tisuća

TIMES AND DATES

day	dan
week	tjedan
month	mjesec
year	godina
today	danas
tomorrow	sutra
yesterday	jučer
the day after tomorrow	prekosutra
the day before yesterday	prekjučer
in the morning	ujutro
in the afternoon	popodne
in the evening	uvečer
early	rano
late	kasno
what time is it?	koliko je sati?
hour	sat
minute	minuta
10 o'clock	deset sati
10.15	deset i petnaest
10.30	deset i trideset or pola jedanaest
10.45	petnaest do jedanaest
Monday	ponedjeljak
Tuesday	utorak
Wednesday	srijeda
Thursday	četvrtak
Friday	petak
Saturday	subota
Sunday	nedjelja
holiday	praznik
church holiday, saint's day	blagdan
January	siječanj
February	veljača
March	ožujak
April	travanj
May	svibanj
June	lipanj
July	srpanj
August	kolovoz
September	rujan
October	listopad
November	studeni
December	prosinac
spring	proljeće
summer	ljeto
autumn	jesen
winter	zima

FOOD AND DRINK

BASIC TERMS

hrana	food
jelovnik	menu
račun	bill
doručak/zajutrak	breakfast
gableci/marenda	brunch
ručak	lunch
večera	dinner
tanjur	plate
pladanj	platter
nož	knife
viljuška	fork
žlica	spoon
čaša	glass
šalica	cup
dobar tek!	bon appetit!
živjeli!/nazdravje!	cheers!

COOKING TERMS

ispod peke/ pod pekom	baked under a lid covered with hot embers
kuhano/lešo	boiled
na ražnju	spit roasted
na roštilju/na žaru	grilled
pečeno/u pećnici	baked
pohani	fried in breadcrumbs
prženo	fried

BASIC FOODS

burek	greasy pastry, usually filled with cheese
jaje	egg
jogurt	yoghurt
kifla	breakfast pastry, croissant
kruh	bread
maslac	butter
masline	olives
maslinovo ulje	olive oil
med	honey
mlijeko	milk
ocat	vinegar
omlet	omelette
papar	pepper
pašteta	pâté
pekmez	jam
riža	rice
salata	salad
šalša	tomato sauce
šećer	sugar
sir	cheese
sol	salt

umak sauce
vrhnje cream

SOUPS (JUHE) AND STARTERS (PREDJELA)

fažol bean soup from Istria
grah soup made from haricot beans
jota bean-and-sauerkraut soup
kobasica sausage
kozji sir goat's cheese
kulen spicy paprika-flavoured pork-and-beef salami from Slavonia
maneštra bean-and-vegetable soup from Istria
punjene paprike stuffed peppers
ovčji sir sheep's cheese
paški sir hard piquant cheese from the island of Pag
pršut home-cured ham
sir iz ulja hard yellow cheese with piquant rind, kept under olive oil
sir s vrhnjem cream cheese
škripavac mild yellow cheese
šunka ham
vrat cured pork neck

VEGETABLES (POVRĆE) AND PASTA (TJESTENINE)

ajvar spicy relish made from puréed aubergines and peppers
bijeli luk garlic
blitva Swiss chard (eaten with fish)
češnjak garlic
đuveđ/đuveč ratatouille-style mixture of vegetables and rice, heavily flavoured with paprika
fuži pasta twirls
gljiva mushroom
grah beans; also bean soup
grašak peas
hren horseradish
kapulica spring onion
kiseli kupus sauerkraut
krastavac cucumber, gherkin
krumpir potato
kukuruz corn on the cob
kupus cabbage
luk onion
miješana salata mixed salad
mlinci ragged sheets of baked pasta dough
mrkva carrot
njoki gnocchi
paprika pepper, paprika
paradajz/pomidor/rajčica tomato
patlidžan aubergine
repa turnip
šampinjoni champignon mushrooms
šparoga asparagus
štrukli dough blobs stuffed with cheese
šurlice pasta twirls
tartufi truffles
zelena salata green salad (usually lettuce)

FISH (RIBA)

bakalar cod (often dried)
barbun mullet
brancin sea bass
brodet/brudet fish stew
buzara wine and garlic sauce used for scampi, mussels and other seafood
cipal golden grey mullet
crni rižot squid risotto
dagnje mussels
girice small fish like whitebait, usually deep-fried whole
grdobina frogfish
hobotnica octopus
iglica garfish
inćun anchovy
jakopove kapice scallops
jastog lobster
jegulja eel
kalamari squid
kamenice oysters
komarča gilt-head sea bream
kapica clam
kovač John Dory
lignje squid
list sole
lubin sea perch
mušule mussels
orada gilt-head sea bream
oslić hake

ostrige oysters
pastrva trout
plava riba "oily fish"; ie anchovies, sardines, mackerel, etc
rak crab
ribice whitebait, sprats
riblja salata literally "fish salad", usually octopus
šaran carp
sipa cuttlefish
škampi scampi
školjke mussels
škrpina/škarpina groper, sea scorpion
skuša mackerel
smuđ pike-perch
som catfish
srdele anchovies
štuka pike
trilja striped or red mullet
žablji kraci frogs' legs
zubatac dentex

MEAT (MESO), POULTRY (PERAD) AND GAME (DIVLJAČ)

arambašica cabbage leaves stuffed with meat and rice
bečki odrezak Wiener schnitzel
bubrezi kidneys
buncek pork hock
ćevapčići/ćevapi grilled mincemeat rissoles
čobanac paprika-flavoured meat stew
govedina beef
gulaš goulash
guska goose
janjetina lamb
jetra liver
junetina young, tender beef (but not veal)
koljenica pork knuckle
kotlet cutlet, chop
kunić rabbit
lungić lean, boneless and tender pork chop
mješano meso mixed-meat grill
nogice pigs' trotters
odrezak escalope of veal or pork
ombolo Istrian pork chop
panceta bacon
pariški odrezak veal cutlet in batter
pašticada beef cooked in wine, vinegar and prunes
patka duck
piletina chicken
pljeskavica hamburger-style minced-meat patty
punjene paprike peppers stuffed with rice and meat
puretina turkey
purica s mlincima turkey with baked pasta sheets
ražnjići pieces of pork grilled on a skewer; kebab
sarma cabbage leaves stuffed with rice and meat
slanina bacon
srneći gulaš venison goulash
srnetina venison
svinjetina pork
teletina veal
zagrebački odrezak schnitzel stuffed with ham and cheese and fried in breadcrumbs

DESSERTS (DESERTI)

čokolada chocolate
fritule or uštipci deep-fried dough balls dusted with icing sugar
kolač cake
kremšnita cream cake or custard slice
krafna doughnut
kroštule deep-fried twists of pastry
makovnjača poppy-seed cake
orehnjača walnut cake
palačinke pancakes
rožata crème-caramel-style custard from Dubrovnik
savijača or štrudla strudel
sladoled ice cream
torta cake

FRUIT (VOĆE)

ananas pineapple
banana banana
breskva peach
dinja melon
grožđe grapes
jabuka apple
jagoda strawberry
kruška pear
limun lemon
lubenica watermelon
marelica apricot
naranča orange
šljiva plum

smokva	fig
trešnja	cherry
višnja	sour cherry

DRINKS (PIĆA)

bambus	red wine and cola
bermet	bitter stomach-settling spirit from Samobor
bevanda	wine mixed with water
bijelo vino	white wine
biska	mistletoe-flavoured brandy
borovnica	blueberry juice/liqueur
čaj	tea
crno vino	red wine
crveno vino	rosé wine
džus or đus	juice
gemišt	white wine and still water
kava	coffee
led/s ledom/bez leda	ice/with ice/without ice
limunada	lemonade
loza/lozovača	grape brandy
maraskino	cherry liqueur
medica	honey-flavoured brandy
mineralna voda	mineral water
orahovača	walnut-flavoured brandy
pelinkovac	bitter juniper-based aperitif
pivo	beer
pjenušac	sparkling wine
pščenično pivo	wheat beer
rakija	brandy
rogačica	carob-flavoured brandy
šljivovica	plum brandy
sok	juice
špricer	white wine and soda
svjetlo pivo	light, lager-style beer
tamno pivo	dark beer, porter
topla čokolada	hot chocolate
travarica	herb-based spirit, similar to Italian grappa
viljamovka	pear brandy
voda	water
vodka	vodka

GLOSSARY OF GENERAL TERMS

autocesta motorway
Beč Vienna
Beograd Belgrade
brdo/brijeg hill
buk waterfall
bura strong northerly wind that blows across the coastal mountains to the Adriatic Sea
centar centre
cesta road
crkva church
dolac dell (in karst areas, a small cultivable area enclosed by wall)
dolina valley
donji grad lower town
draga vale, bay
dvor palace, court, courtyard
dvorac castle
dvorište yard, courtyard
fortica fortress
gaj grove
gat quay
gostiona restaurant, inn
gornji grad upper town
grad town
gradska vijećnica town hall
groblje graveyard
hram temple, church
Jadran Adriatic Sea
jama pit, cave
jezero lake
jugo southerly wind that blows along the coast, frequently associated with wet weather and bad moods
kafič café
kamenjar stony, infertile land; used to describe the arid areas of Hercegovina and inland Dalmatia
kaštel castle, fortress
kavana café
kolo folk dance
kolodvor station
konoba inn, tavern, folksy restaurant
korzo evening promenade
krčma inn, tavern
kuća house
lučka kapetanija harbourmaster's office
luka port
lungomare shoreline road or promenade
Maestral Mild northwesterly wind
Magistrala Highway running the length of the Adriatic coast
mandrać inner harbour for small boats
Mleci Venice
more sea
most bridge
obala shore, quayside
oluja storm
otok island
palača palace

park prirode nature park, nature reserve
pekara or pekarnica bakery
perivoj park, public garden
plaža beach
poljana field, meadow
polje field
poluotok peninsula
put road, way
rat/rt cape
restoran restaurant
rijeka river
riva seafront
riznica treasury
samoposluga supermarket
samostan monastery
selo village
šetalište walkway, promenade
škoj small island
škor/škver shipyard or part of fishing village where boats are repaired
stajalište autobusa bus stop
stari grad (i) old town; (ii) castle
staza path
slastičarnica patisserie
spilja cave
šuma forest, wood
toranj tower
trg square
tržnica market
tvrđava fortress
ulica street
uvala bay
varoš central residential quarter of an old town
vijećnica council chamber, town hall
vikendica holiday house or cottage
vodopad waterfall
vrata gate, door
vrh peak
vrt garden
žal beach
zaljev bay, gulf
zdenac well
ždrilo gorge
zidine walls
županija county
zvonik bell tower, campanile

GLOSSARY OF POLITICAL AND HISTORICAL TERMS

Austria-Hungary Official name adopted by the Habsburg Empire in 1867, designed to make the Hungarians feel that they were equal partners with the Austrians in the imperial enterprise.

AVNOJ Literally "anti-fascist council of national liberation of Yugoslavia", a provisional parliament established by the Partisans during World War II, first convened in Jajce, Bosnia-Hercegovina, in 1943.

Ban Governor or viceroy. Title given to rulers of Croatia appointed by Hungarian (later Austrian) monarchs.

Blijesak "Flash". Name given to the Croatian Army offensive that drove Serbian forces out of western Slavonia in 1995.

Bošnjak Bosnian Muslim.

Četnik Serbian irregular fighter. The term was first coined during the anti-Ottoman struggles of the nineteenth century and subsequently used to describe nationalist anti-communists in World War II, then Serbian forces active in Croatia and Bosnia in 1991–95.

Domovinski rat Homeland War. Official Croatian name for the 1991–95 conflict.

Frankopans Aristocratic family long associated with the island of Krk.

Glagolitic The script used by the Croatian Church in the early Middle Ages. Survived in some areas of Istria and the Kvarner region until the early nineteenth century, when it was replaced by the Latin script.

Habsburg Empire The central European state ruled by the Habsburg family, who first gained control of parts of Austria in the early thirteenth century, and went on to control an empire comprising – among others – Germans, Italians, Czechs, Slovaks, Hungarians, Slovenes and Croats. The empire was broken up in 1918.

Hajduk Brigand. Romantically associated with popular struggles against the Ottoman Turks, the term has positive connotations for Croats, Serbs, Bulgarians and other southeast European peoples.

HDZ Croatian Democratic Union. Right-of-centre pro-independence political movement formed in 1989 and led by Franjo Tuđman. The governing party in Croatia from 1990 to 2000.

Hrvatski narodni preporod Croatian National Renaissance. Name given to the mid-nineteenth-century upsurge in Croatian culture, language and consciousness.

HSLS Croatian Social Liberal Party. Croatia's main centre party; in opposition 1991–2000, briefly shared power with the SDP (see p.449) 2000–02.

HVO Croatian Defence Council. Formed by Croats in Bosnia-Hercegovina to organize themselves militarily against the Serbs (and subsequently Muslims) in the Bosnian war of 1992–95.

Illyria Roman name for the territories that are nowadays roughly covered by the states of Croatia, Bosnia-Hercegovina, Serbia and Albania. The term was resurrected by Napoleon in 1805 with the creation of the Illyrian Provinces, which stretched from Villach in southern Austria to Dubrovnik in Dalmatia. Some Western writers continued to use the term "Illyria" to describe the South Slav lands throughout the nineteenth century.

Illyrianism Early nineteenth-century Croatian cultural movement which stressed the linguistic affinities of Croats and Serbs.

JNA Yugoslav People's Army. Official title of Yugoslavia's army from 1945 to 1991. Generally sided with the Serbs during the 1991–92 conflict.

Knez Prince, duke or (in Dubrovnik and other Dalmatian towns) city governor or rector.

Kralj King

Military frontier (Vojna krajina in Croatian; Militärgrenze in German). Belt of territory running along Croatia's border with Ottoman-controlled Bosnia-Hercegovina, created in the early sixteenth century and finally dismantled in the mid-nineteenth. Designed to prevent Ottoman expansion, it was under the direct rule of Habsburg military bodies in Graz or Vienna.

NDH Puppet Croatian state established under Nazi auspices 1941–45.

Non-Aligned Movement Created by Tito, Nehru and Nasser to give a voice to countries that existed outside the East–West divisions of the Cold War.

Oluja "Storm". The Croatian offensive of August 1995 which finally defeated secessionist Serb forces and brought an end to the war in Croatia.

Partisan Anti-fascist fighter in World War II.

Ragusa Old name for Dubrovnik.

RS Republika Srpska. Name adopted by Serbian-controlled areas of Bosnia after 1992.

RSK Republic of the Serbian Krajina. Serbian name for the territories controlled by Serbian secessionists in Croatia 1991–95.

Sabor Assembly, parliament.

SDP Social Democratic Party. Successor to the SKH, principal opposition party from 1990 to 2000, and leading partner in the coalition elected to power in January 2000.

SKH Croatian League of Communists.

SKJ Yugoslav League of Communists.

Uskok Sixteenth-century freebooters operating out of the port of Senj (see p.222).

Ustaša (plural Ustaše). Croatian Nazi movement, formed by Ante Pavelić, which came to power with German help in 1941, forming the NDH.

Small print and index

A ROUGH GUIDE TO ROUGH GUIDES

Published in 1982, the first Rough Guide – to Greece – was a student scheme that became a publishing phenomenon. Mark Ellingham, a recent graduate in English from Bristol University, had been travelling in Greece the previous summer and couldn't find the right guidebook. With a small group of friends he wrote his own guide, combining a highly contemporary, journalistic style with a thoroughly practical approach to travellers' needs.

The immediate success of the book spawned a series that rapidly covered dozens of destinations. And, in addition to impecunious backpackers, Rough Guides soon acquired a much broader readership that relished the guides' wit and inquisitiveness as much as their enthusiastic, critical approach and value-for-money ethos.

These days, Rough Guides include recommendations from budget to luxury and cover more than 200 destinations around the globe, as well as producing an ever-growing range of eBooks and apps.

Visit **roughguides.com** to see our latest publications.

Rough Guide credits

Editor: Edward Aves
Layout: Anita Singh, Ankur Guha, Nikhil Agarwal
Cartography: Rajesh Mishra
Picture editor: Rhiannon Furbear
Proofreader: Anita Sach
Managing editor: Monica Woods
Assistant editor: Jalpreen Kaur Chhatwal
Production: Charlotte Cade
Cover design: Nicole Newman, Dan May, Anita Singh
Editorial assistant: Olivia Rawes
Photographers: Tim Draper, Martin Richardson
Senior pre-press designer: Dan May
Design director: Scott Stickland
Travel publisher: Joanna Kirby
Digital travel publisher: Peter Buckley
Reference director: Andrew Lockett
Operations coordinator: Becky Doyle
Publishing director (Travel): Clare Currie
Commercial manager: Gino Magnotta
Managing director: John Duhigg

Publishing information

This sixth edition published March 2013 by
Rough Guides Ltd,
80 Strand, London WC2R 0RL
11, Community Centre, Panchsheel Park,
New Delhi 110017, India
Distributed by the Penguin Group
Penguin Books Ltd,
80 Strand, London WC2R 0RL
Penguin Group (USA)
345 Hudson Street, NY 10014, USA
Penguin Group (Australia)
250 Camberwell Road, Camberwell,
Victoria 3124, Australia
Penguin Group (NZ)
67 Apollo Drive, Mairangi Bay, Auckland 1310,
New Zealand
Penguin Group (South Africa)
Block D, Rosebank Office Park, 181 Jan Smuts Avenue,
Parktown North, Gauteng, South Africa 2193
Rough Guides is represented in Canada by Tourmaline
Editions Inc. 662 King Street West, Suite 304, Toronto,
Ontario M5V 1M7
Printed in Singapore

480pp includes index
A catalogue record for this book is available from the British Library
ISBN: 978-1-40936-265-4

3 5 7 9 8 6 4

Help us update

We've gone to a lot of effort to ensure that the sixth edition of **The Rough Guide to Croatia** is accurate and up-to-date. However, things change – places get "discovered", opening hours are notoriously fickle, restaurants and rooms raise prices or lower standards. If you feel we've got it wrong or left something out, we'd like to know, and if you can remember the address, the price, the hours, the phone number, so much the better.

Please send your comments with the subject line "**Rough Guide Croatia Update**" to mail@uk.roughguides.com. We'll credit all contributions and send a copy of the next edition (or any other Rough Guide if you prefer) for the very best emails.

Find more travel information, connect with fellow travellers and book your trip on roughguides.com

ABOUT THE AUTHOR

Jonathan Bousfield first took his bucket and spade to the Adriatic coast in 1975 and has been making regular visits to Croatia ever since. He is the author of the Rough Guides to Croatia and the Baltic States, and the co-author of the Rough Guides to Austria, Bulgaria and Poland. He has also authored DK Eyewitness guides to Bulgaria, Slovenia and Tallinn. In between times he has been a rock critic for a UK newspaper, has edited a listings magazine in Bulgaria, and has resided at various times in Kraków, Riga, Vilnius and Zagreb. He writes extensively about society and culture in Central and Eastern Europe for *Time Out* and Croatian daily *Jutarnji List*.

Acknowledgements

Jonathan Bousfield would like to order double *rakijas* all round for Marina Blagajić and family, Mirjana Darrer, Dorjan Dragojević, Neva and Dan Jelovac, Sanja and Jonathan Kawaguchi, Robert Loher, Toni Lozica, Dubravka Mićić, Ivica Miličević, Vanja Mohorović, Igor Prikaski, Erik Walker and Nevenko Žuvela. And thanks to Gordana for sharing the best bits of chapters 1, 3, 4 and 7.

Stiff drinks are also due to Edward Aves for helping the author across the finishing line, Rajesh Mishra for painstaking labours in preparing new maps, Anita Sach for meticulous proofreading, Rhiannon Furbear for tracking down the wonderful images and Anita Singh, Ankur Guha and Nikhil Agarwal for adroit typesetting.

Readers' letters

Thanks to all the readers who have taken the time to write in with comments and suggestions (and apologies if we've inadvertently omitted or misspelt anyone's name):

John Blackgrove, Greg Caplan, Andrea Cuman, Frieja Current, Malcolm Curtis, J Fraser Muirhead, Helene Jewell, Tracy Lean, John Pindar, Paddy Stone (Mrs), Jeff White.

Photo credits

All photos © Rough Guides except the following:
(Key: t-top; c-centre; b-bottom; l-left; r-right)

p.1 Getty Images: Otto Stadler
p.2 4Corners: Bildagentur Huber
p.4 Corbis: Guido Cozzi
p.5 4Corners: Huber Johanna
p.10 4Corners: Fantuz Olimpio
p.11 Alamy: Hemis (t); imagebroker (c); Jason Wallengren Photography (b)
p.12 Corbis: John Harper
p.15 SuperStock: Juan Carlos (t); Corbis: Rene Mattes (b)
p.16 SuperStock: Josel Azel (t); Alamy: Hemis b)
p.17 Alamy: imagebroker (tl); SuperStock: Alvaro Leiva (tr)
p.18 Getty Images: Alan Cookson (t); SuperStock: Axiom Photographic (bl)
p.19 Alamy: Eye Ubiquitous (b)
p.22 Alamy: Nik Wheeler (t); Terraneo (b)
p.23 Corbis: Owen Franken (t)
p.56 SuperStock: Latitude Stock
p.69 Alamy: Paul Williams (t); Corbis: Graham Lawrence (br)
p.94 Corbis: Guido Cozzi
p.175 Alamy: LOOK Die Bildagentur der Fotografen GmbH (b)
p.203 Corbis: Russell Young (tr)
p.231 SuperStock: Funkystock (t)
p.240 SuperStock: Photononstop
p.243 Corbis: Jean-Pierre Lescourret
p.251 SuperStock: Gunter Kirsch (t)
p.271 Alamy: Borna Cavrag (t)
p.283 SuperStock: Bjanka Kadic
p.353 SuperStock: Photononstop (t)
p.375 Photoshot: Franco Banfi (tl); SuperStock: Raymond Forbes (b)
p.384 SuperStock: Axiom Photographic
p.401 AWL Images: Christian Kober (tr)
p.423 SuperStock: Photononstop (t)

Front cover: Dubrovnik © Johanna Huber/4Corners
Back cover: Pula amphitheatre © Rough Guides (t); Zagorje village © Rough Guides (bl); Sardines © Sensi Images/Alamy (br)

Index

Maps are marked in grey

S

Map symbols

The symbols below are used on maps throughout the book

- Airport
- Bus/taxi
- Parking
- Internet café/access
- Post office
- Tourist office
- Museum
- Hospital
- Place of interest
- Cave
- Statue
- Ruins
- Monastery
- Gardens/fountain
- Petrol station
- Waterfall
- Synagogue
- Fortress/castle
- Mountain peak
- Mountain range
- Mountain hut
- Bridge
- Cable car
- Funicular
- Gate
- Steps
- Wall
- Church
- Market
- Building
- Stadium
- Park/national park
- Beach
- Cemetery
- Marshland
- River
- Ferry route

Listings key

- Accommodation
- Eating and drinking
- Nightlife
- Shop

ROUGH
GUIDES

RECOMMENDED BY
ROUGH
GUIDES